C000212106

STREET ATLAS

Northamptonshire

First published in 1999 by

Philip's, a division of
Octopus Publishing Group Ltd
2-4 Heron Quays, London E14 4JP

Second edition 2003
Third impression with revisions 2005

ISBN-10   0-540-08287-2 (spiral)
ISBN-13   978-0-540-08287-2 (spiral)

© Philip's 2005

O/S Ordnance Survey®

This product includes mapping data licensed
from Ordnance Survey® with the permission of
the Controller of Her Majesty's Stationery Office.
© Crown copyright 2005. All rights reserved.
Licence number 100011710.

Printed and bound in Spain
by Cayfosa-Quebecor

Contents

III	**Key to map symbols**
IV	**Key to map pages**
VI	**Route planning**
VIII	**Administrative and Postcode boundaries**
1	**Street maps** at 3½ inches to 1 mile
240	**Town maps** of Banbury, Buckingham, Rugby and Stamford
242	**Index** of towns and villages
243	**Index** of streets, hospitals, industrial estates, railway stations, schools, shopping centres, universities and places of interest

Digital Data

The exceptionally high-quality mapping found in this atlas is available as digital data in TIFF format, which is easily convertible to other bitmapped (raster) image formats.

The index is also available in digital form as a standard database table. It contains all the details found in the printed index together with the National Grid reference for the map square in which each entry is named.

For further information and to discuss your requirements, please contact Philip's on 020 7644 6932 or james.mann@philips-maps.co.uk

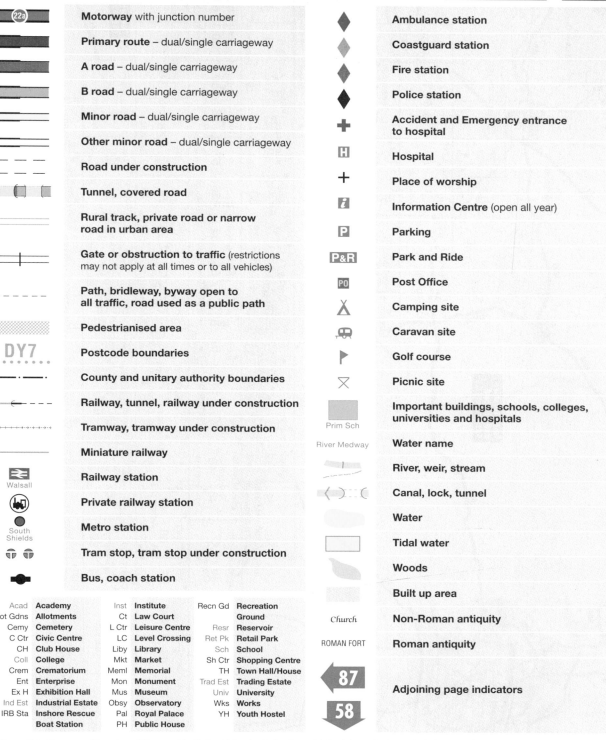

Motorway with junction number		◆	Ambulance station
Primary route – dual/single carriageway		◇	Coastguard station
A road – dual/single carriageway		◆	Fire station
B road – dual/single carriageway		◆	Police station
Minor road – dual/single carriageway		✚	Accident and Emergency entrance to hospital
Other minor road – dual/single carriageway		H	Hospital
Road under construction		✛	Place of worship
Tunnel, covered road		𝑖	Information Centre (open all year)
Rural track, private road or narrow road in urban area		P	Parking
Gate or obstruction to traffic (restrictions may not apply at all times or to all vehicles)		P&R	Park and Ride
Path, bridleway, byway open to all traffic, road used as a public path		PO	Post Office
Pedestrianised area		Ⲭ	Camping site
DY7 Postcode boundaries		⛺	Caravan site
County and unitary authority boundaries		▶	Golf course
Railway, tunnel, railway under construction		⊠	Picnic site
Tramway, tramway under construction		Prim Sch	Important buildings, schools, colleges, universities and hospitals
Miniature railway		River Medway	Water name
Railway station			River, weir, stream
Private railway station			Canal, lock, tunnel
Metro station			Water
Tram stop, tram stop under construction			Tidal water
Bus, coach station			Woods
			Built up area
		Church	Non-Roman antiquity
		ROMAN FORT	Roman antiquity

Acad	Academy	Inst	Institute	Recn Gd	Recreation Ground
Allot Gdns	Allotments	Ct	Law Court		
Cemy	Cemetery	L Ctr	Leisure Centre	Resr	Reservoir
C Ctr	Civic Centre	LC	Level Crossing	Ret Pk	Retail Park
CH	Club House	Liby	Library	Sch	School
Coll	College	Mkt	Market	Sh Ctr	Shopping Centre
Crem	Crematorium	Meml	Memorial	TH	Town Hall/House
Ent	Enterprise	Mon	Monument	Trad Est	Trading Estate
Ex H	Exhibition Hall	Mus	Museum	Univ	University
Ind Est	Industrial Estate	Obsy	Observatory	Wks	Works
IRB Sta	Inshore Rescue Boat Station	Pal	Royal Palace	YH	Youth Hostel
		PH	Public House		

◀ 87
▼ 58 Adjoining page indicators

■ The small numbers around the edges of the maps identify the 1 kilometre National Grid lines

■ The dark grey border on the inside edge of some pages indicates that the mapping does not continue onto the adjacent page

The scale of the maps on the pages numbered in blue is 5.52 cm to 1 km • 3½ inches to 1 mile • 1: 18103

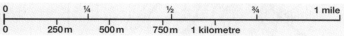

Symbols shown in left margin column: Walsall (Railway station), South Shields (Metro station)

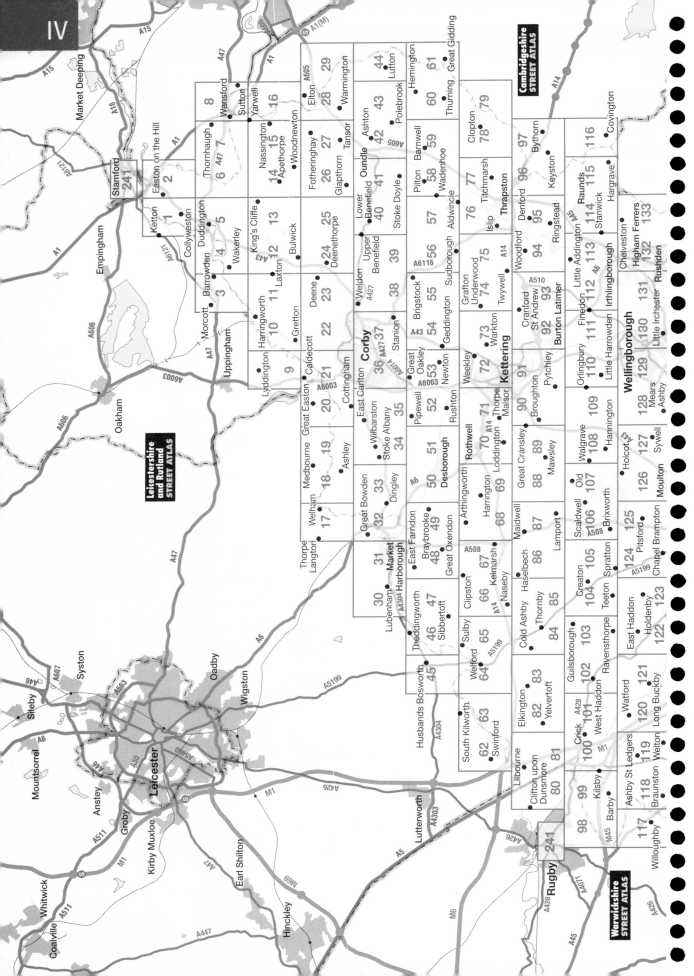

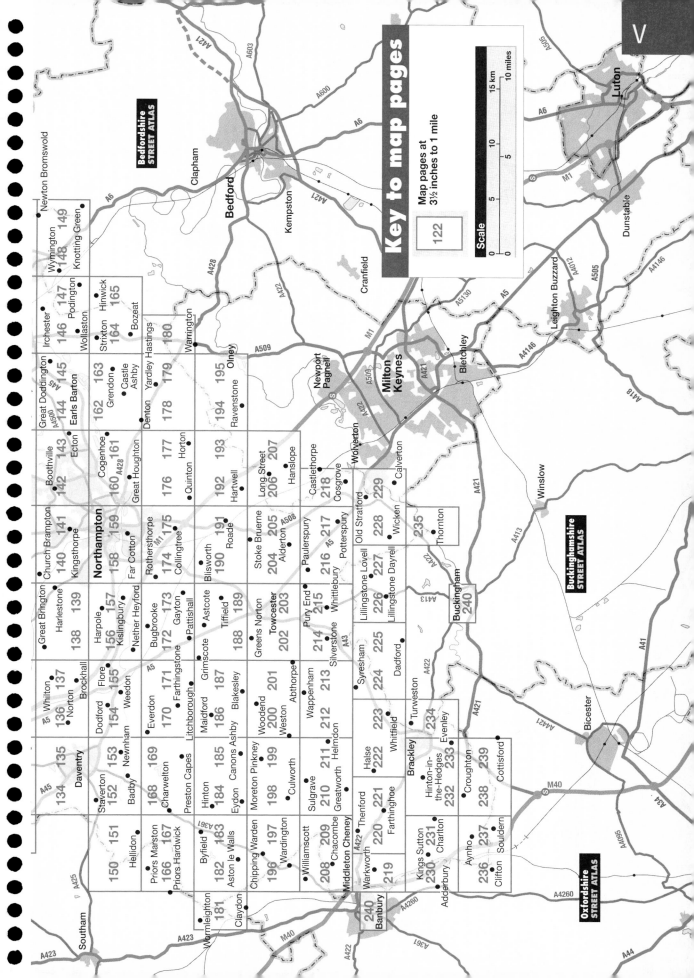

Key to map pages

Map pages at
3½ inches to 1 mile

122

Scale
0   5   10
0   5   10 miles
0   5   10   15 km

V

Bedfordshire STREET ATLAS
Buckinghamshire STREET ATLAS
Oxfordshire STREET ATLAS

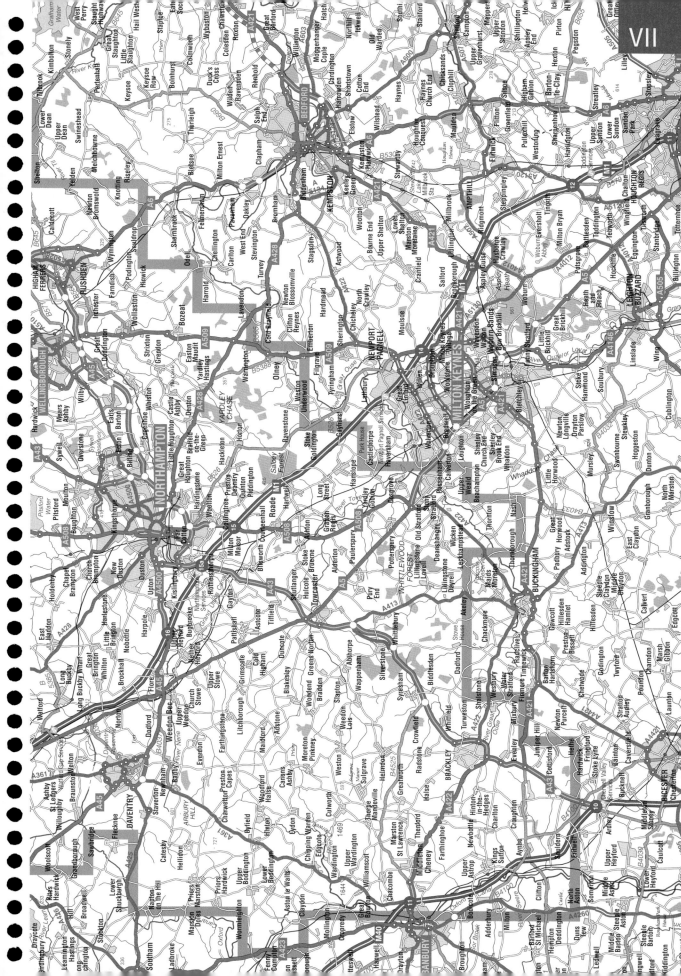

Major administrative and Postcode boundaries

- County and unitary authority boundaries
- District boundaries
- Postcode boundaries
- Area covered by this atlas

Scale

| 0 | 5 | 10 | 15 km |
| 0 | | 5 | 10 miles |

Lincolnshire

SK TF

Rutland

City of Peterborough

SK SP

Leicestershire

Easton on the Hill
PE9
LE15
Wakerley
Wansford PE6 TF
PE5 TL
Lyddington
LE15
King's Cliffe
NN17
Deene
Warmington
PE7

Market Harborough
LE16
Wilbarston
Corby
Corby
Great Oakley
NN18
PE8
Oundle
East Northamptonshire

Braybrooke
Desborough
Brigstock
Rothwell
Kettering
NN16
Kettering
Woodford
Thrapston
PE28

LE17
Welford
Maidwell
NN15
Burton Latimer

Warwickshire
CV21
CV22
Yelvertoft
Guilsborough
NN6
Raunds
NN9
Irthlingborough
Higham Ferrers
Cambridgeshire

CV23 Barby
Brixworth
Northamptonshire
Wellingborough
NN8
Rushden
NN10

Daventry
Moulton
Wellingborough
Daventry
NN2
NN3
Wollaston
Harpole
NN5 NN1
NN29

CV47
NN11
Bugbrooke
Northampton
NN4
Bozeat

Byfield
NN7
Hackleton
Roade
MK46

South Northamptonshire
MK16
Towcester
NN12
MK19
Milton Keynes
Bedfordshire

Culworth
Silverstone
Cosgrove
MK12
OX17
Syresham
Stony Stratford
MK11

OX16
Farthinghoe
Brackley
MK18
NN13
Kings Sutton
Croughton
MK17

OX15
OX27
OX25
Herts

Oxfordshire
Buckinghamshire
Luton

SP TL

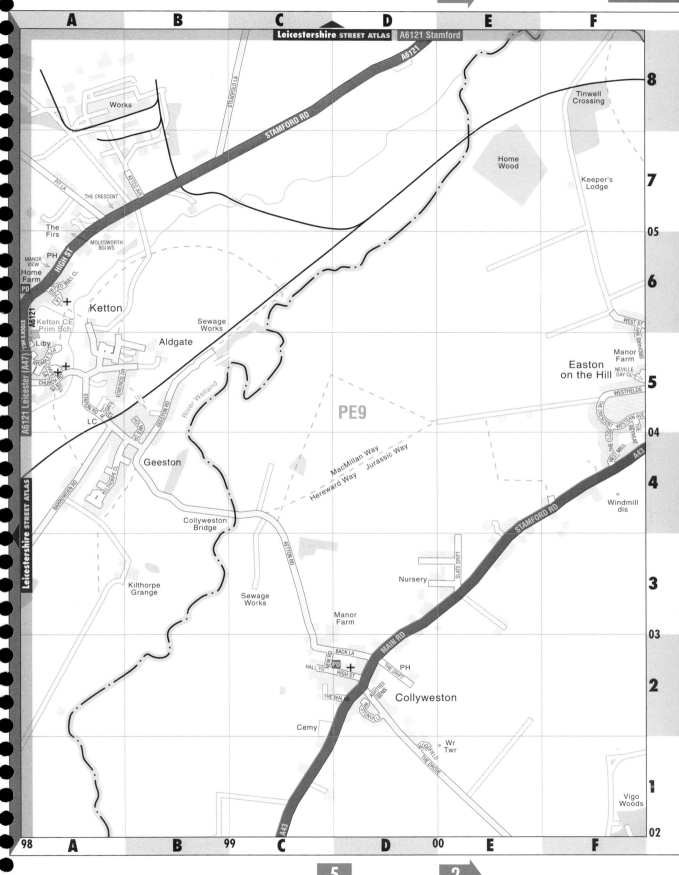

Leicestershire STREET ATLAS | A6121 Stamford

A | B | C | D | E | F

8

Works

STAMFORD RD

A6121

STEADFOLD LA

Tinwell
Crossing

7

Home
Wood

Keeper's
Lodge

THE CRESCENT

KETTO AVE

PIT LA

05

The
Firs

MOLESWORTH
BGLWS

PH

MANOR
VIEW

HIGH ST

Home
Farm

PO

6

PIED BULL CL

Ketton

Sewage
Works

WEST ST
ORCHARD WAY

A6121

Ketton CE
Prim Sch

SCHOOL HILL

Aldgate

Manor
Farm

NEVILLE
DAY CL

Easton
on the Hill

5

Liby

REDMILES LA

CHAPEL RD

CHURCH ST

A6121 Leicester (A47)

River Welland

WESTFIELDS

STATION RD

ALDGATE

EDMUNDS DR

GEESTON RD

PE9

THE CRESCENT

THE CLOSE

WESTERN AVE

THE
RETREAT

LC

HOLMES LA

04

KELTHORPE CL

Geeston

MacMillan Way

Jurassic Way

WEST MILL

A43

Leicestershire STREET ATLAS

BARROWDEN RD

Hereward Way

Collyweston
Bridge

STAMFORD RD

Windmill
dis

4

Kilthorpe
Grange

KETTON RD

SLATE DRIFT

Nursery

3

Sewage
Works

Manor
Farm

MAIN RD

03

BACK LA

NEW RD

PO

THE DRIFT

PH

HALL YD

HIGH ST

2

THE WALKS

ASHTREE GDNS

STONVALE

Collyweston

Cemy

WOODFIELD

Wr
Twr

THE BROOK

1

Vigo
Woods

A43

02

98 | A | B | 99 | C | D | 00 | E | F

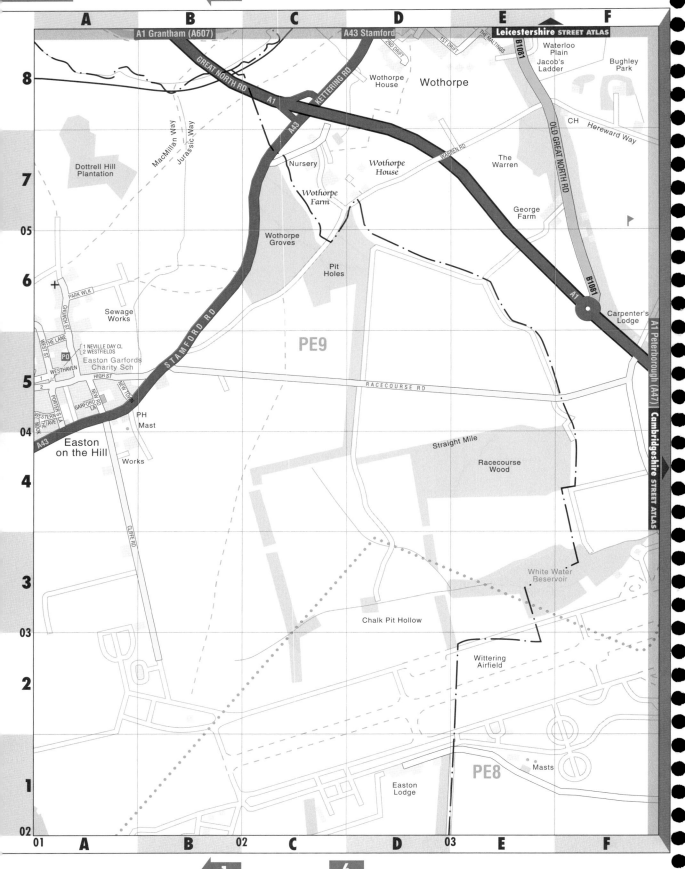

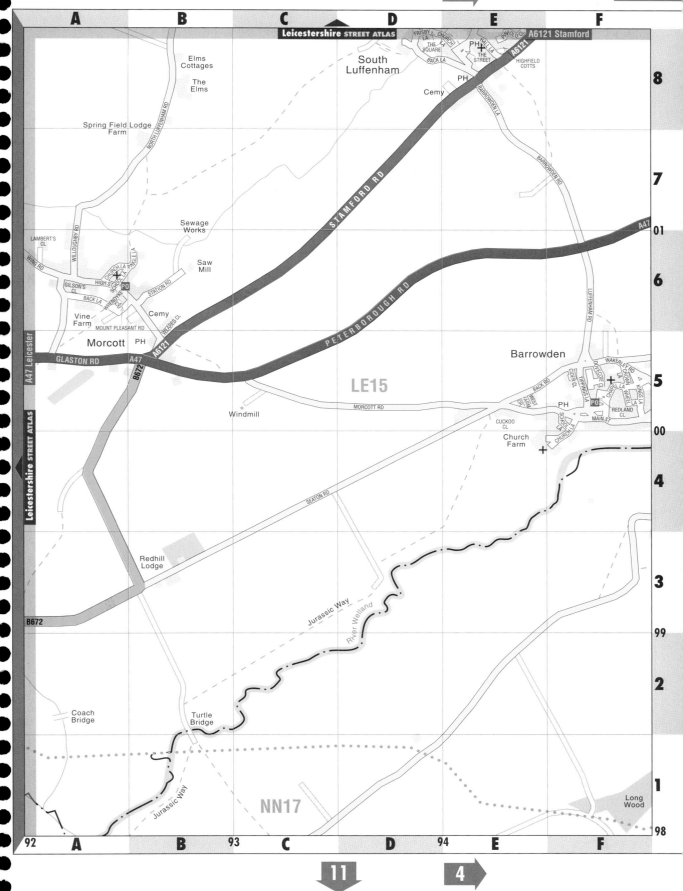

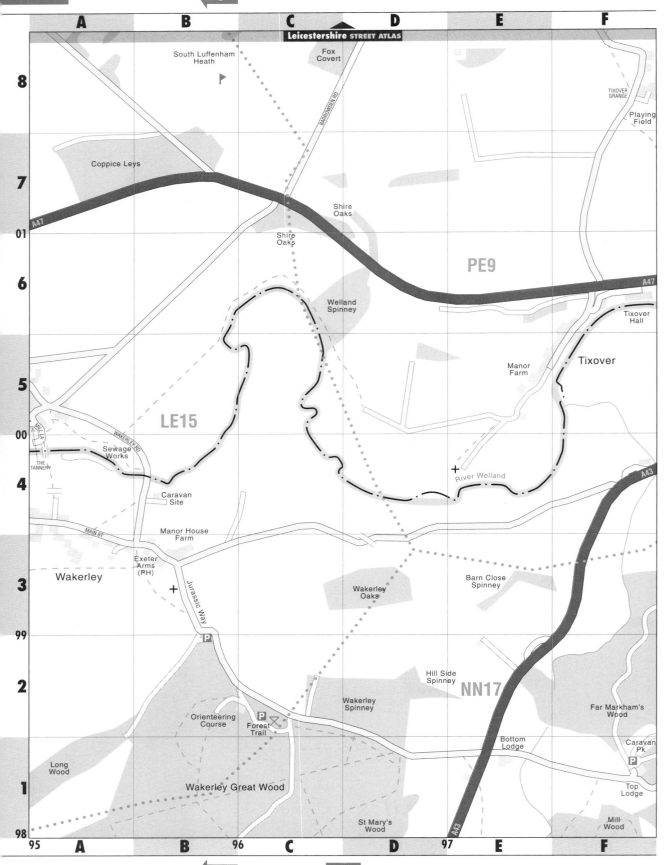

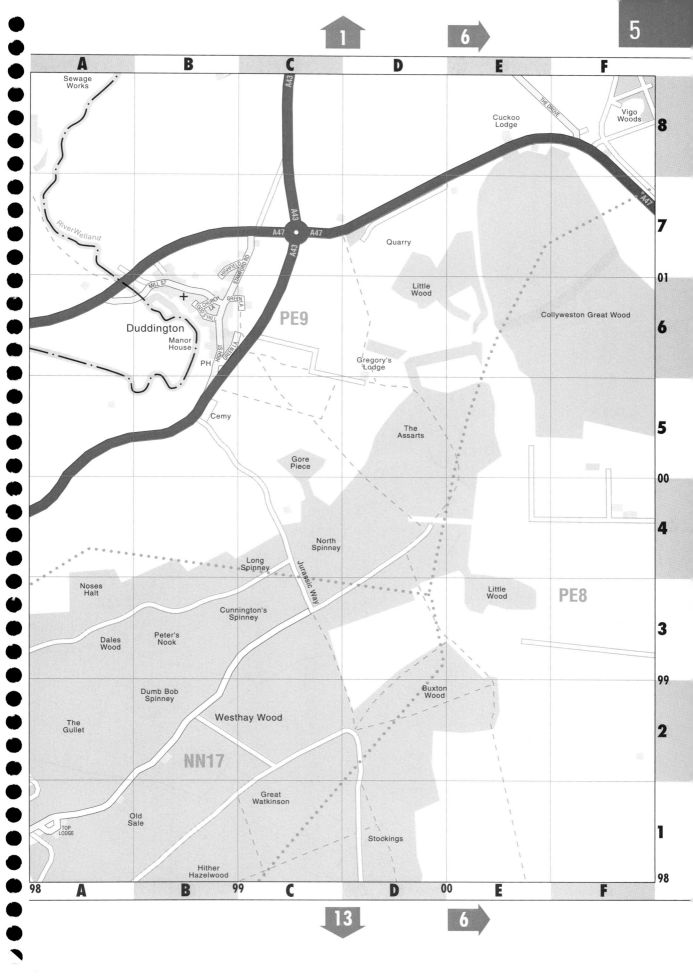

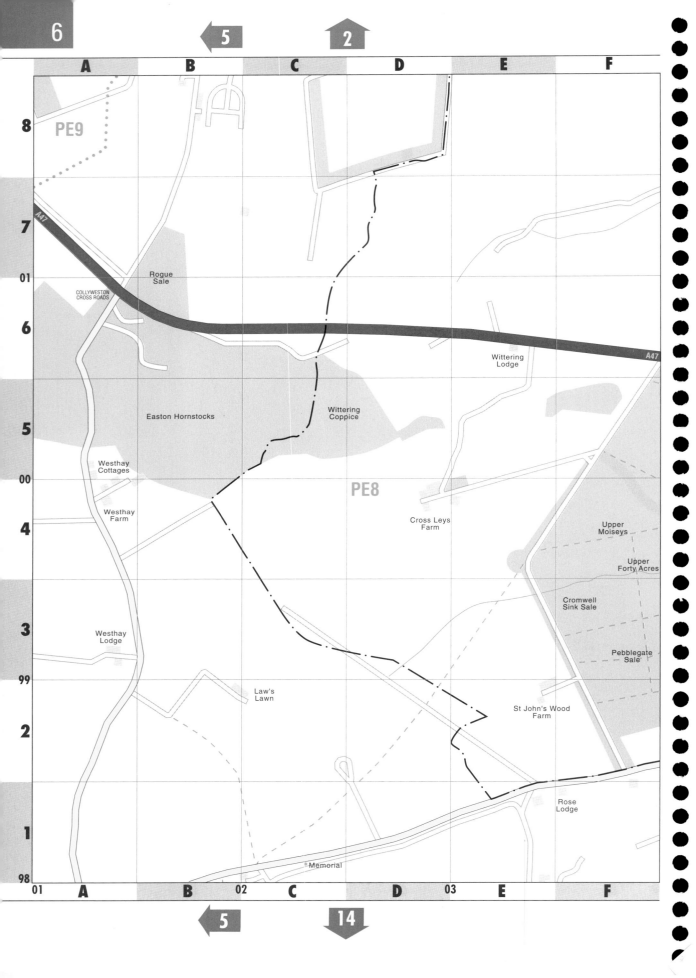

Cambridgeshire STREET ATLAS

Wittering

Bonemills
Cottages

Bonemills
Farm

Elms
Farm

A1 Stamford

Wittering
Cottages

8

Sewage
Works

HALL LA
WOODROFFE RD
CHURCH PK
TRENT RD
ECCLES RD
CLIFFE RD
PARKER RD
PG RD

Diamond Jubilee
Plantation

Lound
Wood

Abbot's
Wood

7

OLD OUNDLE RD

Wittering
Grange

West
Wood

01

Manor
House

6

Thornhaugh
Hall

The
Oaks

Home Farm
House

Home
Farm

Thornhaugh
Cottages

RUSSELL HILL

+

The
Bedlams

Toll Bar
Cottage

Oaks
Cottage

MEADOW LA

Croft
Farm

Thornhaugh

5

North Gate
Sale

Sibberton
Lodge

00

Cook's
Hole

A47

4

PE8

The Old
Pump House

Lower
Moiseys

Bedford Purlieus

Lower
Forty Acres

Cocker
Wood

3

Leedsgate
Farm

99

St John's
Wood

Forest
Lodge

2

Sulehay
Cottages

WANSFORD RD

Works

SULEHAY RD

Old Sulehay
Forest

Old Sulehay
Lodge

1

98

A | B | C | D | E | F

Cambridgeshire **STREET ATLAS**

Nature Reserve

Cambridgeshire STREET ATLAS

Lady Wood

Deardon Wood

Southorpe Bottom

8

Gazley Lodge

PE9

Beech Spinney

Wall Spinney

Crow Spinney

Sutton Wood

7

01

Research Centre

A1

Sacrewell Lodge

PE6

6

OLD RECTORY DR.
RUSSELL HILL
WINDGATE WAY

Jubilee Spinney

Thornhaugh

Sacrewell Farm & Country Centre

Hereward Way

5

Mill House

Top Field Spinney

Hell Corner

A47 Peterborough

00

THACKERS CL.
OLD NORTH RD

PE8

4

Black Swan Hill

A47

A6118

Black Swan Spinney

SWAN CL.
PH

Wansford

Mast

Nene Way

Heath House

PE5

River Nene

ROBINS WOOD
ROBINS FIELD
THE STABLES
OLD LEICESTER RD
NENE CL.
PETERBOROUGH RD
SIDE RD
NENE SPINNEY
A6118
OLD NORTH RD

Deep Springs

A47

3

WANSFORD RD
YARWELL RD
BRIDGE END

The Bungalow

THE DRIFT

Wansford Bridge

Hotel

Stibbington Hall

Sutton

NENE WAY

Manor Farm

99

LONDON RD
PH A6118
PO
CHAPEL LA.
B671

GREAT NORTH RD

OLD GREAT NORTH RD

CHURCH

Manor Farm

LOVERS LA.
MANOR RD
GRAEME RD

The Grange

2

ROMAN DR.

Stibbington

Bunkers Hill

Field Studies Centre

ELTON RD

Stibbington House

Nene Way

1

NEW LA.

Depot

Sewage Farm

OLD GREAT NORTH RD

Ship End Pits

B671

Toll Bar Spinney

A1

Nene Valley Railway

98

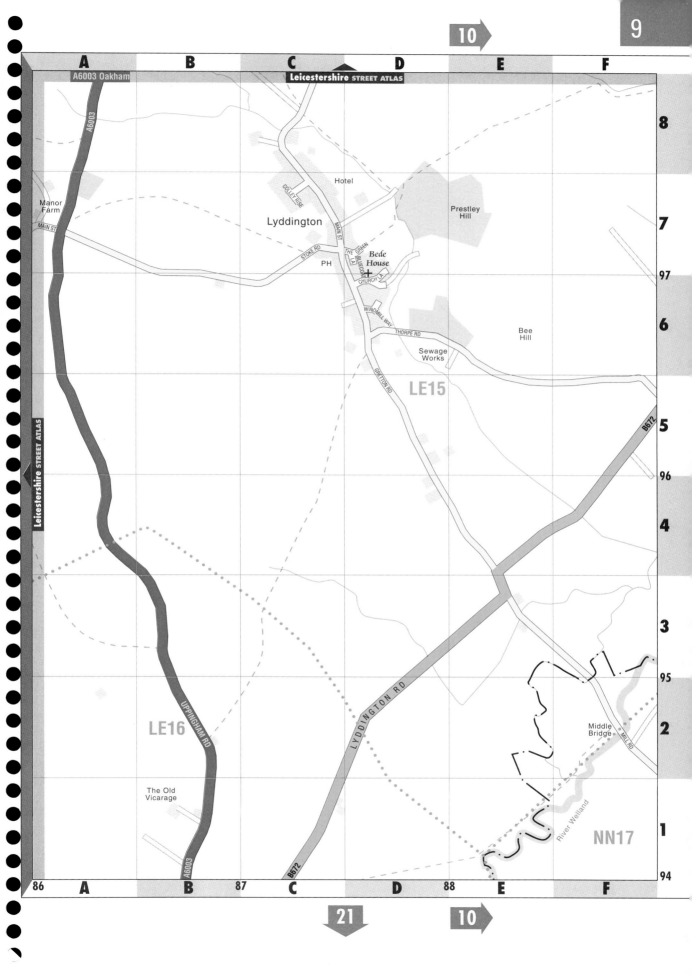

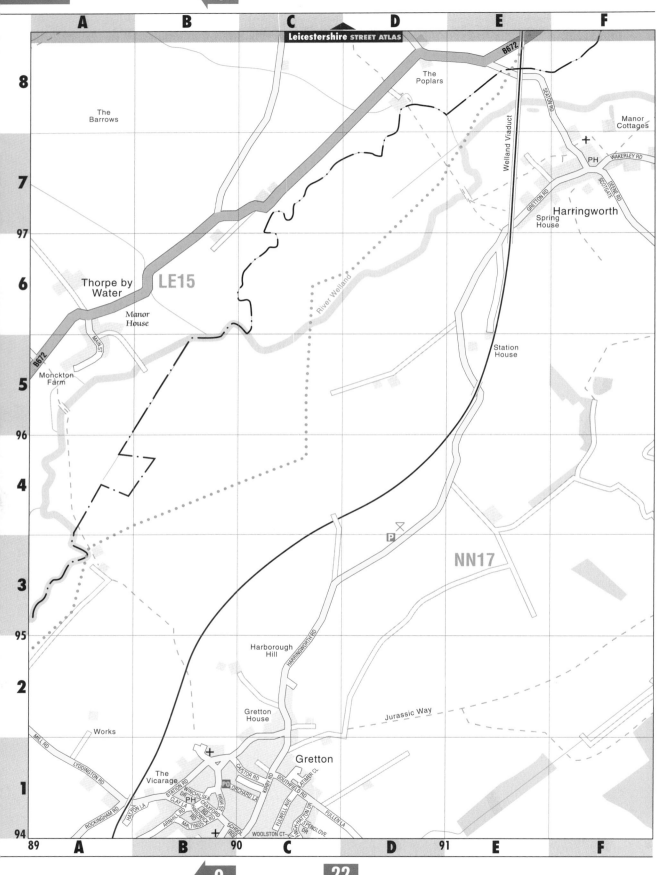

Leicestershire STREET ATLAS

The Barrows

The Poplars

Manor Cottages

Welland Viaduct

SEATON RD

PH

WAKERLEY RD

GRETTON RD

DRENE RD

SCOTGATE

Harringworth

Spring House

LE15

Thorpe by Water

Manor House

River Welland

Station House

B672

Monckton Farm

NN17

Harborough Hill

HARRINGWORTH RD

Jurassic Way

Gretton House

Works

Gretton

The Vicarage

PH

PO

MILL RD

LYDDINGTON RD

ROCKINGHAM RD

HALTON LA

STATION RD

WINCHILSEA

CHAXFORD

CLAY LA

HARDING RD

ARNHILL RD

MALTINGS

RDG

HIGH ST

CASTOR RD

KIRBY RD

ORCHARD LA

FULWELL LANE

SOUTHFIELD RD

LATIMER CL

WINCHILHATON DR

SPENDLOVE DR

WOOLSTON CT

SCHOOL RD

FULLEN LA

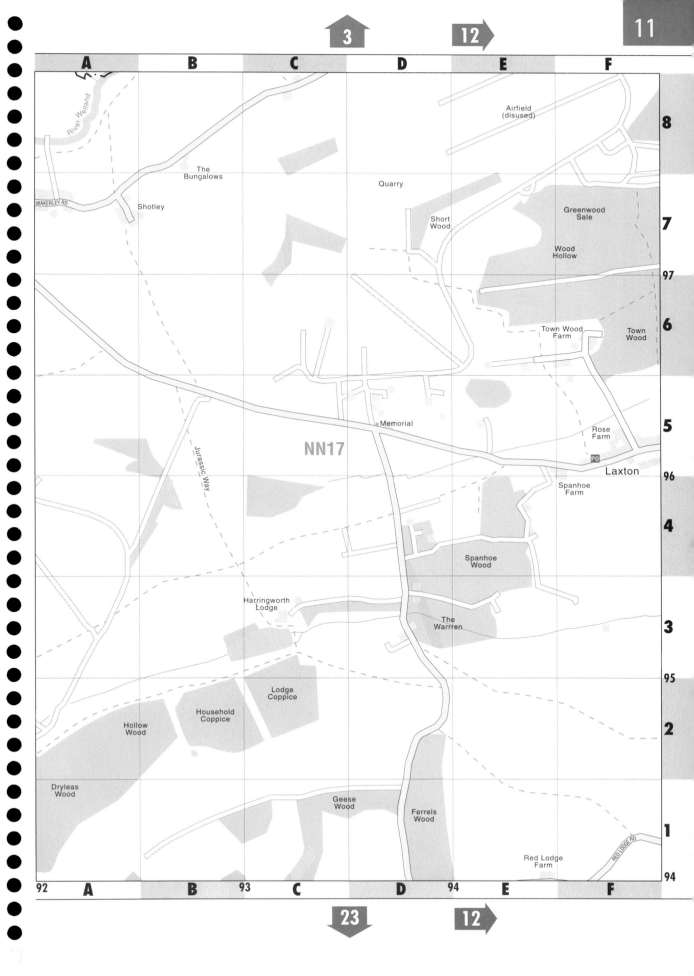

River Welland

WAKERLEY RD

Shotley

The Bungalows

Quarry

Airfield
(disused)

Short
Wood

Greenwood
Sale

Wood
Hollow

Town Wood
Farm

Town
Wood

Memorial

NN17

Jurassic Way

Rose
Farm

Laxton

Spanhoe
Farm

Spanhoe
Wood

Harringworth
Lodge

The
Warrren

Lodge
Coppice

Household
Coppice

Hollow
Wood

Dryleas
Wood

Geese
Wood

Ferrels
Wood

Red Lodge
Farm

RED LODGE RD

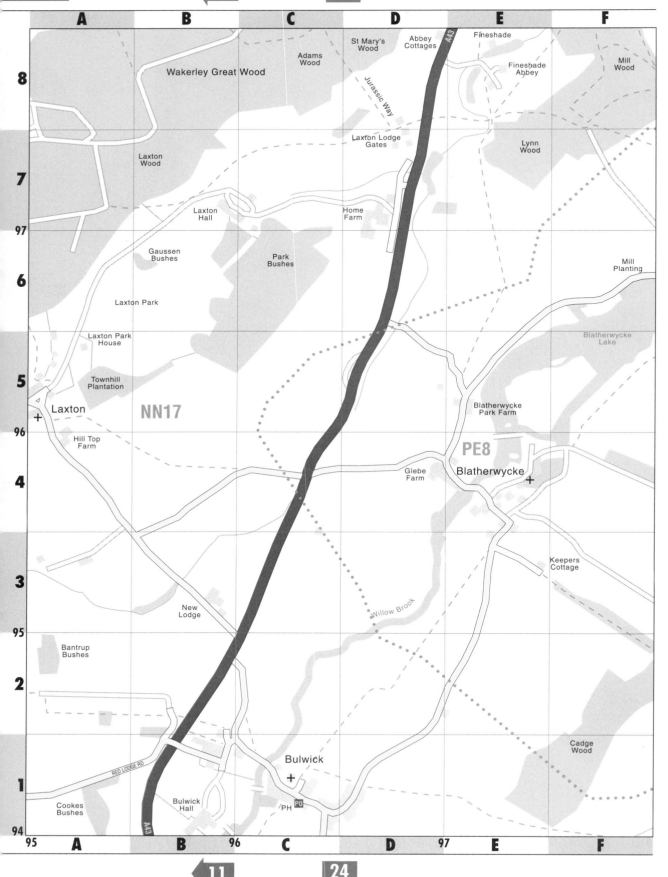

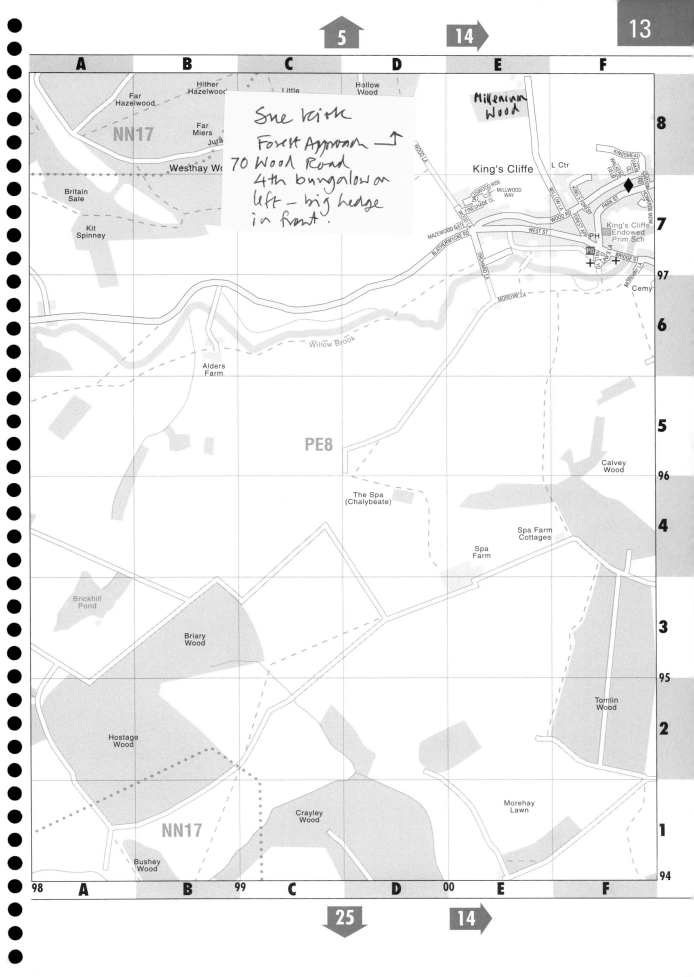

A   B   C   D   E   F

8

Rosary Farm

Huskisson's Lodge

Airfield (disused)

Great Byards Sale

Jack's Green

PARK CL

PARK ST

Sewage Works

7

Cornforth Holmes

Great Morton Sale

BRIDGE ST

97

Cemy

6

Bluefield Farm

Quarry Cottages

PE8

Bushrubs Wood

APETHORPE RD

5

Willowbrook Lodge

96

KINGS CLIFFE RD

4

PH

MANOR FARM

BRIDGE ST

Priors Haw

THE ORCHARD

MAIN ST

HUNTING LAUNDRY WAY RD

Apethorpe

3

Apethorpe Hall

Willow Brook

95

2

New Wood

Conegar Farm

Woodnewton

ST MARYS CL

ST MARYS HILL

ORCHARD CRES

PRIORMERE CL

MEADOW GATE

ORCHARD LA

THE PADDOCK

Cheeseman's Wood

THE MAIN ST

PH

WADES CL

LINDSEY CL

MASSINGTON RD

1

Lodge Farm

Willowbrook Farm

DUNDLE RD

94

Fisher's Close Spinney

Sewage Works

01   A   B   02   C   D   03   E   F

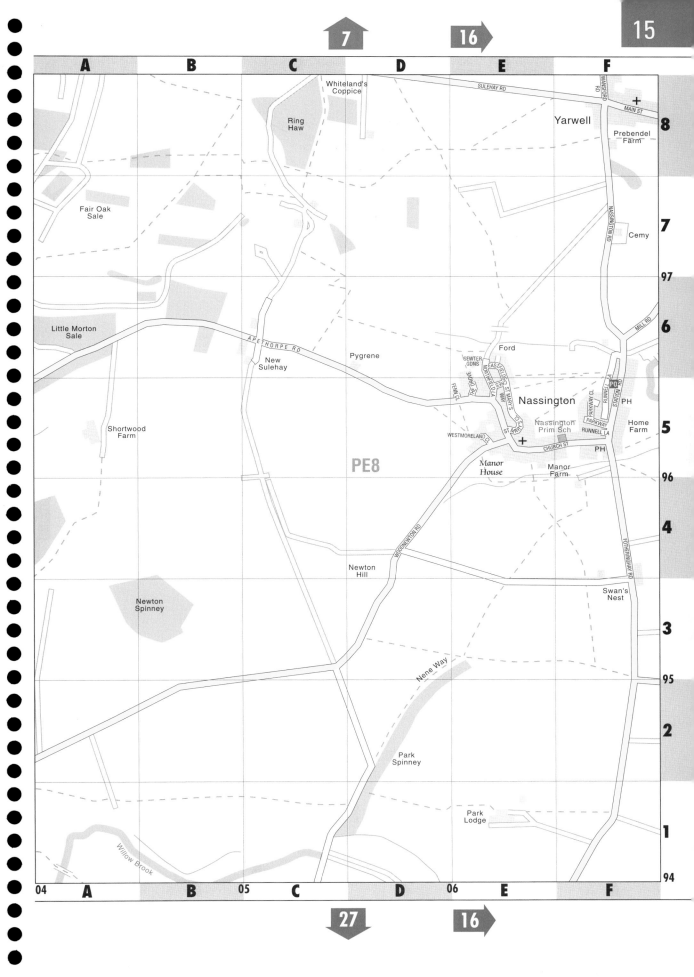

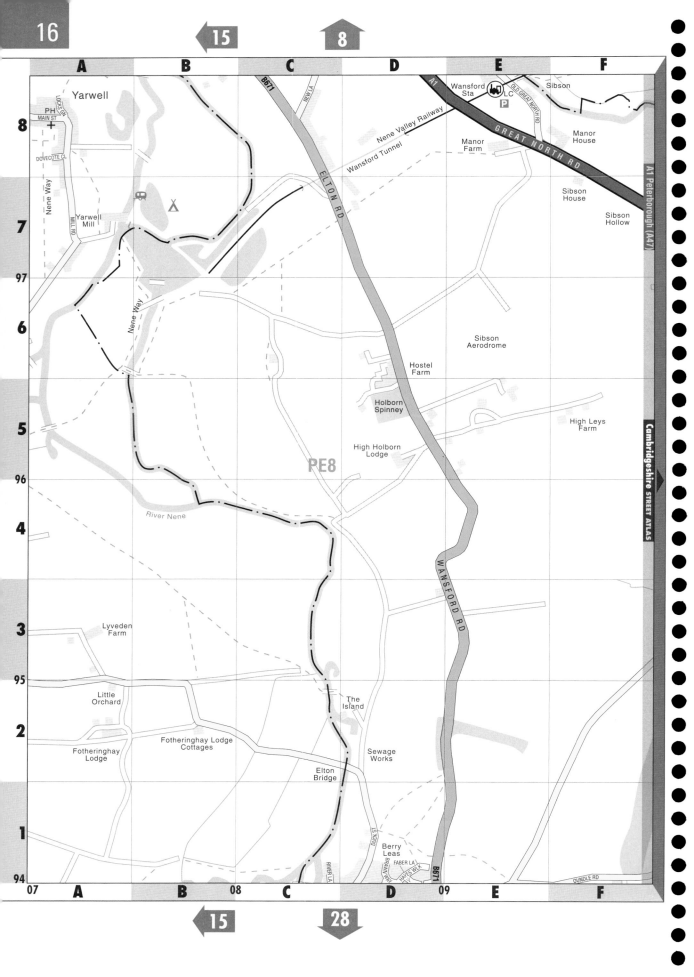

Yarwell

Nene Valley Railway
Wansford Tunnel
Wansford Tunnel

Wansford Sta
LC
P
Sibson

Manor House

Sibson House

Sibson Hollow

Manor Farm

GREAT NORTH RD

A1

ELTON RD

B671

LOCKS LN

PH

MAIN ST

DOVECOTE CL

Nene Way

MILL RD

Yarwell Mill

Nene Way

Nene Way

River Nene

PE8

Sibson Aerodrome

Hostel Farm

Holborn Spinney

High Holborn Lodge

High Leys Farm

WANSFORD RD

Lyveden Farm

Little Orchard

Fotheringhay Lodge

Fotheringhay Lodge Cottages

Elton Bridge

The Island

Sewage Works

Berry Leas

BRAMLEY WAY

KING ST

FABER LA

HAYES WLK

B671

RIVER LA

OUNDLE RD

OLD GREAT NORTH RD

07   08   09

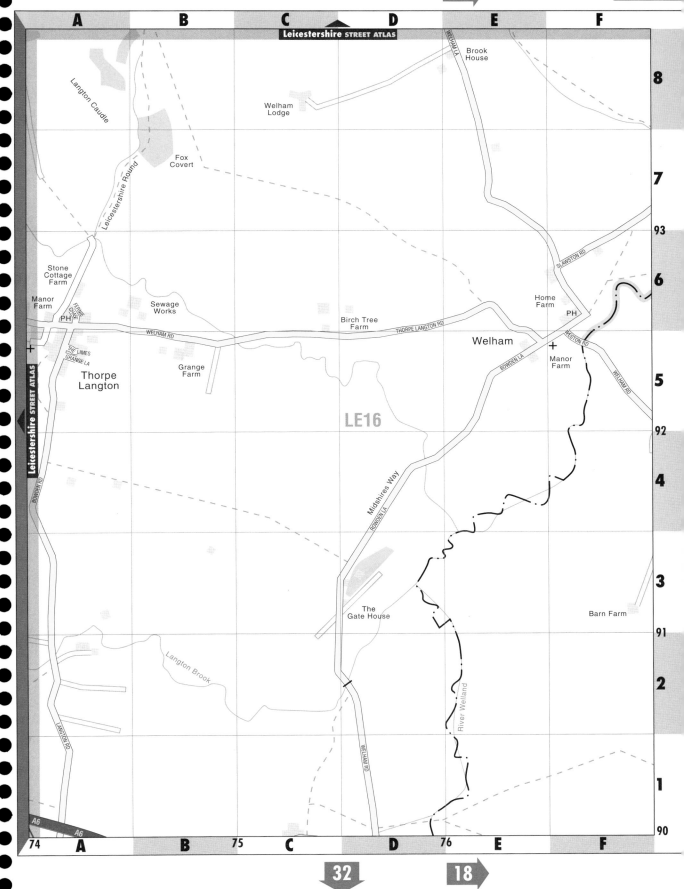

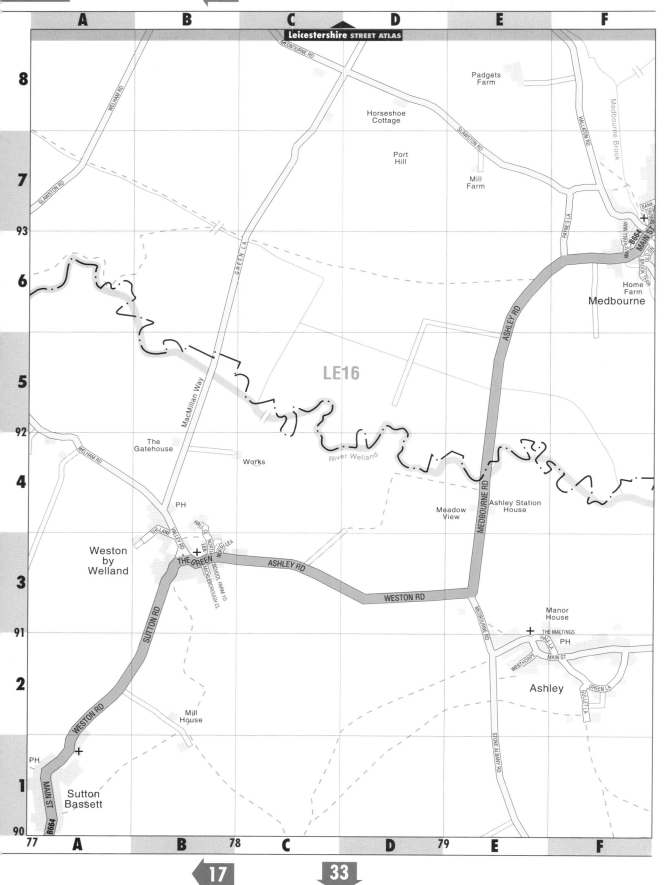

LE16

Medbourne

Padgets Farm

Horseshoe Cottage

Port Hill

Mill Farm

Home Farm

SLAWSTON RD

WELHAM RD

PAYNE'S LA

HALLATON RD

Medbourne Brook

MAIN ST

BANK

B664

ASHLEY RD

GREEN LA

MacMillan Way

The Gatehouse

Works

River Welland

Meadow View

Ashley Station House

MEDBOURNE RD

Weston by Welland

PH

THE LANE

VALLEY RD

HALL CL

WORTH LEA

SAXON LEA

THE GREEN

SCHOOL FARM YD

MICKLEBOROUGH CL

ASHLEY RD

WESTON RD

WELHAM RD

SUTTON RD

Manor House

THE MALTINGS

PH

HALL LA

MAIN ST

WESTHORPE

GREEN LA

GULLET LA

Ashley

MEDBOURNE RD

STOKE ALBANY RD

Mill House

WESTON RD

PH

Sutton Bassett

MAIN ST

B664

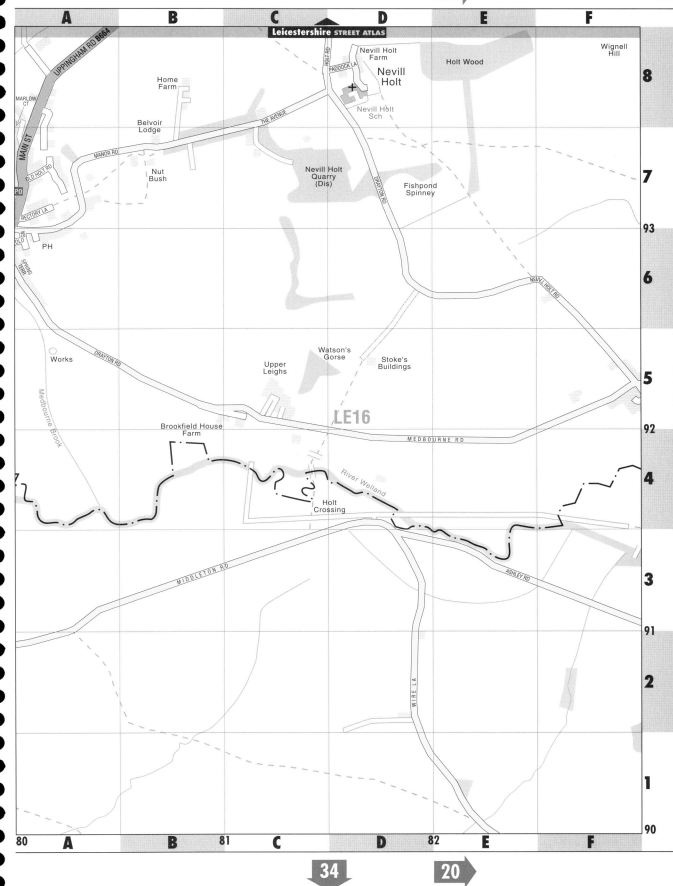

19

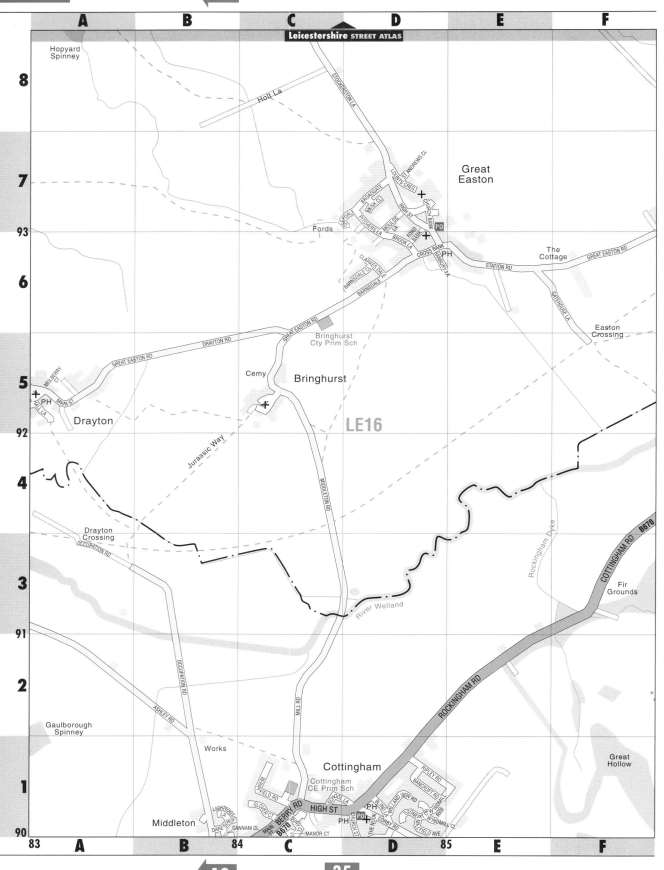

Leicestershire STREET ATLAS

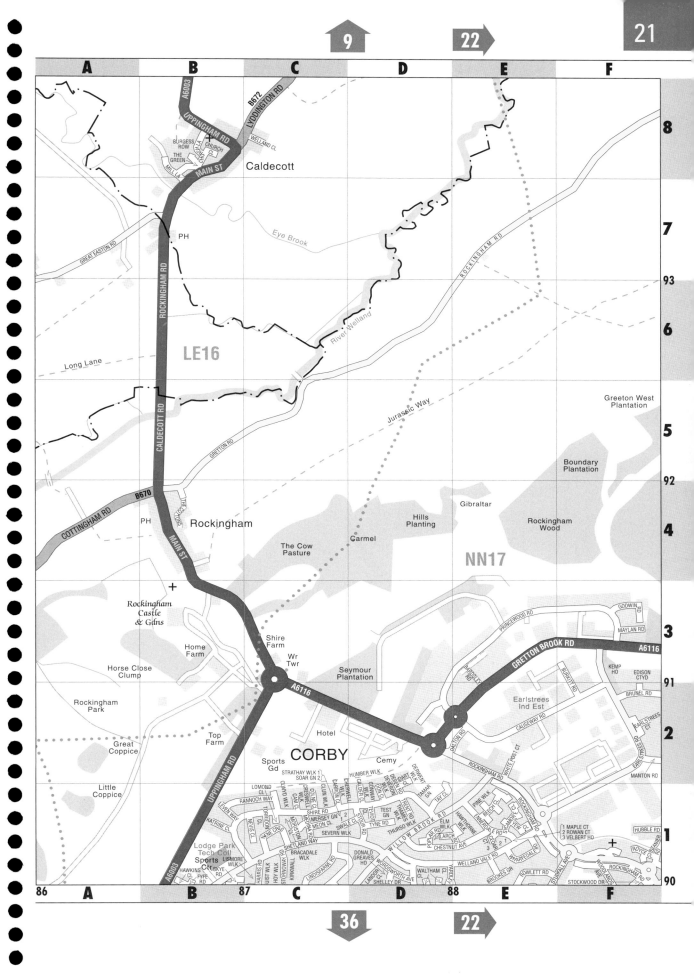

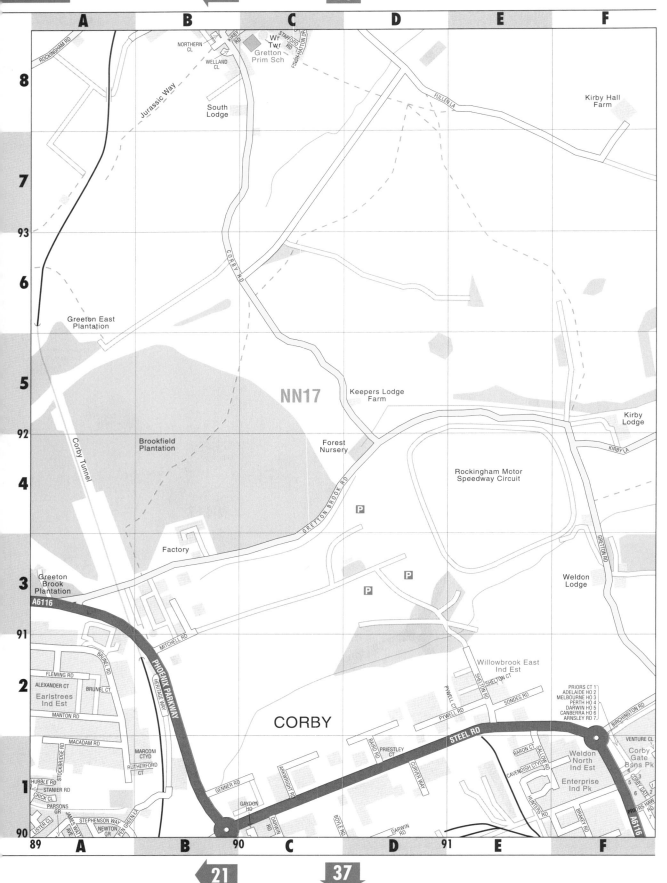

A B C D E F

8

7

93

6

Greeton East
Plantation

5

NN17

92

4

3

2

1

90

89 A B 90 C D 91 E F

ROCKINGHAM RD

NORTHERN CL

WELLAND CL

KIRBY RD

STAFFORD RD

FINCH HATTON DR

Wr Twr

Gretton Prim Sch

Jurassic Way

South Lodge

FULLEN LA

Kirby Hall Farm

CORBY RD

Corby Tunnel

Keepers Lodge Farm

Kirby Lodge

Brookfield Plantation

Forest Nursery

KIRBY LA

GRETTON BROOK RD

Rockingham Motor Speedway Circuit

GRETTON RD

P

P

P

Factory

Weldon Lodge

Greeton Brook Plantation

A6116

MITCHELL RD

Willowbrook East Ind Est

PHOENIX PARKWAY

HERITAGE WAY

BRUNE RD

BRUNEL RD

FLEMING RD

BRUNEL CT

ALEXANDER CT

Earlstrees Ind Est

MANTON RD

STOCKBRIDGE RD

MACADAM RD

MARCONI CTYD

RUTHERFORD CT

HUBBLE RD

STANIER RD

CRICK CL

PARSONS GR

LISTER CT

JAMES WATT AVE

STEPHENSON WAY

NEWTON GR

PEN GREEN LA

CORBY

PYWELL CT

SHELTON RD

SHELTON CT

BAIRD RD

PRIESTLEY CT

ARKWRIGHT RD

PYWELL RD

SONDES RD

CULVERT WAY

GENNER RD

GAYDON HO

DARWIN RD

BOYLE RD

DARWIN RD

STEEL RD

BARON CT

SALLOW RD

CAVENDISH CTYD

HUNTERS RD

Weldon North Ind Est

BRAMEY RD

Enterprise Ind Pk

PRIORS CT 1
ADELAIDE HO 2
MELBOURNE HO 3
PERTH HO 4
DARWIN HO 5
CANBERRA HO 6
ARNSLEY RD 7

BIRCHINGTON RD

VENTURE CL

Corby Gate Bsns Pk

CORBY GATE

PRIORS HAW RD

A6116

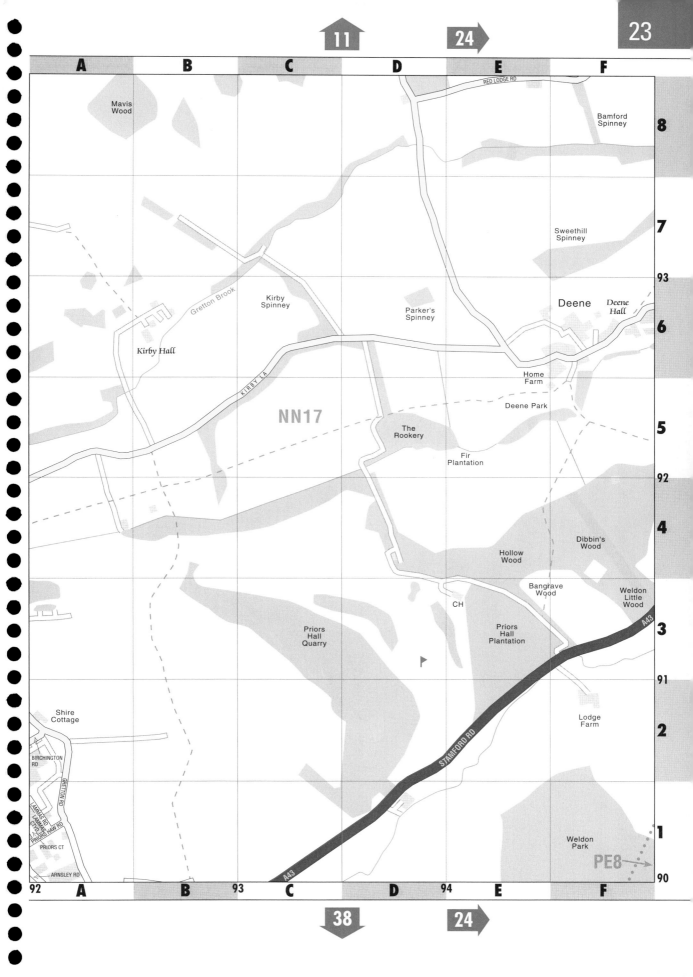

23
12

A B C D E F

8

Kennel
Coppice

Gretton Brook

A43

7

Great
Spinney

NN17

Bulwick
Lodge

93

Glebe
Farm

6

+

The
Lake

Barratt's
Coppice

Rough
Close

DEENETHORPE LA

5

NEW
COTTS

OSIER BED LA

92

Forest
Lodge

4

Deenethorpe

BENEFIELD RD

Burn
Coppice

STAMFORD RD

A43

3

Home
Farm
Lodge

91

Langley
Coppice

2

Airfield
(dis)

PE8

1

Mast

90

95 A B 96 C D 97 E F

23
39

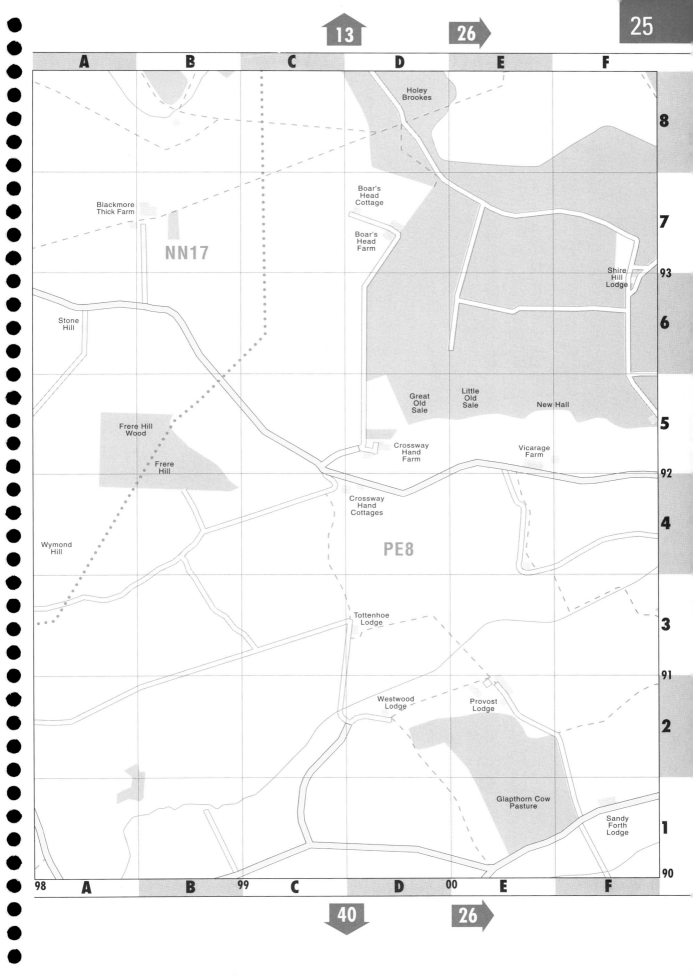

A   B   C   D   E   F

8

Holey
Brookes

Boar's
Head
Cottage

7

Blackmore
Thick Farm

NN17

Boar's
Head
Farm

93

Shire
Hill
Lodge

6

Stone
Hill

Frere Hill
Wood

Great
Old
Sale

Little
Old
Sale

New Hall

5

Frere
Hill

Crossway
Hand
Farm

Vicarage
Farm

92

Crossway
Hand
Cottages

Wymond
Hill

PE8

4

Tottenhoe
Lodge

3

91

Westwood
Lodge

Provost
Lodge

2

Glapthorn Cow
Pasture

Sandy
Forth
Lodge

1

90

98   A   B   99   C   D   00   E   F

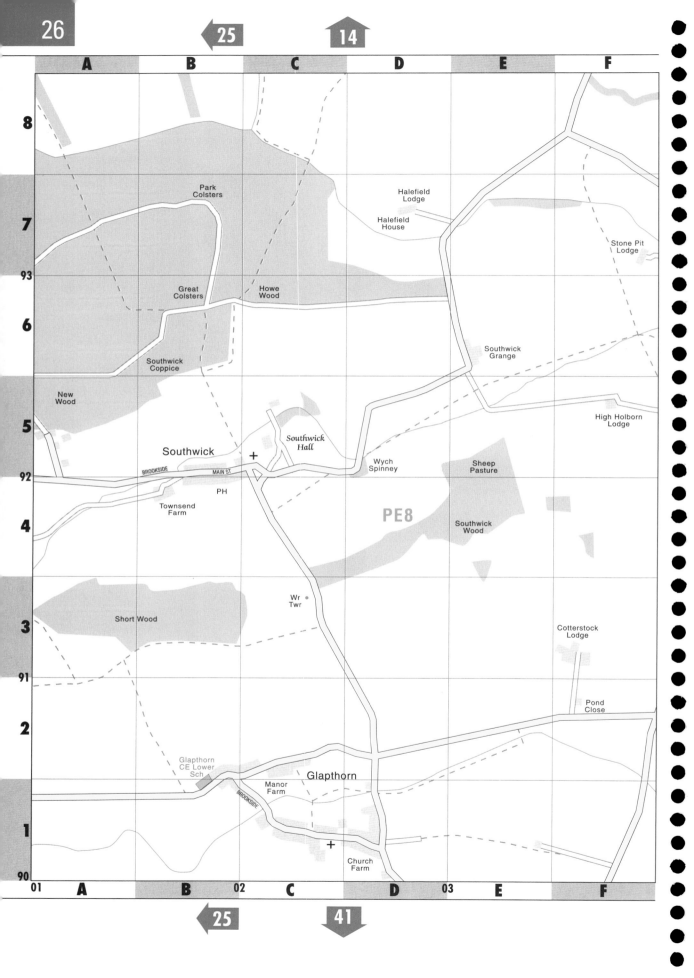

25
14

A   B   C   D   E   F

8

7

93

6

Park
Colsters

Halefield
Lodge

Halefield
House

Stone Pit
Lodge

Great
Colsters

Howe
Wood

Southwick
Coppice

Southwick
Grange

New
Wood

High Holborn
Lodge

5

92

Southwick

Southwick
Hall

Wych
Spinney

Sheep
Pasture

BROOKSIDE   MAIN ST

PH

Townsend
Farm

PE8

Southwick
Wood

4

Short Wood

Wr
Twr

Cotterstock
Lodge

3

91

Pond
Close

2

Glapthorn
CE Lower
Sch

Glapthorn

Manor
Farm

BROOKSIDE

1

90

Church
Farm

01   A   B   02   C   D   03   E   F

25
41

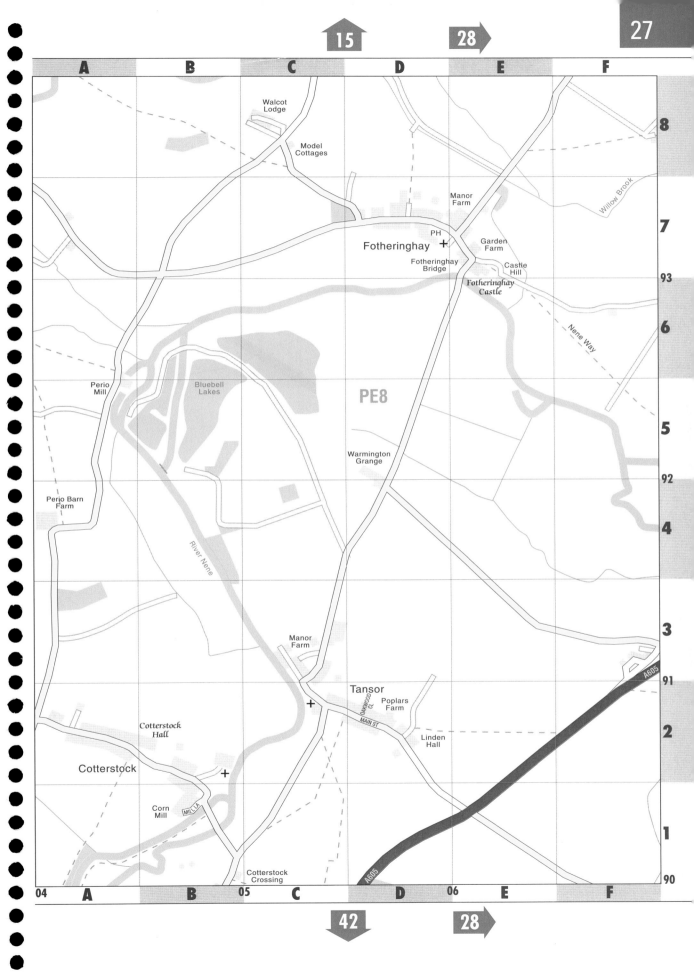

A B C D E F

8

7

93

6

5

92

4

3

91

2

1

90

Walcot Lodge

Model Cottages

Manor Farm

PH
Fotheringhay

Garden Farm

Fotheringhay Bridge

Castle Hill

Fotheringhay Castle

Willow Brook

Nene Way

Perio Mill

Bluebell Lakes

PE8

Warmington Grange

Perio Barn Farm

River Nene

Manor Farm

Tansor

OAKWOOD CL
MAIN ST
Poplars Farm

Linden Hall

Cotterstock Hall

Cotterstock

Corn Mill

MILL LA

Cotterstock Crossing

A605

A605

04 A B 05 C D 06 E F

27
16

A B C D E F

8

7

93

6

5

92

4

3

91

2

1

90

Middle Lodge

River Nene

Mill
River End
Highgate
BRAWN WAY
HAYES WLK
HIGHGATE GN
BACK LA
DUCK ST
RIVER LA
CHAPEL LA
MIDDLE ST
PO
1
2
SCHOOL LA
RECTORY FARM CT 1
RECTORY FARM MEWS 2
Elton CE Prim Sch
VINCO TERR
B671 WANSFORD RD
OUNDLE RD
Elton
Proby Farm
Greenhill
GREENHILL RD

PH
OVEREND
Over End
Carrs Farm

Elton Park

ST BOTOLPH GN
B671
Dairy Farm
A605

Elton Hall

The Oaks

Crow Spinney

The Ferns

Oak Plantation
Blue Bell Spinney

Stock Hill

PE8

Ashpole Spinney

Sewage Works

A605

Eaglethorpe PH

PETERBOROUGH RD

SHORT CL
MERRY WAY
BOSWORTH CL
BUNTING'S LA

Ashdown Farm

Beanhill Spinney

Little Green
BEVAN CL
CHAPEL ST
STAMFORD LA
PO
HAUTBOY LA
SCHOOL LA
ORCHARD CL
BIG GN
PIERCE CRES
DRAPER'S CL
Warmington

Davey's Lodge

Elms Farm

Springfield Farm

Nene Way
SPINNEY CL
CHURCH ST
LONG LA
LARGE MEAD
Warmington Sch
BROADGATE WAY
Cemy
Long Lane Farm
TAYLORS GN

Villa Farm

Lodge Farm

Tansor Grange

07 A 08 B C 08 D 09 E F

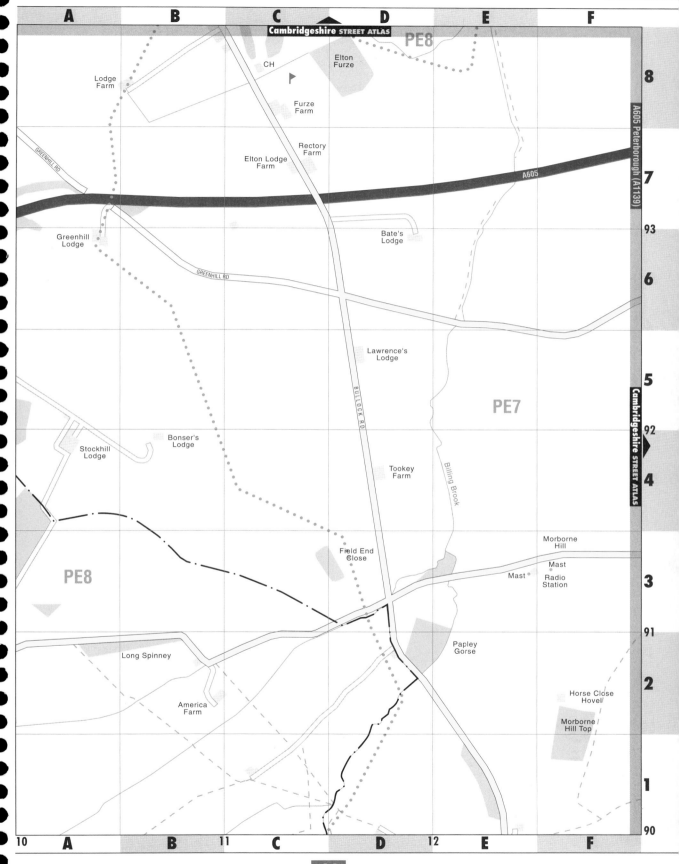

PE8

A B C D E F

8

Lodge
Farm

CH

Elton
Furze

Furze
Farm

A605 Peterborough (A1139)

Rectory
Farm

Elton Lodge
Farm

A605

7

93

Greenhill
Lodge

Bate's
Lodge

GREENHILL RD

6

Lawrence's
Lodge

BULLOCK RD

PE7

5

Cambridgeshire STREET ATLAS

92

Stockhill
Lodge

Bonser's
Lodge

Tookey
Farm

Billing Brook

4

Morborne
Hill

Mast

PE8

Field End
Close

Mast

Radio
Station

3

91

Long Spinney

Papley
Gorse

America
Farm

Horse Close
Hovel

2

Morborne
Hill Top

1

90

10 A B 11 C D 12 E F

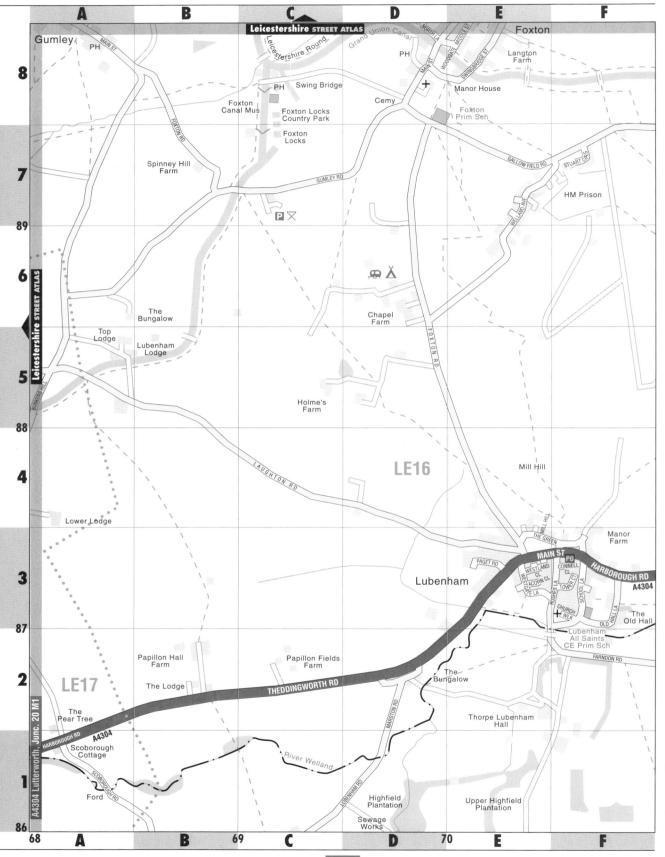

Gumley

Foxton

Leicestershire Round

Grand Union Canal

PH

PH

PH

Swing Bridge

Foxton
Canal Mus

Cemy

Manor House

Foxton
Locks
Country Park

Foxton
Prim Sch

Foxton
Locks

GALLOW FIELD RD

STUART CRES

Spinney Hill
Farm

GUMLEY RD

HM Prison

WELLAND AVE

The
Bungalow

Chapel
Farm

FOXTON RD

Top
Lodge

Lubenham
Lodge

Holme's
Farm

LE16

Mill Hill

LAUGHTON RD

Lower Lodge

MILL HILL

THE GREEN

Manor
Farm

PAGET RD

MAIN ST

PO

HARBOROUGH RD

CONNELL
CL

WESTLAND
CL

RUSHES LA

ACORN CL

TOWER CT

SCHOOL LA

A4304

Lubenham

WESTGATE LA

VALL LA

OLD

The
Old Hall

CHURCH
WLK

Lubenham
All Saints
CE Prim Sch

FARNDON RD

Papillon Hall
Farm

Papillon Fields
Farm

The
Bungalow

LE17

The Lodge

THEDDINGWORTH RD

MARSTON RD

Thorpe Lubenham
Hall

The
Pear Tree

HARBOROUGH RD

A4304

Scoborough
Cottage

River Welland

SCOBOROUGH RD

Ford

LUBENHAM RD

Highfield
Plantation

Upper Highfield
Plantation

Sewage
Works

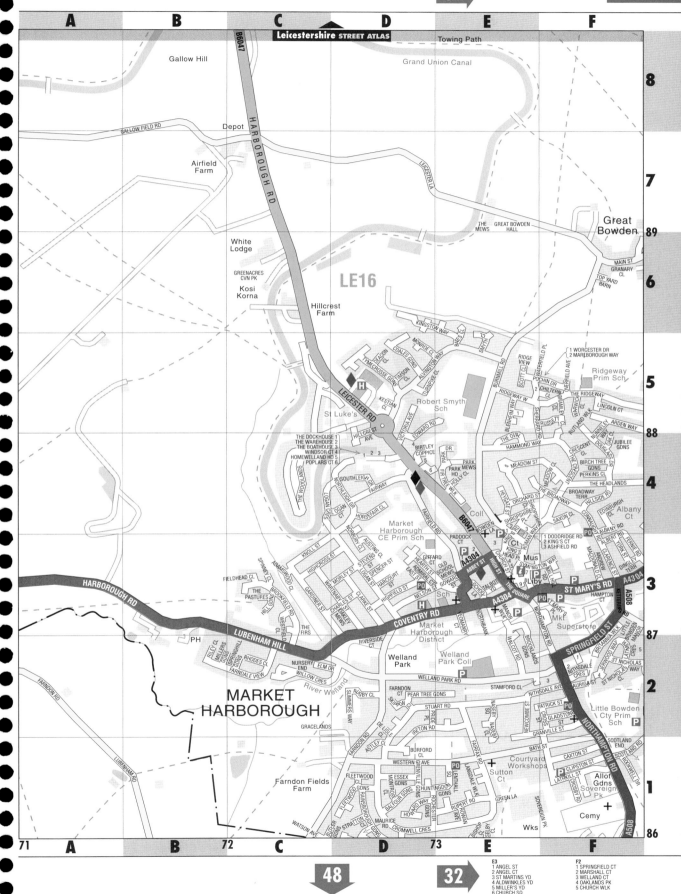

Leicestershire STREET ATLAS

LE16

MARKET HARBOROUGH

E3
1 ANGEL ST
2 ANGEL CT
3 ST MARTINS YD
4 ALDWINKLES YD
5 MILLER'S YD
6 CHURCH SQ
7 FOX YD
8 ADAM AND EVE ST
9 FACTORY LA

F2
1 SPRINGFIELD CT
2 MARSHALL CT
3 WELLAND CT
4 OAKLANDS PK
5 CHURCH WLK

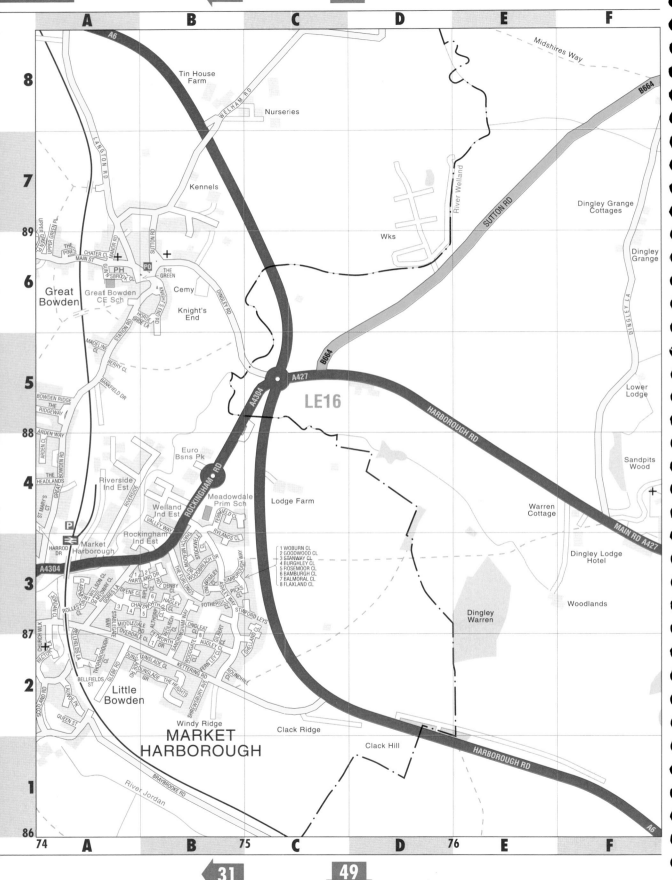

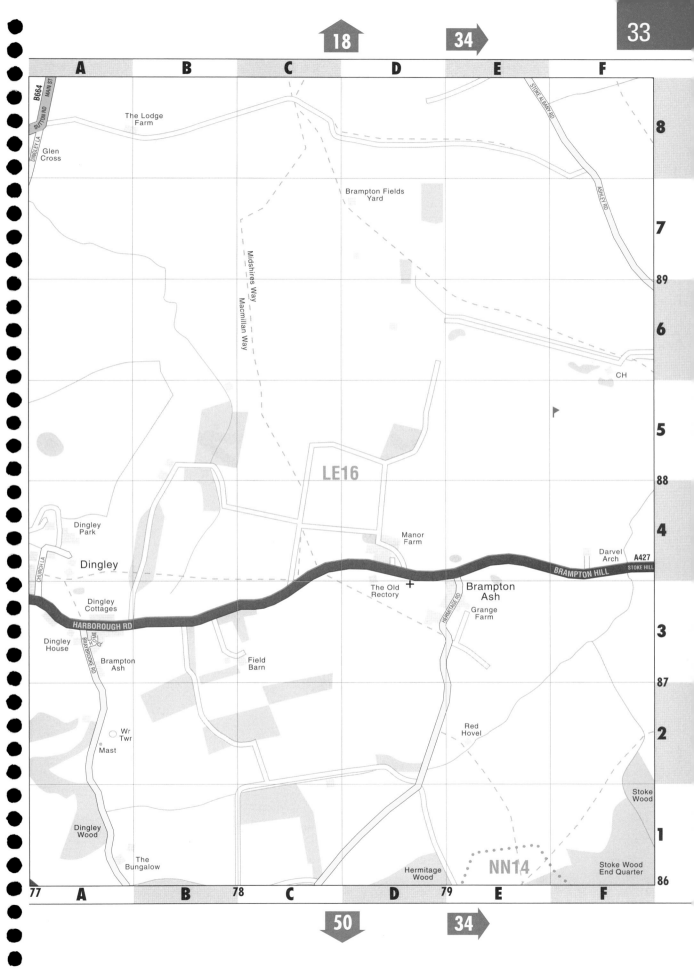

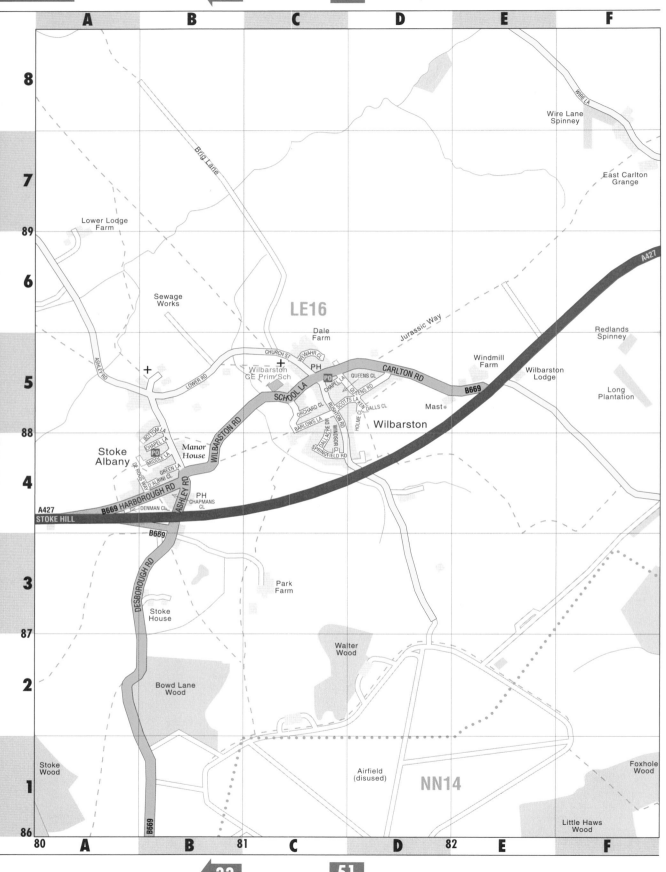

A   B   C   D   E   F

8

7

89

6

LE16

5

88

4

STOKE HILL

3

87

2

1

86

80   A   81   B   C   82   D   E   F

Brig Lane

Wire Lane
Spinney

East Carlton
Grange

Lower Lodge
Farm

Sewage
Works

Jurassic Way

Dale
Farm

Redlands
Spinney

ASHLEY RD

LOWER RD

CHURCH ST

WE-NAHR CL

Wilbarston
GE Prim Sch

PH

PO

CHAPEL LA

CARLTON RD

QUEENS CL

QUEENS RD

Windmill
Farm

Wilbarston
Lodge

B669

Long
Plantation

A427

SCHOOL LA

ORCHARD CL

RUSHTON RD

SCOTTS LA

HOLME CL

DALLS CL

Mast

Wilbarston

BARLOWS LA

WINDSOR CL

DALLACRE DR

SPRINGFIELD RD

WILBARSTON RD

BOTTOM LA

CHAPEL LA

PO

MIDDLE LA

GREEN LA

Manor
House

Stoke
Albany

DE ROOS WAY

D'ALBINI CL

ASHLEY RD

B669 HARBOROUGH RD

PH
CHAPMANS
CL

DENMAN CL

A427

B669

DESBOROUGH RD

Stoke
House

Park
Farm

Walter
Wood

Bowd Lane
Wood

Stoke
Wood

Airfield
(disused)

NN14

Foxhole
Wood

Little Haws
Wood

B669

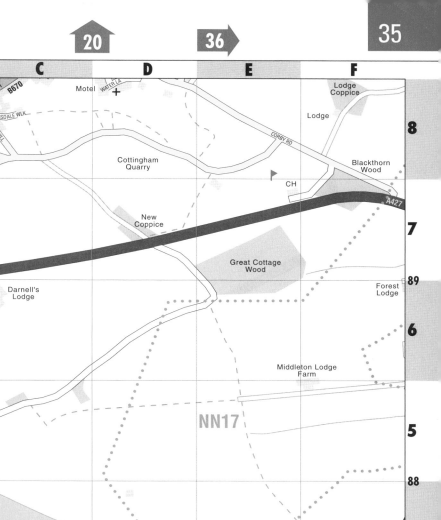

A B C D E F

8

Shoulder of Mutton
Plantation

Middleton

MAIN ST
B670
ASHLEY RD
PEAKE CL
PH
CAMSDALE WLK
SCHOOL HILL
THE HILL

Motel

WATER LA

Lodge
Coppice

Lodge

Jurassic Way

East Carlton
Countryside Park

Cottingham
Quarry

CORBY RD

CH

Blackthorn
Wood

Home
Farm

East Carlton
Hall

New
Coppice

A427

7

WIRE LA

Almshouses

EAST
CARLTON
PK

EAST CARLTON PK

Darnell's
Lodge

Great Cottage
Wood

89

Church La

SN
THE GROVE

East
Carlton

B670

LE16

Forest
Lodge

6

Pipewell Rd

Middleton Lodge
Farm

East Carlton
Lodge

NN17

5

88

Ash
Coppice

4

A6003

Carlton Purlieus

Pipewell Rd

Wood
Farm

Broad
Angle

DANESHOLME RD
DENMARK CL
OLDENBURG RD
OSLO GDNS
BRANDENBURG RD
VIKING WAY

3

87

Askershaw Wood

Bar
Coppice

Swinawe Barn
Plantation

NN18

BRUNSWICK GDNS

HERFORD CL

UPPINGHAM RD

2

Woodlands
Farm

Swinawe
Wood

MINDEN CL
CRESDEN CL
COPENHAGEN RD

NN14

Barrowdykes
Wood

Hedgerow
Spinney

SAXON WAY
NORTH FOLDS
SHIELING CT
Oakley
Hay
Ind Est
GREAT FOLDS RD
A6003

1

Pipewell Wood

86

Monks Arbour
Wood

Rawshaw
Wood

83 A B 84 C D 85 E F

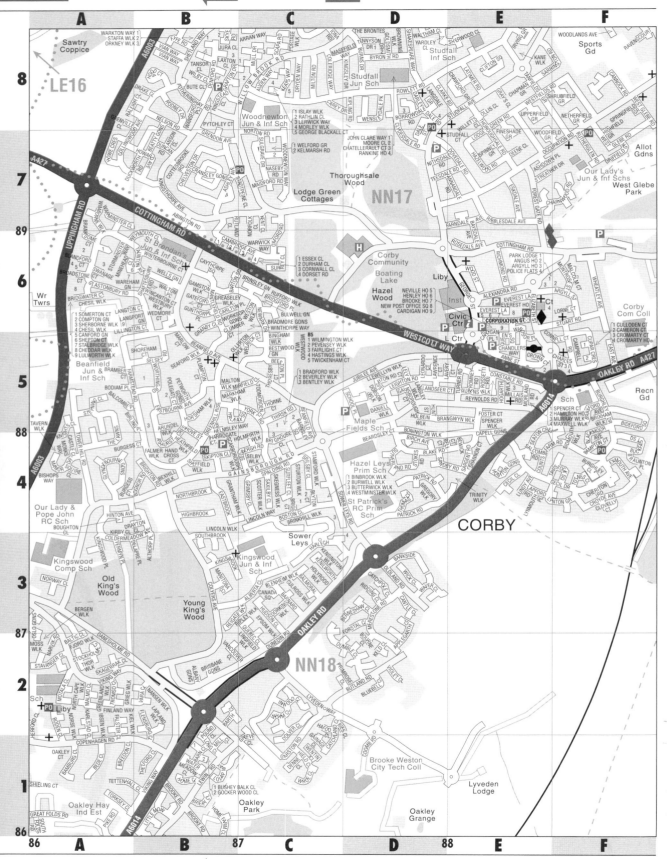

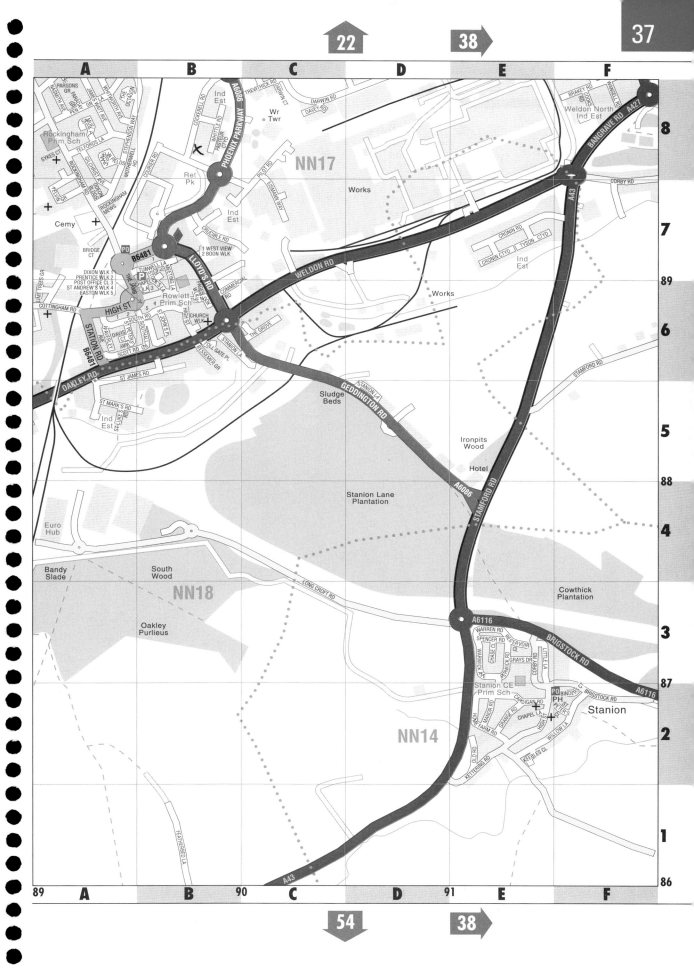

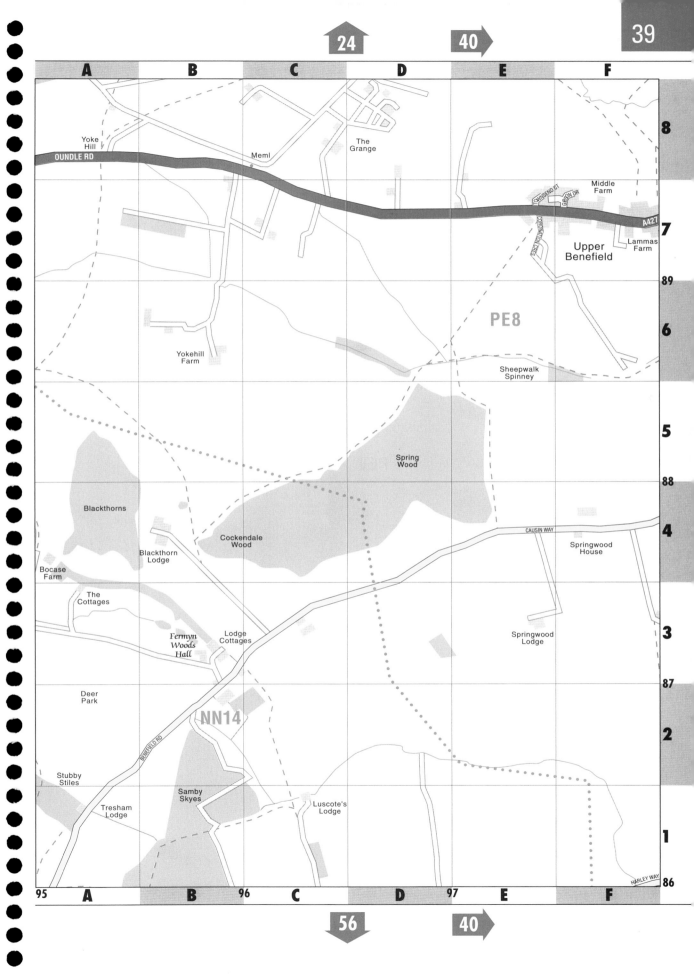

A   B   C   D   E   F

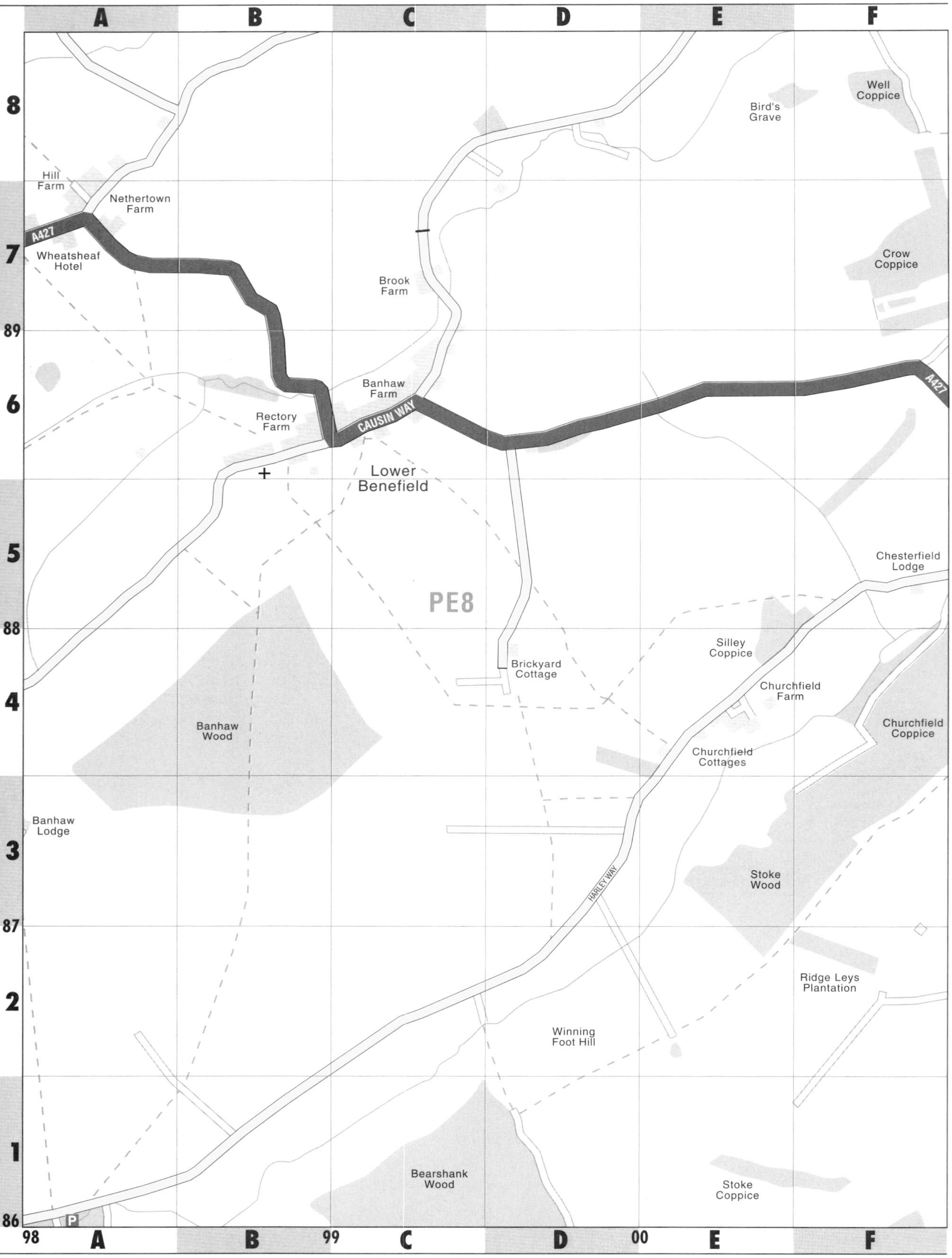

8

Well
Coppice

Bird's
Grave

Hill
Farm

Nethertown
Farm

A427

7

Wheatsheaf
Hotel

Crow
Coppice

Brook
Farm

A427

89

6

Banhaw
Farm

CAUSIN WAY

Rectory
Farm

Lower
Benefield

Chesterfield
Lodge

5

PE8

88

Silley
Coppice

Churchfield
Farm

4

Brickyard
Cottage

Churchfield
Coppice

Banhaw
Wood

Churchfield
Cottages

Banhaw
Lodge

Stoke
Wood

3

HARLEY WAY

87

Ridge Leys
Plantation

2

Winning
Foot Hill

1

Bearshank
Wood

Stoke
Coppice

86

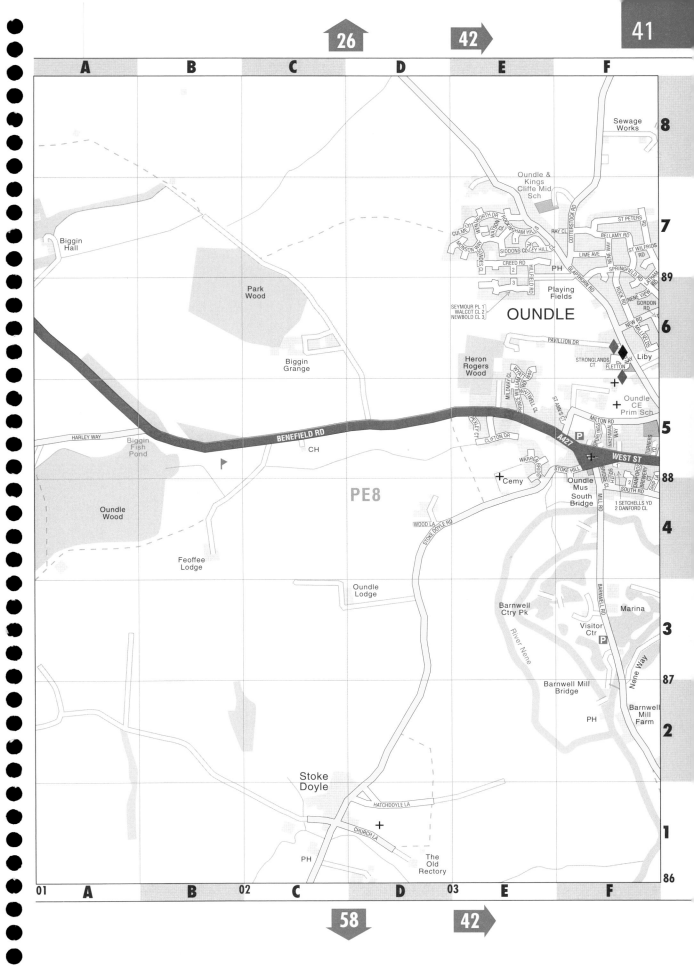

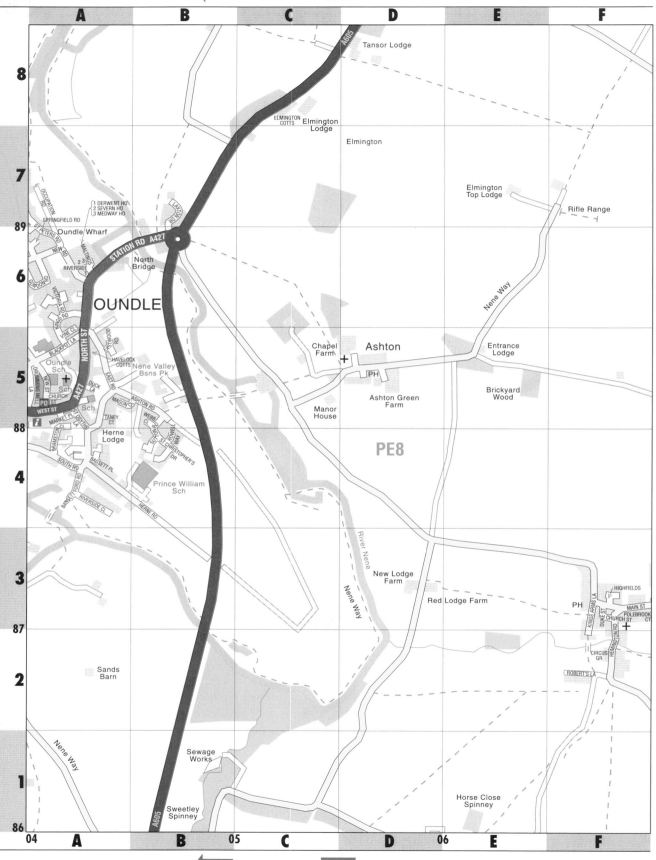

A B C D E F

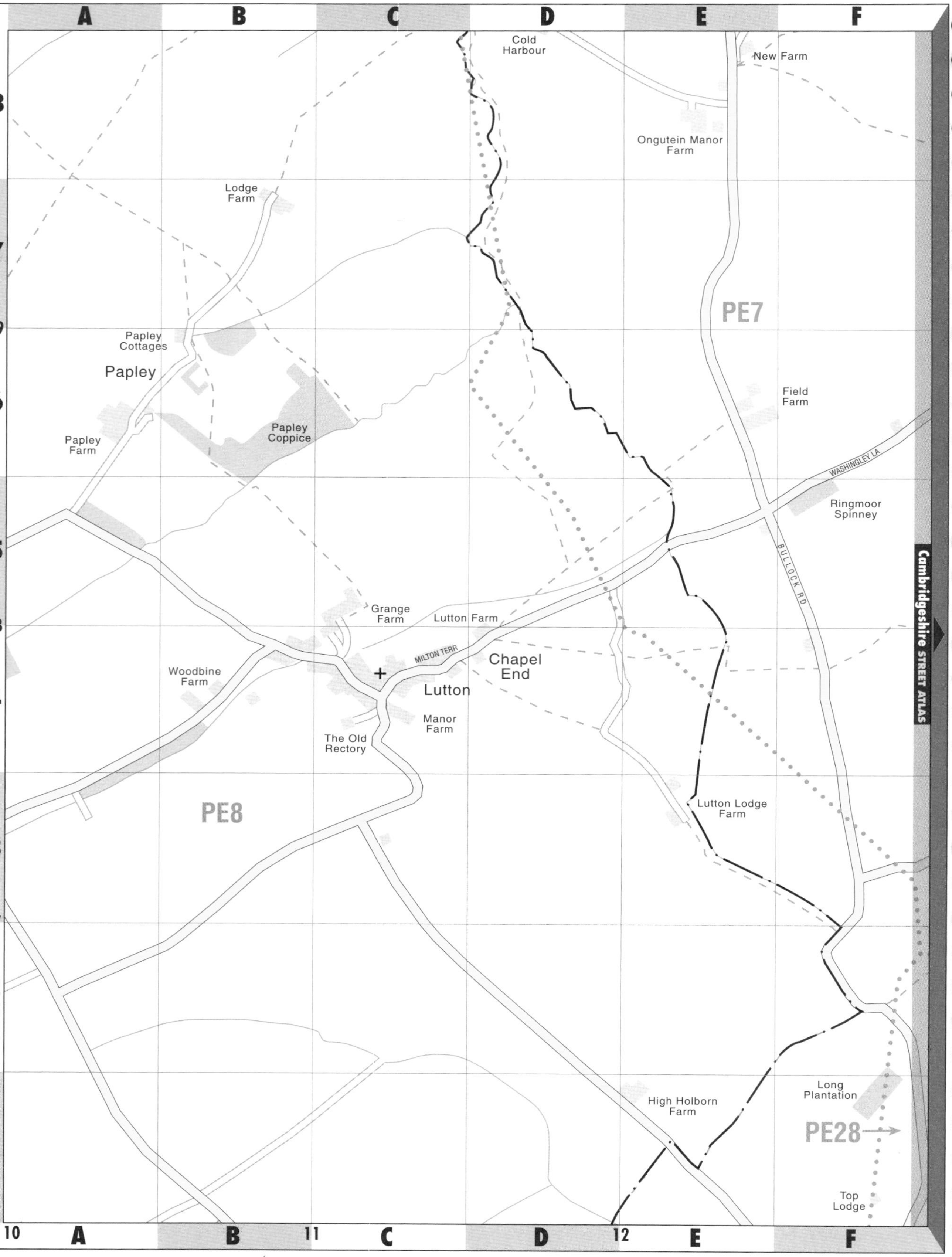

8

7

89

6

5

88

4

3

87

2

87

1

86

Cold
Harbour

New Farm

Ongutein Manor
Farm

PE7

Lodge
Farm

Field
Farm

Papley
Cottages

Papley

Papley
Coppice

WASHINGLEY LA

Ringmoor
Spinney

Papley
Farm

BULLOCK RD

Grange
Farm

Lutton Farm

Chapel
End

MILTON TERR

Woodbine
Farm

Lutton

PE8

Manor
Farm

The Old
Rectory

Lutton Lodge
Farm

High Holborn
Farm

Long
Plantation

PE28→

Top
Lodge

10 A 11 B C 12 D E F

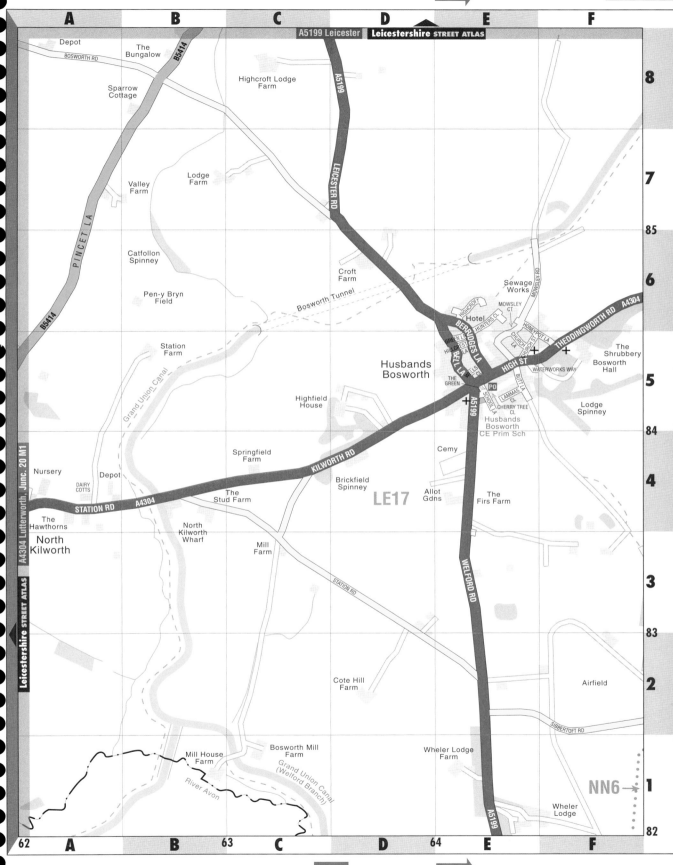

Depot

BOSWORTH RD

The Bungalow

B5414

Sparrow Cottage

Highcroft Lodge Farm

A5199

8

Valley Farm

Lodge Farm

PINCET LA

LEICESTER RD

7

Catfollon Spinney

85

Pen-y Bryn Field

Croft Farm

6

Bosworth Tunnel

Sewage Works

MOWSLEY RD

A4304

THEDDINGWORTH RD

B5414

Station Farm

Grand Union Canal

Hotel

HIGHCROFT

MOWSLEY CT

HUNTERS CL

HONEY POT LA

CHURCH ST

The Shrubbery

Bosworth Hall

GREEN LA

HILLCREST

BERRIDGES LA

BELL LA

Husbands Bosworth

HIGH ST

WATERWORKS WAY

Highfield House

THE GREEN

BUTT LA

PO

LAMMAS CL

CHERRY TREE CL

Lodge Spinney

5

A5199

Springfield Farm

KILWORTH RD

Brickfield Spinney

LE17

Husbands Bosworth CE Prim Sch

Cemy

84

Nursery

Depot

DAIRY COTTS

The Stud Farm

Allot Gdns

The Firs Farm

4

A4304 Lutterworth, Junc. 20 M1

Leicestershire STREET ATLAS

The Hawthorns

STATION RD

A4304

North Kilworth Wharf

North Kilworth

Mill Farm

STATION RD

WELFORD RD

3

83

Cote Hill Farm

Airfield

2

SIBBERTOFT RD

Mill House Farm

Bosworth Mill Farm

Grand Union Canal (Welford Branch)

Wheler Lodge Farm

NN6 →

River Avon

A5199

Wheler Lodge

1

82

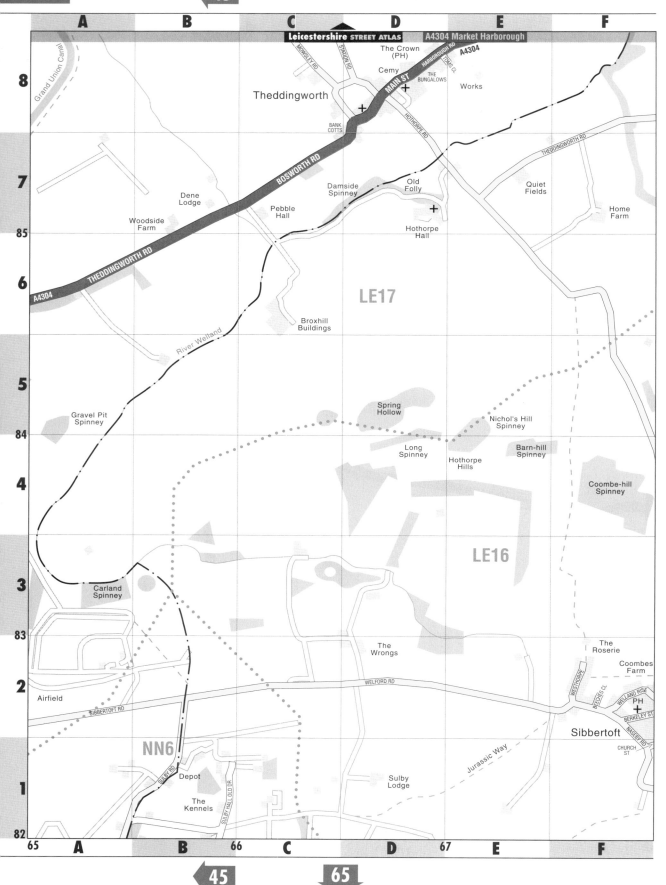

Leicestershire STREET ATLAS

A4304 Market Harborough

Theddingworth

The Crown (PH)

Cemy

Main St

THE BUNGALOWS

Works

BANK COTTS

BOSWORTH RD

MOWSLEY RD

STATION RD

HARBOROUGH RD

HOTHORPE RD

TOMS CL

A4304

Dene Lodge

Pebble Hall

Damside Spinney

Old Folly

Quiet Fields

Home Farm

THEDDINGWORTH RD

Woodside Farm

THEDDINGWORTH RD

Hothorpe Hall

A4304

LE17

Broxhill Buildings

River Welland

Gravel Pit Spinney

Spring Hollow

Nichol's Hill Spinney

Barn-hill Spinney

Long Spinney

Hothorpe Hills

Coombe-hill Spinney

LE16

Carland Spinney

The Wrongs

The Roserie

Coombes Farm

WESTHORPE

BEECHES CL

WELLAND RISE

PH

BERKELEY ST

Airfield

SIBBERTOFT RD

WELFORD RD

Sibbertoft

NASEBY RD

CHURCH ST

NN6

Jurassic Way

SULBY RD

SULBY HALL OLD DR

Depot

Sulby Lodge

The Kennels

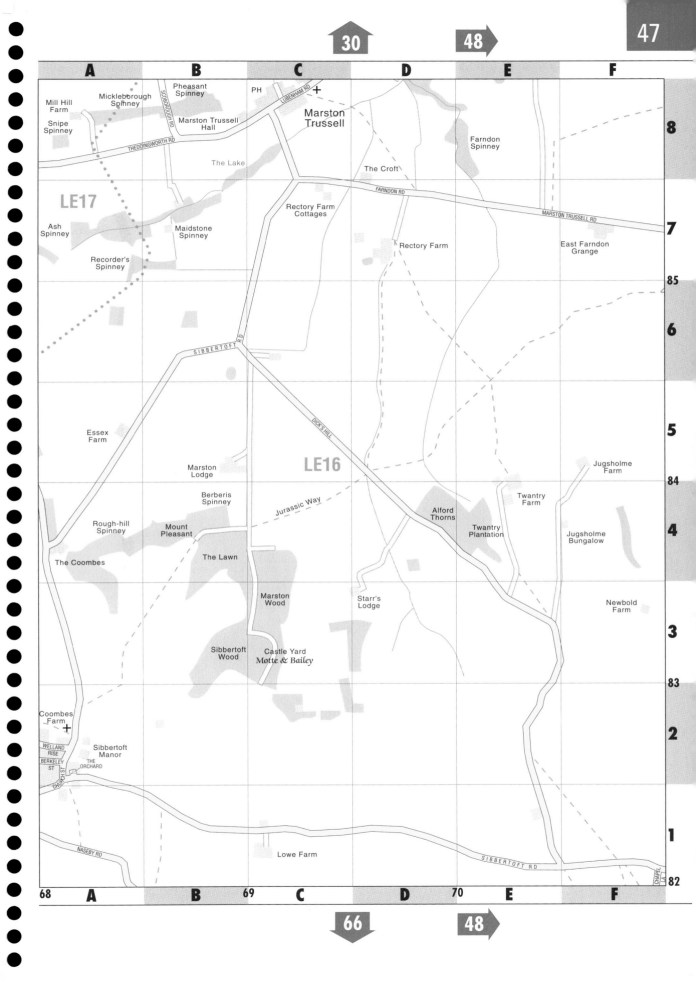

A **B** **C** **D** **E** **F**

8

Luberham Rd
The Sealand
Council Ho's
Harborough Rd

Brierley Farm

Watson Ave
Harrison Cl
Maurice Rd
Barnard Gdns
Gerrard Gdns
Hopton Fields
Rainsborough Gdns
Lindsey Gdns
Ritchie Pk
Jackson Cl
Bishop Cl
Kirby Cl
Argyle Pk
Dallison Cl
Vaughan Cl

Leisure Ctr

Northampton Rd A508

New House Farm

Farndon Fields Prim Sch

7

Marston Trussell Rd
Back La
Main St

Oxendon Lodge Farm

Oxendon Lodge Cottages

Justin Park

The Dales
East Farndon Hall

85
East Farndon

Jurassic Way

CH

6
+ Rectory Ct

Farn Wood

Oxendon Rd
Jurassic Way

Allot Gdns

5

The Lodge

Little Oxendon

LE16

84

Clipston Rd

Farndon Rd

+
Waterloo House

Harborough Rd

4

The Spinney

Mews Cotts
Oxendon Hall

PH

Harborough Rd

3
West End

Main St

Braybrooke Rd

Clipston La

Oxendon House

Great Oxendon

Midshires Way

83

2
Harborough Rd

Clipston Rd

1
Oxendon Rd

Sewage Works

Station Cottage

Oxendon Rd

82
Sibbertoft Rd

A508

71 **A** **B** **72** **C** **D** **73** **E** **F**

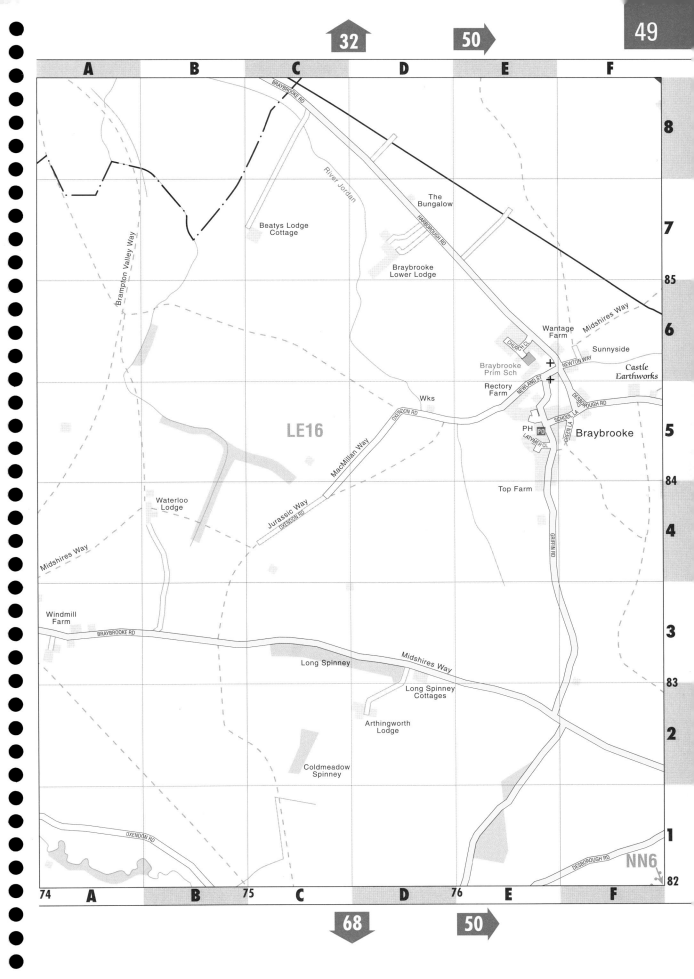

49
33

A   B   C   D   E   F

8 Commons Farm

Midshires Way

Hermitage Wood

Birch Quarter

Rogues Quarter

Brampton Wood

Pond Quarter

Hermitage Cottages

The Hermitage

B576

7 HARBOROUGH RD

A6

Tires Quarter

Jurassic Way
Midshires Way
MacMillan Way

Eckland Lodge

Hotel

Glebe Cottage

BRAMPTON WOOD LA

85 Park Hill Farm

Eckland Lodge Farm

Garden Ctr

Dob Hall Farm

6

Factory

B669

STOKE RD

5 The Bungalow

Smallholding

The Grange

LE16

Wyndie Rydge Farm

NN14

84 Lodge Farm

Humfrey's Lodge

ASHFORD LEA 1
BIRCHVALE CT 2
EDALE GN 3
HEATHCOTE GR 4
TIDESWELL CL 5
CHELMORTON VALE 6
HATHERSAGE CL 7
DOVEDALE GR 8
HOWDEN GN 9

B576

4

Upper Lodge

BRIDGE RD
Wr Twr
GAPSTILE CL

PETRIE PL
ASH GR
HILLTOP AVE
HILLTOP CL
OAKHAM CL
RUTLAND CL
PEASLANDS
LINLEY DRI

WORTHINGWORTH RD
CASTLETON
BUXTON DR
MATLOCK WAY
THE RIDINGS
BRAYBROOKE RD
CASTLETON
EYAM CL
ASHBOURNE DR
LANGDALE
Loatlands Prim Sch

GRINDLEFORD CL
STERNDALE CL
UPPER DENE
OAK TREE CL

BLEAKLOW CL
WHITEHILL RD
HARRINGTON RD
ALEXANDRA RD

3 Lodge Farm

GREEN LA

CYPRESS CL
NEVILLE WAY
ADDISON RD

COAL PORT CL
MINTON CL

MEISSENE AVE
PRINCE RUPERT AVE

AYNSLEY CL
DOULTON CL
WEDGWOOD CL

83

Works

2 Manor Farm

WOODWELL HILL
FEDERATION AVE

WINDSOR AVE
PIONEER AVE

NN6

DESBOROUGH RD

1

Loatland Lodge Farm

A6

82

77   A   B   78   C   D   79   E   F

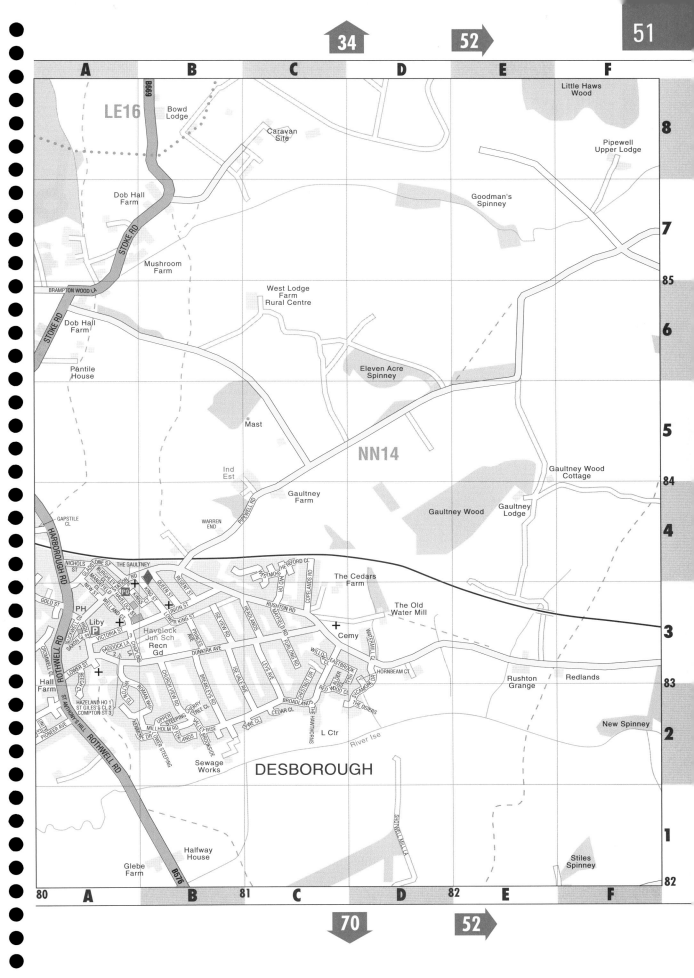

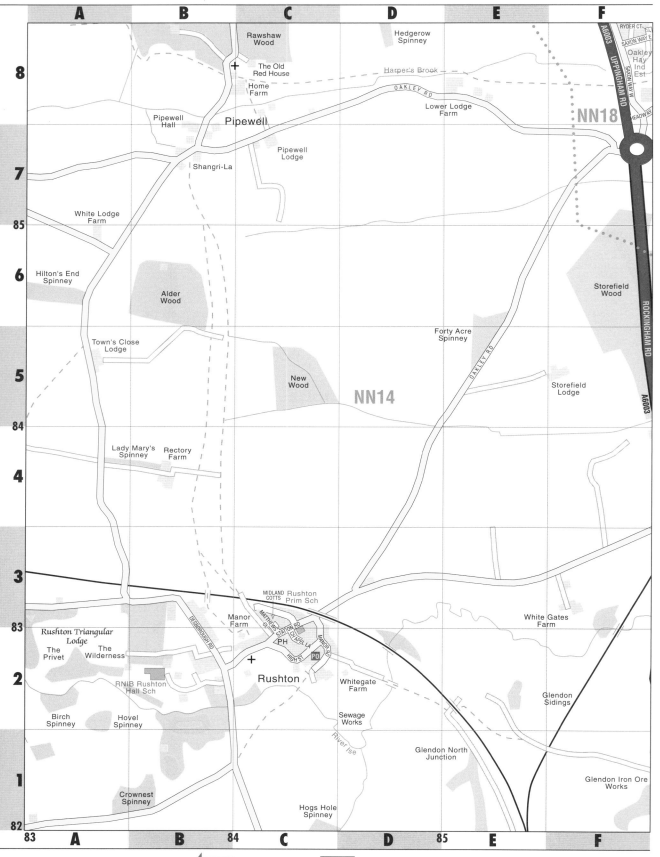

A   B   C   D   E   F

8

Rawshaw
Wood

Hedgerow
Spinney

The Old
Red House

Harper's Brook

OAKLEY RD

Home
Farm

Lower Lodge
Farm

NN18

Pipewell
Hall

Pipewell

7

Shangri-La

Pipewell
Lodge

85

White Lodge
Farm

6

Hilton's End
Spinney

Storefield
Wood

Alder
Wood

Forty Acre
Spinney

Town's Close
Lodge

5

New
Wood

Storefield
Lodge

NN14

OAKLEY RD

84

Lady Mary's
Spinney

Rectory
Farm

4

3

MIDLAND
COTTS

Rushton
Prim Sch

83

DESBOROUGH RD

Manor
Farm

MATTHEWS CL

STATION RD

CHAPEL LA

MANOR RD

White Gates
Farm

Rushton Triangular
Lodge

The
Privet

The
Wilderness

PH

HIGH ST

PO

RNIB Rushton
Hall Sch

Rushton

2

Whitegate
Farm

Glendon
Sidings

Birch
Spinney

Hovel
Spinney

Sewage
Works

Glendon North
Junction

1

Crownest
Spinney

River Ise

Hogs Hole
Spinney

Glendon Iron Ore
Works

82

83   A   B   84   C   D   85   E   F

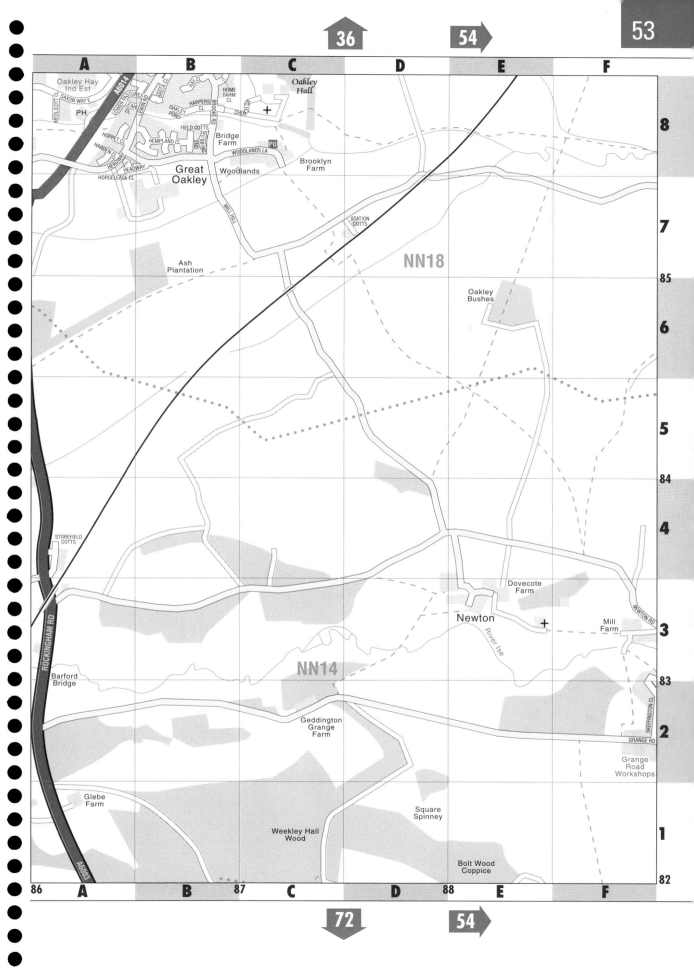

53
37

A B C D E F

8

The Manor Farm

Moat Farm

Little Oakley

Rising Bridge

A43

FEATHERBED LA

7 NN18

Start Wood

Great Hames Sale

Birch Tree Lawn

85

Cobley Lodge Farm

Woodlands

Great Brand

Geddington Chase

Pedlar's Wells

6

Crab Tree Hills

Langley Quarter

Newton Spinney

Little Brand

Pale Hill

5

Chase Lodge

STAMFORD RD

Clay Dick

84

Cotton Hills

Lardours Wood

4

Bright Trees

Red House

NN14

BRIGHT TREES RD

3 NEWTON RD

CHASE VIEW RD

FERN DALE CL

THE WOODLANDS

WOOD ST

Geddington

1 LEE'S WAY
2 WORMLEIGHTON WAY
3 BAKEHOUSE HILL
4 CHURCH HILL
5 CASTLE GDNS

QUEEN ELEANOR RD

WEST ST

MALTING LA

HALL'S CL

MAGDALENE CL

83 DALLINGTON CL

Queen Eleanor's Cross PH

BRIDGE ST

CHASE FARM

Round Coppice

Pitmans Sale

Sedge Hills

SKEFFINGTON CL

CHAPEL LA

PRIORY CL

Geddington CE Prim Sch

GRAFTON RD

2

NEW RD

QUEEN ST

PO

Sawmill

Kennel Quarter

Boughton Wood

GRANGE RD

MILBY LA

THOMAS RIPPIN CL

Bancroft Wood

1 KETTERING RD

Sewage Works

New Ground Spinney

Boughton Wood Lodge

Thorny Coppice

82 A43 STAMFORD RD

89 A 90 B C D 91 E F

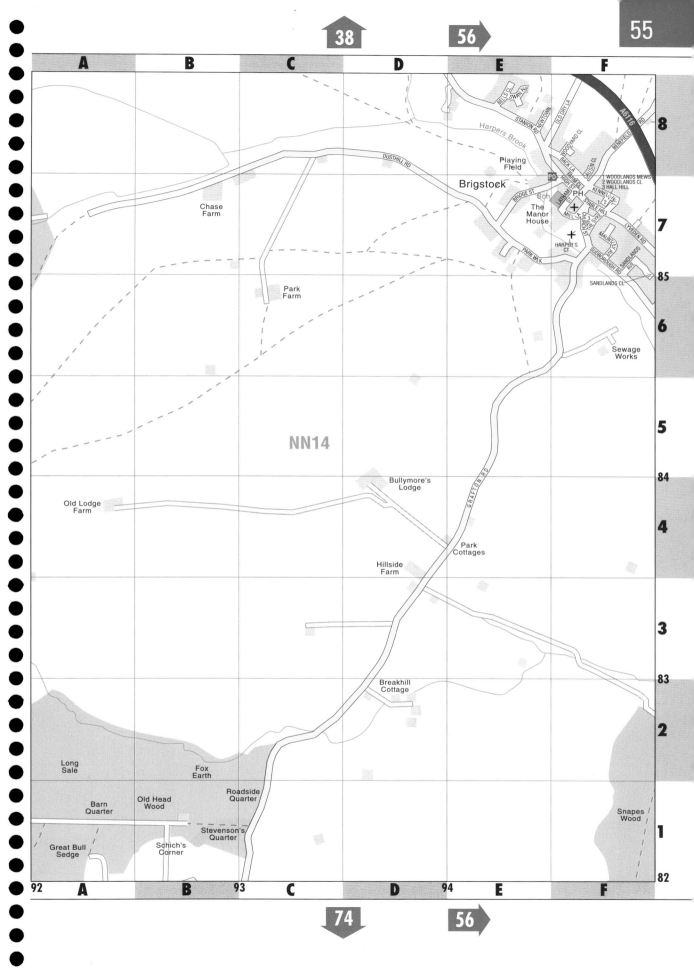

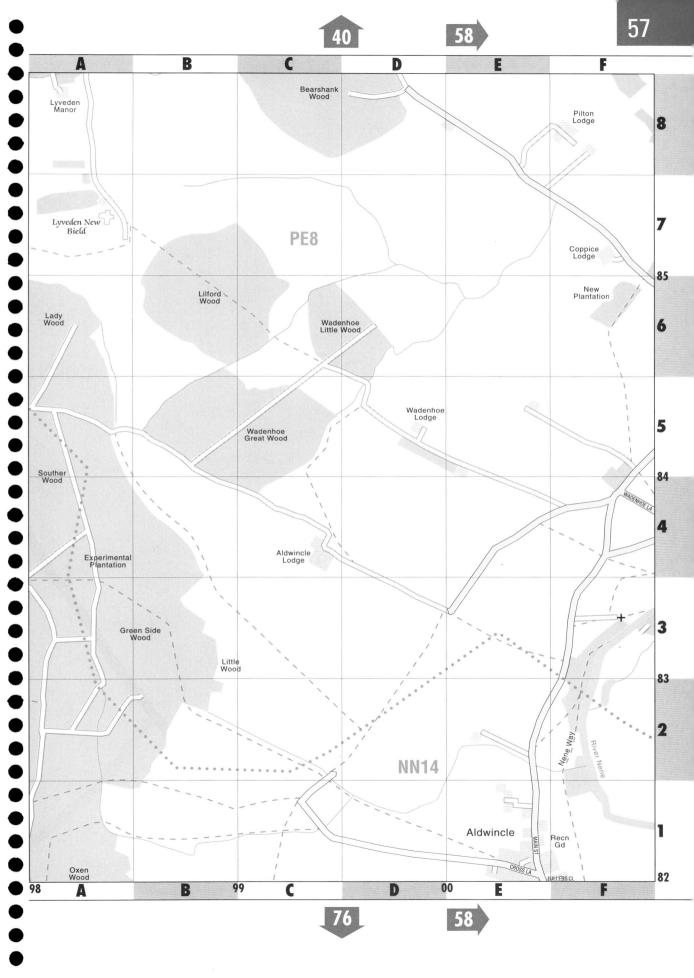

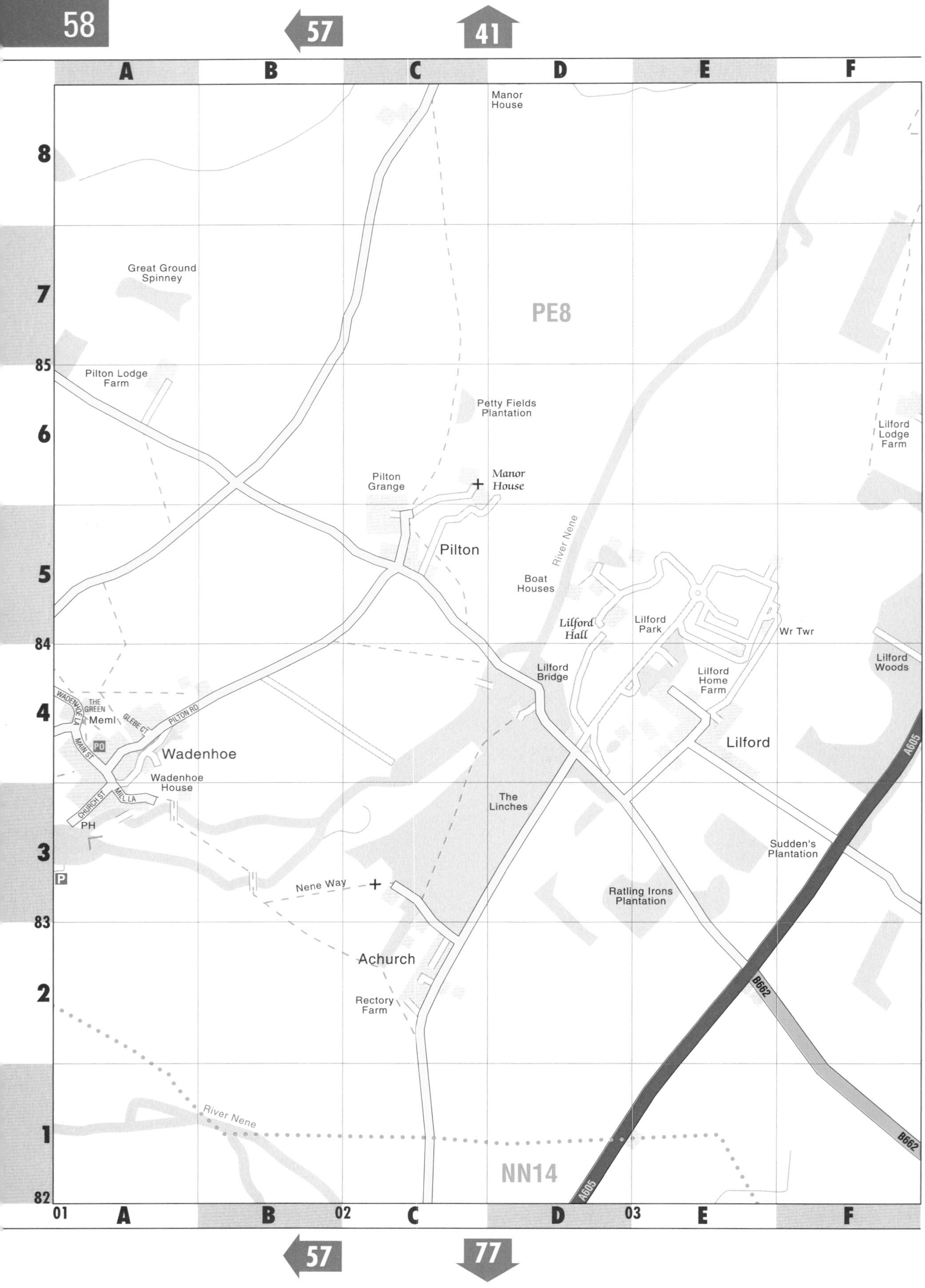

57
41

A **B** **C** **D** **E** **F**

Manor House

8

Great Ground Spinney

7

PE8

85

Pilton Lodge Farm

6

Petty Fields Plantation

Lilford Lodge Farm

Pilton Grange

Manor House

Pilton

River Nene

5

Boat Houses

Lilford Park

Wr Twr

Lilford Hall

84

Lilford Woods

Lilford Bridge

Lilford Home Farm

WADENHOE LA
THE GREEN
GLEBE CT
PILTON RD

4

Meml

PO

Wadenhoe

MAIN ST

Lilford

Wadenhoe House

MILL LA

CHURCH ST

PH

The Linches

3

Sudden's Plantation

P

Nene Way

Ratling Irons Plantation

83

Achurch

2

Rectory Farm

B662

River Nene

1

A605

NN14

B662

82

A 01 **B** 02 **C** 03 **D** **E** **F**

57
77

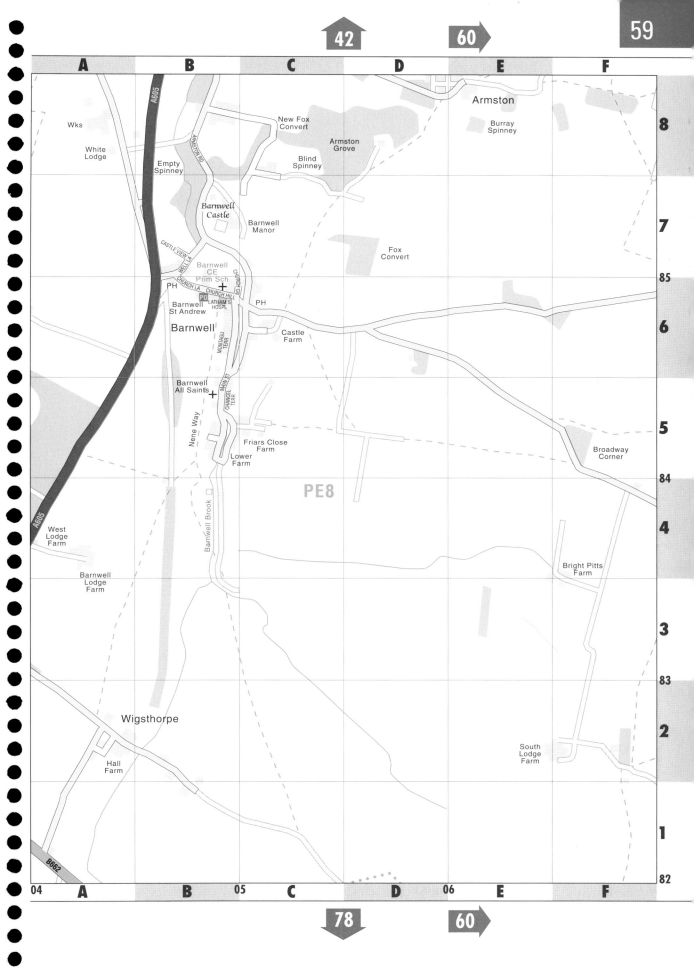

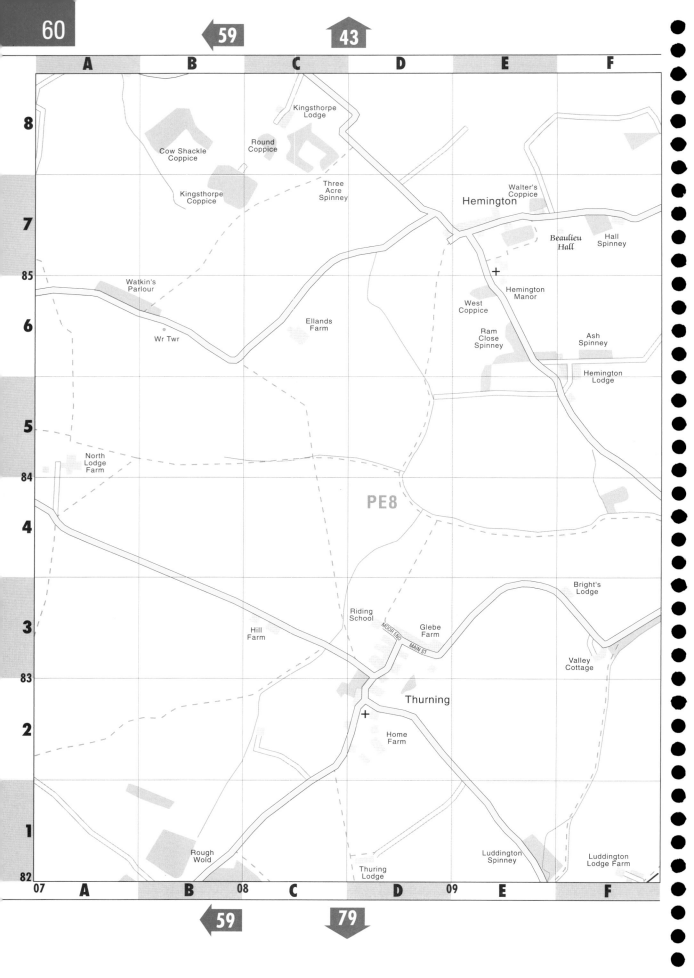

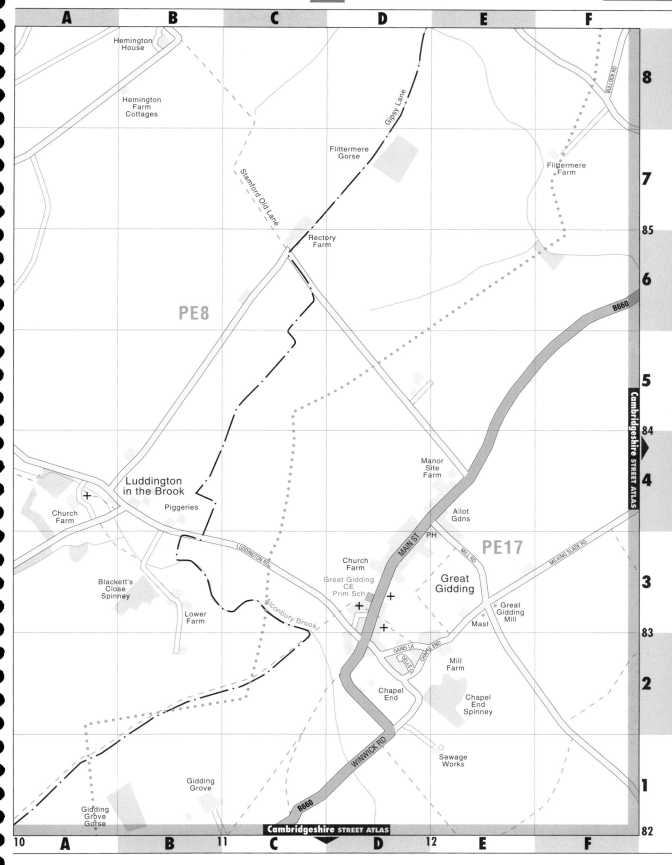

A   B   C   D   E   F

8

Hemington House

Hemington Farm Cottages

Gipsy Lane

BULLOCK RD

7

Flittermere Gorse

Stamford Old Lane

Flittermere Farm

85

6

Rectory Farm

PE8

B660

5

84

Manor Site Farm

4

Luddington in the Brook

Piggeries

Allot Gdns

PE17

Church Farm

Church Farm

Great Gidding CE Prim Sch

MAIN ST

PH

MILL RD

MILKING SLADE RD

Great Gidding

Great Gidding Mill

3

Blackett's Close Spinney

LUDDINGTON RD

Alconbury Brook

Mast

83

Lower Farm

GAINS LA

CHAPEL END

BELL'S CL

Mill Farm

2

Chapel End

Chapel End Spinney

WINWICK RD

Sewage Works

Gidding Grove

1

B660

Gidding Grove Gorse

82

10   A   B   11   C   D   12   E   F

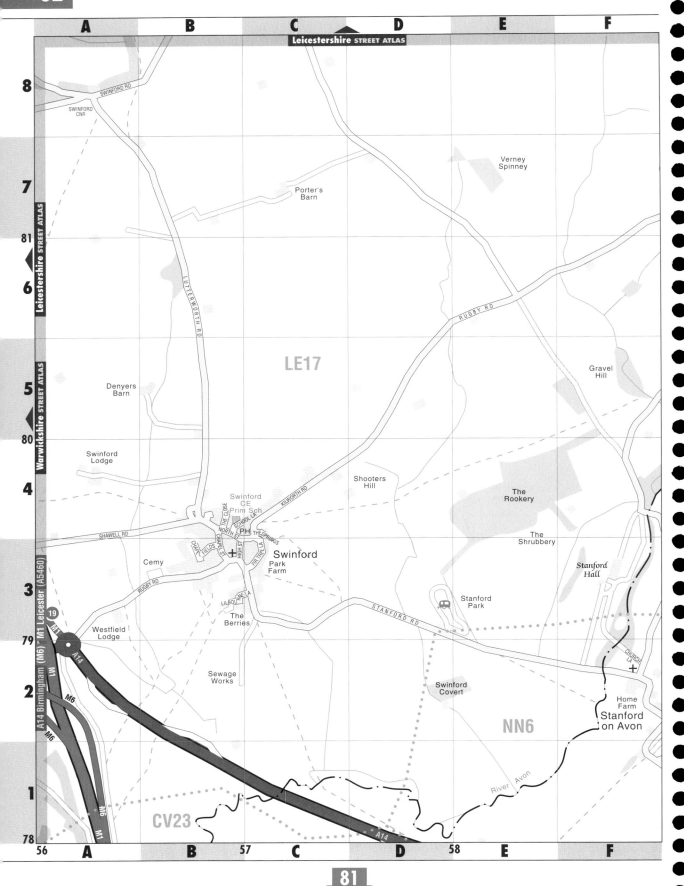

Leicestershire STREET ATLAS

Warwickshire STREET ATLAS

SWINFORD RD

SWINFORD CNR

Porter's Barn

Verney Spinney

LUTTERWORTH RD

RUGBY RD

LE17

Gravel Hill

Denyers Barn

Swinford Lodge

Shooters Hill

The Rookery

KILWORTH RD

The Shrubbery

Swinford CE Prim Sch

SCHOOL LA

Stanford Hall

THE CLOSE

PH

THE SPRINGS

SHAWELL RD

NORTH ST

HIGH ST

Swinford Park Farm

CHAPEL ST

CHAP- FIELDS

FIR TREE LA

Cemy

RUGBY RD

LILBOU- NE LA

The Berries

Stanford Park

STANFORD RD

A14 Birmingham (M6) ° M1 Leicester (A5460)

M1 Leicester

19

M1

A14

Westfield Lodge

Sewage Works

Swinford Covert

CHURCH

M6

Home Farm

Stanford on Avon

NN6

M6

River Avon

M1

CV23

A14

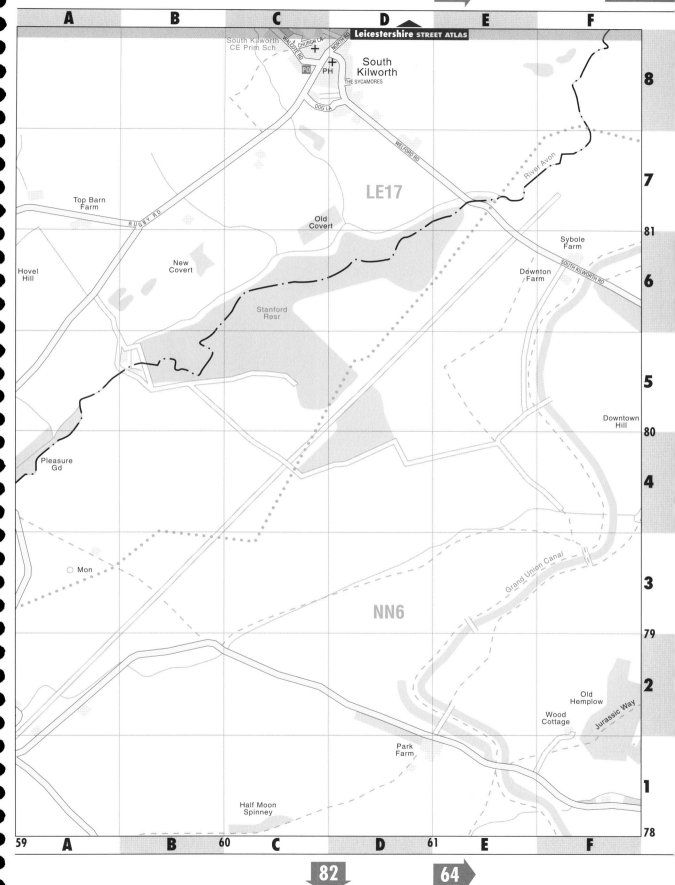

Leicestershire STREET ATLAS

63
45

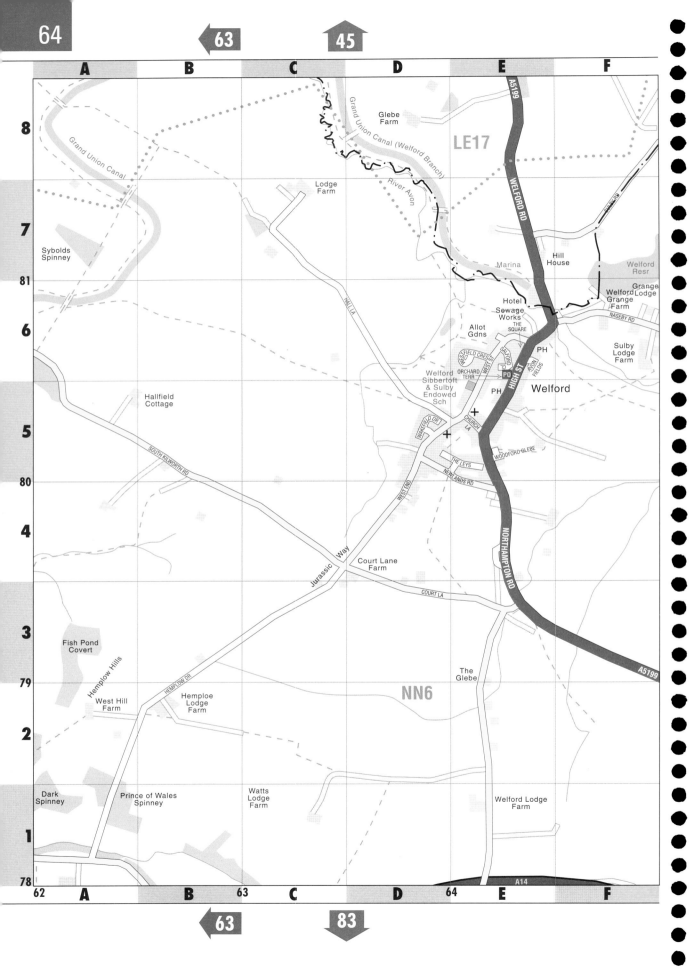

63
83

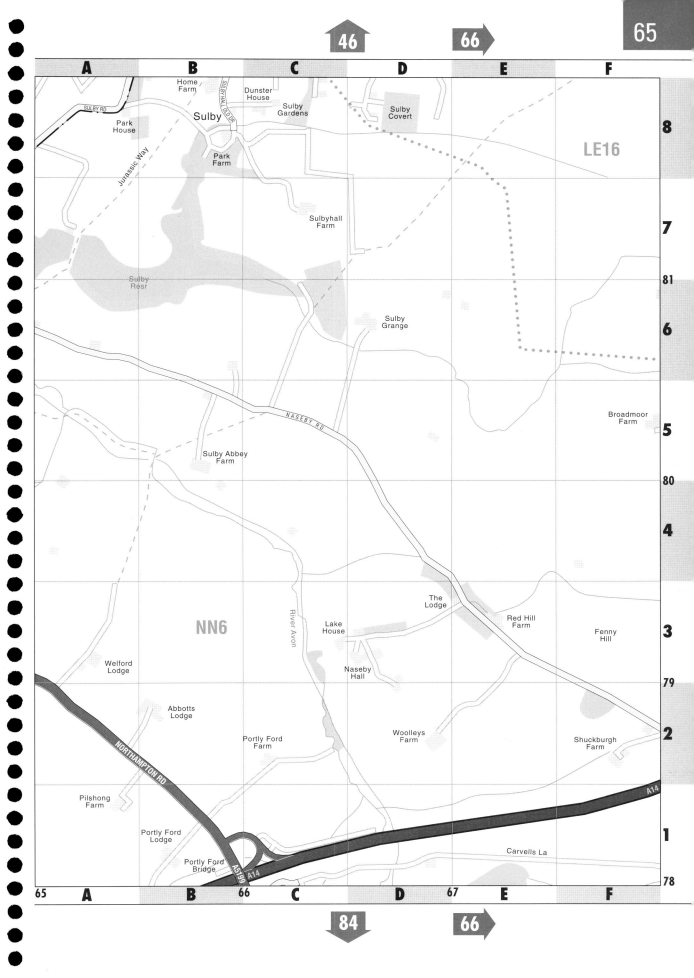

A B C D E F

8 7 81 6 5 80 4 79 3 2 1 78

The Paddocks

NASEBY RD

Longhold Lodge

LE16

Clipston

The Old Manse

NOBOLD CT

CHAPEL LA

GOLD ST

PEG'S LA

NASEBY RD

MARECROFT

The Chestnuts

Prince Rupert's Farm

Dust Hill

Dust Hill Farm

Long Hold Spinney

Mon

P

Naseby Covert

The Plantation

Paisnell Spinney

Naseby Field

Mill Hill

New-House Farm

A14

Mast

Mill Hill Farm

NN6

Clothill Spinney

Obelisk

HALL CL

NEWLANDS

A14

Naseby

PH

Naseby CE Prim Sch

CHURCH ST

HIGH ST

Carvells La

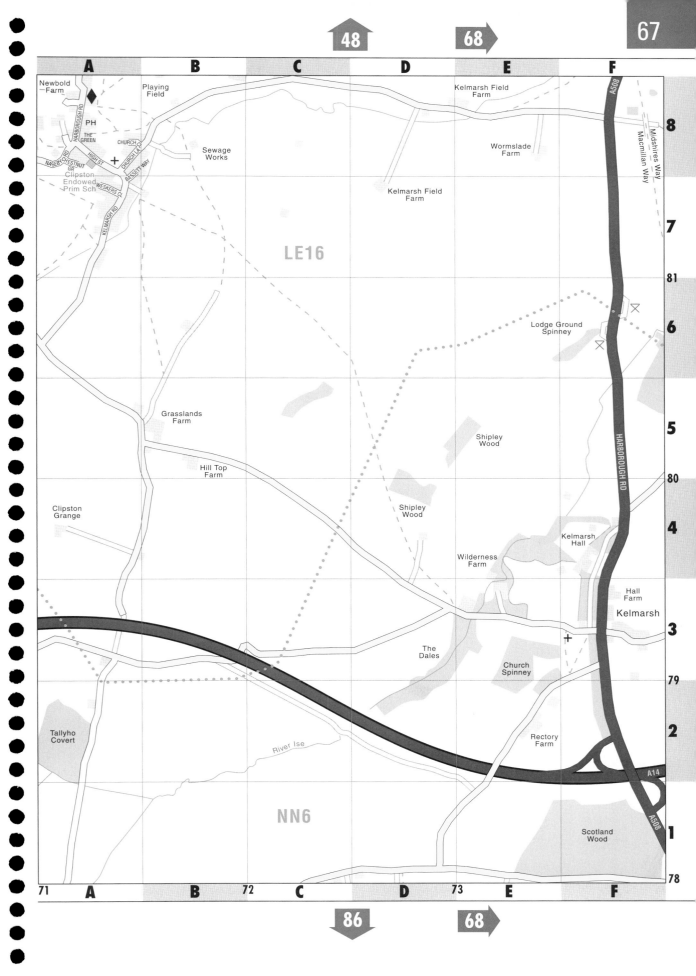

48

68

A B C D E F

Newbold Farm

Playing Field

Kelmarsh Field Farm

PH

THE GREEN

HARBOROUGH RD

CHURCH CL

Sewage Works

Wormslade Farm

8

NASEBY

CHESTNUT GR

HIGH ST

BASSETT WAY

CHURCH LA

Clipston Endowed Prim Sch

WESKERS CL

KELMARSH RD

Kelmarsh Field Farm

Midshires Way

Macmillan Way

A508

LE16

7

81

Lodge Ground Spinney

6

Grasslands Farm

Shipley Wood

HARBOROUGH RD

5

Hill Top Farm

80

Clipston Grange

Shipley Wood

Kelmarsh Hall

4

Wilderness Farm

Hall Farm

Kelmarsh

3

The Dales

Church Spinney

79

Tallyho Covert

River Ise

Rectory Farm

A14

2

NN6

Scotland Wood

A508

1

78

67
49

A **B** **C** **D** **E** **F**

8

Arthingworth

OXENDON RD

Manor House

DESBOROUGH RD

BRAYBROOKE RD

PO

HALL CL

HOME FARM

GR

CHURCH FARM WAY

INN YARD CT

PH

7

Arthingworth Lodge

LE16

KELMARSH RD

Sidom's Ford

81

River Ise

6

Clark's Spinney

Warren Hill Farm

Langborough Wood

PH

Rabbithill Spinney

Midshires Way

Warren Hill

5

Midshires Way
Macmillan Way

80

Far Hill

Sunderland Wood

4

New Covert

Tunnels

Wheatfield Lodge Farm

3

Top Lodge

Johnson's Covert

NN6

Warth Lodge

A14

79

Aviation Mus

2

Sewage Works

Blue Covert

A14

Cobdell

1

Scotland Wood Farm

Green Lane Crossing

Draughton Lodge

HARBOROUGH RD

A508

78

67
87

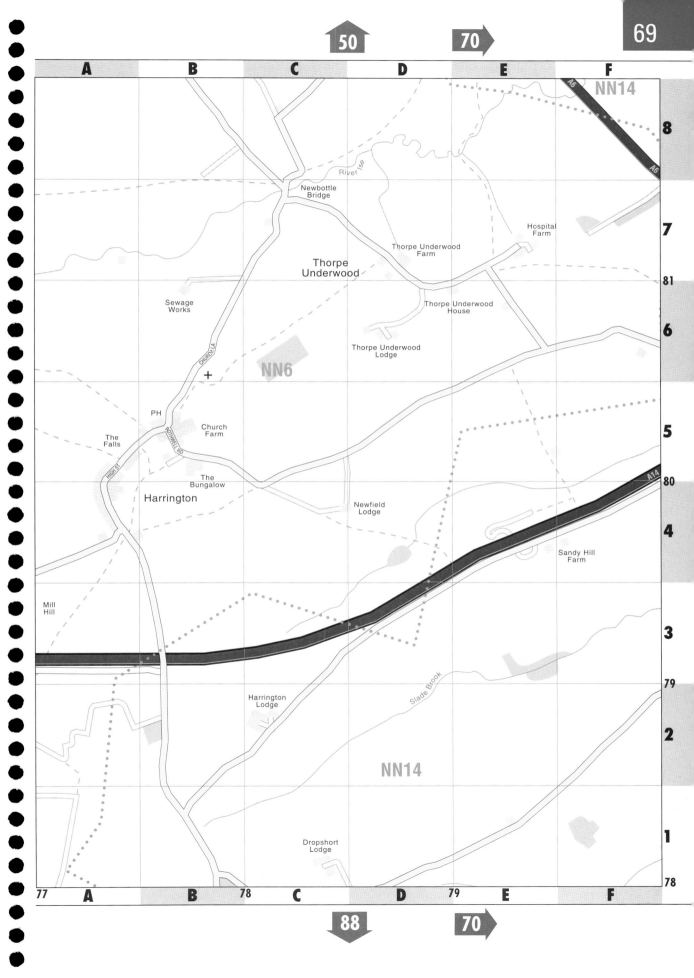

A B C D E F

8

7

81

6

5

80

4

3

79

2

1

78

ROTHWELL

Grange Farm

Hospital Farm

Styles Lodge

Suffolk Villa

SHOTWELL MILL LA

RUSHTON RD

CAMBRIDGE ST

Allot Gdns Wr Twr

SCOTT AVE

TEBBUTT CL

DESBOROUGH RD

Rothwell Jun Sch

OXFORD ST

SPENCER ST

BUSWELL RISE

DRAKE CL

NELSON

CONNOLLY DR

Montsaye Com Coll

NUNNERY AVE

KINGSLEY RD

Rothwell Victoria Inf Sch

CECIL ST

THE AVENUE

LITTLEWOOD ST

JOHN SMITH AVE

TEGG WAY

PLAYFORD CL

CONNOLLY CL

GREENING RD

TENNYSON RD

GLADSTONE ST

MADAMS GDN

NEW ST

CROSS ST

NORTON ST

UPTON

GLEN VALLEY AVE

BALFOUR DR

BARLOW

ADAMS DR

LEWIN CL

THE MALTINGS 1 WHITEMAN LA 2 NEWHAM CL 3

ASHGATE ST

Liby

BELL HILL

CRISPIN ST

STANLEY ST

LANCASTER RD

LIVINGSTONE CL

GIBBONS DR

TESBY RD

SHARMAN WAY

BUTLIN

MAUNSELL RISE

MANOR RD

CROWN LA

HIGH MILL AVE

HIGH ST

SCHOOL LA

CASTLE HILL

TRESHAM ST

HOSPITAL HILL

ROCK HILL

CHURCHILL

RAGSDALE

GLENDON RD

RALEIGH CL

BEVERLEY CL

UNDERWOOD RD

CHARLES

TRINITY RD

FOX ST

GROVE CT

BRIDGE ST

BRIDGE HO

SPRING

CORONATION AVE

BAFFIN

CHICHESTER

ROSE CL

BURDITT CL

VICKERS CL

MATSON CL

DAISY BANK AVE

COGAN

MOORFIELD RD

MOORFIELD GDN

TRINITY RD

HARRINGTON RD

ELIZABETH RD

GLOUCESTER CT

THE CRESCENT

MEETING LA

EDSON RD

SUN HILL

FLOOD LA

GORDON ST

JUBILEE ST

KETTERING RD

PONDER ST

NARREL HILL

WELL LA

MYH

HANS CL

DAVIS

GREENVILLE

CABOT CL

COLUMBUS CRES

BLYTHE CL

TASMAN WAY

LARSEN CL

MAGELLAN CL

1 WHEELWRIGHT HO 2 FORGE HO 3 AUSTIN HO

MEADOW RD

EDINBURGH CL

JOHN BEVERLY MEWS 1 HOBBS HILL 2 CLIPSTONE CT 3

B576

B576

Factory

Cemy

KETTERING RD

Nunnery Farm

A6

A14

A14

Rothwell Lodge

NN16

Slade Brook

NN14

Orton

Bay House Farm

MAIN ST

Manor Farm

Orton Lodge

Thorpe Malsor Resr

The Cedar House

Three Chimneys

Loddington

ORTON RD

RICHARDSONS LA

Uplands Farm

STERLING CT

MAIN ST

PH

Prim Sch

STABLE YD

PARK

NOS CL

HARRINGTON RD

CRANSLEY RD

Loddington Hall

HALL GDNS

HARRINGTON RD

MANSLEY LA

Nus Hill Lodge

Cransley Resr

B576

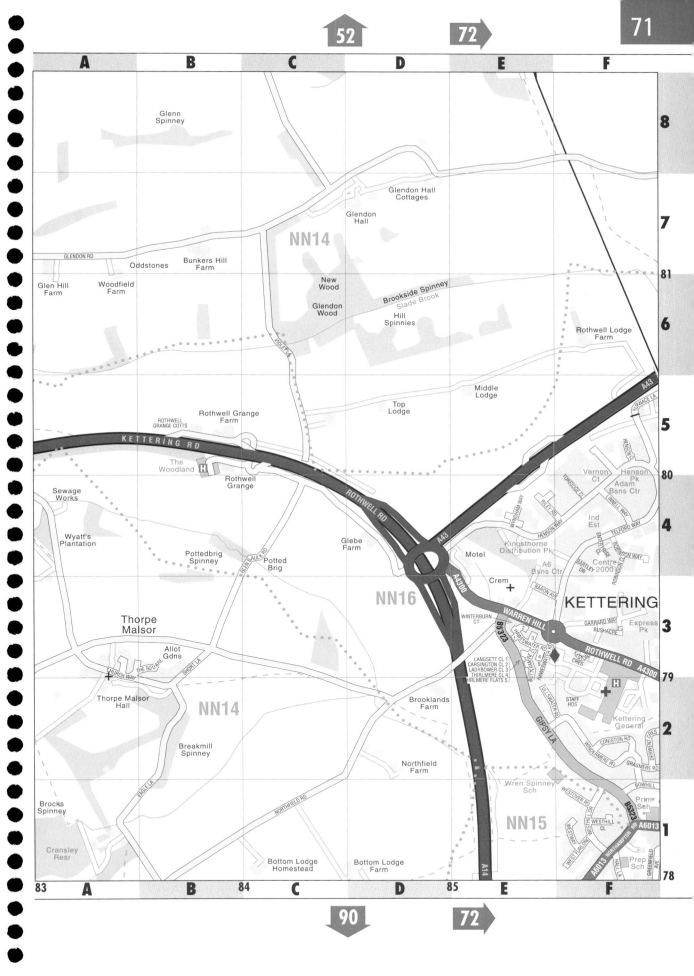

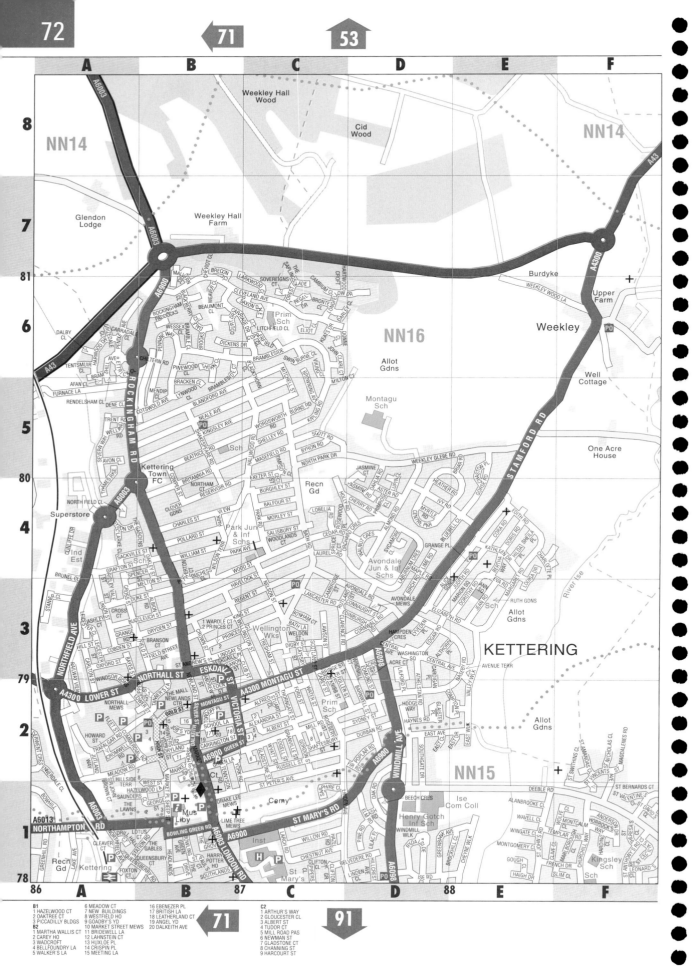

71
53

NN14

NN14

8

Weekley Hall
Wood

Cid
Wood

7

NN14

Glendon
Lodge

Weekley Hall
Farm

81

Burdyke

Upper
Farm

6

Weekley

DALBY
CL

NN16

Well
Cottage

Allot
Gdns

Montagu
Sch

One Acre
House

5

80

Recn
Gd

4

Superstore

Kettering
Town
FC

Ind
Est

Park Jun
& Inf
Schs

Avondale
Jun & Inf
Schs

Allot
Gdns

KETTERING

3

Avenue Terr

Allot
Gdns

79

A4300 LOWER RD

NORTHALL ST

ESKDALE ST

A4300 MONTAGU ST

A6008

Prim
Sch

NN15

2

The Mall
Northall
Mews

Prim
Sch

Henry Gotch
Inf Sch

Ise
Com Coll

Kingsley
Sch

1

A6013
NORTHAMPTON RD

Mus
Liby

ST MARY'S RD

Inst

78

Recn
Gd

Kettering

St
Mary's

71

91

86   A   87   B   C   87   D   88   E   F

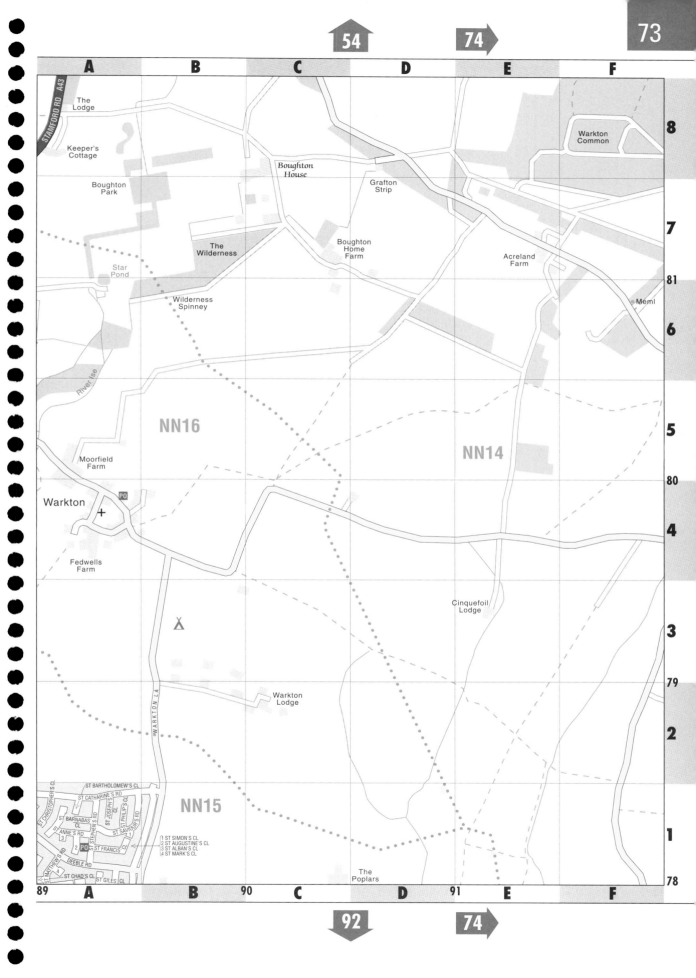

A B C D E F

8

Round
Green

Long
Lown
Wood

7

Grafton Park
Wood

81

Ekens'
Copse

6

Freer
Wood

Little
Green
Wood

Park
Lodge

Keeper's
Cottage

Sale
Hill
Wood

Grafton
Park
Farm

PO

5

Grafton
Underwood

NN14

Whitehouse
Farm

The
Manor
House

80

Kirtley
Barn

Kirtley
Coppice

4

Sewage
Works

3

Cranford
Wood

79

Glebe
Farm

Bushy
Covert

SLIPTON LA

2

GORDON TERR

HIGH ST

THE
HOMESTEAD

1

78

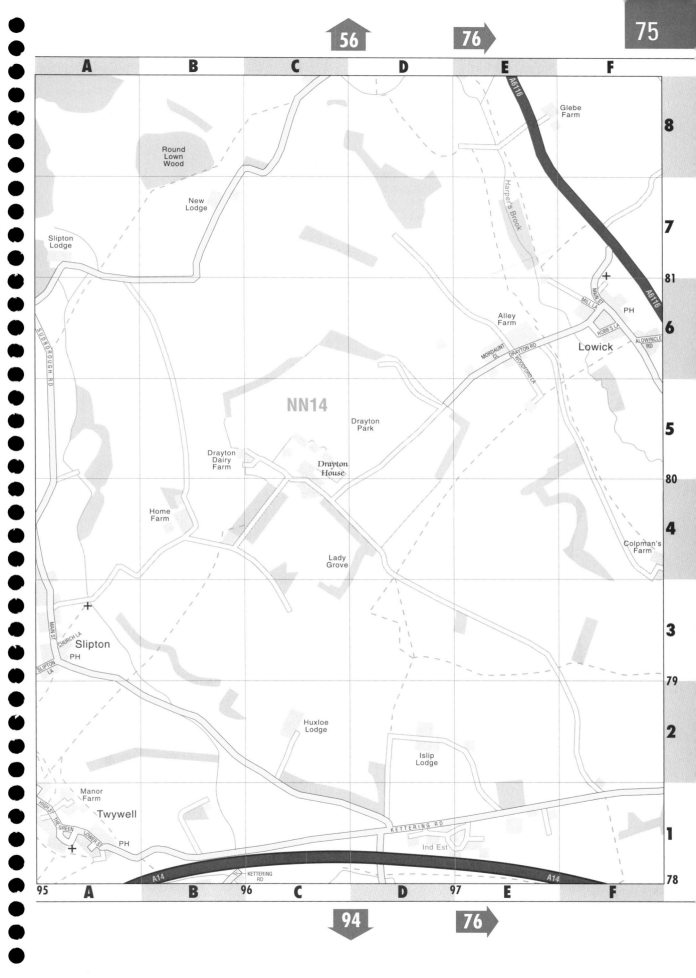

75 57

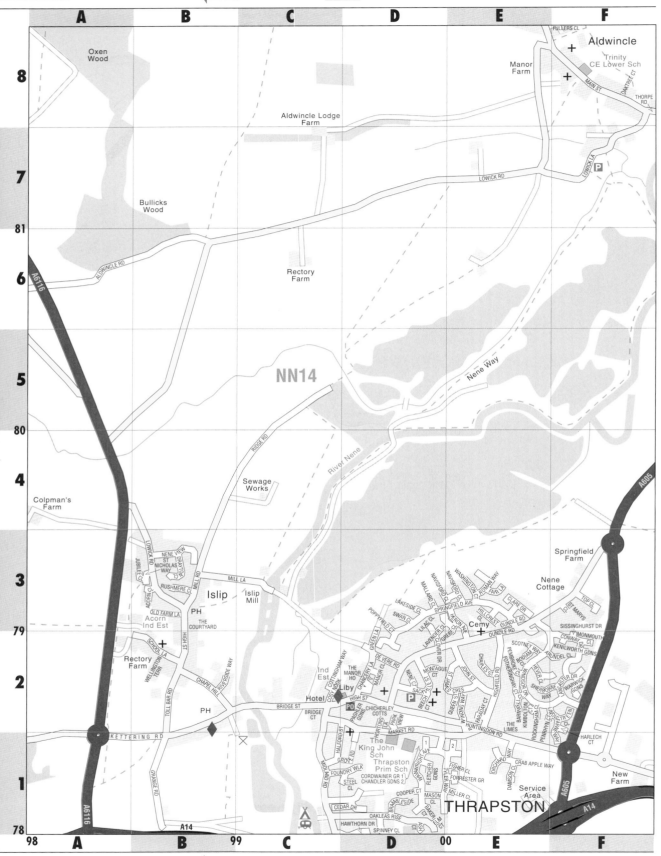

8

Oxen
Wood

FULLERS CL

Aldwincle

Manor
Farm

Trinity
CE Lower Sch

OAKTREE CT

MAIN ST

THORPE
RD

Aldwincle Lodge
Farm

7

LOWICK RD

LOWICK LA

P

81

Bullicks
Wood

ALDWINCLE RD

A6116

6

Rectory
Farm

NN14

Nene Way

5

80

River Nene

RIDGE RD

Springfield
Farm

Nene
Cottage

4

Colpman's
Farm

Sewage
Works

A605

3

LOWICK RD

NENE
VIEW

ST
NICHOLAS
WAY

DRAYTON
CL

MILL RD

MILL LA

Islip

Islip
Mill

NAVISFORD CL

NAVISFORD CL

ROTMAN WAY

WASHINGTON CL

CLARE RD

SPRINGFIELD AVE

TOP CL

ST MARYS

SISSINGHURST DR

MONMOUTH
CL

JUBILEE
CL

ACORN CL

RUSHMERE CL

OLD FARM LA

PH

THE
COURTYARD

LAKESIDE CL

SWAN CL

POPPYFIELD CL

LILAC CL

LAVENDER CL

CLOVER DR

ACORN RD

GREEN LA

HILLCREST
CL

Cemy

OUNDLE CL

OUNDLE RD

CONWAY
CL

SCOTNEY WAY

KENILWORTH GDNS

79

Acorn
Ind Est

CHASE CL

BODIAM

FOTHERINGHAY CL

PEMBROKE CL

HEVER CL

ARUNDEL CL

2

Rectory
Farm

SCHOOL LA

WELLINGTON
TERR

HIGH ST

CHAPEL HILL

RIVERSIDE WAY

Ind
Est

COTTINGHAM WAY

THE
MANOR
HO

CHANCERY LA

DE VERE RD

NENE CT

MONTAGUE
CT

JOHN ST

QUEEN ST

CRES

WINDING WAY

JOHN ST

SHERBORNE
CT

ANCASTER DR

WARWICK
GDNS

TOLL BAR RD

PH

Hotel

Liby

PO

BRIDGE ST

PASHLER

GDNS

BRIDGE
CT

HIGH ST

SACKVILLE ST

BEECH

CHICHERLEY
COTTS

LA PARK
VIEW

FARADAY CT

BARNWELL

KIMBOLTON

ROCKINGHAM CL

PENRHYN CL

HUNTINGDON RD

THE
LIMES

HARLECH
CT

1

KETTERING RD

ORANGE RD

MIDLAND RD

HALFORD ST

THE

GROVE

FOUNDRY WLK

STEEL
CL

COOPER CT

CEDAR DR

The
King John
Sch

Thrapston
Prim Sch

MARKET RD

CORDWAINER GR 1
CHANDLER GDNS 2

WAINWRIGHT

1

2

FLETCHER
GDNS

DAMSON CL

ORCHARD
WAY

FISHER CL

FORRESTER GR

MILLER CL

MASON
CL

BRAMBLESIDE

DANGER CL

ASK

CRAB APPLE WAY

Service
Area

New
Farm

A605

THRAPSTON

78

A6116

A14

HAWTHORN DR

OAKLEAS RISE

SPINNEY CL

A14

75 95

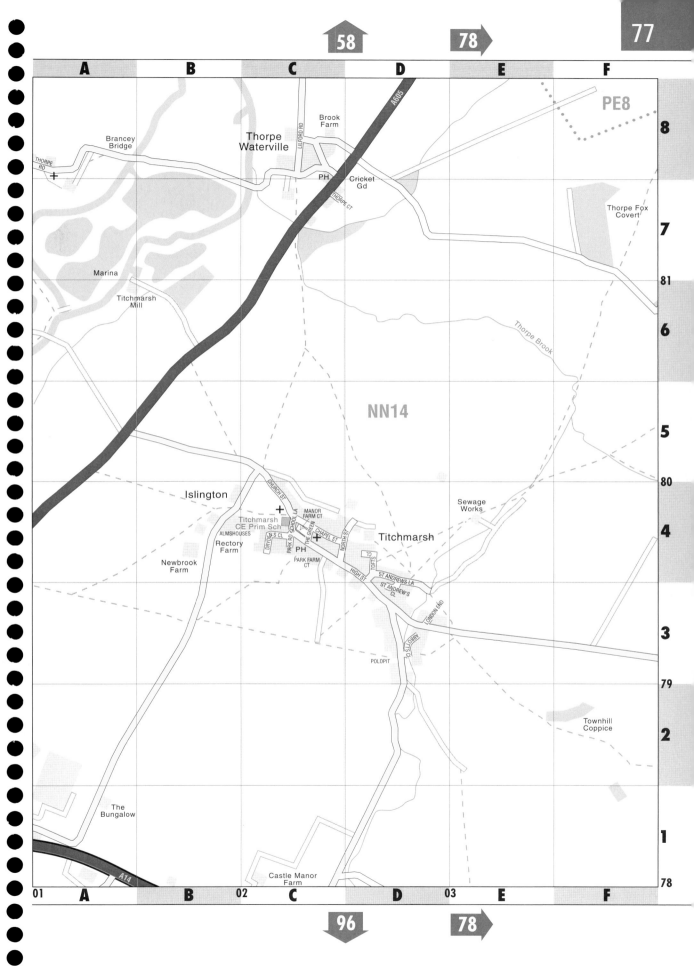

A B C D E F

PE8

8

Brancey
Bridge

Brook
Farm

A605

LILFORD RD

Thorpe
Waterville

Thorpe Fox
Covert

THORPE
RD

PH

Cricket
Gd

THORPE CT

7

Marina

81

Titchmarsh
Mill

Thorpe Brook

6

NN14

5

80

Islington

CHURCH ST

Sewage
Works

MANOR
FARM CT

Titchmarsh
CE Prim Sch

4

ALMSHOUSES

CHAPEL ST

NORTH ST

PARK RD

Titchmarsh

Rectory
Farm

DRYDEN'S CL

PH

THE GREEN

Newbrook
Farm

SCHOOL LA

ST ANDREWS LA

PARK FARM
CT

TOFTS

HIGH ST

ST ANDREW'S
CL

LONDON END

3

TO ABBEY

POLOPIT

79

Townhill
Coppice

2

The
Bungalow

1

A14

Castle Manor
Farm

78

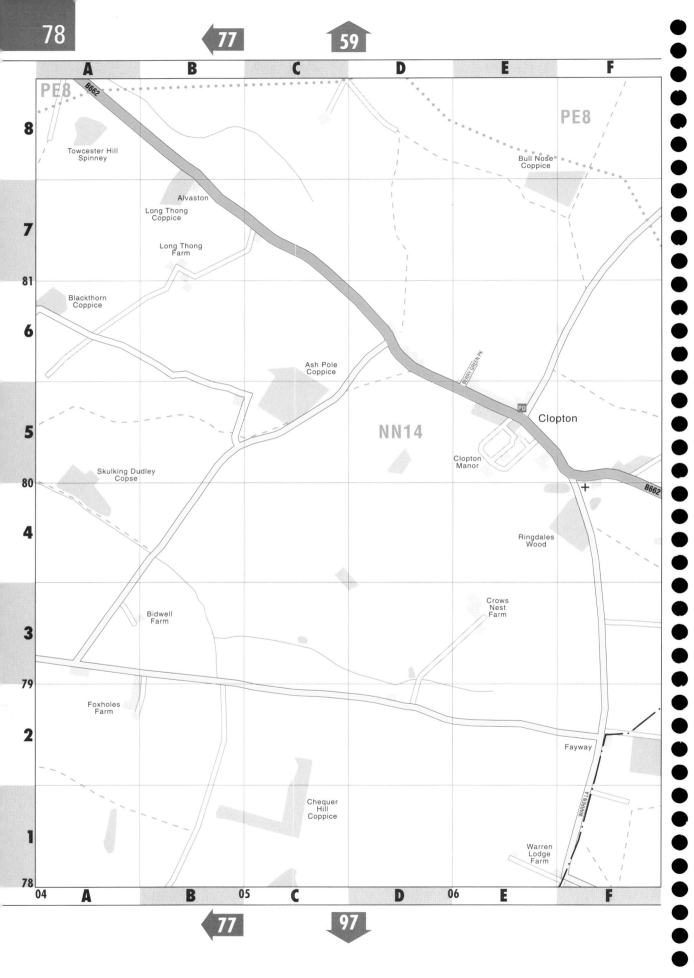

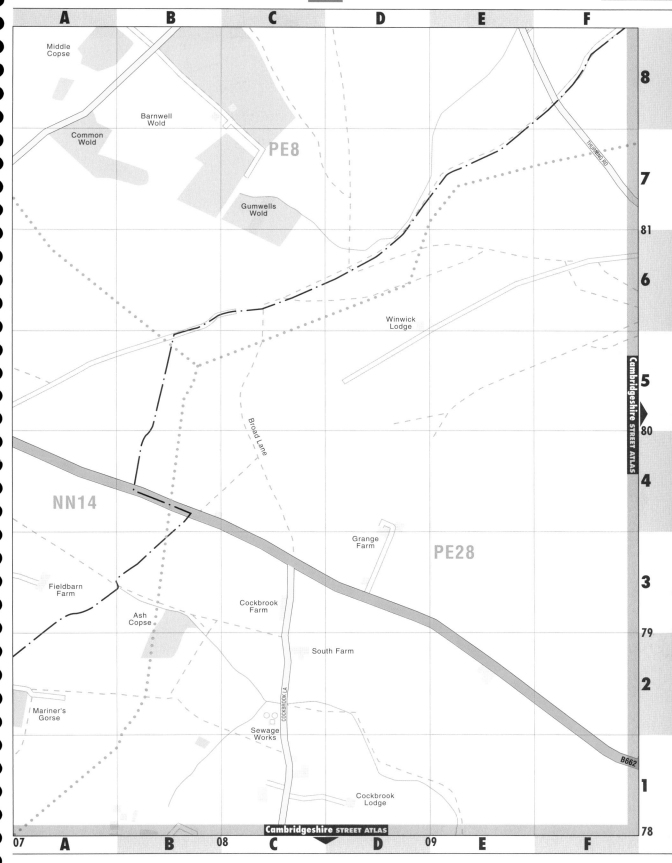

A B C D E F

8

7

81

6

PE8

Middle
Copse

Barnwell
Wold

Common
Wold

Gumwells
Wold

THURNING RD

Winwick
Lodge

Broad Lane

5

80

4

NN14

Grange
Farm

PE28

Fieldbarn
Farm

Ash
Copse

Cockbrook
Farm

South Farm

3

79

Mariner's
Gorse

COCKBROOK LA

Sewage
Works

2

B662

Cockbrook
Lodge

1

78

07 A B 08 C D 09 E F

Cambridgeshire STREET ATLAS

LE17

Dow Bridge

River Avon

Mill Farm

St Thomas Cross (PH)

NEWTON RD

B5414

Lilbourne Furze

Dunsmore Farm

Lilbourne Gorse

RUGBY RD

Cemy

Clifton upon Dunsmore

BUCKWELL LA

Dunsmore

Almond Bank

Magpie Lodge Farm

Manor Farm

NORTH RD

MANOR LA

ROBERT LN

CHURCH ST

HAYARD CL

B5414

PH

MAIN ST

ALLANS CL

ORWELL CL

EVERARD CL

GOODACRE CL

ALLANS LA

SOUTH RD

ALLANS DR

LILBOURNE RD

HILLMORTON LA

Dunsmore House

Clifton Hall Farm

CV23

Masts

Dunsmore Home Farm

Hotel

Clifton Hall

HILLMORTON LA

The Meadows

Grange Farm House

Home Farm

Masts

Clifton Brook

75

A5

Oxford Canal

CV21

Oxford Canal Walk

A1
1 BROMWICH RD
2 PETTIVER CRES
3 WIGSTON RD
4 THE MEWS
5 LOWER HILLMORTON RD

THE KENT

RUGBY

WAVERLEY RD

THE LOCKS

ROBERT HILL CL

PINE GR

Hillmorton Locks

THE KENT

BRINDLEY RD

Rugby Radio Station

FEATHERBED LA

JENKINS RD

COTON RD

CLEVER RD

SCHOOL ST

GAINSBOROUGH CRES

CONSTABLE RD

Normandy Farm

Masts

GIBSON DR

DYSON CL

JACKSON RD

SCHOOL GDNS

FOX CL

LOWER ST

REYNOLDS

1 BONNINGTON CL
2 LANDSEER CL

LOWER ST

Warwickshire STREET ATLAS

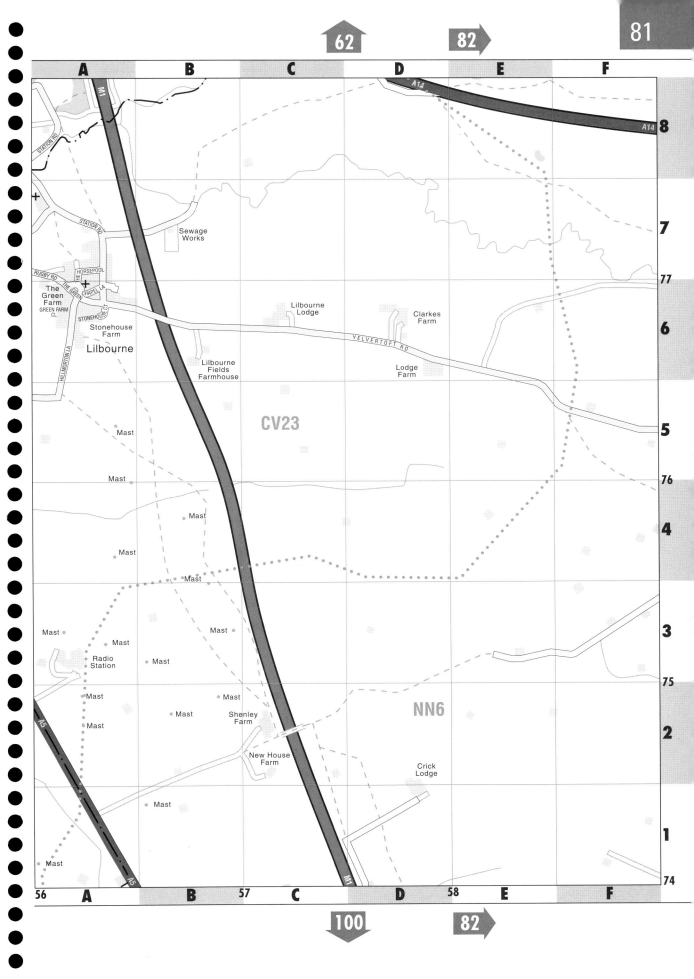

81
63

A B C D E F

8

A14

Stanford Mear

Pages Lodge Farm

Jurassic Way

A14

7

Manor Farm

77

Manor Farm

Clay Coton

Blackdown Farm

Rectory Farm

PH

Willow Farm Cottage

6

Buffs Farm

Elkington Farm Cottage

5

YELVERTOFT RD

Yelvertoft Fieldside Covert

Mountain Barn

76

Sewage Works

BROOKSIDE CL 1
ORCHARD CL 2
BROOKSIDE MEWS 3

NN6

Grand Union Canal

Hall

4

Yelvertoft Prim Sch

2 3

TARRY'S END

SCHOOL LA

ASHWELLS LA

BRIDGEND

ELLINGTON RD

Yelvertoft

Glebe Farm

HILLMORTON LA

SCHOOL CL

KINGS LA

BWINNERTONS LA

ELKINS CL

MERRYCOT LA

KIRKHAMS CL

Winwick Manor Farm

HIGH ST

STYLES PL

WARDS LA

PH

3

PO

Cemy

Grand Union Canal

75

2

CRICK RD

Flint Hill Farm

New House Farm

1

Winwick Grange

74

59

A

B

60

C

D

61

E

F

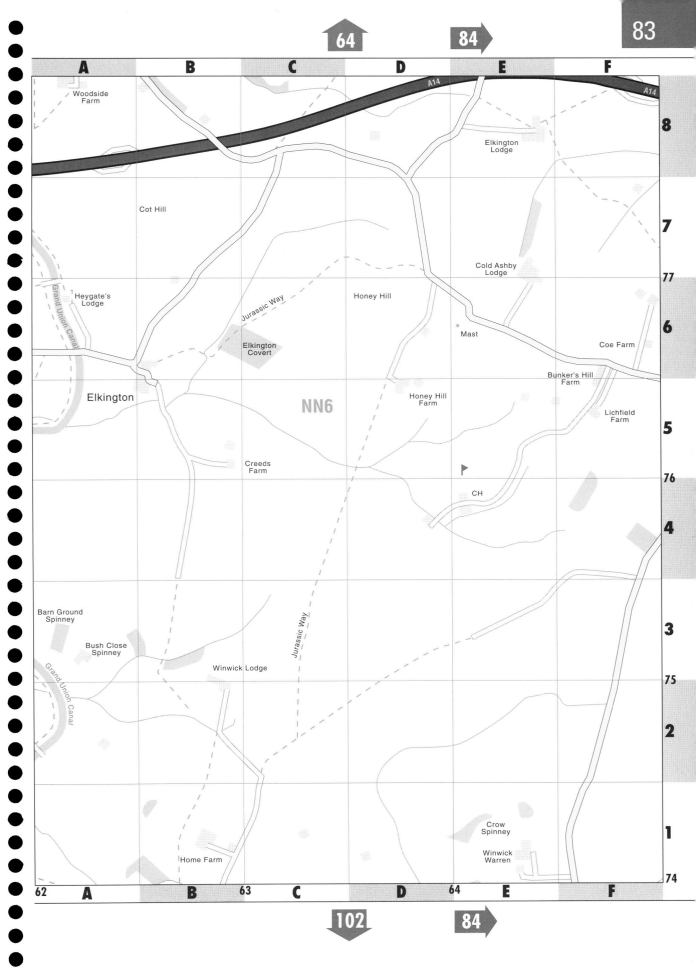

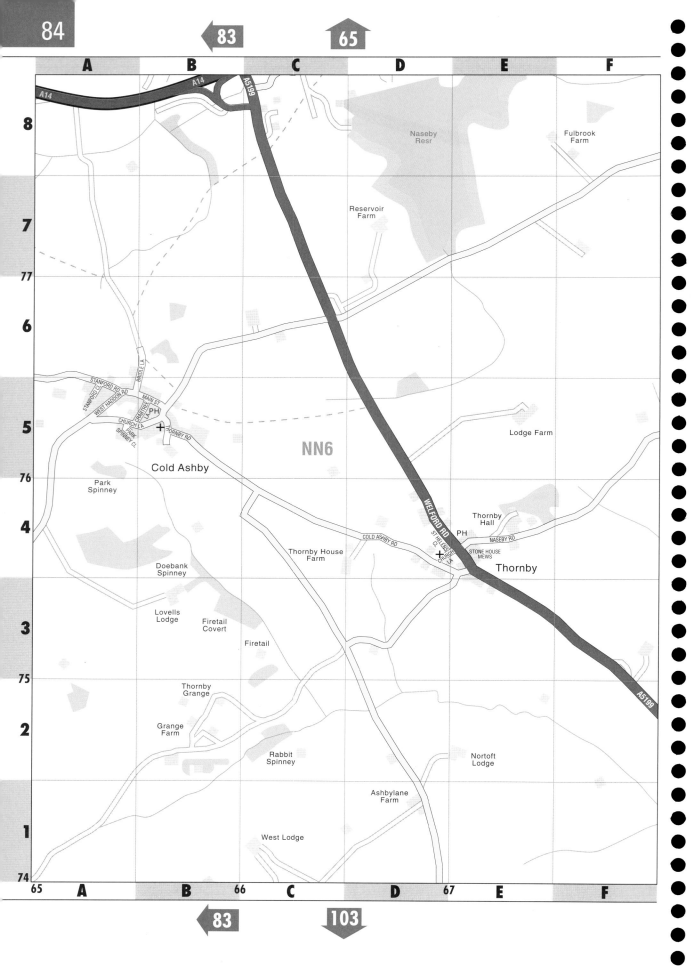

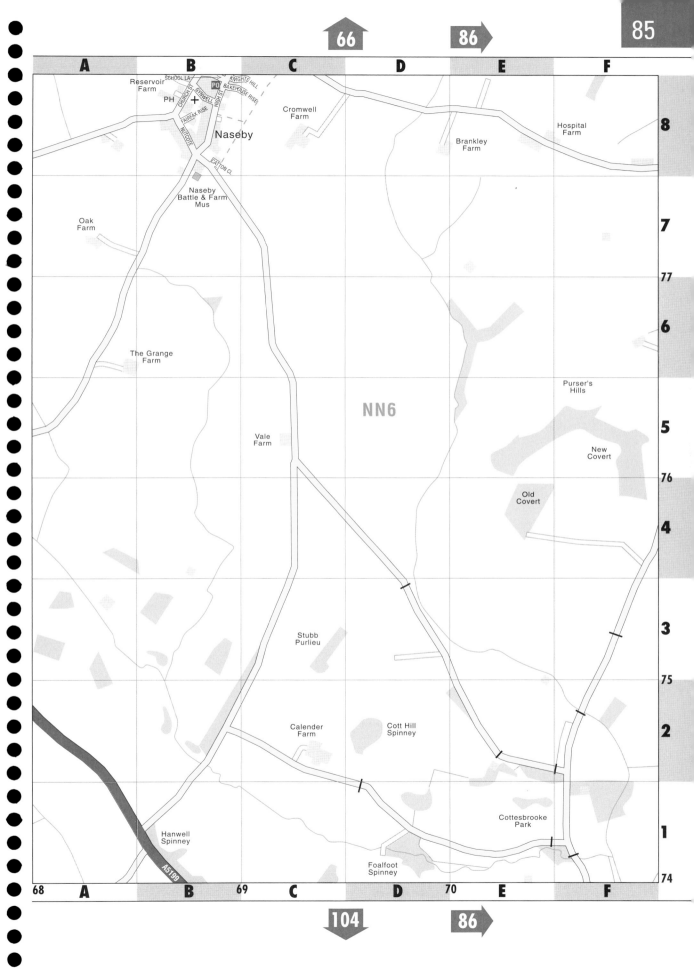

	A	B	C	D	E	F	

Reservoir Farm

SCHOOL LA

KNIGHTS HILL

PO

BAKEHOUSE RISE

CHURCH ST

GYNWELL

HIGH ST

PH

FAIRFAX RISE

NUTCOTE

Naseby

Cromwell Farm

Brankley Farm

Hospital Farm

8

CATTON CL

Naseby Battle & Farm Mus

Oak Farm

7

77

6

The Grange Farm

Purser's Hills

NN6

Vale Farm

New Covert

5

76

Old Covert

4

Stubb Purlieu

3

75

Calender Farm

Cott Hill Spinney

2

Cottesbrooke Park

Hanwell Spinney

1

A5199

Foalfoot Spinney

74

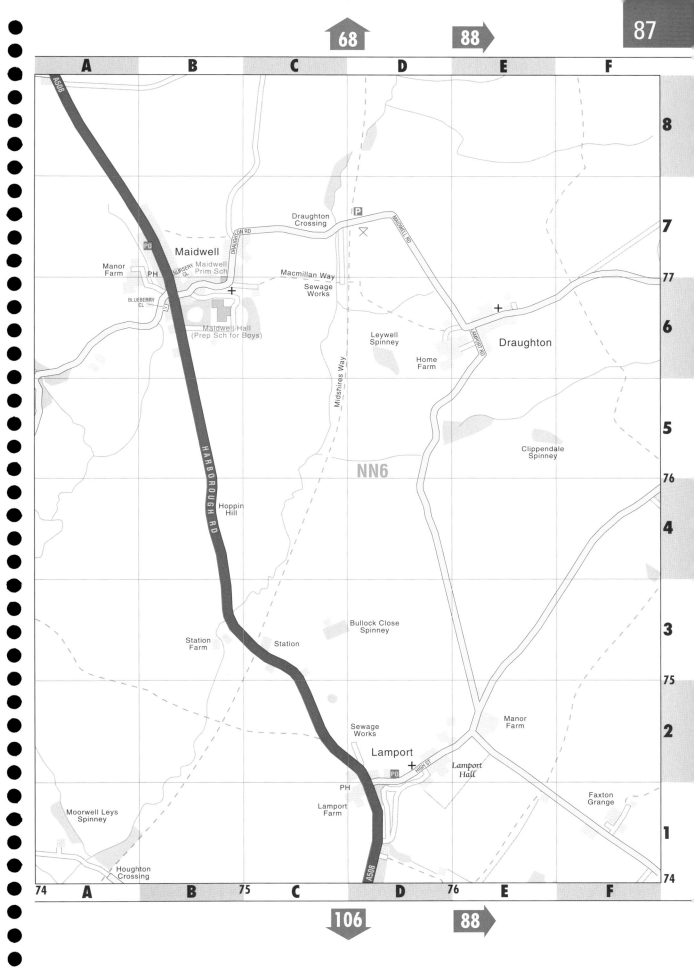

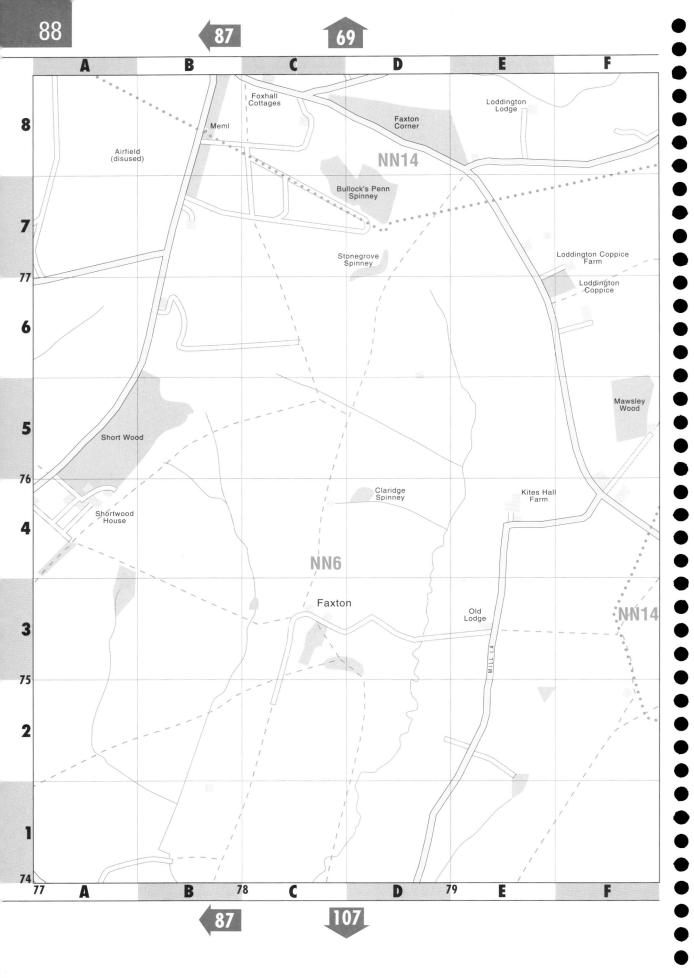

A   B   C   D   E   F

8

Foxhall
Cottages

Loddington
Lodge

Meml

Faxton
Corner

Airfield
(disused)

NN14

7

Bullock's Penn
Spinney

77

Stonegrove
Spinney

Loddington Coppice
Farm

Loddington
Coppice

6

Mawsley
Wood

5

Short Wood

76

Claridge
Spinney

Kites Hall
Farm

4

Shortwood
House

NN6

Faxton

Old
Lodge

NN14

3

MILL LA

75

2

1

74

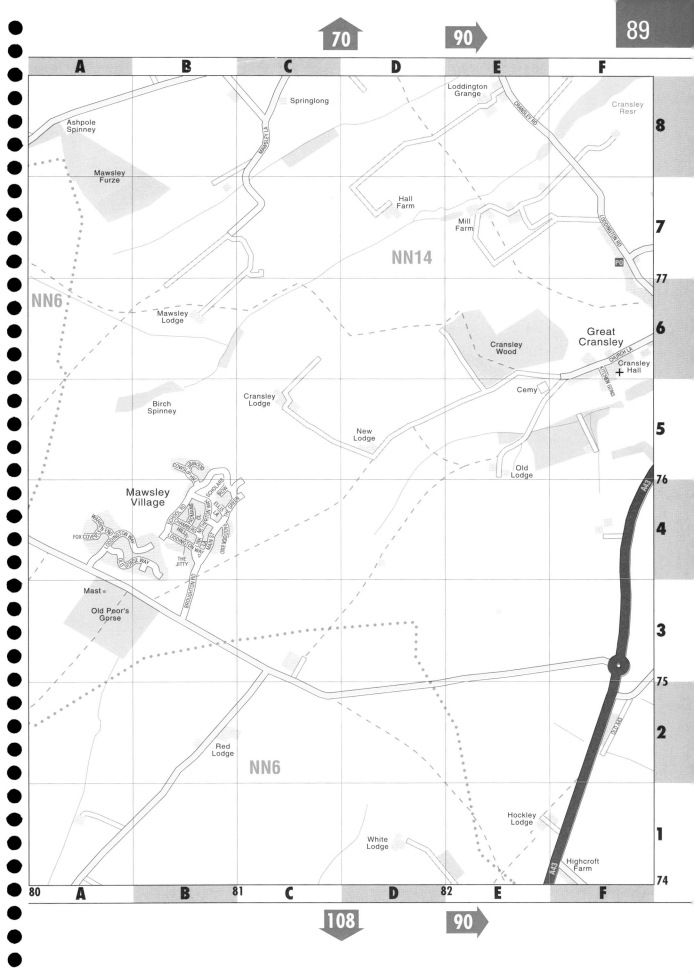

A B C D E F

8
7
77
6
5
76
4
3
75
2
1
74

Ashpole
Spinney

Mawsley
Furze

Springlong

Loddington
Grange

Cransley
Resr

CRANSLEY RD

LODDINGTON RD

PO

Hall
Farm

Mill
Farm

NN14

NN6

Mawsley
Lodge

Great
Cransley

Cransley
Wood

CHURCH LA

Cransley
+ Hall

KITCHEN GDNS

Cemy

Birch
Spinney

Cransley
Lodge

New
Lodge

Old
Lodge

A43

ELSWOOD
COWSLIP HL

SCHOLARS
ROW

Mawsley
Village

SCHOOL RD
PADMANS
CHAMBERS
CL
NETHERTON WK
THE GREEN

WARREN END
LODDINGTON WK
HILLS
LINK
MAIN ST
PADDOCK END

FOX COVERT

OLD GORSE WAY

THE
JITTY

LODDINGTON WAY

BROUGHTON RD

Mast

Old Poor's
Gorse

Red
Lodge

NN6

OLD A43

Hockley
Lodge

White
Lodge

A43

Highcroft
Farm

80 A 81 B C 81 82 D E 82 F

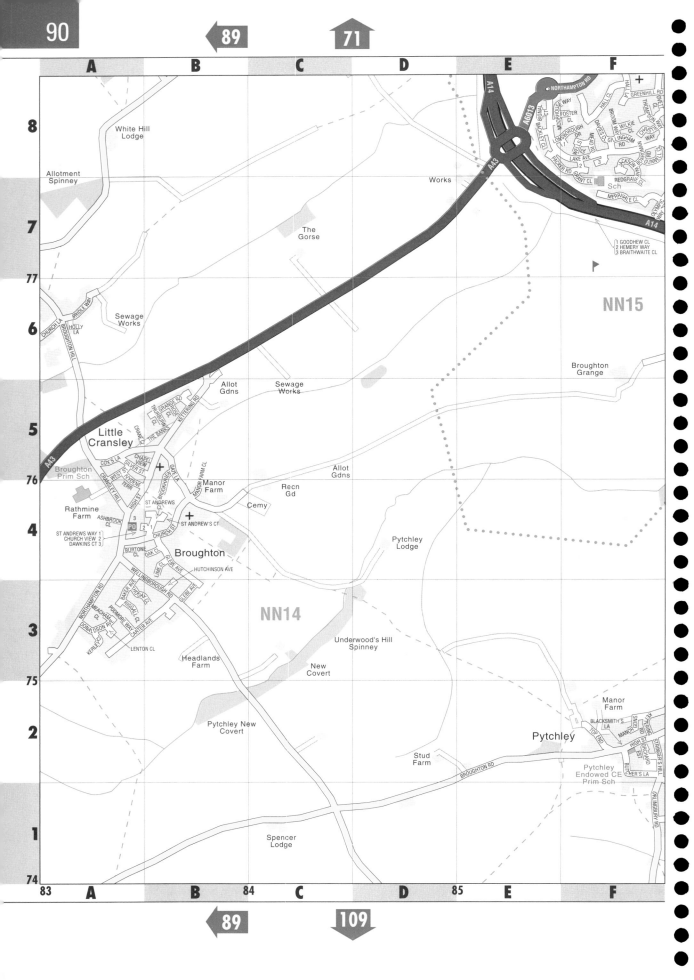

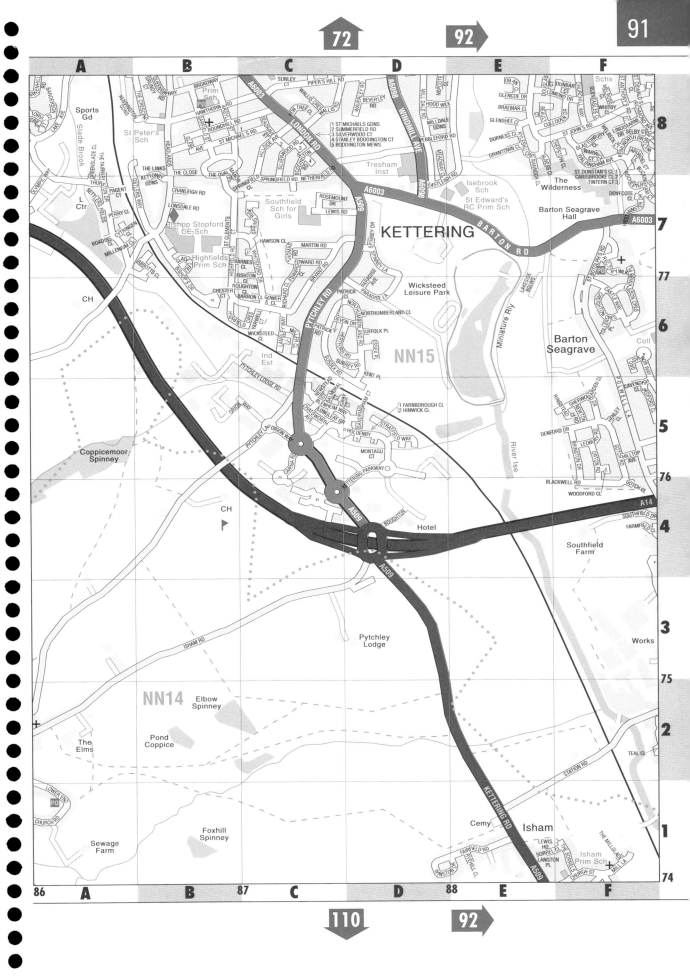

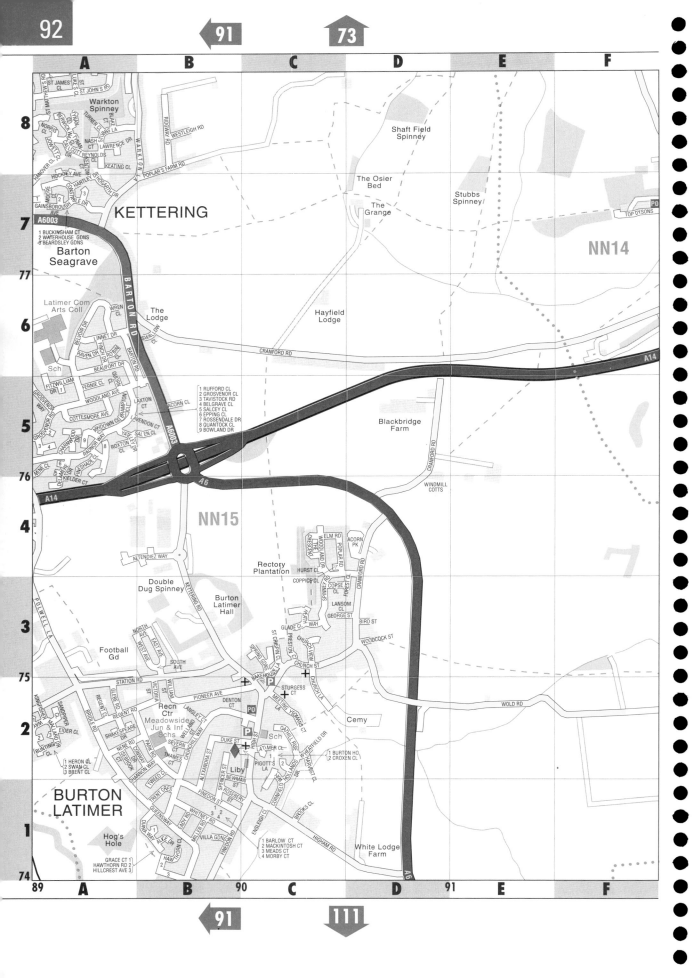

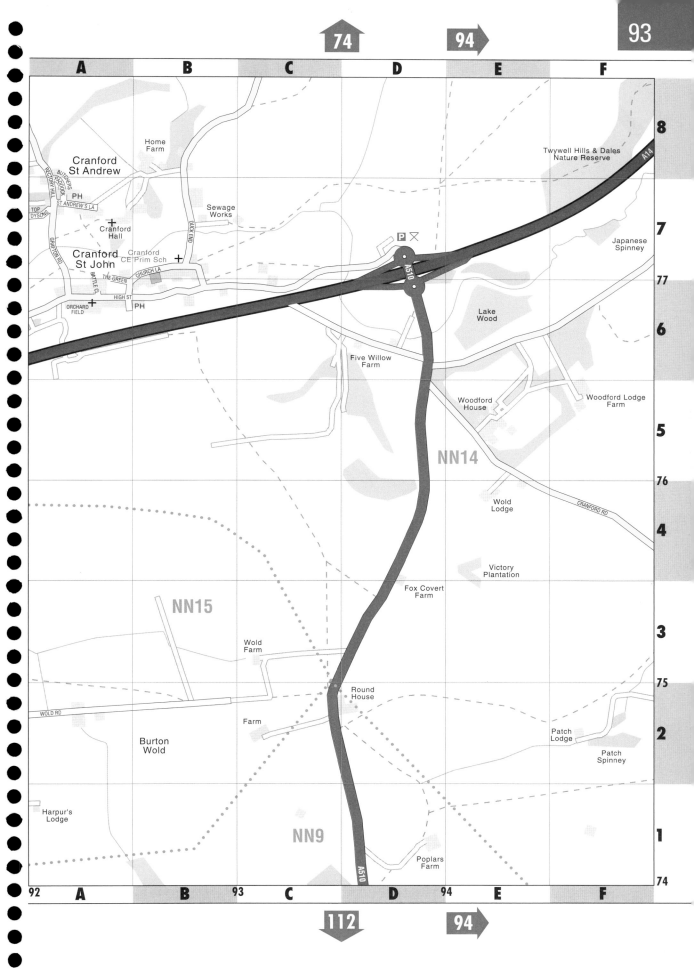

A   B   C   D   E   F

8

Home Farm

Cranford St Andrew

Twywell Hills & Dales Nature Reserve

A14

PH

St Andrew's La

Cranford Hall

Sewage Works

Japanese Spinney

7

Butchers Paddock

Top Dysons

Rectory Hill

Cranford CE Prim Sch

P ✕

A510

77

Cranford St John

Grafton Rd

Battle Cl

The Green

Church La

Lake Wood

6

High St

Orchard Field

PH

Duck End

Five Willow Farm

Woodford House

Woodford Lodge Farm

5

NN14

Wold Lodge

CRANFORD RD

76

4

Victory Plantation

NN15

Fox Covert Farm

3

Wold Farm

75

Round House

Wold Rd

Farm

Patch Lodge

2

Burton Wold

Patch Spinney

Harpur's Lodge

NN9

1

A510

Poplars Farm

74

92   A   B   93   C   D   94   E   F

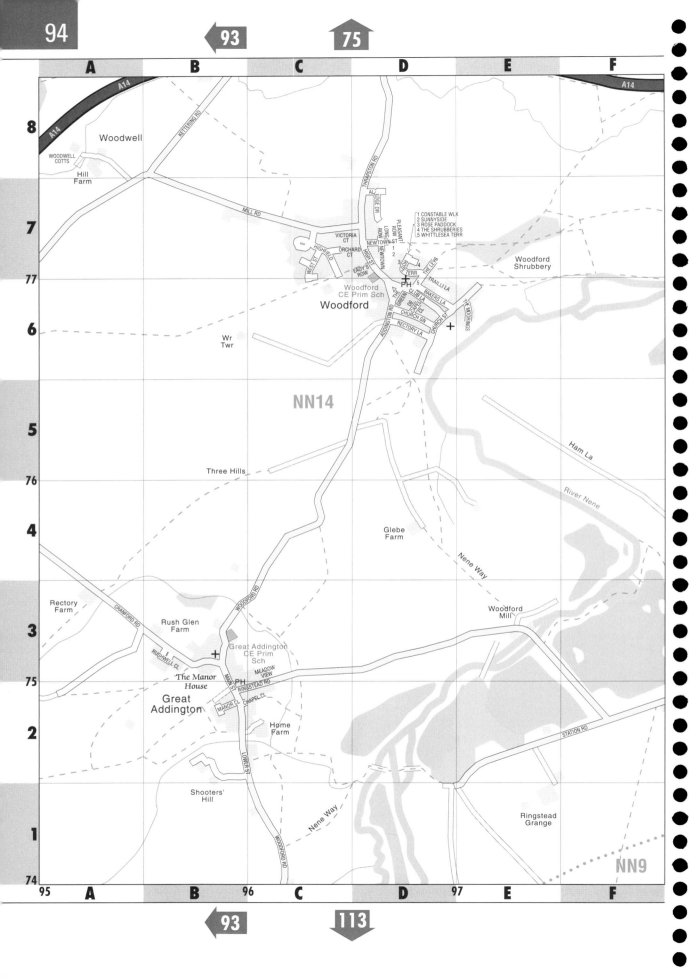

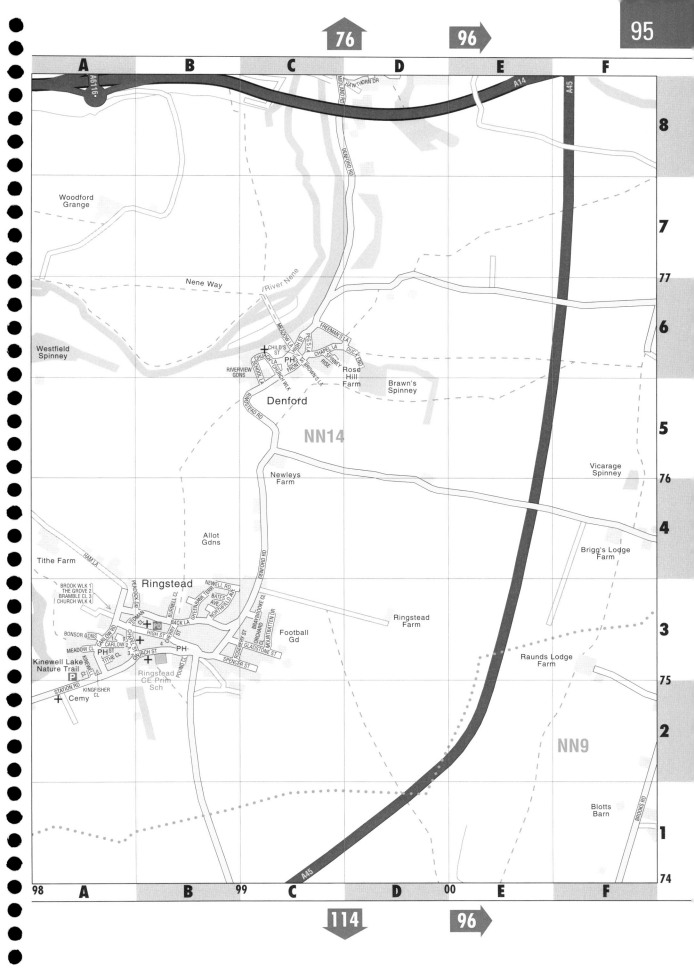

76
96
114
96

A   B   C   D   E   F

8
7
77
6
5
76
4
3
75
2
1
74

98   A   B   99   C   D   00   E   F

A6116

A14

A45

MIDLAND RD
HAWTHORN DR

RAINFORD RD

Woodford
Grange

Nene Way
River Nene

Westfield
Spinney

MEADOW LA
HIGH ST
PEG S LA
CHILD'S ST
CHURCH LA
SCHOOL LA
CHURCH WLK
FRONT ST
BROWN'S LA
PH
FREEMAN'S LA
CHAPEL LA
SPINNEY
RISE
DUCK END

RIVERVIEW
GDNS

Rose
Hill
Farm

Brawn's
Spinney

RINGSTEAD RD

Denford

NN14

Newleys
Farm

Vicarage
Spinney

Allot
Gdns

DENFORD RD

Brigg's Lodge
Farm

Tithe Farm

HAM LA

Ringstead

BROOK WLK 1
THE GROVE 2
BRAMBLE CL 3
CHURCH WLK 4

PEACOCK DR
NEWELL RD
BATES
AVE
GREENBANK TERR
BURNELL CL
NORTHFIELD AVE

Ringstead
Farm

BONSOR GDNS
CARLOW RD
CARLOW 2
CARLOW 3
CHAPEL ST
YEOMAN CL
PO
HIGH ST
BACK LA
CHERRY ST
ROSEBERY ST
ORCHARD
GLADSTONE ST
BRAYBROOKE CL
MOUNTBATTEN DR

Football
Gd

MEADOW CL
PH
TITHE CL
CHURCH ST
PH
SPENCER ST

Raunds Lodge
Farm

Kinewell Lake
Nature Trail
P

KINEWELL CL
STATION RD
KINGFISHER CL
Cemy
Ringstead
CE Prim
Sch
POUND CL

NN9

Blotts
Barn

BROOKS RD

A45

A14

Top Lodge

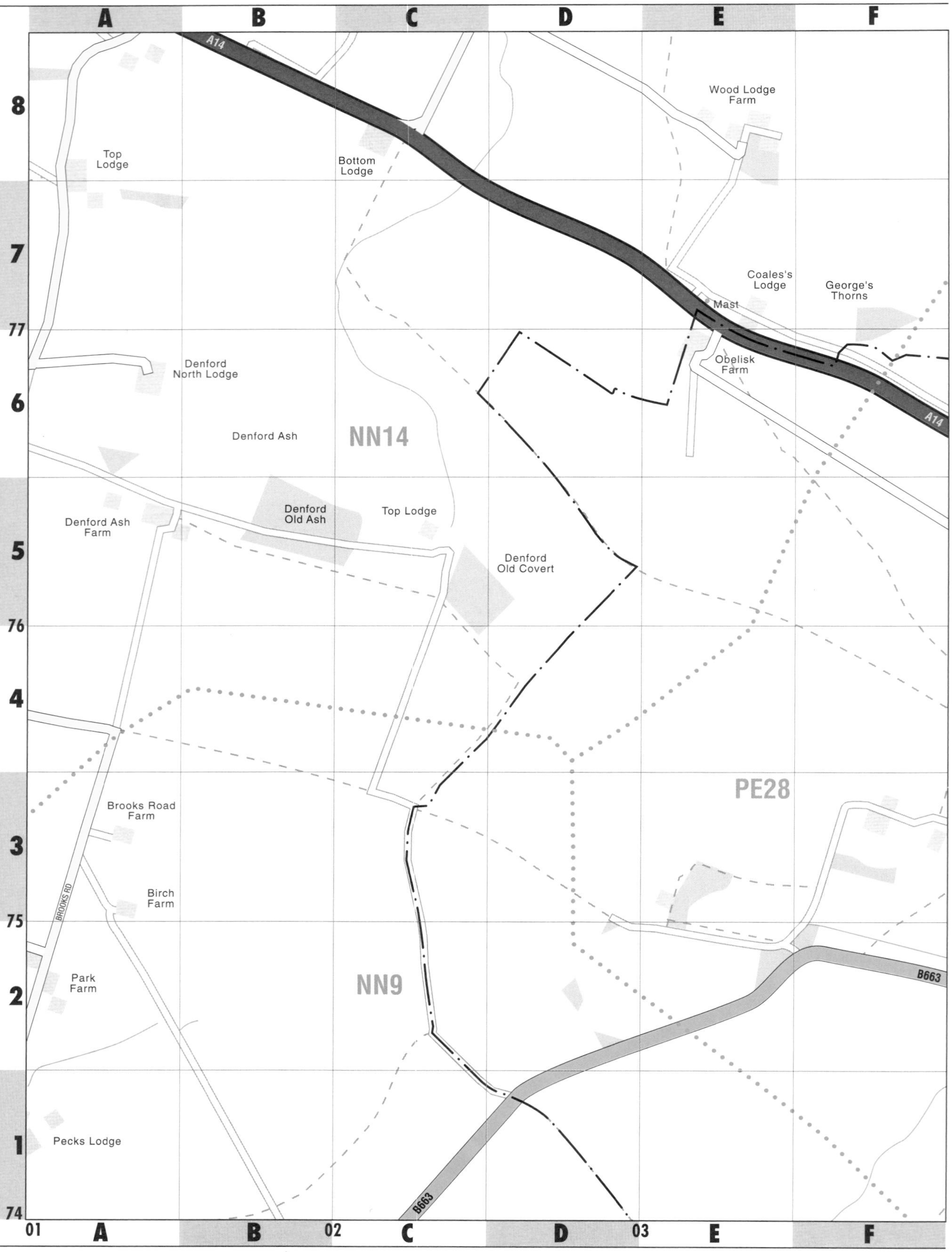

Bottom Lodge

Wood Lodge Farm

Coales's Lodge

George's Thorns

Mast

Denford North Lodge

Obelisk Farm

Denford Ash

NN14

Denford Ash Farm

Denford Old Ash

Top Lodge

Denford Old Covert

A14

PE28

Brooks Road Farm

Birch Farm

BROOKS RD

NN9

B663

Park Farm

B663

Pecks Lodge

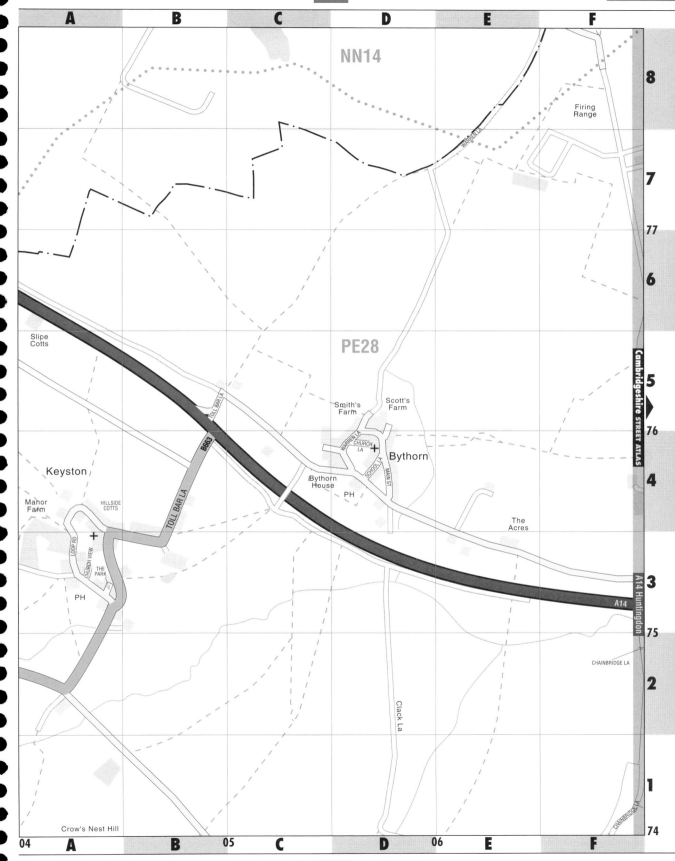

NN14

PE28

Firing Range

WARREN LA

Slipe Cotts

Smith's Farm

Scott's Farm

WARREN LA

CHURCH LA

Bythorn

Keyston

Bythorn House

SCHOOL LA

MAIN ST

PH

Manor Farm

HILLSIDE COTTS

TOLL BAR LA

B663

TOLL BAR LA

The Acres

LOOP RD

CHURCH VIEW

THE PARK

PH

A14

A14 Huntingdon

CHAINBRIDGE LA

Clack La

CHAINBRIDGE LA

Crow's Nest Hill

Cambridgeshire STREET ATLAS

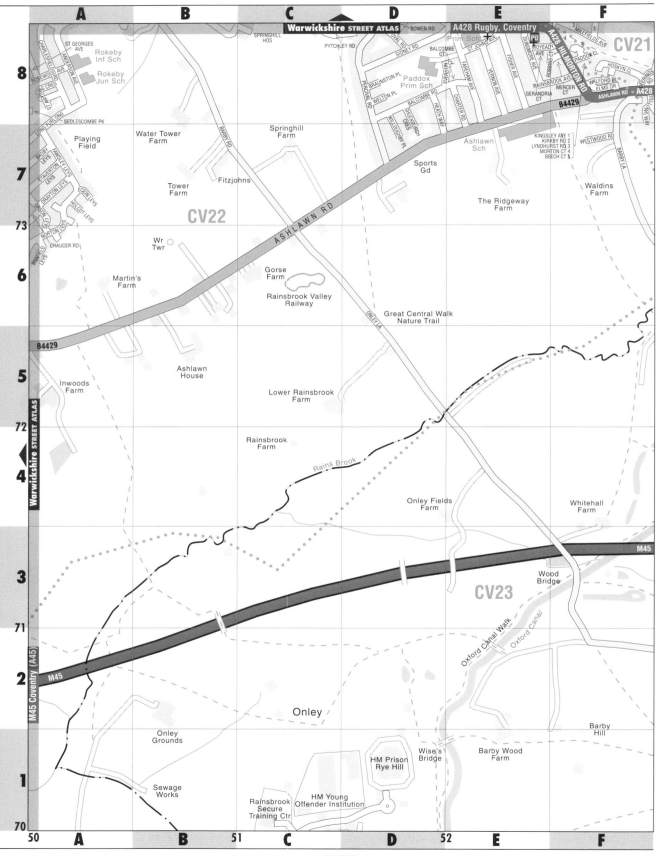

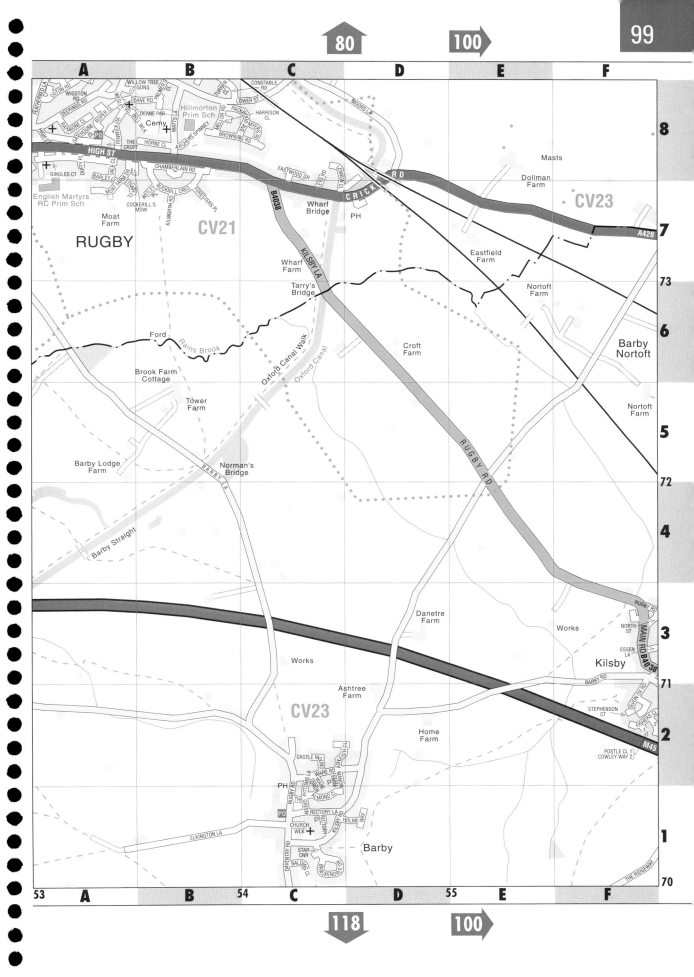

A   B   C   D   E   F

8

7

73

6

5

72

4

3

71

2

1

70

FEATHERBED LA
COTON RD
WIGSTON RD
WILLOW TREE GDNS
DEANE RD
DEERINGS RD
PALMER'S CL
TURNER CL
CONSTABLE RD
LOWER ST
HIGH
GATEHOUSE RD
FAIRBONE CL
ROPER DR
DEANE PAR
BELL WLK
Cemy
WATTS LA
MELLOR RD
PACKWOOD AVE
MYERS RD
HARRISON CL
MOORS LA

Hillmorton
Prim Sch

HORNE CL
THE CROFT
BROWNING RD

RUGBY

HIGH ST

GINGLES CT
DUFFY PL
BARLEY
VALE CL
ASTLEY PL
MOAT FARM DR
CHAMBERLAIN RD
BUCKNILL CRES
FORESTERS PL
EASTWOOD GR
LENNOX CL
CRICK   R D
CRICK
Masts

Dollman
Farm

CV23

English Martyrs
RC Prim Sch

Moat
Farm

KILWORTH RD
COCKERILL'S MDW

CV21

B4038
Wharf
Bridge

PH

A428

Eastfield
Farm

Nortoft
Farm

KILSBY LA
Wharf
Farm

Tarry's
Bridge

Barby
Nortoft

Ford
Rains Brook

Oxford Canal Walk
Oxford Canal

Croft
Farm

Nortoft
Farm

Brook Farm
Cottage

Tower
Farm

Barby Lodge
Farm

BARBY LA
Norman's
Bridge

RUGBY RD

Barby Straight

Works
RUGBY RD

Danetre
Farm

NORTH ST
ESSEN LA
MAIN RD B4038

Works

Kilsby

BARBY RD

Works

Ashtree
Farm

CV23

STEPHENSON CT
FISHERS CL

M45

Home
Farm

POSTLE CL 1
COWLEY WAY 2

CASTLE MO
WARE RD
TOWNLEY LA
VIDGE
MANOR
FARM CL
ALMOND CL

PH
RUGBY RD
THE GREEN
PITFIELD
CHURCH
RECTORY LA
HOLME WAY

PO

CHURCH
WLK

ELKINGTON LA

DAVENTRY RD
BALDWIN CL
STAR CNR
BRACKENDALE DR

Barby

THE RIDGEWAY

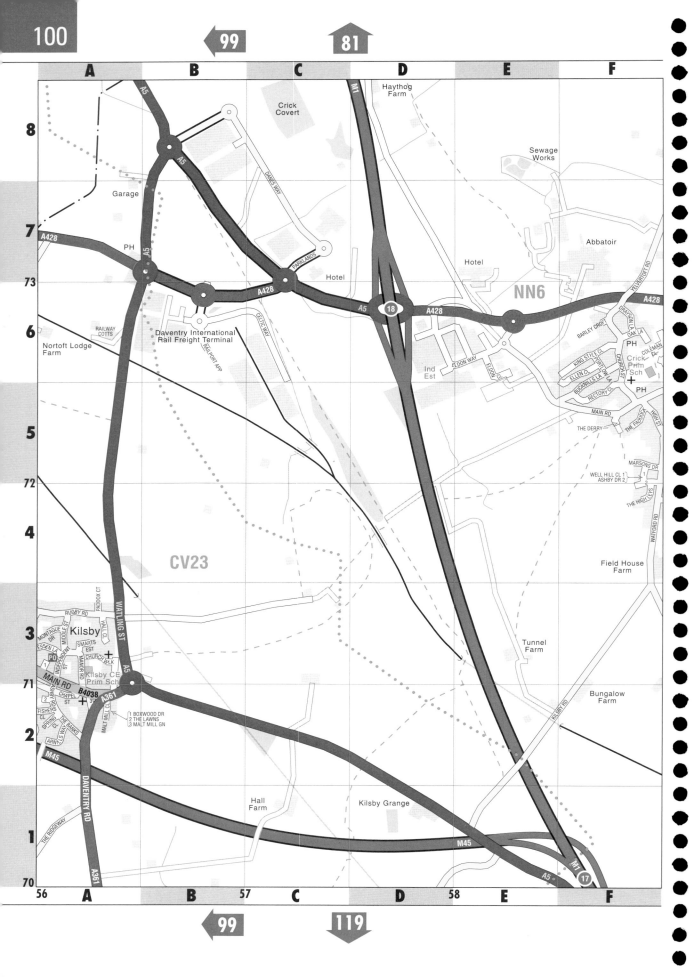

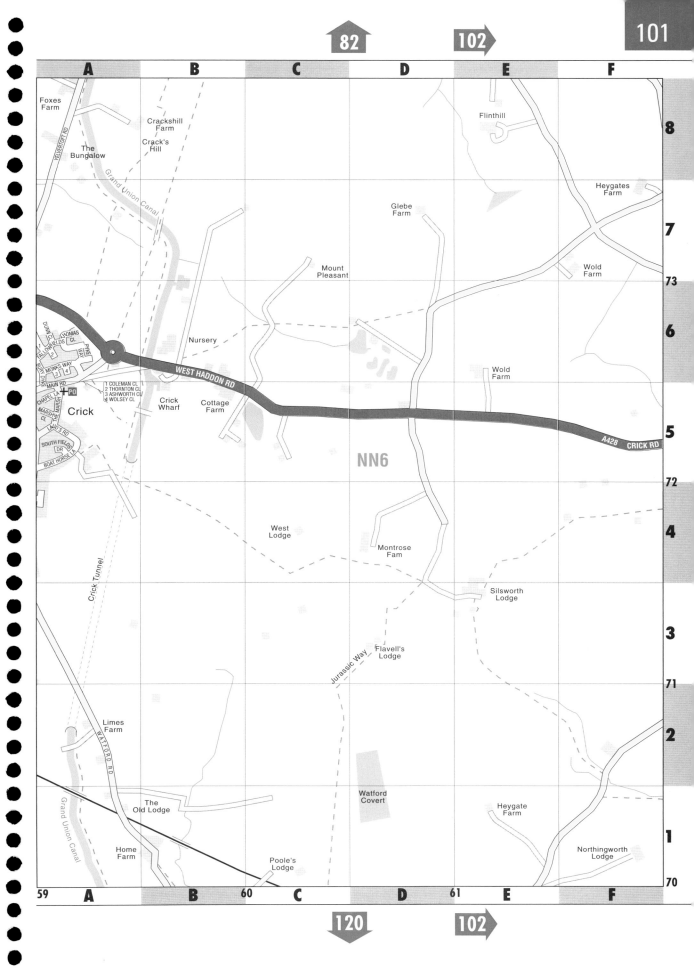

82
102

A B C D E F

8

Foxes
Farm

YELVERTOFT RD

The
Bungalow

Crackshill
Farm

Crack's
Hill

Grand Union Canal

7

73

Flinthill

Heygates
Farm

Wold
Farm

Glebe
Farm

Mount
Pleasant

6

Nursery

DUNN CL
THOMAS CL
FALLOWFIELDS
MONKS WAY
PYKE WAY

WEST HADDON RD

1 COLEMAN CL
2 THORNTON CL
3 ASHWORTH CL
4 WOLSEY CL

Wold
Farm

MAIN RD
CHAPEL LA
THE MARSH
PO

Crick

MARSHAL
CL

Crick
Wharf

Cottage
Farm

5

A428 CRICK RD

LAND'S RD
SOUTH FIELDS DR
BOAT HORSE LA

NN6

72

Crick Tunnel

West
Lodge

Montrose
Fam

4

Silsworth
Lodge

3

Jurassic Way

Flavell's
Lodge

71

Limes
Farm

WATFORD RD

2

The
Old Lodge

Watford
Covert

Heygate
Farm

Grand Union Canal

Home
Farm

Poole's
Lodge

Northingworth
Lodge

1

70

120
102

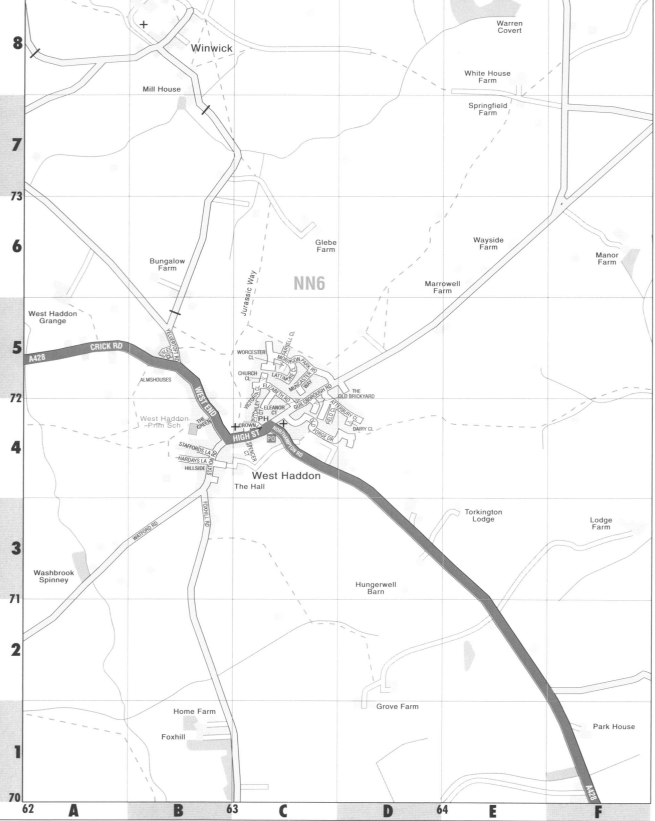

A   B   C   D   E   F

8

7

73

6

Winwick

Warren Covert

White House Farm

Mill House

Springfield Farm

Glebe Farm

NN6

Jurassic Way

Wayside Farm

Manor Farm

Bungalow Farm

Marrowell Farm

5

West Haddon Grange

72

A428

CRICK RD

ALMSHOUSES

WELFORD RD

WEST END

WORCESTER CL

PARTWELL CL

MORETON PARK RD

LATTIMORE CL

CHURCH CL

ELIZABETH RD

MUNCASTER WAY

GUILSBOROUGH RD

THE OLD BRICKYARD

4

West Haddon Prim Sch

THE GREEN

HIGH ST

VICTORY CL

PITCHLEY CL

ELEANOR CT

CROWN

PH

PO

SPENCER CT

NORTHAMPTON RD

ATTERBURY CL

FIELD CL

FORGE DR

DAIRY CL

STAFFORDS LA RD

HARDAYS LA

HILLSIDE

STATION RD

West Haddon

The Hall

WATFORD RD

FOXHILL RD

Torkington Lodge

Lodge Farm

3

Washbrook Spinney

71

Hungerwell Barn

2

Grove Farm

Home Farm

Foxhill

Park House

1

70

A428

62   A   B   63   C   D   64   E   F

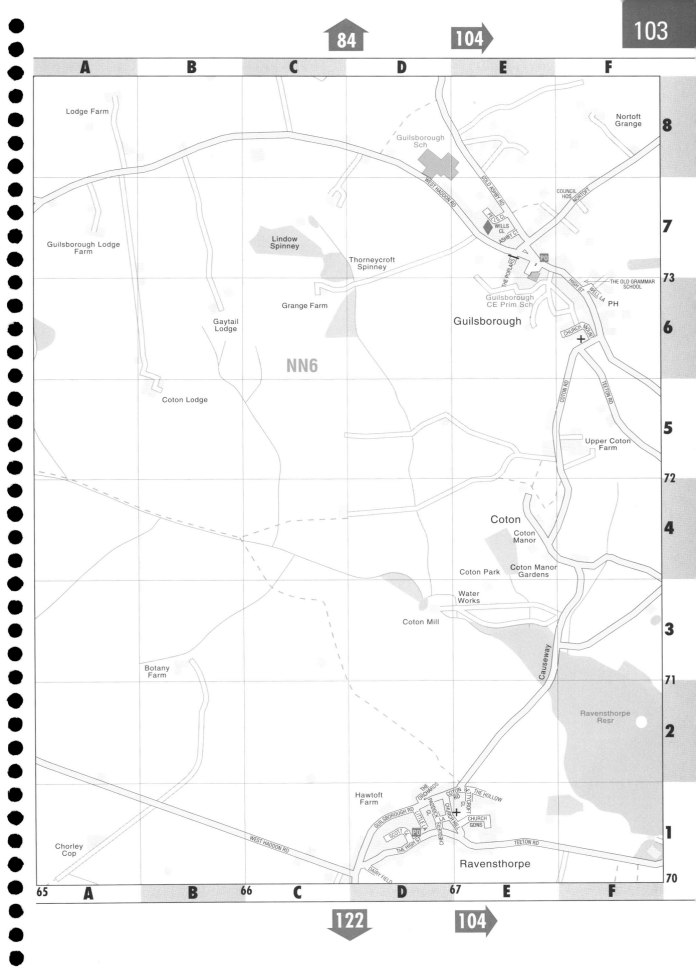

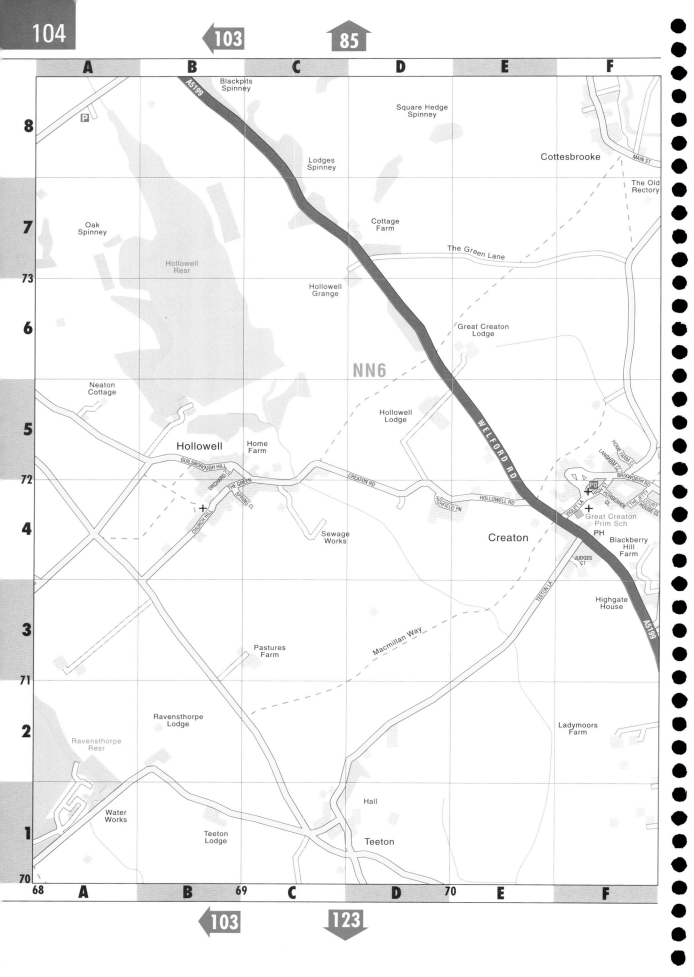

103
85

A   B   C   D   E   F

8

Blackpits
Spinney

Square Hedge
Spinney

A5199

Lodges
Spinney

Cottesbrooke

MAIN ST

The Old
Rectory

7

Oak
Spinney

Cottage
Farm

The Green Lane

Hollowell
Resr

73

Hollowell
Grange

6

Great Creaton
Lodge

NN6

Neaton
Cottage

Hollowell
Lodge

5

Hollowell

Home
Farm

HOME FARM CL

LANGHAM CL

GUILSBOROUGH HILL

CREATON RD

BRIXWORTH RD

72

ORCHARD CL

THE GREEN

HOLLOWELL RD

HIGH ST

HORSESHOE CL

THE JETTY

COURT CL

THE HOUSE CL

SPRING CL

HOTHFIELD PK

PO

4

CHURCH HILL

Sewage
Works

Creaton

VIOLET LA

Great Creaton
Prim Sch

PH

Blackberry
Hill
Farm

JUDGES
CT

3

Pastures
Farm

Macmillan Way

TEETON LA

Highgate
House

71

Ravensthorpe
Lodge

2

Ravensthorpe
Resr

Ladymoors
Farm

A5199

1

Water
Works

Teeton
Lodge

Hall

Teeton

70

68   A   B   69   C   D   70   E   F

103
123

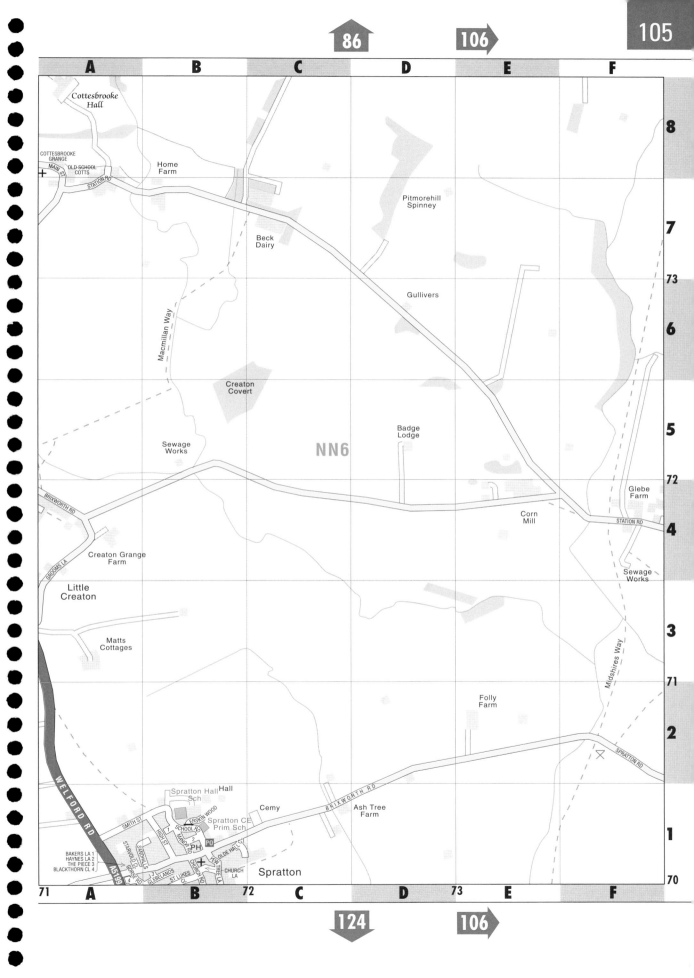

A B C D E F

Cottesbrooke
Hall

COTTESBROOKE
GRANGE
OLD SCHOOL
COTTS
MAIN ST
STATION RD
Home
Farm

Pitmorehill
Spinney

Beck
Dairy

Gullivers

Macmillan Way

Creaton
Covert

Badge
Lodge

NN6

Sewage
Works

Glebe
Farm

Corn
Mill

STATION RD

BRIXWORTH RD

GROOMS LA

Creaton Grange
Farm

Little
Creaton

Sewage
Works

Matts
Cottages

Midshires Way

Folly
Farm

WELFORD RD

A5199

SPRATTON RD

Spratton Hall
Sch
Hall

Cemy

BRIXWORTH RD

Ash Tree
Farm

ERSKIN WOOD

SMITH ST

Spratton CE
Prim Sch

SCHOOL RD

MANOR RD

HIGH ST

PH

PO

STARVOLD CL

GORSE RD

SANDHILLS

GLEBELANDS

ST LUKES
CL

CHURCH RD

OLDE HALL CL

KEN TREE LA

CHURCH LA

Spratton

BAKERS LA 1
HAYNES LA 2
THE PIECE 3
BLACKTHORN CL 4

71 A B 72 C D 73 E F

8
7
73
6
5
72
4
3
71
2
1
70

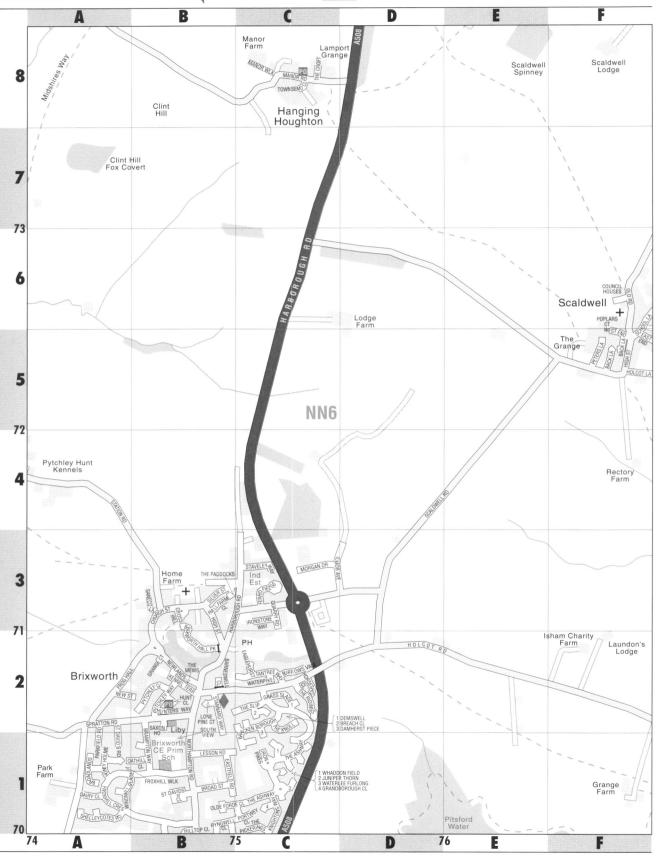

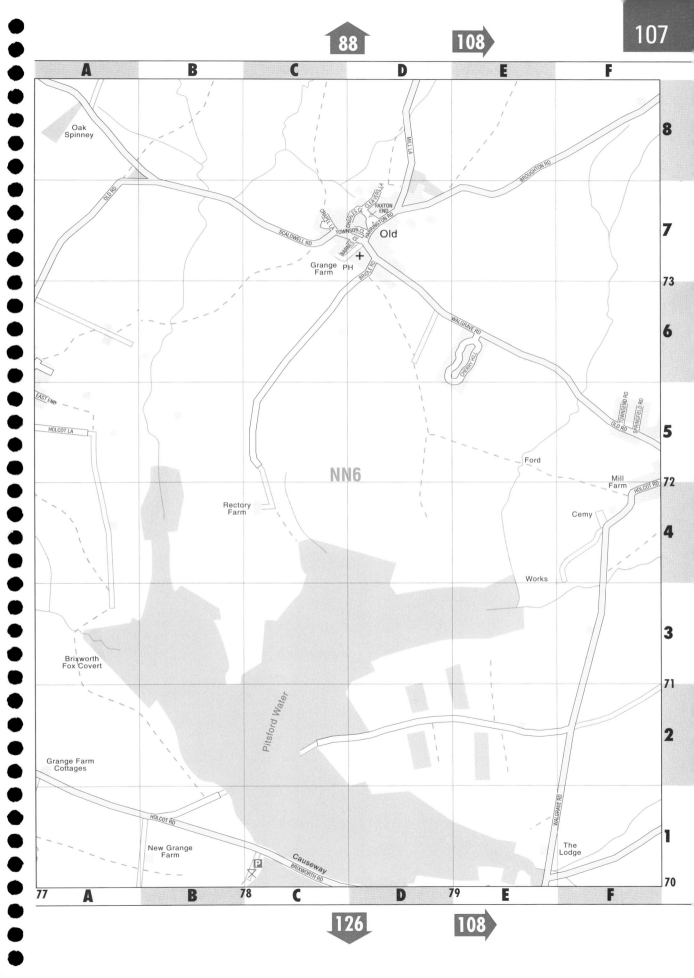

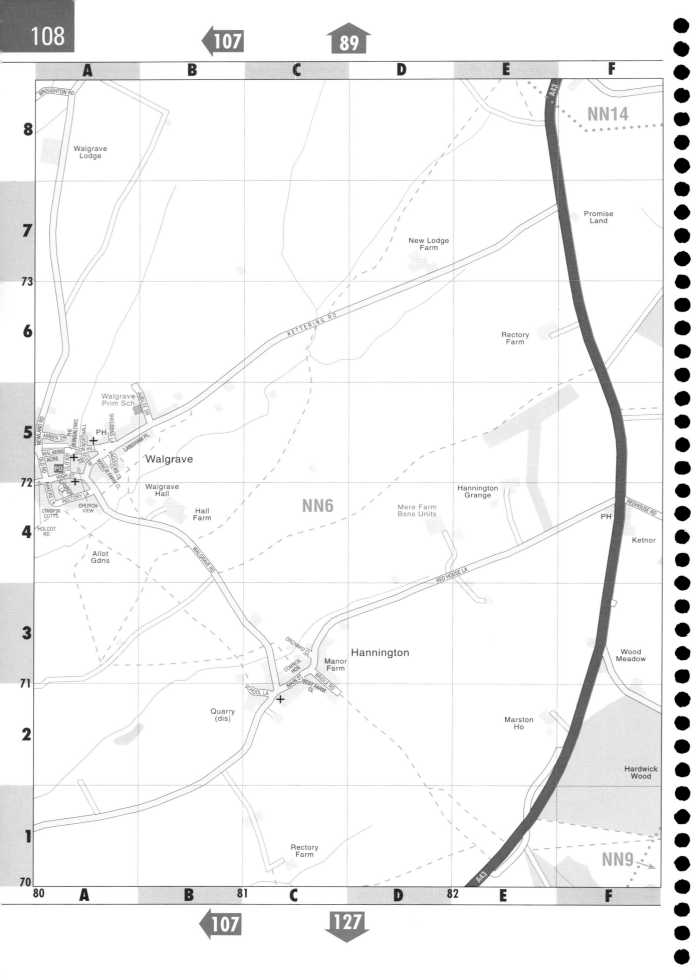

107
89

NN14

A   B   C   D   E   F

8

Walgrave
Lodge

7

73

Promise
Land

New Lodge
Farm

KETTERING RD

6

Rectory
Farm

BROUGHTON RD

Walgrave
Prim Sch

JUBILEE DR

5

PH

NEWLAND RD

AMBER DR

SHELDONS LA

THE BUNGALOWS

NORTHALL

ZION HILL

LANGHAM PL

Walgrave

Hannington
Grange

WALKERS
ACRE

OLD CLO

SILVER ST

PADDOCKS CL

MANOR FARM CL

72

PO

Mere Farm
Bsns Units

HIGH ST

BAKERS LA

CHURCH LA

RECTORY LA

Walgrave
Hall

NN6

REDHOUSE RD

PH

CHURCH VIEW

CRISPIN
COTTS

Hall
Farm

Ketnor

HOLCOT
RD

4

WALGRAVE RD

RED HOUSE LA

Allot
Gdns

3

Wood
Meadow

ORCHARD CL

Hannington

Manor
Farm

71

COUNCIL
HOS

MAIN ST

WEST FARM CL

BRIDLE RD

SCHOOL LA

Quarry
(dis)

2

Marston
Ho

Hardwick
Wood

NN9

1

Rectory
Farm

A43

70

80   A   B   81   C   D   82   E   F

107
127

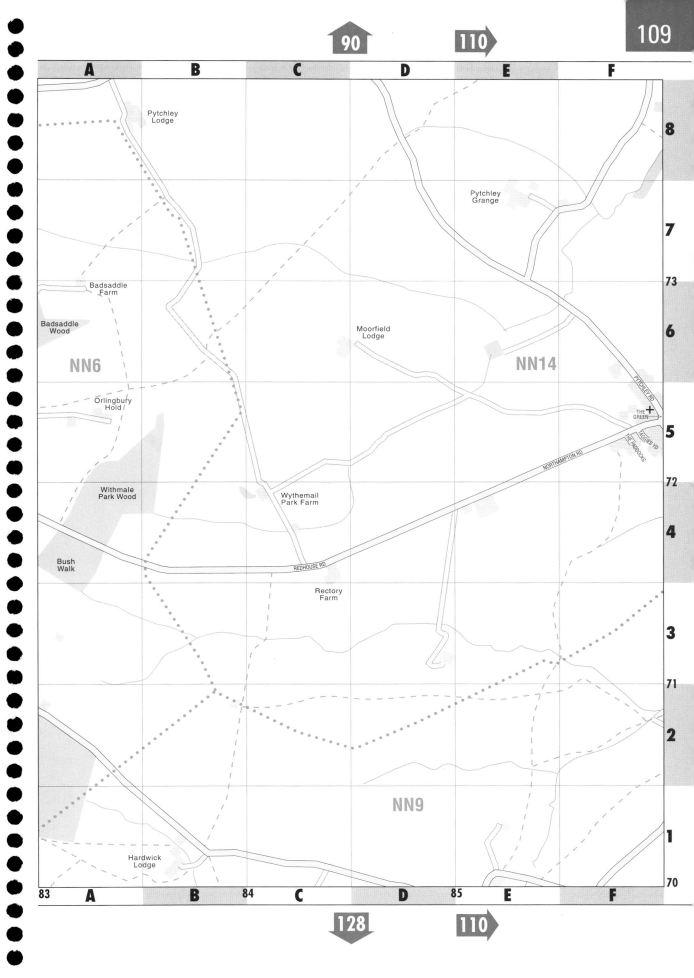

A B C D E F

8

NN14

7

73

6

Isham

North Lodge

Ryehill Farm

ORLINGBURY RD

Big Covert

Glebe Farm

Manor Farm

A509

KETTERING RD

MIDDLE ST

HIGH ST

CHURCH ST

SOUTH ST

MANOR CL

JUBILEE TERR

PO

ORMOND PL

WELLINGBOROUGH RD

Isham South Bridge

Ashpole Plantation

FINEDON STATION RD

Cock o Roost Spinney

North End Farm

PH

THE LEYS

ISHAM RD

THE ORCHARD

PO

DOVECOTE YD

RECTORY LA

LAMMAS CL

Orlingbury

THE GLEBE

HARROWDEN RD

5

Orlingbury Hall

Lammas Spinney

B574

KETTERING RD

FURNACE LA

HILL TOP

72

Roadside Spinney

NN9

HILL TOP RD

Allot Gdns

Little Harrowden Com Prim Sch

Sander's Barn

HILLSIDE

The Gables

4

Orlingbury Rd

Willow Farm

Little Harrowden

SCHOOL LA

ALBION CT

MAIN ST

SMITHS YD

KING'S LA

CHAPEL LA

MANOR CT

BARN CT

PH

PO

BANK HILL VIEW

PH

B574

WELLINGBOROUGH RD

WILLOWS

SIX WILLOWS

THE WILLOWS

WESTFIELDS

HARDWICK RD

MEADOWLANDS

3

71

Stonebrig La

ORLINGBURY RD

DARK LA

MANOR CL

B574

Manor Farm

Great Harrowden

Wentworth Farm

CH

GREAT HARROWDEN HALL

THE SLIPS

Finedon Road Ind Est

2

Red Hill

NN8

WELLINGBOROUGH RD

A509

GRANGE RD

HOLME CL

GILBEY CL

THE MEADOWS

THE DOWNS

THE FAIRWAY

THE PASTURES

REDHILL WAY

THE BANKS

THE GLADE

APPLEBY CL

THE OAK VIEW

1

NN8

70

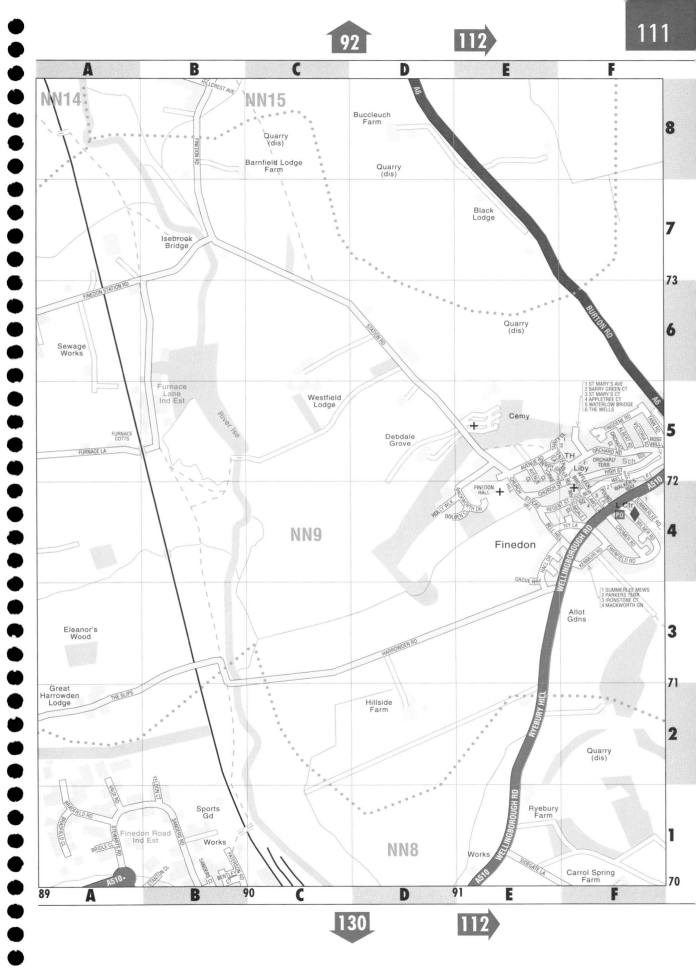

111 93

A B C D E F

8

7

73

6

5

72

4

3

71

2

1

70

NN14

Finedon Poplars

A510

Poplar's Bungalow

Finedon Lodge

Poplar Lodge

THRAPSTON RD

Burrows Barn

Mast

Allot Gdns

Bank Farm

Finedon

NN9

Knightlands

HYDE DR
ROCKLEIGH
ALLINGTAN
A6 BURTON RD
MILLER'S CL
EASTLANDS RD
HYDE RD
CASTLE CRES
WENTWORTH RD
HIGHFIELD
ROCK RD
ALLEN RD
HAYDEN AVE
FREEMAN WAY
OXFORD ST

A510

HIGH ST

OBELISK RD

ROSE HILL

MULSO RD

HAWTHORNE RD

WILLOW RD

UNION ST

SUBLI RD

CHERRY

IRTHLINGBOROUGH RD

Finedon Mulso CE Jun Sch

Wr Twr

Townside Farm

Garrow Close Spinney

Poplar Barn Farm

TURNBROOK CL

By Pass Farm

FINEDON RD

A6

B5348

LOUIS INGRE

WICKLEY CL
RINGWELL CL
LONG ACRES DR
MOUNTFIELD RD
MIDDLE GRASS
KNIGHTLANDS RD
DRAYTON RD
TITTWELL CL
PERI PRD RD
DRAY CL
MEREFIELDS CL
HIGHFIELD RD
SPRING TERR
SPRING CL
LILLEY TERR
ADDINGTON RD

B571

Nevilles Lodge

Huxlow Sch

FINEDON RD

GATES CL

PIPERS CL

SCHARPWELL

NURSERY GDNS

B5348

STATION RD

IRTHLINGBOROUGH

Irthlingborough Cty Jun & Inf Schs

EXCELSIOR CT

MARKET CROSS

B571

Liby

LIME ST

NENE VIEW

THE FLATLETS

MALTHOUSE CL

Cricket Gd

MANTON RD

SCARBOROUGH ST

COLLEGE ST

SWANSPOOL

CHURCH ST

NENE

OAK TERR

WAY WLK

7
8
9
10
11
12

SPINNEY TERR

THE CLOSE

Liby

MEADOW WAY

Nene Way

NN8

MUSSON ST

QUEEN ST

WINDMILL RD

JUBILEE ST

LEES RD

VICTORIA ST

GEORGE ST

CHERRY ST

BAKER ST

STANLEY SON

STANLEY RD

SPENCER RD

WHILES RISE

NICHOLAS RD

JOHN PYEL RD

HAYWAY

MEADOWVALE

F2
1 BROOK TERR
2 ARCHFIELD TERR
3 EASTFIELD RD
4 SPRING ST
5 CHURCH WLK
6 OAK TERR
7 THE LOUISA LILLEY HOMES
8 SPINNEY TERR
9 MEADOW WLK
10 GORSEHOLM CT
11 THE LIMES
12 LOVELL CT

SHERIFF HO

NICHOLAS LA

Factory

B571 WELLINGBOROUGH RD

COWPER CL 1
MARRIOTT CL 2

EBBW VALE RD

ALLEN RD

92 A B 93 C D 94 E F

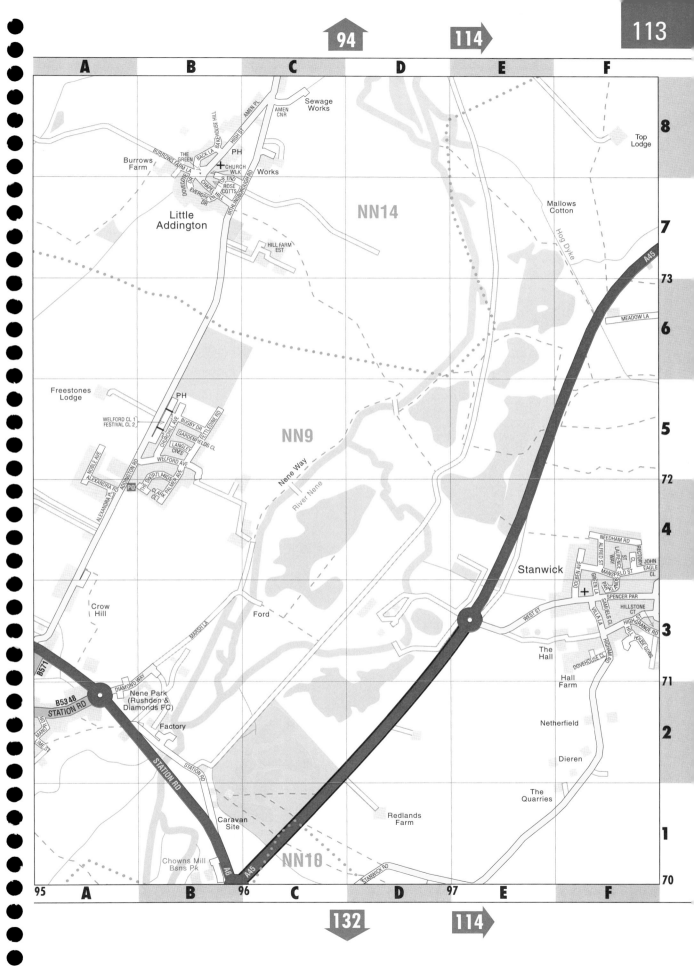

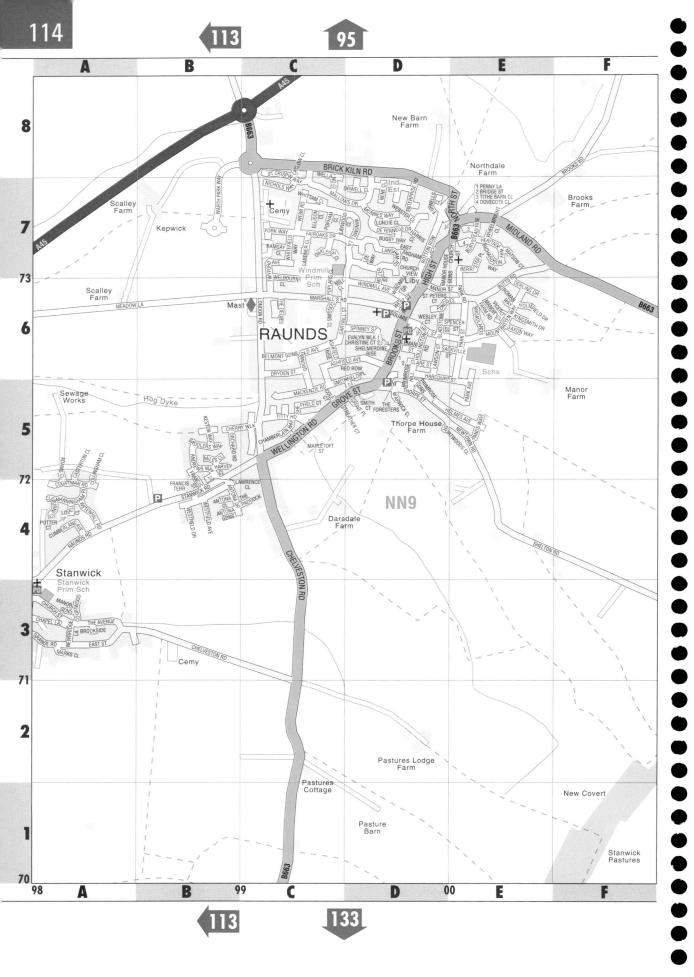

A B C D E F

8

7

73

6

RAUNDS

5

72

4

Stanwick

3

71

2

1

70

98 A 99 B C 00 D E F

NN9

New Barn Farm

Northdale Farm

Brooks Farm

Scalley Farm

Kepwick

Scalley Farm

Sewage Works

Hog Dyke

Darsdale Farm

Manor Farm

Thorpe House Farm

Stanwick Prim Sch

Cemy

Pastures Lodge Farm

Pastures Cottage

Pasture Barn

New Covert

Stanwick Pastures

BRICK KILN RD

MIDLAND RD

WELLINGTON RD

GROVE ST

CHELVESTON RD

CHELVESTON RD

A45

B663

B663

B663

1 PENNY LA
2 BRIDGE ST
3 TITHE BARN CL
4 DOVECOTE CL

Windmill Prim Sch

Cemy

Mast

Meadow La

Shelton Rd

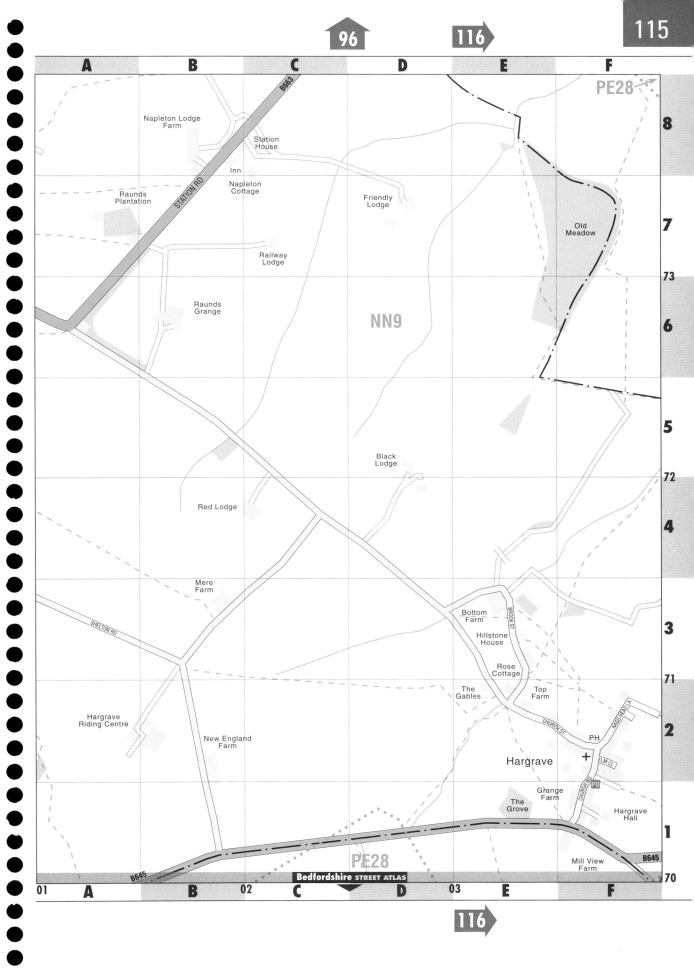

PE28

8

Napleton Lodge
Farm

Station
House

7

Inn

Napleton
Cottage

Friendly
Lodge

Old
Meadow

73

Raunds
Plantation

Railway
Lodge

6

Raunds
Grange

NN9

5

Black
Lodge

72

Red Lodge

4

Mere
Farm

Bottom
Farm

BROOK ST

3

SHELTON RD

Hillstone
House

Rose
Cottage

71

The
Gables

Top
Farm

2

Hargrave
Riding Centre

New England
Farm

CHURCH ST

PH

Hargrave

ELM CL.

CHURCH RD

PO

The
Grove

Grange
Farm

Hargrave
Hall

1

PE28

Mill View
Farm

B645

B645

70

Cambridgeshire STREET ATLAS

Crow's Nest Hill

Manchester Lodge

Clack La

Clack Barn

CHAINBRIDGE LA

Molesworth Lodge Farm

MICKLE HILL

Mickle Hill

Hunt's Close Gorse

Mickle Hill Farm

PE28

Cleaver's Lodge Farm

Three Shires Way

Three Shires Way

NN9

Three Shires Way

Grange Farm

Rookery Farm

CROSS ST

CHURCH LA

PH

Covington

THE PENTELOWES

Three Shire House

Wr Twr

Covington Lodge

Bottom Farm

KEYSTON RD

Covington Gorse

Three Shire Stone

B645

B645

PE28

04   05   06

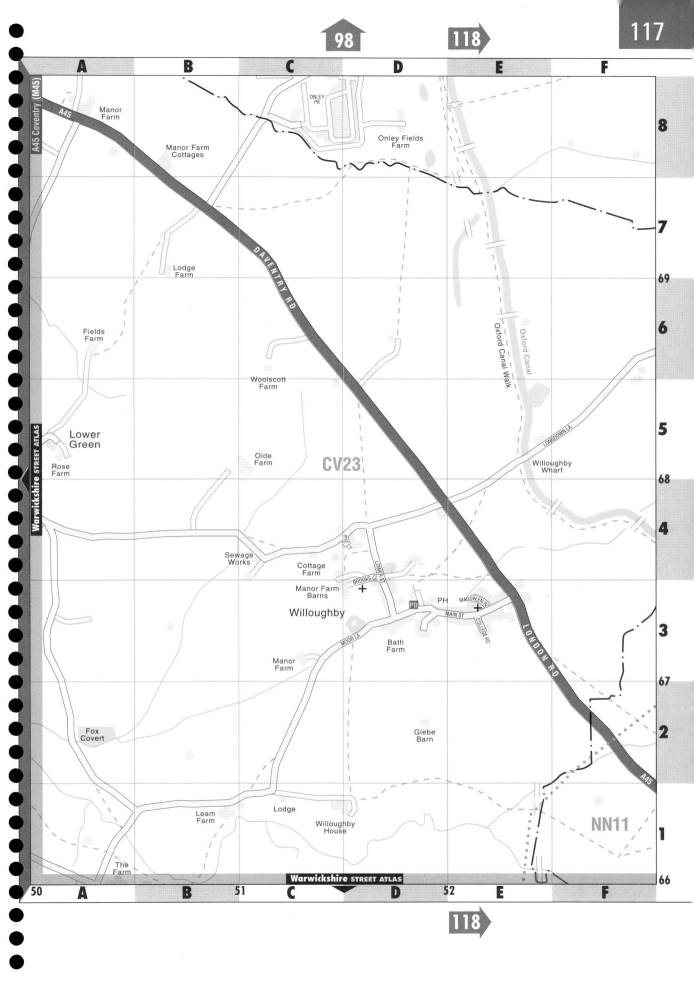

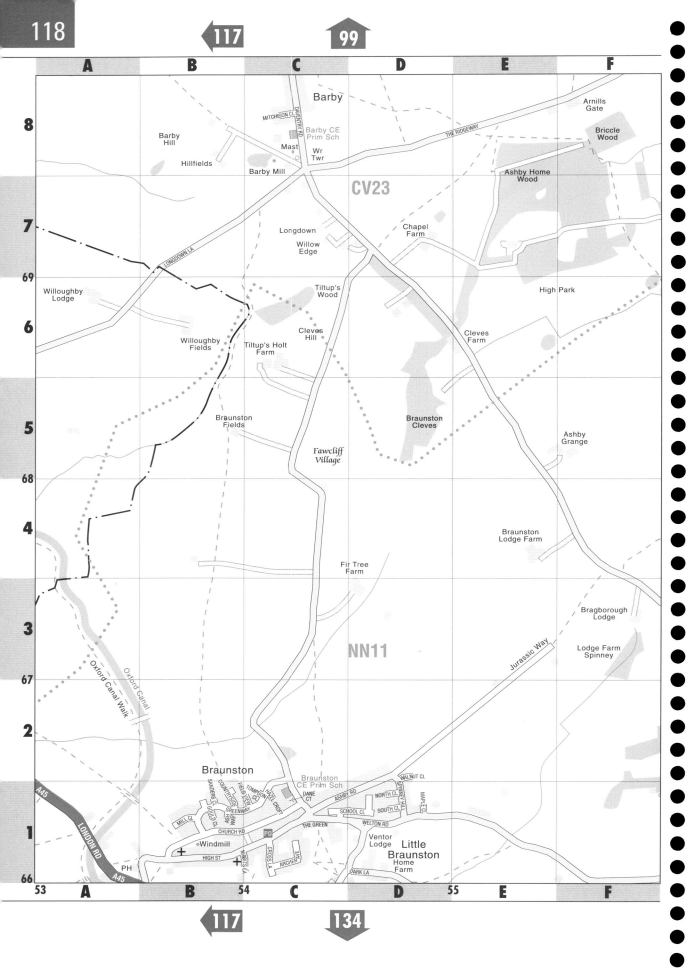

A B C D E F

8
7
69
6
5
68
4
3
67
2
1
66

53 A B 54 C D 55 E F

Barby

MITCHISON CL
DAVENTRY RD

Barby CE
Prim Sch

Barby
Hill

Hillfields

Barby Mill

Mast

Wr
Twr

THE RIDGEWAY

Arnills
Gate

Briccle
Wood

Ashby Home
Wood

CV23

LONGDOWN LA

Longdown

Willow
Edge

Chapel
Farm

High Park

Willoughby
Lodge

Willoughby
Fields

Tiltup's
Wood

Cleves
Hill

Tiltup's Holt
Farm

Cleves
Farm

Ashby
Grange

Braunston
Fields

Fawcliff
Village

Braunston
Cleves

Braunston
Lodge Farm

Fir Tree
Farm

Bragborough
Lodge

Lodge Farm
Spinney

NN11

Jurassic Way

Oxford Canal Walk

Oxford Canal

Braunston

Braunston
CE Prim Sch

Walnut Cl

A45
LONDON RD

SANDERS CL
G GUILD CL
ASH WAY
GREENWAY
MILL CL
COUNTRYSIDE
FIELD VIEW
TOMPSON
HAZEL CROFT

DANE
CT

ASHBY RD

SCHOOL CL

NORTH CL
SOUTH CL

SPINNEY HILL
MAPLE CL

CHURCH RD

THE GREEN

WELTON RD

Windmill

HIGH ST

NIBBITS LA
CROSS LA
ARCHER

PO

PH

DARK LA

Ventor
Lodge

Little
Braunston
Home
Farm

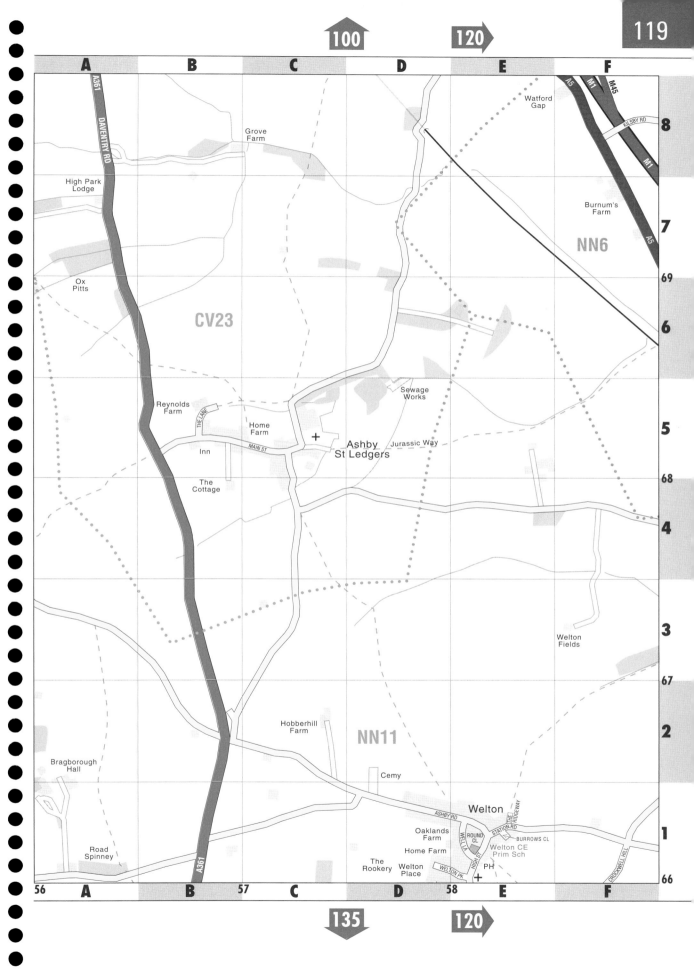

119
101

A B C D E F

8

WATFORD RD

Long Spinney

Barleypiece Spinney

Watford Lodge Farm

KILSBY RD

7

WEST HADDON RD

Cemy

69

Bluebell Spinney

WOODLANDS CT

CHURCH ST

Park House

Jurassic Way

MAIN ST

6

Marina

PARK LA

HENLEY CT

Watford Locks

PARK CL

PO

Grand Union Canal

Watford

Sewage Works

STATION RD

Watford Lodge

LONG BUCKBY RD

5

Foxholes

PH

NN6

Mast

Murcott

B5385

FOG COTTS

Watford Gap Service Area

68

Brockhill Lodge

B5385

4

Langborough Barn

Welton Lodge Farm

Mill House

3

NN11

67

Sewage Works

2

Welton Grange

Ryehill Lodge

White Barn Farm

1

Welton Hythe Marina

Greenhill Farm

66

A5

M1

59   A   B   60   C   D   61   E   F

119
136

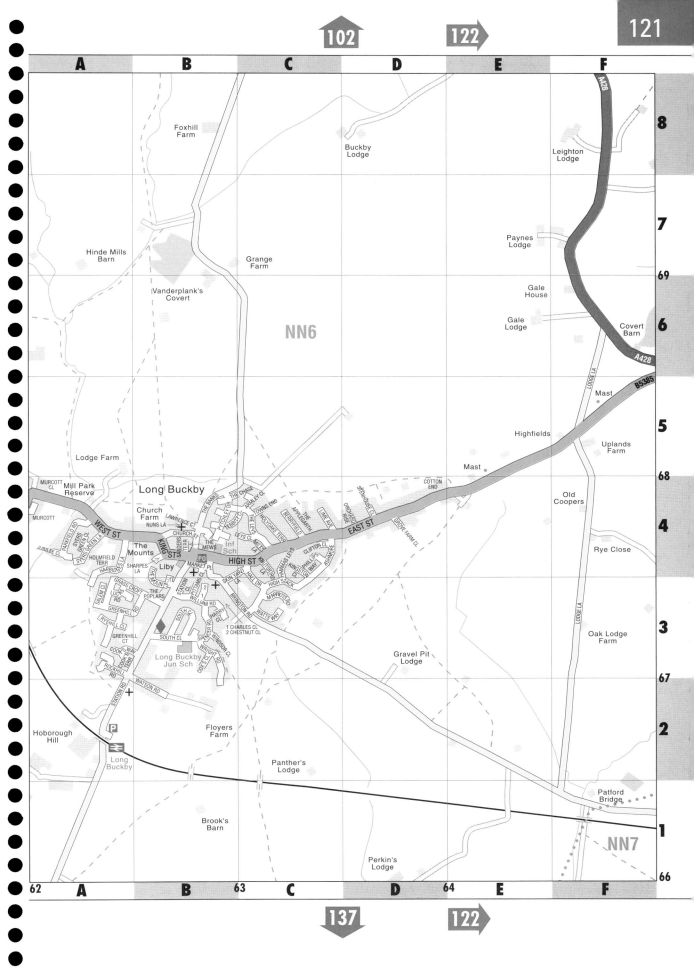

102
122

A B C D E F

8

Foxhill Farm

Buckby Lodge

Leighton Lodge

A428

7

Hinde Mills Barn

Paynes Lodge

69

Grange Farm

Gale House

Vanderplank's Covert

NN6

Gale Lodge

Covert Barn

6

A428

B5385

Mast

5

Lodge Farm

Highfields

Uplands Farm

Mast

68

MURCOTT CL Mill Park Reserve

Long Buckby

COTTON END

Old Coopers

MURCOTT

PARKFIELD RD SYRES GREEN LA Church Farm LAWRENCE CT NUNS LA THE BANKS THE CHASE ARMLEY CL PITCHLEY DR TERRDY CT CHURCH ST TOWINS END THE LEYS HOLYOAKE TERR BERRYFIELD THE APPLEGARTH SPINNDSEL CL ORCHARD RISE GROVE FARM CL

WEST ST KING ST SANDERS TERR THE MEWS Inf Sch LEYS CL MYERS CLIFTON CL LIME AVE EAST ST

4

JUBILEE CL SYRES GREEN LA The Mounts Liby MARKET PL PO HIGH ST KNUTSFORD ASHMORE KINGSTON WAY PHILLIPS WAY

HOLMFIELD TERR HARBIDS SHARPES LA SALEM CL LUCY RD STATION CL PITLINS CL SKIN YARD LA HALL DR HIGH STACK HAMMAS LEYS

Rye Close

GRASS CROFT The Mounts THE POPLARS WILLIAM RD BRINGTON RD MARKIOTS RD

GREENHILL RD SOUTH CL HARRY CL WATTS WAY

RYEHILL CL GREEN-HILL CT SOUTH CL OLD WINDSOR CL SPENCE RD WRIGHT RD 1 CHARLES CL 2 CHESTNUT CL

Oak Lodge Farm

3

COOK'S WAY ROCKHILL RD Long Buckby Jun Sch COTS CL

Gravel Pit Lodge

STATION RD WATSON RD

67

Hoborough Hill

Floyers Farm

2

P

Long Buckby

Panther's Lodge

Patford Bridge

Brook's Barn

1

NN7

Perkin's Lodge

66

62 A B 63 C D 64 E F

137
122

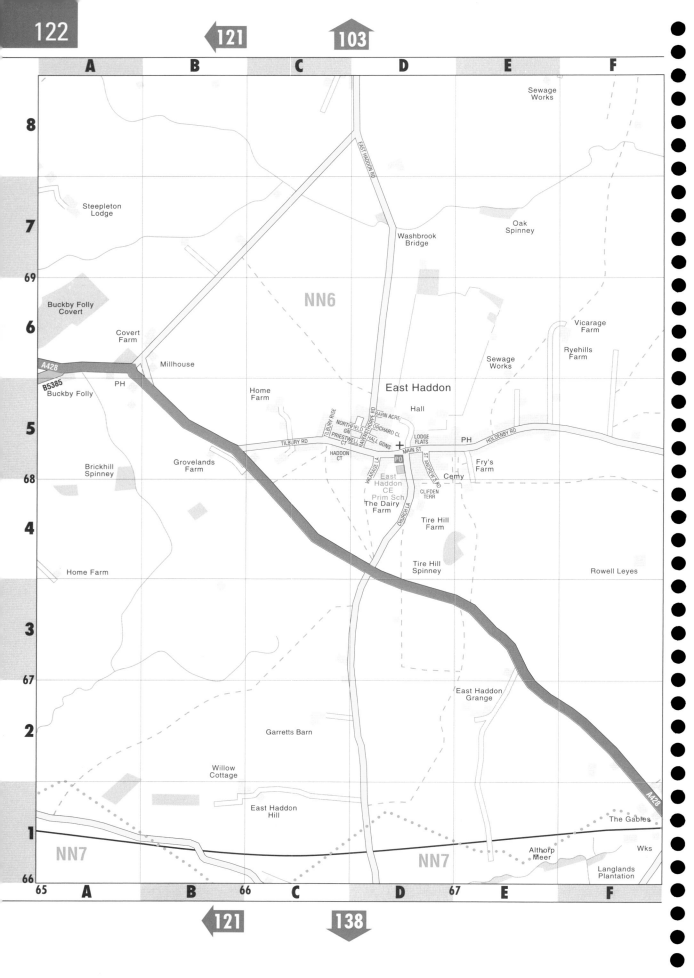

A   B   C   D   E   F

8

7

69

6

NN6

Sewage
Works

Steepleton
Lodge

Washbrook
Bridge

EAST HADDON RD

Oak
Spinney

Buckby Folly
Covert

Covert
Farm

Vicarage
Farm

Ryehills
Farm

A428

Millhouse

Sewage
Works

B5385

PH

East Haddon

Buckby Folly

Home
Farm

Hall

5

TILBURY RISE

BARN ACRE

ORCHARD CL

Grovelands
Farm

NORTHFIELD
GN

RAISTHORPE

HALL GDNS

PRIESTWELL
CT

TILBURY RD

LODGE
FLATS

PH

HOLDENBY RD

Brickhill
Spinney

HADDON
CT

MAIN ST

ST ANDREW'S RD

Fry's
Farm

68

VICARAGE LA

PO

East
Haddon
CE
Prim Sch

Cemy

CLIFDEN
TERR

4

The Dairy
Farm

CHURCH LA

Tire Hill
Farm

Home Farm

Tire Hill
Spinney

Rowell Leyes

3

67

East Haddon
Grange

2

Garretts Barn

Willow
Cottage

A428

East Haddon
Hill

The Gables

1

NN7

Althorp
Meer

NN7

Wks

Langlands
Plantation

66

65   A   B   66   C   D   67   E   F

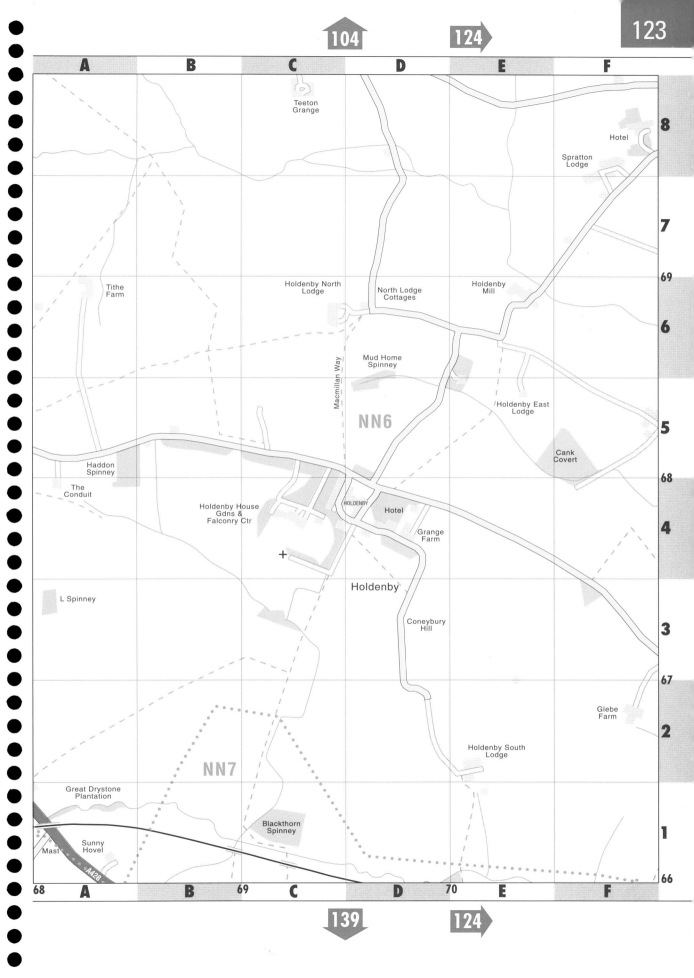

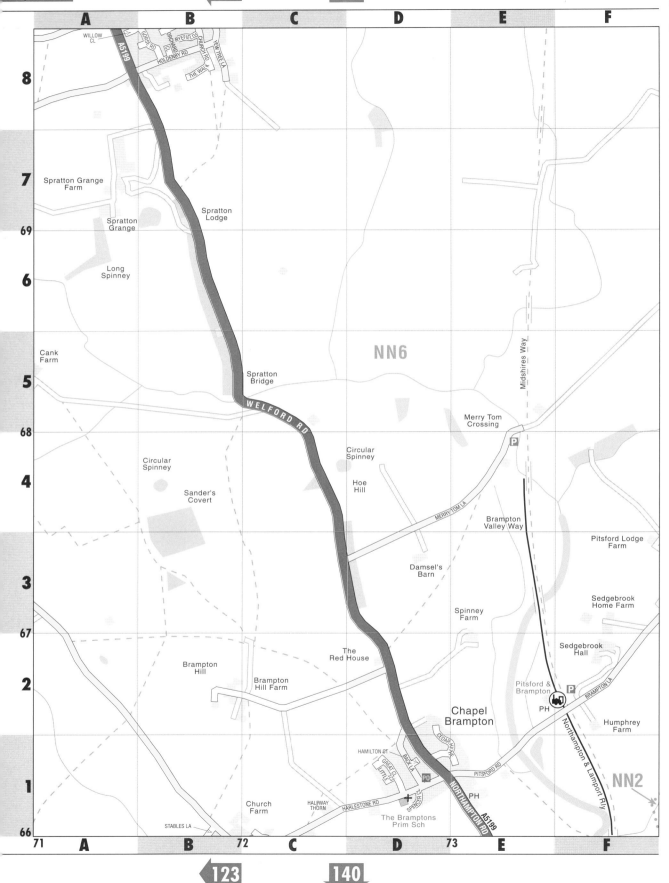

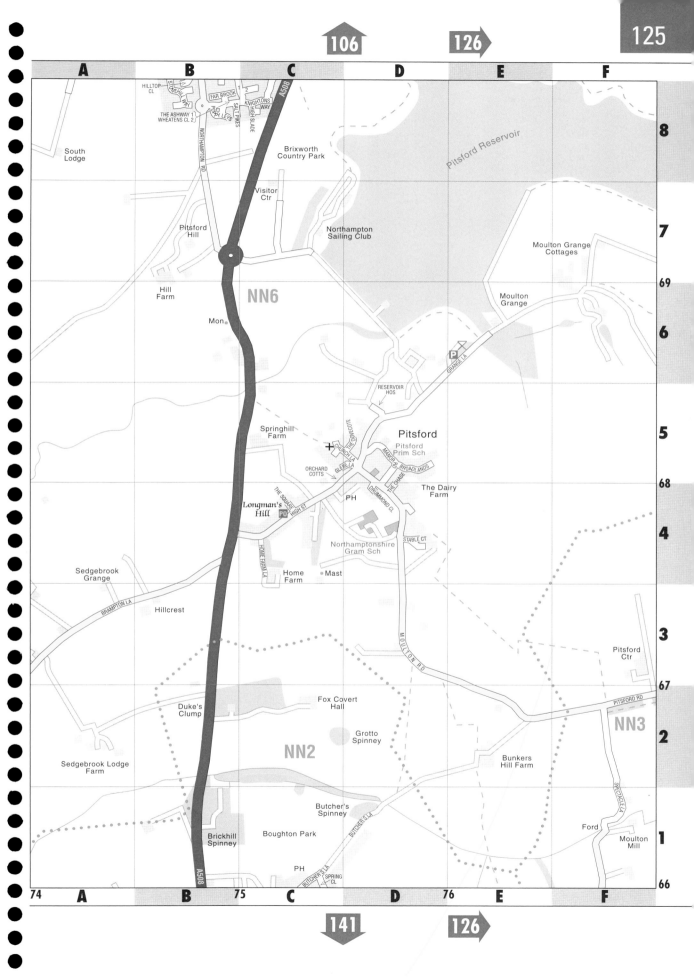

125
107

A   B   C   D   E   F

8

Lower Brixworth
Lodge

Pitsford Reservoir

NN6

Brixworth Rd

Walgrave Rd

Rectory La   Main St   PO
Farm Cl   Polars La   PH

Manor
Farm   Glebe Cl

Back La   Sunny
Bank   Holcot

The
Hawthorns

Sywell Rd   Equestrian
Ctr

7

North
Fields

Moulton Grange
Farm

Moulton Rd

Tithe Cl

69

Hillcrest

Moulton Lodge
Farm

6

North
Farm

Tithe
Farm

South
Lodge

5

Overstone
Old Rectory

68

Slade
Farm

Holcot Rd

Grange
Cottages

Overstone
Grange

4

Moulton
Lodge

Boughton Fair La

NN3

3

Hog Hole
Spinney

Marsh
Spinney

A43

Kettering Rd

67

Pitsford Rd

2

Holcot
Centre

Cemy

Browns Cl

The Grove

Grove
Farm

Grove Farm La

Sandy Hill
Farm

Sandy Hill La

Park View

NN6

Moulton

The Hollies

Church View

Church La

Overstone
Farm

Stewart Cl

The Laurels

Moulton
Coll

Moulton
Prim Sch

Church
Mews

Church Hill

The Parade

Albone Cl

Pytchley
View

Tarrant Way

Tarrant Cl

Overstone Rd

Park
View Cl

1

Sewage
Works

Arnsby Cres

Jefes Cl   Eynon Cl

Pound
Ct

West St

The Paddocks

2

School La

Church Hill

Honey Cross St

High St

Homestead Cl

Siddons Way

The Crescent

Prince Of Wales Row

Ashley La

Wantage Cl

Park
View Cl

Overstone La

A43   Park View

Overstone La

Carey Ct

Carey

Boughton Rd

Pound La

Lunchfield
Ct

Lunchfield
Gdns

Northampton La

Ashby Cl

5   Lunchfield

3

Oakley La

Liby

Dove La

The Avenue

Billing La

Sywell Rd

Moulton
Sch

66

77   A   78   B   C   78   D   79   E   F

125
142

C1
1 LEONARD LA
2 BLUEBELL PK CVN PK
3 THE NURSERIES
4 ASHBY GDNS
5 CHAPPELL HO
6 WELLS CT
7 LUNCHFIELD WLK

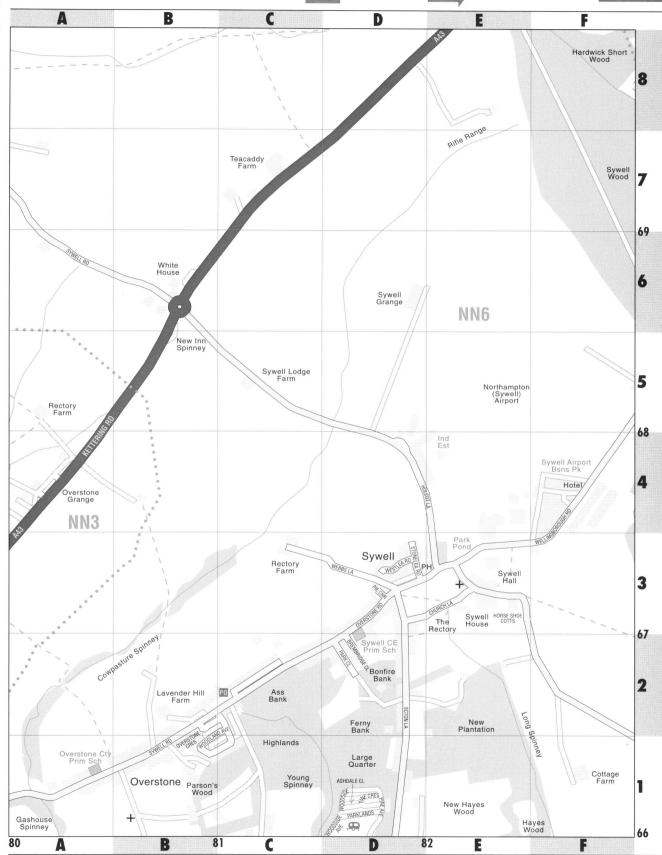

108
128

A B C D E F

8
7
69
6
5
68
4
3
67
2
1
66

Hardwick Short Wood

Rifle Range

Sywell Wood

Teacaddy Farm

A43

SYWELL RD

White House

Sywell Grange

NN6

New Inn Spinney

Sywell Lodge Farm

Northampton (Sywell) Airport

Rectory Farm

KETTERING RD

Ind Est

Sywell Airport Bsns Pk

Hotel

Overstone Grange

NN3

A43

WELLINGBOROUGH RD

Park Pond

Rectory Farm

Sywell

HOLCOT LA

STONE LA RD

PH

Sywell Hall

WEBBS LA

WEST LEA RD

Sywell House

HORSE SHOE COTTS

Cowpasture Spinney

PIE CNR

OVERSTONE RD

CHURCH LA

The Rectory

Sywell CE Prim Sch

BREAMBRIDGE CL

PARK CL

Bonfire Bank

ECTON LA

Lavender Hill Farm

PO

Ass Bank

Ferny Bank

New Plantation

Long Spinney

Overstone Cty Prim Sch

SYWELL RD

OVERSTONE CRES

WOODLAND AVE

Highlands

Large Quarter

Cottage Farm

Overstone

Parson's Wood

Young Spinney

ASHDALE CL

New Hayes Wood

Gashouse Spinney

WOODSIDE AVE

PINE CRES

PINE AVE

PARKLANDS

Hayes Wood

80 A B 81 C D 82 E F

143
128

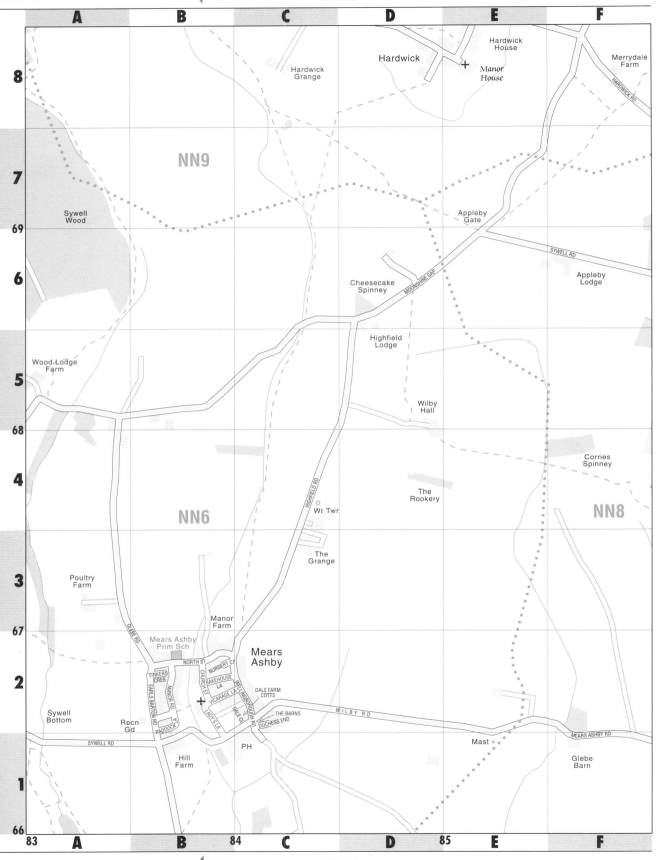

A B C D E F

8

NN9

7

69

6

Sywell
Wood

Hardwick
Grange

Hardwick

Hardwick
House

Manor
House

Merrydale
Farm

HARDWICK RD

Appleby
Gate

SYWELL RD

Appleby
Lodge

Cheesecake
Spinney

MOONSHINE GAP

5

68

Wood Lodge
Farm

Highfield
Lodge

Wilby
Hall

Corries
Spinney

4

NN6

HIGHFIELD RD

Wr Twr

The
Rookery

NN8

3

67

Poultry
Farm

Manor
Farm

The
Grange

2

GLEBE RD

Mears Ashby
Prim Sch

NORTH ST

TINKERS
CRES

EARLS BARTON RD

MANOR RD

PADDOCK

CHURCH ST

NURSERY CT

BAKEHOUSE
LA

VICARAGE LA

LADY'S LA

DALE CL

WELLINGBOROUGH RD

Mears
Ashby

DALE FARM
COTTS

THE BARNS

DUCHESS END

WILBY RD

Mast

MEARS ASHBY RD

Glebe
Barn

1

Sywell
Bottom

Recn
Gd

SYWELL RD

Hill
Farm

PH

66

83 A B 84 C D 85 E F

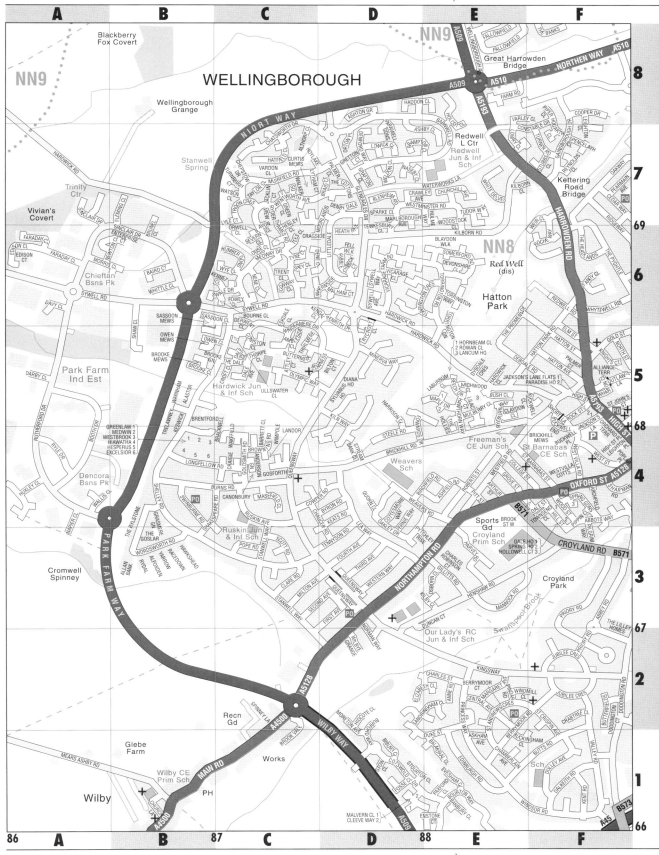

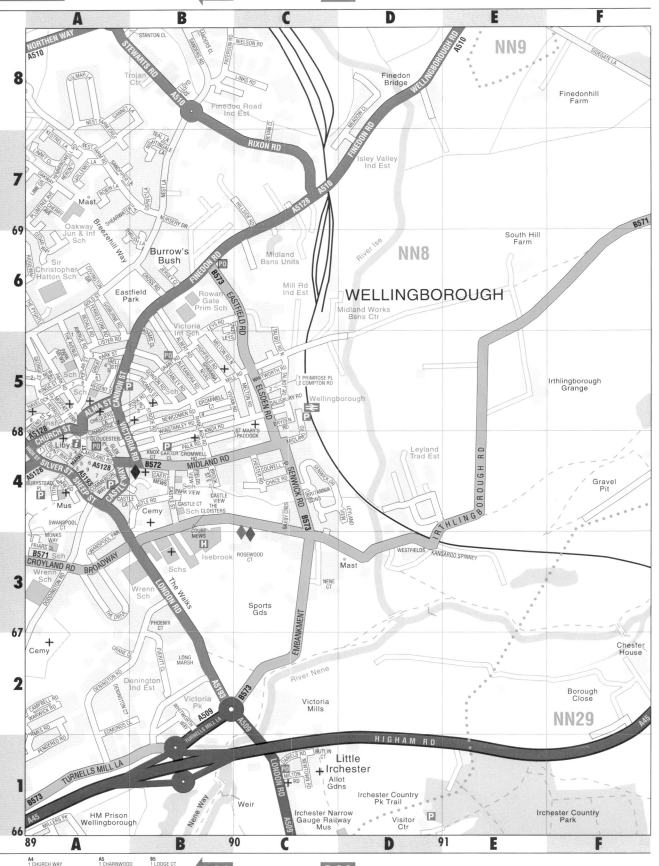

WELLINGBOROUGH

NN9

NN8

NN29

Finedonhill Farm

Finedon Bridge

Irthlingborough Grange

Chester House

Borough Close

Little Irchester

Irchester Country Park

HM Prison Wellingborough

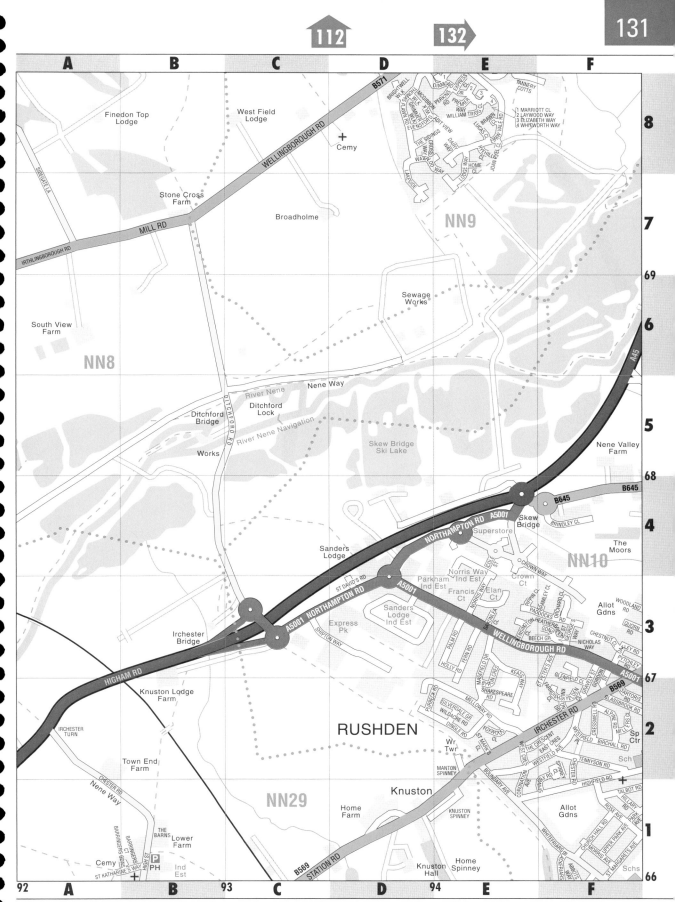

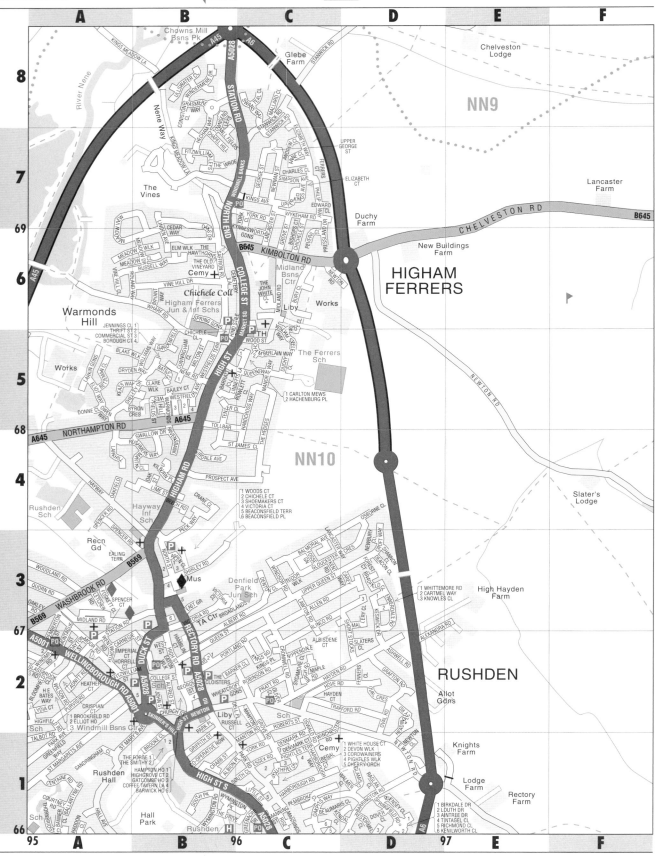

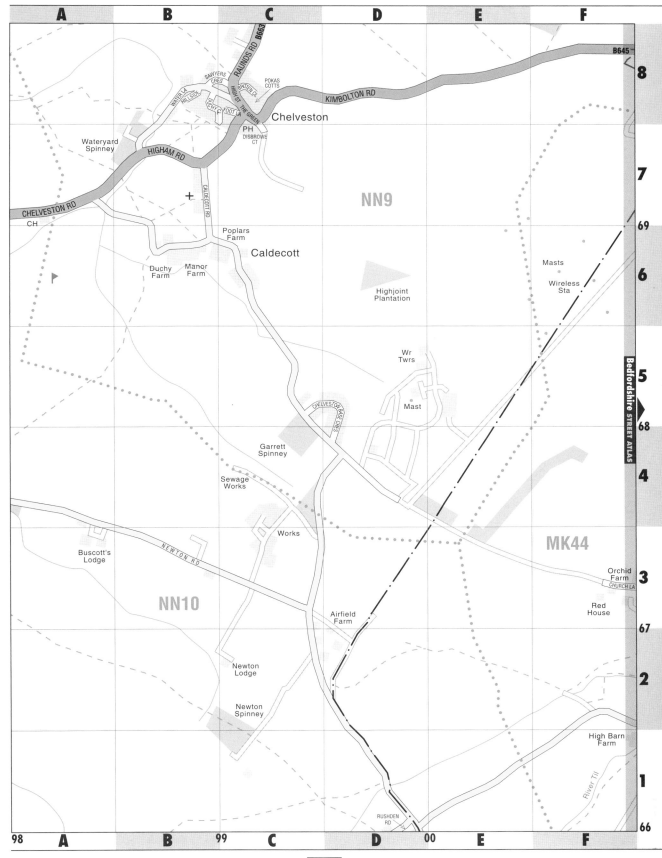

A B C D E F

B645

RAUNDS RD B663

SAWYERS CRES
WATER LA
MILLSIDE
HIGH ST
SPITTEN CL
POKAS COTTS
THE GREEN
DUCHY C
FOOT LA

KIMBOLTON RD

Chelveston

PH
DISBROWE CT

Wateryard
Spinney

HIGHAM RD

NN9

CHELVESTON RD

CH

CALDECOTT RD

+

Poplars
Farm

Caldecott

Duchy
Farm
Manor
Farm

Highjoint
Plantation

Masts

Wireless
Sta

Wr
Twrs

Mast

CHELVESTON BASE CRES

Garrett
Spinney

Sewage
Works

Bedfordshire STREET ATLAS

Buscott's
Lodge

NEWTON RD

Works

MK44

Orchid
Farm
CHURCH LA

NN10

Red
House

Newton
Lodge

Airfield
Farm

Newton
Spinney

High Barn
Farm

River Til

RUSHDEN
RD

98 A B 99 C D 00 E F

8 7 69 6 5 68 4 3 67 2 1 66

118

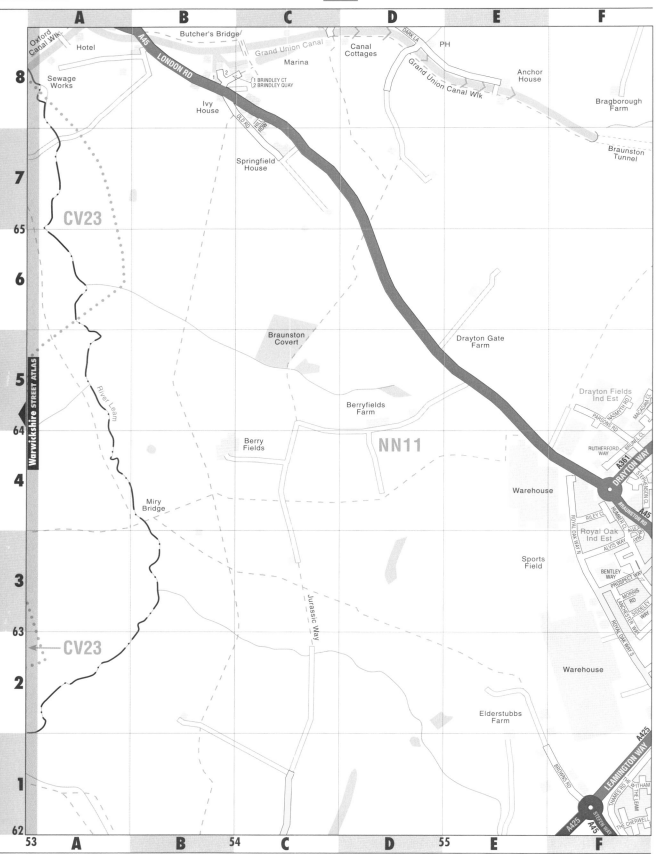

Oxford Canal Wlk
Hotel
Butcher's Bridge
A45
LONDON RD
Grand Union Canal
Marina
Canal Cottages
DARK LA
PH
Grand Union Canal Wlk
Anchor House
Bragborough Farm

Sewage Works
Ivy House
1
2
1 BRINDLEY CT
2 BRINDLEY QUAY

Braunston Tunnel

OLD RD
HILL ROW

Springfield House

CV23

River Leam

Braunston Covert

Drayton Gate Farm

Drayton Fields Ind Est
NASMYTH RD
PARSONS RD
MACADAM CL

Berryfields Farm

NN11

RUTHERFORD WAY
BROWNE CL
STEPHENSON CL

Berry Fields

A361
DRAYTON WAY
A45
BRAUNSTON RD

Warehouse

RILEY CL
HUMBER RD
AUSTIN CL

Miry Bridge

Royal Oak Ind Est
ROYAL OAK WAY N
ALVIS WAY

Sports Field

BENTLEY WAY
PROSPECT WAY
MORRIS RD
SIDDELEY WAY
LANCHESTER WAY
ROYAL OAK WAY S

Jurassic Way

Warwickshire STREET ATLAS

CV23

Warehouse

Elderstubbs Farm

A425
LEAMINGTON WAY

BROWNS RD

THAMES RD
THE WITHAM
THE LEAM
THE CHERWELL

A425
A45
SEVERN WAY

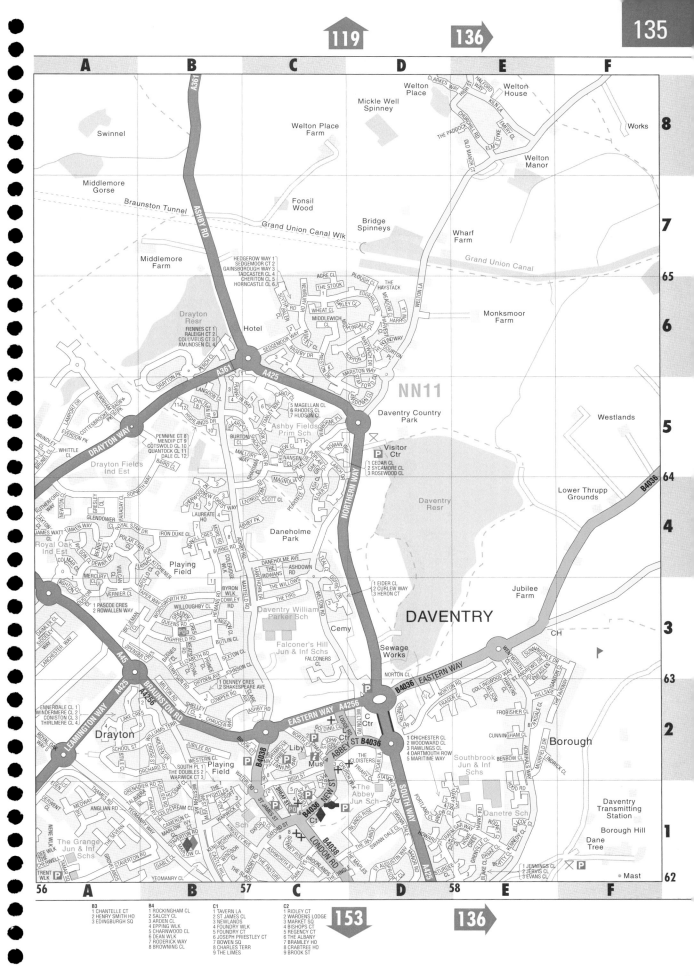

135
120

A B C D E F

8

7

65

6

5

64

4

3

63

2

1

62

Crockwell Farm

Cornerhill Spinney

Norton Junction

Grand Union Canal

Grand Union Canal Wlk

Swing Bridge

PH

Buckby Top Lock

Rye Hill Farm

NN6

NEWBRIDGE

THE COUNCIL HOS

Surney Cottage

Surney Farm

Thrupp Grounds

Thrupp Lodge

B4036

Long Buckby Wharf

Thrupp Covert

Norton Lodge Farm

Whilton Lodge

Whilton Locks

B4036

NN11

Marina

Sewage Works

DAVENTRY RD

Beehive Lodge

EAGLESFIELD
HOME FARM CT
BAKERS

MANOR GDNS

Norton Hall Farm

Pant Y Owen Farm

Watling Lodge

PH

WEEDON LA

THE BROADWAY

Norton

Allot Gdns

Noborough Lodge

Mast

Borough Hill Plantation

Underhill Spinney

Noborough Farm

Noborough Spinney

The Woodyard
Heart of The Shires
Sh Village

NN7

Ivy House Farm

A5

M1

59 A B 60 C D 61 E F

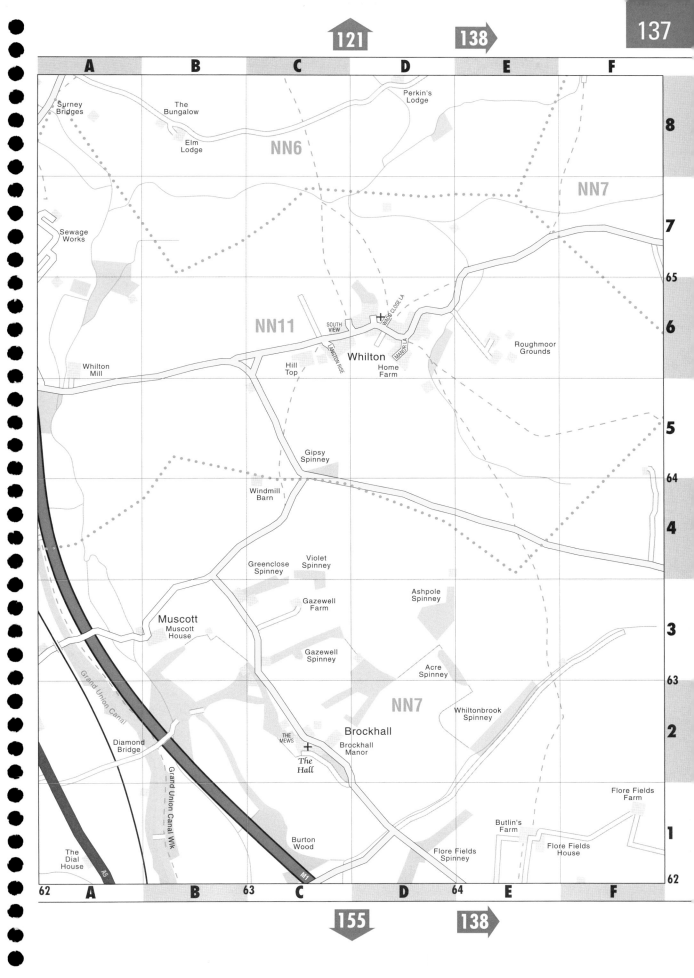

121
138

A B C D E F

8

NN7

7

65

6

5

64

4

3

63

2

1

62

Surney Bridges

The Bungalow

Perkin's Lodge

Elm Lodge

NN6

Sewage Works

NN11

Whilton Mill

SOUTH VIEW

WADD CLOSE LA

Whilton

Home Farm

MANOR LA

LANGTON RISE

Hill Top

Roughmoor Grounds

Gipsy Spinney

Windmill Barn

Greenclose Spinney

Violet Spinney

Ashpole Spinney

Gazewell Farm

Muscott
Muscott House

Gazewell Spinney

Acre Spinney

NN7

Whiltonbrook Spinney

Grand Union Canal

Grand Union Canal Wlk

THE MEWS

Brockhall

Brockhall Manor

Diamond Bridge

The Hall

Flore Fields Farm

Burton Wood

Butlin's Farm

Flore Fields Spinney

Flore Fields House

The Dial House

A5

M1

62 A B 63 C D 64 E F

137 122

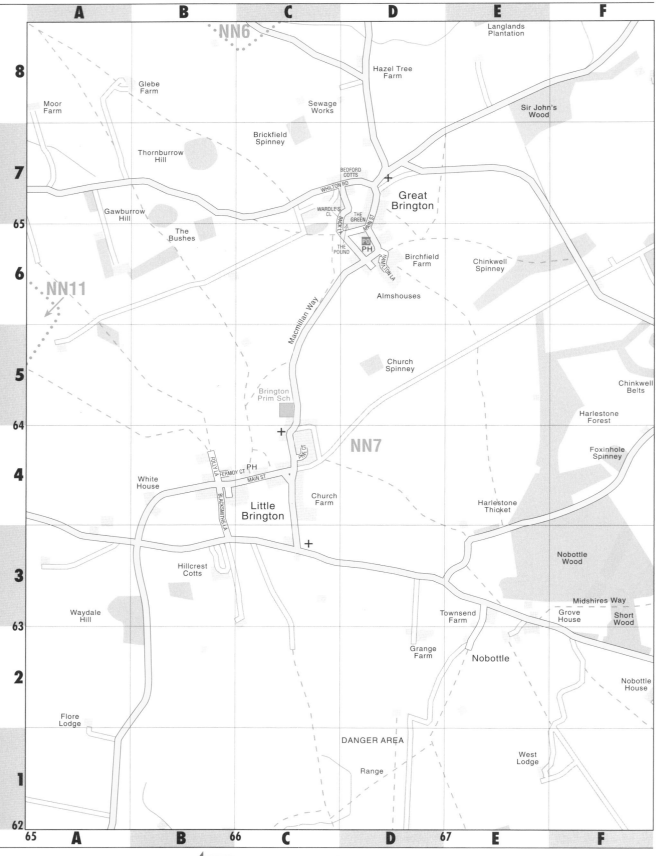

NN6

Langlands Plantation

Hazel Tree Farm

Moor Farm

Glebe Farm

Sewage Works

Sir John's Wood

Brickfield Spinney

Thornburrow Hill

BEDFORD COTTS

WHILTON RD

Great Brington

Gawburrow Hill

WARDLE'S CL

THE GREEN

BACK LA

MAIN ST

The Bushes

THE POUND

PO PH

Birchfield Farm

Chinkwell Spinney

HAMILTON LA

NN11

Macmillan Way

Almshouses

Church Spinney

Chinkwell Belts

Brington Prim Sch

Harlestone Forest

NN7

Foxinhole Spinney

FOLLY LA

PH

FERMOY CT

PRIORY CT

White House

MAIN ST

Church Farm

Harlestone Thicket

BLACKSMITHS LA

Little Brington

Hillcrest Cotts

Nobottle Wood

Waydale Hill

Midshires Way

Townsend Farm

Grove House

Short Wood

Grange Farm

Nobottle

Nobottle House

Flore Lodge

DANGER AREA

West Lodge

Range

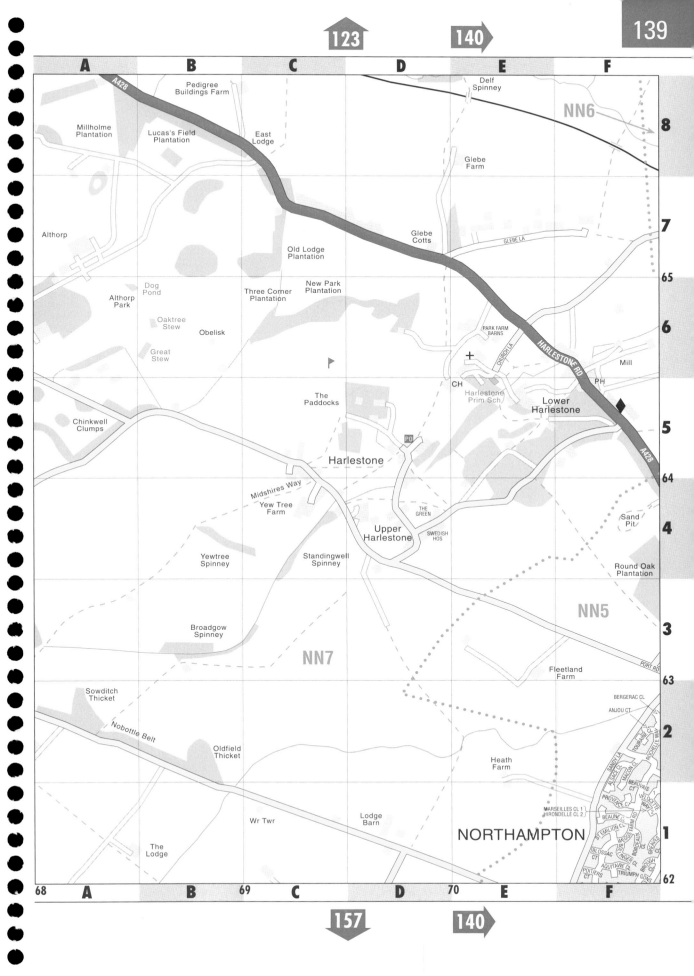

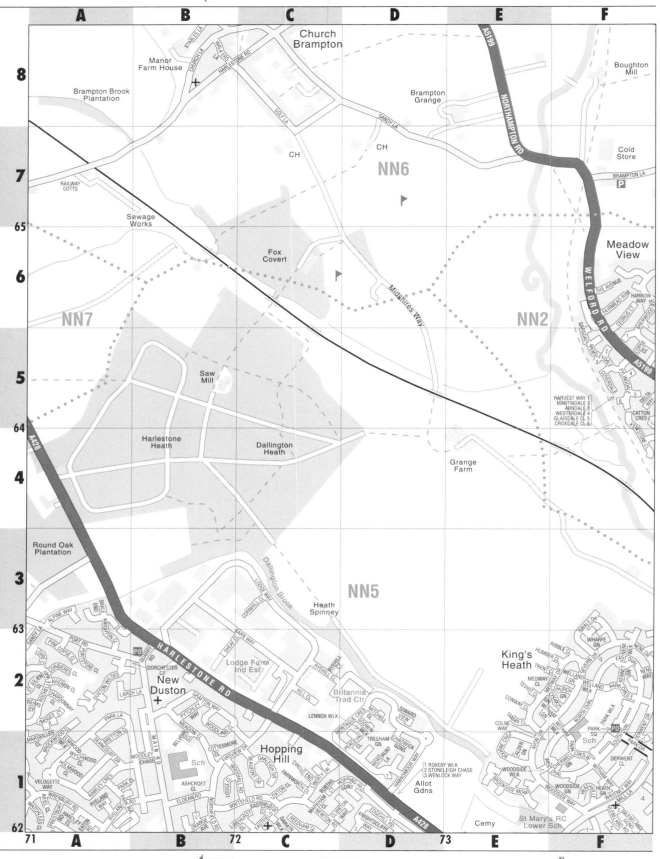

139
124

Church Brampton

Manor Farm House

Brampton Brook Plantation

Brampton Grange

Boughton Mill

Cold Store

NN6

RAILWAY COTTS

Sewage Works

Fox Covert

Meadow View

NN7

NN2

Saw Mill

Harlestone Heath

Dallington Heath

Grange Farm

HARVEST WAY 1
MARTINDALE 2
ARNDALE 3
WESTERDALE 4
GLAISDALE CL 5
CROXDALE CL 6

Round Oak Plantation

NN5

Dallington Brook

Heath Spinney

King's Heath

Lodge Farm Ind Est

New Duston

Britannia Trad Ctr

Hopping Hill

1 ROKEBY WLK
2 STONELEIGH CHASE
3 WENLOCK WAY

Allot Gdns

St Mary's RC Lower Sch

Cemy

139
158

F1
1 THE CROFT
2 THE BARTONS CL
3 ST MARGARET'S GDNS
4 KG House Bsns Ctr

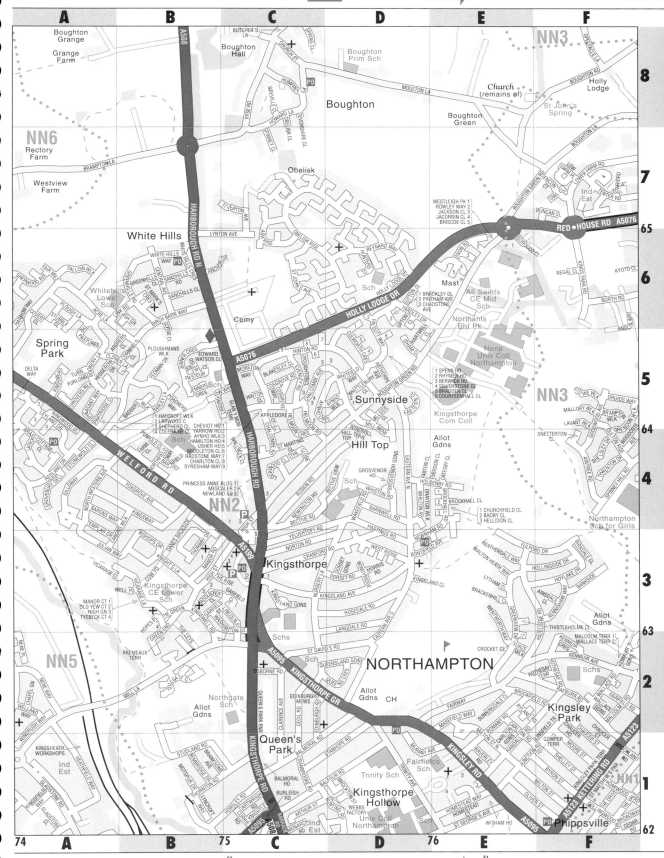

125
142
159
142

C3
1 CRANFORD HO
2 Kingsthorpe Sh Ctr
3 ETON CT
4 STABLE CT
5 ALEXANDRA TERR

E1
1 BETHANY HOMESTEAD
2 DARDIS CL
3 KINGSLEY GDNS
4 METHODIST HOMESTEAD

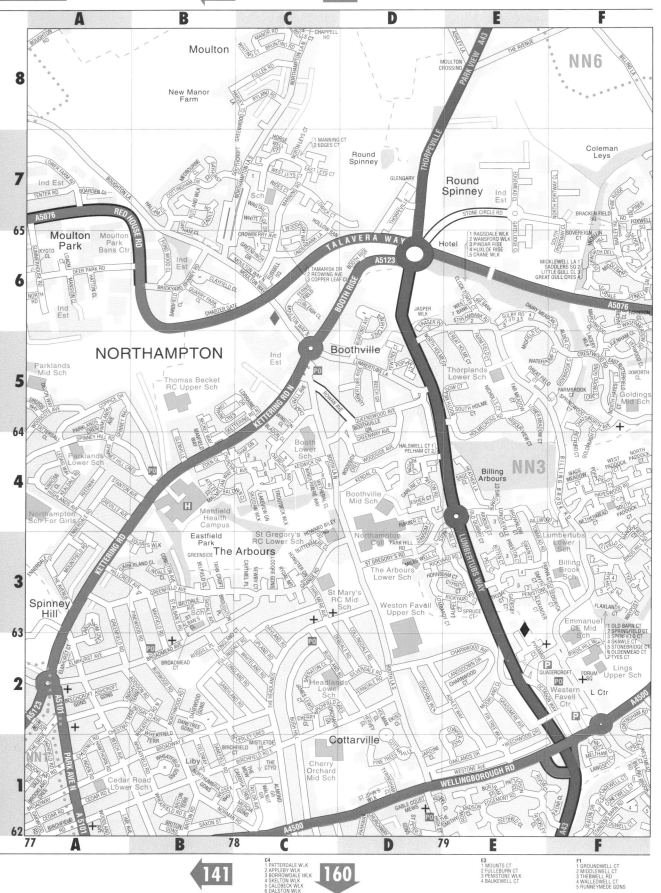

C4
1 PATTERDALE WLK
2 APPLEBY WLK
3 BORROWDALE WLK
4 SKELTON WLK
5 CALDBECK WLK
6 DALSTON WLK
7 KIRKSTONE WLK
8 LANERCOST WLK
9 AMBLESIDE CL

E3
1 MOUNTS CT
2 FULLEBURN CT
3 PENISTONE WLK
4 BAUKEWELL CT

F1
1 GROUNDWELL CT
2 MIDDLEWELL CT
3 THEBWELL RD
4 WALLEDWELL CT
5 RUNNEYMEDE GDNS

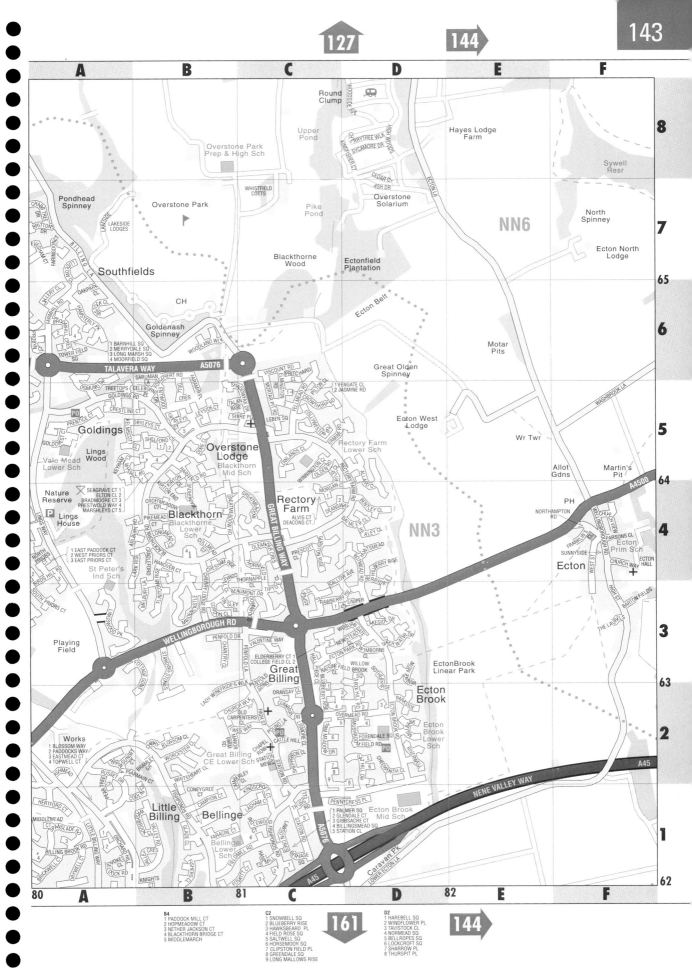

A B C D E F

8 7 65 6 5 64 4 3 63 2 1 62

80 81 82

Round Clump
WOODSIDE AVE
Upper Pond
Hayes Lodge Farm
CHERRYTREE WLK
KINGFISHER CT
SYCAMORE DR
HIGH WOODS
Sywell Resr
Overstone Park Prep & High Sch
WHISTFIELD COTTS
CEDAR CY
ASH DR
Overstone Solarium
ECTON LA
NN6
North Spinney
Pondhead Spinney
CRABB TREE DR
BRITTONS DR
LAKESIDE
LAKESIDE LODGES
Overstone Park
Pike Pond
Ecton North Lodge
ELSHAM CL
FARRINGTON
BILLING LA
Southfields
Blackthorne Wood
Ectonfield Plantation
ARTILLERY CL
FARMHILL RD
BROOMHILL CRES
HAMSTERLY PK
DUCK CL
CH
Ecton Belt
TOWER FIELD SQ
PHOENIX
Goldenash Spinney
WOODLAND WLK
1 BARNHILL SQ
2 MERRYDALE SQ
3 LONG MARSH SQ
4 MOORFIELD SQ
Motar Pits
TALAVERA WAY A5076
VISCOUNT RD
PRITCHARD
SARUMAN
ROBERT RD
FARWAY PK
Great Olden Spinney
OSMUNS
TREETOPS
CELEBORN
FLEETWOOD
GOLDINGS RD
DEL CRES
SHADOWAX LA
TALAN RISE
SHIRE PL
LEBEN SQ
WASHBROOK LA
1 FENGATE CL
2 JASMINE RD
PRENTICE CT
CRESTLINE CT
Goldings
DRYLEYS CT
SHELFORD CT
LEYSIDE CT
DOWLANDS CL
WINNINGTON CL
OLDEN RD
Ecton West Lodge
Wr Twr
GOLDCREST
Lings Wood
KENHAM
SALL RD
Overstone Lodge
RECTORY FARM RD
ALLARD RD
Allot Gdns
Martin's Pit
Vale Mead Lower Sch
KEYHAM
Blackthorne Mid Sch
Rectory Farm Lower Sch
A4500
64
Nature Reserve
SEAGRAVE CT 1
ELTON CL 2
BRADMOORE CT 3
PRESTWOLD WAY 4
MARSHLEYS CT 5
CROFTMEAD
ARLBURY RD
MIRTON END
HUSBORNE
GREATMEADOW
GREATMEADOW
MORGAN CL
BENTLEY CT
DEANSWAY
PH
NORTHAMPTON RD
FRANKLINS
WEST ST
PARSONS CL
Ecton Prim Sch
Lings House
PIKEMEAD
Blackthorn Lower Sch
OLD MILL RD
ALVIS CT
DEACONS CT
DAIMLER CL
SUNNYSIDE
CHURCH WAY
Ecton Hall
NORTH PRIORS
BIRDS HILL CT
1 EAST PADDOCK CT
2 WEST PRIORS CT
3 EAST PRIORS CT
HANOVER CT
OLEAN RISE
THORNE CL
CRESTON RISE
MARTSMEAD
HIGH ST
Ecton
BARTON FIELDS
LINGSWOOD PK
St Peter's Ind Sch
MELBURY RD
FLINTOME RISE
LARK RISE
CHESHAM PK
TIPTON
SALLOW AVE
JERRY RISE
BERYLON
THE LAURELS
SOUTH PRIORS CT
MASON CASTLE
THORNAPPLE CL
BEAUMONT DR
RAWBERRY HILL
JUNIPER
Playing Field
COTTAGE GDNS
STIRLING STANES
CODON CL
SLEY CL
Wellingborough Rd
LAKESIDE DR
DEER WATER DR
Great Billing
WELLINGBOROUGH RD
PENFOLD DR
VALENTINE WAY
WOBURN CL
NEWSTEAD CL
WIMBORNE CL
ECTON PARK RD
EctonBrook Linear Park
PENFOLD LA
CHANTRY CL
ELDERBERRY CT 1
COLLEGE FIELD CL 2
HALL
BLUEBERRY RISE
PIECE
RATSING FIELD CL
WILLOW BROOK
SOTTERBY RISE
Ecton Brook
Works
1 BLOSSOM WAY
2 PADDOCKS WAY
3 EASTMEAD CT
4 TOPWELL CT
LADY WINEFRIDE'S WLK
ORANSAY CL
CUMBRE DR
BLUEBERRY RISE
ROXHILL
MUSHROOM FIELD RD
SPINNEY MEADOW
PARADISE
Ecton Brook Lower Sch
BRAMLEY GR
BLOSSOM CL
OLD CARPENTERS CL
CHURCH WLK
HIGH ST
POND LA
ELWES WAY
CATTLE HILL CL
OVERMEAD RD
ECTON BROOK RD
CHMEAD
APPLE
SUNSET
WORCESTER CT
WHITEHEART CT
CHAPEL ROW
NELSON CL
FOXENDALE SQ
PO
1 PALMER SQ
2 GLENDALE CT
3 GIBBSACRE CT
4 BILLINGSMEAD SQ
Ecton Brook Mid Sch
HERTFORD CT
RUSSEL DR
PEARMAIN CT
Great Billing CE Lower Sch
STATION MEWS
CONEYGREE CT
KINGSCROFT
CAMBERLEY CL
KINGSLEY
TRUSS
CHEDWORTH RD
A45
MIDDLEMEAD
CODLIN
CAMPION CT
LASHAM SQ
STATION RD
PENNYCRESS PL
NENE VALLEY WAY
Little Billing
SPINSLADE DR
Bellinge
FABACRE CT
ELMWOOD
FIELDGATE CT
LANSDOWNE CRES
Caravan Pk
BILLING BROOK RD
LITTLE BILLING WAY
VALLEY RD
FELDON CL
Bellinge Lower Sch
FELDMILL RD
HAREHILL RD
FOSKITT CT
A5076
LOWER ECTON LA
BRICKWELL CT
ORYWELL CT
BELDOCK RD
WOKES CT
KNIGHTS

NN3
Ecton Brook
Bellinge
Great Billing

143
128

A B C D E F

8

Trafalgar Covert

Ward's Barn

Field Barn

NN8

Sywell Resr Country Park

Hockerhill Farm

Brookhill House

7

Brookhill Farm

A4500

Visitors Ctr

P

WASHBROOK LA

Sandpit Barn

65

Sandwell Spinney

Mainroad Farm

MEARS ASHBY RD

6

White House Ind Est

MAIN RD

Cemy

Allot Gdns

Ecton East Lodge

Copplemore Barn

EARLS BARTON TURN

B573

The Grange

WELLINGBOROUGH RD

TITLEY BAWK AVE

BARTON AVE

Ind Est

Grange Farm

Ash Spinney

New Lodge

NORTHAMPTON RD

MALLARD BROOKES

THE PYGHTLE

HORNBY RD

KING ST

VICTORIA ST

New Barton

5

Earls Barton Bridge

Elizabeth Way

GRANGE CL

STRETTON WAY

TWINLEY WAY

WHITE WAY

Elizabeth CL

Victoria CL

MANOR RD

NORTH R'ST

PRINCE

Stevens Ct

Ecton Lodge

BERRY CL

QUEEN ST

64

A4500

Dutch Walk

WEST WAY

HARROWICK LA

WHITWORTH

KNIGHTS CL

HIGH ST

MANOR HOUSE CL

CHURCHILL RD

MILL S CL

SPENCER CL

ST CRISPIN RD

Nightingale Walk

NN6

AUSTINS YD

THE SQUARE

Earls Barton Jun & Inf Schs

FAIRWAY

FIRS CL

CLARKE CT

The Clump

Kemshead Farm

LEY'S RD

TEBBUTTS CL

WEST ST

B573

PO

Liby

DODDINGTON RD

B573

The Wilderness

AGGATE WAY

PARK CL

PARK ST

PARK LA

HARCOURT SQ

BROAD ST

NEW ST

4

SUNNY SIDE

LONDON END

Mus

SAXON RISE

DOWTHORPE END

SPRING GDNS

MOUNT PLEASANT

CORDON CRES

KEATS CL

Earls Barton

South Lodge

WK SOM WAY

BARKER RD

SHURVILLE CL

CLARE CL

OXFORD CL

BALMORAL CL

MILBURY

3

Ryehill Spinney

Nene Way

ALLBONE RD

SHEFIELD

DOWTHORPE HILL

Robersacks Spinney

CUMPTON AVE

STATION RD

63

Blackthorn Spinney

THORPE RD

Crow Spinney

A45

2

A45

B573

Sewage Works

Comander's Spinney

GRENDON RD

NN3

STATION RD

1

Wind Spinney

Sports Ground

NN7

62

83 A B 84 C D 85 E F

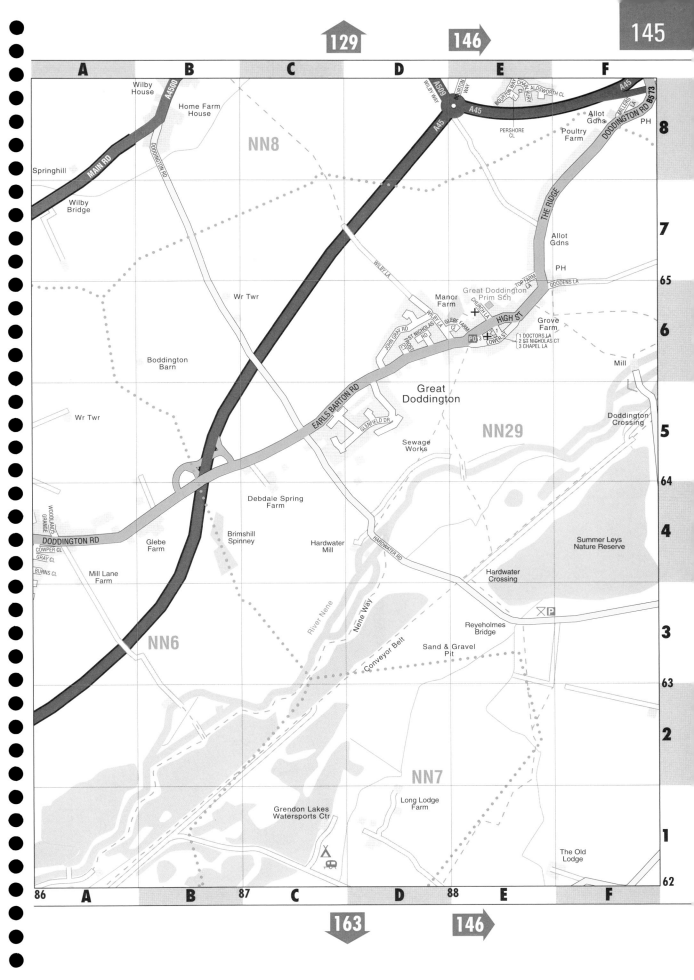

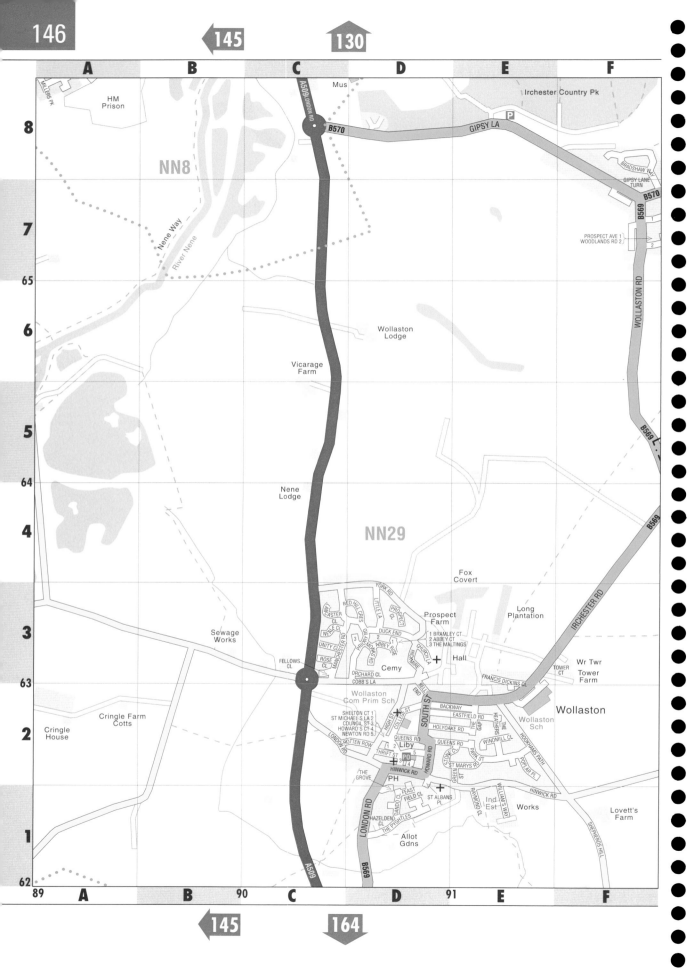

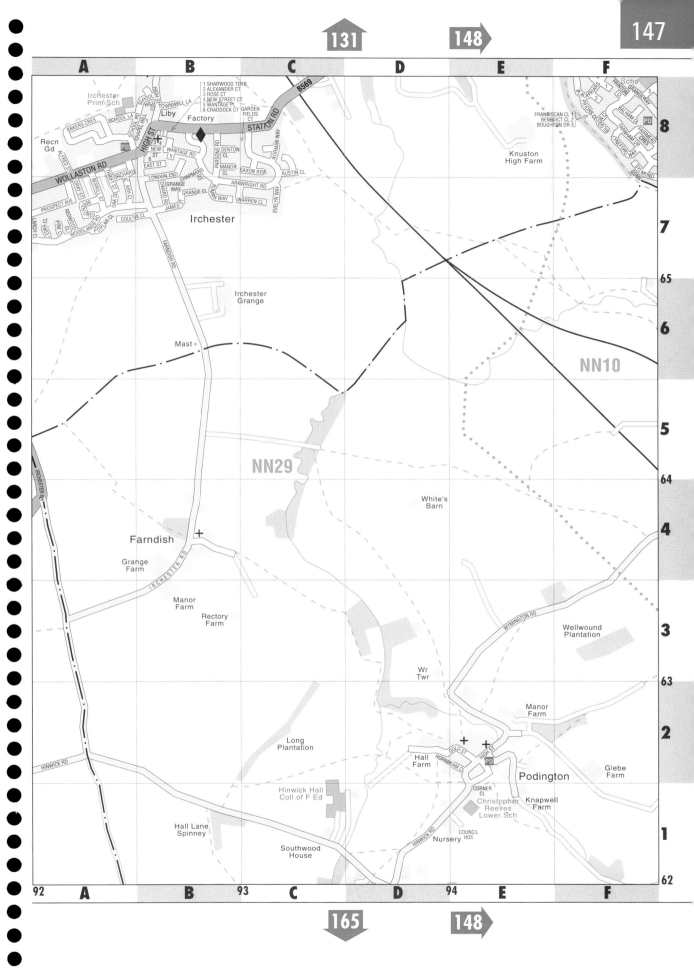

131
148

A B C D E F

1 SHARWOOD TERR
2 ALEXANDER CT
3 ROSE CT
4 NEW STREET CT
5 WANTAGE PL
6 CRADDOCK CT

B569

Schs
FRINTON
GRANGEWAY

FRANCISCAN CL 1
BENEDICT CL 2
BOUGHTON DR 3

BLACK FRIARS
PRIORS CLOSE
BALHAM CL
FARNHAM CL
FAIRMEAD
CRES
RECTORY
ST OSMOND
GDNS

PO

Irchester
Prim Sch

SCHOOL HILL
HIGH ST
TOWNWELL LA

Liby

Factory

GARDEN
FIELDS
CT

STATION RD

NORMAN WAY

Knuston
High Farm

8

BAKERS CRES

SCHOOL LA
CHAPEL HILL
SCHOOL RD

PO

WOLLASTON RD

ALFRED ST

NEW
ST
WANTAGE RD
EAST ST

PARSONS RD
CHAPMANS CL

MANOR
CL

SAXON RISE

DENTON
CL

AUSTIN CL

Recn
Gd

ORCHARD
ASH CL

LONDON END

GRANGE
WAY

GRANGE CL

RYMON WAY

ARKWRIGHT RD

WARREN CL

EVELYN WAY

PROSPECT AVE
GRAY ST
THRIFT RD
OAK CL

JAMES ST
EDWARD RD

Irchester

LARCH CL
PINE CL
REDWOOD
WOODLANDS RD
POPLAR RD

COULON CL

FARNDISH RD

7

Irchester
Grange

65

6

NN10

Mast

NN29

5

64

White's
Barn

Farndish

4

Grange
Farm

IRCHESTER RD

Manor
Farm

Rectory
Farm

WYMINGTON RD

Wellwound
Plantation

3

63

Wr
Twr

Manor
Farm

2

Long
Plantation

Hall
Farm

HORNBEAM CL
GOLD ST
HIGH ST

PO

Podington

Glebe
Farm

IRCHESTER RD

HINWICK RD

Hall Lane
Spinney

Hinwick Hall
Coll of F Ed

CORNER
CL

Christopher
Reeves
Lower Sch

Knapwell
Farm

1

Southwood
House

HINWICK RD

Nursery

COUNCIL
HOS

62

92 A B 93 C D 94 E F

165
148

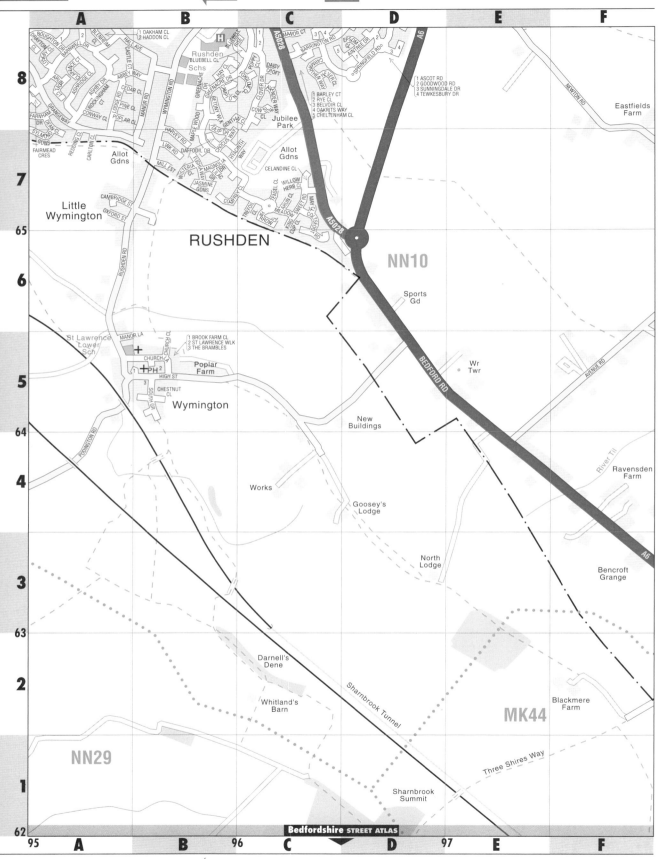

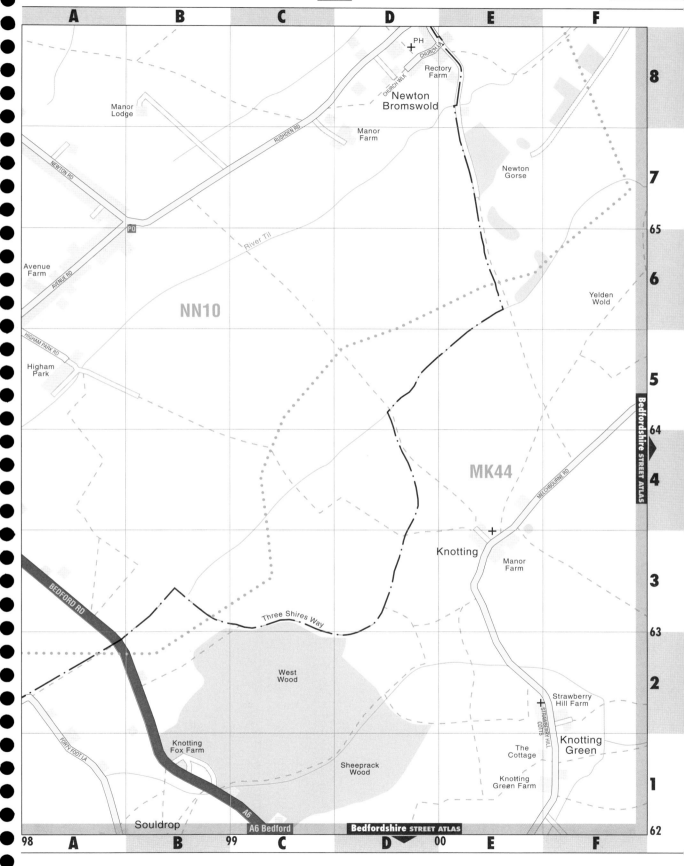

A B C D E F

8

Manor
Lodge

PH
+

CHURCH WLK

CHURCH LA

Rectory
Farm

Newton
Bromswold

NEWTON RD

RUSHDEN RD

Manor
Farm

Newton
Gorse

7

65

River Til

Avenue
Farm

AVENUE RD

NN10

Yelden
Wold

6

HIGHAM PARK RD

Higham
Park

5

64

Bedfordshire STREET ATLAS

MK44

MELCHBOURNE RD

4

Knotting

+

Manor
Farm

BEDFORD RD

3

Three Shires Way

63

West
Wood

2

FORTY FOOT LA

Knotting
Fox Farm

Sheeprack
Wood

Strawberry
Hill Farm

+

STRAWBERRY HILL COTTS

The
Cottage

Knotting
Green

Knotting
Green Farm

1

Souldrop

A6

A6 Bedford

Bedfordshire STREET ATLAS

62

98 A B 99 C D 00 E F

Shuckburgh Park

Home Farm

Long Hill Wood

Upper Shuckburgh

Lodge Hill

Shuckburgh Hills

Sandpit Spinney

NN11

Beacon Hill

Park Farm

Halls Barn Farm

Old Fox Covert

Napton on the Hill

DOG LA

In Meadow Gate

CV47

Northfields Farms

Potash Farm

Nedge Hill Farm

Priory Farm

Marston Hill

Warwickshire STREET ATLAS

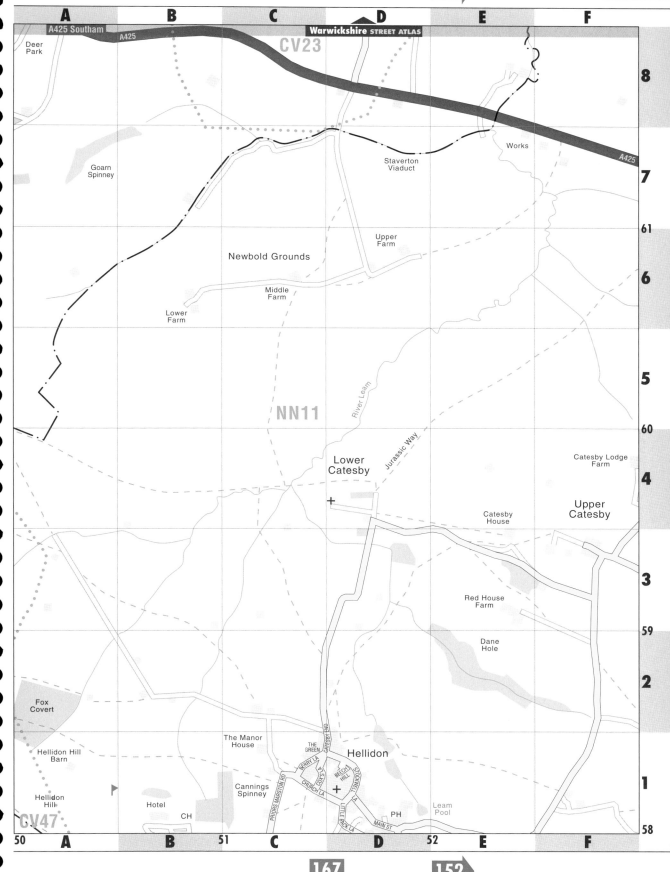

A B C D E F

8

WELLAND CL 1
THAMES RD 2
A45
TYNE RD
STEFFEN WAY
A425
STAVERTON RD
Drayton Lodge

Hall

Woodhollow Cottages

Stepnell Spinney

Hall Farm

CH

Oak Spinney

Sewage Works

Hotel

Staverton CE Prim Sch

Manor House

HOME CL

BRAUNSTON LA

CROFT LA

GLEBE LA

OAKHAM LA

MANOR RD

WELL LA

THE WOODLANDS

THE GREEN

THE ORCHARD

PH

DAVENTRY RD

A425

Compton Cottage

Staverton Wood

Staverton Clump

Staverton Hill Farm

Mast

Big Hill

Pond Spinney

1 WINDMILL LA
2 WINDMILL GDNS
3 CHURCH FIELDS

PO

CHURCH

DAVENTRY RD

Staverton

7

61

Staverton Acres

Broiler Breeder Farm

Bates Farm

Jurassic Way

Vine Tree Farm

Sports Gd

Badby Lodge Farm

Staverton Fields

6

Badby Fields

Markleys

NN11

5

60

Bridge Hill Farm

A361

4

Studborough Hill

Studborough Clump

Longridge Farm

3

Staverton Lodge

Barehill Farm

AVENUE SIDE CL

PINFOLD BN

PH

ORCHARD CL

Badby Sch

SCHOOL LA

MAIN ST

PO

59

Arbury Hill

STONEWAY HILL

VICARAGE HILL

BUNKERS HILL

CHURCH HILL

2

Haycock Hill Farm

Konigssee Farm

Highfield Farm

The Beeches

Badby Plantation

1

A361

Badby Down

58

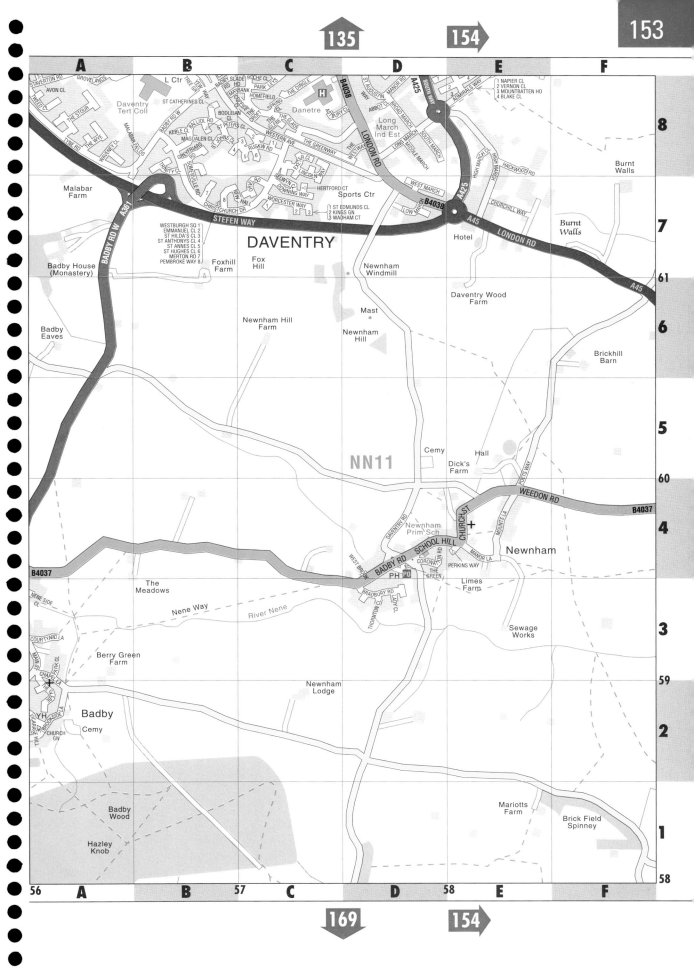

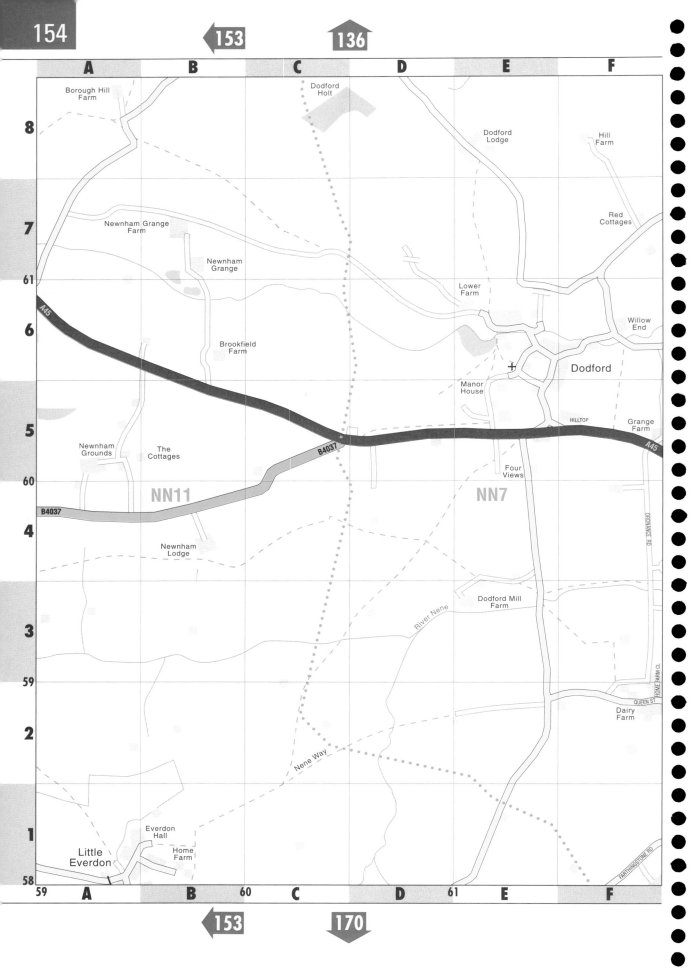

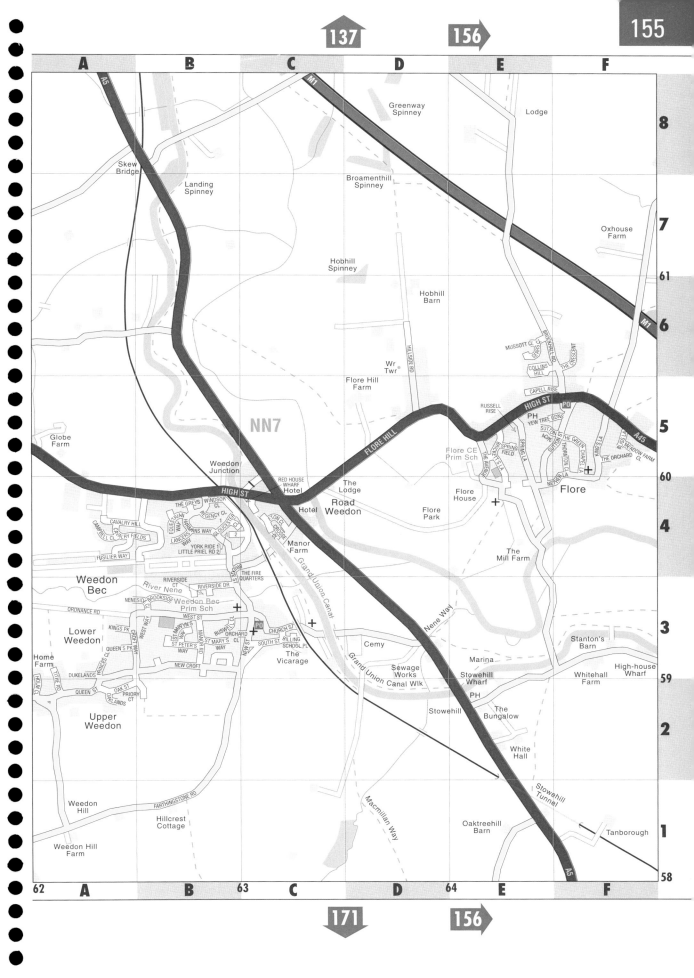

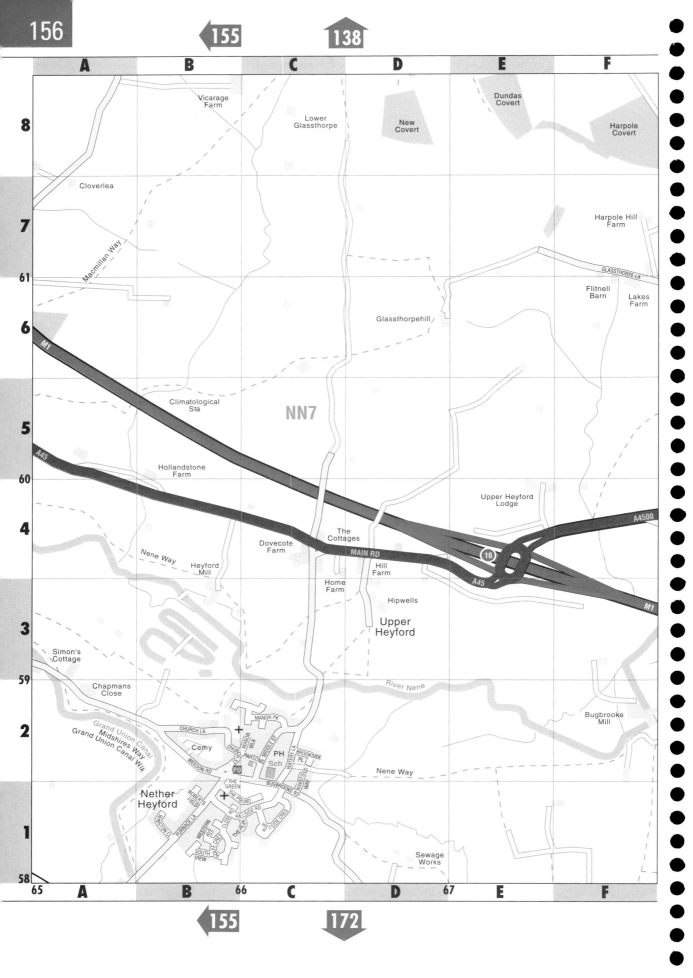

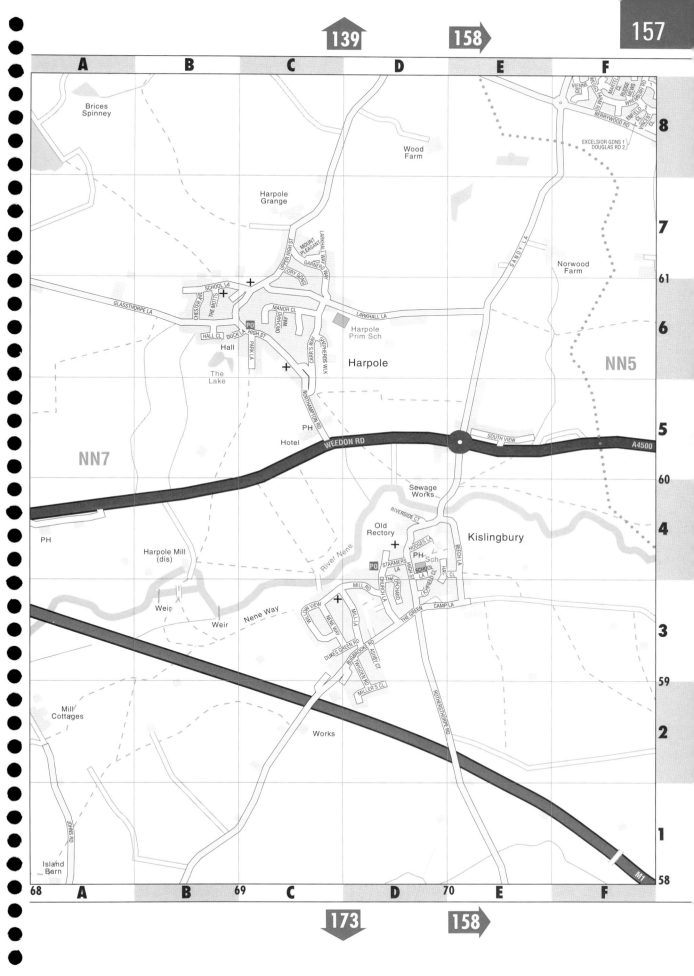

139
158

A B C D E F

8

Brices
Spinney

Wood
Farm

VIENNE
CL
WEISS FARM RD
MARTEL
CL
BUDGE
MEWS
WREYBURY RD
ENFIELD
BERRYWOOD RD
VINCENT CL

EXCELSIOR GDNS 1
DOUGLAS RD 2

Harpole
Grange

7

Norwood
Farm

UPPER HIGH ST
MOUNT
PLEASANT
LARKHALL WAY
LARKHALL WAY
GARNER
CORY GDNS

SANDY LA

61

SCHOOL LA
CHESTER AVE
THE MOTTS
MANOR CL
ORCHARD
WAY
CADS WAY
SHEPHERDS WLK

GLASSTHORPE LA

LARKHALL LA

NN5

6

HALL CL
DUCK LA
HIGH ST
PO

Hall

PARK LA

Harpole
Prim Sch

Harpole

The
Lake

NORTHAMPTON RD

5

NN7

PH

Hotel

WEEDON RD

SOUTH VIEW

A4500

60

PH

Sewage
Works

4

Harpole Mill
(dis)

RIVERSIDE CT

River Nene

Old
Rectory

PO

STARMERS
LA

HODGES LA
HIGH ST
RIVERSIDE CT
PH
Sch
SCHOOL
LA
BEECH LA
HALL CL
LICHFIELD CL

Kislingbury

Weir

Nene Way

Weir

MILL RD

THE
ORCHARD
CHURCH LA

THE GREEN

CAMP LA

3

WILLOW VIEW
NENE WAY
MILL LA

DUKES GREEN RD
BIGBROOKE RD
TWIGDEN RD
ASHBY CT

ROTHERSTHORPE RD

59

MILLER'S CL

Mill
Cottages

Works

2

JOHNS RD

1

Island
Barn

M1

58

173
158

157 140
157 174

F8
1 GLEBELAND WLK
2 DALLINGTON GN
3 TENNYSON CL
4 CARDIGAN CL
5 DALLINGTON HAVEN

Grid columns: A B C D E F (top)
Grid rows: 8 7 61 6 5 60 4 3 59 2 1 58

Ryelands Mid Sch
Duston Upper Sch
Galahad Ct
Cemy
Berry Wood
Hospital Farm
Upton Lodge
Princess Marina
Park House
Upton Hall Farm
Bottom Spinney
Upton Mill
NN7
Bly La
River Nene
Pineham Barn
SWAN VALLEY WAY

Duston
1 BEECHWOOD RD
2 POND FARM CL
3 STARMER'S YD
4 SQUIRREL LA
5 GOUGHS COTTS

1 EDINBURGH HO
2 LIMEHURST SQ
3 WINDSOR HO
4 GIFFORD CT
5 STEPHEN BENNETT CL
6 ROSETTE CL

St Luke's CE Lower Sch
Millway Mid Sch
Quinton House Sch
Upton
NN5
Nene Way
Works
Duston Mill (dis)

TOWER HILL CL 1
TALLYFIELD END 2
CHEVIOT CT 3
LANGLEY CL 4
LIMLOW CL 5

Chiltern Lower Sch
Dallington
WARWICK HO 1
HARLESTONE CT 2
HARLESTONE RD
Lyncrest Lower Sch
The Bsns Ctr
Ind Est
Superstore
Sixfields L Complex
Sixfields Stad
Northampton Town FC
Hotel
WEEDON RD
UPTON WAY

Grand Union Canal Northampton Arm
Grand Union Canal Wlk

NEWSTONE CRES
RAINSBOROUGH CRES
Briar Hill
Sch
NN4
DANES CAMP WAY
Hunsbury Hill Spinney
Camp Hill
Hunsbury Hill
Mus
Hunsbury Park Lower Sch
Hunsbury Hill Country Park

MILLSTONE CL 1
COBBLESTONE CT 2
BRINDLESTONE CT 3
DAPPLESTONE CL 4
QUARTERSTONE 5

MILLER HILL 1
FARRAXTON SQ 2

WHITESANDS WAY 6
CAULDECOTT CL 7
LYNMORE CL 8
KEYSTONE 9

F2
1 ARCHANGEL SQ
2 ARCHANGEL RD
3 MARNOCK SQ
4 HASELRIG SQ
5 DAYRELL SQ
6 BENJAMIN SQ
7 PLANTAGENET SQ
8 BROCADE CL
9 ROTHERHITHE CL

F3
1 SPRINGER STRAIGHT
2 FRENSHAM CL
3 ROSENELLA CL
4 DICKSON CL

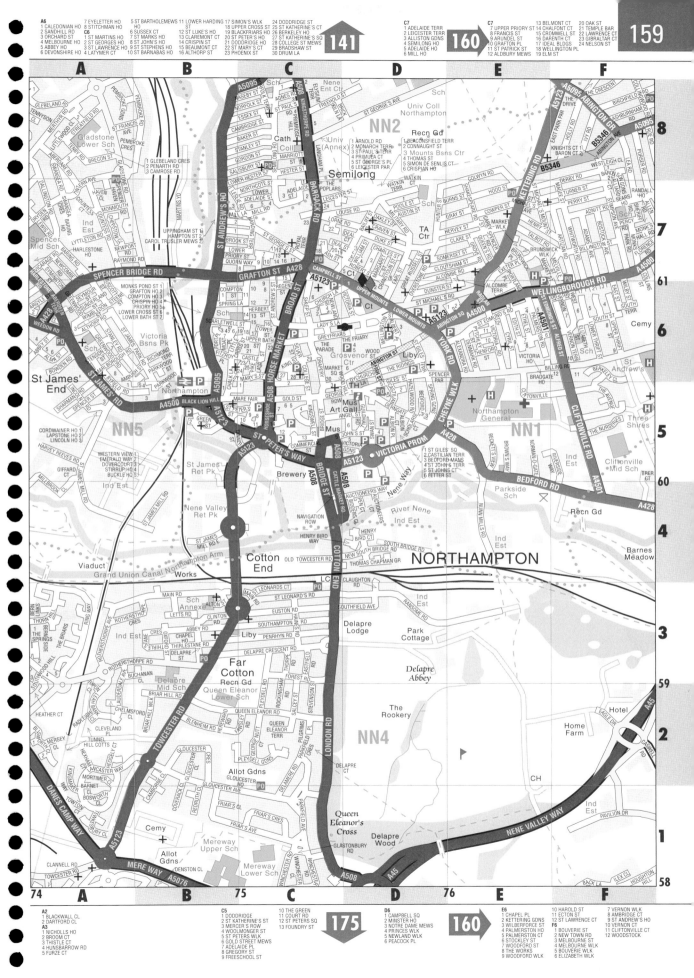

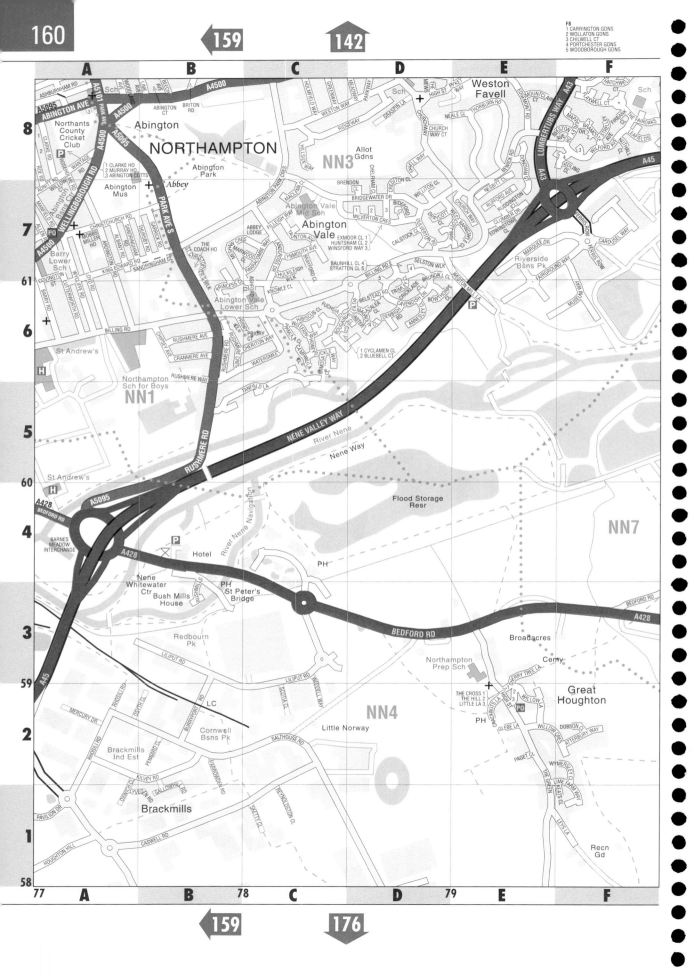

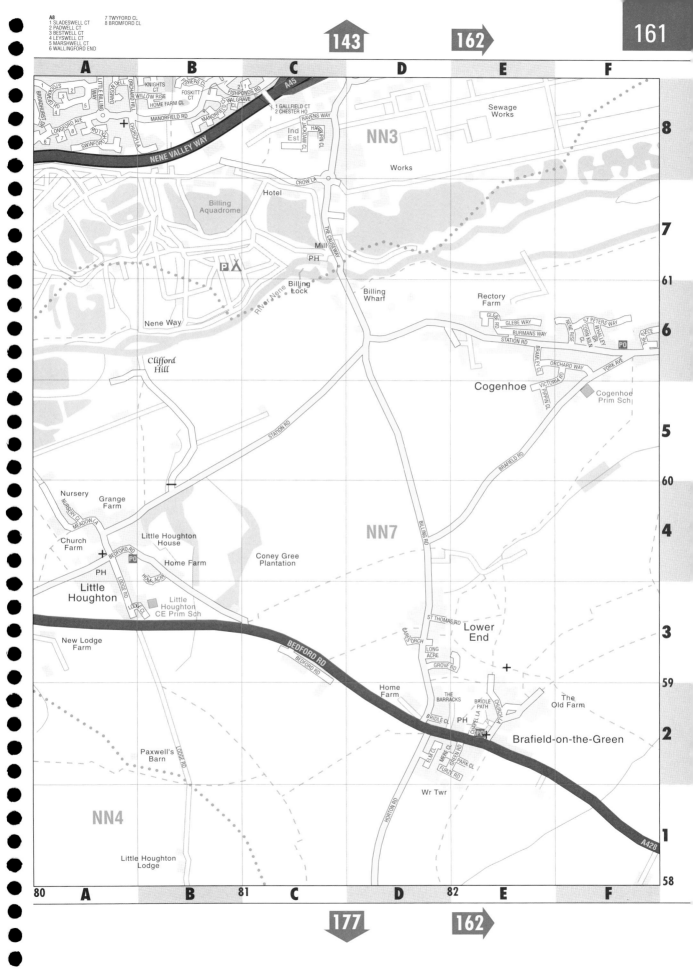

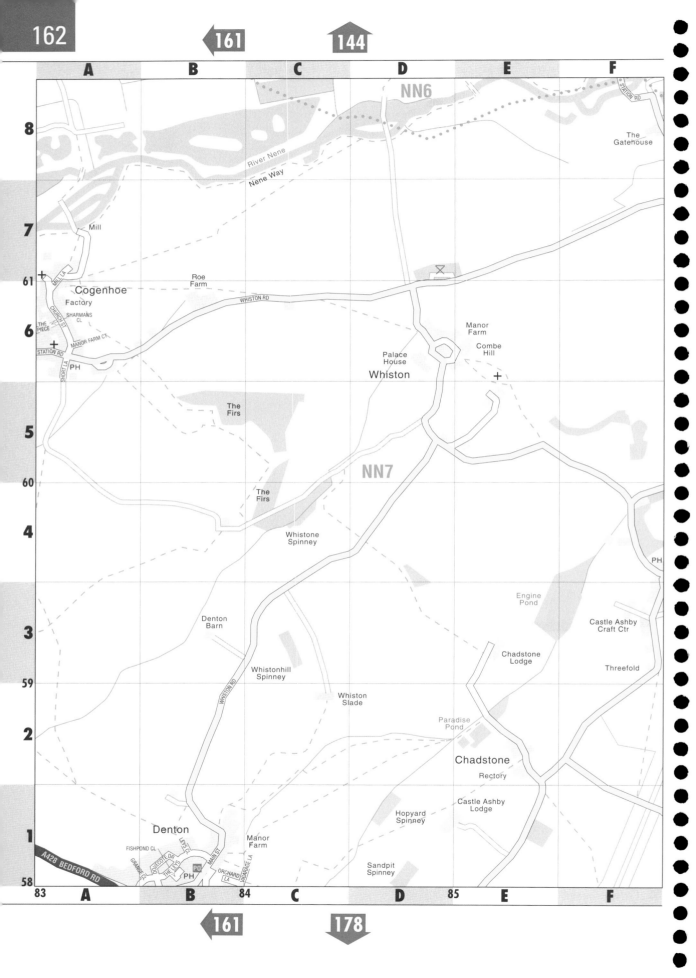

NN6

8

River Nene

Nene Way

The Gatehouse

STATION RD

7

Mill

Roe Farm

61

Cogenhoe

WHISTON RD

MILL LA

CHURCH ST

Factory

SHARMANS CL

Manor Farm

6

THE PIECE

MANOR FARM CT.

STATION RD

SHORT LA

PH

Palace House

Whiston

Combe Hill

The Firs

NN7

5

60

The Firs

Whistone Spinney

4

Engine Pond

Castle Ashby Craft Ctr

Denton Barn

3

Chadstone Lodge

Threefold

Whistonhill Spinney

59

WHISTON RD

Whiston Slade

Paradise Pond

2

Chadstone

Rectory

Castle Ashby Lodge

Hopyard Spinney

Denton

FISHPOND CL

LEYS CL

SIDCOTE DR

GRANGE CL

THE LEYS

MAIN ST

Manor Farm

VICARAGE LA

PH

PO

ORCHARD LA

Sandpit Spinney

1

A428 BEDFORD RD

58

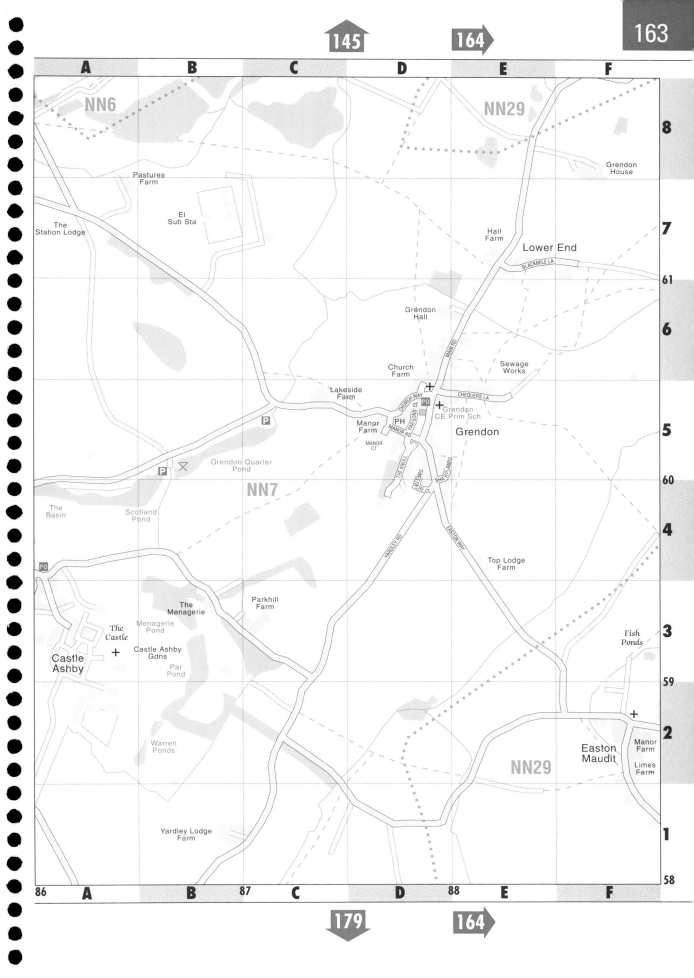

145
164

NN6

NN29

8

Grendon
House

Pastures
Farm

El
Sub Sta

7

The
Station Lodge

Hall
Farm

Lower End

BLACKMILE LA

61

Grendon
Hall

6

Church
Farm

Sewage
Works

Lakeside
Farm

CHURCH WAY

MAIN RD

CHEQUERS LA

PARSONS CL

Grendon
CE Prim Sch

Manor
Farm

PH

Grendon

MANOR RD

5

MANOR
CT

THE KNOLL

SHARPLANDS

SWEET...

...RE CL

NN7

60

The
Basin

Scotland
Pond

Grendon Quarter
Pond

YARDLEY RD

EASTON WAY

Top Lodge
Farm

4

Fish
Ponds

The
Menagerie

Parkhill
Farm

3

Menagerie
Pond

The
Castle

Castle Ashby
Gdns

Par
Pond

59

Castle
Ashby

PO

Easton
Maudit

Manor
Farm

2

Warren
Ponds

Limes
Farm

NN29

Yardley Lodge
Farm

1

58

86   87   88

179
164

163
146

A **B** **C** **D** **E** **F**

8

Hillmount
Spinney

Manor
Farm

Chruch
Farm

Lodge
Farm

Strixton

Shepherds Hill

7

Strixton
Plantation

Poplars
Farm

61

6

NN7

Greenfield
Lodge

5

60

WOLLASTON RD

4

NN29

WOLLASTON RD

Red Gables
Farm

FULLWELL RD

HOPE ST

COUNCIL ST

BULL CL

ALLENS HILL

Bozeat

1 CHURCH FARM CL
2 PUDDING BAG LA
3 THE ORCHARD
4 BURTON TERR

Glebe
Farm

Three Fields
Farm

3

Slype
Farm

Church
Farm

PEAR
TREE
CL

Spring Vale
Farm

CHURCH WLK

HENSMANS LA

MILE ST

HAROLD RD

Bozeat Com
Prim Sch

Cemy

LONDON RD

CHURCH LA

MANOR CL

DYCHURCH LA

59

Park
Farm

EASTON LA

PH

HIGH ST

STONEY
PIECE
CL

SELBY
GDNS

ST HEWLETT'S

MARY'S RD

WYMAN CL

KNIGHTS CL

PO

BROOKSIDE

East Farm

Spring Hill Farm

2

QUEEN ST

ABBEY CL

MILL RD

FIR TREE GR

THISTLE

CLAYLAND
CL

ROBERTS ST

LITTLE CL

5 WARNERS HILL
6 CAMDEN SQ
7 WHEELWRIGHTS YD

Easton
Low

1

Home
Farm

White House
Farm

58

89 **A** **B** 90 **C** **D** 91 **E** **F**

163
180

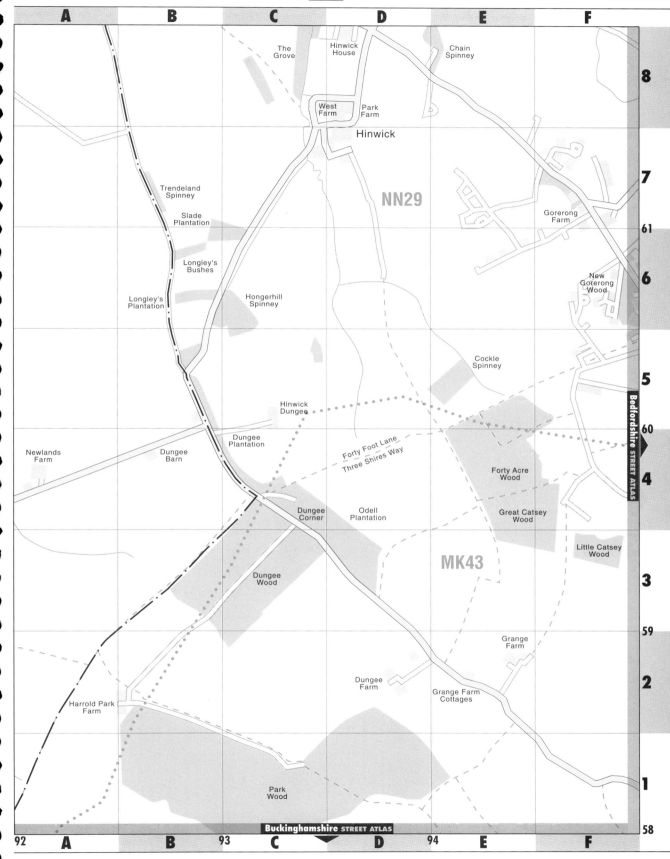

A · B · C · D · E · F

8

The Grove
Hinwick House
Chain Spinney

West Farm
Park Farm

Hinwick

NN29

7

Trendeland Spinney

Slade Plantation

Gorerong Farm

61

Longley's Bushes

New Gorerong Wood

6

Longley's Plantation

Hongerhill Spinney

Cockle Spinney

5

Hinwick Dungee

60

Dungee Plantation

Forty Foot Lane
Three Shires Way

Forty Acre Wood

4

Newlands Farm

Dungee Barn

Dungee Corner

Odell Plantation

Great Catsey Wood

Little Catsey Wood

Dungee Wood

MK43

3

59

Grange Farm

Dungee Farm

2

Harrold Park Farm

Grange Farm Cottages

Park Wood

1

58

92 A · B · 93 C · D · 94 E · F

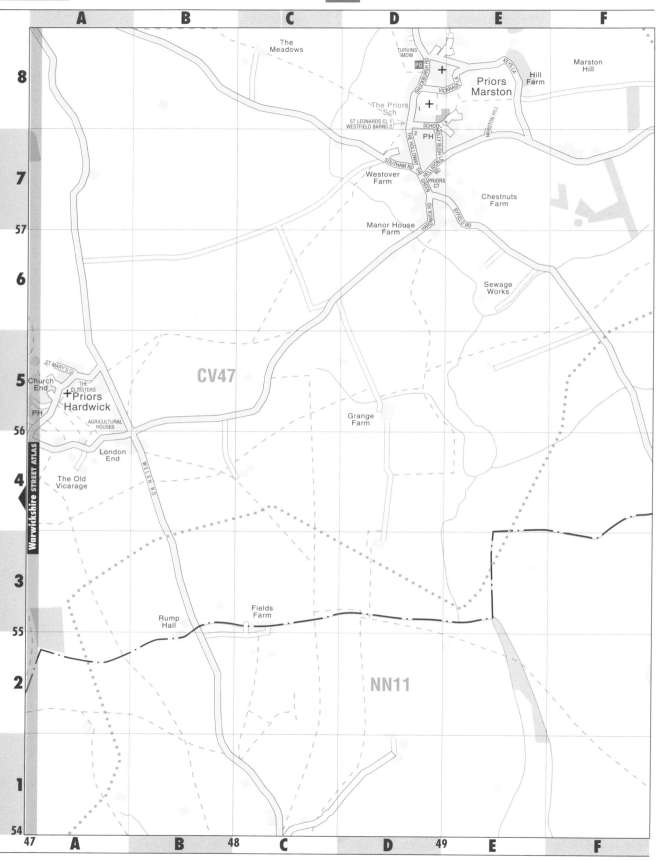

A B C D E F

8

7

57

6

5

56

4

3

55

2

1

54

Warwickshire STREET ATLAS

The Meadows

TURVINS
MDW

PO

Priors
Marston

Hill
Farm

Marston
Hill

SHUCKBURGH RD

VICARAGE

KEYSLA

The Priors
Sch

ST LEONARDS CL 1
WESTFIELD BARNS 2

SCHOOL

PH

MARSTON HILL

SOUTHAM RD

THE HOLLOWAY

THE GREEN

HOLLY BUSH LA

HELLIDON RD

Westover
Farm

PRIORS
CT

Manor House
Farm

HARDWICK RD

BYFIELD RD

Chestnuts
Farm

Sewage
Works

CV47

ST MARY'S CL

THE
CLOISTERS

Church
End

+Priors
Hardwick

PH

AGRICULTURAL
HOUSES

London
End

The Old
Vicarage

WELSH RD

Grange
Farm

Rump
Hall

Fields
Farm

NN11

47 A 48 B C 49 D E F

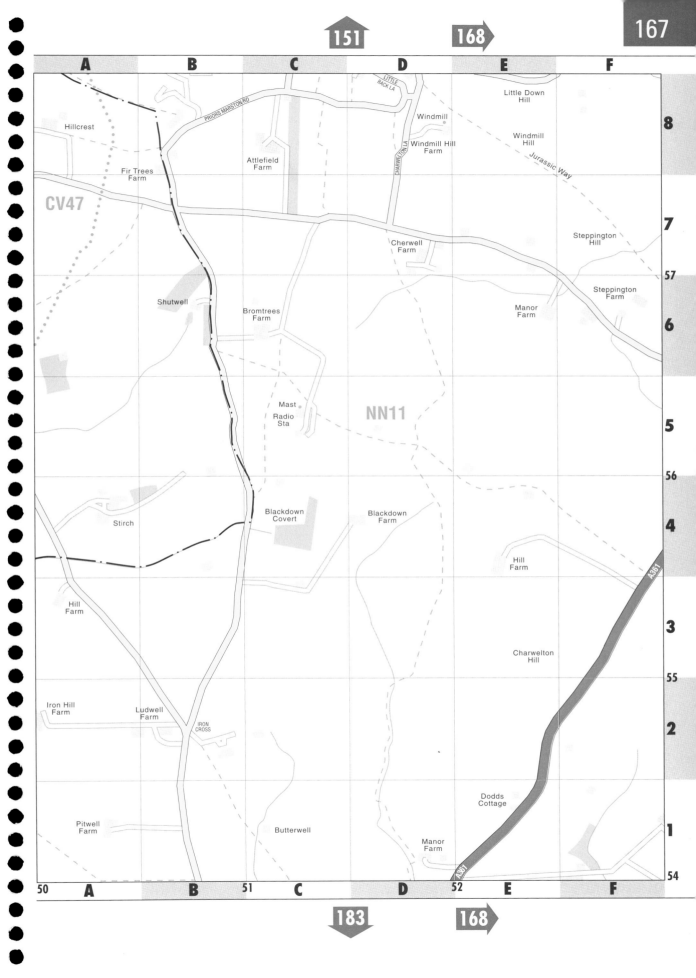

167
152

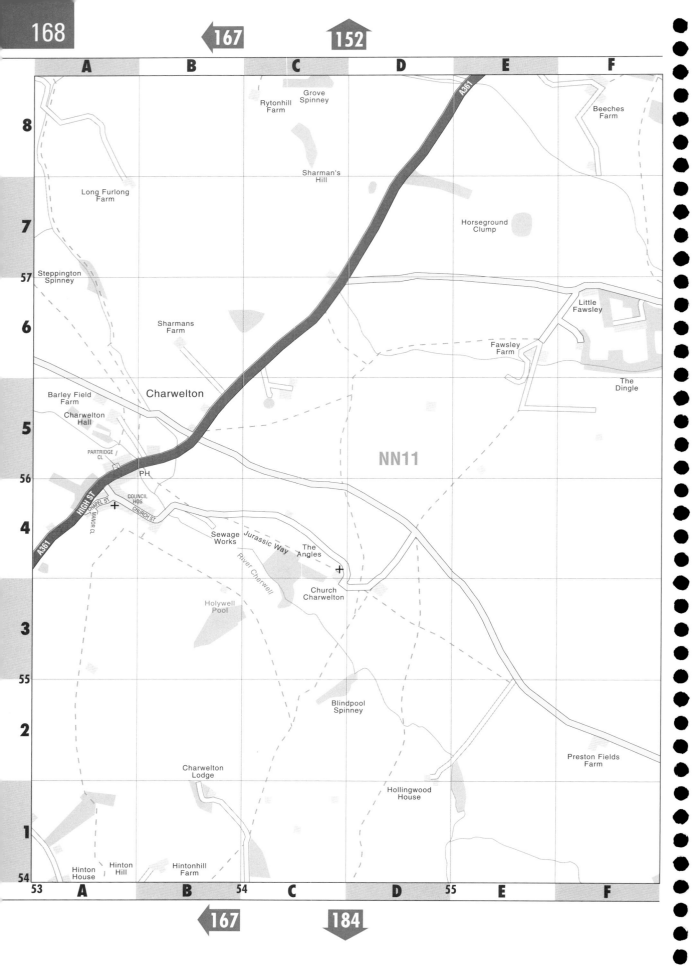

A B C D E F

8

Beeches
Farm

Rytonhill
Farm

Grove
Spinney

A361

Long Furlong
Farm

Sharman's
Hill

7

Horseground
Clump

57

Steppington
Spinney

Little
Fawsley

6

Sharmans
Farm

Fawsley
Farm

The
Dingle

Charwelton

Barley Field
Farm

NN11

Charwelton
Hall

5

PARTRIDGE
CL

56

PH

COUNCIL
HOS

HIGH ST

MANOR CL

CHAPEL ST

CHURCH ST

Sewage
Works

Jurassic Way

The
Angles

4

A361

River Cherwell

Church
Charwelton

Holywell
Pool

3

55

Blindpool
Spinney

2

Preston Fields
Farm

Charwelton
Lodge

Hollingwood
House

1

54

Hinton
House

Hinton
Hill

Hintonhill
Farm

53 A 54 B C 54 D 55 E F

167
184

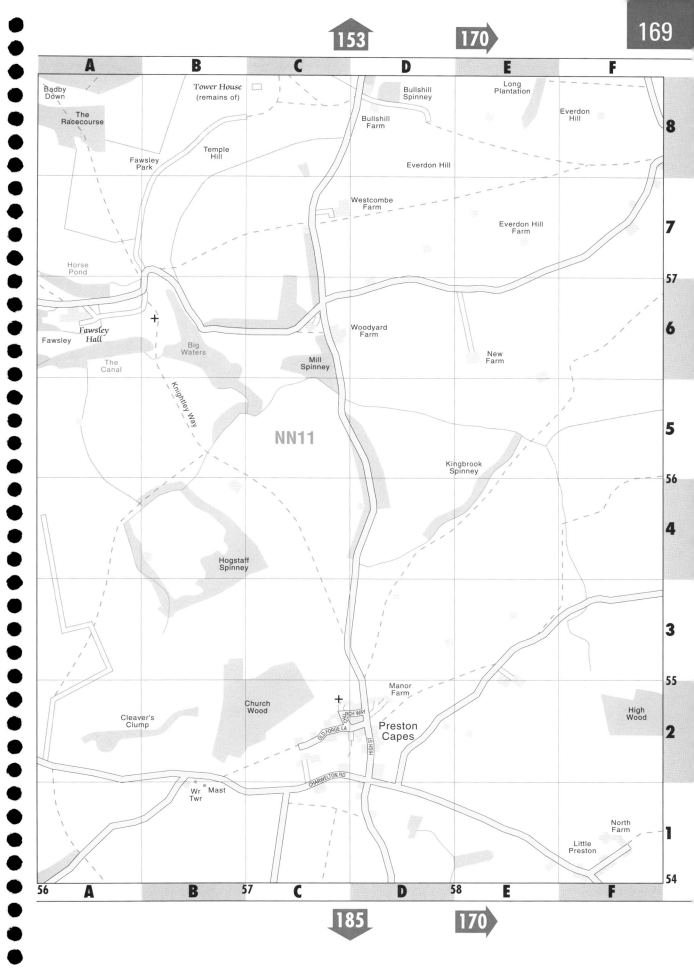

169 154

A B C D E F

Nene Way

Weedon Villa

Fern Hollow

NN7

8

Sewage Works

Weedon Lodge Cottage

Everdon

Weedon Lodge

LONG ROW CL.

THE GREEN

FAWSLEY RD

SCHOOL LA

HIGH ST

WELL LA

BETHEL LA

PH

College Farm

STUBBS RD

The Manor House

Wood Farm

FARTHINGSTONE RD

7

Joban

57

Everdon Wood

Castle Dykes

6

Snorscomb Mill

Everdon Stubbs Nature Trail

Everdon Stubbs Woodland Trust Wood

Castle Dykes Farm

Meg Spinney

NN11

Wr Twr

Farthingstone Heath

Snorscomb

5

56

Snorscomb Farm

Cockcrow Spinney

4

Fernhill Lodge

Hen Wood

Manor Farm

COUNCIL HOS 1
MANOR GDNS 2
CATTLE END 3

WEEDON RD

LITCHBOROUGH RD

3

Mantles Heath

Knightley Way

NN12

Park Farm

EVERDON RD

1 2 3

Earls Farm

Hotel

CH

PH

MAIN ST

Farthingstone

55

Church Farm

High Wood

Macmillan Way

Little Court

MAIDFORD RD

Littlecourt Yard

2

Little Court Farm

Knightley Wood

Cemy

Glebe Farm

1

54

59 A 60 C 61 E F
B D

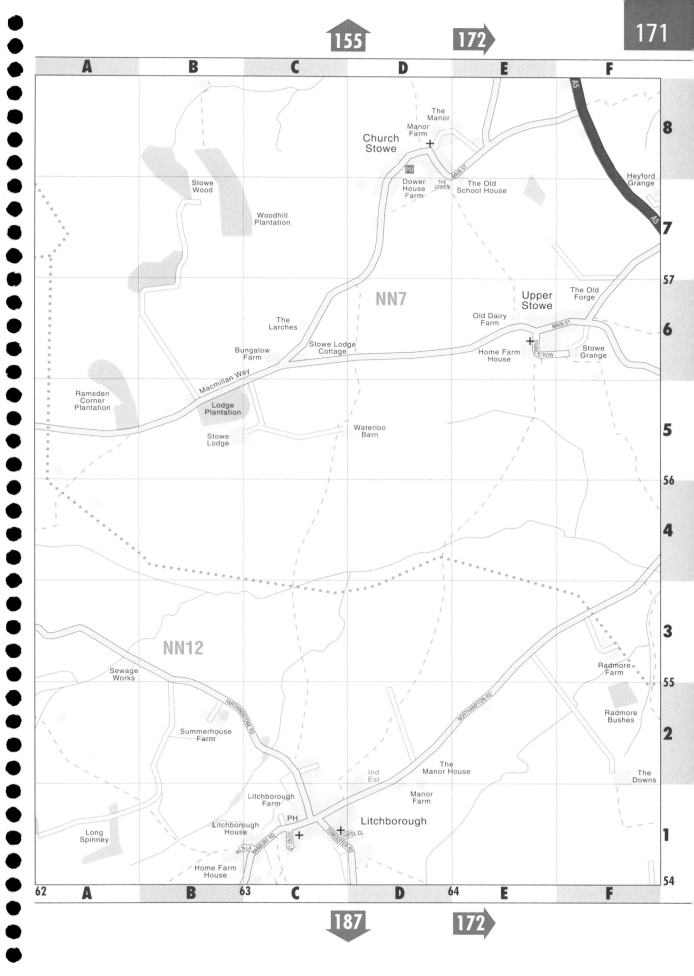

155
172
187
172

A B C D E F

8
7
57
6
5
56
4
3
55
2
1
54

62 A B 63 C D 64 E F

The Manor
Manor Farm
Church Stowe
PO
Dower House Farm
THE GREEN
MAIN ST
The Old School House

A5
Heyford Grange

Stowe Wood
Woodhill Plantation

NN7

Upper Stowe
The Old Forge
Old Dairy Farm
MAIN ST
FRANCIS ROW
Home Farm House
Stowe Grange

The Larches
Stowe Lodge Cottage
Bungalow Farm
Macmillan Way

Ramsden Corner Plantation
Lodge Plantation
Stowe Lodge

Waterloo Barn

NN12

Sewage Works
FARTHINGSTONE RD
Summerhouse Farm

Radmore Farm

Radmore Bushes

Northampton Rd
The Manor House
Manor Farm

The Downs

Ind Est
Litchborough Farm
PH
Litchborough House
KILN LA BANBURY RD IVENS LA
TOWCESTER RD
CHAPEL CL
Litchborough

Long Spinney
Home Farm House

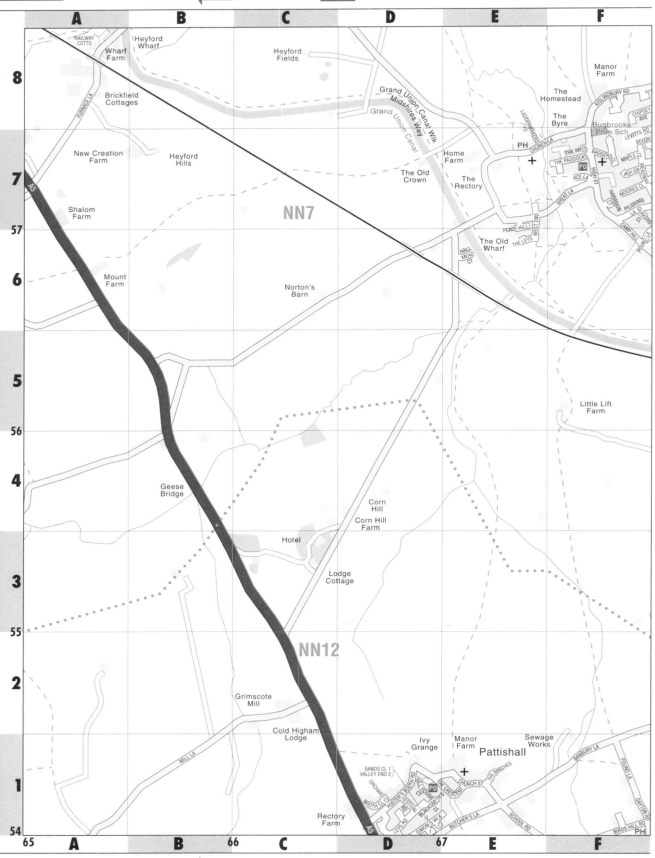

171
156
171
188

Railway Cotts
Wharf Farm
Heyford Wharf
Heyford Fields

Brickfield Cottages

Grand Union Canal Wlk
Midshires Way
Grand Union Canal

Manor Farm
The Homestead
KISLINGBURY RD
The Byre
CHIPSEY AVE
Bugbrooke Prim Sch
LEVITTS RD
BEECH
FURNACE LA

New Creation Farm
Heyford Hills

PH
CHURCH LA
THE ANVIL
BADGERS CL
MAPLE CL
ASH GR
MEADWAY
THE PADDOCKS
PO
ACE LA
HIGH ST
HARRISON
MOORES CL
PILGRIMS

NN7

Home Farm
The Old Crown
The Rectory

Shalom Farm

The Old Wharf
PEACE HILL
WEST END
THE LEYS
GREAT LA
CAMP HILL
POUND LA

Mount Farm

Norton's Barn

HALL MEAD CT

Little Lift Farm

Geese Bridge

Corn Hill
Corn Hill Farm

Hotel

Lodge Cottage

NN12

Grimscote Mill

Cold Higham Lodge

Ivy Grange
Manor Farm
Sewage Works
Pattishall
BANBURY LA

MILL LA

SANDS CL 1
VALLEY END 2
ORCHARD CL
BOOTH
ROSTER'S BOOTH RD
FESTIVAL
LEYS RD
PO
THE CRESCENT
BLACKSMITHS CL
SIMON'S WLK
CHURCH ST
THE BEECHES
BUTCHER'S LA
SCHOOL RD
POUND LA
GAYTON RD
BIRDS HILL RD
PH

Rectory Farm

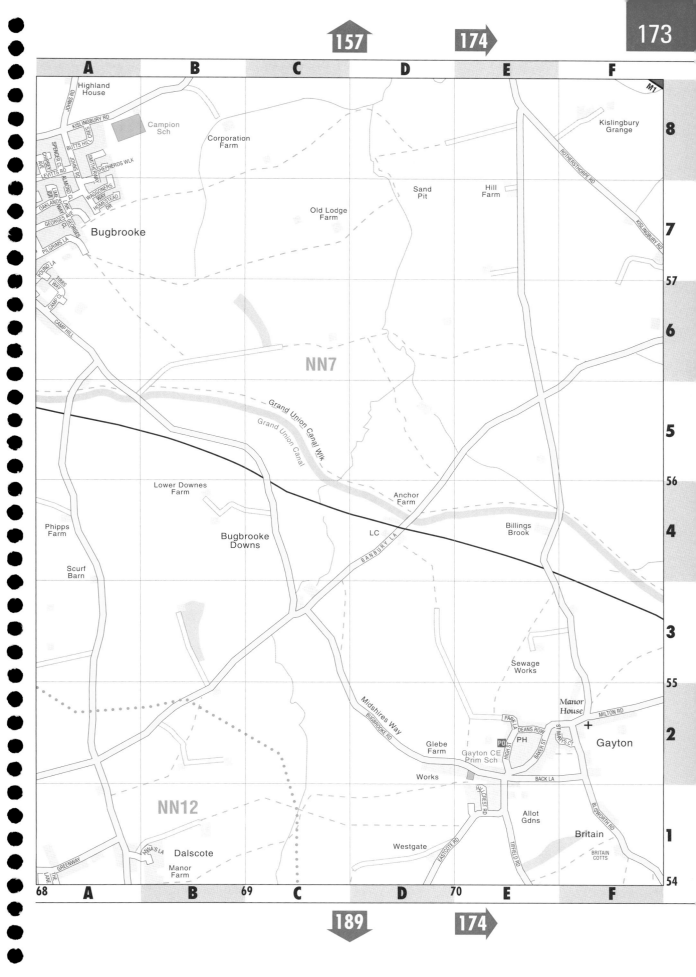

A   B   C   D   E   F

Highland House
Campion Sch
Corporation Farm

Kislingbury Grange

8

JOHNS RD
KISLINGBURY RD
BUTTS HILL
JOHNS RD

Sand Pit

Hill Farm

ROTHERSTHORPE RD

SPENCER CL
CHIPSEY AVE
LEVITTS CL
ALMOND CL
SMITHERWAY
SHEPHERDS WLK
WAGGONERS WAY
HOMESTEAD DR
OAKLANDS
THE MAWN
LINK

Old Lodge Farm

KISLINGBURY RD

7

GEORGES AVE
GEORGES

Bugbrooke

PILGRIMS LA

57

POUND LA
TIBBS WAY
CAMP CL

6

CAMP HILL

NN7

Grand Union Canal Wlk
Grand Union Canal

5

Lower Downes Farm

Anchor Farm

Billings Brook

56

Phipps Farm

Bugbrooke Downs

LC

4

BANBURY LA

Scurf Barn

3

Sewage Works

55

Midshires Way

Manor House

MILTON RD

2

BUGBROOKE RD

Glebe Farm

PARK LA
DEANS ROW
PO
PH
BACK ST
ST MARYS CT

Gayton

Gayton CE Prim Sch

HIGH ST

Works

BACK LA

Allot Gdns

BLISWORTH RD

NN12

CREST RD

Britain

1

Dalscote

Westgate

EASTCOTE RD

TIFFIELD RD

BRITAIN COTTS

ANNA'S LA

Manor Farm

THE GREENWAY
THE LANE

54

68   A   B   69   C   D   70   E   F

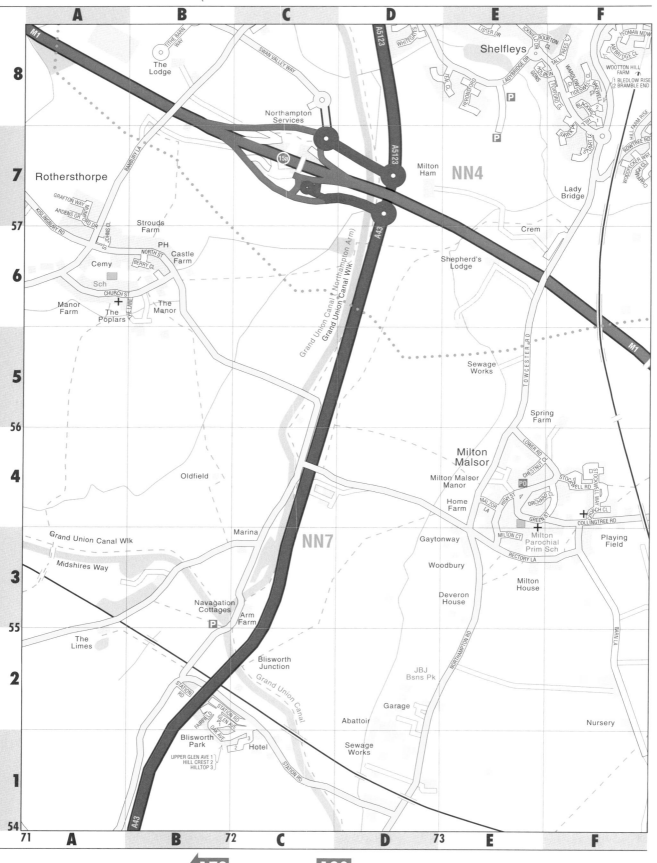

A B C D E F

8

7

57

6

5

56

4

3

55

2

1

54

71 A B 72 C D 73 E F

M1

Rothersthorpe

The Lodge

TITHE BARN WAY

SWAN VALLEY WAY

Northampton Services

15a

Milton Ham

NN4

Shelfleys

LISTER DR

ICKNIELD CL

BOURTON CL

TALL TREES CL

FOXFORD CL

WOOTTON HILL FARM
1 BLEDLOW RISE
2 BRAMBLE END

YEOMAN MDW

AULTBRIDGE CL

HILL FARM RISE

BOWTREE CL

WOODPECKER WAY

WOODFORD CL

Lady Bridge

A5123

Crem

Shepherd's Lodge

Sewage Works

M1

Spring Farm

Milton Malsor

Milton Malsor Manor

Home Farm

Gaytonway

Woodbury

Deveron House

Milton House

LOWER RD

CHESTNUT CL

STOCKWELL RD

STOCKWELL WAY

SCH CL

COLLINGTREE RD

Milton Parochial Prim Sch

Playing Field

MALZOR LA

HIGH ST

ORCHARD CL

GREEN ST

MILTON CT

RECTORY LA

NORTHAMPTON RD

TOWCESTER RD

BARN LA

JBJ Bsns Pk

Garage

Abattoir

Sewage Works

Nursery

NN7

Grand Union Canal Wlk

Midshires Way

The Limes

Oldfield

Marina

Navagation Cottages

Arm Farm

Blisworth Junction

Grand Union Canal

STATION RD

STATION RD

FAIRFIELD

GLEN AVE

OAK AVE

STATION RD

Blisworth Park

UPPER GLEN AVE 1
HILL CREST 2
HILLTOP 3

Hotel

A43

Grand Union Canal (Northampton Arm)

Grand Union Canal Wlk

A43

A5123

GRAFTON WAY

ARDENS GR

CRO DR

KISLINGBURY RD

ST JOHNS CL

BANBURY LA

Strouds Farm

PH

Castle Farm

NORTH ST

BERRY CL

Cemy

Sch

CHURCH ST

THE LANE

Manor Farm

The Poplars

The Manor

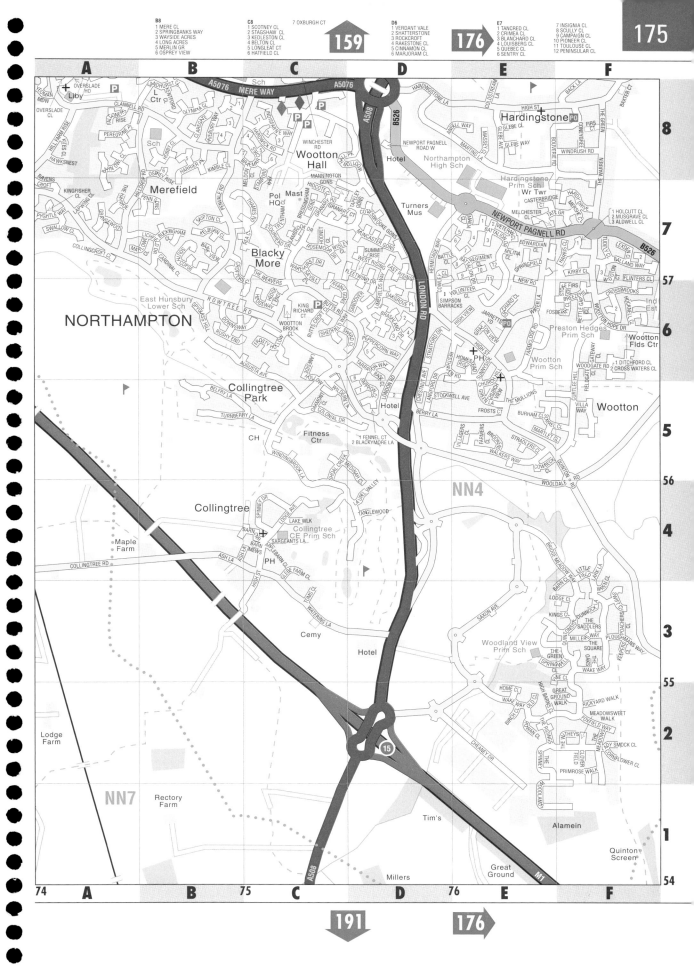

A B C D E F

8

SALTHOUSE RD

Saucebridge

NN4

7

Hardingstone Lodge

B526

57
GNELL CT

Ind Est

BROOK CL

HIGH GREEVE
MIDDLE GREEVE
LOW GREEVE

BEDDOES CL
LORDSWOOD
MORTONS BCH

6
WOOTTON HOPE DR
WOOLDALE RD
WHITTLES CROSS
MILTON BRIDGE
THRUPP BRIDGE
RICKERY DENE
LADY HOLLOW DR
LONG MDW
THE ASHES
THE CHOAKLES

1 COPYMOOR CL
2 EARLSFIELD CL
3 LITTLE GREEVE WAY

Preston Lodge Farm

Preston Lodge Cottages

NEWPORT PAGNELL RD

5

Grange Farm

The Grange

56

4

Hall

Nursery

Woodlands

Preston Deanery

B526

3

NN7

Rookery Farm Cottage

Sewage Works

55

Lower Farm

Rookery Farm

Fox Field

Lower Farm

Wood Cottage

Rookery New Farm

2

WOOTTON RD

Rookery Farm

Glebe Cottage

1

Glebe Farm

PRESTON DEANERY RD
PRESTON DEANERY RD

SCHOOL LA

Quinton

Preston wood

The Risings

The Lodge

Park Farm

54

77 A B 78 C D 79 E F

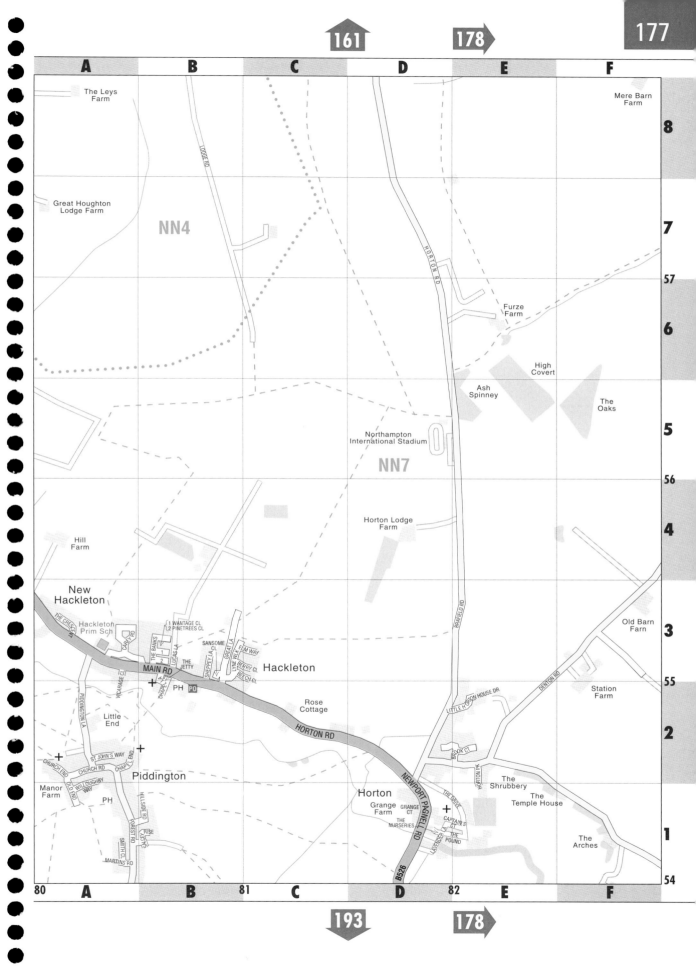

A B C D E F

The Leys Farm

Mere Barn Farm

8

Great Houghton Lodge Farm

NN4

7

LODGE RD

57

HORTON RD

Furze Farm

6

High Covert

Ash Spinney

The Oaks

5

Northampton International Stadium

NN7

56

Horton Lodge Farm

4

Hill Farm

Old Barn Farm

New Hackleton

THE CRESCENT

3

Hackleton Prim Sch

CAREY RD

1 WANTAGE CL
2 PINETREES CL

THE BANKS

LUCAS LA

SANSOME CL

GREAT LA

SHEPPEY LA

LYNE WLK

ELM WAY

BERRY CL

BEECH CL

Hackleton

BRAFIELD RD

Station Farm

DENTON RD

55

MAIN RD

VICARAGE CL

CHAPEL RD

THE JETTY

PH

PO

LITTLE HORTON HOUSE DR

Rose Cottage

PIDDINGTON LA

Little End

HORTON RD

BROOK CT

2

St John's Way

CHAPEL END

HORTON PK

The Shrubbery

CHURCH END

CHURCH RD

Piddington

NEWPORT PAGNELL RD

The Temple House

Manor Farm

OLD END

WILLOUGHBY WAY

PH

HILLSIDE RD

Horton

THE DRIVE

Grange Farm

GRANGE CT

THE NURSERIES

LAVENDER LA

CAPTAIN'S CL

THE POUND

The Arches

1

FOREST RD

SMITH CL

RISE

MARTINS RD

54

80 A B 81 C D 82 E F

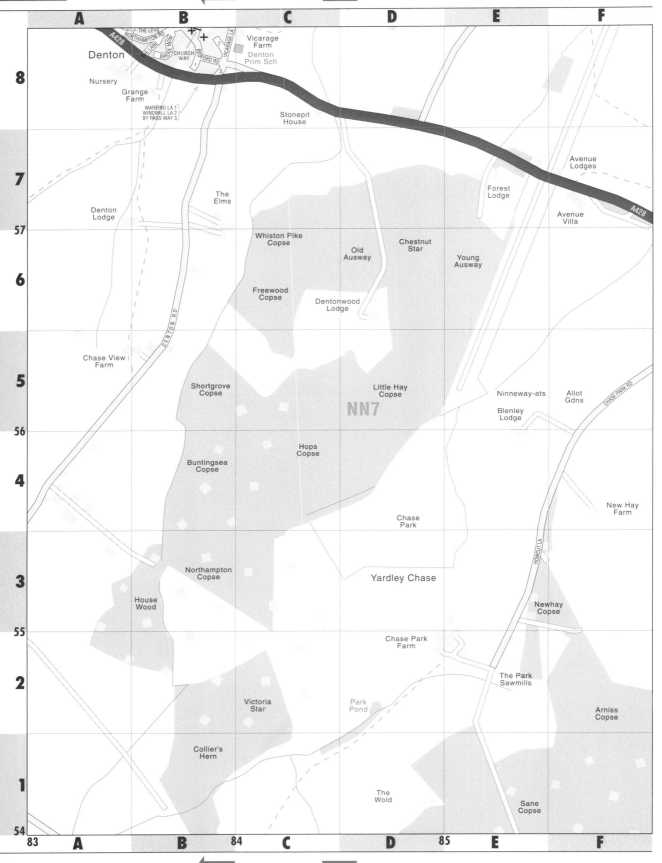

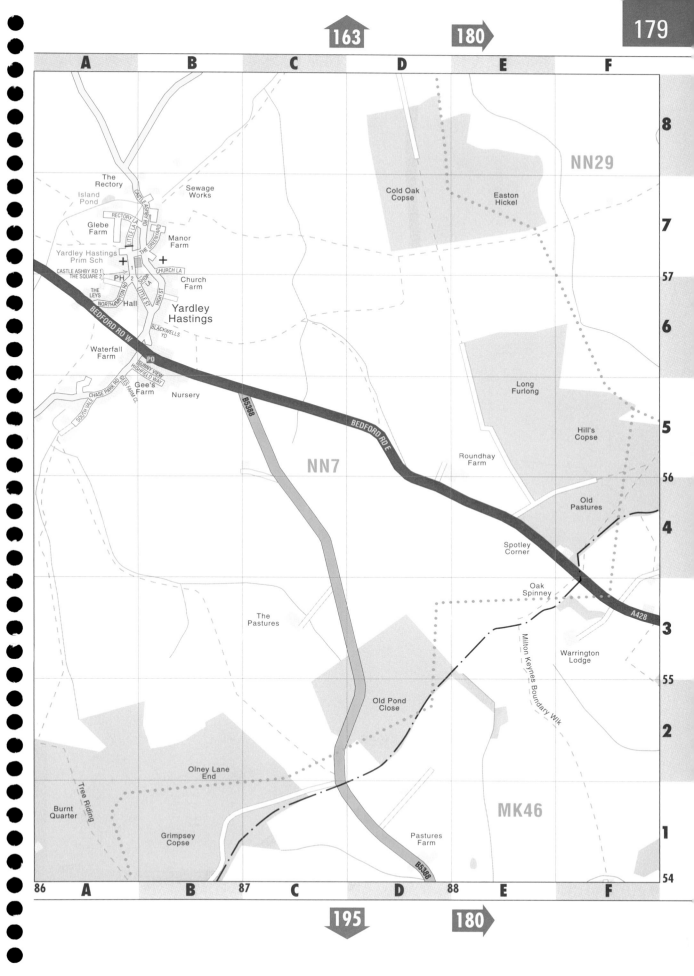

179
164

A
B
C
D
E
F
8
7
57
6
5
56
4
3
55
2
1
54
89
90
91
Horn Wood
Stocking Hollow
The Belts
A509
NN29
Wold Barn
Santon Barn
The Lodge
Bozeat Wood
Bozeat Grange
The Slipe
Northey Farm
The Oaks Wood
Nunwood Barn
Milton Keynes Boundary Wlk
Three Shires Way
Nun Wood
Threeshire Wood
New Pastures Farm
Lavendon Lodge Farm
Barslay Spinney
MK43
A428
Broadlane Spinney
Warrington House
Nursery
Park Farm
Nuniron Spinney
Nunirons
MK46
Castle Farm
The Nest Farm
Lower Farm
CASTLE RD
Brickfield Plantation
Warrington House Farm
Home Farm
Warrington
Lavendon
A509 Milton Keynes
Buckinghamshire STREET ATLAS
A428 Bedford
Bedfordshire STREET ATLAS

179

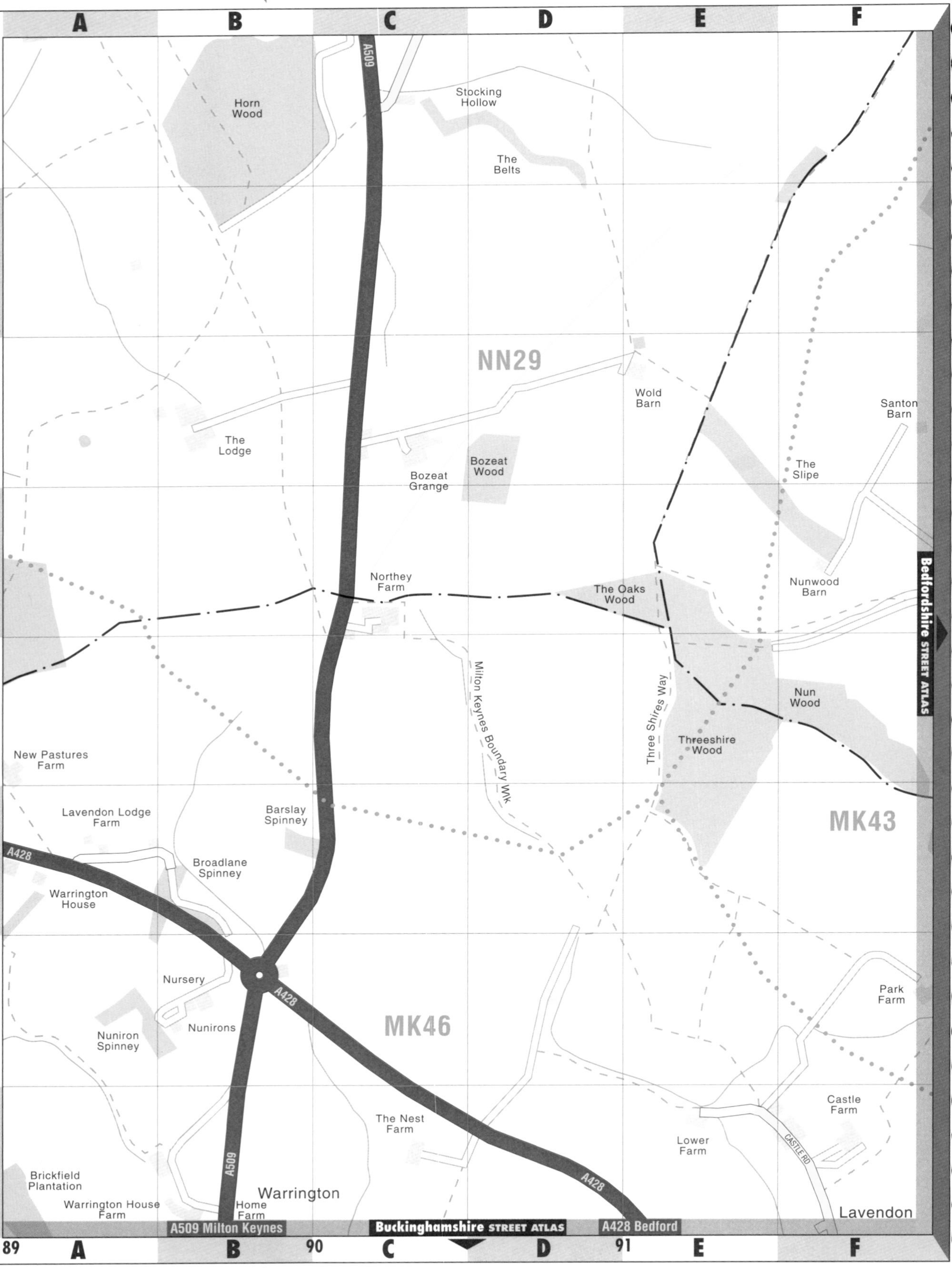

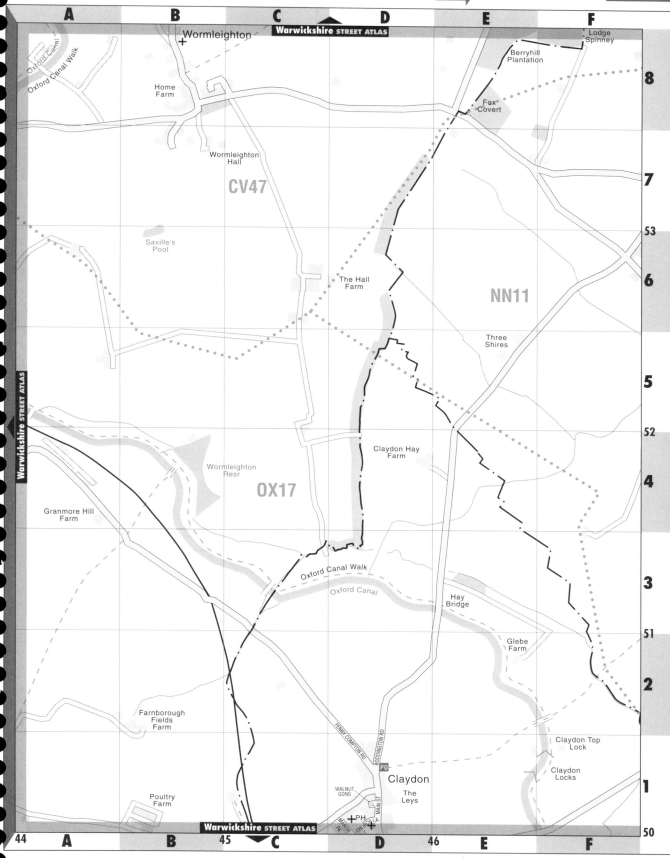

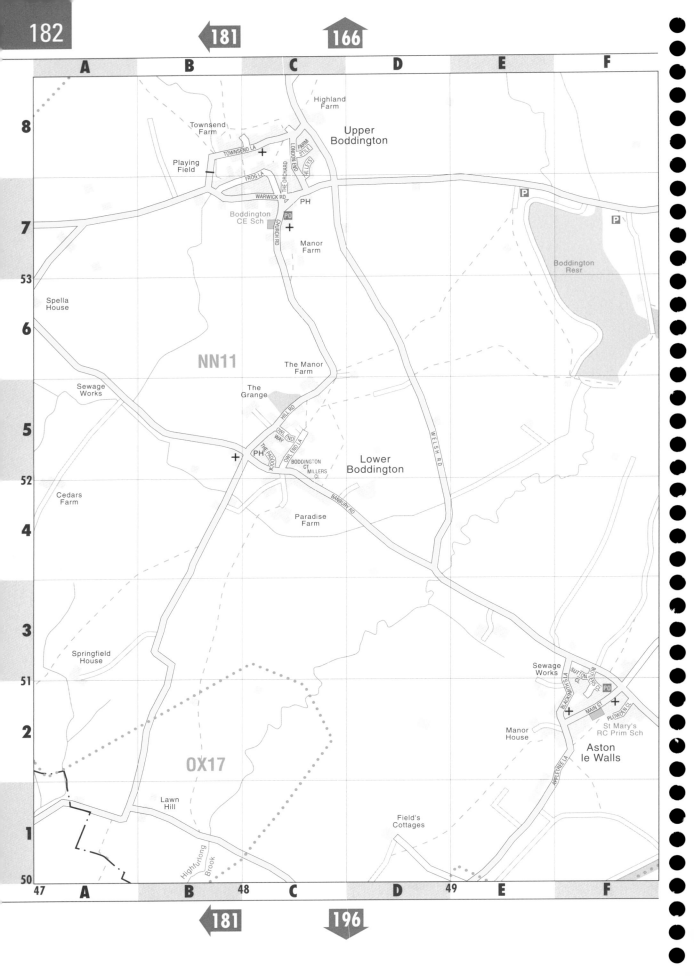

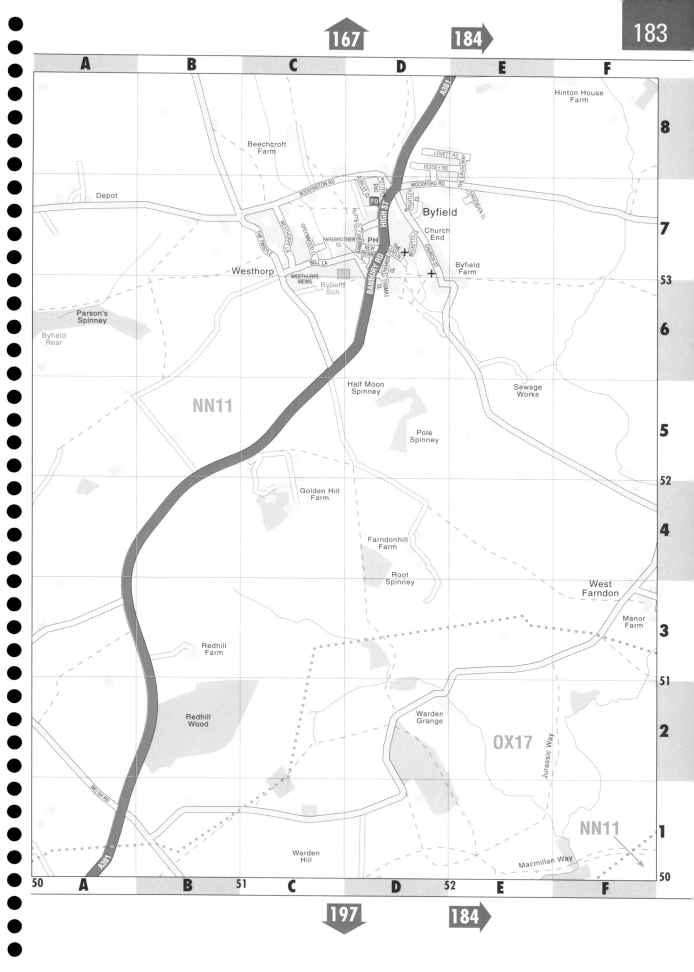

A B C D E F

8

Hinton House Farm

Beechcroft Farm

Depot

BODDINGTON RD

LOVETT RD

FESSEY RD

THE CAUSEWAY

WOODFORD RD

KIRBY CL

BRIGHTLEY CL

POTTERS END

JUBILEE CL

HIGH ST

Byfield

7

THE THISTLE

WESTHORPE LA

GREENWOOD CL

BELL LA

FAREBROTHER CL

HUTTS CL

ASHBY RD

PH

NEW TERR

BECKETTS CL

Church End

CHURCH ST

53

Westhorp

WESTHORPE MEWS

Byfield Sch

BANBURY RD

EDWARDS CL

THE GREEN

ST THOMAS CL

Byfield Farm

Parson's Spinney

Byfield Resr

6

Half Moon Spinney

Sewage Works

NN11

Pole Spinney

5

52

Golden Hill Farm

Farndonhill Farm

4

Root Spinney

West Farndon

Redhill Farm

Manor Farm

3

51

Warden Grange

OX17

2

Redhill Wood

Jurassic Way

NN11

1

WELSH RD

A361

Warden Hill

Macmillan Way

50

A B C D E F

8

7

53

6

5

52

4

3

51

2

1

50

BLUEBELL CL

THE BEAVER CTR

RAL WAY

Mast

BYFIELD RD

GREAT CE

FAY CL

AVE

WHITECROFT

GDNS

CENTR

TOWNSEND

CLOVE AVE

DRYDEN CL

MANOR RD

GORSE RD

MANOR CL

NELSON AVE

PRIMROSE WLK

Woodford Halse

Liby

PO

SCHOOL ST

SCRIVENS HILL

Foxhill Farm

MENZIES WAY

BROOKSIDE

WILLOW

BEECHER

ANSCOMBE WAY

GREBE CL

SWAN CL

MALLARD CL

HERON CL

PHIPPS CL

CASTLE RD

SIDNEY RD

PERCY RD

CHURCH ST

PARSONS ST

MOUNT PLEASANT

Woodford Halse CE Prim Sch

HIGH ST

CHESTNUT CL

ELM CL

MAPLE CL

ROWAN WAY

SYCAMORE CL

BIRCH

BARKER PL

ADAMS RD

LABURNUM CL

KINGFISHER CL

CHERWE

BANKSIDE

QUINTON LA

Hinton

HAWTHORNE CL

ASH WAY

OAK

CHERRY LA

WILD

HINTON CT

TOP FARM CT

HINTON MANOR CT

STATION RD

STATION GDNS

CHERRY LA

PH

SOUTH ST

Woodford Hill Farm

HINTON RD

POOL ST

1 EBONY CT
2 WINSTON CL

FARNDON RD

BROMLEY FARM CT

Bromley's Farm

River Cherwell

Gravel Farm

Woodford Hill

Sewage Works

Jurassic Way

Gravelfield Barn

Dairy Farm

NN11

Cherry Tree

Moors Farm

Eydonhill

Tile Barn

OX17

Cedars Farm

Ashby's Farm

Crockwell Farm

PRESTON RD

BYFIELD RD

MANITOBA WAY

WAY

HILL VIEW

MORETON RD

PARTRIDGE LA

PO

Eydon

LIME AVE

DOCTORS LA

HIGH ST

BLACKSMITHS LA

PH

Macmillan Way

Cemy

HOLLOW WAY

SCHOOL LA

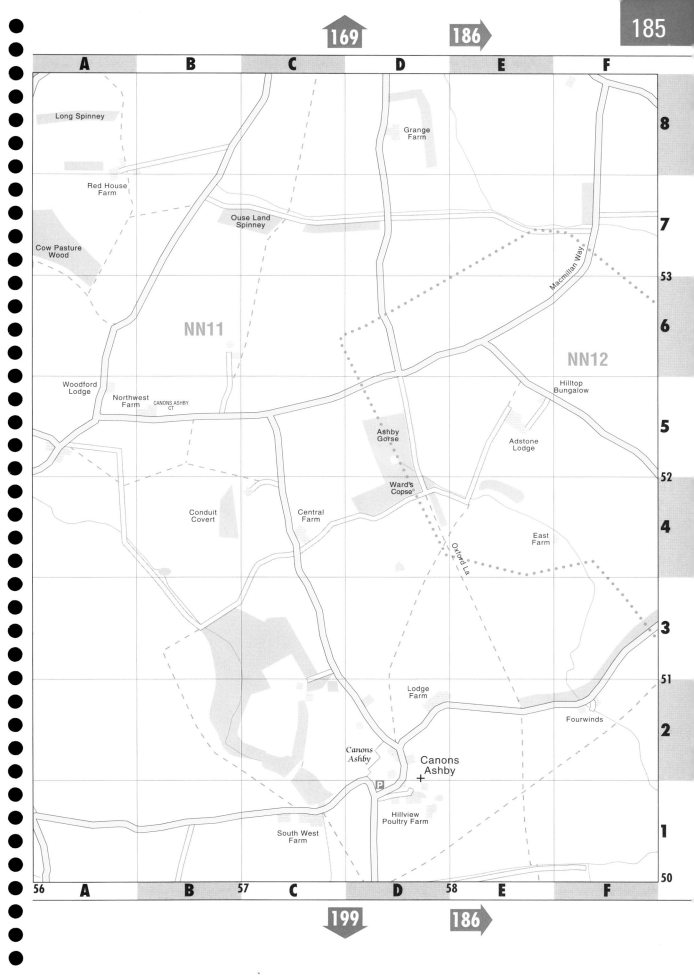

169
186

A   B   C   D   E   F

8

Long Spinney

Grange
Farm

Red House
Farm

7

Ouse Land
Spinney

53

Cow Pasture
Wood

NN11

6

Macmillan Way

NN12

Woodford
Lodge

Hilltop
Bungalow

Northwest
Farm
CANONS ASHBY
CT

5

Ashby
Gorse

Adstone
Lodge

52

Ward's
Copse

Conduit
Covert

Central
Farm

East
Farm

4

Oxford La

3

Lodge
Farm

51

Fourwinds

2

Canons
Ashby

Canons
Ashby

P

Hillview
Poultry Farm

1

South West
Farm

50

56   A   B   57   C   D   58   E   F

199
186

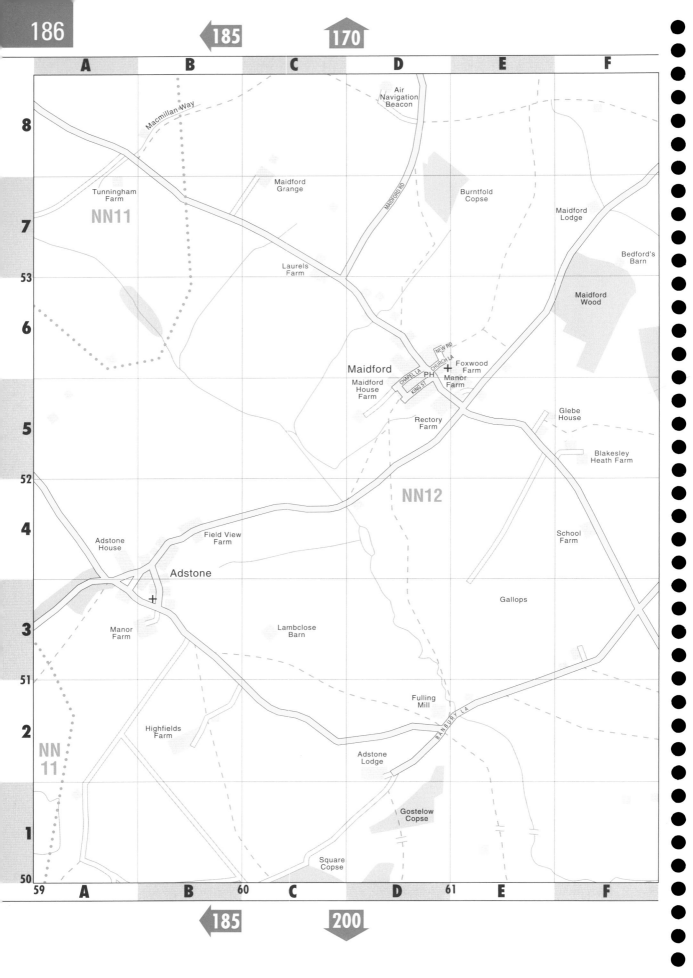

185
170

A B C D E F

8

7

NN11

53

6

5

52

4

3

51

2

NN 11

1

50

59 A B 60 C D 61 E F

185
200

Macmillan Way

Tunningham Farm

Maidford Grange

Air Navigation Beacon

MAIDFORD RD

Burntfold Copse

Maidford Lodge

Bedford's Barn

Maidford Wood

Laurels Farm

NEW RD

CHURCH LA

Maidford

CHAPEL LA

PH

Foxwood Farm

Manor Farm

Maidford House Farm

KING ST

Glebe House

Rectory Farm

Blakesley Heath Farm

NN12

Field View Farm

School Farm

Adstone House

Adstone

Gallops

Manor Farm

Lambclose Barn

Fulling Mill

Highfields Farm

BANBURY LA

Adstone Lodge

Gostelow Copse

Square Copse

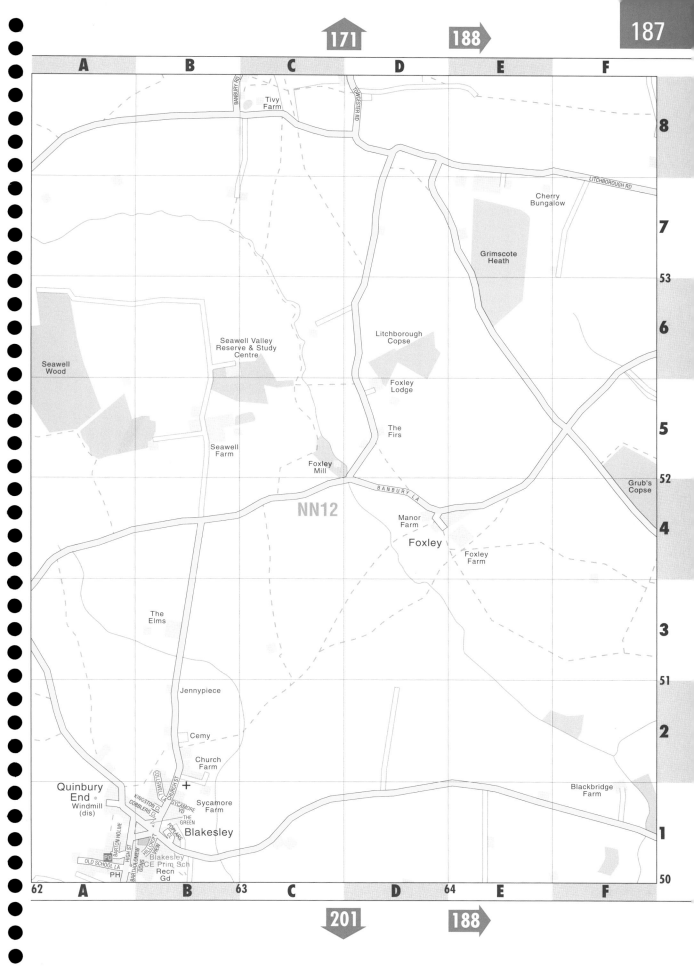

171
188
201
188

A B C D E F

8
7
53
6
5
52
4
3
51
2
1
50

Tivy Farm

BANBURY RD

TOWCESTER RD

LITCHBOROUGH RD

Cherry Bungalow

Grimscote Heath

Litchborough Copse

Foxley Lodge

Seawell Valley Reserve & Study Centre

Seawell Wood

The Firs

Seawell Farm

Foxley Mill

NN12

BANBURY LA

Grub's Copse

Manor Farm

Foxley

Foxley Farm

The Elms

Jennypiece

Cemy

Church Farm

Blackbridge Farm

Quinbury End
Windmill (dis)

KINGSTON CL
COBBLERS CL
COLLSWELL LA
CHURCH ST
SYCAMORE YD
Sycamore Farm
THE GREEN
POPLARS CL
Blakesley

BARTON HOLME
HIGH ST
BARTHOLOMEW GDNS
HILLCROFT VIEW
PO
OLD SCHOOL LA
PH
Blakesley CE Prim Sch
Recn Gd

62 A B 63 C D 64 E F

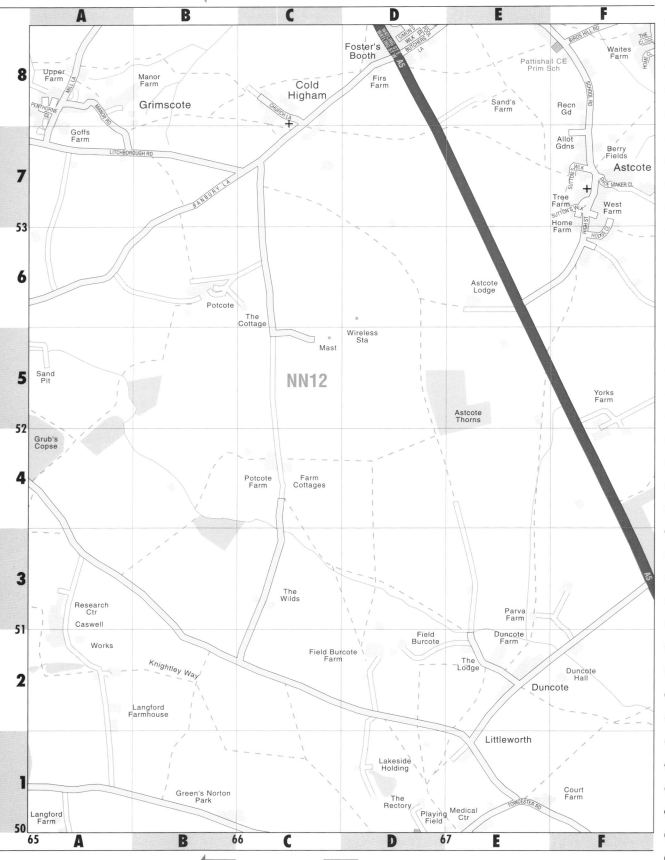

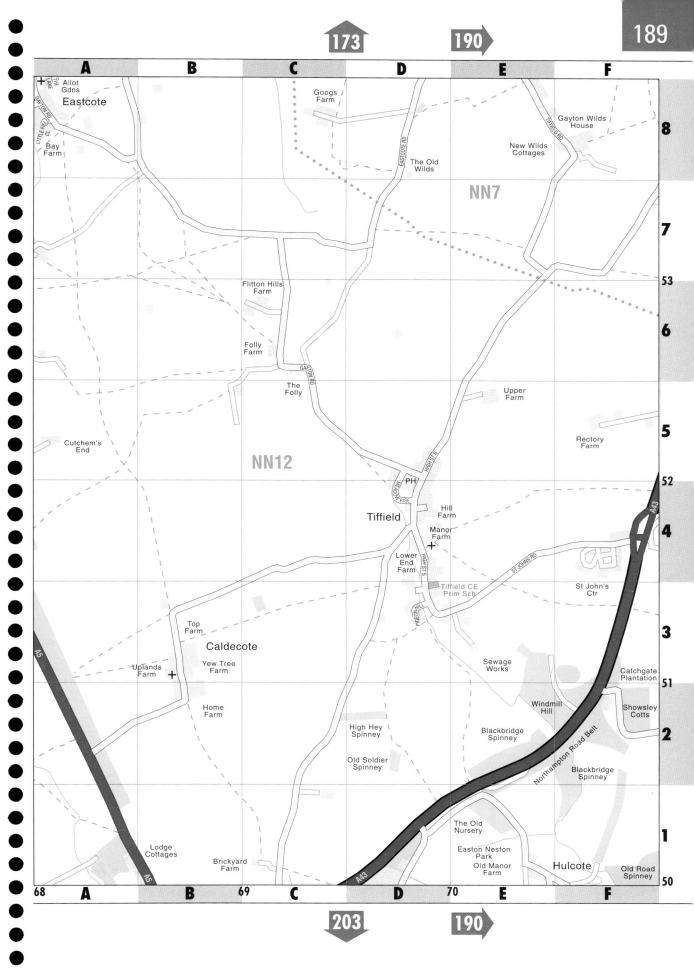

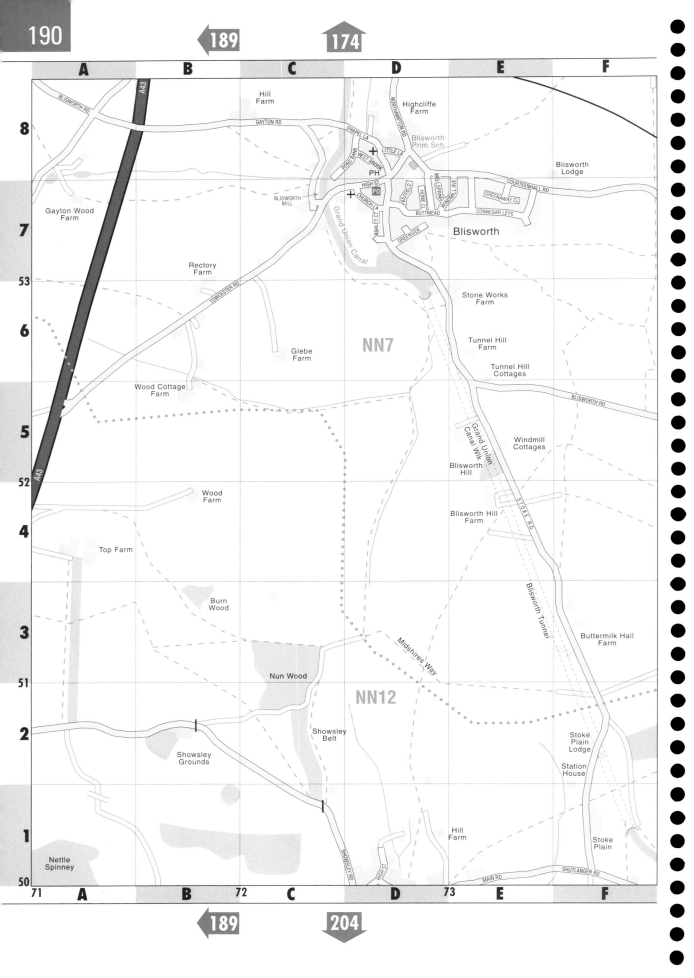

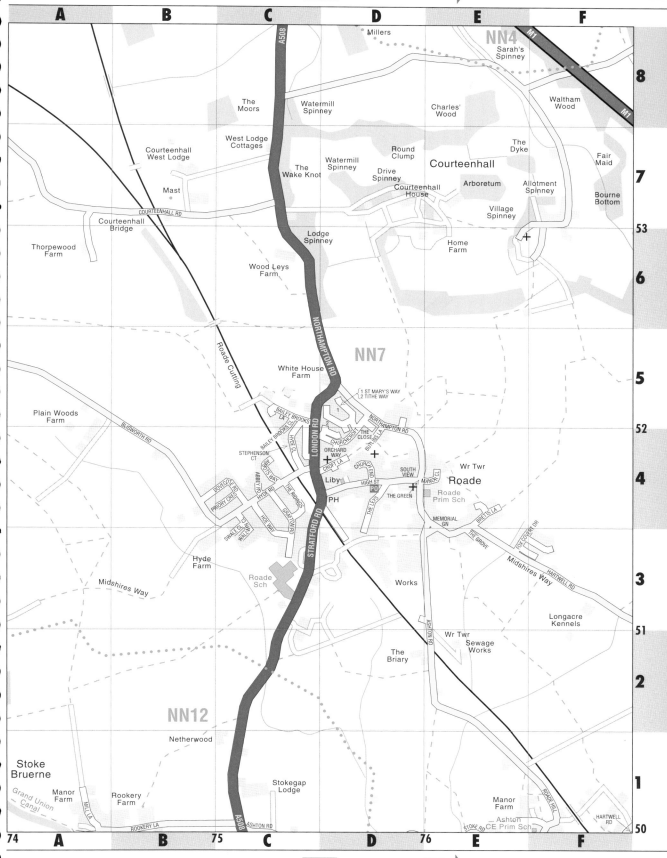

Millers
NN4
Sarah's Spinney
Waltham Wood
M1

The Moors
Watermill Spinney
Charles' Wood
The Dyke
Fair Maid

Courteenhall West Lodge
West Lodge Cottages
The Wake Knot
Watermill Spinney
Round Clump
Courteenhall
The Dyke
Bourne Bottom

Mast
COURTEENHALL RD
Drive Spinney
Courteenhall House
Arboretum
Allotment Spinney

Courteenhall Bridge
Lodge Spinney
Village Spinney
53

Thorpewood Farm
Home Farm
6

Wood Leys Farm
NORTHAMPTON RD

Roade Cutting
NN7

White House Farm
5

Plain Woods Farm
BLISWORTH RD
BAILEY BROOKS LA
1 ST MARY'S WAY
2 TITHE WAY
52

STEPHENSON CT
BAILEY BROOKS CL
HYDE CL
CHURCHCROFT
ORCHARD WAY
THE CLOSE
NORTHAMPTON RD
BUTT LA

DOVECOT CL
ABBEY RD
BRITTS WAY
HYDE RD
CROFT LA
CHURCH END
Liby
LONDON RD
SOUTH VIEW
MANOR
Wr Twr
Roade
4

PRIORY CRES
THE RIDINGS
HIGH ST
PO
Roade Prim Sch

SWALE CL
HOE WAY
GRAFTON RD
THE LEYS
PH
THE GREEN

Hyde Farm
STRATFORD RD
MEMORIAL GN
BRETTS LA

Midshires Way
Roade Sch
FOX COVERT DR
HARTWELL RD

Works
THE GROVE
Midshires Way
3

51
Longacre Kennels

NN12
The Briary
ASHTON RD
Wr Twr
Sewage Works
2

Netherwood

Stoke Bruerne
Stokegap Lodge
Manor Farm
Ashton CE Prim Sch
ROADE HILL
HARTWELL RD
1

Grand Union Canal
Manor Farm
MILL LA
Rookery Farm
ROOKERY LA
ASHTON RD
A508
STOKE RD
50

74   75   76

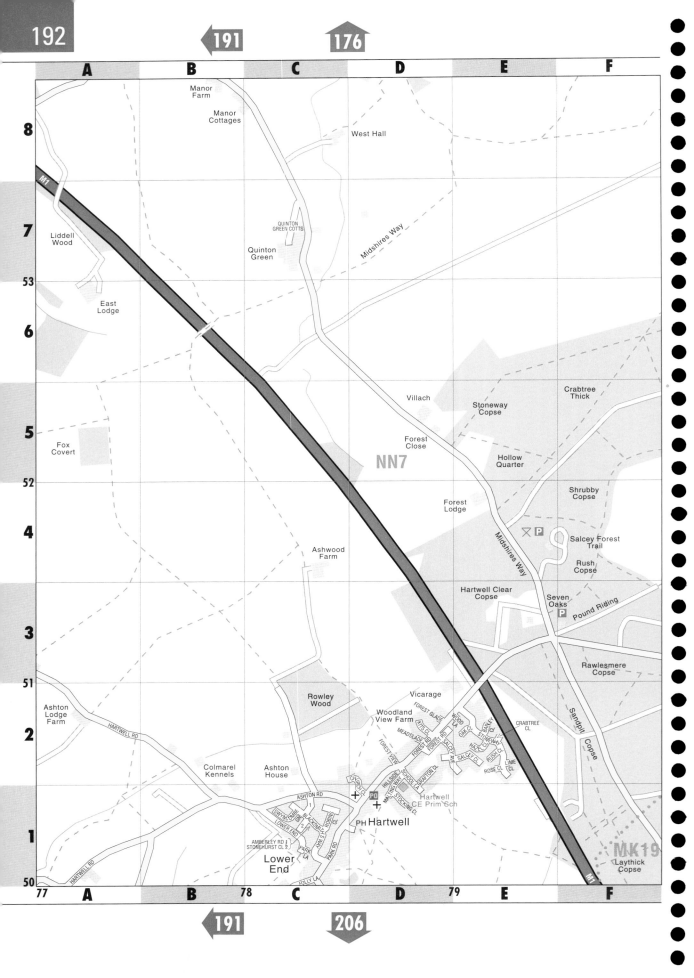

8

7

53

6

5

52

4

3

51

2

1

50

A   B   C   D   E   F

Manor Farm
Manor Cottages
West Hall
Liddell Wood
Quinton Green Cotts
Quinton Green
Midshires Way
East Lodge
Villach
Crabtree Thick
Stoneway Copse
Fox Covert
Forest Close
NN7
Hollow Quarter
Shrubby Copse
Forest Lodge
Salcey Forest Trail
Ashwood Farm
Midshires Way
Rush Copse
Hartwell Clear Copse
Seven Oaks
Pound Riding
Ashton Lodge Farm
Rowley Wood
Vicarage
Rawlesmere Copse
Hartwell Rd
Woodland View Farm
FOREST GLADE
WOOD LA
CRABTREE CL
Sandpit Copse
Colmarel Kennels
Ashton House
MEADSLADE CL
FOREST
KITS CL
FOREST RD
BARLEY
OAK CL
STONEWAY
RUSH CL
LIME CL
ROSE CL
SALCEY AVE
HAZEL
SALCEY CL
FOREST VIEW
Ashton Rd
HILLSIDE
SCHOOL LA
BRAFTON CL
MALTING WAY
STOCKING CL
Hartwell CE Prim Sch
SWYNCOMBE
BLACKSMITHS
ROBINS CL
LOWER END
PARK LA
PARK RD
AMBERLEY RD
STONEHURST CL
PH Hartwell
Lower End
FOLLY LA
Laythick Copse
MK19

77   A   B   78   C   D   79   E   F   50

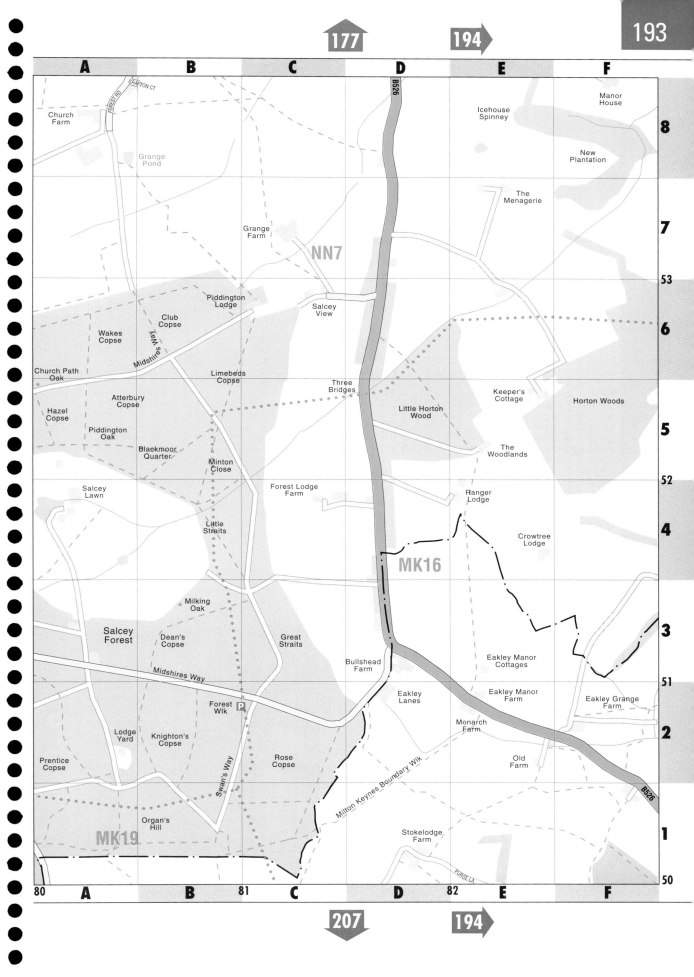

193
178

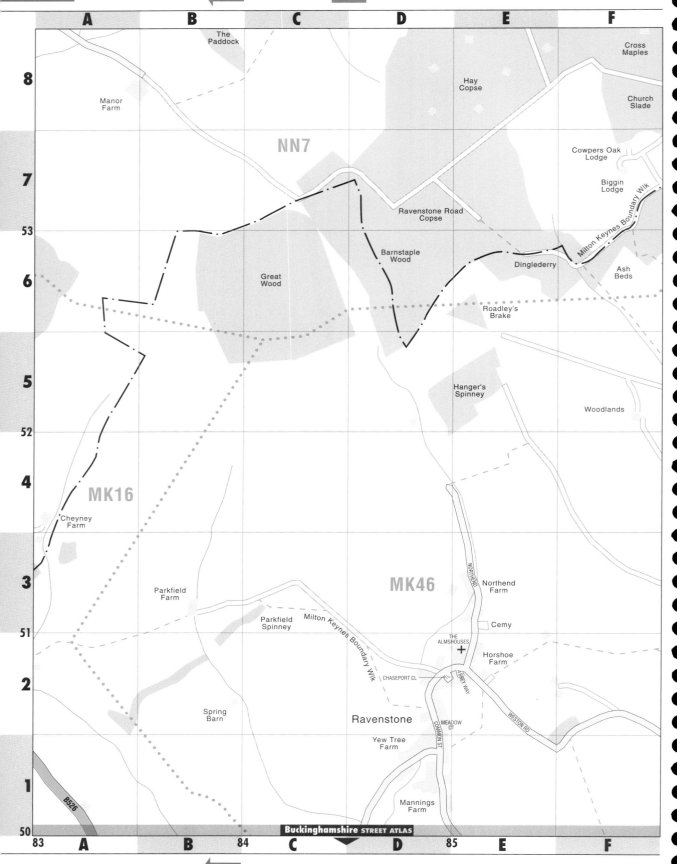

8

7

53

6

5

52

4

3

51

2

1

50

The Paddock

Cross Maples

Hay Copse

Church Slade

Manor Farm

NN7

Cowpers Oak Lodge

Biggin Lodge

Ravenstone Road Copse

Milton Keynes Boundary Wlk

Barnstaple Wood

Dinglederry

Ash Beds

Great Wood

Roadley's Brake

Hanger's Spinney

Woodlands

MK16

Cheyney Farm

Parkfield Farm

MK46

Northend

Northend Farm

Cemy

Parkfield Spinney

Milton Keynes Boundary Wlk

THE ALMSHOUSES

Horshoe Farm

CHASEPORT CL

ABBEY WAY

WESTON RD

Spring Barn

Ravenstone

COMMON ST

MEADOW CT

Yew Tree Farm

Mannings Farm

B526

83 A B 84 C D 85 E F

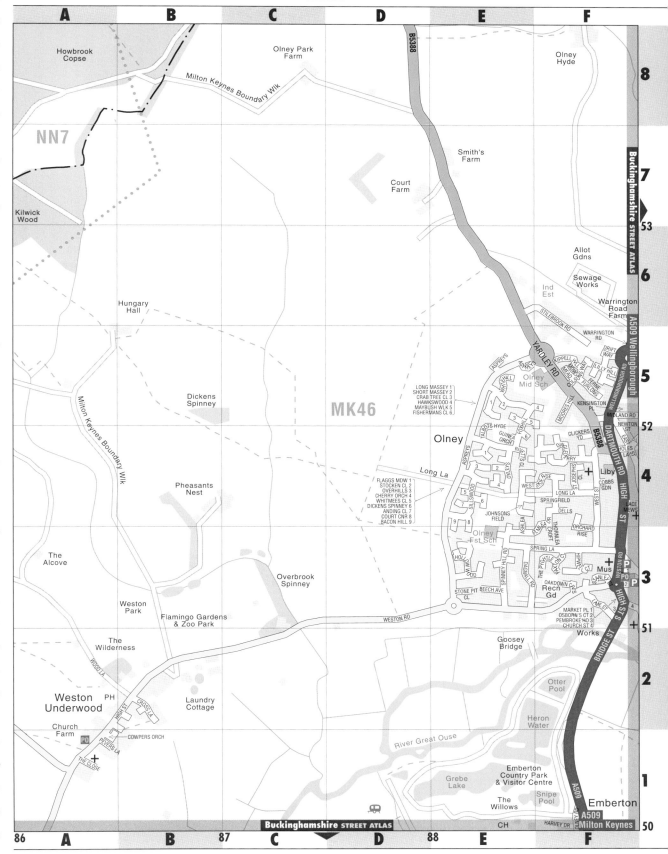

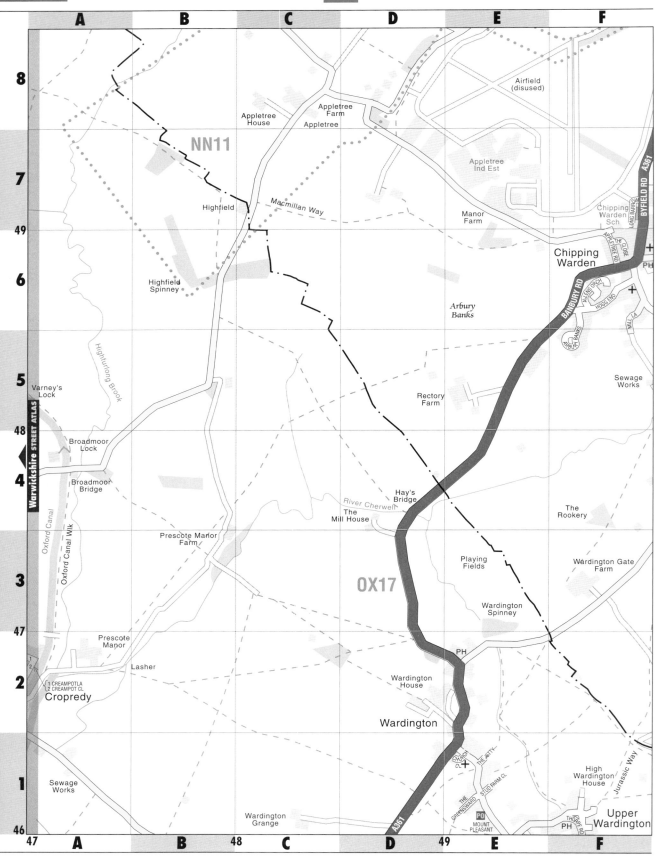

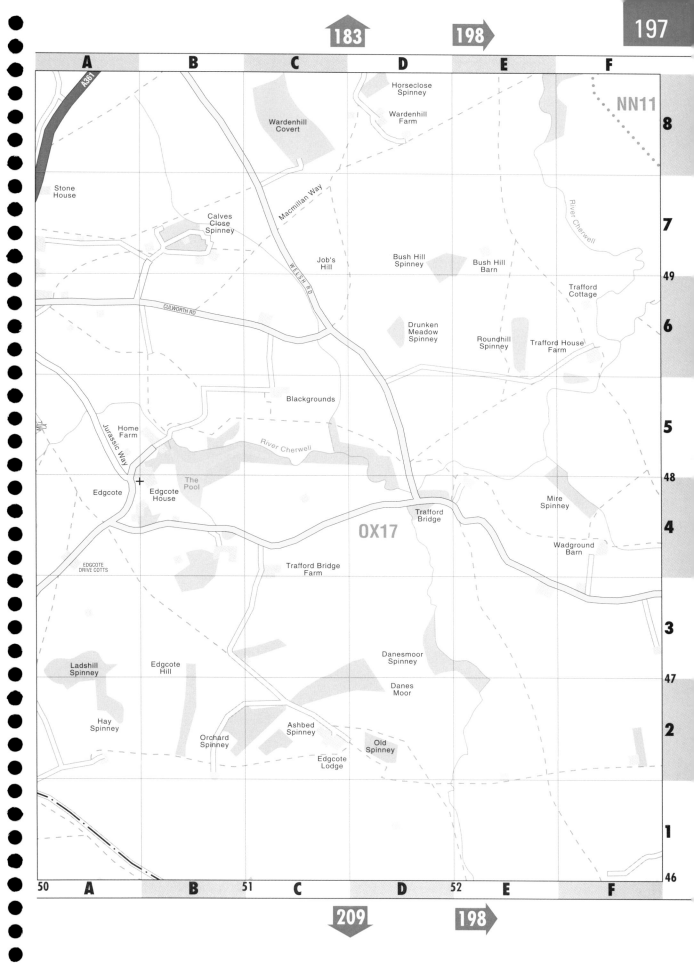

183
198
209
198

NN11

A361

Horseclose
Spinney

Wardenhill
Farm

Wardenhill
Covert

Stone
House

Macmillan Way

Calves
Close
Spinney

Job's
Hill

Bush Hill
Spinney

Bush Hill
Barn

River Cherwell

Trafford
Cottage

WELSH RD

CULWORTH RD

Drunken
Meadow
Spinney

Roundhill
Spinney

Trafford House
Farm

Blackgrounds

Home
Farm

River Cherwell

Jurassic Way

Edgcote

Edgcote
House

The
Pool

Mire
Spinney

Trafford
Bridge

OX17

Wadground
Barn

Trafford Bridge
Farm

EDGCOTE
DRIVE COTTS

Danesmoor
Spinney

Ladshill
Spinney

Edgcote
Hill

Danes
Moor

Hay
Spinney

Ashbed
Spinney

Orchard
Spinney

Old
Spinney

Edgcote
Lodge

A B C D E F
8 7 49 6 5 48 4 3 47 2 1 46
50 A B 51 C D 52 E F

A   B   C   D   E   F

8

Hall Farm

Eydon Hall

The Rookery

Foxhill Farm

Eydon Park

Fox Covert

7

Blackbird Hill Spinney

Lawnhill Farm

Macmillan Way

Long Spinney

Little Close

49

NN11

6

Blackbird Hill Farm

Rye Hill Farm

5

Fulford Spinney

Zig-Zag Farm

48

Lodge Farm

Pewitt Farm

4

Fulford Farm

Adwell Farm

3

Culworth

OX17

HIGH ST

Culworth Hall

Banbury La

Barrow Hill

THE GREEN

PH

47

Culworth CE Sch

QUEENS ST

WALNUT CL

BARL

Culworth Fields

PO

2

BUTTS CL

THE LODGE

Sewage Works

Culworth House

SULGRAVE RD

Sulgrave Farm

1

BANBURY LA

Culworth Grounds Farm

46

53   A   B   54   C   D   55   E   F

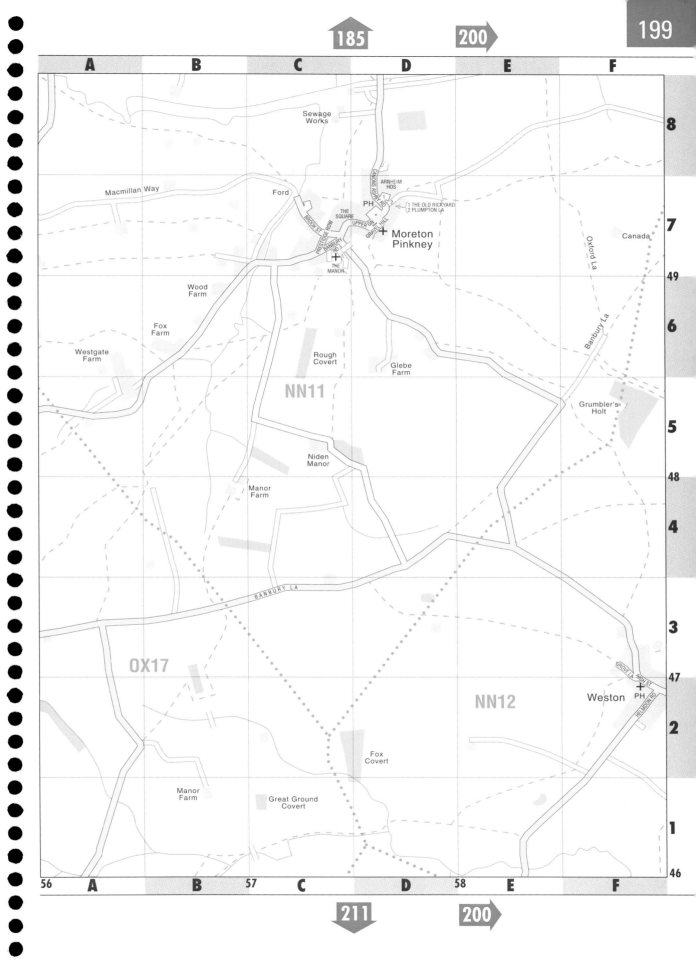

A B C D E F

8

7

49

6

5

48

4

3

47

2

1

46

Sewage Works

Macmillan Way

Ford

THE SQUARE

CANONS ASHBY RD

ARNHEIM HOS

PH

1 THE OLD RICKYARD
2 PLUMPTON LA

BROOK ST ROW

PRESTIDGE ROW

BANBURY RD

UPPER GR

GRAVEL HILL

THE MANOR

Moreton Pinkney

Oxford La

Canada

Banbury La

Wood Farm

Fox Farm

Westgate Farm

Rough Covert

NN11

Glebe Farm

Grumbler's Holt

Niden Manor

Manor Farm

BANBURY LA

OX17

NN12

Weston

GROVE LA

HIGH ST

PH

HELMDON RD

Manor Farm

Great Ground Covert

Fox Covert

56 A B 57 C D 58 E F

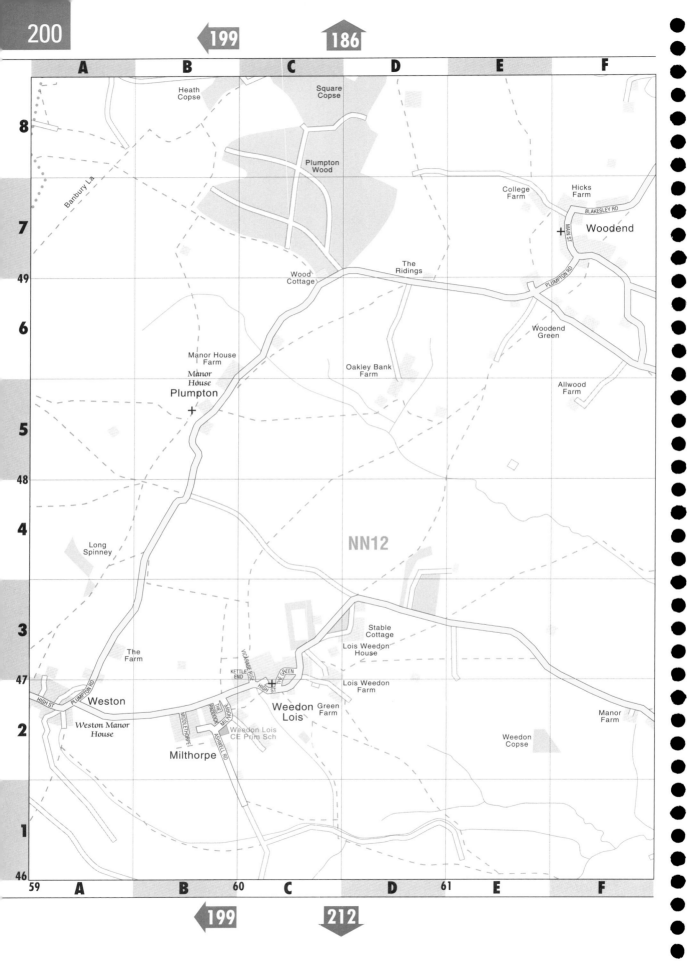

199
186

Heath Copse

Square Copse

Plumpton Wood

8

Banbury La

College Farm

Hicks Farm

BLAKESLEY RD

7

MAIN ST

Woodend

49

Wood Cottage

The Ridings

PLUMPTON RD

6

Manor House Farm

Manor House

Oakley Bank Farm

Woodend Green

Plumpton

Allwood Farm

5

48

4

Long Spinney

NN12

3

The Farm

Stable Cottage

Lois Weedon House

47

VICARAGE RISE

KETTLE END

THE GREEN

Lois Weedon Farm

PLUMPTON RD

HIGH ST

Weston

Weedon Lois

Green Farm

Manor Farm

2

HIGH ST

Weston Manor House

MIDDLETHORPE

THE PADDOCKS

MILL LA

ASHWELL RD

Weedon Lois CE Prim Sch

Weedon Copse

Milthorpe

1

46

59   60   61

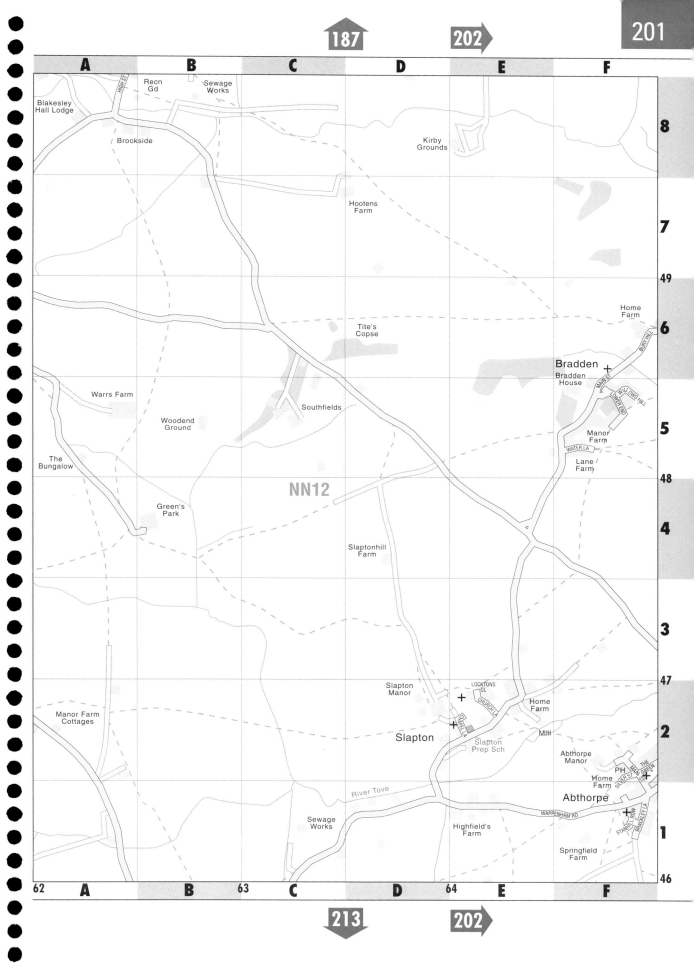

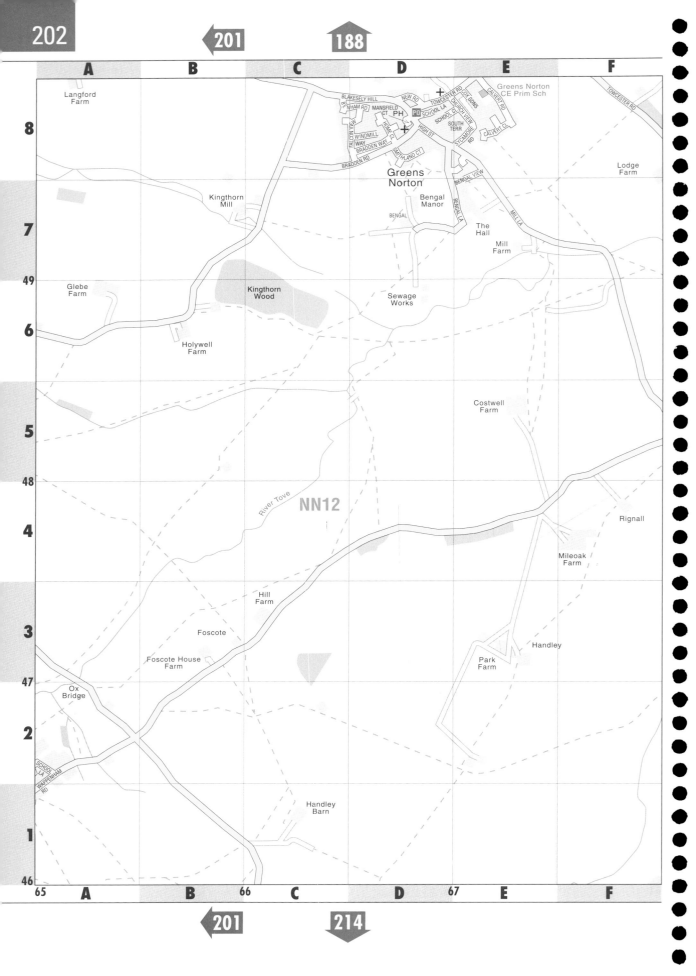

A   B   C   D   E   F

8

7

49

6

5

48

4

3

47

2

1

46

65   A   B   66   C   D   67   E   F

Langford
Farm

Greens Norton
CE Prim Sch

TOWCESTER RD

BLAKESELY HILL
BENHAM RD
NEW RD
MANSFIELD
CT   PH
PO
SCHOOL LA
TOWCESTER RD
FOX GDNS
CALVERT RD
SCHOOL CL
CHURCH VIEW
HIGH ST
SOUTH
TERR
SYCAMORE
RD
CALVERT CL
FALCON VIEW
WINDMILL
WAY
HOME CL
BRADDEN WAY
BRADDEN RD
SMITHLAND CT

Lodge
Farm

Kingthorn
Mill

Greens
Norton

Bengal
Manor

BENGAL

BENGAL VIEW
BENGAL LA

MILL LA

The
Hall

Mill
Farm

Glebe
Farm

Kingthorn
Wood

Sewage
Works

Costwell
Farm

Holywell
Farm

River Tove   NN12

Rignall

Mileoak
Farm

Hill
Farm

Foscote

Handley

Park
Farm

Foscote House
Farm

Ox
Bridge

SCHOOL LA
WAPPENHAM RD

Handley
Barn

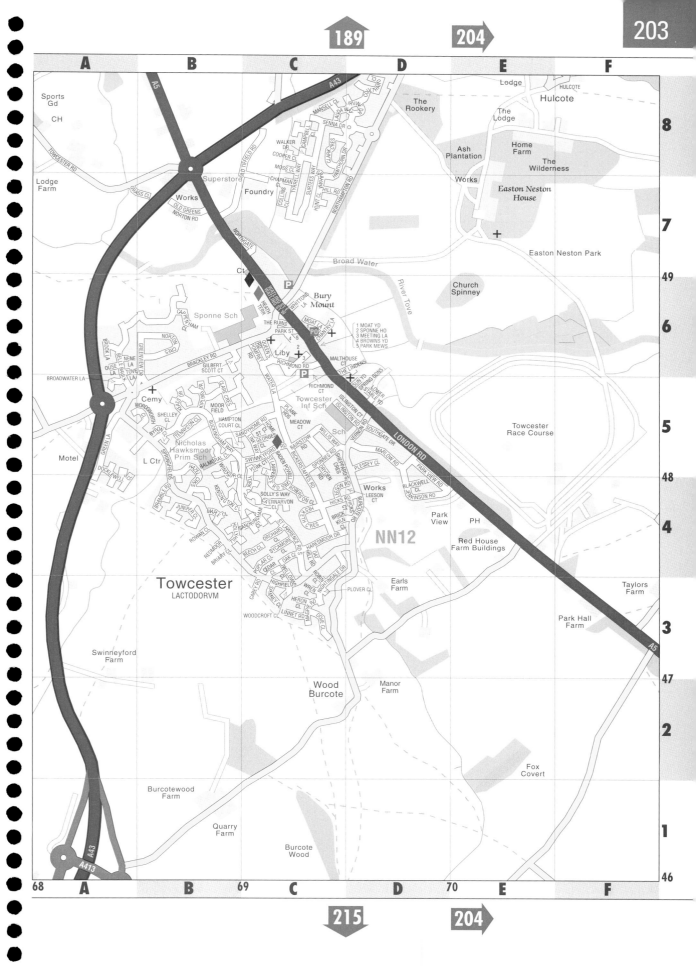

A   B   C   D   E   F

8

Nettle Spinney

Millers Belt
Plantation

SHUTLANGER
RD

WENTWORTH WAY

HIGH ST
SHOSLEY RD

THE
PADDOCKS

BAKER'S
LA

BLACKSMITHS
GN

MAIN RD

TWITCH
HILL

WATER LA

The
Monastery

PH

Alexanders
Plantation

Shutlanger

7

Magpie
Plantation

Radsmore
Plantation

Stokepark
Wood

Blagden

The Longwater

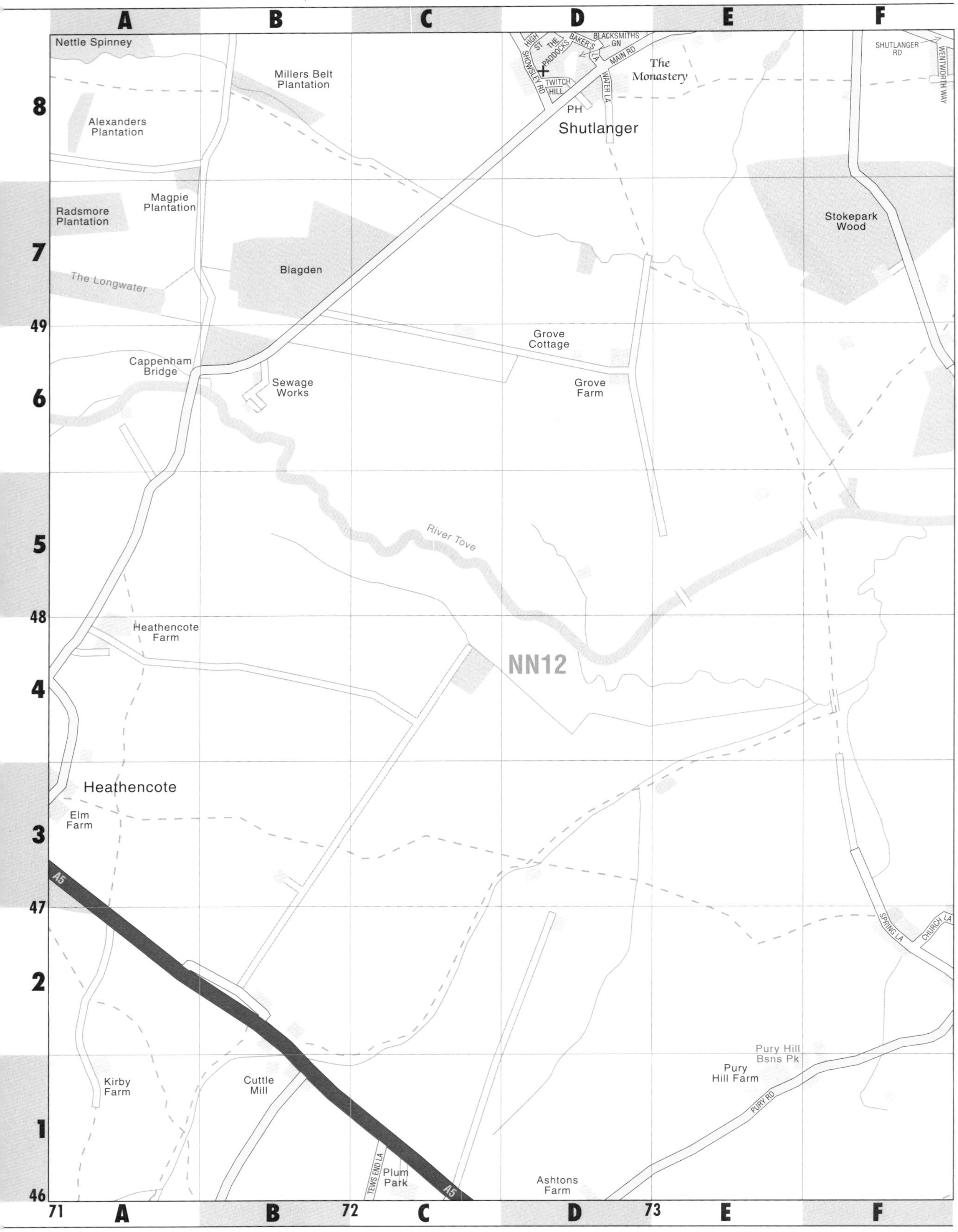

49

Grove
Cottage

Cappenham
Bridge

Sewage
Works

Grove
Farm

6

River Tove

5

48

Heathencote
Farm

NN12

4

Heathencote

Elm
Farm

3

A5

47

TWITCH

SPRING LA

CHURCH ST

2

Pury Hill
Bsns Pk

Pury
Hill Farm

Kirby
Farm

Cuttle
Mill

PURY RD

1

TEWS END LA

Plum
Park

A5

Ashtons
Farm

46

71   A   B   72   C   D   73   E   F

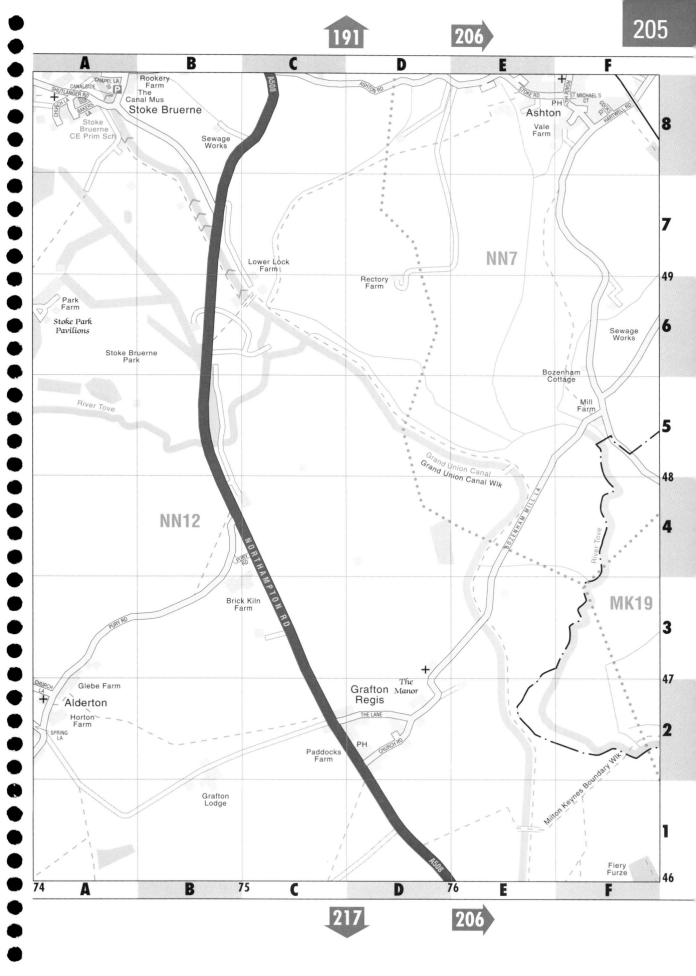

191
206
206

A   B   C   D   E   F

8

7

49

6

5

48

4

47

2

1

46

NN7

NN12

MK19

Hartwell Park Farm

Ravenshead Farm

FOLLY LA

PARK RD

Elms Farm

Hartwell End Farm

Hartwell End House

M1

Chapel Farm

Stonepit Farm

Milton Keynes Boundary Wlk

Gorden's Lodge

Roselane Farm

Glebe Farm

Wr Twr

FOREST RD

Model Farm

Long Street

GLEBE LA

HARTWELL RD

PH +

Milton Keynes Boundary Walk

Chantry Farm

RHYMER CL

HOLIDAY LA

Pindon Manor

Pindon End

Folly Farm

Halfway Houses

LONG STREET RD

New Farm

Pindon Manor Farm

HIGHAM CROSS RD

Sewage Works

Mast

Higham Cross

Badger's Balney

WILLIAMS CL

Green End La

CASTLETHORPE RD

Grange Farm

Cuckoo Hill Farm

Huntgate End

Huntgate End Farm

River Tove

Cuckoos' Hill

Maltmill Lane Farm

Lincoln Lodge Cottage

77   A   B   78   C   D   79   E   F

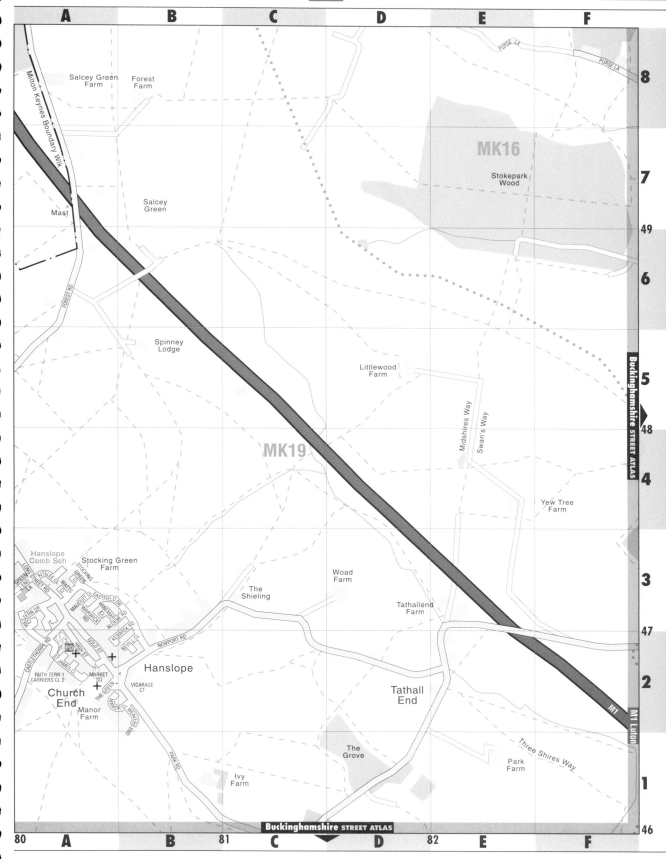

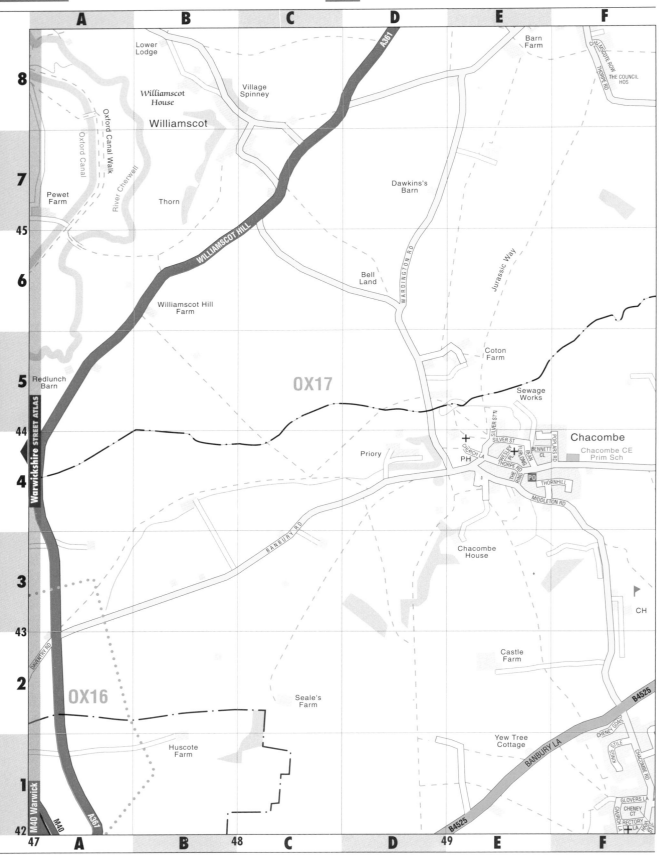

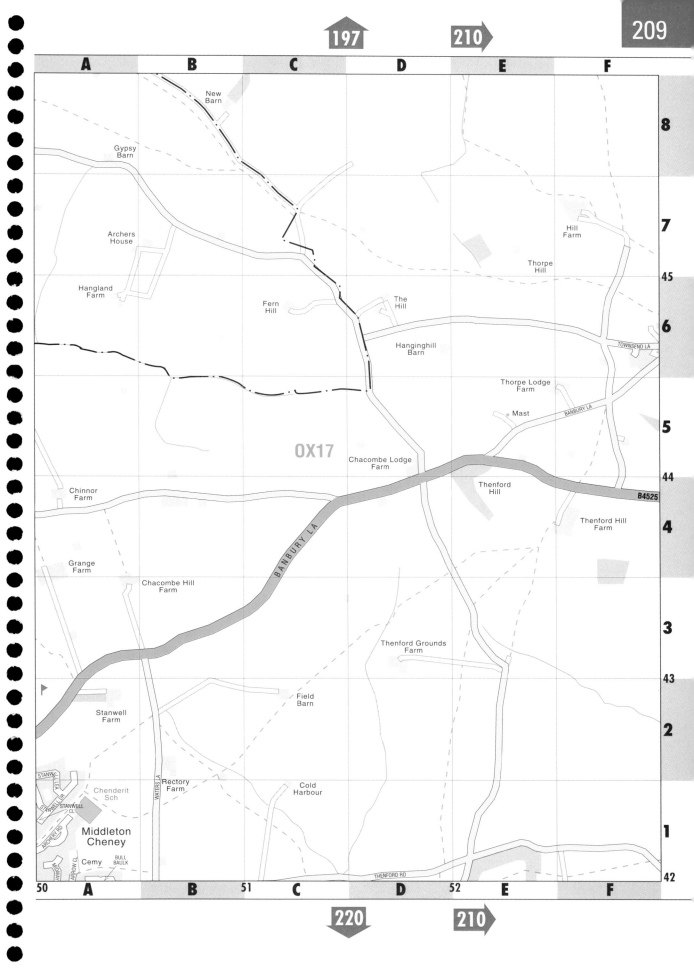

197
210
220
210

New Barn

Gypsy Barn

Archers House

Hangland Farm

Fern Hill

The Hill

Hanginghill Barn

Hill Farm

Thorpe Hill

TOWNSEND LA

Thorpe Lodge Farm

Mast

BANBURY LA

OX17

Chacombe Lodge Farm

Thenford Hill

B4525

Chinnor Farm

Thenford Hill Farm

Grange Farm

BANBURY LA

Chacombe Hill Farm

Thenford Grounds Farm

Stanwell Farm

Field Barn

STANW
WAY LEA
STANW
STANWELL CL
ARCHERY RD
Chenderit Sch
Rectory Farm
WATERS LA

Cold Harbour

Middleton Cheney

Cemy
BULL BAULK
MIDWAY
ARROW CL

THENFORD RD

A B C D E F

50 51 52

8 7 45 6 5 44 4 3 43 2 1 42

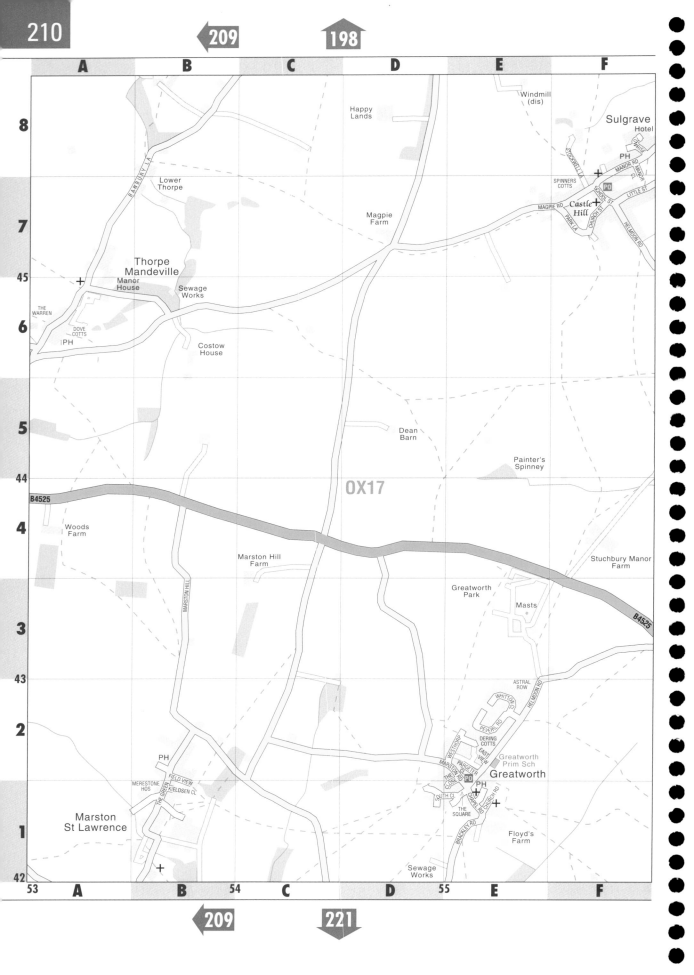

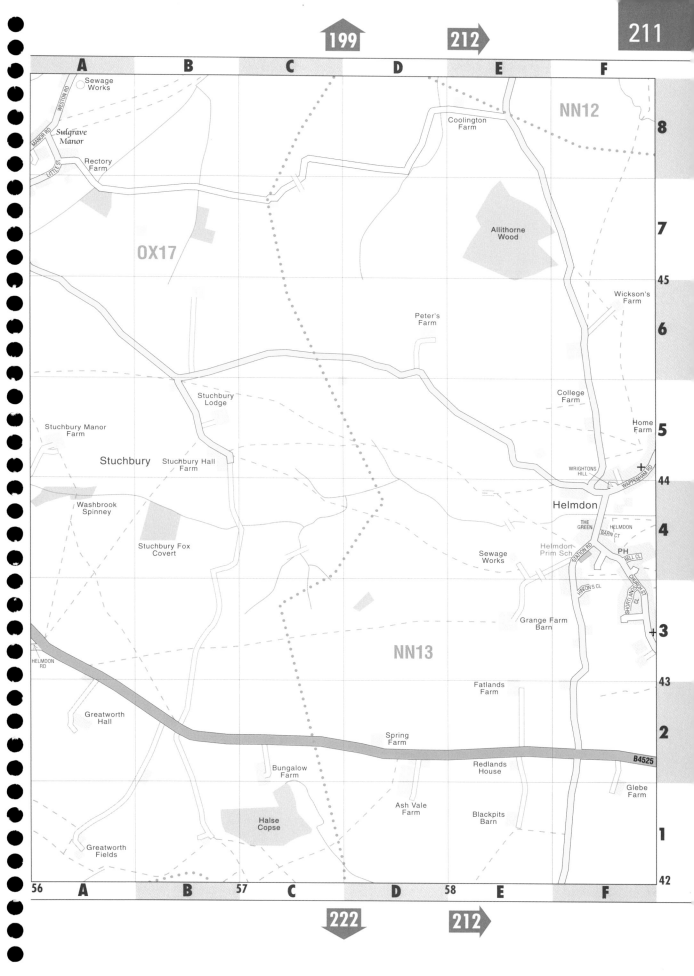

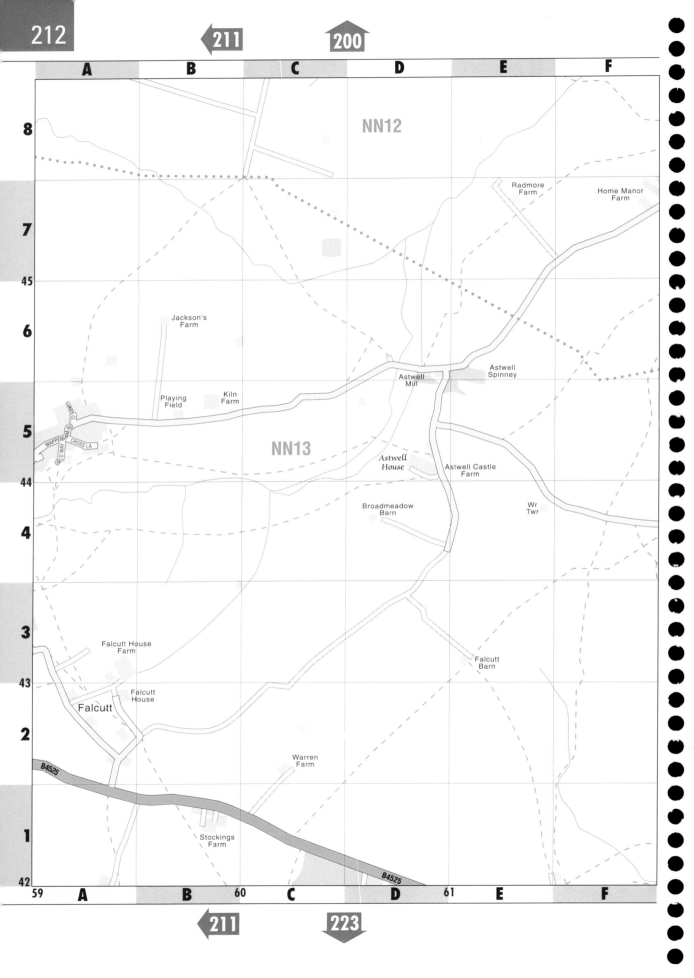

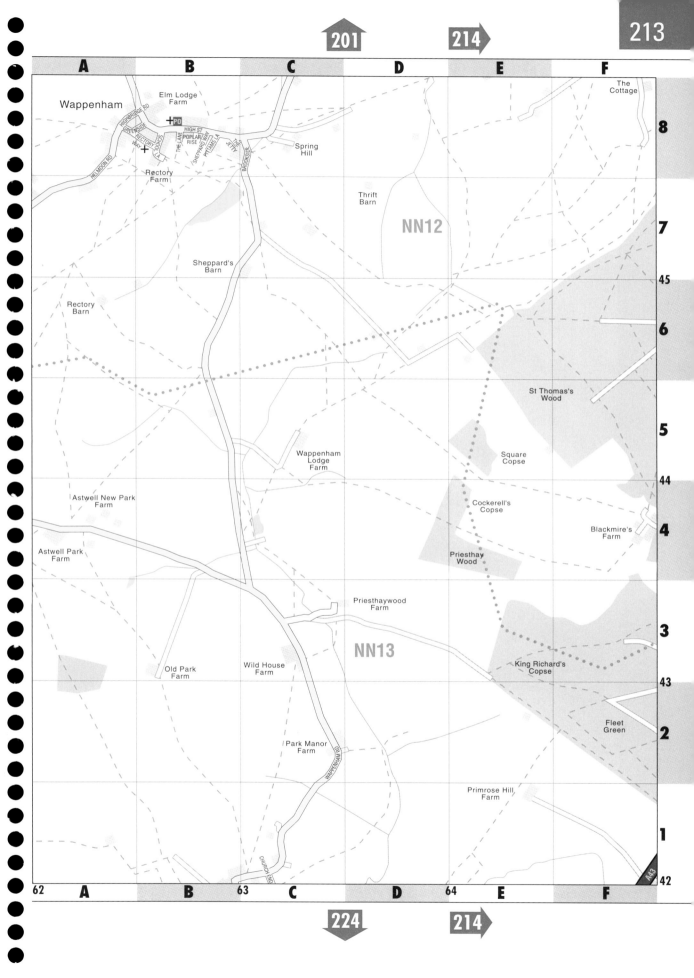

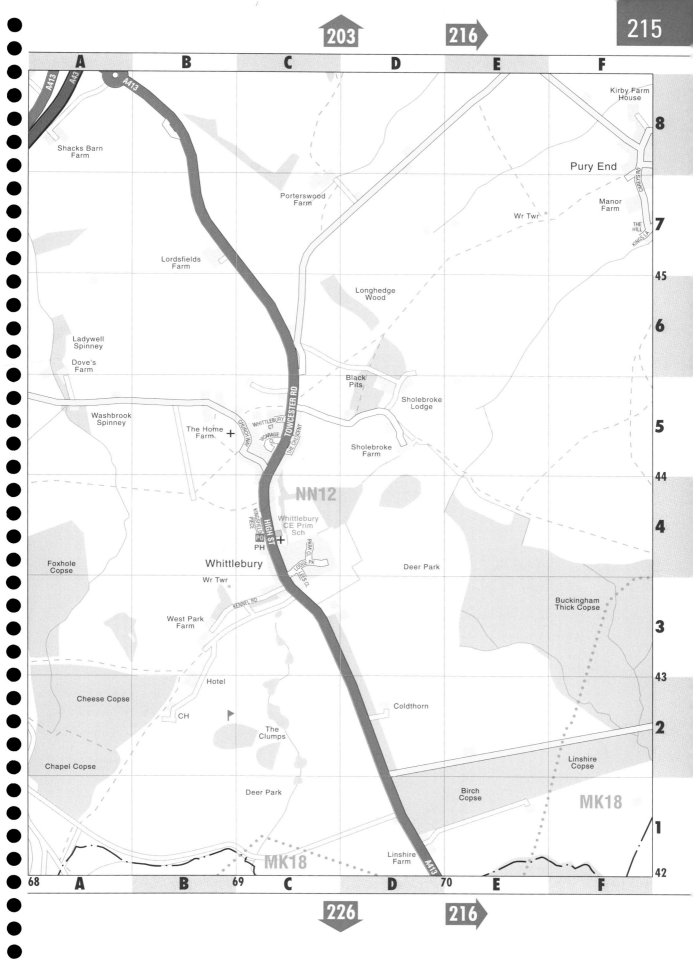

215
204

A   B   C   D   E   F

8

Tew's End

Paulerspury CE Prim Sch

PH

Paulerspury

Tew's End

LONGCROFT LA

A5

PURY RD

GRAYS CL
GRAYS LA

Plum Park

Grafton Park

7

CAREYS RD

SCRIVENERS LA

LOWER ST

PO

THE GREEN

PARK LA

NEW ROW CL

FAIRFIELD RD

LUMBER RD LA

STONY HILL

HIGH ST

Kingstons Farm

PLUM PARK LA

Plumpton End

45

Plum Park Farm

6

Park Farm

Stollage Farm

Bradlem Pond

The Gullet

A5

5

NN12

King's Copse

44

Bear's Copse

Lady Copse

4

Say's Copse

Old Tun Copse

3

Smalladine Copse

THE KENNELS

KENNELS DR

43

Wakefield Lawn

2

MK18

Whittlewood Forest

Wakefield Lodge

MAIN DR

Home Farm

The Pheasantry

DEANSHANGER DR

1

Briary Wood

Hill Copse

42

71   A   B   72   C   D   73   E   F

215
227

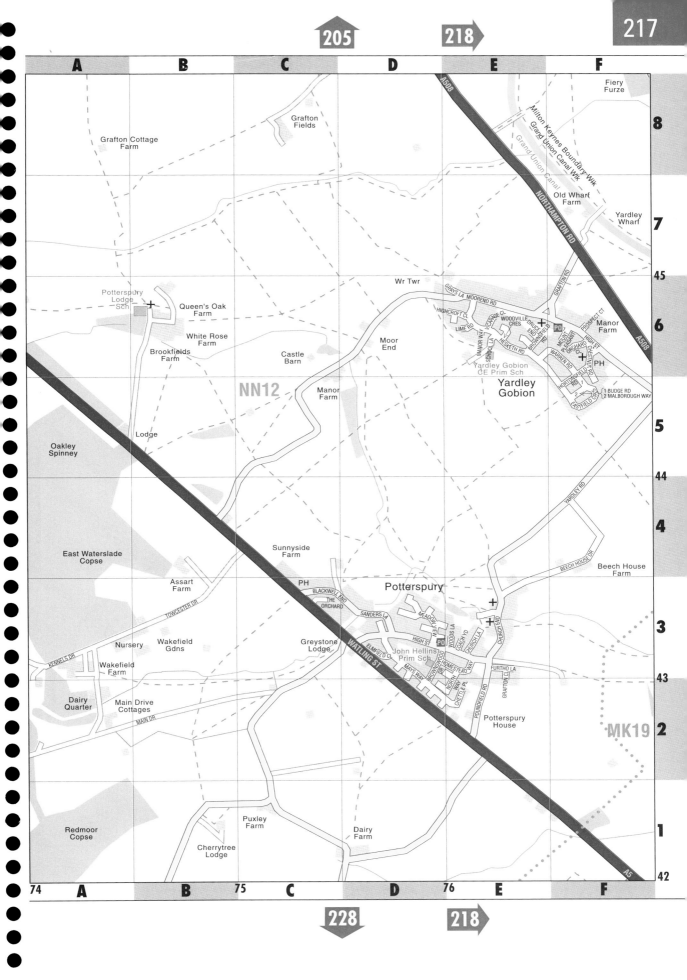

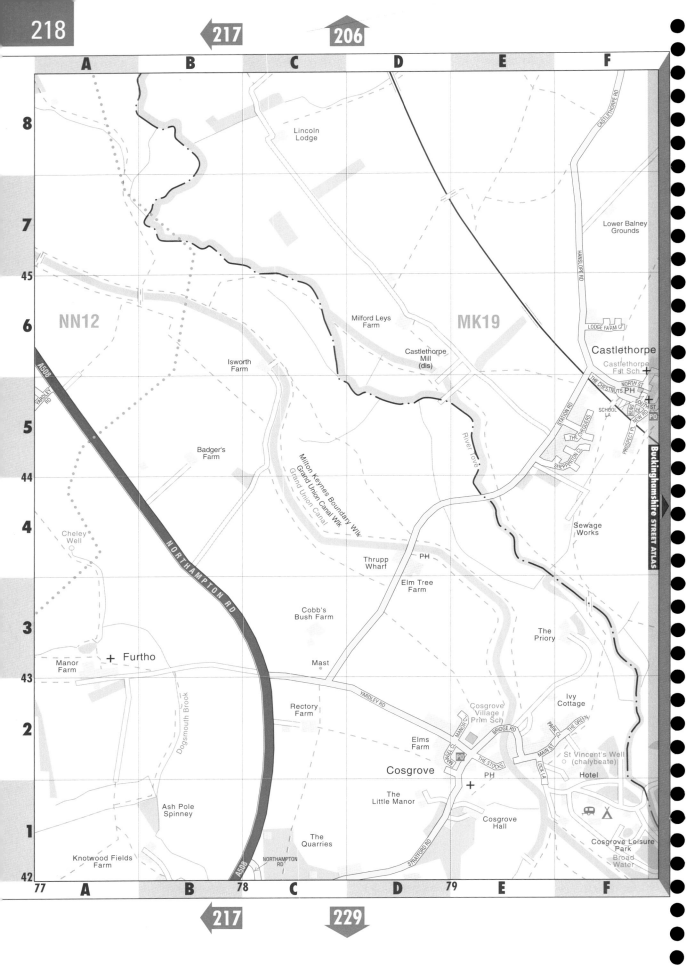

A **B** **C** **D** **E** **F**

8

Lincoln
Lodge

7

Lower Balney
Grounds

45

6 **NN12** Milford Leys **MK19**
Farm

Castlethorpe
Mill
(dis)

Castlethorpe

Isworth
Farm

Castlethorpe
Fst Sch

PH

5

THE CHEQUERS

SCHOOL LA

Badger's
Farm

44

Milton Keynes Boundary Wlk
Grand Union Canal Wlk
Grand Union Canal

River Tove

4 Cheley
Well

Sewage
Works

Thrupp
Wharf

PH

Elm Tree
Farm

3 Cobb's
Bush Farm

The
Priory

Furtho
Manor
Farm

Mast

43

Yardley Rd

Ivy
Cottage

THE GREEN

2

Rectory
Farm

Cosgrove
Village
Prim Sch

BRIDGE RD

Elms
Farm

MAIN ST

St Vincent's Well
(chalybeate)

Cosgrove **Cosgrove** PH

Hotel

The
Little Manor

1

Ash Pole
Spinney

Cosgrove
Hall

Cosgrove Leisure
Park

Broad
Water

42 Knotwood Fields
Farm

The
Quarries

NORTHAMPTON
RD

STRATFORD RD

A508

NORTHAMPTON RD

YARDLEY RD

A508

Dogsmouth Brook

77 **A** **B** **78** **C** **D** **79** **E** **F**

Buckinghamshire STREET ATLAS

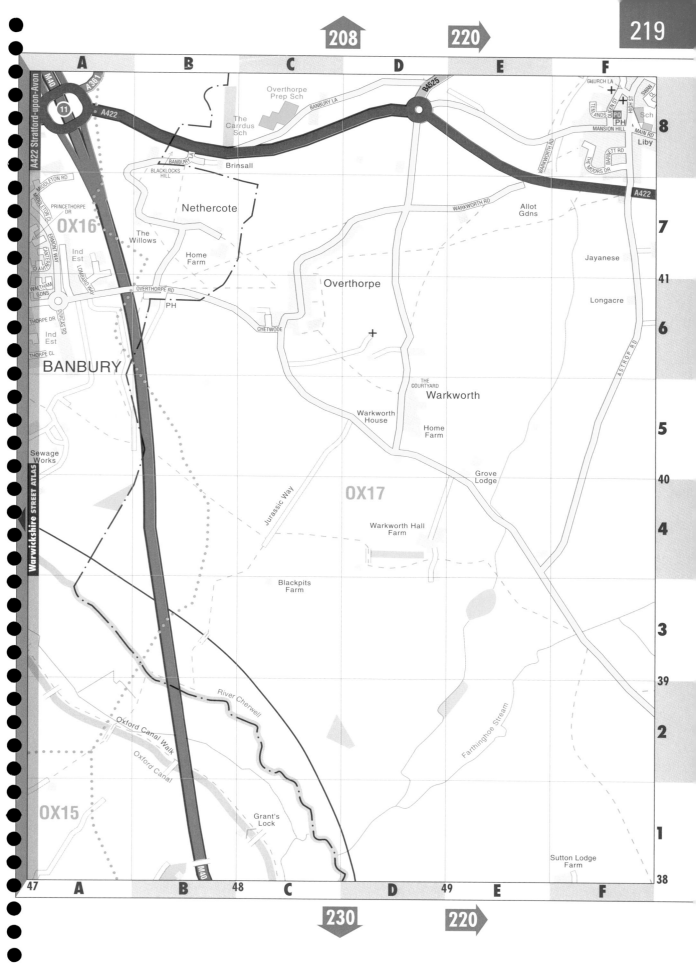

208
220

A B C D E F

M40
A422 Stratford-upon-Avon
A361
11
A422
MIDDLETON RD
PRINCETHORPE DR
MIDDLETON CL
OX16
Ind Est
EAMONT WAY
CANTERBURY WAY
WALTHAM GDNS
LOMBARD WAY
THORPE DR
DORCAS RD
Ind Est
THORPE CL
BANBURY
Sewage Works

Overthorpe Prep Sch
BANBURY LA
The Carrdus Sch
Brinsall
BLACKLOCKS HILL
BANBURY LA
Nethercote
The Willows
Home Farm
OVERTHORPE RD
PH
CHETWODE

B4525
Overthorpe
+
WARWORTH RD

CHURCH LA
QUEEN ST
TEN ANDS
PO PH
Sch
SWAN
HIGH ST
MAIN RD
MANSION HILL
Liby
THE MOORS DR
BARK TT RD
A422

Allot Gdns
Jayanese
Longacre
ASTROP RD

THE COURTYARD
Warkworth
Warkworth House
Home Farm
Grove Lodge

Jurassic Way
OX17
Warkworth Hall Farm
Blackpits Farm

River Cherwell
Oxford Canal Walk
Oxford Canal
Farthinghoe Stream

OX15
Grant's Lock
M40

Sutton Lodge Farm

8
7
41
6
5
40
4
3
39
2
1
38

47 A B 48 C D 49 E F

230
220

219 209

A B C D E F

8

Bull Baulk
Bowman Cl
Midway
Arrow Cl
Peacock's Cl
Yew Tree Cl
Dands Dr
Dands Cl
The Avenue
Horton Cres
Main Rd La
Rose Hall La
Poplars Cl
Braggington Dr
Akyn Oak Cl
Slade Leas La
Lexton Gdns
Waters La
Ash Tree Ct
Thenford Rd
Longburges
Longhoyalong Cl
Salmons La
Manor Cl
Hailsham Ct
Ashlade Dr
Washle Dr
Kingston Cl
Horton Dr
Horton Cl
Horton Rd
Horton

Lower Middleton Cheney

Thenford House
Gardener's Cottage
Thenford
+

A422
Tulbrook Stones
Sewage Works
Burgess Farm

Thenford Lodge

7

41

OX17

Middleton Lodge Farm

Thenford Grange

6

PURSTON CROSS RDS

Avenue Bridge

Works

5

Farthinghoe Stream

Baldwin's Spinney

40

A422

4

Great Purston

NN13

Farthinghoe Park

3

Little Purston

39

Buston Farm

2

Buston Farm Cottages

Sandy La

Astrophill Farm

Coldharbour

1

Rosamond's Bower

38

50 A B 51 C D 52 E F

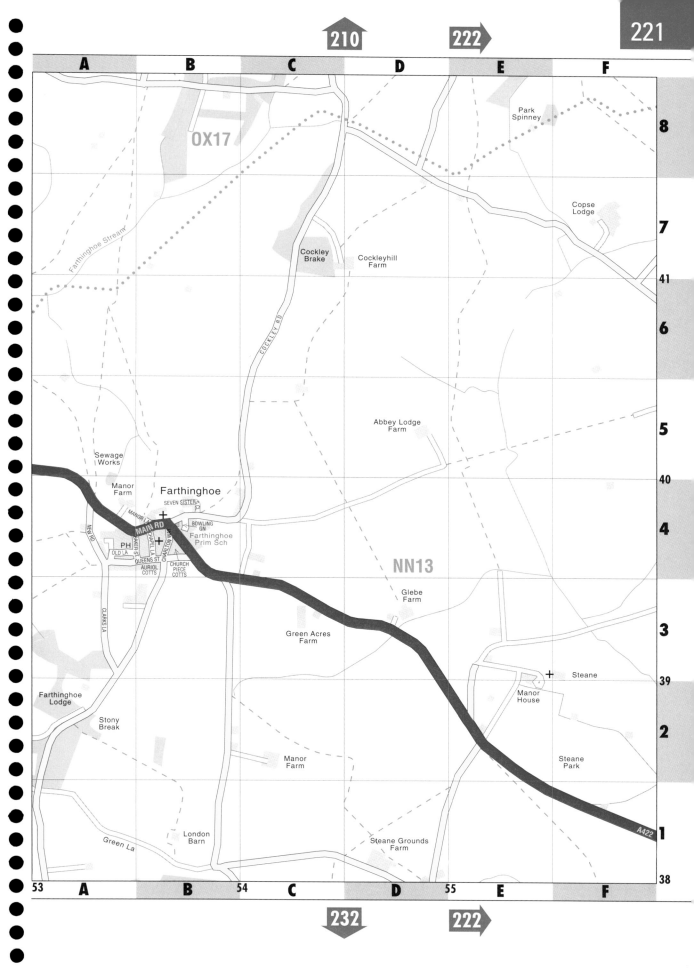

210
222
232
222

A B C D E F

8 7 41 6 5 40 4 3 39 2 1 38

Park Spinney

OX17

Copse Lodge

Cockley Brake

Cockleyhill Farm

COCKLEY RD

Farthinghoe Stream

Abbey Lodge Farm

Sewage Works

Manor Farm

Farthinghoe

SEVEN SISTERS

MANOR LA

MAIN RD

BOWLING GN

Farthinghoe Prim Sch

NN13

NEW RD

CHAPEL ST

CHAPEL LA

QUEENS ST

CHARLTON RD

PH

OLD LA

AURIOL COTTS

CHURCH PIECE COTTS

Glebe Farm

CLARKS LA

Green Acres Farm

Steane

Manor House

Farthinghoe Lodge

Stony Break

Manor Farm

Steane Park

Green La

London Barn

Steane Grounds Farm

A422

53 54 55

A B C D E F

221
211

A B C D E F

8

7

41

6

5

40

4

3

39

2

1

38

OX17

Halse
Copse

Halsecope
Farm

Halse
Grange

Wr
Twr

Halse

Lower
Farm

NN13

Radstone

Manor
Farm

Hall
Farm

The Worlidge

Hill
Farm

Fox
Covert

Ash
Spinney

Brackley
Grange

Brackley Fields
Farm

Old Glebe
Farm

BRACKLEY

Gooseholm
Copse

Brackley
Gorse

A422

A422

SWAN CL
FALCON WAY
WOODPECKER
WREN CL
HERON
GOLDCREST WAY
HUMPHRIES RD
PRICES WAY
BREWIN
CL

NIGHTINGALE
CL
KINGFISHER
DR
CHAFFINCH
WAY
ROBIN LN
KESTREL CRES
THRUSH
WAY
FORRESTER DR 1
BISHOPS CL 2
EYNARD IMPASSE 3

CEDAR CL
BLACKBIRD
CL
SWALLON CL
HOLDGATE
WODMAN CL
ASHWIN CL
DE QUINCEY CL
DE MONTFORT
CT
SPRINGFIELD
WAY

WR ASH
OAK ASH
DR
BECHTOR
DR
HALSE RD
BOLTONS
L Ctr
PAVILIONS WAY

MAPLE CL
CHESTNUT
DR
ELM CL
Cemy

RADSTONE RD

WALNUT

EDGEWOOD
JOHN CLARK
HAWTHORN DR
HOLLY CL
HAZEL CL
BRIAR CL
BRIDGEWATER RD
ELESMERE CRES
ELESMERE CL
ELESMERE
CL
ELESMERE RD
WORDSWORTH CL

Bracken Leas
Prim Sch

56 57 58

221
233

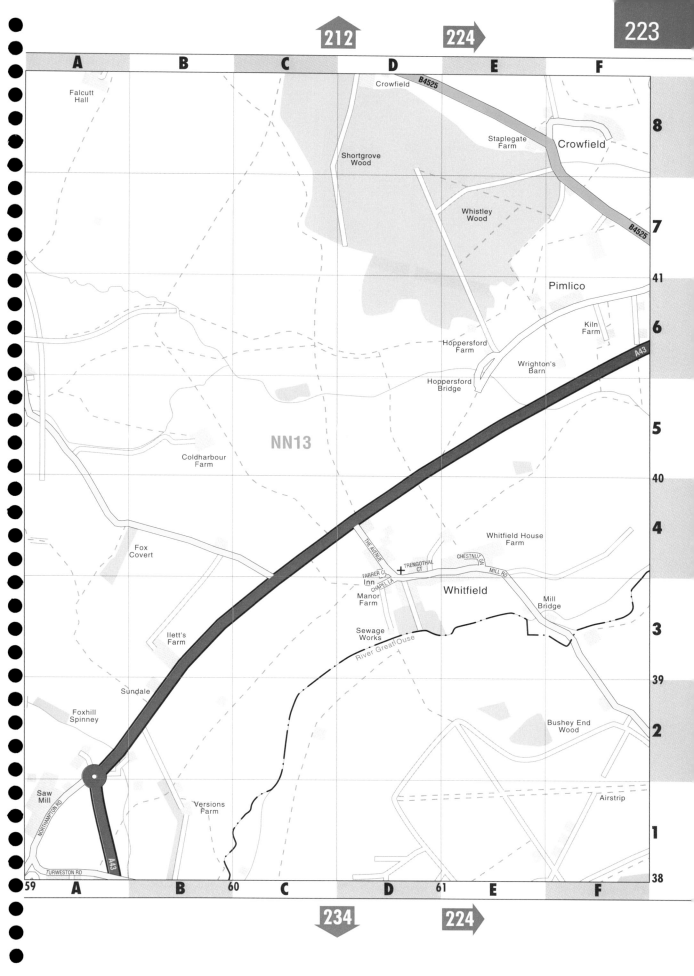

212
224
234
224

Crowfield
B4525
Staplegate Farm
Crowfield
Shortgrove Wood
Whistley Wood
Falcutt Hall

Pimlico
Kiln Farm
Hoppersford Farm
Wrighton's Barn
Hoppersford Bridge
A43

NN13
Coldharbour Farm

Whitfield House Farm
CHESTNUT DR
MILL RD
THE AVENUE
FARRER CL
TRENGOTHAL CT
Inn
CHAPEL LA
Whitfield
Manor Farm
Mill Bridge
Fox Covert

Ilett's Farm
Sewage Works
River Great Ouse
Bushey End Wood

Sundale
Foxhill Spinney
Versions Farm
Airstrip

Saw Mill
NORTHAMPTON RD
A43
TURWESTON RD

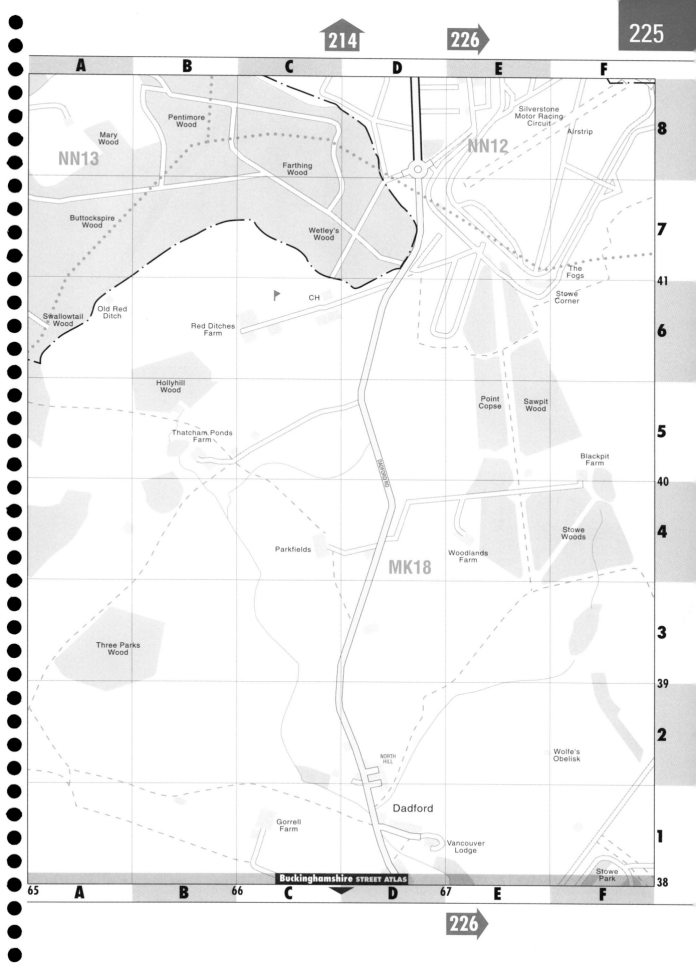

A B C D E F

8

Silverstone
Motor Racing
Circuit
Airstrip

NN12

Pentimore
Wood

Mary
Wood

NN13

Farthing
Wood

7

Buttockspire
Wood

Wetley's
Wood

The
Fogs

41

Stowe
Corner

Swallowtail
Wood

Old Red
Ditch

CH

Red Ditches
Farm

6

Hollyhill
Wood

Point
Copse

Sawpit
Wood

5

Thatcham Ponds
Farm

Blackpit
Farm

40

Stowe
Woods

4

DADFORD RD

Parkfields

MK18

Woodlands
Farm

Three Parks
Wood

3

39

2

Wolfe's
Obelisk

NORTH
HILL

Dadford

Gorrell
Farm

1

Vancouver
Lodge

Stowe
Park

38

65 A B 66 C D 67 E F

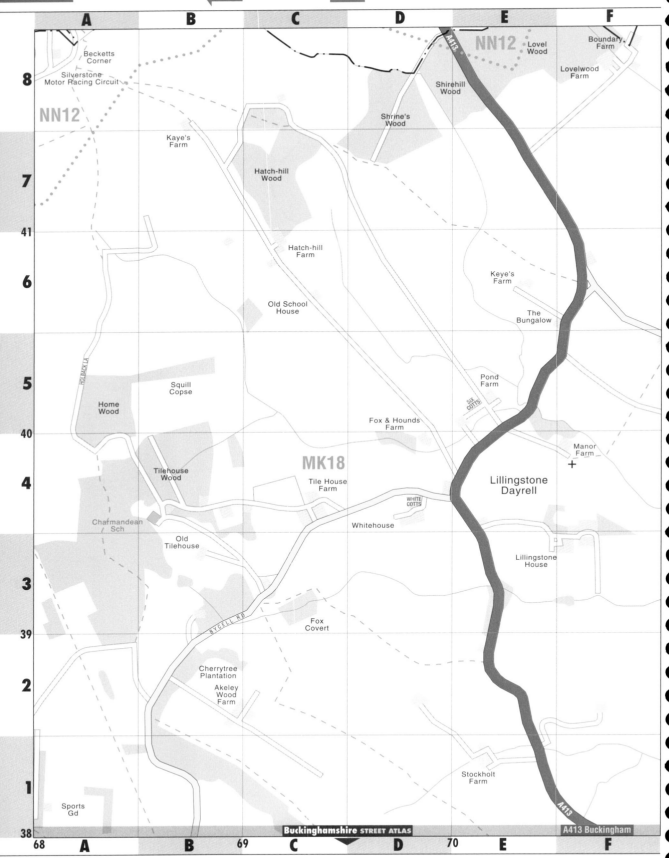

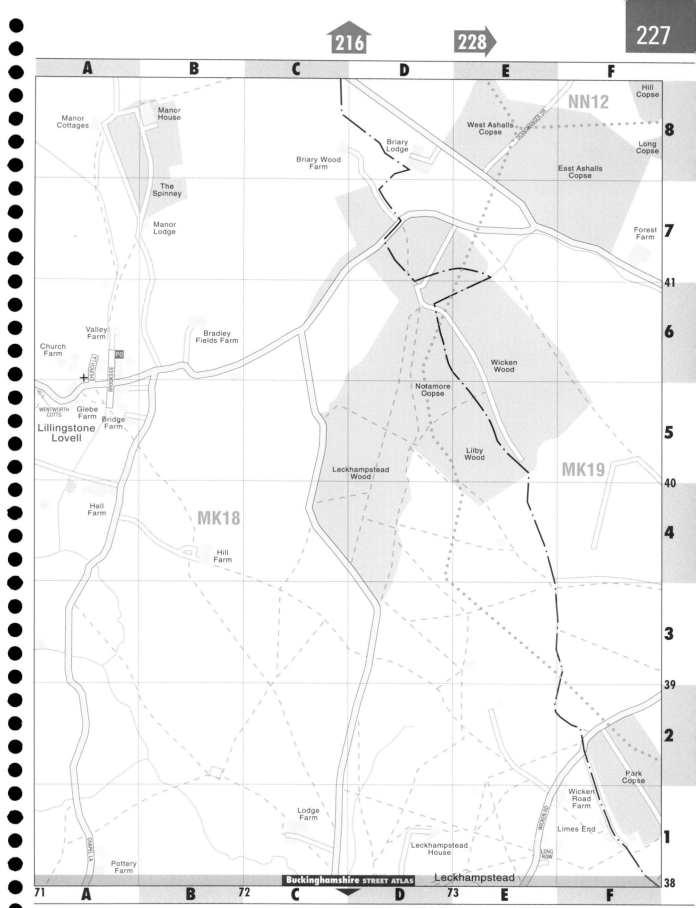

← 227
↑ 217

A B C D E F

8

7

41

6

5

40

4

3

39

2

1

38

74 A B 75 C D 76 E F

MK19

Green Farm

Grange Farm

Shrob Spinney

Puxley

NN12

Hanger Lodge

Poultry Farm

Stollage Lodge

Point's Copse

Steeple Oak

Old Copse Spinney

Hurst Farm

Hurst Cottage

Folly Fields Farm

The Folly

Wr Twr

HIGH VW

GLEBE RD

NORTH WAY

PUXLEY RD

RIDGMONT

RIDGMONT CL

THE RIDING

ELM DR

WESTFIELD AVE

COD CL

CANNIM

CRISWELL

BROOK WAY

HONEY HILL DR

KINGSHILL

PARKS CL

GOOSEMERE

SIMS RD

Northfields

PORTER'S CL

Liby

SPRINGFIELD GDNS

LITTLE LONDON

BOSWELL

WOODMANS CL

ROBERTS CL

Wks

FOLLY RD

Deanshanger

HIGH ST

BROOKWAY

CHURCH LA

PD

P

PATRON'S LA

PH

STRATFORD RD

Kingsbrook Sch

DOVEHOUSE CT

THE GREEN

THE BEECHES

Deanshanger Prim Sch (dis)

Hotel

POUND ST

ST JOHN'S LA

CHURCH LA

CHURCH

PH

CROSS TREE RD

DEANSHANGER RD

QUARRY GREEN CL

Silver Spinney Farm

Dagnall Cottages

Home Farm

Wicken

MK19

LECKHAMPSTEAD RD

WICKEN PARK RD

Sparrow Lodge

Dagnall Farm

Grand Union Canal Buckingham Arm (dis)

BUCKINGHAM RD

Hotel

A422

Pightle Farm

MK18

Akeley Wood Jun Sch

Jack's Copse

Bedlam Copse

A422

Mount Mill Cottages

New Barn

A5

← 227
↓ 235

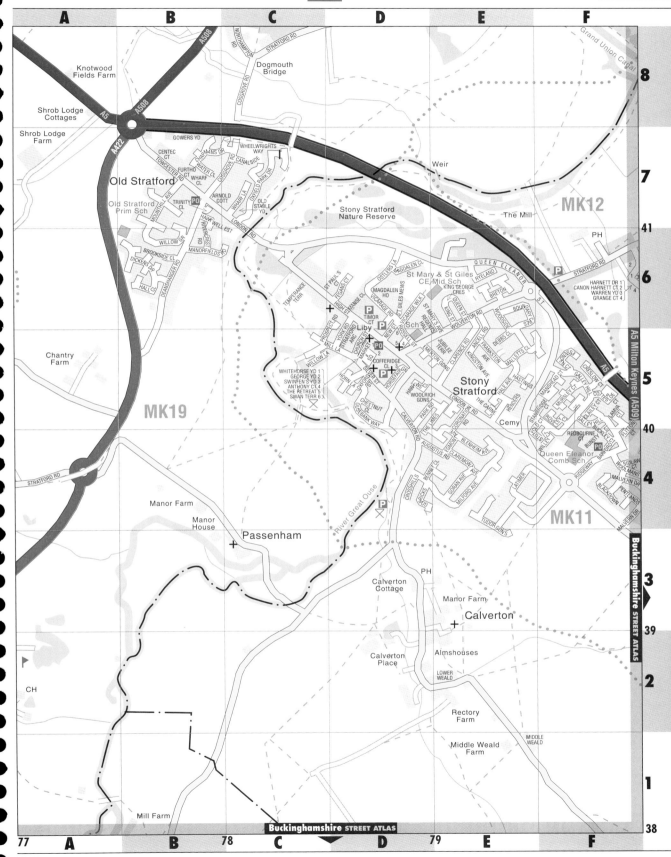

A B C D E F

8

Knotwood
Fields Farm

Dogmouth
Bridge

Grand Union Canal

Shrob Lodge
Cottages

Weir

MK12

Shrob Lodge
Farm

The Mill

7

GOWERS YD

WHEELWRIGHTS
WAY

41

Old Stratford

PH

Stony Stratford
Nature Reserve

P

Stratford Rd

Old Stratford
Prim Sch

TRINITY
CL

2

CENTEC
CT

HARNETT DR 1
CANON HARNETT CT 2
WARREN YD 3
GRANGE CT 4

6

FURTHO
CT

BROOKSIDE CL

St Mary & St Giles
CE Mid Sch

Queen Eleanor

DICKENS DR

HALL CL

MANORFIELDS

MAGDALEN
HO

KING GEORGE
CRES

TEMPERANCE
TERR

Chantry
Farm

Liby

MK19

P

Stony
Stratford

A5 Milton Keynes (A509)

5

WHITEHORSE YD 1
GEORGE YD 2
SWINFEN S YD 3
ANTHONY CT 4
THE RETREAT 5
SWAN TERR 6

WOOLRICH
GDNS

REDBOURNE
CT

40

Queen Eleanor
Comb Sch

Manor Farm

MK11

4

Manor
House

Buckinghamshire STREET ATLAS

Passenham

River Great Ouse

P

PH

Calverton
Cottage

Manor Farm

3

39

CH

Calverton

Calverton
Place

Almshouses

LOWER
WEALD

MIDDLE
WEALD

2

Rectory
Farm

Middle Weald
Farm

1

Mill Farm

38

77 A 78 B C 78 D 79 E F

219

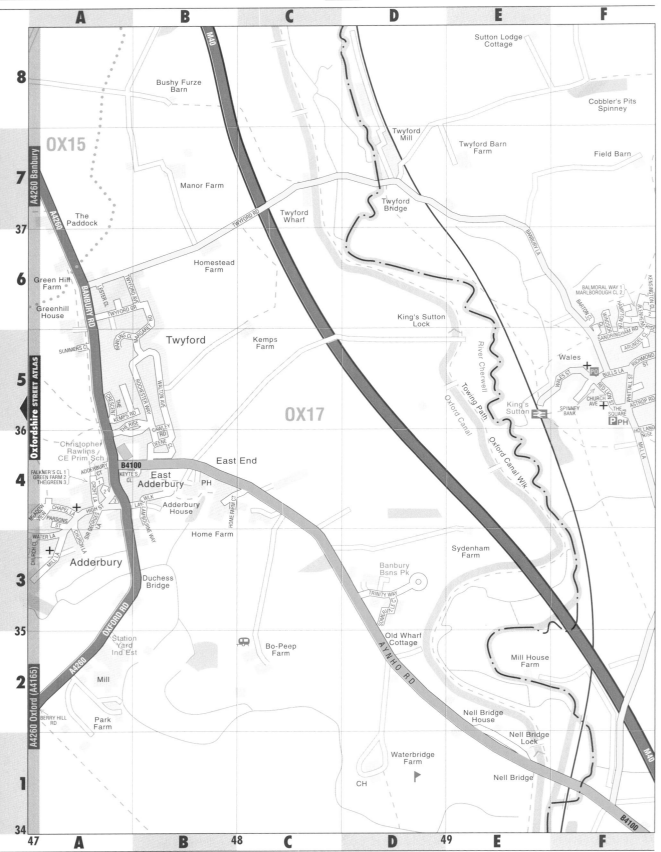

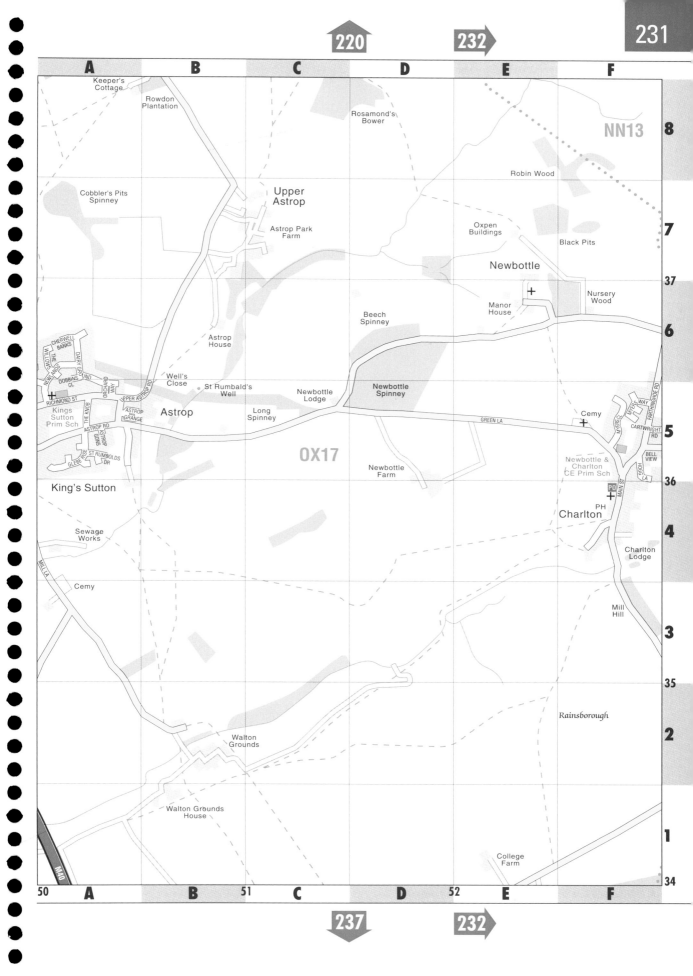

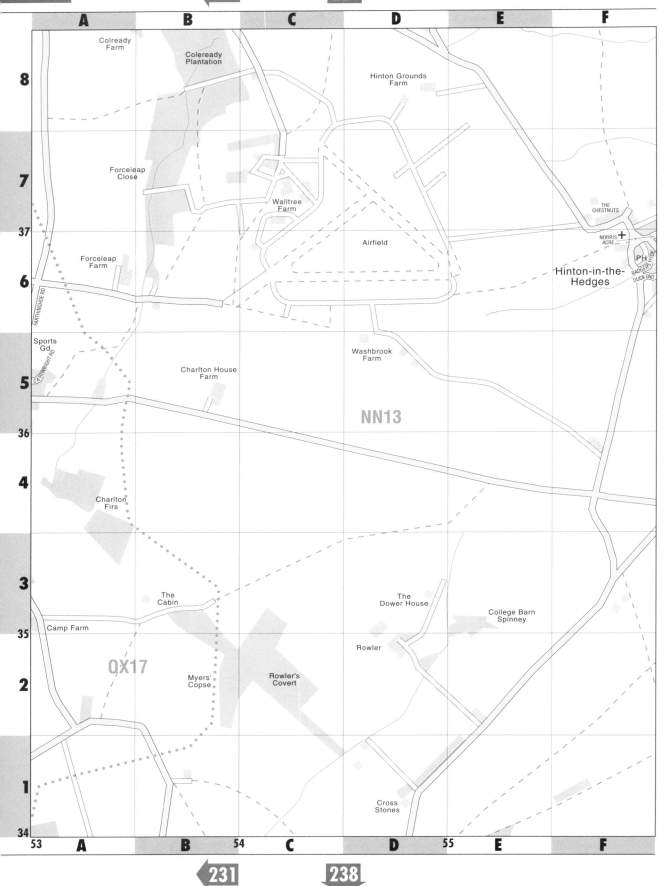
A B C D E F

8 Colready Farm

Coleready Plantation

Hinton Grounds Farm

7 Forceleap Close

Walltree Farm

THE CHESTNUTS

37 Airfield NORRIS ACRE

6 Forceleap Farm

Hinton-in-the-Hedges

FARTHINGHOE RD

Sports Gd

Washbrook Farm

5 Charlton House Farm

CARTWRIGHT RD

NN13

36

4 Charlton Firs

3 The Cabin The Dower House

College Barn Spinney

35 Camp Farm Rowler

OX17 Myers' Copse Rowler's Covert

2

1

Cross Stones

34

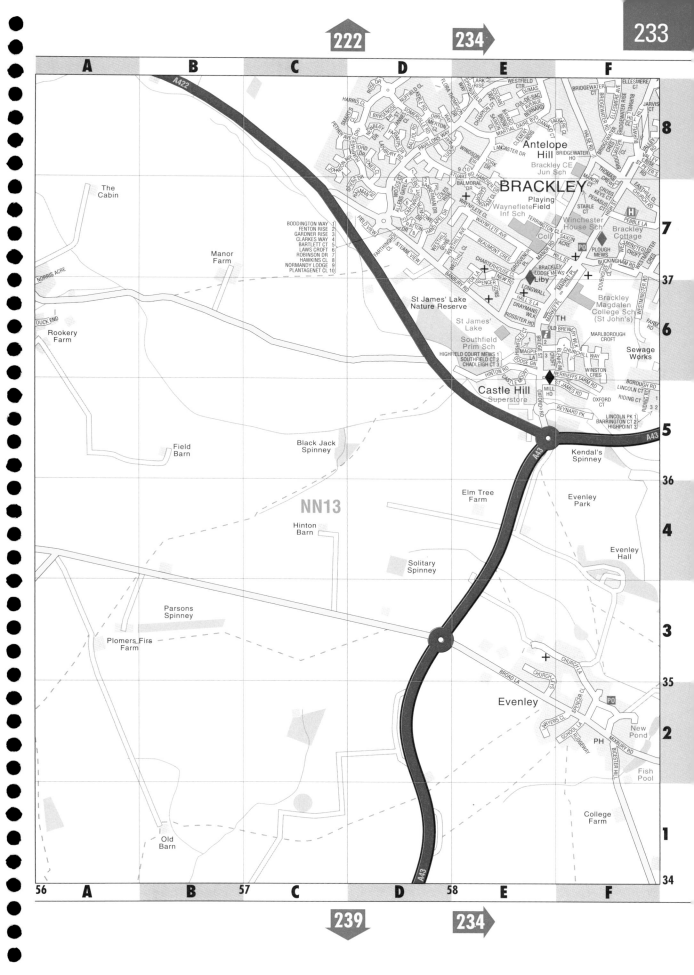

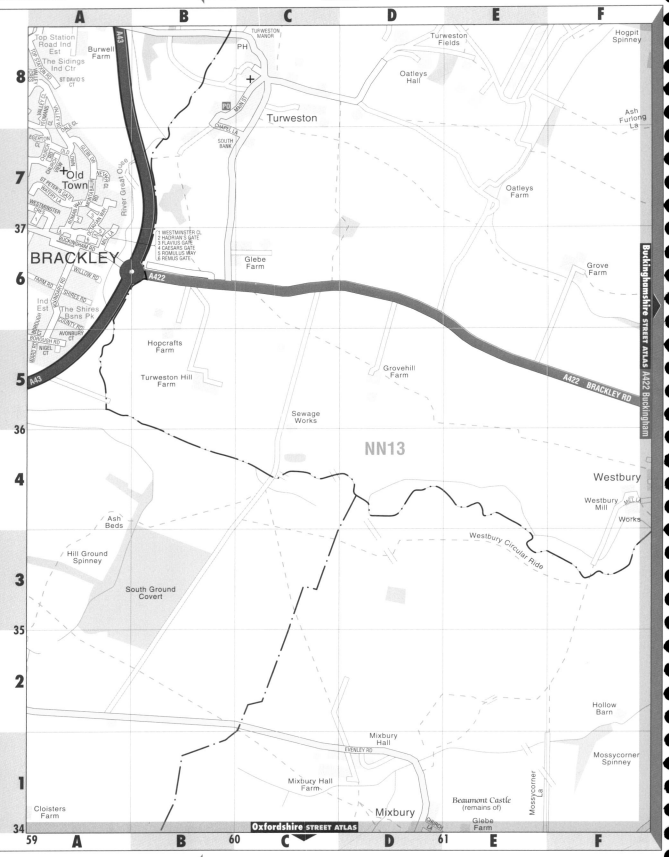

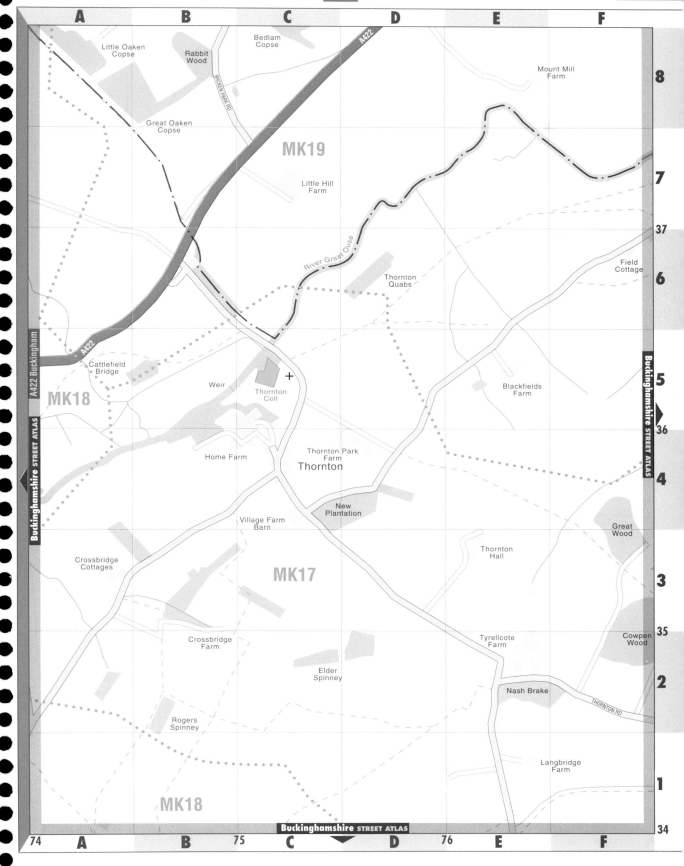

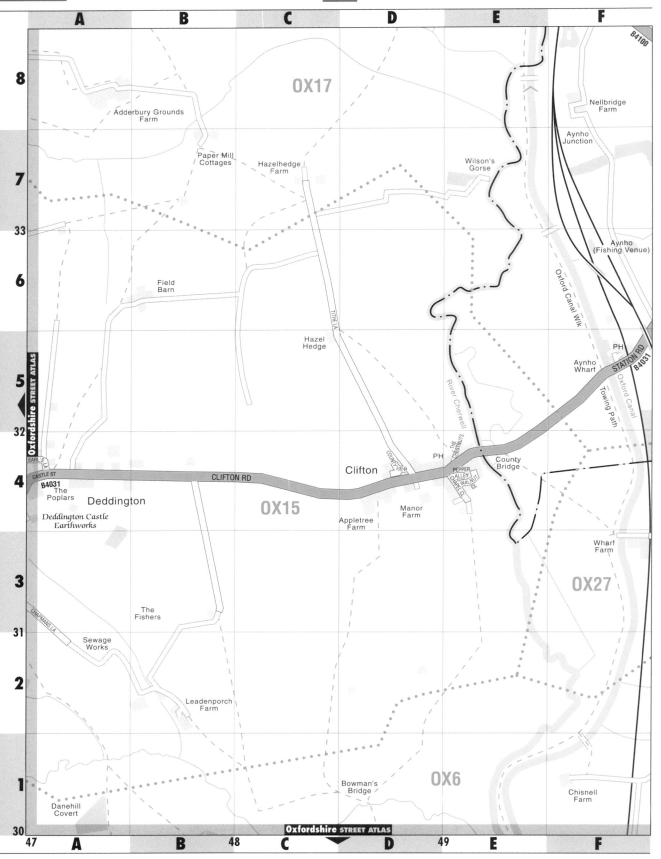

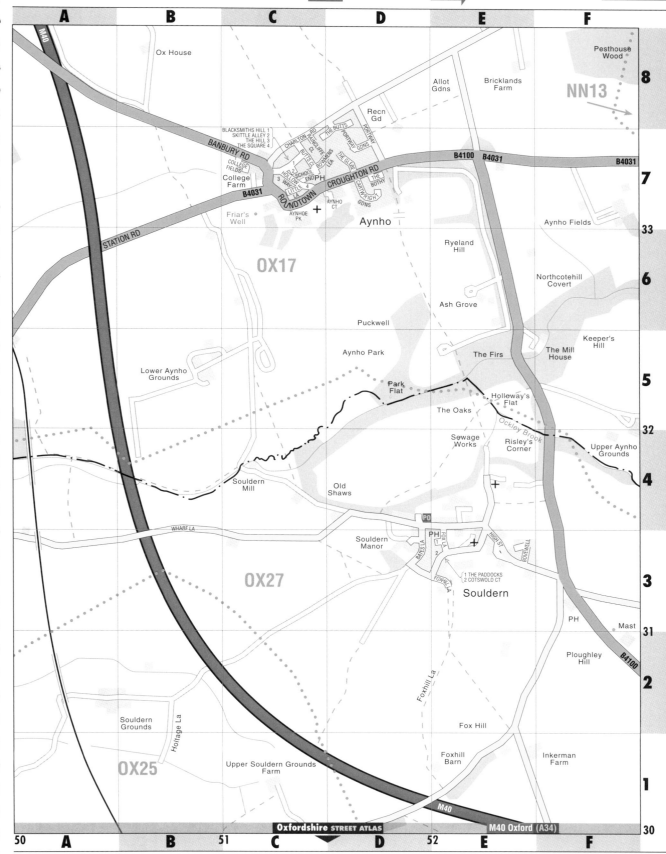

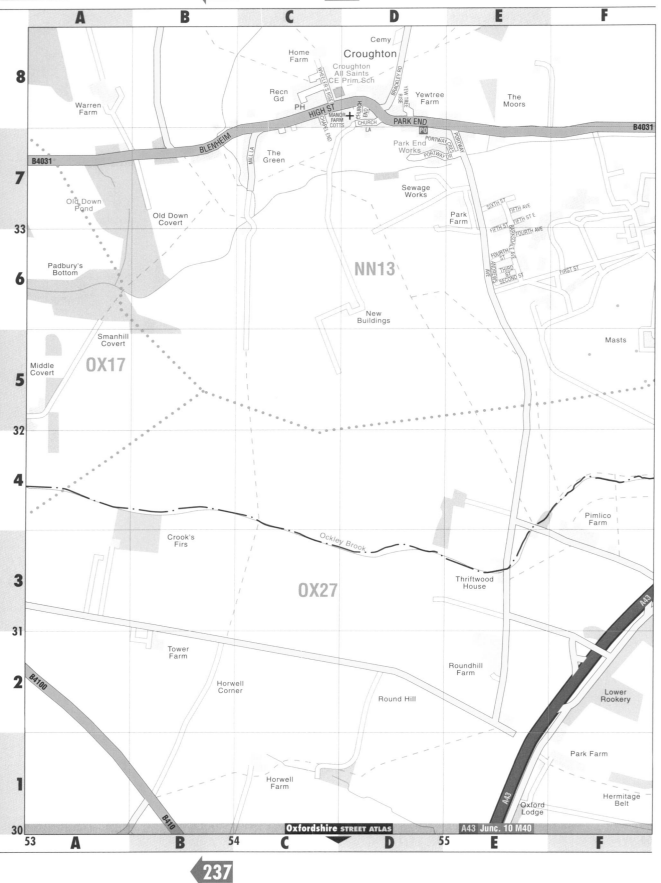

Croughton

Cemy

Home
Farm

Croughton All Saints
CE Prim Sch

Recn
Gd

PH

HIGH ST

Warren
Farm

BLENHEIM

B4031

Old Down
Pond

Old Down
Covert

The Green

MILL LA

WHEELER'S RISE

CHAPEL END

MANOR
FARM
COTTS

CHURCH END

CHURCH
LA

BRACKLEY RD

YEW TREE
RISE

Yewtree
Farm

PARK END

PO

The
Moors

B4031

Park End
Works

PORTWAY RISE

PORTWAY

PORTWAY DR

Sewage
Works

Park
Farm

SIXTH ST

FIFTH AVE

FIFTH ST

FIFTH ST E

BARNSDALE AVE

FOURTH AVE

FOURTH
ST

ST ANDREW'S
AVE

THIRD
ST

SECOND ST

FIRST ST

NN13

33

Padbury's
Bottom

Smanhill
Covert

OX17

Middle
Covert

New
Buildings

Masts

5

32

4

Crook's
Firs

Ockley Brook

OX27

Pimlico
Farm

Thriftwood
House

A43

3

31

Tower
Farm

Horwell
Corner

Round Hill

Roundhill
Farm

Lower
Rookery

2

B4100

B410

Horwell
Farm

Park Farm

Hermitage
Belt

A43

Oxford
Lodge

1

30

Oxfordshire STREET ATLAS

A43 Junc. 10 M40

53   A   B   54   C   D   55   E   F

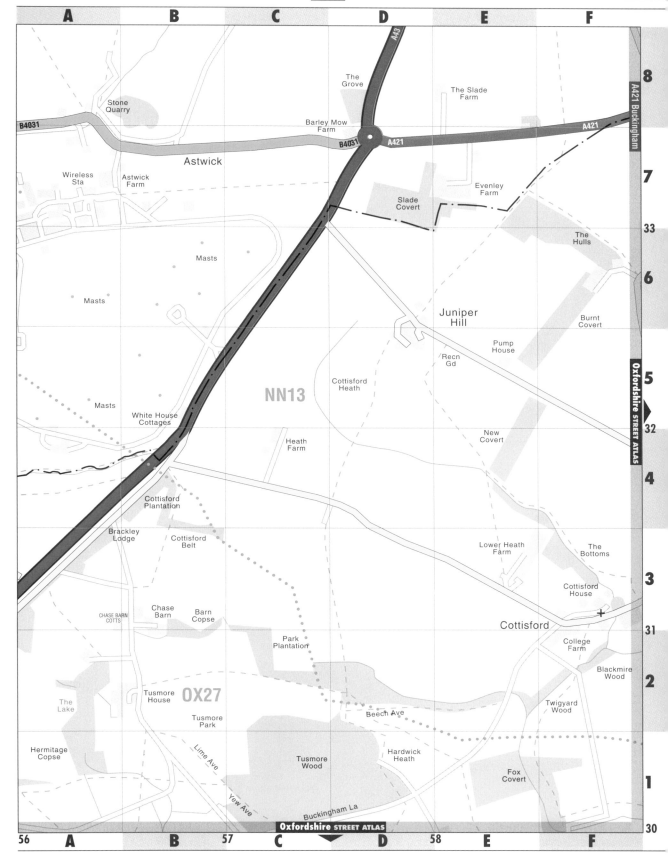

A B C D E F

8
7
33
6
5
32
4
3
31
2
1
30

Stone Quarry
B4031
Astwick
Wireless Sta
Astwick Farm
Masts
Masts
Masts
Masts
White House Cottages
Cottisford Plantation
Brackley Lodge
Cottisford Belt
CHASE BARN COTTS
Chase Barn
Barn Copse
Tusmore House
OX27
Tusmore Park
The Lake
Hermitage Copse
Lime Ave
Yew Ave
Buckingham La
Tusmore Wood
Park Plantation

The Grove
A43
Barley Mow Farm
B4031
A421
The Slade Farm
Evenley Farm
Slade Covert
A421
A421 Buckingham
The Hulls
Juniper Hill
Burnt Covert
Pump House
Recn Gd
Cottisford Heath
NN13
New Covert
Heath Farm
Lower Heath Farm
The Bottoms
Cottisford House
Cottisford
College Farm
Blackmire Wood
Twigyard Wood
Beech Ave
Hardwick Heath
Fox Covert

Oxfordshire STREET ATLAS

56 A B 57 C D 58 E F

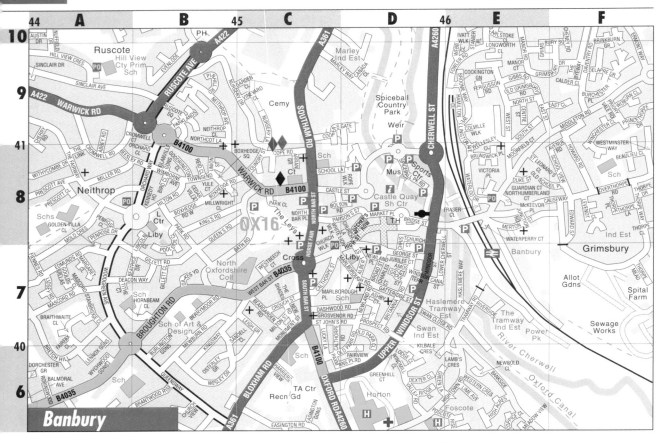

Banbury

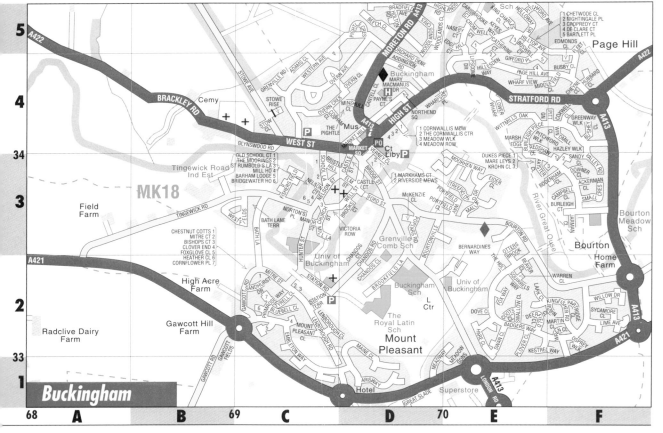

Buckingham

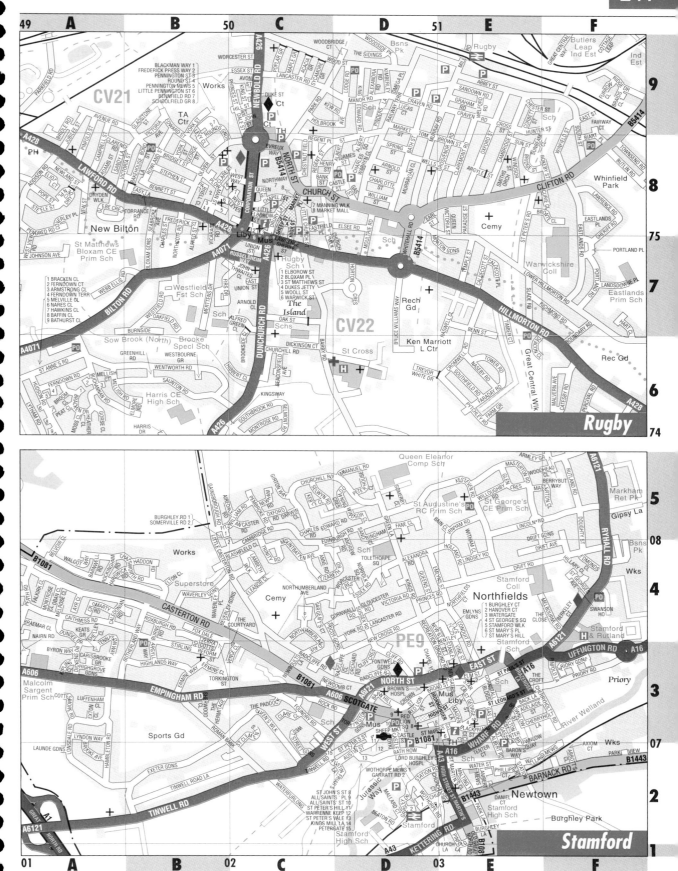

241

Rugby

Stamford

Index

Church Rd 6 Beckenham BR2..........**53** C6

Place name	Location number	Locality, town or village	Postcode district	Page and grid square
May be abbreviated on the map	Present when a number indicates the place's position in a crowded area of mapping	Shown when more than one place has the same name	District for the indexed place	Page number and grid reference for the standard mapping

Public and commercial buildings are highlighted in magenta   **Places of interest** are highlighted in blue with a star ★

Abbreviations used in the index

Acad	**Academy**	Comm	**Common**	Gd	**Ground**	L	**Leisure**
App	**Approach**	Cott	**Cottage**	Gdn	**Garden**	La	**Lane**
Arc	**Arcade**	Cres	**Crescent**	Gn	**Green**	Liby	**Library**
Ave	**Avenue**	Cswy	**Causeway**	Gr	**Grove**	Mdw	**Meadow**
Bglw	**Bungalow**	Ct	**Court**	H	**Hall**	Meml	**Memorial**
Bldg	**Building**	Ctr	**Centre**	Ho	**House**	Mkt	**Market**
Bsns, Bus	**Business**	Ctry	**Country**	Hospl	**Hospital**	Mus	**Museum**
Bvd	**Boulevard**	Cty	**County**	HQ	**Headquarters**	Orch	**Orchard**
Cath	**Cathedral**	Dr	**Drive**	Hts	**Heights**	Pal	**Palace**
Cir	**Circus**	Dro	**Drove**	Ind	**Industrial**	Par	**Parade**
Cl	**Close**	Ed	**Education**	Inst	**Institute**	Pas	**Passage**
Cnr	**Corner**	Emb	**Embankment**	Int	**International**	Pk	**Park**
Coll	**College**	Est	**Estate**	Intc	**Interchange**	Pl	**Place**
Com	**Community**	Ex	**Exhibition**	Junc	**Junction**	Prec	**Precinct**

Prom	**Prom**
Rd	**Road**
Recn	**Recreation**
Ret	**Retail**
Sh	**Shopping**
Sq	**Square**
St	**Street**
Sta	**Station**
Terr	**Terrace**
TH	**Town Hall**
Univ	**University**
Wk, Wlk	**Walk**
Wr	**Water**
Yd	**Yard**

Index of localities, towns and villages

Abthorpe 201 F1
Adderbury 230 A3
Alderton 205 A2
Aldwincle 76 F8
Apethorpe 14 C3
Arthingworth 68 C8
Ashby St Ledgers 119 D5
Ashley 18 E2
Ashton 205 E8
Astcote 188 F7
Aston le Walls 182 F2
Aynho 237 D7
Badby 153 A2
Banbury 219 A6
Barby 99 D1
Barnwell 59 B6
Barrowden 3 F5
Biddlesden 224 D5
Blakesley 187 B1
Blisworth 190 E7
Boughton 141 D8
Bozeat 164 D3
Brackley 233 E7
Bradden 201 F6
Brafield-on-the-Green 161 E2
Brampton Ash 33 E3
Braunston 118 B2
Braybrooke 49 F5
Brigstock 55 E7
Bringhurst 20 C5
Brixworth 106 A2
Brockhall 137 D2
Broughton 90 B4
Bugbrooke 173 A7
Bulwick 12 C1
Burton Latimer 92 A1
Byfield 183 D7
Bythorn 97 D4
Caldecott 21 C8
Canons Ashby 185 D2
Castlethorpe 218 F6
Chacombe 208 F4
Chapel Brampton 124 E2
Charlton 231 F4
Charwelton 168 B5
Chelveston 133 C8
Chipping Warden ...196 F6
Church Brampton ...140 C8
Church Stowe 171 D8
Claydon 181 D1
Clifton 236 D4
Clifton upon Dunsmore .80 A6
Clipston 66 F8
Clopton 78 E5
Cogenhoe 162 A6
Cold Ashby 84 B5
Cold Higham 188 C8
Collyweston 1 D1
Corby 36 E4
Cosgrove 218 D2
Cottesbrooke 104 F8
Cottingham 20 D1
Cottisford 239 E3
Covington 116 D2

Cranford 93 A7
Creaton 104 E4
Crick 101 A5
Cropredy 196 A2
Croughton 238 D8
Culworth 198 C3
Dadford 225 D1
Daventry 135 D3
Deanshanger 228 B2
Deddington 236 A4
Deene 23 F6
Deenethorpe 24 B4
Denford 95 C5
Denton 178 A8
Desborough 51 C2
Dingley 33 A4
Dodford 154 F6
Draughton 87 A6
Drayton 20 A5
Duddington 5 B6
Earls Barton 144 F3
East Carlton 35 A7
Eastcote 189 A8
East Farndon 48 B7
East Haddon 122 D5
Easton on the Hill ...2 A4
Ecton 143 F4
Elton 28 E8
Emberton 195 F1
Evenley 233 E2
Everdon 170 B8
Eydon 184 C1
Farthinghoe 221 B4
Farthingstone 170 F2
Finedon 111 E4
Flore 155 F4
Fotheringhay 27 D7
Foxton 30 E8
Gayton 173 F2
Geddington 54 B3
Glapthorn 26 C2
Grafton Regis 205 D2
Great Addington 94 B2
Great Bowden 32 A6
Great Brington 138 D7
Great Doddington ..145 D5
Great Easton 20 E7
Great Gidding 61 E3
Great Harrowden ...110 D2
Great Houghton 160 F2
Great Oxendon 48 E3
Greatworth 210 E2
Greens Norton 202 D8
Grendon 163 E5
Gretton 10 C1
Grimscote 188 B8
Guilsborough 103 E6
Gumley 30 A8
Hackleton 177 C3
Hanging Houghton ..106 C8
Hannington 108 D3
Hanslope 207 B2
Hargrave 115 F2
Harpole 157 D6

Harrington 69 B4
Harringworth 10 F7
Hartwell 192 D1
Hellidon 151 D1
Helmdon 211 F4
Higham Ferrers 132 D6
Hinton 184 A6
Hinton-in-the-Hedges .232 F6
Holcot 126 E8
Holdenby 123 D3
Hollowell 104 B5
Horton 177 D1
Husbands Bosworth ..45 D5
Irchester 147 B7
Irthlingborough ...112 D2
Isham 110 E8
Islip 76 B3
Kelmarsh 67 F3
Kettering 72 E3
Ketton 1 A6
Keyston 97 A4
Kilsby 100 A3
King's Cliffe 13 E8
King's Sutton 231 D1
Kislingbury 157 E4
Knotting Green 149 F1
Lamport 87 D2
Lavendon 180 F1
Leckhampstead 227 E1
Lilbourne 81 A6
Lillingstone Dayrell ..226 E4
Lillingstone Lovell ..227 A5
Litchborough 171 D1
Little Addington ...113 B7
Little Brington ...138 C4
Little Harrowden ..110 B4
Little Houghton ...161 A3
Little Irchester ...130 C1
Loddington 70 C2
Long Buckby 121 B4
Long Buckby Wharf .136 E7
Lower Benefield 40 C6
Lower Boddington ..182 D5
Lower Harlestone ..139 F5
Lowick 75 F6
Lubenham 30 E3
Lutton 44 C4
Lyddington 9 C7
Maidford 186 D6
Maidwell 87 B7
Market Harborough ..31 C2
Marston St Lawrence ..210 A1
Marston Trussell ...47 C8
Mawsley Village 89 B4
Mears Ashby 128 C2
Medbourne 18 F6
Middleton 35 B8
Middleton Cheney ..209 A1
Milton Malsor 174 E4
Mixbury 234 D1
Morcott 3 A5
Moreton Pinkney ...199 D2
Moulton 126 C2
Napton on the Hill .150 A7

Naseby 66 B1
Nassington 15 E5
Nether Heyford 156 B1
New Hackleton 177 A3
Newnham 153 E4
Newton Bromswold .149 D8
Northampton 159 D4
North Kilworth 45 A3
Norton 136 C4
Old 107 D7
Old Stratford 229 E7
Olney 195 E4
Orlingbury 110 A5
Orton 70 A3
Oundle 42 A6
Overstone 127 B1
Pattishall 172 E1
Paulerspury 216 C8
Piddington 177 B2
Pitsford 125 D5
Podington 147 E2
Polebrook 43 A3
Potterspury 217 D3
Preston Capes 169 D2
Priors Hardwick ...166 A5
Priors Marston 166 E8
Pury End 215 F8
Pytchley 90 F2
Quinton 176 B1
Raunds 114 C6
Ravensthorpe 103 E1
Ravenstone 194 D2
Ringstead 95 B3
Roade 191 E4
Rockingham 21 B4
Rothersthorpe 174 A7
Rothwell 70 D8
Rugby 99 A7
Rushden 132 E2
Rushton 52 C2
Scaldwell 106 F6
Shutlanger 204 D8
Sibbertoft 46 F2
Silverstone 214 D4
Slapton 201 D2
Slipton 75 A3
Souldern 237 E3
Souldrop 149 B1
South Kilworth 63 D8
South Luffenham 3 D8
Southwick 26 B5
Spratton 105 C1
Stanion 37 F2
Stanwick 113 E4
Staverton 152 C7
Stibbington 8 D2
Stoke Albany 34 A4
Stoke Bruerne 205 B8
Stoke Doyle 41 C1
Stony Stratford ...229 E5
Sulgrave 210 F8
Sutton 8 F2
Sutton Bassett 18 A1
Swinford 62 C3

Syresham 224 B8
Sywell 127 D3
Tansor 27 D2
Theddingworth 46 C8
Thornby 84 E4
Thornhaugh 7 F5
Thornton 235 C4
Thorpe by Water 10 A6
Thorpe Langton 17 A5
Thorpe Malsor 71 B3
Thorpe Mandeville .210 B7
Thorpe Waterville ..77 C8
Thrapston 76 E1
Thurning 60 D2
Tiffield 189 D4
Titchmarsh 77 D4
Towcester 203 B3
Turweston 234 C8
Twyford 230 B5
Twywell 75 A1
Upper Benefield 39 F7
Upper Boddington ..182 D4
Upper Harlestone ..139 D4
Upper Heyford 156 D1
Upper Stowe 171 E6
Wadenhoe 58 A4
Wakerley 4 A3
Walgrave 108 B5
Wansford 8 B4
Wappenham 213 A8
Wardington 196 D2
Warmington 28 C3
Watford 120 C6
Weedon 155 A3
Weedon Lois 200 C2
Weldon 38 C8
Welford 64 E5
Welham 17 E5
Wellingborough ...130 D6
Welton 119 C3
Westbury 234 F4
West Haddon 102 C4
Weston 200 A2
Weston by Welland ..18 A3
Weston Underwood .195 A2
Whilton 137 D6
Whitfield 223 E3
Whittlebury 215 C4
Wicken 228 B3
Wilbarston 34 D5
Wilby 129 A1
Willoughby 117 C3
Wittering 7 D8
Wollaston 146 F2
Woodend 200 F7
Woodford 94 D6
Woodford Halse ...184 C6
Woodnewton 14 F2
Wothorpe 2 D8
Wymington 148 B5
Yardley Gobion 217 E5
Yardley Hastings ..179 B6
Yarwell 16 A8
Yelvertoft 82 C4

1

1st Drift PE9 ....2 D8

2

2nd Drift PE9 ....2 D8

A

A6 Bsns Ctr NN16 ......71 E4
Abbey Cl NN29 ......164 C2
Abbey Ct NN29 ......146 D3
Abbey Ho 5 NN5 ......159 A6
Abbey Jun Sch The
 NN11 ......135 D1
Abbey Lodge NN3 ......160 C7
Abbey Rd Banbury OX16 ..240 A9
 Northampton NN4 ......159 B3
 Roade NN7 ......191 C4
 Syresham NN13 ......224 C7
 Wellingborough NN8 ......129 F3
Abbey Rise NN29 ......146 D3
Abbey St Daventry NN11 ..135 C2
 Market Harborough LE16 ..31 E3
 Northampton NN5 ......159 A6
 Rugby CV21 ......241 E9
Abbey Way
 Ravenstone MK46 ......194 E2
 Rushden NN10 ......148 A8
Abbot Cl NN11 ......153 D8
Abbots Way
 Northampton NN5 ......158 F6
 Roade NN7 ......191 C4
 Rushden NN10 ......131 F1
 Wellingborough NN8 ......129 F4
Abbott's Cl PE9 ......241 E2
Abbotts Cl Kettering NN15 ..91 B7
 Titchmarsh NN14 ......77 D3
Aberdare Rd NN5 ......159 A8
Aberdeen Terr NN5 ......159 A6
Abingdon Ave NN3 ......160 C7
Abington Bsns Ctr NN1 ..160 A7
Abington Cotts NN1 ......160 A7
Abington Ct NN3 ......160 B8
Abington Gr NN1 ......159 F8
Abington Mus* NN1 ......160 A7
Abington Park Cres
 NN3 ......160 C7
Abington Rd NN17 ......36 B7
Abington Sq NN1 ......159 E6
Abington St NN1 ......159 D6
Abington Vale Lower Sch
 NN3 ......160 C6
Abington Vale Mid Sch
 NN3 ......160 C6
Abthorpe Ave NN2 ......141 D5
Acacia Gr CV21 ......241 C9
Ace La NN7 ......172 F7
Ackerman Cl MK18 ......240 F3
Acorn Cl Islip NN14 ......76 B3
 Kettering NN15 ......92 B5
 Lubenham LE16 ......30 E3
Acorn Ind Est NN14 ......76 B3
Acorn Pk NN15 ......92 D4
Acorn Way NN12 ......214 E4
Acre Cl NN11 ......135 C6
Acre Ct NN16 ......72 D3
Acre La NN2 ......141 A6
Acre St NN16 ......72 D3
Acremead PE8 ......28 B3
Adam & Eve St 8 LE16 ..31 E3
Adam Bsns Ctr NN16 ......71 F5
Adams Ave NN1 ......159 F7
Adams Cl
 Buckingham MK18 ......240 C4
 Stanwick NN9 ......114 A5
 Wellingborough NN8 ......130 B5
Adams Dr NN14 ......70 B7
Adams Rd NN11 ......184 B6
Adams St CV21 ......241 A8
Adamswood Cl LE16 ......31 C3
Adderbury Ct OX17 ......230 A4
Addington Rd
 Buckingham MK18 ......240 D4
 Irthlingborough NN9 ......113 A5
 Woodford NN14 ......94 D6
Addison Rd
 Desborough NN14 ......50 F3
 Northampton NN3 ......142 B2
 Rugby CV21 ......241 A8
Addlecroft Cl NN2 ......141 B3
Adelaide Ho Corby NN17 ..22 F1
 5 Northampton NN2 ......159 C7
Adelaide Pl 7 NN1 ......159 C5
Adelaide St
 Northampton NN2 ......159 C7
 Stamford PE9 ......241 E3
Adelaide Terr 1 NN2 ..159 C7
Adit View NN9 ......131 D8
Admiral Cl LE16 ......31 D3
Admirals Way NN11 ......135 E2
Adnitt Rd
 Northampton NN1 ......159 F7
 Rushden NN10 ......132 A2
Afan Cl NN16 ......72 A5
Affleck Bridge NN9 ......111 F4
Aggate Way NN6 ......144 D4
Agnes Rd NN2 ......159 C8
Agricultural Houses
 CV47 ......166 A5
Ainsdale Cl NN2 ......141 F3
Aintree Dr NN10 ......148 D8
Aintree Rd NN3 ......141 F4
Airedale Rd PE9 ......241 C5

Akeley Wood Jun Sch
 MK19 ......228 A1
Akister Cl MK18 ......240 E3
Alanbrooke Cl NN15 ......72 E1
Alastor NN8 ......129 B5
Albany Ct LE16 ......31 F4
Albany Gdns NN18 ......36 B2
Albany Rd
 Market Harborough LE16 ..31 F4
 Northampton NN1 ......160 A7
Albany The 6 NN11 ......135 C2
Albert Pl NN1 ......159 D6
Albert Rd Finedon NN9 ..111 F5
 Market Harborough LE16 ..31 F3
 Rushden NN10 ......132 B3
 Stamford PE9 ......241 E3
 Wellingborough NN8 ......130 B5
Albert Sq CV21 ......241 D8
Albert St Banbury OX16 ..240 D7
 3 Kettering NN16 ......72 C2
 Rugby CV21 ......241 D8
Alberta St NN18 ......36 C3
Albion Ct
 Little Harrowden NN9 ......110 C4
 Northampton NN1 ......159 D5
Albion Pl
 Northampton NN1 ......159 D5
 Rushden NN10 ......132 B1
Albion Rd NN16 ......72 B3
Albisdene Ct NN10 ......132 C2
Alcombe Rd NN1 ......159 E7
Alcombe Terr NN1 ......159 E7
Aldbury Mews 12 NN1 ..159 C7
Aldene Rd MK19 ......207 B3
Alder Cl NN14 ......51 C3
Alder Ct NN3 ......142 F5
Alderley Cl NN5 ......158 B8
Aldgate Ct PE9 ......1 A5
Aldsworth Cl NN8 ......145 E8
Aldwell Cl NN4 ......175 F7
Aldwincle Rd NN14 ......76 A6
Aldwinkles Yd 4 LE16 ..31 E3
Alexander Ct Corby NN17 ..22 A2
 Irchester NN29 ......147 B8
 Northampton NN3 ......142 E3
Alexandra Rd Corby NN17 ..36 E6
 Desborough NN14 ......50 F3
 Little Addington NN9 ......113 A4
 Northampton NN1 ......159 E6
 Rugby CV21 ......241 D9
 Stamford PE9 ......241 D4
 Wellingborough NN8 ......130 B5
Alexandra St
 Burton Latimer NN15 ......92 B2
 Kettering NN16 ......72 C2
Alexandra Terr 5 NN1 ..141 C3
Alfoxden NN8 ......129 B3
Alfred Green Cl CV22 ..241 C7
Alfred St Irchester NN29 ..147 A8
 Kettering NN16 ......72 C2
 Northampton NN1 ......159 F6
 Rugby CV21 ......241 B8
 Stanwick NN9 ......113 F4
Alfred Street Jun Sch
 NN10 ......132 B2
Alibone Cl NN3 ......126 D1
Alice Dr NN16 ......92 B1
Alice Gdns NN16 ......72 D3
Alington Cl NN14 ......112 A5
All Saints CE Mid Sch
 NN2 ......141 E6
All Saints' CE Prim Sch
 NN8 ......130 B4
All Saints' Pl PE9 ......241 D3
All Saints' St PE9 ......241 D3
Allan Bank NN8 ......129 B3
Allans Cl CV23 ......80 A5
Allans Dr CV23 ......80 A5
Allard Cl NN14 ......143 D4
Allebone Rd NN6 ......144 E3
Alledge Dr NN14 ......94 D7
Allen Rd Finedon NN9 ..112 A5
 Irthlingborough NN9 ......112 E1
 Northampton NN1 ......160 A7
 Rushden NN10 ......132 C3
Allens Gate NN13 ......233 D7
Allens Hill NN29 ......164 D3
Allens Orch OX17 ......196 F6
Alliance Ct 2 NN8 ......130 A5
Alliance Terr NN8 ......129 F5
Alliston Gdns 3 NN2 ..159 C7
Alma St
 Northampton NN5 ......159 A6
 Wellingborough NN8 ......130 A5
Almond Cl Barby CV23 ..99 C1
 Bugbrooke NN7 ......173 A4
Almond Gr NN3 ......142 A7
Almond Rd NN16 ......72 D4
Almshouses
 Titchmarsh NN14 ......77 B4
 West Haddon NN6 ......102 B5
Almshouses The MK46 ..194 E2
Alness Cl NN15 ......91 E8
Alpine Rd NN10 ......131 F2
Alpine Way NN5 ......140 A3
Alsace Cl NN5 ......139 C2
Altendiez Way NN15 ......92 B4
Althorp* NN7 ......139 A7
Althorp Cl
 Market Harborough LE16 ..32 B3
 Wellingborough NN8 ......129 C7
Althorp Pl NN18 ......36 B3
Althorp Rd NN5 ......159 A6
Althorp St 16 NN1 ......159 C6
Althorpe Pl NN16 ......72 D3
Alton St NN4 ......159 B3

Alvington Way LE16 ......31 D5
Alvis Ct NN3 ......143 C4
Alvis Way NN11 ......134 F3
Amber Dr NN6 ......108 A5
Amberley Rd NN7 ......192 C1
Ambleside Cl
 9 Northampton NN3 ......142 C4
 Wellingborough NN8 ......129 C5
Ambridge Cl NN4 ......174 F8
Ambridge Ct 8 NN1 ......159 F6
Ambush St NN5 ......159 B6
Amen Cnr NN14 ......113 C8
Amen Pl NN14 ......113 C8
Amos Ct OX16 ......240 D7
Amundsen Ct NN11 ......135 B5
Ancaster Rd PE9 ......241 C5
Ancell Rd MK11 ......229 E5
Anchor Dr NN2 ......141 B6
Anderson Ave CV22 ......98 A8
Anderson Dr NN15 ......72 F1
Anderson Gn NN8 ......129 C4
Anding Cl NN10 ......132 C7
Andrew Cl NN10 ......132 C7
Andrew Macdonald Cl
 LE16 ......31 F3
Andrew Rd PE9 ......241 D4
Andrews Ave NN13 ......238 E6
Andrews Way NN9 ......114 B5
Angel Ct 2 LE16 ......31 E3
Angel La 2 NN8 ......130 A4
Angel St
 1 Market Harborough
 LE16 ......31 E3
 Northampton NN1 ......159 D5
Angel Yd 19 NN16 ......72 B2
Anglia Way NN3 ......141 F6
Anglian Rd NN11 ......135 B1
Angus Ho NN17 ......36 E6
Anjou Ct NN5 ......139 F2
Ann Sq NN16 ......72 E3
Anna's La NN12 ......173 B1
Annandale Rd NN7 ......36 E7
Anne Rd Stamford PE9 ..241 C4
 Wellingborough NN8 ......129 E2
Anne St NN16 ......72 C5
Annesley Cl NN3 ......160 D6
Anscomb Way NN11 ......184 B6
Ansell Way NN4 ......175 E8
Anson Cl Corby NN17 ......36 B7
 Daventry NN11 ......135 D1
Anthony Ct MK11 ......229 D5
Antona Cl NN9 ......114 B4
Antona Dr NN9 ......114 B4
Antona Gdns NN9 ......114 B4
Anvil The NN7 ......172 F7
Apethorpe Rd PE8 ......15 C6
Apollo Cl NN11 ......135 B3
Applebarn Cl NN4 ......175 C4
Appleby Cl NN5 ......110 F1
Appleby Wlk 2 NN3 ......142 C4
Appledore Cl NN2 ......141 C4
Applegarth Cl NN18 ......36 D3
Applegarth The NN6 ......121 C4
Appletree Ct NN9 ......111 F5
Appletree Ind Est OX17 ..196 E7
Appletree La NN11 ......182 C7
Appletree Rd OX17 ......196 F6
Approach The NN5 ......158 F6
Aquitaine Cl NN5 ......139 F1
Arbour Cl NN3 ......142 E4
Arbour View Ct NN3 ......142 E5
Arbours Lower Sch The
 NN3 ......142 D3
Arbury Banks OX17 ......196 F5
Archangel Rd 2 NN4 ......158 F2
Archangel Sq 1 NN4 ......158 F2
Archer Ave NN11 ......118 C1
Archers Cl NN2 ......141 B5
Archers Spinney CV21 ..99 B8
Archery Rd OX17 ......209 A1
Archfield NN8 ......129 F4
Archfield Terr 2 NN9 ..112 F2
Arden Cl
 3 Daventry NN11 ......135 B4
 Kettering NN15 ......91 F5
 Market Harborough LE16 ..32 A4
Arden Way LE16 ......31 F5
Ardens Gr NN7 ......174 A7
Ardington Rd NN1 ......160 A7
Argyle Pk LE16 ......48 E8
Argyle St
 Northampton NN5 ......159 A6
 Rugby CV21 ......241 E8
Argyll Ho NN17 ......36 E6
Argyll St Corby NN17 ......36 F6
 Kettering NN15 ......91 B8
Argyll Way PE9 ......241 B3
Ariel Cl NN5 ......140 A1
Aris Way MK18 ......240 D1
Arkwright Rd Corby NN17 22 C1
 Irchester NN29 ......147 C2
Arlbury Rd NN3 ......143 B4
Armley Cl NN6 ......121 C4
Armley Gr PE9 ......241 E5
Armston Rd PE8 ......59 B8
Armstrong Cl CV22 ......241 A6
Arndale NN2 ......140 F5
Arnheim Hos NN11 ......199 D7
Arnhill Rd NN17 ......10 B1
Arnills Way CV23 ......100 A2
Arnold Cl CV22 ......241 C7
Arnold Cott MK19 ......229 B7
Arnold Rd NN2 ......159 C8
Arnold St CV21 ......241 D8
Arnsby Cres NN3 ......126 B1
Arnull Cres NN11 ......135 B4

Arran Gr OX16 ......240 C8
Arran Way NN17 ......36 C8
Arrow Cl OX17 ......220 A8
Arrow Head Rd NN4 ......158 F3
Arthingworth Rd NN14 ..50 E4
Arthur St
 Northampton NN2 ......141 C1
 Wellingborough NN8 ......129 E4
Arthur's Way 1 NN16 ..72 C2
Artizan Rd NN1 ......159 F7
Arun Cl NN10 ......148 C7
Arundel Cl
 Kings Sutton OX17 ......230 F5
 Thrapston NN14 ......76 F2
Arundel Ct Kettering NN15 ..91 F8
 Rushden NN10 ......148 A8
Arundel St 9 NN1 ......159 C7
Arundel Wlk NN18 ......36 B5
Ascot Rd NN10 ......148 D8
Ash Cl Daventry NN11 ..135 C4
 Irchester NN29 ......147 A7
Ash Ct NN14 ......76 D1
Ash Dr Brackley NN13 ..222 F1
 Sywell NN6 ......143 D7
Ash Gr Bugbrooke NN7 ..172 F7
 Desborough NN14 ......50 E4
 Northampton NN2 ......141 B6
Ash La NN4 ......175 B4
Ash Rd NN15 ......72 C1
Ash Rise NN2 ......141 C6
Ash St NN1 ......159 C7
Ash Tree Ct OX17 ......220 B8
Ash Way Braunston NN11 118 B1
 Hinton NN11 ......184 A6
Ashbourne Dr NN14 ......50 E4
Ashbrook Cl NN14 ......90 A4
Ashbrow Rd NN4 ......158 F3
Ashburnham Rd NN1 ..159 F8
Ashby Cl NN8 ......129 E7
Ashby Ct Banbury OX16 ..240 D7
 Guilsborough NN6 ......103 E7
 Kislingbury NN7 ......157 D3
 Moulton NN3 ......126 C1
Ashby Dr Crick NN6 ......100 F5
 Rushden NN10 ......148 A8
Ashby Fields Prim Sch
 NN11 ......135 C5
Ashby Gdns 4 NN3 ......126 C1
Ashby Pk NN11 ......135 C4
Ashby Rd
 Braunston NN11 ......118 C1
 Daventry NN11 ......135 B4
 Daventry NN11 ......135 B7
 Daventry NN11 ......135 C2
 Kilsby CV23 ......100 A2
 Welton NN11 ......119 D1
Ashcroft Cl NN5 ......140 B1
Ashcroft Gdns NN14 ......142 A2
Ashdale Cl NN6 ......127 D1
Ashdown Cl NN15 ......92 A5
Ashdown Pl NN17 ......36 E7
Ashdown Rd NN11 ......135 C4
Ashes The
 Northampton NN4 ......176 B6
 Weldon NN17 ......38 C8
Ashfield Rd
 Market Harborough LE16 ..31 E4
 Wellingborough NN8 ......129 E4
Ashfield Rise NN9 ......114 C6
Ashford Cl NN3 ......160 C6
Ashford Lea NN14 ......50 E4
Ashgate Ct NN14 ......70 C7
Ashlade OX17 ......220 B7
Ashlawn Rd CV22 ......98 C7
Ashlawn Sch CV22 ......98 C7
Ashlea MK46 ......195 E3
Ashleigh Cl CV23 ......99 C2
Ashley Ave NN17 ......36 B7
Ashley Ct Blisworth NN7 ..190 D7
 Kettering NN16 ......72 A3
Ashley La NN3 ......126 D1
Ashley Rd Medbourne LE16 18 E6
 Middleton LE16 ......20 B2
 Stoke Albany LE16 ......34 A5
 Weston by W LE16 ......18 C3
Ashley Way
 Market Harborough LE16 ..32 B3
 Northampton NN3 ......142 E2
Ashmead NN3 ......143 A2
Ashmore Cl NN6 ......121 C4
Ashpole Spinney NN4 ..158 C2
Ashridge Cl NN10 ......148 A8
Ashton CE Prim Sch
 NN7 ......191 F1
Ashton Cl NN11 ......135 A3
Ashton Gr NN8 ......129 C8
Ashton Rd Hartwell NN7 ..192 C1
 Oundle PE8 ......42 B5
 Roade NN7 ......191 E2
 Stoke Bruerne NN12 ......205 D8
Ashtree Gdns PE9 ......1 D2
Ashtree Way NN5 ......158 C7
Ashurst Cres NN18 ......36 B4
Ashway The
 Brixworth NN6 ......106 C1
 Brixworth NN6 ......125 B8
Ashwell Rd
 Rushden NN10 ......132 D2
 Weedon Lois NN12 ......200 B2
Ashwells La NN6 ......82 B4
Ashwin Cl NN13 ......222 E1
Ashwood Rd NN5 ......158 C2
Ashworth Cl NN6 ......101 A6
Ashworth St NN11 ......135 C1
Askham Ave NN8 ......129 C1
Aspen Cl
 Northampton NN3 ......143 C3

Aspen Cl continued
 Rushden NN10 ......132 B3
Aspreys MK46 ......195 E4
Astbury Cl NN11 ......153 C8
Aster Cl NN3 ......160 D6
Aster Rd NN16 ......72 D4
Astley Cl LE16 ......31 D1
Astley Pl CV21 ......99 B7
Aston Rise NN5 ......158 B8
Astral Row NN7 ......210 C2
Astrop Gdns OX17 ......231 A5
Astrop Grange OX17 ..231 A5
Astrop Rd
 King's Sutton OX17 ......231 A5
 Middleton Cheney OX17 ..219 F6
Athelstan Rd NN16 ......72 D2
Atterbury Cl NN6 ......102 D4
Atterbury Way NN4 ......160 F2
Attlee Cl NN3 ......142 B4
Attley Ct NN8 ......129 C5
Auctioneers Ct NN1 ......159 D4
Auctioneers Way NN1 ..159 D4
Auden Way NN17 ......36 C8
Audley Cl LE16 ......32 B2
Augusta Ave NN4 ......175 C6
Augustus Rd MK11 ......229 E4
Auriga St LE16 ......31 F2
Auriol Cotts NN13 ......221 B4
Austin Dr NN29 ......147 C8
Austin Dr OX16 ......240 A10
Austin Friar's La PE9 ..241 D2
Austin Ho NN14 ......70 D7
Austin St
 Northampton NN1 ......159 D7
 Stamford PE9 ......241 E3
Austin Way NN11 ......134 F4
Austins Cl LE16 ......31 D3
Austins Pl NN12 ......214 E4
Austins Yd NN16 ......144 E4
Avalon Cl NN14 ......70 E7
Avebury Way NN4 ......175 B8
Avenue Bernard NN13 ..233 E8
Avenue Cl NN9 ......111 E5
Avenue Inf Sch The
 NN8 ......130 A5
Avenue Rd Banbury OX16 240 F8
 Finedon NN9 ......111 E5
 Rugby CV21 ......241 A9
 Rushden NN10 ......148 B5
 Wellingborough NN8 ......130 A5
Avenue Terr NN16 ......72 E3
Avenue The Flore NN7 ..155 E5
 Medbourne LE16 ......19 C8
 Middleton Cheney OX17 ..220 A8
 Moulton NN3 ......142 E8
 Northampton NN1 ......159 F5
 Northampton, Dallington
 NN5 ......158 F7
 Northampton,Meadow View
 NN2 ......140 F6
 Northampton,Spinney Hill
 NN3 ......142 A3
 Rothwell NN14 ......70 D7
 Stanwick NN9 ......114 A3
 Wellingborough NN8 ......130 A5
 Whitfield NN13 ......223 D4
Aviemore Gdns NN4 ......158 E1
Avignon Cl NN5 ......140 A2
Avon Cl Daventry NN11 ..153 A8
 Kettering NN16 ......72 A5
 Wellingborough NN8 ......129 C6
Avon Dr NN5 ......140 E1
Avon Fields NN6 ......64 E6
Avon St CV21 ......241 C9
Avonbury Ct NN13 ......234 A5
Avondale Jun & Inf Schs
 NN16 ......72 D4
Avondale Mews NN16 ..72 D3
Avondale Rd NN16 ......72 D3
Axe Head Rd NN4 ......158 F4
Axiom Ct PE9 ......241 D2
Aynho (Fishing Venue)*
 OX17 ......236 F6
Aynho Cres NN2 ......141 C5
Aynho Ct OX17 ......237 D7
Aynho Rd OX17 ......230 D2
Aynho Wlk NN2 ......141 D5
Aynhoe Pk OX17 ......237 C7
Aynsley Ct NN14 ......50 F3
Ayr Cl PE9 ......241 A4
Azalea Cl NN3 ......160 D6

B

Back La Brigstock NN14 ..55 F8
 Chapel Brampton NN6 ..124 D1
 Collyweston PE8 ......1 D2
 East Farndon LE16 ......48 B7
 Elton PE8 ......28 D8
 Gayton NN7 ......173 E2
 Great Brington NN7 ......138 C6
 Holcot NN6 ......126 E8
 Little Addington NN14 ..113 B8
 Morcott LE15 ......3 A6
 Northampton NN4 ......175 E8
 Ringstead NN14 ......95 B3
 Scaldwell NN6 ......106 F5
 South Luffenham LE15 ..3 D8
 Stamford PE9 ......241 E3
Back Rd LE15 ......3 E5
Backley Cl NN15 ......90 E8
Backway NN29 ......146 D2
Bacon Hill MK46 ......195 E4
Badby Cl NN2 ......141 E4

Badby Leys CV22 ....98 A7
Badby Pk NN11 ....135 A5
Badby Rd Daventry NN11 135 C1
Newnham NN11 ....153 D4
Badby Rd W
Daventry NN11 ....153 A4
Daventry NN11 ....153 B8
Badby Sch NN11 ....152 F3
Baden Powell Cres
NN12 ....203 C4
Badgers Cl NN7 ....172 F7
Badgers Hyde NN13 ....232 F6
Badgers Way MK18 ....240 E2
Badgers Wlk NN2 ....141 B5
Baffin Cl Rothwell NN14 ...70 E7
Rugby CV22 ....241 A6
Bailey Brooks Cl NN7 ..191 C5
Bailey Brooks La NN7 ..191 C5
Bailey Ct NN10 ....132 B5
Bailiff St NN1 ....159 D7
Bain Cl PE9 ....241 E5
Baird Ave NN5 ....158 D4
Baird Cl NN11 ....135 B5
Baird Ct NN8 ....129 B6
Baird Rd NN17 ....22 D1
Bairstow Rd NN12 ......203 C5
Bakehouse Hill
Geddington NN14 ....54 A3
Little Addington NN14 ....113 B8
Bakehouse La
Burton Latimer NN15 ....92 A3
Mears Ashby NN6 ....128 B2
Rugby CV21 ....241 B8
Bakehouse Rise NN6 ....85 B8
Baker Ave NN14 ....90 A3
Baker Ct NN14 ....76 D1
Baker St
Farthinghoe NN13 ....221 B4
Gayton NN7 ....173 E2
Irthlingborough NN9 ....112 E1
Northampton NN2 ....159 C8
3 Wellingborough NN8 ..130 A5
Baker's La NN12 ....204 D8
Bakers Cres NN29 ......147 A8
Bakers La Norton NN11 ..136 C4
Spratton NN6 ....105 B1
Stoke Bruerne NN12 ....205 A8
Walgrave NN6 ....108 A4
Woodford NN14 ....94 D6
Bakewell Cl NN4 ....174 F8
Balcombe Ct CV22 ......98 E8
Balcombe Pl NN18 ......36 A5
Balcombe Rd CV22 ......98 D8
Balding Cl CV23 ....99 C1
Baldwin Cl NN3 ....142 B4
Baler Cl NN11 ....135 C6
Balfour Dr NN14 ....70 E7
Balfour Gdns LE16 ......31 C1
Balfour Rd NN2 ....141 D1
Balfour St NN16 ....72 C4
Balham Cl NN10 ....147 F8
Balland Way NN4 ....175 F7
Ballantyne Rd NN10 ....132 A1
Balliol Rd Brackley NN13 233 D8
Daventry NN11 ....153 B8
Balmoral NN18 ....36 C3
Balmoral Ave
Banbury OX16 ....240 A6
Rushden NN10 ....132 C3
Balmoral Cl
Earls Barton NN6 ....144 F3
Market Harborough LE16 ..32 B2
Towcester NN12 ....203 B5
Wellingborough NN8 ....129 E1
Balmoral Ct NN15 ....91 C5
Balmoral Dr NN13 ......233 E7
Balmoral Ho NN2 ....141 C1
Balmoral Rd NN2 ....141 C1
Balmoral Way OX17 ....230 F6
Baltic Cl NN18 ....36 A2
Bamburg Cl NN18 ......36 A1
Bamburgh Cl LE16 ......32 B3
Bampton Ct NN18 ......36 F4
Banbury Bsns Pk OX17 230 D3
Banbury Cl
Northampton NN4 ....158 D2
Wellingborough NN8 ....129 E1
Banbury La
Banbury OX17 ....219 B8
Banbury OX17 ....219 C8
Blakesley NN12 ....186 D2
Byfield NN11 ....183 D7
Cold Higham NN12 ......188 B7
Culworth OX17 ....198 E3
Gayton NN7 ....173 D4
Great Easton LE16 ....20 D6
Kings Sutton OX17 ......230 E6
Middleton Cheney OX17 ..209 C4
Northampton NN4 ....158 D1
Rothersthorpe NN7 ......174 C1
Thorpe Mandeville OX17 ..210 B8
Weston NN12 ....199 C3
Banbury Mus OX16 ....240 D8
Banbury Rd Aynho OX17 237 C2
Brackley NN13 ....233 E6
Byfield NN11 ....183 D7
Chacombe OX17 ....208 C3
Chipping Warden OX17 ..196 F6
Litchborough NN12 ......171 C1
Lower Boddington NN11 ..182 C4
Moreton Pinkney NN11 ..199 C7
Twyford OX17 ....230 A6
Banbury Sch OX16 ......240 A6
Banbury Sta OX16 ......240 E7
Bancroft Rd LE16 ....20 D1

Bangrave Rd NN17 ......37 F8
Bank Hill View NN9 ....110 C4
Bank St CV21 ....241 C8
Bank View NN4 ....175 B7
Bankfield Dr LE16 ......32 A5
Banks The
Broughton NN14 ....90 B5
Hackleton NN7 ....177 B3
Kilsby CV23 ....100 A2
Long Buckby NN6 ....121 B4
Wellingborough NN9 ....129 F8
Bankside Banbury OX16 240 E6
Corby NN18 ....36 D3
Northampton NN2 ....141 F3
Woodford Halse NN11 ..184 C6
Banner Cl NN10 ....132 A1
Bannerman Dr NN13 ....233 D7
Bants La NN5 ....158 E7
Barby CE Prim Sch
CV23 ....118 C8
Barby La CV23 ....99 B5
Barby Rd Kilsby CV23 ....99 F3
Rugby CV22 ....241 C6
Rugby CV22 ....98 B7
Bardsley Rd NN17 ......21 E3
Barford MK11 ....229 F4
Barham Lodge MK18 ....240 C3
Baring Ho NN5 ....159 A7
Baring Rd NN5 ....159 A7
Barker Cl NN10 ....132 C2
Barker Rd NN6 ....144 E3
Barksdale Ave NN13 ....238 E6
Barley Cl Daventry NN11 135 C6
Hartwell NN7 ....192 C2
Rugby CV21 ....99 A8
Barley Croft NN6 ....100 F6
Barley Ct NN10 ....148 C8
Barley Hill OX17 ....198 D2
Barley Hill Rd NN3 ......142 F6
Barley La NN7 ....141 B5
Barlow Cl NN14 ....70 B7
Barlow Ct NN15 ....92 B1
Barlow La NN3 ....126 C1
Barlows La LE16 ....34 C5
Barn Acre NN6 ....122 D5
Barn Cl Corby NN18 ....36 B1
Northampton NN4 ....175 F3
Barn Cnr NN4 ....175 C4
Barn Ct Helmdon NN13 ..211 F4
Little Harrowden NN9 ....110 C4
Barn Hill PE9 ....241 D3
Barn La NN7 ....174 F2
Barn Mews NN4 ....175 C4
Barn Owl Cl NN4 ....175 A8
Barnack Rd PE9 ....241 E2
Barnard NN14 ....36 C3
Barnard Cl NN5 ....158 B8
Barnard Gdns LE16 ......48 D8
Barnard's Way NN14 ....56 A6
Barnes Cl Daventry NN11 135 B3
Kettering NN15 ....91 B7
Old NN6 ....107 D7
Barnes Mdw* NN4 ......159 F4
Barnes Meadow Intc
NN4 ....160 A4
Barneswell Ct NN6 ......106 B2
Barnet Cl NN4 ....159 A2
Barnett Cres NN15 ......184 B6
Barnett Rd OX17 ....219 F8
Barnfield Cl NN2 ....141 B4
Barnhill Sq NN3 ....143 A6
Barns The
Irchester NN29 ....131 B1
Mears Ashby NN6 ....128 C2
Barnsdale LE16 ....20 D6
Barnsdale Cl LE16 ......20 D6
Barnsley Sq NN18 ......36 C4
Barnstaple Cl NN3 ......160 E7
Barnwell CE Prim Sch
PE8 ....59 B6
Barnwell Cl NN14 ....76 E2
Barnwell Ctry Pk* PE8 .41 E3
Barnwell Ctry Pk Visitor Ctr*
PE8 ....41 F3
Barnwell Dr NN10 ....148 A8
Barnwell Gdns NN8 ......129 D7
Barnwell Rd
Northampton NN2 ....141 D4
Oundle PE8 ....41 F3
Stamford PE9 ....241 A4
Wellingborough NN8 ....129 E7
Barnwell St NN16 ....72 D2
Baron Ave
Earls Barton NN6 ....144 F6
Kettering NN16 ....71 E3
Baron Ct Corby NN17 ....22 E1
Northampton NN1 ....159 F8
Barons Way NN2 ....141 A4
Baronson Gdns NN1 ....159 F8
Barrack Rd NN1,NN2 ....159 C7
Barracks The NN7 ......161 D2
Barratt Cl NN10 ....132 B5
Barratt Cl NN8 ....129 C4
Barringers Ct NN19 ....159 C7
Barringers Gdns NN29 ..131 B1
Barrington Ct NN13 ....233 F5
Barrington Rd NN10 ....148 C8
Barron Cl NN15 ....91 C6
Barrowden La LE15 ......3 E8
Barrowden Rd
Barrowden PE9 ....4 C8
Ketton PE9 ....1 A4
South Luffenham LE15 ....3 F7
Barry Green Ct NN9 ....111 F5
Barry Lower Sch NN1 ..160 A7
Barry Rd NN1 ....160 A6
Barth Cl NN18 ....36 B2

Bartholomew Gdns
NN12 ....187 A1
Bartlett Ct NN13 ....233 D7
Bartlett Pl MK18 ....240 E4
Bartley Dr NN16 ....71 F4
Barton Cl OX17 ....230 F6
Barton Fields NN6 ......143 F3
Barton Holme NN12 ....187 A1
Barton Rd NN15 ....91 E7
Barton Seagrave Prim Sch
NN15 ....92 A6
Barton Sq NN18 ....36 B6
Bartons Cl The 2 NN5 ..140 C1
Barwick Ho NN10 ....132 B2
Basil Cl NN4 ....175 D6
Bassett Ford Rd PE8 ....42 A4
Bassett Pl PE8 ....42 A4
Bassett Way LE16 ....67 A8
Bates Ave NN14 ....95 B3
Bates Cl
Higham Ferrers NN10 ....132 B5
Market Harborough LE16 ..31 E5
Bates La OX27 ....237 D3
Bath La
Buckingham MK18 ....240 C3
Kettering NN16 ....72 C3
Bath Lane Terr MK18 ....240 C3
Bath Rd Banbury OX16 ..240 C7
Kettering NN16 ....72 C4
Bath Row PE9 ....241 D2
Bath St
Market Harborough LE16 ..31 E1
Rugby CV21 ....241 D8
Bathurst Cl CV22 ......241 A6
Battalion Dr NN4 ....175 E7
Battle Cl Cranford NN14 ..93 A6
Northampton NN4 ....175 D7
Baukewell Ct 4 NN3 ..142 E3
Baunhill Cl NN3 ....160 D7
Baxter Cl NN4 ....175 F8
Bayard Brow NN13 ......233 E8
Bayes St NN16 ....72 A3
Baysdale Ave NN17 ......36 E6
Beacon Cl NN4 ....175 D7
Beaconsfield Ave CV22 241 C6
Beaconsfield Pl NN10 ..132 B3
Beaconsfield Terr
Northampton NN1 ....159 D7
Rushden NN10 ....132 B3
Bean Furlong OX17 ......208 E4
Beanfield Ave NN18 ......36 B5
Beanfield Jun & Inf Sch
NN18 ....36 A5
Beardsley Ct NN18 ......36 D5
Beardsley Gdns NN15 ..92 A7
Beargarden Rd OX16 ....240 C7
Beatrice Dr OX16 ....240 B7
Beatrice Rd NN16 ....72 B5
Beatty Cl NN11 ....135 E1
Beatty Gdns NN7 ....36 B7
Beaufort Dr
Kettering NN15 ....92 A6
Northampton NN5 ....140 C1
Beaulieu Cl OX16 ....240 F8
Beauly Cl NN15 ....91 E8
Beaumaris Cl NN10 ......132 C1
Beaumont Cl NN16 ......72 B6
Beaumont Cres NN13 ..233 E7
Beaumont Ct 15 NN1 ..159 C6
Beaumont Dr NN3 ......143 C3
Beaune Cl NN5 ....139 F1
Beauvais Ct NN5 ....139 F1
Beaver Cl MK18 ....240 E2
Beaver Ctr The NN18 ..184 C7
Beck Ct NN8 ....129 D6
Becket Way NN3 ....142 B4
Beckett's View NN1 ....159 E5
Becketts Cl NN11 ....183 D7
Bective Rd NN2 ....141 C4
Bective View NN2 ......141 D4
Bedale Rd NN8 ....130 A6
Beddoes Cl NN4 ....176 A6
Bede Cl Corby NN18 ....36 A1
Higham Ferrers NN10 ....132 C5
Bede Ho* LE15 ....9 D7
Bedford Cl NN15 ....91 F5
Bedford Cotts NN7 ......138 D7
Bedford Mans NN1 ......159 D5
Bedford Pl NN1 ....159 D5
Bedford Rd Denton NN7 ..178 B8
Little Houghton NN7 ......160 F3
Northampton NN1 ....159 E4
Rushden NN10 ....148 D5
Bedford Rd E NN7 ......179 D5
Bedford Rd W NN7 ......179 A6
Beech Ave
Northampton NN3 ....142 A1
Olney MK46 ....195 E3
Beech Cl
Buckingham MK18 ....240 D5
Bugbrooke NN7 ....172 F7
Corby NN17 ....21 E1
Desborough NN14 ....51 A3
Hackleton NN7 ....177 B3
Towcester NN12 ....203 C4
Beech Cres
Irchester NN29 ....147 A7
Kettering NN15 ....72 C6
Beech Ct Rugby CV22 ..98 F8
Thrapston NN14 ....76 D2
Beech Dr Brackley NN13 222 E1
Hinton NN11 ....184 B6
Wellingborough NN8 ....129 E5
Beech Gr
Northampton NN3 ....142 D5
Rushden NN10 ....131 F3
Beech Hill NN11 ....151 D1
Beech House Dr NN12 ..217 F4

Beech La NN7 ....157 E4
Beech Rd NN10 ....132 B4
Beechcroft Gdns NN3 ..142 A2
Beeches Cl LE16 ....46 F2
Beeches The
Deanshanger MK19 ......228 E3
Pattishall NN12 ....172 A1
Beechwood Dr NN3 ......142 E1
Beechwood Rd NN5 ....158 C7
Beesley Rd OX16 ....240 A8
Beeston Ave NN3 ....160 F8
Beeston Pl NN18 ....36 C5
Belfield Cl NN3 ....142 B3
Belfry La NN4 ....175 B5
Belgrave Ct NN15 ....92 A5
Bell Cl NN13 ....211 F4
Bell Ct Corby NN18 ....36 D4
5 Wellingborough NN8 130 A5
Bell End NN29 ....146 D2
Bell Hill Finedon NN9 ..111 E4
Rothwell NN14 ....70 D7
Bell La Byfield NN11 ....183 D7
Husbands Bosworth LE17 ..45 E5
Syresham NN13 ....224 B8
Bell St NN8 ....130 A5
Bell View OX17 ....231 F5
Bell Wlk CV21 ....99 A8
Bellamy Rd PE8 ....41 F7
Belle Baulk NN12 ....203 A6
Bellfields La LE16 ....32 A2
Bellfields St LE16 ....32 A2
Bellfoundry La 4 NN16 ..72 B2
Bellinge Lower Sch
NN3 ....143 B1
Bellropes Sq 5 NN3 ....143 D2
Bells NN14 ....55 E8
Belmont Ct 13 NN1 ....159 C7
Belmont Gdns NN9 ......114 C6
Belmont Rd CV22 ....241 C6
Belstead Rd NN3 ....160 D6
Belton Cl 4 NN4 ....175 D4
Belton St PE9 ....241 E3
Belvedere Cl NN5 ....158 F7
Belvedere Rd NN15 ......72 D1
Belvoir Cl
Northampton NN5 ....140 B1
Rushden NN10 ....148 C8
Stamford PE9 ....241 A4
Belvoir Dr NN15 ....92 A6
Bembridge Dr NN2 ......141 B1
Benbow Cl NN11 ....135 E2
Benedict Cl NN10 ......147 F8
Benefield Rd
Brigstock NN14 ....39 B2
Deenethorpe NN17 ....24 C4
Oundle PE8 ....41 C5
Bengal NN12 ....202 D7
Bengal La NN12 ....202 E7
Bengal View NN12 ......202 E8
Benham Rd NN12 ....202 D8
Benjamin Sq 6 NN4 ....158 F2
Benn St CV22 ....241 E7
Bennet Cl MK11 ....229 D4
Bennett Cl
Chacombe OX17 ....208 E4
Daventry NN11 ....135 A4
Bennett St CV21 ....241 B8
Bennfield Rd CV21 ......241 C8
Bens Cl MK19 ....218 F5
Bentley Cl NN3 ....143 D4
Bentley Cl NN9 ....111 B1
Bentley St PE9 ....241 E4
Bentley Way NN11 ......134 F3
Bentley Wlk NN18 ......36 C5
Bergen Wlk NN18 ....36 A2
Bergerac Cl NN5 ....139 F2
Berkeley Cl NN1 ....159 F6
Berkeley Ct PE9 ....241 F4
Berkeley Ho 26 NN1 ....159 C6
Berkeley St LE16 ....46 F2
Bern Links NN4 ....159 A3
Bern Side NN4 ....159 A3
Bernardines Way MK18 240 E2
Berneshaw Cl NN18 ......36 D3
Berridges La LE17 ......45 E5
Berrill St NN29 ....147 A7
Berrister Pl NN4 ....175 D4
Berry Cl Earls Barton NN6 144 E5
Great Bowden LE16 ....32 A5
Hackleton NN7 ....177 B3
Rothersthorpe NN7 ......174 B6
Berry Field Rd LE16 ......20 C1
Berry Green Pk NN14 ....78 E6
Berry Green Rd NN9 ....111 B5
Berry Hill Rd OX17 ......230 A2
Berry La Hellidon NN11 ..151 C1
Northampton NN4 ....175 D5
Berry Rd LE16 ....20 C1
Berrybut Way PE9 ......241 F5
Berrydale NN3 ....143 D4
Berryfield NN6 ....121 C4
Berrymoor Ct NN8 ......129 C6
Berrymoor Rd
Banbury OX16 ....240 B7
Wellingborough NN8 ....129 C2
Berrywood Rd NN5 ......158 A7
Bertha Way NN16 ....72 E4
Berwick Ho NN2 ....141 D5
Berwick Rd NN16 ....37 E3
Berwick Way NN15 ......92 A8
Bessemer Ct NN18 ......37 B6
Bestwell Ct 3 NN3 ......161 A8
Bestwood Gn NN18 ......36 C5
Bethany Homestead 1
NN2 ....141 E1
Bethel La NN11 ....170 B7
Betjeman Cl
Daventry NN11 ....135 A3

Betjeman Cl continued
Higham Ferrers NN10 ....132 A5
Betony Wlk NN10 ....148 B8
Bettycroft Cl NN6 ....103 E1
Bevan Cl Warmington PE8 ..28 B3
Wellingborough NN8 ....130 C7
Beverley Cl NN14 ....70 B7
Beverley Cres NN3 ......142 C1
Beverley Gdns PE9 ......241 B4
Beverley Rd NN15 ....91 D8
Beverley Wlk NN16 ......36 C5
Bewick Ct NN18 ....36 E4
Bewick Rd NN3 ....160 E8
Bexhill Wlk NN16 ....36 B4
Biart Pl CV21 ....241 F8
Bibury Cl NN8 ....129 D1
Bibury Cres NN3 ....142 D6
Bicester Hill NN13 ......233 F2
Bickerstaffes Rd NN12 ..203 C5
Bidders Cl NN1 ....159 D4
Bideford Cl NN10 ....160 D7
Bideford Sq NN18 ......36 F5
Bies Cl NN18 ....36 C2
Big Gn PE8 ....28 C3
Bignal Ct NN15 ....90 E8
Billing Aquadrome NN7 161 B7
Billing Brook Rd NN3 ..142 F4
Billing Brook Sch NN3 ..142 F3
Billing La Moulton NN6 ..126 F1
Northampton NN3 ....143 A7
Billing Rd
Brafield-on-t-G NN7 ......161 D4
Northampton NN1 ....159 F6
Billing Rd E NN3 ....160 D7
Billing School Pl NN7 ..155 C3
Billing Way NN3 ....143 C5
Billington St NN1 ....159 F7
Bilsdon Cl NN10 ....147 F8
Bilton Ct NN8 ....129 D5
Bilton Rd CV22 ....241 A7
Binbrook Wlk NN18 ......36 C4
Binders Ct NN14 ....37 F2
Bingham Wlk NN18 ......36 C5
Birch Ave NN18 ....36 D4
Birch Barn Way NN2 ....141 B6
Birch Cl Hinton NN11 ..184 B6
Northampton NN10 ......175 E2
Birch Rd Kettering NN16 ..72 D3
Rushden NN10 ....132 C2
Birch Tree Gdns LE16 ....31 F4
Birchall Rd NN10 ....131 F2
Birchfield Cres NN3 ....142 C2
Birchfield Ct NN3 ......142 B3
Birchfield Rd
Northampton NN1,NN3 ..142 A1
Wellingborough NN8 ....129 E4
Birchfield Rd E NN3 ....142 C1
Birchington Rd NN17 ....22 F2
Birchvale Ct NN14 ....50 E4
Bird Cl OX16 ....240 B8
Bird St NN15 ....92 D3
Birds Hill Rd
Eastcote NN12 ....188 F8
Northampton NN3 ....142 F3
Birds Hill Wlk NN3 ......142 F2
Birkdale Cl
Daventry NN11 ....135 E2
Northampton NN2 ....141 F3
Birkdale Dr NN10 ....132 D1
Birling Pl NN18 ....36 B5
Birtley Coppice LE16 ....31 D4
Bishop Cl LE16 ....48 E8
Bishop Stopford CE Sch
NN15 ....91 B7
Bishop Wulstan RC Sch
CV22 ....241 C7
Bishop's Dr NN15 ....91 B6
Bishops Cl NN13 ....222 E1
Bishops Ct
Buckingham MK18 ....240 C2
4 Daventry NN11 ....135 C2
Higham Ferrers NN10 ....132 C7
Bishops Dr NN2 ....141 B3
Bishops Way NN18 ......36 A4
Bitten Ct NN3 ....142 E3
Black Lion Hill NN1 ....159 B5
Black Swan Spinney PE8 38 A4
Blackberry Cl NN16 ......72 B6
Blackberry La NN4 ......158 F3
Blackbird NN13 ....222 E1
Blackdown MK11 ....229 F4
Blackfriars NN10 ....147 F8
Blackfriars Ho 19 NN1 ..159 C6
Blackfriars St PE9 ......241 E3
Blacklocks Hill OX17 ..219 B8
Blackman Way CV21 ....241 B9
Blackmile La NN7 ....163 E7
Blackmires La NN12 ....214 B5
Blackmoor Ave NN18 ....36 F4
Blackpot La PE8 ....42 A5
Blacksmith's Cl NN12 ..172 D1
Blacksmith's La
Aston le W NN11 ....182 F2
Pytchley NN14 ....90 F2
Blacksmith's Way NN12 192 C1
Blacksmiths La NN12 ..204 D8
Blacksmiths Hill OX17 237 C7
Blacksmiths La
Eydon NN11 ....184 C1
Little Brington NN7 ......138 B4
Blackthorn Bridge Ct 4
NN3 ....143 B4
Blackthorn Cl
Kettering NN16 ....72 C6
Spratton NN6 ....105 A1
Blackthorn Mid Sch
NN3 ....143 C5
Blackthorn Rd NN3 ......143 B4

Bla – Bro 245

Blackthorne Lower Sch NN3 143 B4
Blackwall Cl 1 NN4 159 A2
Blackwell Cl NN12 203 D4
Blackwell End NN12 217 C3
Blackwell Hill NN4 174 F8
Blackwell Rd NN15 91 F4
Blackwells Yd NN7 179 B6
Blackymore La NN4 175 D5
Bladon Cl NN3 142 C4
Blake Cl NN11 153 E8
Blake Ct NN15 92 A8
Blake Rd NN18 36 D4
Blake Wlk NN10 132 A5
Blakesely Hill NN12 202 D8
Blakesley CE Prim Sch NN12 187 B1
Blakesley Cl NN2 141 C5
Blakesley Rd NN12 200 F7
Blanchard Cl 3 NN4 175 E7
Blandford Ave NN16 72 B5
Blandford Ct NN18 36 A6
Blashfield Cl PE9 241 C4
Blatherwycke Rd PE8 13 E7
Blaydon Wlk NN8 129 E6
Bleaklow Cl NN14 50 E3
Bledlow Rise NN4 174 F8
Blencowe Dr NN13 233 D7
Blenheim NN13 238 B7
Blenheim Ave MK11 229 E4
Blenheim Cl NN10 148 A8
Blenheim Croft NN13 233 F6
Blenheim Pl NN13 224 C7
Blenheim Rd
Northampton NN4 159 B2
Wellingborough NN8 129 D7
Blenheim Rise OX17 230 F6
Blenheim Way
Kettering NN15 91 C5
Market Harborough LE16 31 E5
Blenheim Wlk NN18 36 C3
Blinco Rd NN10 132 C3
Blind La LE16 20 D1
Bliss Charity Sch The NN7 156 C2
Bliss La NN7 155 F5
Blisworth Cl NN4 159 A2
Blisworth Mill NN7 190 C7
Blisworth Prim Sch NN7 190 D8
Blisworth Rd Gayton NN7 173 F1
Roade NN7 191 B4
Bloomfield Cl NN10 132 A2
Blossac Ct NN5 139 F1
Blossom Way NN3 143 A1
Bloxam Gdns CV22 241 B7
Bloxam Pl CV21 241 C8
Bloxham Rd OX16 240 C6
Bluebell Cl
Buckingham MK18 240 C2
Corby NN18 36 D2
Hinton NN11 184 B7
Kettering NN16 72 E4
Rushden NN10 148 C8
Bluebell Ct NN3 160 C6
Bluebell Pk Cvn Pk 2 NN3 126 C1
Bluebell Rise NN10 148 B8
Blueberry Cl NN6 87 B6
Blueberry Rise 2 NN3 143 C2
Bluecoat La LE15 9 D7
Bluecoat Sch The PE9 241 D4
Blythe Cl NN14 70 E6
Blyton Ct NN18 36 C4
Board St NN9 112 F2
Boarden Cl NN3 142 A7
Boardman Rd NN15 90 F8
Boat Horse La NN6 101 A5
Boathouse The LE16 31 D4
Bobtail Ct NN5 140 C1
Boddington CE Sch NN11 182 C7
Boddington Ct NN11 182 C5
Boddington Mews NN15 91 C8
Boddington Rd
Byfield NN11 183 C7
Claydon OX17 181 D1
Kettering NN15 91 C8
Boddington Way NN13 233 D8
Boden Cl NN18 36 A2
Bodenham Cl MK18 240 F3
Bodiam CL NN14 76 E2
Bodiam Pl NN18 36 A5
Bodleian Cl NN11 153 B8
Bognor Rd NN18 36 B4
Bollinger Cl NN5 139 F1
Bolton Rd OX16 240 C8
Boltons Cl NN13 222 E1
Bond St CV21 241 B8
Bondfield Ave NN2 141 D3
Bonham Ct NN16 72 C3
Bonington Wlk NN18 36 D5
Bonnington Cl CV21 80 B1
Bonsor Gdns NN14 95 A3
Boon Wlk NN17 37 B7
Booth Cl NN12 172 D1
Booth Dr NN8 129 A4
Booth La N NN3 142 C4
Booth La S NN3 142 D2
Booth Lower Sch NN3 142 C4
Booth Meadow Ct NN3 142 E5
Booth Rise NN3 142 D6
Boothville Gn NN3 142 D5
Boothville Mid Sch NN3 142 D4
Bordeaux Cl NN5 139 F1
Borough Ct
Brackley NN13 234 A5
Borough Ct continued
Higham Ferrers NN10 132 B5
Borough Rd NN13 234 A5
Borrowdale Rd NN17 36 D8
Borrowdale Wlk 3 NN3 142 C4
Bostock Ave NN1 159 F7
Boston Cl NN18 36 C4
Boswell Ct MK18 240 E5
Boswell La MK19 228 E4
Bosworth Cl
Northampton NN4 159 A1
Warmington PE8 28 B3
Bosworth Independent Coll NN2 159 C8
Bosworth Rd
Husbands Bosworth LE17 45 A8
Theddingworth LE17 46 C7
Bothy The OX17 237 D7
Botmead Rd NN3 143 D4
Bottom La LE16 34 B5
Bougainvillea Dr NN3 160 C6
Boughton NN15 91 D4
Boughton Cl NN18 36 A4
Boughton Dr NN10 148 A8
Boughton Fair La NN3 126 B4
Boughton Green Rd NN2,NN3 141 D5
Boughton Ho★ NN14 73 A8
Boughton La NN3 141 F7
Boughton Prim Sch NN2 141 D8
Boughton Rd
Boughton NN2,NN3 141 F8
Moulton NN3 126 A1
Boundary Ave NN10 131 E1
Boundary Cres MK11 229 E6
Boundary Rd
Brackley NN13 234 A6
Rugby CV21,CV22 241 F7
Bourne Cl Corby NN18 36 D2
Wellingborough NN8 129 C6
Bourne Cres NN5 140 E1
Bourton Cl NN4 174 E8
Bourton Meadow Sch MK18 240 F3
Bourton Rd MK18 240 E3
Bourton Way NN8 129 E1
Bourtonville MK18 240 D3
Bouverie Rd NN4 175 E8
Bouverie St 1 NN1 159 F6
Bouverie Wlk 5 NN1 159 F6
Bovewell OX27 237 E3
Bow Ct NN4 158 E3
Bowden La
Market Harborough LE16 31 E4
Welham LE16 17 E5
Bowden Rd
Northampton NN5 159 A6
Thorpe Langton LE16 17 A4
Bowden Ridge LE16 32 A5
Bowen Rd CV22 98 D8
Bowen Sq 7 NN11 135 C1
Bowhill NN16 72 A1
Bowland Dr NN15 92 A5
Bowling Gn NN13 221 B4
Bowling Green Ave NN15 72 B1
Bowling Green Rd NN15 72 B1
Bowman Cl OX17 220 A8
Bowmans Cl NN4 158 D1
Bowmens Lea OX17 237 C7
Bowness NN8 129 D5
Bowthorpe Cl NN3 160 D6
Boxhedge Rd OX16 240 B8
Boxhedge Rd W OX16 240 B8
Boxhedge Sq OX16 240 B8
Boxwood Dr CV23 100 A3
Boyle Rd NN17 22 C1
Bozeat Com Prim Sch NN29 164 D3
Bozenham Mill La NN7 205 E4
Brabham Cl NN12 214 D4
Bracadale Wlk NN17 21 C1
Bracken Borough NN6 106 C2
Bracken Cl Kettering NN16 72 B5
Rugby CV22 241 A6
Bracken Dr CV22 241 A6
Bracken Field Sq NN3 142 F7
Bracken Leas Prim Sch NN13 222 E1
Brackendale Dr CV23 99 C1
Brackenhill Cl NN2 141 E3
Brackley CE Jun Sch NN13 233 F8
Brackley Cl NN2 141 D6
Brackley Cottage Hospl NN13 233 F7
Brackley La NN12 201 F1
Brackley Lodge Mews NN13 233 F7
Brackley Magdalen College Sch (St John's) NN13 233 F6
Brackley Magdalen College Sch (Waynflete) NN13 233 E7
Brackley Rd
Buckingham MK18 240 B4
Croughton NN13 238 D8
Greatworth OX17 210 E1
Silverstone NN12 214 D3
Towcester NN12 203 B6
Westbury NN13 234 F5
Brackley Southfield Prim Sch NN13 233 E6
Brackley Waynflete Inf Sch NN13 233 E7
Brackmills Ind Est NN4 160 A2
Bracknell NN8 129 C4
Bradbury Rd NN11 153 D3
Bradden Cl NN2 141 D5
Bradden Rd NN12 202 D8
Bradden Way NN12 202 D8
Bradfield Ave MK18 240 D5
Bradfield Cl
Rushden NN10 132 D3
Wellingborough NN8 111 A1
Bradfield Rd NN8 111 A1
Bradford Wlk NN18 36 C5
Bradgate Ho NN1 159 E6
Bradmoore Ct NN3 143 B5
Bradmore Gdns NN18 36 C6
Bradshaw St 29 NN1 159 C6
Bradshaw Way NN29 146 F8
Braemar Cl
Kettering NN15 91 E8
Stamford PE9 241 A4
Braemar Cres NN4 175 C8
Brafield Leys CV22 98 A6
Brafield Rd
Cogenhoe NN7 161 E5
Horton NN7 177 E3
Bragintons La OX17 220 B8
Braid Ct NN8 129 D7
Braids Cl CV21 241 F9
Braithwaite Cl
Banbury OX16 240 A7
Kettering NN15 90 F8
Brakey Rd NN17 37 F8
Bramber Ct NN18 36 A5
Bramble Cl Kettering NN16 72 B6
Ringstead NN14 95 A3
Bramble End NN4 174 F8
Bramble Rd NN12 203 B4
Brambleside
Kettering NN16 72 C6
Thrapston NN14 76 D1
Brambleside Com Prim Sch NN16 72 C6
Brambleside Ct NN16 72 B6
Bramblewood Rd NN17 38 A8
BraMCote Dr NN3 160 F8
Bramhall Rise NN5 158 B8
Bramley Cl
Cogenhoe NN7 161 E6
Market Harborough LE16 31 F5
Rushden NN10 131 F3
Bramley Ct NN29 146 D3
Bramley Gr NN3 143 B2
Bramley Ho 7 NN11 135 C2
Brammar Ho NN5 158 F7
Brampton Cl
Kettering NN15 92 A5
Wellingborough NN8 129 D7
Brampton Hill LE16 33 F4
Brampton La
Boughton NN2,NN6 141 A7
Chapel Brampton NN6 125 A3
Brampton Valley Way★ NN6 124 E4
Brampton Way NN6 106 B1
Brampton Wlk NN3 141 F5
Brampton Wood La NN14 50 F7
Bramptons Prim Sch The NN6 124 D1
Bramshill Ave NN16 72 A6
Bramston Cl PE8 42 A4
Brandenburg Rd NN18 35 F2
Brangwyn Wlk NN18 36 E5
Branksome Ave NN2 141 B1
Branksome Ct NN18 36 A6
Branson Ct NN16 72 A3
Brantwood Rise OX16 240 B6
Brasenose Dr NN13 233 D8
Brashland Dr NN4 175 D6
Braunston CE Prim Sch NN11 118 C1
Braunston La NN11 152 C8
Braunston Pl CV22 98 D8
Braunston Rd NN11 135 B2
Braunton Pl NN18 36 F4
Brawn Cl NN9 131 E8
Brawn Way PE8 16 D1
Braybrooke Cl NN14 95 C3
Braybrooke Prim Sch LE16 49 E6
Braybrooke Rd
Arthingworth LE16 68 D8
Desborough NN14 50 F4
Dingley LE16 33 A3
Great Oxendon LE16 49 A3
Market Harborough LE16 32 B1
Brayford Ave NN18 36 F5
Brayford Cl NN3 160 C7
Brazenose La PE9 241 E3
Breach Cl NN6 106 C2
Breakleys Rd NN14 51 B2
Breck Cl NN18 53 B8
Brecon Cl NN16 72 B6
Brecon St NN5 159 A8
Breedon Cl NN18 36 A1
Breezehill NN4 175 F6
Brembridge Cl NN6 127 D2
Brendon Cl NN3 160 D7
Brent Cl NN15 92 A2
Brentford NN8 129 B5
Brer Ct NN4 159 F5
Bressingham Gdns NN4 175 C7
Bretch Hill OX16 240 A6
Breton MK11 229 E6
Bretton Cl NN5 140 A1
Bretts La NN7 191 E4
Brewery Ct PE8 41 F4
Brewin Cl NN13 222 D1
Briar Cl NN13 222 F1
Briar Hill Lower Sch NN4 158 F3
Briar Hill Rd NN4 159 B2
Briar Hill Wlk NN4 159 B2
Briar Rd NN16 72 E5
Briars The NN4 159 A3
Briary Cl NN12 203 B4
Brick Kiln Cl NN12 203 D4
Brick Kiln La NN2 159 D8
Brick Kiln Rd NN9 114 D8
Brickett's La NN7 155 E5
Brickhill Mews NN8 129 E4
Brickhill Rd NN8 129 D4
Brickwell Ct NN3 143 A1
Brickyard Spinney Rd NN3 142 B6
Bridewell La 11 NN16 72 B2
Bridge Ct Corby NN17 37 A7
Thrapston NN14 76 C2
Bridge End PE8 8 A3
Bridge Ho NN14 70 D7
Bridge Mdw NN7 178 B8
Bridge Meadow Way NN4 175 F4
Bridge Rd
Cosgrove MK19 218 E2
Desborough NN14 50 F4
Bridge St Apethorpe PE8 14 D4
Banbury OX16 240 D8
Brackley NN13 233 E6
Brigstock NN14 55 E7
Buckingham MK18 240 D3
Geddington NN14 54 A2
Kettering NN16 72 C3
King's Cliffe PE8 14 A7
Northampton NN1 159 C5
Olney MK46 195 F2
Raunds NN9 114 D7
Rothwell NN14 70 D7
Rugby CV21 241 E8
Thrapston NN14 76 C2
Weedon NN7 155 B4
Weldon NN17 38 B8
Bridgend NN6 82 B4
Bridget St CV22 241 B8
Bridgewater Cl NN13 233 F8
Bridgewater Cres NN13 233 F8
Bridgewater Ct NN13 233 F8
Bridgewater Dr NN3 160 D7
Bridgewater Ho
Brackley NN13 233 F8
Buckingham MK18 240 C3
Bridgewater Rd NN13 233 F8
Bridgewater Rise NN13 233 F8
Bridgford Pl NN18 36 C6
Bridgwater Ct NN18 36 A6
Bridle Cl
Brafield-on-t-G NN7 161 D2
Wellingborough NN8 111 A1
Bridle La NN6 84 B6
Bridle Path NN7 161 E2
Bridle Rd
Burton Latimer NN15 92 A2
Hannington NN6 108 C3
Old NN6 107 D7
Rugby CV21 241 A9
Bridle Way NN14 90 A6
Briery Cl NN18 36 B1
Brigg Ct NN18 36 C4
Brighouse Cl NN18 36 C4
Bright Trees Rd NN14 54 B3
Brighton Rd NN18 36 B4
Brightwell Wlk NN9 131 D8
Brigstock Ctry Pk★ NN14 56 A7
Brigstock Latham's CE Prim Sch NN14 55 F7
Brigstock Rd NN14 38 A2
Brindlestone Cl NN4 158 D2
Brindley Cl
Daventry NN11 135 A5
Rushden NN10 131 F4
Brindley Ct NN11 134 B8
Brindley Quay NN11 134 B8
Brindley Rd CV21 80 B1
Bringhurst Cty Prim Sch LE16 20 C6
Brington Dr NN15 91 F5
Brington Prim Sch NN7 138 C5
Brington Rd NN6 121 C3
Brinkburn Gr OX16 240 F10
Brinkhill Wlk NN18 36 C4
Brinsley Gn NN18 36 C6
Brisbane Gdns NN18 36 B2
Briscoe Cl NN2 141 E6
Bristle Hill MK18 240 C3
Britain Cotts NN7 173 F1
Britannia Gdns NN8 130 C4
Britannia Rd
Banbury OX16 240 D7
Kettering NN16 72 B5
Britannia Trad Ctr NN5 140 D2
Britannia Wlk LE16 31 F2
British La 17 NN16 72 B2
Briton Gdns NN3 142 B1
Briton Rd NN3 142 B1
Briton Terr NN3 142 B1
Britten Cl NN9 133 C8
Brittons Dr NN3 143 A7
Brixham Wlk NN18 36 F5
Brixworth CE Prim Sch NN6 106 B1
Brixworth Ctry Pk★ NN6 125 C8
Brixworth Ctry Pk Visitor Ctr★ NN6 125 C7
Brixworth Hall Pk NN6 106 B2
Brixworth Rd
Creaton NN6 104 F4
Holcot NN6 126 D8
Spratton NN6 105 D1
Broad La NN13 233 E3
Broad March NN11 153 D8
Broad St Banbury OX16 240 D7
Brixworth NN6 106 B1
Earls Barton NN6 144 E4
Northampton NN1 159 C6
Stamford PE9 241 D3
Syresham NN13 224 B8
Broadgate LE16 20 D7
Broadgate Way PE8 28 C2
Broadhurst Dr NN3 161 A8
Broadlands
Brixworth NN6 106 A1
Desborough NN14 51 C2
Pitsford NN6 125 D5
Raunds NN9 114 E6
Rushden NN10 132 B3
Broadmead Ave NN3 142 B2
Broadmead Ct NN3 142 B2
Broadstone Ct NN18 36 A6
Broadwater La NN12 203 A5
Broadway Kettering NN15 91 B8
Northampton NN1,NN3 142 A1
Wellingborough NN8 130 A3
Broadway E NN3 142 B1
Broadway Terr LE16 31 F4
Broadway The
Market Harborough LE16 31 F4
Norton NN11 136 C4
Brocade Cl 8 NN4 158 F2
Brockhall Cl NN2 141 E4
Brockhall Rd Flore NN7 155 E6
Northampton NN2 141 E4
Brockhill Cl NN15 72 E1
Brockton St NN2 141 D1
Brockwood Cl NN5 140 A1
Bromford Cl 8 NN3 161 A8
Bromley Farm Ct NN11 184 B5
Bromwich Rd 1 CV21 80 A1
Bronte Cl Kettering NN16 72 C6
Rugby CV21 241 F8
Brontes The NN17 36 D8
Brook Ct Horton NN7 177 E2
Silverstone NN12 214 D5
Brook Farm Cl NN10 148 B5
Brook La
Great Easton LE16 20 D6
Northampton NN5 158 F8
Towcester NN12 203 A6
Brook St
9 Daventry NN11 135 C2
Hargrave NN9 115 E3
Moreton Pinkney NN11 199 C7
Northampton NN1 159 B7
Raunds NN9 114 D6
Brook St E NN8 130 B4
Brook St W NN8 129 F4
Brook Terr
1 Irthlingborough NN9 112 F2
Medbourne LE16 18 F6
Brook Vale NN8 129 C2
Brook Wlk NN14 95 A3
Brooke Ave PE9 241 A2
Brooke Cl Rushden NN10 132 B1
Wellingborough NN8 129 B5
Brooke Gn NN8 129 B5
Brooke Ho NN17 36 E6
Brooke House Sixth Form Coll LE16 31 E4
Brooke Mews NN8 129 B5
Brooke Rd NN18 53 B8
Brooke Specl Sch CV22 241 B6
Brooke Weston City Tech Coll NN18 36 D1
Brookend NN4 175 E5
Brookes Gr NN17 21 E1
Brookes Mews NN6 144 E5
Brookfield La MK18 240 D2
Brookfield Rd
Market Harborough LE16 31 C3
Northampton NN2 141 E2
Rushden NN10 132 A2
Brookhaven NN14 90 B4
Brookland Cres NN1 142 A1
Brookland Rd NN1,NN3 142 A1
Brooklands Cl NN11 135 C1
Brooklands Gdns LE16 31 E2
Brooks Cl
Burton Latimer NN15 92 C1
Willoughby CV23 117 D4
Brooks Ct MK18 240 D3
Brooks Rd NN9 114 F8
Brooksdale Cl NN16 72 B6
Brookside Bozeat NN29 164 D2
Desborough NN14 51 B2
Glapthorn PE8 26 C1
Hinton NN11 184 A6
Lillingstone Lovell MK18 227 A6
Southwick PE8 26 B5
Stanwick NN9 114 A3
Wappenham NN12 213 C8
Weedon NN7 155 B3
Brookside Cl
Old Stratford MK19 229 B6
Rugby CV22 241 C6
Yelvertoft NN6 82 B4
Brookside La NN11 153 A2
Brookside Mdws NN5 140 E1
Brookside Mews NN6 82 B4
Brookside Pl NN7 156 C2
Brookway MK19 228 E4
Broom Cl CV22 241 A6
Broom Ct 2 NN4 159 A3
Broom Way NN15 90 F8
Broome Way OX16 240 E9
Broomhill Cres NN3 143 A6

Brough Cl NN5 ....139 F1
Broughton Hill NN14 ....90 A6
Broughton Pl NN3 ....142 B3
Broughton Prim Sch
　NN14 ....90 A4
Broughton Rd
　Banbury OX16 ....240 B7
　Mawsley Village NN14 ...89 B3
　Old NN6 ....107 E8
　Pytchley NN14 ....90 E2
Brown's La NN14 ....95 C6
Brown's Way NN1 ......159 E5
Browne's Hospl PE9 ...241 D3
Browning Ave NN16 ....72 C5
Browning Cl 8 NN11 ...135 B4
　Wellingborough NN8 ...129 C4
Browning Rd Rugby CV21 ..99 B8
Browning Wlk NN17 ....36 D8
Brownlow Ct NN3 ......142 E4
Brownlow Quay PE9 ....241 E3
Brownlow St PE9 ......241 E3
Browns Cl NN3 ....126 D2
Browns Rd NN11 ....134 F1
Browns Yd NN12 ....203 C6
Brownsfield Rd NN12 ..217 E6
Brownswood Dr NN12 ..217 D3
Bruce St NN5 ....158 F6
Bruce Williams Way
　CV22 ....241 D7
Brundall Cl NN3 ......160 D7
Brunel Cl Daventry NN11 .134 F4
　Kettering NN16 ....72 A3
　Wellingborough NN8 ...129 B6
Brunel Ct NN17 ....22 A3
Brunel Dr NN5 ....158 D5
Brunel Rd NN17 ....22 A4
Brunswick Gdns NN18 ..35 F2
Brunswick Pl
　Banbury OX16 ....240 E8
　Northampton NN1 .....159 E7
Brunswick Wlk NN1 ....159 E7
Brunting Rd NN3 ......142 C8
Bryant Rd NN15 ....91 C7
Bryant Way NN10 ......132 B6
Bsns Ctr The NN5 .....158 F5
Buccleuch St NN16 ....72 B3
Buchanan Cl NN4 .....159 A3
Buchannan Rd CV22 ...241 A6
Buckfast Sq NN14 .....36 F4
Buckingham Cl
　Northampton NN4 .....175 B7
　Wellingborough NN8 ...129 E1
Buckingham Ct NN15 ..91 F7
Buckingham Hospl
　MK18 ....240 D4
Buckingham Prim Sch
　MK18 ....240 E5
Buckingham Rd
　Brackley NN13 ....234 A6
　Deanshanger MK19 ...228 F3
　Buckingham Sch MK18 .240 D2
　Buckingham Way NN12 .203 B5
Buckle Ho NN5 ....159 B5
Buckley Ct MK11 ......229 F4
Bucknell Wood Forest Wlk★
　NN12 ....214 B6
Bucknill Cres CV21 ....99 B7
Bucknills La NN6 ......100 F5
Buckwell Cl
　Desborough NN14 .....51 A3
　Wellingborough NN8 ...129 E5
Buckwell End NN8 .....129 F4
Buckwell La CV23 .....80 B6
Buckwell Pl NN8 ......129 F4
Budge Rd NN12 ....217 F5
Bugbrooke Com Prim Sch
　NN12 ....172 F7
Bugbrooke Rd
　Gayton NN7 ....173 D2
　Kislingbury NN7 .....157 D3
　Nether Heyford NN7 ..156 C1
Bugby Dr NN9 ....113 B5
Bugby Way NN9 ....114 D7
Bull Baulk OX17 ......220 A8
Bull Cl NN29 ....164 D3
Bull La OX17 ....1 A6
Bullock Rd PE7 ....29 C5
Bulls La OX17 ....230 F5
Bulwell Gn NN18 ......36 C6
Bungalows The
　Theddingworth LE17 ..46 D8
　Walgrave NN6 ....108 A5
Bunkers Hill Badby NN11 152 F2
　Gumley LE17 ....30 A5
Bunsty Ct MK11 ....229 F5
Bunting Cl NN15 ......92 A2
Bunting Rd NN2 ....141 D1
Bunting's La PE8 ......28 B3
Burchester Pl OX16 ...240 F9
Burcote Rd NN12 .....203 D4
Burditt Cl NN14 ......70 F6
Burford Ave NN3 .....142 D5
Burford Cl LE16 ......31 D1
Burford Way NN8 .....129 D1
Burgess Ct NN18 .....36 A4
Burgess Row LE16 ....21 B8
Burghley Hill Corby NN18 .36 F4
　Desborough NN14 .....51 A4
　Market Harborough LE16 .32 A3
Burghley Cl PE9 ......241 E3
Burghley Dr NN18 ....36 F5
Burghley La PE9 ......241 E2
Burghley Rd PE9 .....241 B5
Burghley St NN16 ....72 C4
Burham Cl NN4 ....175 E5

Burkitt Rd NN17 ......21 F3
Burleigh Ct MK18 ....240 F3
Burleigh Piece MK18 .240 E4
Burleigh Rd NN2 .....141 C1
Burlington Gdns OX16 .240 B6
Burmans Way NN7 ....161 E6
Burnell Cl NN14 ......95 B3
Burnham Pl NN13 .....224 B8
Burnmill Rd LE16 .....31 E5
Burns Cl NN6 ....145 A4
Burns Dr NN17 ....36 D8
Burns Rd Daventry NN11 135 B4
　Kettering NN16 ......72 C5
　Stamford PE9 ....241 B4
　Wellingborough NN8 ..129 C4
Burns St NN1 ....159 E7
Burnside CV22 ....241 B7
Burrows Cl NN11 .....119 E1
Burrows Ct NN3 ......142 E4
Burrows Farm La NN14 113 B8
Burryport Rd NN4 ....160 B2
Burton Cl NN11 ......135 C5
Burton Ho NN15 ......92 C2
Burton Rd NN9 ....111 F6
Burton Terr NN29 ....164 D3
Burtone Cl NN14 .....90 A4
Burtram Cl NN3 ......142 E1
Burwell Hill NN13 ....233 F8
Burwell Hill Cl NN13 .233 F8
Burwell Wlk NN16 ....36 C4
Burwood Rd NN3 .....142 B2
Bury Cl Cottingham LE16 .20 C1
　Higham Ferrers NN10 .132 C6
Bury Dyke NN6 ....101 A6
Bury Hill NN12 ....201 F6
Burystead Pl NN8 ....130 A4
Burystead Rise NN9 ..114 E7
Busby Cl MK18 ....240 F4
Bush Cl NN8 ....129 E5
Bush Hill NN3 ....142 C2
Bushacre Ct NN16 ....71 F3
Bushey Balk Cl NN16 .36 B1
Bushey Cl MK18 ......240 F4
Bushland Rd NN3 ....142 C2
Buswell Cl NN7 ......155 B3
Buswell Rise NN14 ...70 E7
Butcher's La
　Boughton NN2 ....125 C1
　Pattishall NN12 .....172 E1
　Pytchley NN14 ......90 F2
Butcher's Row OX16 ..240 D8
Butchers Paddock NN14 93 A7
Bute Cl NN17 ....36 B8
Butland Rd NN18 ....36 D2
Butler Gdns LE16 ....31 C1
Butlers Cl NN11 .....182 F2
Butlers Leap Ind Est
　CV21 ....241 F9
Butlin Cl Daventry NN11 135 B3
　Rothwell NN14 ......70 B7
Butlin Ct NN8 ....130 C1
Butlin Rd CV21 ......241 F8
Butlins La NN7 ......191 D4
Butt La LE17 ....45 E5
Butterfields NN8 ....129 F2
Buttermere NN8 .....129 C5
Buttermere Cl
　Kettering NN16 .....71 E3
　Northampton NN3 ...142 C3
Butterwick Wlk NN18 .36 C4
Buttmead NN7 ....190 D7
Butts Cl Aynho OX17 .237 C7
　Culworth NN11 ......198 D2
Butts Croft Cl NN4 ..175 C6
Butts Hill Cres NN7 ..173 A8
Butts Rd
　Northampton NN4 ...175 C6
　Raunds NN9 ....114 E6
　Wellingborough NN8 .129 F1
Butts The OX17 ......237 D8
Buxton Dr NN14 .....50 E4
By Pass Way NN8 ....178 B8
Bycell Rd MK18 .....226 B3
Byeway The OX16 ...240 F9
Byfield Rd
　Chipping Warden OX17 196 F7
　Eydon NN11 ....184 C2
　Hinton NN11 ....184 B7
　Northampton NN5 ...159 A5
　Priors Marston CV47 .166 E7
Byfield Sch NN11 ...183 C7
Byron Cl NN12 ......203 B5
Byron Cres
　Higham Ferrers NN10 132 A5
　Rushden NN10 ......131 E2
Byron Rd Corby NN17 .36 D8
　Kettering NN16 .....72 C5
　Wellingborough NN8 .129 D4
Byron St NN2 ....141 F1
Byron Way PE9 .....241 A3
Byron Wlk NN11 ....135 B3

C

Cabot Cl Daventry NN11 .135 C5
　Rothwell NN14 ......70 E6
Caernarvon Cl NN12 ..203 C4
Caesars Gate NN13 ...234 A6
Caistor Rd NN9 ......10 C1
Caithness Rd PE9 ....241 A4
Caldbeck Wlk 5 NN3 .142 C4
Caldecott Pl CV21 ...241 E7
Caldecott Rd
　Chelveston NN9 .....133 B7
　Rockingham LE16 ....21 B5
Caldecott St CV21,CV22 241 E7

Calder Cl Banbury OX16 .240 F9
　Corby NN17 ....21 D1
Calder Gn NN5 ....140 E1
Caledonian Ho 1 NN5 .159 A6
Callcott Dr NN15 .....92 A8
Calstock Rd NN11 ....160 D7
Calthorpe Rd OX16 ..240 C7
Calthorpe St OX16 ...240 C7
Calvert Cl NN12 .....202 E8
Calvert Rd NN12 ....202 E8
Calverton Rd MK11 ..229 D4
Cam Cl NN17 ....21 C1
Camberley Cl NN3 ...143 B2
Cambium Cl NN16 ...72 C2
Camborne Cl NN4 ...159 B2
Cambria Cres NN3 ...142 C1
Cambridge Ave NN17 .36 B6
Cambridge Rd PE9 ...241 C5
Cambridge St
　Kettering NN16 .....72 C3
　Northampton NN2 ...159 E8
　Rothwell NN14 .....70 D8
　Rugby CV21 ....241 E8
　Wellingborough NN8 .130 A5
　Wymington NN10 ....148 A7
Camden Sq NN29 ....164 D2
Camelot Way NN5 ...158 A7
Cameron Cl
　Daventry NN11 ......135 B1
　Northampton NN5 ...158 E7
Cameron Cres NN5 ..158 E7
Cameron Ct NN17 ...36 F5
Cameron Dr NN5 ....158 E7
Camp Cl NN7 ....173 A6
Camp Hill NN7 .....173 A6
Camp La NN7 ......157 D3
Campaign Cl 9 NN4 .175 E7
Campanula Cl NN3 ..160 C6
Campbell Cl
　Buckingham MK18 ..240 F3
　Towcester NN12 ....203 C8
　Weedon NN7 ....155 A4
Campbell Rd Corby NN17 .36 F5
　Wellingborough NN8 .130 A2
Campbell Sq 1 NN1 .159 D6
Campbell St
　Northampton NN1 ..159 C7
　Rugby CV21 ....241 A8
Campion Cl NN10 ...148 B8
Campion Cl NN3 ....143 B1
Campion Sch NN7 ..173 A8
Camrose Ct NN5 ....159 A8
Camsdale Wlk LE16 ..35 C8
Canada Cl OX16 ....240 D9
Canada Sq NN18 ....36 C3
Canal Mus The★ NN12 205 A8
Canal St OX16 ......240 D7
Canalside
　Old Stratford MK19 .229 C7
　Stoke Bruerne NN12 .205 A8
Canberra Ho NN17 ..22 F1
Candace Ct NN5 ....158 E8
Candleford NN3 ....143 B4
Canford Gn NN18 ...36 A6
Cannam Cl LE16 ....20 B1
Cannock Rd NN17 ..36 F8
Cannon St NN8 .....130 A5
Canon Harnett Ct MK12 229 F6
Canon St NN16 .....72 B3
Canonbury NN8 ....129 C4
Canons Ashby★ NN11 .185 D2
Canons Ashby Rd NN11 .185 B5
Canons Ashby Rd NN11 199 D7
Canons Wlk NN2 ...141 B4
Cantell Cl MK18 ....240 D4
Canterbury Cl OX16 .219 A4
Cantle Cl NN18 .....36 D3
Capell Gdns NN18 ..36 E4
Capell Rise NN7 ....155 E5
Cappenham Cl NN12 203 B6
Captain's Ct NN7 ...177 E1
Cardigan Cl 4 NN5 .158 F8
Cardigan Ho NN17 ..36 E6
Cardigan Pl Corby NN17 .36 E5
　Kettering NN16 ....72 D2
Cardigan Rd NN14 ..37 E2
Cardinal Cl NN4 ....175 B7
Cares Orch NN7 ....161 D2
Carey Cl NN3 ......126 B1
Carey Ct NN3 ......126 B1
Carey Dr NN17 ....36 C8
Carey Ho 2 NN16 ..72 B2
Carey Rd Hackleton NN7 .177 A3
　Towcester NN12 ....203 C3
Carey St Kettering NN16 .72 C3
　Northampton NN1 ..159 E7
Carey Way NN10 ...132 D3
Careys Rd NN12 ...215 F7
Carina Rd NN15 ....91 C5
Carisbrooke Cl NN15 .91 F8
Carisbrooke Ct MK18 240 E5
Carisbrooke Gr PE9 .241 A3
Carline Ct NN3 ....142 D4
Carlow Rd NN14 ...95 A3
Carlow St NN14 ...95 A3
Carlton Cl NN10 ...148 A7
Carlton Gdns NN2 .141 E2
Carlton Mews NN10 132 C5
Carlton Pl NN18 ...36 B6
Carlton Rd
　Northampton NN2 ..141 E2
　Wilbarston LE16 ...34 D5
Carlton St NN16 ...72 A3
Carlyle Ave NN5 ...158 E7
Carmarthen Way NN10 148 C8
Carne The MK11 ...229 E5
Carnegie St NN10 .132 A2

Carol Trusler Mews
　NN2 ....159 B7
Carousel Way NN3 ..160 F7
Carpetbeggar + Northants
　Aviation Mus★ NN6 ..68 F3
Carr's Way NN7 ....157 C6
Carradale Cl NN16 ..72 A6
Carrdus Sch The OX17 219 C8
Carriage Dr NN16 ..72 C6
Carriers Cl MK19 ..207 A2
Carrington Gdns 1
　NN3 ....160 F8
Carrington St NN16 .72 B2
Carron Cl NN17 ....21 C1
Carsington Cl NN16 .71 E3
Carter Ave NN14 ...90 A3
Carter Cl NN8 .....130 B4
Cartmel Pl NN3 ....142 C3
Cartmel Way NN10 .132 D3
Cartrill St NN9 ....114 C6
Cartwright Cres NN13 233 D7
Cartwright Gdns OX17 237 D7
Cartwright Rd
　Charlton OX17 .....231 E5
　Northampton NN2 ...141 C1
Casterbridge Ct NN4 175 E2
Casterton Cl NN16 ..114 A5
Casterton Rd PE9 ...241 B4
Castilian St NN1 ...159 D5
Castilian Terr NN1 .159 D5
Castle Ashby Craft Ctr★
　NN7 ....162 F3
Castle Ashby Gdns★
　NN7 ....163 B3
Castle Ashby Rd NN7 179 B7
Castle Ave NN5 ....158 C8
Castle Bush NN5 ...158 C8
Castle Cl Corby NN18 .36 A4
　Northampton NN5 ..158 C8
Castle Ct
　Buckingham MK18 ..240 D3
　Rushden NN10 .....148 A8
　Wellingborough NN8 130 B4
Castle Dyke PE9 ...241 D3
Castle Gdns NN14 ..54 B3
Castle Hill
　Daventry NN11 .....135 B1
　Rothwell NN14 ....70 D7
Castle La NN8 .....130 B4
Castle Mews NN8 ..130 B4
Castle Mound CV23 .99 C2
Castle Mount NN13 233 E5
Castle Quay Sh Ctr
　OX16 ....240 D8
Castle Rd Lavendon MK46 180 F1
　Wellingborough NN8 130 B4
　Woodford Halse NN11 184 C6
Castle St Banbury OX16 240 D8
　Buckingham MK18 ..240 D3
　Deddington OX15 ...236 A4
　Northampton NN1 ..159 C6
　Rugby CV21 ....241 D8
　Stamford PE9 ......241 D3
　Wellingborough NN8 130 B4
Castle View Barnwell PE8 59 B7
　Wellingborough NN8 130 B4
Castle Way Kettering NN15 91 A4
　Wellingborough NN8 130 A4
Castlethorpe Fst Sch
　MK19 ....218 F5
Castlethorpe Rd MK19 206 F1
Castleton Rd NN14 .50 E4
Caswell Rd NN4 ....160 B1
Catchland Cl NN8 ..36 C2
Catchpole Cl NN18 .36 D3
Catesby Cl NN2 ....141 E4
Catesby End NN11 .151 D1
Catesby Rd Rothwell NN14 70 E7
　Rugby CV22 ....241 B6
Catesby St NN16 ...72 C3
Catherine Ct MK18 .240 E5
Catlow Cl NN9 .....114 C8
Cattle End
　Farthingstone NN12 170 F3
　Silverstone NN12 ..214 C4
Cattle Hill NN3 ....143 C2
Cattle Market Rd NN1 159 C4
Catton Cl NN16 ....85 B8
Catton Cres NN3 ..140 F5
Cauldecott Cl NN4 ..158 D1
Causeway OX16 ....240 F8
Causeway Rd NN17 .21 E2
Causeway The
　Byfield NN11 ......183 E8
　Northampton NN3 ..161 C7
Causin Cl NN14 ....55 F8
Causin Way PE8 ...40 C8
Cavalry Dr NN11 ..135 B1
Cavalry Fields NN7 155 A4
Cavalry Hill NN7 ..155 A4
Cavendish Cl NN15 .91 F5
Cavendish Ctyd NN17 22 E1
Cavendish Dr NN3 ..160 D6
Cawley Rd OX17 ...230 B5
Caxton Cl NN11 ....135 A4
Caxton St LE16 ....31 F1
Caythorpe Sq NN18 .36 B6
Cecil Cl NN14 .....55 F8
Cecil Ct NN18 .....36 F4
Cecil Dr NN18 .....36 F4
Cecil Rd NN2 ......141 C2
Cecil St Kettering NN16 .72 C4
　Rothwell NN14 ....70 D7
Cedar Cl Brackley NN13 222 F2
　Daventry NN11 .....135 C5
　Desborough NN14 ..51 C2
　Irchester NN29 ....147 A7
　Rushden NN10 .....148 A8

Cedar Cl continued
　Sywell NN6 ....143 D8
　Towcester NN12 ....203 C4
Cedar Ct NN11 .....21 E1
Cedar Dr NN14 ....76 D1
Cedar Hythe NN6 ..124 D1
Cedar Rd Kettering NN16 72 C4
　Northampton NN1,NN3 142 A1
Cedar Rd E NN3 ...142 A1
Cedar Road Lower Sch
　NN3 ....142 A1
Cedar Villa OX16 ..240 B8
Cedar Way
　Higham Ferrers NN10 132 B6
　Wellingborough NN8 130 A7
Cedrus Ct NN2 .....140 F6
Celandine Cl NN10 148 C7
Celeborn Pl NN3 ..143 B5
Celtic Way NN6 ...100 C6
Cemetery La NN16 132 B6
Centaine Rd NN10 .132 A1
Centec Ct MK19 ..229 B7
Central Ave Hinton NN11 184 A7
　Kettering NN16 ....72 D3
　Northampton NN2 ..141 B6
　Wellingborough NN8 129 E2
Central Mus & Art Gall★
　NN1 ....159 D5
Centre 2000 NN16 .71 F4
Centre Par NN16 ..72 C4
Centre St OX16 ...240 E9
Chace Rd NN8 ....130 C4
Chacombe CE Prim Sch
　OX17 ....208 F4
Chacombe Rd OX17 208 F1
Chadleigh Ct NN13 233 E6
Chadstone Ave NN2 141 D6
Chadwick Gdns NN5 140 D1
Chaffinch Cl NN4 ..174 F7
Chaffinch Way NN13 222 E1
Chainbridge La PE28 97 F1
Chalcombe Ave NN2 141 C5
Chalcombe Rd NN2 141 C4
Chalfont Ct 14 NN1 159 C7
Chalk La NN1 .....159 B6
Chamberlain Ave NN8 129 E1
Chamberlain Rd CV21 99 B8
Chamberlain Way
　Higham Ferrers NN10 132 C5
　Raunds NN9 ....114 C5
Chambers Hill NN14 89 B4
Champion Ct NN13 233 E8
Chancel Terr PE8 ..59 B5
Chancery La NN14 76 D2
Chandler Gdns NN14 76 E1
Chandlers Way NN17 36 E5
Chandos Cl MK18 ..240 D2
Chandos Ct MK18 ..240 D2
Chandos Rd MK18 ..240 D2
Channing St 8 NN16 72 C2
Chantelle Ct 1 NN11 135 B3
Chantry Cl NN3 ...143 B3
Chantry La NN12 .203 C6
Chapel Cl Clifton OX15 236 E4
　Great Addington NN14 94 B2
　Litchborough NN12 171 C1
　Silverstone NN12 .214 D4
Chapel Ct PE8 ....8 B2
Chapel End
　Croughton NN13 ..238 C8
　Great Gidding PE17 61 D2
　Piddington NN7 ...177 A2
Chapel Fields LE17 62 B3
Chapel Gn NN5 ...141 A2
Chapel Hill
　Higham Ferrers NN10 132 B7
　Irchester NN29 ...147 B8
　Islip NN14 ....76 B2
　Little Addington NN14 113 B7
　Silverstone NN12 .214 D4
Chapel Ho NN4 ...159 B3
Chapel La
　Adderbury OX17 ..230 A4
　Badby NN11 ......153 A3
　Barrowden LE15 ..3 F5
　Blisworth NN7 ...190 D8
　Brafield-on-t-G NN7 161 E2
　Clipston LE16 ....66 F8
　Corby NN17 ......37 B6
　Crick NN6 ....101 A5
　Daventry NN11 ...135 C2
　Denford NN14 ....95 C6
　Elton PE8 ....28 C8
　Farthinghoe NN13 221 B4
　Flore NN7 ....155 F5
　Geddington NN14 .54 A2
　Great Doddington NN29 145 E6
　Hackleton NN7 ..177 B2
　Ketton PE9 ......1 A5
　Lilbourne CV23 ...81 A6
　Lillingstone Lovell MK18 227 A1
　Little Harrowden NN9 110 C4
　Maidford NN12 ..186 D6
　Old NN6 ....107 C7
　Rushton NN14 ...52 C2
　Slapton NN12 ....201 E2
　Stanion NN14 ....37 E2
　Stanwick NN9 ....114 A3
　Stoke Albany LE16 34 B4
　Stoke Bruerne NN12 205 A8
　Turweston NN13 ..234 B7
　Whitfield NN13 ...223 D3
　Wilbarston LE16 ..34 C5
Chapel Rd
　Greatworth OX17 .210 E1
　Weldon NN17 .....38 A8
Chapel Row NN3 ..143 C2

Chapel St
Charwelton NN11 ....168 A4
Kilsby CV23 ....100 A2
Ringstead NN14 ....95 A3
Rugby CV21 ....241 C8
Swinford LE17 ....62 B3
Titchmarsh NN14 ......77 C4
Warmington PE8 ....28 B3
Chapel View NN14 ....90 B5
Chapel Yd PE9 ......241 D3
Chaplins La NN14 .....51 A3
Chapman Cl NN12 ....203 C7
Chapman Gr NN17 ....36 E8
Chapmans Cl
Irchester NN29 ....147 B8
Stoke Albany LE16 .....34 B4
Chapmans Dr MK19 ..229 B7
Chapmans La OX15 ..236 A3
Chappell Ho 5 NN3 ..126 C1
Chardonnay Cl NN5 ..140 D2
Charlbury Cl NN8 .....145 E8
Charles Cl
Higham Ferrers NN10 ..132 C7
Long Buckby NN6 .....121 B3
Old NN6 ....107 D7
Charles Ct OX16 .....240 D7
Charles Rd PE9 ......241 C5
Charles Robinson Ct
NN8 ....129 E3
Charles St Corby NN17 ..36 F5
Kettering NN16 ....72 B4
Market Harborough LE16 ..31 D3
Northampton NN1 .....159 D7
Rothwell NN14 ....70 C6
Rugby CV21 ....241 B8
Thrapston NN14 ....76 E2
Wellingborough NN8 ..129 E2
Charles Terr 8 NN11 ..135 C1
Charles Warren Cl
CV21 ....241 D8
Charlesfield Rd CV22 ..98 A8
Charlotte Pl NN16 ....72 E4
Charlotte St CV21 ....241 D8
Charlton Cl NN2 .....141 C5
Charlton Rd OX17 ....237 C7
Charlton Way NN13 ..221 B4
Charmandean Sch
MK18 ....226 B4
Charnwood 1 NN8 ...130 A5
Charnwood Ave NN3 ..142 E2
Charnwood Cl 5 NN11 ..135 B4
Charnwood Ct NN3 ...142 E2
Charnwood Dr NN15 ..92 A5
Charnwood Rd NN17 ..36 F7
Charter Gate NN3 ....142 B6
Charter Rd CV22 ......98 E8
Charterhouse Cl NN13 ..233 E7
Chartwell Ave NN3 ...142 C5
Charwelton La NN11 ..167 D8
Charwelton Rd NN11 ..169 C2
Chase Barn Cotts OX27 ..239 B3
Chase Cl NN14 ....37 E3
Chase Farm NN14 ....54 B2
Chase Hill NN14 ......54 A3
Chase Park Rd NN7 ..179 A5
Chase The
Long Buckby NN6 .....121 B4
Pitsford NN6 ....125 D4
Chase View Rd NN14 ..54 B2
Chaseport Cl MK46 ..194 D2
Chaston Pl NN16 .....72 E5
Chatellerault Ct NN17 ..36 D8
Chater Cl LE16 ....32 A6
Chatsworth Ave
Kettering NN15 ....91 C5
Northampton NN3 .....142 F5
Chatsworth Dr
Market Harborough LE16 ..32 B3
Wellingborough NN8 ..129 C7
Chatsworth Rd PE9 ..241 B4
Chaucer Ct NN2 .....141 F1
Chaucer Ho NN2 .....141 F2
Chaucer Rd Rugby CV22 ..98 A7
Wellingborough NN8 ..129 D4
Chaucer St NN2 .....141 F1
Chaucer Way NN11 ..135 B2
Cheaney Dr NN4 .....175 E2
Cheddar Cl NN5 .....158 D7
Cheddar Wlk NN18 ....36 A6
Chedworth Cl NN3 ...143 D2
Cheese La 5 NN6 ....130 A4
Chelfham Cl NN3 .....160 D7
Chelmorton Vale NN14 ..50 E4
Chelmscote Row OX17 ..208 C3
Chelmsford Cl NN4 ...159 A2
Cheltenham Cl NN10 ..148 C8
Chelveston Base Cres
NN9 ....133 D5
Chelveston Dr NN17 ..36 B7
Chelveston Rd
Higham Ferrers NN10 ..132 E7
Raunds NN9 ....114 C4
Stanwick NN9 ....114 B3
Chenderit Sch OX17 ..209 A1
Cheney Ct OX17 .....208 F1
Cheney Gdns OX17 ..208 F2
Cheney Rd OX16 .....240 F10
Chepstow Cl
Kettering NN15 ....91 C1
Northampton NN5 .....159 A7
Chepstow Dr NN8 ....129 C7
Chequers La
Grendon NN7 ....163 E5
Ravensthorpe NN6 ....103 D1
Wellingborough NN8 ..130 A5
Chequers The MK19 ..218 F5
Cheriton Cl NN11 ....135 C6
Cheriton Rd NN18 ....36 F4

Cheriton Way NN1 ...160 C6
Cherry Ave NN8 .....130 A7
Cherry Blossom Cl NN3 ..143 B2
Cherry Cl NN3 ....142 C2
Cherry Ct NN9 ....112 E1
Cherry Hill NN6 ......107 E6
Cherry Lodge Rd NN3 ..143 B3
Cherry Orch Olney MK46 ..195 E4
Rushden NN10 ....132 C1
Cherry Orchard Mid Sch
NN3 ....142 C1
Cherry Rd Banbury OX16 ..240 A9
Kettering NN16 ....72 D4
Cherry St
Irthlingborough NN9 ..112 E1
Ringstead NN14 ....95 B3
Cherry Tree Cl
Desborough NN14 .....51 B2
Husbands Bosworth LE17 ..45 E5
Cherry Tree La NN4 ..160 E3
Cherry Wlk NN9 .....114 B5
Cherryholt La PE9 ...241 E3
Cherryholt Rd PE9 ...241 F3
Cherrytree Wlk NN3 ..143 D8
Cherwell Banks OX17 ..231 A6
Cherwell Gn NN5 ....140 F1
Cherwell St OX16 ....240 D9
Cherwell Terr NN11 ..184 C6
Cherwell The NN11 ..134 F1
Cherwell Wlk NN17 ..21 C1
Chesham Rise NN3 ...143 B4
Chesil Wlk NN18 .....36 A6
Chester Ave NN7 ....157 B6
Chester Cl NN15 .....91 B6
Chester Ho NN3 .....161 B8
Chester Rd
Irchester NN29 ....131 A1
Rushden NN10 ....131 F3
Wellingborough NN8 ..130 C4
Chester St CV21 .....241 E9
Chestnut Ave Corby NN17 ..21 D1
Kettering NN15 ....72 C1
Northampton NN4 .....175 D5
Chestnut Cl Hinton NN11 ..184 A6
Long Buckby NN6 .....121 B3
Milton Malsor NN7 ....174 E4
Rushden NN10 ....131 F3
Stony Stratford MK11 ..229 D5
Wymington NN10 .....148 B5
Chestnut Cotts MK18 ..240 C2
Chestnut Dr
Brackley NN13 ....222 F1
Desborough NN14 .....51 C2
Chestnut Field CV21 ..241 C8
Chestnut Gn NN13 ...223 E4
Chestnut Gr LE16 ....67 A8
Chestnut Rd
Northampton NN3 .....142 A1
Yardley Gobion NN12 ..217 F6
Chestnut Terr NN3 ...142 A2
Chestnuts The
Castlethorpe MK19 ...218 F5
Clifton OX15 ....236 E4
Chettle Pl NN12 .....217 E2
Chetwode OX17 .....219 C6
Chetwode Cl MK18 ..240 E5
Cheviot Cl NN16 .....72 B7
Cheviot Ct NN4 ......158 E3
Cheviot Ho NN2 .....141 C5
Chewton Cl NN5 .....158 D7
Cheyne Cl MK18 .....240 E4
Cheyne Wlk
Kettering NN15 ....91 B4
Northampton NN1 .....159 E5
Chichele Cl NN10 ....132 B5
Chichele Coll★ NN10 ..132 B6
Chichele St NN10 ....132 B3
Chichele St NN10 ....132 C6
Chicherley Cotts NN14 ..76 D2
Chichester Cl
Daventry NN11 ....135 D1
Rothwell NN14 ....70 E6
Chieftan Bsns Pk NN8 ..129 A6
Child's St NN14 ......95 C6
Chiltern Ave NN5 ....158 D8
Chiltern Cl
Market Harborough LE16 ..31 F5
Northampton NN5 .....158 D8
Chiltern Lower Sch
NN5 ....158 E8
Chiltern Rd
Daventry NN11 ....135 B5
Kettering NN16 ....72 B6
Chiltern Way NN5 ...158 E8
Chilwell Ct 3 NN3 ...160 F8
Chipping Warden Sch
OX17 ....196 F7
Chipsey Ave
Bugbrooke NN7 ....172 F8
Northampton NN1 .....160 B6
Choakles The NN4 ...176 B6
Chowns Mill Bsns Pk
NN9 ....113 B1
Christchurch Cl OX16 ..240 D8
Christchurch Dr NN11 ..153 B7
Christchurch Rd NN1 ..160 A7
Christie Way NN15 ....90 F8
Christine Ct NN9 .....114 D6
*Christopher Rawlins CE Prim
Sch* OX17 ....230 A4
*Christopher Reeves Lower
Sch* NN29 ....147 E1
Chulmleigh Wlk NN3 ..160 C7
Church Ave OX17 ....230 D5
Church Bank LE16 ....20 D7
Church Cl
Adderbury OX17 ......230 A3
Braybrooke LE16 .....49 E6

Church Cl *continued*
Caldecott LE16 ....21 B8
Clipston LE16 ....67 A8
Hartwell NN7 ....192 D2
Milton Malsor NN7 ....174 F4
Wardington OX17 .....196 E1
West Haddon NN6 ....102 C5
Wicken MK19 ....228 B3
Wymington NN10 .....148 B5
Church Ct PE9 ......241 D2
Church Dr NN18 .....53 C8
Church End
Croughton NN13 ......238 D8
Piddington NN7 ....177 A2
Pottersbury NN12 ....217 E3
Roade NN7 ....191 D4
Syresham NN13 ......224 C8
Church Farm Cl NN29 ..164 D3
Church Farm Way LE16 ..68 C7
Church Fields NN11 ..152 C7
Church Gdns NN6 ...103 E1
Church Gn Badby NN11 ..153 A2
Barnwell PE8 ....59 B6
Northampton NN5 .....140 F2
Woodford NN14 ......94 D6
Church Hall Rd NN10 ..131 F1
Church Hill Badby NN11 ..152 F1
Barnwell PE8 ....59 B6
Finedon NN9 ....111 E4
Geddington NN14 .....54 A3
Hollowell NN6 ....104 B4
Moulton NN3 ....126 C1
Northampton NN4 ....175 E6
Ravensthorpe NN6 ...103 D1
Church La
Adderbury OX17 ......230 A3
Alderton NN12 ....204 F2
Banbury OX16 ....240 D8
Barnwell PE8 ....59 B6
Barrowden LE15 ......3 F4
Blisworth NN7 ....190 D7
Bozeat NN29 ....164 D3
Brafield-on-t-G NN7 ..161 E2
Broughton NN14 ......89 F6
Bugbrooke NN7 ......172 E7
Burton Latimer NN15 ..92 C2
Bythorn PE28 ....97 D4
Caldecott LE16 ....21 B8
Caldecott MK44 ......133 F3
Chacombe OX17 .....208 E4
Church Brampton NN6 ..140 B8
Claydon OX17 ....181 D1
Clipston LE16 ....67 A8
Cold Ashby NN6 .....84 A5
Cold Higham NN12 ...188 C8
Covington PE18 ......116 C2
Cranford NN14 ....93 B7
Croughton NN13 .....238 D8
Deanshanger MK19 ..228 E4
Denford NN14 ....95 C6
Dingley LE16 ....33 A4
Duddington PE9 ......5 B6
East Carlton LE16 ....35 A7
East Haddon NN6 ....122 D4
Evenley NN13 ....233 F3
Great Doddington NN29 ..145 E6
Harrington NN6 ......69 B6
Hellidon NN11 ....151 C1
Husbands Bosworth LE17 ..45 E5
Kislingbury NN7 ......157 D3
Lillingstone Lovell MK18 ..227 A6
Lower Harlestone NN7 ..139 E6
Lyddington LE15 .....9 D6
Maidford NN12 ......186 D6
Middleton Cheney OX17 ..208 F1
Morcott LE15 ....3 A6
Nether Heyford NN7 ..156 B2
Newton Bromswold NN10 ..149 D8
Northampton NN1 ....159 C6
Northampton,Billinge NN3 ..161 A8
Pitsford NN6 ....125 D5
Pottersbury NN12 ....217 E3
Slapton NN12 ....201 E2
Slipton NN14 ....75 A3
South Kilworth LE17 ..63 C8
South Luffenham LE15 ..3 E8
Spratton NN6 ....105 B1
Stamford PE9 ....241 E2
Stibbington PE8 .....8 D2
Stoke Bruerne NN12 ..205 A8
Stoke Doyle PE8 .....41 D1
Swinford NN6 ....62 F2
Sywell NN6 ....127 E3
Thornby NN6 ....84 D4
Walgrave NN6 ....108 A4
Warmington PE8 .....28 B3
Welford NN6 ....64 E5
Wicken MK19 ....228 B3
Wilby NN8 ....129 B1
Wollaston NN29 .....146 D3
Wymington NN10 ....148 B5
Yardley Hastings NN7 ..179 B7
Church Leys NN13 ..233 E3
Church Mount NN6 ..103 D6
Church Piece Cotts
NN13 ....221 B4
Church Pk PE8 ......7 D8
Church Rd Brackley NN13 ..233 F7
Braunston NN11 .....118 B1
Grafton Regis NN12 ..205 D2
Greatworth OX17 ....210 E1
Hargrave NN9 ....115 F1
Ketton PE9 ....1 A5
Piddington NN7 ......177 A2
Pytchley NN14 ....91 A1
Spratton NN6 ....124 B8
Upper Boddington NN11 ..182 C7
Church Sq 6 LE16 ...31 E3

Church St
Blakesley NN12 ......187 B1
Boughton NN2 ....141 C8
Brigstock NN14 ......55 F7
Brixworth NN6 ....106 B3
Broughton NN14 .....90 B4
Buckingham MK18 ..240 C3
Burton Latimer NN15 ..92 C3
Byfield NN11 ....183 D7
Charwelton NN11 ....168 B4
Clifton u D CV23 ....80 A5
Cogenhoe NN7 ......162 A6
Cottingham LE16 ....20 D1
Crick NN6 ....100 F6
Easton o t H PE9 ....2 A6
Finedon NN9 ....111 E4
Hargrave NN9 ....115 E2
Helmdon NN13 ......211 F3
Husbands Bosworth LE17 ..45 E5
Irthlingborough NN9 ..112 F2
Isham NN14 ....91 F1
Long Buckby NN6 ...121 B4
Market Harborough LE16 ..31 E3
Mears Ashby NN6 ...128 B2
Moulton NN3 ....126 C1
Naseby NN6 ....85 B8
Nassington PE8 .....15 F5
Nether Heyford NN7 ..156 B2
Newnham NN11 .....153 E4
Olney MK46 ....195 F4
Oundle PE8 ....42 A5
Pattishall NN12 .....172 C1
Polebrook PE8 ......42 F3
Raunds NN9 ....114 E7
Ringstead NN14 .....95 B3
Rothersthorpe NN7 ..174 A6
Rugby CV21 ....241 C8
Rushden NN10 ......132 B2
Sibbertoft NN6 ......47 A2
Silverstone NN12 ...214 D5
Stamford PE9 ....241 E2
Stanwick NN9 ....114 A3
Staverton NN11 .....152 C1
Stony Stratford MK11 ..229 D5
Sulgrave OX17 ......210 F7
Titchmarsh NN14 ...77 C4
Wadenhoe PE8 .....58 A3
Warmington PE8 ....28 B2
Watford NN6 ....120 C6
Weedon NN7 ....155 C3
Weldon NN17 ....38 B7
Wellingborough NN8 ..130 A4
Wilbarston LE16 ....34 C5
Woodford NN14 ....94 D6
Woodford Halse NN11 ..184 C6
Church View
Banbury OX16 ......240 B6
Brackley NN13 ......234 A7
Broughton NN14 ....90 A4
Burton Latimer NN15 ..92 C3
Ecton NN6 ....143 F4
Greens Norton NN12 ..202 E8
Keyston PE28 ......97 A3
Moulton NN3 ....126 C2
Northampton NN4 ...175 E5
Raunds NN9 ....114 D7
Walgrave NN6 ......108 A5
Weldon NN17 ......38 B7
Church View Rd NN14 ..51 B2
Church Way Denton NN7 ..178 B8
Ecton NN6 ....143 F4
Grendon NN7 ....163 D5
Northampton NN3 ...160 E7
Preston Capes NN11 ..169 D2
Thorpe Malsor NN14 ..71 A3
1 Wellingborough NN8 ..130 A4
Whittlebury NN12 ...215 C5
Church Way Ct NN3 ..160 D8
Church Wlk
Banbury OX16 ......240 C7
Barby CV23 ....99 C1
Bozeat NN29 ....164 D3
Corby NN17 ....37 B6
Daventry NN11 .....135 C2
Denford NN14 ......95 C6
5 Irthlingborough NN9 ..112 F2
Kettering NN16 .....72 B6
Kilsby CV23 ....100 A3
Little Addington NN14 ..113 B8
Lubenham LE16 ....30 F3
Market Harborough LE16 ..32 A2
Newton Bromswold NN10 ..149 D8
Northampton NN3 ...143 B2
Ringstead NN14 ....95 B3
Rugby CV21,CV22 ..241 C7
Weldon NN17 ......38 B7
Churchcroft NN7 ...191 D4
Churchfield NN2 ....141 E4
Churchill Ave
Irthlingborough NN9 ..113 B5
Northampton NN3 ...142 B4
Wellingborough NN8 ..129 E2
Churchill Cl NN14 ...70 E7
Churchill Rd
Earls Barton NN6 ...144 F4
Rugby CV22 ....241 C6
Stamford PE9 ......241 C5
Welton NN11 ....135 E8
Churchill Way
Brackley NN13 ......233 F6
Burton Latimer NN15 ..92 B2
Daventry NN11 .....153 E7
Kettering NN15 .....72 F1
Churchway NN3 ....160 D8
Cider Cl LE15 ......3 F5
Cinnamon Cl 5 NN4 ..175 D6
Circus End NN5 ....140 C1
Circus Gr PE8 ......42 F2

Cissbury Rd NN4 ...158 F4
Clailey Ct MK11 ....229 F5
Clannell Rd NN4 ....175 A8
Clare Ave NN11 ....135 C2
Clare Cl Earls Barton NN6 ..144 F3
Stamford PE9 ....241 C3
Clare Cres NN12 ...203 B5
Clare Ct CV21 ......241 B8
Clare Dr NN14 .....76 E3
Clare Rd NN8 ......129 C3
Clare St
Northampton NN1 ...159 E7
Raunds NN9 ....114 D6
Clare Wlk NN10 ....132 B5
Claregate NN4 .....175 B8
Claremont Ave MK11 ..229 E4
Claremont Ct 13 NN1 ..159 C6
Claremont Dr LE16 ..32 A3
Claremont Rd CV21 ..241 E8
Clarence Ave NN2 ..141 C2
Clarence Ct NN10 ..148 A8
Clarence Rd
Kettering NN16 .....72 C3
Rugby CV21 ....241 E8
Stony Stratford MK11 ..229 E5
Clarence St LE16 ..31 F3
Clark Cl NN9 ......113 B4
Clark Cres NN12 ..203 C8
Clarke Cl NN16 ...72 A4
Clarke Cl NN6 ....144 F4
Clarke Ho NN1 ...160 A8
Clarke Rd Corby NN17 ..36 D8
Northampton NN1 ..160 A8
Clarke St LE16 ...31 D3
Clarkes Dale LE16 ..20 D6
Clarkes Way
Brackley NN13 .....233 D7
Welton NN11 ......135 D8
Clarks La NN11 ...221 A3
Claughton Rd NN4 ..159 D3
Clay La NN17 .....10 B1
Claydon Cl NN8 ...129 E5
Clayfield Cl NN3 ..142 B6
Clayland Cl NN29 ..164 C2
Claystones NN4 ...158 D2
Cleaver Ct NN15 ..72 A1
Cleavers La NN6 ..107 D7
Cleburne Cl NN9 ..114 A4
Clee Rise NN5 ....158 D8
Cleeve Way NN8 ..129 D1
Clement Bois NN13 ..233 E8
Cleveland Ave NN16 ..72 C6
Cleveland Pl NN4 ..159 A2
Clickers Yd MK46 ..195 F4
Clifden Terr NN6 ..122 D4
Cliff Cres PE9 ....241 D3
Cliff Rd PE9 ......241 D3
Cliffe Rd PE9 .....2 A3
Clifton Cl Kettering NN15 ..72 C1
Long Buckby NN6 ..121 C4
Clifton Dr PE8 ....41 E5
Clifton Gr NN15 ..72 C1
Clifton Rd
Deddington OX15 ..236 B4
Rugby CV21 ....241 F8
Clifton Sq NN17 ..36 E8
Cliftonville NN1 ..159 E5
Cliftonville Ct 11 NN1 ..159 F6
Cliftonville Mid Sch
NN1 ....159 F5
Cliftonville Rd NN1 ..159 F5
Clinton Rd NN4 ...159 B3
Clipston Endowed Prim Sch
LE16 ....67 A8
Clipston Field Pl 7
NN3 ....143 C2
Clipston La LE16 ..48 E3
Clipston Rd
East Farndon LE16 ..48 B4
Great Oxendon LE16 ..48 D2
Clipston St LE16 ..31 F1
Clipston Way NN5 ..140 D1
Clipstone Ct NN14 ..70 C6
Clive Cl NN15 ....72 E1
Clock Tower Ct NN3 ..142 E6
Cloisters The
Daventry NN11 ....135 D2
Priors Hardwick CV47 ..166 A5
Rushden NN10 .....132 B2
Wellingborough NN8 ..130 B4
Close Rd NN7 ....156 B1
Close The
Chipping Warden OX17 ..196 F6
Eastcote NN12 ....188 F8
Easton o t H PE9 ..1 F4
Greatworth OX17 ..210 E1
Irthlingborough NN9 ..112 F1
Kettering NN15 ....91 B8
Northampton NN2 ..141 C4
Roade NN7 ....191 D4
Stamford PE9 .....241 E4
Swinford LE17 ....62 B4
Weston Underwood MK46 ..195 A1
Cloutsham St NN1 ..159 E7
Clovelly Ct NN18 ..36 F4
Clover Dr Rushden NN10 ..148 C8
Thrapston NN14 ...76 D2
Clover End MK18 ..240 C2
Clover Field NN4 ..175 F2
Clover Gdns NN16 ..72 B4
Clover La NN2 ....141 B5
Club La NN14 ....94 D6
Club St NN16 ....72 C3
Clumber Ct NN18 ..36 B6
Clumber Dr NN3 ..160 E7

Clun Wlk NN17 . . . . .21 C1
Clwyd Wlk NN17 . . . . .21 C1
Clydesdale Rd NN17 . . . .36 D7
Co-operative Row
NN10 . . . . .132 B1
Coach Ho The NN3 . . . . . . .160 B7
Coach Yd NN12 . . . . .217 E3
Coaching Wlk NN3 . . . . . . .142 D2
Coales Gdns LE16 . . . . .31 D5
Coalport Cl NN14 . . . . .50 F3
Cob Dr NN4 . . . . .158 B1
Cobb's La NN29 . . . . .146 D3
Cobblers Cl NN12 . . . . . . .187 B1
Cobblestone Ct NN4 . . . . .158 D2
Cobbs Gdn MK46 . . . . .195 F4
Cobden St NN16 . . . . .72 A3
Cobham Cl MK18 . . . . .240 C4
Cockbrook La PE17 . . . . .79 C2
Cockerell Rd NN17 . . . . .37 B8
Cockerill's Mdw CV21 . . . . . .99 A8
Cockington Gn OX16 . . . . .240 E9
Cockley Rd NN13 . . . . .221 C6
Codlin Cl NN3 . . . . .143 B1
Coffee Tavern La NN10 . . .132 B2
Cofferidge Cl MK11 . . . . . .229 D5
Cogan Cres NN14 . . . . .70 B6
Cogenhoe Prim Sch
NN7 . . . . .161 F5
Coggins Cl NN9 . . . . .114 C6
Cold Ashby Rd
Guilsborough NN6 . . . . .103 E7
Thornby NN6 . . . . .84 D4
Coldermeadow Ave
NN18 . . . . .36 A1
Coldstream Cl NN15 . . . . .135 B1
Coldstream La NN4 . . . . . .175 A6
Cole Ct NN10 . . . . .114 C5
Cole St NN10 . . . . .131 E4
Coleman Cl NN6 . . . . .101 A6
Coleman St NN9 . . . . .114 D6
Coleraine Cl NN2 . . . . .141 A5
Coleridge Way NN17 . . . . . .36 C8
Coleridge Wlk NN11 . . . . .135 B4
Coles Rise NN13 . . . . .233 D7
College Field Cl NN3 . . . . .143 C3
College Fields OX17 . . . . . .237 C7
College Rd CV23 . . . . .117 E3
College St
Higham Ferrers NN10 . . . . . .132 C5
Irthlingborough NN9 . . . . . . .112 F2
Northampton NN1 . . . . .159 C6
Rushden NN10 . . . . .132 B4
Wellingborough NN8 . . . . . .129 E4
Wollaston NN29 . . . . .146 D2
College St Mews 28
NN1 . . . . .159 C6
Colley Rise LE15 . . . . .9 C7
Collingcroft Cl NN4 . . . . . .175 A4
Collingdale Rd NN3 . . . . . .142 D2
Collingham Cl NN9 . . . . . . .114 A5
Collingtree CE Prim Sch
NN4 . . . . .175 C4
Collingtree Rd NN4,NN7 175 A4
Collingwood Ave NN17 . . . .36 A7
Collingwood Rd NN1 . . . . .141 F1
Collingwood Way NN11 . . .135 E3
Collins Cl NN12 . . . . .203 C7
Collins Hill NN7 . . . . .155 E6
Collins St NN1 . . . . .159 F7
Collmead St NN3 . . . . .143 B4
Collswell La NN12 . . . . . . .187 B1
Collyweston Cross Roads
PE8 . . . . .6 A6
Collyweston Rd NN3 . . . . .143 C5
Colmar Cl NN11 . . . . .135 A4
Colne Cl NN17 . . . . .21 C1
Colne Way NN5 . . . . .140 E1
Colonial Dr NN4 . . . . .175 C5
Colsons Way MK46 . . . . . . .195 F5
Coltsfoot Rd NN10 . . . . . . .148 C2
Columbus Cres NN14 . . . . . .70 E6
Columbus St NN11 . . . . . . .135 B5
Colville Wlk OX16 . . . . .240 E9
Colwell Rd NN8 . . . . .130 C4
Colwyn Rd NN1 . . . . .159 E8
Colyers Ave NN18 . . . . .36 B3
Comfrey Cl NN10 . . . . .148 B7
Commercial Rd
Corby NN17 . . . . .37 B6
Kettering NN16 . . . . .72 B2
Commercial St
Higham Ferrers NN10 . . . . . .132 B5
Northampton NN1 . . . . .159 C5
Commercial Way NN8 . . . .130 A4
Common St MK46 . . . . .194 D1
Compton Gn NN18 . . . . .36 A6
Compton Ho NN1 . . . . .159 B6
Compton Pl NN16 . . . . .72 C2
Compton Rd NN8 . . . . .130 C5
Compton St
Desborough NN14 . . . . .51 A4
Northampton NN1 . . . . .159 B6
Compton Way NN6 . . . . . . .144 E4
Conduit Rd PE9 . . . . .241 E4
Coneygree NN4 . . . . .175 F6
Coneygree Ct NN3 . . . . . . .143 B1
Coneywell Ct NN3 . . . . . . .142 F1
Conifer Rise NN3 . . . . .142 E1
Coniston Ave NN3 . . . . . . .142 B3
Coniston Cl
Daventry NN11 . . . . .135 B2
Higham Ferrers NN10 . . . . . .132 B5
Wellingborough NN8 . . . . . .129 C5
Coniston Rd NN16 . . . . .71 F2
Connaught Rd LE16 . . . . . . .31 F4

Connaught St
Kettering NN16 . . . . .72 D3
Northampton NN1 . . . . .159 D7
Connegar Leys NN7 . . . . . .190 E7
Connell Cl LE16 . . . . .30 F3
Connell Ct NN17 . . . . .36 F5
Connolly Cl NN14 . . . . .70 F7
Connolly Dr NN14 . . . . .70 F7
Constable Dr
Kettering NN15 . . . . .92 A7
Wellingborough NN8 . . . . . .129 F7
Constable Rd Corby NN18 .36 E5
Rugby CV21 . . . . .80 B1
Constable Wlk NN14 . . . . . .94 D7
Conway Cl
Northampton NN5 . . . . .140 E7
Rushden NN10 . . . . .148 A8
Wellingborough NN8 . . . . . .129 C6
Conway Dr
Burton Latimer NN15 . . . . . .92 B2
Thrapston NN14 . . . . .76 F2
Conway Wlk NN17 . . . . .21 C1
Conyngham Rd NN3 . . . . . .142 F2
Cook Cl Daventry NN11 . . .135 C5
Rothwell NN14 . . . . .70 E6
Cook's Terr NN6 . . . . .121 A3
Cook's Way NN6 . . . . .121 A3
Cooks Cl NN7 . . . . .205 F8
Cooks Way NN7 . . . . .37 F8
Coomb Rd NN18 . . . . .36 D1
Cooper Cl NN12 . . . . .203 C8
Cooper Ct NN14 . . . . .76 D1
Cooper Dr NN8 . . . . .129 F8
Coopers Gate OX17 . . . . . .240 C9
Coots Cl MK18 . . . . .240 C2
Cope Rd OX16 . . . . .240 C8
Copelands Rd NN14 . . . . . .51 C3
Copenhagen Rd NN18 . . . . .36 A1
Copper Leaf Cl NN3 . . . . . .142 C6
Copperfield Cl NN14 . . . . . .72 C6
Coppice Cl Banbury OX16 240 E6
Burton Latimer NN15 . . . . . .92 C4
Daventry NN11 . . . . .153 C8
Coppice Dr NN3 . . . . .142 A5
Copse Cl
Burton Latimer NN15 . . . . . .92 C3
Northampton NN2 . . . . .140 F5
Copymoor Cl NN4 . . . . .176 A6
Cora Rd NN16 . . . . .72 E4
Corbett St CV21 . . . . .241 E9
Corbieres Cl NN5 . . . . .140 A2
Corby Com Coll NN17 . . . . .36 F6
Corby Com Hospl NN17 . . .36 D6
Corby Gate NN17 . . . . .22 F1
Corby Gate Bsns Pk
NN17 . . . . .22 F1
Corby Rd Cottingham LE16 .35 E8
Gretton NN17 . . . . .22 B6
Stanion NN14 . . . . .37 E3
Weldon NN17 . . . . .38 A7
Cordon Cl NN3 . . . . .143 B3
Cordon Cres NN16 . . . . . . .144 F4
Cordwainer Gr NN14 . . . . . .76 D1
Cordwainer Ho NN5 . . . . . .159 A5
Cordwainers NN10 . . . . . . .132 C1
Corn Kiln Cl NN7 . . . . .161 F6
Corn La 7 NN8 . . . . .130 A4
Corner Cl NN29 . . . . .147 E1
Cornfield Cl NN2 . . . . .141 B5
Cornfield Way NN15 . . . . . .92 C1
Cornflower Cl NN14 . . . . . .175 F2
Cornflower Pl MK18 . . . . . .240 C2
Cornhill Cl NN5 . . . . .140 C3
Cornstall Bldgs PE9 . . . . . .241 E3
Cornwall Cl NN17 . . . . .36 C6
Cornwall Rd
Kettering NN16 . . . . .72 D3
Stamford PE9 . . . . .241 D4
Cornwalls Ctr The
MK18 . . . . .240 D4
Cornwalls Mdw MK18 . . . .240 D4
Cornwell Bsns Pk NN4 . . .160 B2
Coronation Ave
Rothwell NN14 . . . . .70 D7
Rushden NN10 . . . . .131 E1
Coronation Rd
Newnham NN11 . . . . .153 D4
Stony Stratford MK11 . . . . .229 E5
Corporation St
Corby NN17 . . . . .36 E6
Rugby CV21 . . . . .241 E8
Corran Cl NN5 . . . . .158 E8
Cory Gdns NN7 . . . . .157 C7
Cosgrove L Pk* MK19 .218 F1
Cosgrove Rd
Northampton NN2 . . . . .141 C5
Old Stratford MK19 . . . . . . .229 C2
Cosgrove Village Prim Sch
MK19 . . . . .218 E2
Cosgrove Way NN2 . . . . . . .141 C5
Cosy Nook NN14 . . . . .76 C2
Coton NN6 . . . . .103 E1
Coton Manor Gdns*
NN6 . . . . .103 E4
Coton Rd
Guilsborough NN6 . . . . .103 F5
Rugby CV21 . . . . .80 A1
Cotswold Ave
Kettering NN16 . . . . .72 B5
Northampton NN5 . . . . .158 D8
Cotswold Cl NN11 . . . . . . .135 B5
Cotswold Ct OX27 . . . . .237 C5
Cotswold Dr NN8 . . . . .129 D1
Cottage Cl NN2 . . . . .141 A4
Cottage Gdns NN3 . . . . . . .143 B3
Cottage Leap CV21 . . . . . .241 F9
Cottages The NN13 . . . . . .224 C5

Cottagewell Ct NN3 . . . . . .142 F1
Cottarville NN3 . . . . .142 D1
Cotterstock Rd PE8 . . . . . . .41 F7
Cottesbrooke Gdns
NN4 . . . . .175 D7
Cottesbrooke Grange
NN6 . . . . .105 A8
Cottesbrooke Hall*
NN6 . . . . .105 A8
Cottesbrooke Pk NN11 . . .135 A5
Cottesbrooke Rd NN17 . . . .36 B7
Cottesloe Ct MK11 . . . . . . .229 F5
Cottesmore Ave NN15 . . . .92 A5
Cottesmore Cl NN5 . . . . . .140 B1
Cottesmore Rd PE9 . . . . . .241 A3
Cottesmore Way NN8 . . . .129 D6
Cottingham CE Prim Sch
LE16 . . . . .20 C1
Cottingham Dr NN3 . . . . . .142 B7
Cottingham Rd
Corby NN17 . . . . .36 E6
Corby NN18 . . . . .36 B7
Rockingham LE16 . . . . .21 A4
Cottingham Way NN14 . . . .76 C2
Cotton End
Long Buckby NN6 . . . . .121 D4
Northampton NN4 . . . . .159 C4
Cottons The
Rockingham LE16 . . . . .21 B4
Wellingborough NN8 . . . . . .129 D7
Coulon Cl NN29 . . . . .147 A2
Coulthard Cl NN12 . . . . . . .203 D8
Council Ho's LE16 . . . . .48 B8
Council Hos
Farthingstone NN12 . . . . . . .170 E3
Guilsborough NN6 . . . . .103 F7
Hannington NN6 . . . . .108 C3
Podington NN29 . . . . .147 E1
Council Hos The
Long Buckby Wharf NN6 . . .136 E7
Wardington OX17 . . . . .208 F8
Council Houses NN6 . . . . . .106 F6
Council St Bozeat NN29 . . .164 D4
Wollaston NN29 . . . . .146 D2
Countess Ct NN5 . . . . .159 A7
Countess Rd NN5 . . . . .159 A7
Countryside NN11 . . . . . . .118 B1
Counts Farm Rd NN18 . . . .36 F4
County Rd NN13 . . . . .234 A6
County View OX15 . . . . . . .236 D4
Courier Rd NN17 . . . . .37 B8
Court Cnr MK46 . . . . .195 E4
Court Dr NN16 . . . . .72 B6
Court House Cl NN6 . . . . . .104 F4
Court La NN6 . . . . .64 D3
Court Mews NN8 . . . . .130 B4
Court Rd 11 NN1 . . . . .159 C5
Courteenhall Cl NN2 . . . . .143 D6
Courteenhall Rd NN7 . . . . .191 A7
Courtman Rd NN9 . . . . .114 A4
Courtney Rd NN10 . . . . . . .132 A1
Courtwood NN9 . . . . .114 A3
Courtyard La NN11 . . . . . . .153 A3
Courtyard The Islip NN14 .76 B3
Middleton Cheney OX17 . . .219 D5
Stamford PE9 . . . . .241 C3
Courtyard Workshops
LE16 . . . . .31 E1
Coventry Rd LE16 . . . . .31 D3
Coverack Cl NN4 . . . . .159 B1
Coverdale NN7 . . . . .140 F5
Coverley Pl CV22 . . . . .241 A8
Covert Cl NN2 . . . . .141 A6
Covington Gr NN8 . . . . . . .130 A6
Covington St NN1 . . . . .160 A7
Cow Yd NN2 . . . . .141 B3
Cowbeck Cl NN4 . . . . .175 E5
Cowgill Cl NN3 . . . . .143 B3
Cowley Cl NN4 . . . . .175 D6
Cowley Rd NN11 . . . . .135 B3
Cowley Way CV23 . . . . .99 F2
Cowper & Newton Mus The*
MK46 . . . . .195 F3
Cowper Rd
Earls Barton NN6 . . . . .145 A4
Irthlingborough NN9 . . . . . . .112 D1
Cowper St Kettering NN16 .72 B4
Northampton NN1 . . . . .159 E7
Cowper Terr NN2 . . . . .141 F1
Cowpers Orch MK46 . . . . .195 A1
Cowslip Cl NN10 . . . . .148 C8
Cowslip Hill NN14 . . . . .89 B5
Cox Gdns NN12 . . . . .202 E8
Cox's Cl NN6 . . . . .121 B3
Cox's La NN14 . . . . .90 A5
Cox's La NN11 . . . . .151 C1
Coxwell Cl MK18 . . . . .240 F4
Crab Apple Way NN14 . . . . .76 E1
Crab Tree Cl MK46 . . . . . . .195 E5
Crabb St NN10 . . . . .132 B1
Crabb Tree Dr NN3 . . . . . . .143 A7
Crabtree Cl Hartwell NN7 .142 F2
Wellingborough NN8 . . . . . .129 F2
Crabtree Ho 8 NN11 . . . .135 C2
Crabtree La NN14 . . . . .84 B5
Cracknuts La NN4 . . . . .160 E2
Craddock Ct NN29 . . . . . . .147 B8
Cragside NN8 . . . . .129 C6
Craigie NN3 . . . . .129 C4
Cranbrooke Rd NN2 . . . . . .141 C1
Crane Cl Broughton NN14 .70 C7
Rushden NN10 . . . . .132 B4
Wellingborough NN8 . . . . . .130 A2
Crane Wlk NN3 . . . . .142 C6

Cranford CE Prim Sch
NN14 . . . . .93 B7
Cranford Ho 1 NN2 . . . . .141 C3
Cranford Rd
Burton Latimer NN15 . . . . . .92 D4
Great Addington NN14 . . . . . .94 A4
Kettering NN15 . . . . .92 C6
Northampton NN2 . . . . .141 C3
Cranleigh Rd NN15 . . . . . . .91 B7
Cranmere Ave NN1 . . . . . . .160 B6
Cransley Gdns NN11 . . . . . .36 C7
Cransley Hill NN14 . . . . . . .90 A4
Cransley Rd NN14 . . . . .70 E1
Cranstoun St NN1 . . . . .159 D7
Craven Cl CV21 . . . . .241 E9
Craven St NN1 . . . . .159 D7
Crawford Ave NN5 . . . . . . .158 E7
Crawford Gr NN17 . . . . .36 E8
Crawford Rd NN17 . . . . .10 B1
Crawley Ave NN8 . . . . .129 D7
Craxford Rd NN17 . . . . .10 B1
Creampot Cl OX17 . . . . . . .196 A2
Creampot La OX17 . . . . . . .196 A2
Creaton Rd NN6 . . . . .104 D5
Crediton Cl NN3 . . . . .160 D7
Creed Rd PE8 . . . . .41 E7
Creighton Cres NN15 . . . . . .91 F6
Crescent Cl LE16 . . . . .31 F4
Crescent The
Burton Latimer NN15 . . . . . .92 C4
Easton o t H PE9 . . . . .1 F5
Flore NN7 . . . . .155 F6
Hackleton NN7 . . . . .177 A3
Kettering NN15 . . . . .91 B8
Ketton PE9 . . . . .1 A7
Market Harborough LE16 . . . .31 F4
Moulton NN3 . . . . .126 D1
Northampton NN1 . . . . .159 F8
Pattishall NN12 . . . . .172 E1
Rothwell NN14 . . . . .70 C6
Rushden NN10 . . . . .131 E2
Twyford OX17 . . . . .230 A5
Whittlebury NN12 . . . . .215 C5
Creslow Ct MK11 . . . . .229 F5
Cresswell Rd NN10 . . . . . . .131 F2
Crestline Ct NN3 . . . . .143 A6
Crestwood Gdns NN3 . . . .142 F5
Crestwood Rd NN3 . . . . . . .142 F5
Creswell Wlk NN17 . . . . . . .21 C1
Crick Cl NN17 . . . . .22 A1
Crick Prim Sch NN6 . . . . . .100 F6
Crick Rd Rugby CV21,CV23 .99 D7
West Haddon NN6 . . . . .102 A3
Yelvertoft NN6 . . . . .82 A2
Cricketers Gn NN17 . . . . . .38 C8
Cricklade Cl NN3 . . . . .160 D6
Crickley Cres NN8 . . . . . . .158 E3
Crimea Cl 2 NN4 . . . . . . .175 E7
Crispian Cl NN10 . . . . .132 A2
Crispian Ho NN1 . . . . .159 D7
Crispin Cl NN6 . . . . .108 A4
Crispin Ho NN1 . . . . .159 B6
Crispin Pl 14 NN16 . . . . . .72 B2
Crispin St
14 Northampton NN1 . . . . .159 C6
Rothwell NN14 . . . . .70 E7
Crispin Way St NN9 . . . . . .114 C8
Crocket Cl NN2 . . . . .141 E2
Crockwell Hill NN11 . . . . . .119 F1
Crocus Way NN10 . . . . .148 B7
Croft Cl NN8 . . . . .129 C5
Croft La Adderbury OX17 .230 A4
Roade NN7 . . . . .191 D4
Staverton NN11 . . . . .152 B7
Croft The Daventry NN11 . .153 C8
Hanging Houghton NN6 . . . .106 C8
1 Northampton NN5 . . . . . .140 F1
Rugby CV21 . . . . .99 A8
Stamford PE9 . . . . .241 E3
Croft Way Rushden NN10 132 D3
Weedon NN7 . . . . .155 A3
Crofters Cl NN4 . . . . .175 B7
Croftmeadow Ct NN3 . . . .143 B4
Cromarty Ct NN17 . . . . .36 F5
Cromarty Ho NN17 . . . . . . .36 F5
Cromarty Rd PE9 . . . . .241 A4
Cromer Rd NN9 . . . . .111 F4
Cromwell Cl NN14 . . . . .51 A3
Cromwell Cres LE16 . . . . . .31 D1
Cromwell Ct
Banbury OX16 . . . . .240 B9
Buckingham MK18 . . . . . . .240 E5
Wellingborough NN8 . . . . . .130 B5
Cromwell Ho NN8 . . . . .130 B4
Cromwell Rd
Banbury OX16 . . . . .240 A8
Kettering NN16 . . . . .72 A2
Rugby CV22 . . . . .241 E6
Rushden NN10 . . . . .132 C2
Cromwell St 15 NN1 . . . . .159 C7
Cronin Ctyd NN18 . . . . .37 E7
Cronin Rd NN18 . . . . .37 E7
Cropredy Ct MK18 . . . . . . .240 E5
Crosby Rd LE16 . . . . .31 F1
Cross Bank LE16 . . . . .20 D6
Cross Cl NN16 . . . . .72 A3
Cross Hill NN6 . . . . .106 B3
Cross Keys Ct NN13 . . . . . .233 F7
Cross La Aldwincle NN14 . .57 E1
Braunston NN11 . . . . .118 C1
Helmdon NN13 . . . . .212 A5
Weston Underwood MK46 . .195 B6
Cross Rd NN8 . . . . .130 B6
Cross St Covington PE18 . .116 D2
Daventry NN11 . . . . .135 B2
Kettering NN16 . . . . .72 A3
Market Harborough LE16 . . . .31 F2
Moulton NN3 . . . . .126 C1
Rothwell NN14 . . . . .70 E7

Cross St continued
Rugby CV21 . . . . .241 E9
Cross The NN4 . . . . .160 E2
Cross Tree Rd NN18 . . . . . .228 B3
Cross Waters Cl NN4 . . . . .175 F6
Cross Way NN9 . . . . .131 D8
Crossbrooks NN4 . . . . .175 F6
Crosse Cl NN7 . . . . .155 C4
Crosshills MK11 . . . . .229 D4
Crouch Rd NN9 . . . . .112 F1
Crouch St OX16 . . . . .240 C7
Croughton All Saints CE Prim
Sch NN13 . . . . .238 C8
Croughton Cl NN2 . . . . . . .141 C5
Croughton Rd OX17 . . . . . .237 D7
Crow La NN3 . . . . .161 C7
Crowberry Ave NN3 . . . . . .142 C6
Crown Ct Corby NN18 . . . . .36 E5
Rushden NN10 . . . . .131 E3
Crown La Barrowden LE15 . .3 F5
Rothwell NN14 . . . . .70 C7
West Haddon NN6 . . . . .102 C4
Crown St Kettering NN16 . .72 B3
Stamford PE9 . . . . .241 D3
Crown Way NN10 . . . . .131 E4
Crownsmead NN4 . . . . .158 D1
Crowthorp Rd NN3 . . . . . . .143 C5
Croxdale Cl NN2 . . . . .140 F5
Croxen Cl NN15 . . . . .92 C2
Croyde Ave NN18 . . . . .36 F4
Croyland Hall Her Ctr Mus*
NN8 . . . . .130 A4
Croyland Prim Sch NN8 . .129 E3
Croyland Rd NN8 . . . . .129 F3
Crucible Rd NN17 . . . . .37 B7
Ctyd The NN3 . . . . .142 C1
Cubleigh Cl NN3 . . . . .142 C6
Cuckoo Cl LE15 . . . . .3 E5
Cullahill Ct NN4 . . . . .158 E2
Culloden Ct NN17 . . . . .36 F5
Culloden Dr NN15 . . . . .91 F8
Culme Cl PE8 . . . . .41 E7
Culross Wlk NN18 . . . . .36 C3
Culworth CE Sch CV37 . . .198 C2
Culworth Cres NN2 . . . . . .141 D5
Culworth Rd OX17 . . . . . . .197 B6
Cumberland Ave NN9 . . . .114 A4
Cumberland Cl NN3 . . . . . .142 A3
Cumbrae Dr NN3 . . . . .143 C2
Cunliffe Dr NN16 . . . . .72 A4
Cunningham Cl
Daventry NN11 . . . . .135 E2
Higham Ferrers NN10 . . . . . .132 B5
Cupar Cres NN17 . . . . .36 F5
Curgenven Cl NN11 . . . . . .183 E7
Curie Cl CV21 . . . . .241 F8
Curlbrook Cl NN4 . . . . .176 A6
Curlew Way NN11 . . . . .135 C3
Currie Rd NN2 . . . . .141 C1
Curtis Mews NN8 . . . . .129 C2
Curtlee Hill NN4 . . . . .175 F5
Curver Way NN17 . . . . .22 D1
Cyclamen Cl NN14 . . . . . . .50 F3
Cypress Cl NN14 . . . . .50 F3
Cypress Ct NN3 . . . . .142 E3
Cyril St NN1 . . . . .159 E6
Cytringen Cl NN15 . . . . . . .91 A7

D

D'albini Cl LE16 . . . . .34 B4
Da Vinci Cl NN5 . . . . .158 C5
Dadford Rd NN12,MK18 . . .225 D5
Daffodil Dr NN10 . . . . .148 B7
Dagnall Rd MK46 . . . . .195 E3
Dahlia Rd NN16 . . . . .72 D4
Daimler Cl
Daventry NN11 . . . . .135 A3
Northampton NN3 . . . . .143 D4
Dairy Cl Brixworth NN6 . . .106 A1
West Haddon NN6 . . . . .102 D4
Dairy Cotts LE17 . . . . .45 A4
Dairy Field NN6 . . . . .103 D1
Dairy Ground OX17 . . . . . .231 A6
Dairy Meadow Ct NN3 . . .142 F6
Dairy Way NN9 . . . . .131 E8
Daisy Bank Ave NN14 . . . . .70 C7
Daisy Croft NN10 . . . . .148 C8
Dakin Cl PE8 . . . . .13 F8
Dalby Cl NN16 . . . . .72 A6
Dale Ave NN8 . . . . .129 C5
Dale Cl Brackley NN13 . . . .234 A7
Daventry NN11 . . . . .135 B5
Mears Ashby NN6 . . . . .128 C2
Wellingborough NN8 . . . . . .129 C5
Dale Ho NN8 . . . . .129 F4
Dale St Corby NN17 . . . . . . .36 D7
Rugby CV21 . . . . .241 C9
Wellingborough NN8 . . . . . .129 F4
Dale The NN8 . . . . .129 C5
Dalestones NN4 . . . . .158 D2
Daleswood Rise PE8 . . . . . .13 E7
Dalkeith Ave 20 NN16 . . . .72 B2
Dalkeith Pl NN16 . . . . .72 B2
Dalkeith Rd NN16 . . . . .129 F1
Dallacre Dr LE16 . . . . .34 C4
Dallington Cl NN14 . . . . . . .54 A2
Dallington Gn 2 NN5 . . . .158 F8
Dallington Haven 5
NN5 . . . . .158 F8
Dallington Park Rd NN5 158 F8
Dallington Rd NN5 . . . . . . .159 A7
Dallison Cl LE16 . . . . .48 E8
Dalston Wlk 6 NN3 . . . . . .142 C4
Dalton Rd NN17 . . . . .21 E2
Damherst Piece NN6 . . . . .106 C2

Damson Cl NN14 . . . . .76 E1
Damson Dell NN3 . . . . .161 A8
Dando Cl NN29 . . . . .146 D1
Dands Cl OX17 . . . . .220 A8
Dands Dr OX17 . . . . .220 A8
Dane Ct NN11 . . . . .118 C1
Dane Ridge NN5 . . . . .158 C6
Danefield Rd NN3 . . . . .142 B1
Daneholme Ave NN11 . . . .135 C4
Danes Backside NN2 . . . . . .141 B3
Danes Camp Way NN4 . . . .158 E3
Danes Way NN6 . . . . .100 C7
Danesholme Jun & Inf Sch
  NN18 . . . . .36 A2
Daneholme Rd NN18 . . . . . . .36 A2
Danetre Comp Sch
  NN11 . . . . .135 E1
Danetre Dr NN11 . . . . .135 E1
Danetre Hospl NN11 . . . . . .153 C8
Danetree Gdns NN3 . . . . . .142 B2
Danewood Gdns NN3 . . . . .142 B2
Danford Cl PE8 . . . . .41 F4
Danfords PE8 . . . . .41 F5
Daniaud Ct NN13 . . . . .233 E8
Daniel Ct PE9 . . . . .241 C5
Daniell Wlk NN18 . . . . .36 D5
Daniels Rd NN8 . . . . .130 C1
Dapplestone Cl NN4 . . . . . .158 D2
Darby Cl NN8 . . . . .129 A5
Dardis Cl 2 NN2 . . . . .141 E1
Darenth Cl 16 NN1 . . . . . .159 C2
Darescroft LE16 . . . . .20 B1
Dark La Braunston NN11 . . .118 B7
  Great Harrowden NN9 . . . . .110 D2
Darley Cl NN16 . . . . .72 C6
Darley Dale Rd NN17 . . . . . .36 D8
Dart Cl NN11 . . . . .21 D2
Dartford Cl 2 NN4 . . . . . .159 A2
Dartmouth Rd MK46 . . . . .195 F4
Dartmouth Row NN11 . . . .135 D1
Darwin Cl PE9 . . . . .241 C5
Darwin Ct NN17 . . . . .37 C8
Darwin Ho NN17 . . . . .22 F1
Darwin Rd NN17 . . . . .37 C8
Darwin Wlk NN5 . . . . .140 C1
Dash Farm Cl NN17 . . . . . . .38 A8
Dashwood Rd OX16 . . . . . .240 C7
Daventry Country Pk★
  NN11 . . . . .135 D5
Daventry Rd
  Banbury OX16 . . . . .208 A2
  Banbury OX16 . . . . .240 F9
  Barby CV23 . . . . .118 C6
  Kilsby CV23 . . . . .100 A1
  Newnham NN11 . . . . .153 D4
  Norton NN11 . . . . .136 C5
  Staverton NN11 . . . . .152 B7
  Staverton NN11 . . . . .152 C7
  Willoughby CV23 . . . . .117 C7
Daventry Tert Coll
  NN11 . . . . .153 B8
Daventry William Parker Sch
  NN11 . . . . .135 C3
Davey Rd NN17 . . . . .37 C8
Davies Cl NN15 . . . . .90 F8
Davis Cl NN14 . . . . .70 E6
Davis Ct NN17 . . . . .37 A6
Davy Cl NN8 . . . . .129 A6
Dawkins Ct NN14 . . . . .90 A4
Dayrell Rd NN4 . . . . .158 F2
Dayrell Sq 5 NN4 . . . . . . .158 F2
Dayton St NN10 . . . . .132 A2
De Capel Cl NN14 . . . . .94 D6
De Clare Ct MK18 . . . . .240 E4
De Ferneus Dr NN4 . . . . . .114 D7
De Lisle Cl LE16 . . . . .31 D2
De Montfort Ct NN13 . . . . .222 E1
De Quincey Cl NN11 . . . . . .222 E1
De Roos Way LE16 . . . . . . .34 B4
De Vere Rd NN14 . . . . .76 D2
Deacon Cl
  Market Harborough LE16 . . .31 D5
  Rugby CV22 . . . . .241 E6
  Rushden NN10 . . . . .132 D3
Deacon Way OX16 . . . . . . .240 A7
Deacons Ct NN3 . . . . .143 C4
Deal Ct NN1 . . . . .159 D7
Deal St NN1 . . . . .159 C7
Dean Cl NN10 . . . . .148 A8
Dean Wlk 6 NN11 . . . . . . .135 B4
Deancourt Dr NN5 . . . . . . .140 A1
Deane Par CV21 . . . . .99 A8
Deane Rd CV21 . . . . .99 B8
Deans Row NN7 . . . . .173 E2
Deanshanger Dr NN12 . . . .216 F1
Deanshanger Prim Sch
  MK19 . . . . .228 E3
Deanshanger Row
  Old Stratford MK19 . . . . . .229 B6
  Wicken MK19 . . . . .228 B3
Deansway NN3 . . . . .143 C4
Debbs Cl MK11 . . . . .229 E5
Debdale Rd
  Northampton NN3 . . . . .142 D2
  Wellingborough NN8 . . . . . .129 F5

Deer Park Rd NN3 . . . . . . .142 A6
Deerfield Cl MK18 . . . . . . .240 E2
Deerings Rd CV21 . . . . .99 A8
Delamere Dr NN15 . . . . . . .92 A5
Delamere Rd NN4 . . . . .159 C2
Delapre Abbey★ NN4 . . . .159 D3
Delapre Cres NN4 . . . . .159 C3
Delapre Crescent Rd
  NN4 . . . . .159 C3
Delapre Ct NN4 . . . . .159 C2
Delapre Dr OX16 . . . . .240 F9
Delapre Mid Sch NN4 . . . . .159 B3
Delapre Mid Sch Annexe
  NN4 . . . . .159 B3
Delapre Pl NN18 . . . . .36 A3
Delapre St NN4 . . . . .159 B3
Dell Cres NN13 . . . . .143 B5
Dell Pl NN10 . . . . .132 C2
Dells MK46 . . . . .195 F4
Dells Cl PE17 . . . . .61 D2
Delta Way NN2 . . . . .141 A5
Delves The NN9 . . . . .114 C6
Dempsey Dr NN14 . . . . .70 F6
Demswell NN6 . . . . .106 C2
Denbigh Rd NN3 . . . . .160 D6
Denby Dale NN8 . . . . .129 C7
Dencora Bsns Pk NN8 . . . .129 A4
Dene Cl Kettering NN16 . . . .72 A5
  Wellingborough NN8 . . . . . .129 C6
Denethorpe La NN17 . . . . . .24 B5
Denfield Park Jun Sch
  NN10 . . . . .132 C3
Denford Dr NN15 . . . . .91 F5
Denford Rd Corby NN17 . . . .36 B8
  Ringstead NN14 . . . . .95 C4
  Thrapston NN14 . . . . .95 D8
Denford Way NN8 . . . . .129 D7
Denington Ct NN8 . . . . .130 A1
Denington Ind Est NN8 . . . .130 B2
Denington Rd NN8 . . . . .130 A2
Denman Cl LE16 . . . . .34 A4
Denmark Cl NN18 . . . . .35 F3
Denmark Ct NN10 . . . . .132 C1
Denmark Rd
  Northampton NN1 . . . . .159 E6
  Rushden NN10 . . . . .132 C1
Denne Cl NN18 . . . . .36 C1
Denney Cres NN11 . . . . . . .135 B2
Denston Cl NN4 . . . . .159 B1
Denton Cl
  Irchester NN29 . . . . .147 B8
  Rushden NN10 . . . . .132 C3
Denton Ct NN15 . . . . .92 B2
Denton Rd NN7 . . . . .178 B6
Denton Prim Sch NN7 . . . . .178 C8
Derby Rd NN1 . . . . .159 E6
Dering Cotts OX17 . . . . . . .210 C2
Derling Dr NN9 . . . . .114 E6
Derngate NN1 . . . . .159 D5
Derry The NN6 . . . . .100 F5
Derwent Cl
  Daventry NN11 . . . . .135 A1
  Northampton NN5 . . . . .140 F1
  Wellingborough NN8 . . . . . .129 C6
Derwent Cres NN16 . . . . . . .71 C7
Derwent Dr NN5 . . . . .140 F2
Derwent Ho PE8 . . . . .42 A6
Derwent Wlk NN17 . . . . . . .21 D1
Desborough Sch
  Arthingworth LE16 . . . . .49 F1
  Braybrooke LE16 . . . . .49 F5
  Rothwell NN14 . . . . .70 C7
  Rushton NN14 . . . . .52 B2
  Stoke Albany LE16 . . . . . . .34 B3
Deveron Wlk NN17 . . . . . . .21 D1
Devon Dr NN15 . . . . .91 D6
Devon Ox Rd CV23 . . . . .99 F2
Devon Way NN3 . . . . .142 A5
Devon Wlk NN10 . . . . .132 C1
Devonshire Cl
  Boughton NN2 . . . . .141 C8
  Wellingborough NN8 . . . . . .129 C6
Devonshire Ho 6 NN5 . . . .159 A6
Dewar Dr NN11 . . . . .135 A4
Dexter Cl OX16 . . . . .240 D6
Dexter Way PE8 . . . . .28 B3
Diamond Dr NN9 . . . . .131 E8
Diamond Way NN9 . . . . . . .113 A2
Diana Ho NN8 . . . . .129 D5
Diana Way NN15 . . . . .92 B1
Dibbin Cl NN17 . . . . .38 B8
Dick's Hill LE16 . . . . .47 C5
Dickens Dr Kettering NN16 .72 D6
  Old Stratford MK19 . . . . . .229 B6
  Stamford PE9 . . . . .241 A3
Dickens Spinney MK46 . . . .195 C6
Dickinson Ct CV22 . . . . . . .241 C6
Dickson Cl 4 NN4 . . . . . . .158 F3
Digby St NN11 . . . . .72 C3
Dimock Sq NN4 . . . . .158 F2
Dingle Rd NN10 . . . . .131 E2
Dingle The NN18 . . . . .35 F2
Dinglederry MK46 . . . . . . .195 F4
Dingley La LE16 . . . . .32 F6
Dingley Rd LE16 . . . . .32 B6
Dingley Terr LE16 . . . . .31 F3
Disbrowe Ct NN9 . . . . .133 C7
Diswell Brook Way
  MK19 . . . . .228 E5
Ditchford Cl NN4 . . . . .175 C6
Ditchford Rd NN8 . . . . .131 C5
Dixon Rd NN2 . . . . .141 E6
Dixon Wlk NN17 . . . . .37 A6
Dobbins Cl OX17 . . . . .231 A6
Dobson Cl NN4 . . . . .160 F2
Dobson Wlk NN18 . . . . .36 D5
Dockhouse The LE16 . . . . . .31 D4
Docklewell Cl NN12 . . . . . .203 A4

Doctors La Eydon NN11 . . .184 C1
  Great Doddington NN29 . . .145 E6
Doddington Ct NN8 . . . . . .129 F2
Doddington Rd
  Earls Barton NN6 . . . . .145 A4
  Wellingborough NN8 . . . . . .129 F2
  Wellingborough NN8 . . . . . .145 F8
  Wilby NN8 . . . . .145 B8
Dog La
  Napton on t H CV47 . . . . . .150 A7
  South Kilworth LE17 . . . . . . .63 C8
Dolben Ave NN9 . . . . .113 E4
Dolben Cl NN9 . . . . .111 E4
Dolben Sq NN9 . . . . .111 F4
Dolver Cl NN18 . . . . .36 C2
Don Cl NN17 . . . . .21 D1
Donald Greaves Ho
  NN17 . . . . .21 D1
Donaldson Ave NN14 . . . . . .90 A3
Donellan Gn NN3 . . . . .142 F6
Donne Cl
  Higham Ferrers NN10 . . . . .132 A5
  Kettering NN16 . . . . .72 C6
Donovan Ct NN3 . . . . .160 E8
Dorcas Rd OX16 . . . . .219 A6
Dorchester Ct NN5 . . . . . . .140 B2
Dorchester Gr OX16 . . . . . .240 A6
Dore Cl NN3 . . . . .143 B5
Doris Rd NN16 . . . . .72 E4
Dorking Wlk NN18 . . . . .36 C3
Dorothy Rd NN16 . . . . .72 E3
Dorset Gdns NN2 . . . . .141 D3
Dorset Rd Corby NN17 . . . . .36 C6
  Northampton NN2 . . . . .141 D3
Doubles The NN11 . . . . . . .135 B1
Doughty St PE9 . . . . .241 F5
Douglas Ct NN15 . . . . .91 E8
Douglas Rd NN5 . . . . .157 F8
Douglass Dr LE16 . . . . .31 F4
Doulton Cl NN14 . . . . .50 F3
Dove Cl
  Buckingham MK18 . . . . . . .240 E2
  Towcester NN12 . . . . .203 C3
Dove Cotts OX17 . . . . .210 A6
Dove's La NN3 . . . . .126 D1
Dovecote Cl
  Barrowden LE15 . . . . .3 F5
  Kettering NN15 . . . . .91 F5
  Raunds NN9 . . . . .114 C7
  Yarwell PE8 . . . . .16 A8
Dovecote Dr Denton NN7 .162 B1
  Little Addington NN14 . . . . .113 B7
Dovecote Rd NN7 . . . . .191 C4
Dovecote The NN6 . . . . . . .125 D5
Dovecote Yd NN14 . . . . . . .110 A5
Dovedale Gr NN14 . . . . .50 E4
Dovedale Rd NN17 . . . . .36 E7
Dovehouse Cl
  Brackley NN13 . . . . .233 F7
  Stanwick NN9 . . . . .113 F3
Dovehouse Ct MK19 . . . . . .228 E4
Dover Cl NN10 . . . . .132 D1
Dovercourt NN5 . . . . .159 B5
Downer Cl MK18 . . . . .240 F3
Downing Cres PE9 . . . . . . .241 D5
Downing Way NN11 . . . . . .153 C2
Downs The NN9 . . . . .110 E1
Downsway NN4 . . . . .175 B6
Downwood Cl NN3 . . . . . . .143 C3
Dowthorpe End NN6 . . . . . .144 F4
Dowthorpe Hill NN6 . . . . . .144 F3
Drake Cl Corby NN17 . . . . . .36 B8
  Daventry NN11 . . . . .135 E1
  Rothwell NN14 . . . . .70 E7
Drake Lee Mews NN16 . . . .72 B1
Draper's Cl PE8 . . . . .28 C3
Drapery NN1 . . . . .159 C6
Draughton Rd NN6 . . . . .87 B7
Draycott Cl NN3 . . . . .160 D7
Drayman's Wlk NN13 . . . . .233 E6
Drayson La NN6 . . . . .100 F6
Drayton Cl Corby NN18 . . . .36 B4
  Islip NN14 . . . . .76 B3
  Rushden NN10 . . . . .148 A8
Drayton Fields Ind Est
  NN11 . . . . .135 A5
Drayton Leys CV22 . . . . . . .98 A4
Drayton Pk NN11 . . . . .135 B5
Drayton Pl NN9 . . . . .112 F3
Drayton Rd
  Bringhurst LE16 . . . . .20 B5
  Drayton LE16 . . . . .19 D7
  Irthlingborough NN9 . . . . . .112 F3
  Lowick NN14 . . . . .75 E6
  Medbourne LE16 . . . . .19 A5
Drayton Way NN11 . . . . . . .135 A5
Drayton Wlk NN2 . . . . .141 D4
Dresden Cl NN18 . . . . .35 F2
Driffield Gr NN17 . . . . .36 F7
Drift Ave PE9 . . . . .241 F4
Drift Gdns PE9 . . . . .241 E5
Drift Rd PE9 . . . . .241 E4
Drift The Collyweston PE9 . . .1 D2
  Sutton PE5 . . . . .8 F3
Drift Way MK46 . . . . .195 F5
Drill Hall Ct NN15 . . . . .72 A1
Drive The Horton NN7 . . . . .177 E1
  Kettering NN15 . . . . .72 B1
  Northampton, Duston NN5 .158 A7
  Northampton,Phippsville
    NN1 . . . . .141 F1
  Rushden NN10 . . . . .132 C1
  Wellingborough NN8 . . . . . .130 A3
Droue Ct NN14 . . . . .70 C7

Drove The Collyweston PE9 . .1 D1
  Nassington PE8 . . . . .15 E5
Drovers Wlk NN2 . . . . .141 A5
Druce End NN12 . . . . .217 E6
Druids Way NN3 . . . . .141 F5
Drum La 30 NN1 . . . . .159 C6
Drumming Well La PE8 . . . . .42 A5
Drummond Cl NN6 . . . . . . .125 D4
Drury La CV21 . . . . .241 C8
Drydale Ave NN3 . . . . .142 B3
Dryden Ave NN11 . . . . .135 B2
Dryden Cl NN11 . . . . .184 A7
Dryden Pl CV22 . . . . .241 A8
Dryden Rd
  Northampton NN5 . . . . .158 F7
  Towcester NN12 . . . . .203 C5
  Wellingborough NN8 . . . . . .130 C5
Dryden St Kettering NN16 .72 B3
  Higham Ferrers NN10 . . . . .132 B5
Dryden Way Corby NN17 . . .36 F7
Dryden Wlk CV22 . . . . .241 A8
Dryden's Cl NN14 . . . . .77 C4
Dryland Rd NN3 . . . . .142 C2
Dryland St NN16 . . . . .72 B2
Dryleys Ct NN3 . . . . .143 B5
Drywell Ct NN3 . . . . .143 A1
Duchess Cl NN16 . . . . .72 B4
Duchess End NN6 . . . . .128 C2
Duchy Cl Chelveston 133 B8
  Higham Ferrers NN10 . . . . .132 C5
Duck End Cranford NN6 . . . .93 B7
  Denford NN14 . . . . .95 D6
  Hinton-in-t-H NN13 . . . . . . .232 F6
  Wollaston NN29 . . . . .146 D3
Duck La Harpole NN7 . . . . .157 C6
  Oundle PE8 . . . . .42 A5
Duck St Elton PE8 . . . . .16 D1
  Rushden NN10 . . . . .132 B2
Duckham Dell NN3 . . . . . . .142 F6
Duckworth Rd NN17 . . . . . . .36 B7
Duffy Cl CV21 . . . . .99 A8
Duke St Banbury OX16 . . . .240 E8
  Burton Latimer NN15 . . . . . .92 B2
  Kettering NN16 . . . . .72 B3
  Northampton NN1 . . . . .159 D7
  Polebrook PE8 . . . . .42 F3
  Rugby CV21 . . . . .241 C9
  Wellingborough NN8 . . . . . .129 E1
Dukelands NN7 . . . . .155 A3
Dukes Green Rd NN7 . . . . .157 D3
Dukes Jetty CV21 . . . . .241 C8
Dukes Piece MK18 . . . . . . .240 F3
Dulce Rd NN5 . . . . .158 C8
Dulley Ave NN8 . . . . .129 F1
Dulverton Rd NN3 . . . . .160 D7
Dumas Cul-De-Sac
  NN13 . . . . .233 E8
Dumble Cl NN18 . . . . .36 D2
Dunbar Ct NN15 . . . . .91 F8
Duncan Cl NN3 . . . . .141 F7
Duncan Ct NN8 . . . . .129 D3
Duncan Rd NN17 . . . . .36 B7
Dunchurch Rd CV22 . . . . . .241 C6
Dundee Dr PE9 . . . . .241 A4
Dundee St NN5 . . . . .158 F6
Dunedin Rd NN18 . . . . .36 C2
Dunkirk Ave NN14 . . . . .51 B3
Dunn Cl NN6 . . . . .101 A6
Dunnock La NN4 . . . . .175 F3
Dunslade Cl NN18 . . . . .32 B2
Dunslade Gr LE16 . . . . .32 B2
Dunslade Rd LE16 . . . . .32 A2
Dunsmore Ave CV22 . . . . . .98 E8
Dunster St NN1 . . . . .159 D6
Durban Rd NN16 . . . . .72 D2
Durham Cl NN17 . . . . .36 B6
Durness Cl NN15 . . . . .91 E8
Duston Cl NN11 . . . . .135 A3
Duston Eldean Lower Sch
  NN5 . . . . .140 B1
Duston Mill La NN5 . . . . . . .158 D4
Duston Rd NN5 . . . . .158 E6
Duston Upper Sch NN5 . . . .158 A8
Duston Wildes NN5 . . . . . . .140 A2
Dybdale Cres NN8 . . . . .129 E5
Dychurch La
  Bozeat NN29 . . . . .164 E3
  Northampton NN1 . . . . .159 D6
Dyson Cl CV21 . . . . .80 A1
Dyson Dr NN16 . . . . .72 A4

E

Eady Rd NN15 . . . . .92 B1
Eady's Row NN14 . . . . .94 D7
Eagle Dr NN4 . . . . .159 F2
Eagle La NN14 . . . . .71 B1
Eaglehurst NN6 . . . . .106 C2
Eaglesfield NN11 . . . . .136 C4
Ealing Terr NN11 . . . . .132 A3
Earl St Northampton NN1 . .159 D7
  Rugby CV21 . . . . .241 D8
Earl's La OX15 . . . . .236 A8
Earls Barton Inf Sch
  NN6 . . . . .144 E4
Earls Barton Jun Sch
  NN6 . . . . .144 E4
Earls Barton Mus★
  NN6 . . . . .144 E4
Earls Barton Rd
  Great Doddington NN29 . . .145 C5
  Mears Ashby NN6 . . . . .128 B2
Earlsfield Cl NN4 . . . . .176 A6
Earlstoke Cl OX16 . . . . .240 E10
Earlstrees Ct NN17 . . . . . . .21 F2

Earlstrees Ind Est NN17 . . .21 E2
Earlstrees Rd NN17 . . . . . . .21 F2
Easington Gdns OX16 . . . .240 C6
Easington Rd OX16 . . . . . . .240 C6
East Ave
  Burton Latimer NN15 . . . . . .92 B3
  Corby NN17 . . . . .36 F5
  Kettering NN15 . . . . .72 D2
East Bank NN3 . . . . .142 E6
East Butterfield Cl NN3 . . .142 F5
East Carlton Countryside
  Pk★ LE16 . . . . .35 B8
East Carlton Pk LE16 . . . . . .35 B7
East Cl Banbury OX16 . . . . .240 F9
  Kettering NN15 . . . . .72 D2
East Cres Rushden NN10 . .131 F2
  Weldon NN17 . . . . .38 C8
East Dr NN15 . . . . .72 E2
East End NN6 . . . . .106 F5
East Gr NN10 . . . . .132 B3
East Haddon CE Prim Sch
  NN6 . . . . .122 D5
East Haddon Rd NN6 . . . . .122 D8
East Hunsbury Lower Sch
  NN4 . . . . .175 B6
East Langham Rd NN9 . . . .114 D7
East Leys Ct NN3 . . . . .142 C7
East Oval NN5 . . . . .140 F2
East Paddock Ct NN3 . . . . .143 A4
East Park Par NN1 . . . . . . .159 F8
East Priors NN3 . . . . .143 A4
East Rd PE8 . . . . .42 A5
East Rising NN4 . . . . .175 D7
East St Banbury OX16 . . . . .240 E9
  Irchester NN29 . . . . .147 B8
  Long Buckby NN6 . . . . .121 D4
  Market Harborough LE16 . . .31 D3
  Northampton NN1 . . . . .159 F6
  Olney MK46 . . . . .195 F4
  Rugby CV21 . . . . .241 F9
  Stamford PE9 . . . . .241 E3
  Stanwick NN9 . . . . .114 A3
East Union St CV22 . . . . . .241 C7
East View OX17 . . . . .210 C2
East Wlk NN15 . . . . .72 E2
Eastbourne Ave NN18 . . . . .36 B5
Eastbrook NN18 . . . . .36 B4
Eastbrook Hill NN14 . . . . . . .51 C3
Eastcote Rd NN7 . . . . .189 D8
Eastern Ave N NN2 . . . . . .141 D4
Eastern Ave S NN2 . . . . . .141 D3
Eastern Cl NN2 . . . . .141 D5
Eastern Way NN11 . . . . . . .135 C2
Eastfield NN7 . . . . .190 D7
Eastfield Cl NN5 . . . . .140 C1
Eastfield Cres
  Finedon NN9 . . . . .112 A5
  Yardley Gobion NN12 . . . . .217 F5
Eastfield Dr MK19 . . . . . . .207 A3
Eastfield Lower Sch
  NN3 . . . . .142 B3
Eastfield Pl CV21 . . . . .241 C8
Eastfield Rd
  Brixworth NN6 . . . . .106 B1
  3 Irthlingborough NN9 . . . .112 F2
  Northampton, Duston NN5 .158 B8
  Northampton,Far Cotton
    NN4 . . . . .159 C3
  Wellingborough NN8 . . . . . .130 C4
  Wollaston NN29 . . . . .146 E2
Eastfields Cres PE8 . . . . . . .15 E6
Easthill Cl NN13 . . . . .233 F7
Eastlands Pl CV21 . . . . . . .241 F8
Eastlands Prim Sch
  CV21 . . . . .241 F7
Eastlands Rd
  Finedon NN9 . . . . .112 A5
  Rugby CV21 . . . . .241 F8
Eastleigh Rd NN15 . . . . .91 D7
Eastmead NN3 . . . . .143 A1
Easton Garfords Charity Sch
  PE9 . . . . .2 A5
Easton La NN29 . . . . .164 C3
Easton Way NN7 . . . . .163 E4
Easton Wlk NN17 . . . . .37 B6
Eastwood Gr CV21 . . . . .99 C8
Eastwood Rd PE8 . . . . .42 A5
Easy La CV21 . . . . .241 B8
Eaton Rd NN5 . . . . .158 A8
Eaton Wlk NN10 . . . . .132 B2
Ebbw Vale Rd NN9 . . . . . . .131 E8
Ebenezer Pl 16 NN16 . . . . .72 B2
Ebony St NN11 . . . . .184 D5
Eccles Rd PE8 . . . . .7 D8
Ecton Brook Lower Sch
  NN3 . . . . .143 D2
Ecton Brook Mid Sch
  NN3 . . . . .143 D1
Ecton Brook Rd NN3 . . . . . .143 D2
Ecton Hall NN6 . . . . .143 F4
Ecton La NN6 . . . . .127 D2
Ecton Leys CV22 . . . . .98 A2
Ecton Park Rd NN3 . . . . . . .143 C3
Ecton Prim Sch NN6 . . . . . .143 F4
Ecton St 11 NN1 . . . . .159 E6
Edale Gn NN14 . . . . .50 E4
Eden Cl Daventry NN11 . . . .135 A1
  Northampton NN3 . . . . .142 B4
Eden St NN16 . . . . .72 B2
Edgar Rd NN16 . . . . .72 D3
Edgcote Drive Cotts
  OX17 . . . . .197 A4
Edge Hill Ct MK18 . . . . . . .240 E6
Edgehill Dr NN11 . . . . .135 D6
Edgehill Rd NN5 . . . . .140 D1

Edgell St NN16 . . . . .72 C2
Edgemead Cl NN3 . . . . . .142 E7
Edgemont Rd NN3 . . . . . .142 E1
Edges Ct NN3 . . . . .142 C7
Edgewood NN13 . . . . . . .222 F1
Edinburgh Cl
  Market Harborough LE16 . .31 C3
  Rothwell NN14 . . . . .70 C6
Edinburgh Ho NN5 . . . . .158 C8
Edinburgh Mews NN2 . . .141 C2
Edinburgh Rd
  Kettering NN16 . . . . .72 D3
  Northampton NN2 . . . . . . .141 C2
  Stamford PE9 . . . . .241 D5
  Wellingborough NN8 . . . . .129 E1
Edinburgh Sq 🖪 NN11 . .135 B4
Edison Cl NN8 . . . . .129 A6
Edison Ct NN8 . . . . .129 A6
Edison Ctyd NN17 . . . . . . .21 F3
Edison Dr NN5 . . . . .158 D4
Edith Rd NN16 . . . . .72 E4
Edith St NN1 . . . . .159 E6
Edmonds Cl
  Buckingham MK18 . . . . . .240 F4
  Stamford PE9 . . . . .241 F4
  Wellingborough NN8 . . . . .130 A2
Edmonds Dr PE9 . . . . .1 A5
Edmund St NN16 . . . . .72 D2
Edmunds Rd OX16 . . . . . .240 A7
Edward Cl
  Higham Ferrers NN10 . . . .132 C7
  Kettering NN15 . . . . .91 C7
Edward Rd
  Irchester NN29 . . . . .147 B7
  Kettering NN15 . . . . .91 C7
  Market Harborough LE16 . .31 D5
  Stamford PE9 . . . . .241 D5
Edward St Banbury OX16 . .240 F4
  Rugby CV21 . . . . .241 B9
Edward Watson Cl NN2 . .141 B5
Edwardian Cl NN4 . . . . . .175 E7
Edwards Cl NN11 . . . . . .183 D7
Edwards Dr NN11 . . . . . .129 D5
Edwinstowe Cl NN3 . . . . .160 E7
Egerton Cl NN13 . . . . . . .234 A6
Egmont Ave MK11 . . . . . .229 E4
Eider Cl
  Buckingham MK18 . . . . . .240 E3
  Burton Latimer NN15 . . . . .92 A2
  Daventry NN11 . . . . .135 C3
Eismann Way NN17 . . . . . .37 C7
Ekins Cl NN3 . . . . .142 D2
Elan Ct NN10 . . . . .131 E3
Elborow St CV21 . . . . . . .241 C8
Eldean Rd NN5 . . . . .140 B1
Elder Dr NN11 . . . . .135 C3
Elderberry Ct NN3 . . . . . .143 C3
Eldon Cl NN6 . . . . .100 E6
Eldon Way NN6 . . . . .100 E6
Eleanor Cl PE9 . . . . .241 C4
Eleanor Ct NN6 . . . . .102 C4
Elgin St NN5 . . . . .158 F6
Eliot Cl NN16 . . . . .72 C6
Eliot Ct CV22 . . . . .241 A6
Eliot Way NN10 . . . . .132 A5
Elizabeth Cl
  Earls Barton NN6 . . . . . . .144 E5
  Wellingborough NN8 . . . . .129 D2
Elizabeth Ct NN10 . . . . . .132 C2
Elizabeth Rd
  Daventry NN11 . . . . .135 B3
  Kettering NN16 . . . . .72 D3
  Rothwell NN14 . . . . .70 C6
  Stamford PE9 . . . . .241 C5
  West Haddon NN6 . . . . . .102 C5
Elizabeth St Corby NN17 . . .36 B4
  Northampton NN1 . . . . . . .159 F6
Elizabeth Way
  Earls Barton NN6 . . . . . . .144 E5
  Higham Ferrers NN10 . . . .132 C7
  Irthlingborough NN9 . . . . .131 E8
Elizabeth Wlk 🖪 NN1 . .159 F6
Elkington La CV23 . . . . . . .99 B1
Elkington Rd NN6 . . . . . . .82 B4
Elkins Cl NN6 . . . . .82 B4
Ellen Cl NN6 . . . . .100 F6
Ellesmere Ave
  Brackley NN13 . . . . .233 B4
  Northampton NN5 . . . . . . .158 E7
Ellesmere Cl NN13 . . . . . .222 F1
Ellesmere Cres NN13 . . . .222 F1
Ellesmere Rd NN13 . . . . . .233 B4
Ellesmere Rd NN11 . . . . . .222 F1
Ellfield Ct NN3 . . . . .142 F3
Elliot Ho NN10 . . . . .132 A4
Ellis La NN14 . . . . .89 B4
Ellison Cl NN9 . . . . .114 C7
Elm Cl
  Brafield-on-t-G NN7 . . . . .161 D2
  Hargrave NN9 . . . . .115 F2
Elm Ct NN14 . . . . .76 C1
Elm Dr Brackley NN13 . . . .222 F1
  Deanshanger MK19 . . . . . .228 D3
  Hinton NN11 . . . . .184 A6
  Market Harborough LE16 . .31 C5
Elm Rd
  Burton Latimer NN15 . . . . .92 C4
  Kettering NN15 . . . . .72 D1
Elm St Buckingham MK18 . .240 D3
  🖪 Northampton NN1 . . . .159 C7
  Stamford PE9 . . . . .241 E3
  Wellingborough NN8 . . . . .129 F5
Elm Way NN7 . . . . .177 C3
Elm Wlk Corby NN17 . . . . .21 C1
  Higham Ferrers NN10 . . . .132 B6

Elmfield Cl NN12 . . . . . . .217 D3
Elmhurst Ave NN3 . . . . . .142 A2
Elmhurst Cl NN3 . . . . . . .142 A2
Elmington Cotts PE8 . . . . .42 C8
Elmington Rd NN3 . . . . . .143 C5
Elmlea Dr MK46 . . . . .195 F4
Elmore Rd CV22 . . . . . . .241 B6
Elms Dr CV22 . . . . .98 F4
Elms Dyke NN11 . . . . . . .135 E8
Elmwood Wlk NN5 . . . . . .140 A1
Elsden Rd NN8 . . . . .130 C5
Elsee Rd CV21 . . . . .241 D8
Elton CE Prim Sch PE8 . . . .28 D8
Elton Cl
  Northampton NN3 . . . . . . .143 B5
  Stamford PE9 . . . . .241 B4
Elton Hall ★ PE8 . . . . .28 D6
Elton Rd PE8 . . . . .16 C7
Elwes Way NN3 . . . . .143 B2
Elysium Terr NN2 . . . . . . .159 C8
Embankment NN8 . . . . . .130 C2
Emberton Ctry Pk & Visitor
  Ctr ★ MK46 . . . . .195 F4
Embleton Way MK18 . . . .240 C2
Emerald Way NN11 . . . . . .159 B5
Emerton Gdns MK11 . . . .229 D5
Emery Cl NN11 . . . . .135 E8
Emley Cl NN3 . . . . .142 F1
Emlyns Gdns PE9 . . . . . . .241 E4
Emlyns St PE9 . . . . .241 D4
Emmanuel CE Mid Sch
  NN3 . . . . .142 F2
Emmanuel Cl NN11 . . . . . .153 C8
Emmanuel Rd PE9 . . . . . .241 D5
Empingham Rd PE9 . . . . . .241 B3
Encon Ct NN3 . . . . .141 F7
Enfield Cl NN5 . . . . .157 F8
English Martyrs RC Prim Sch
  CV21 . . . . .99 A7
Ennerdale Cl
  Daventry NN11 . . . . .135 A2
  Kettering NN16 . . . . .72 A2
  Northampton NN3 . . . . . . .142 A3
Ennerdale Rd Corby NN17 . .21 E1
  Northampton NN3 . . . . . . .142 A4
  Rushden NN10 . . . . .132 D3
Ensleigh Cl NN15 . . . . .92 C1
Enstone Ct NN8 . . . . .129 C1
Enterprise Cl NN16 . . . . . .71 F4
Enterprise Ct NN8 . . . . . .129 B6
Enterprise Ind Pk NN17 . .22 F1
Enterprise Rd NN9 . . . . . .114 D7
Entwood Dr NN3 . . . . . . .143 B5
Epping Cl NN15 . . . . .92 A5
Epping Wlk 🖪 NN11 . . . .135 B4
Epsom Cl NN10 . . . . .148 D8
Epsom Wlk NN18 . . . . .36 C3
Equestrian Way NN7 . . . .155 B4
Ericsson Cl NN11 . . . . . . .135 C5
Ermine Cl PE9 . . . . .241 B3
Ermine Rd NN3 . . . . .143 C5
Ermine Way PE9 . . . . . . .241 B3
Ermont Way
  Banbury OX16 . . . . .219 A7
  Banbury OX16 . . . . .240 F9
Erskin Wood NN6 . . . . . . .105 B1
Esher Cl NN3 . . . . .142 D4
Eskdaill Pl NN16 . . . . .72 B3
Eskdaill St NN16 . . . . .72 B3
Eskdale Ave Corby NN17 . . .36 F2
  Northampton NN3 . . . . . . .142 B3
Eskdale Cl NN8 . . . . .129 C6
Essen La CV23 . . . . .100 A3
Essenden Ct MK11 . . . . . .229 F5
Essex Cl NN17 . . . . .36 B6
Essex Gdns LE16 . . . . .31 D1
Essex Pl NN15 . . . . .91 D6
Essex Rd Rushden NN10 . .132 C1
  Stamford PE9 . . . . .241 D4
Essex St
  Northampton NN2 . . . . . . .159 C8
  Rugby CV21 . . . . .241 C9
Ethel St NN1 . . . . .159 E6
Eton Cl NN7 . . . . .155 C4
Eton Ct 🖪 NN2 . . . . .141 C3
Ettrick Cl NN16 . . . . .72 A6
Euro Bsns Pk LE16 . . . . . . .32 B4
Euro Hub NN18 . . . . .37 A4
Euston Rd NN4 . . . . .159 C3
Eva Rd NN16 . . . . .72 E3
Evalyn Wlk NN9 . . . . . . .114 D6
Evans Cl NN11 . . . . .135 C1
Evelyn Way NN29 . . . . . .147 C7
Evenley Rd
  Mixbury NN13 . . . . .234 D1
  Northampton NN2 . . . . . . .141 C5
Evenlode OX16 . . . . .240 B9
Evensford Wlk NN9 . . . . .131 D8
Everard Ct CV23 . . . . .80 A5
Everdon Cl
  Northampton NN2 . . . . . . .141 A4
  Rugby CV22 . . . . .98 E8
Everdon Pk NN11 . . . . . . .135 A5
Everdon Rd NN12 . . . . . . .170 E3
Everdon Stubbs Nature
  Trail ★ 170 C6
Everdon Stubbs Woodland
  Trust Wood ★ NN11 . . . .170 D6
Everest Ho NN17 . . . . .36 E6
Everest La NN17 . . . . .36 E6
Evergreen Dr NN14 . . . . .113 D4
Everitt Cl NN8 . . . . .130 B2
Evesham Cl NN8 . . . . . . .129 E1
Evesham Ct NN3 . . . . .143 A4
Evison Rd NN14 . . . . .70 C6
Evreux Way CV21 . . . . . .241 C8
Ewenfield Rd NN9 . . . . . .111 F4
Excalibur Cl NN5 . . . . . . .158 A7

Excelsior NN8 . . . . .129 B4
Excelsior Ct NN9 . . . . . . .112 E2
Excelsior Gdns NN5 . . . . .157 F8
Exeter Cl NN11 . . . . .153 C8
Exeter Gdns PE9 . . . . . . .241 B2
Exeter Jun & Inf Sch
  NN8 . . . . .36 F5
Exeter Pl NN1 . . . . .159 E7
Exeter St NN16 . . . . .72 C5
Exmoor Cl NN3 . . . . .160 D7
Exmouth Ave NN18 . . . . . .36 F4
Express Cl NN9 . . . . .131 E8
Express Pk Kettering NN16 .71 D3
  Rushden NN10 . . . . .131 D3
Exton Cl PE9 . . . . .241 A3
Eyam Cl NN11 . . . . .135 A4
Eyeletter Ho 🖪 NN5 . . . .159 A6
Eynard Impasse NN13 . . .222 E1
Eynon Rd NN3 . . . . .126 B1

F

Factory La 🖪 LE16 . . . . . .31 E3
Fair La NN14 . . . . .76 E3
Fair Mile NN2 . . . . .141 A6
Fairfax Cl OX16 . . . . .240 A6
Fairfax Rd LE16 . . . . .31 E1
Fairfax Rise NN6 . . . . .85 B8
Fairfield NN7 . . . . .174 B2
Fairfield Rd Isham NN14 . . .91 C2
  Market Harborough LE16 . .31 D4
  Northampton NN2 . . . . . . .141 F2
  Paulerspury NN12 . . . . . . .216 B7
Fairfields Sch NN2 . . . . . .141 E1
Fairground Way NN3 . . . .160 E7
Fairhurst Way NN6 . . . . . .144 F4
Fairlight Ct 🖪 NN3 . . . . . .36 B5
Fairmead Cres NN10 . . . .147 F8
Fairmead Rise NN10 . . . . .140 F6
Fairoaks Dr NN9 . . . . . . .114 C7
Fairoaks The NN3 . . . . . .160 F8
Fairview Rd OX16 . . . . . . .240 D6
Fairway
  Market Harborough LE16 . .31 D4
  Northampton NN2 . . . . . . .141 E2
Fairway Ct CV21 . . . . . . .241 F9
Fairway The
  Banbury OX16 . . . . .240 A8
  Daventry NN11 . . . . .135 C3
  Kettering NN15 . . . . .91 A8
  Wellingborough NN9 . . . . .110 E1
Faith Terr MK19 . . . . .207 A2
Falcon View NN12 . . . . . .202 D8
Falcon Way NN13 . . . . . . .222 D2
Falconer's Hill Jun & Inf Schs
  NN11 . . . . .135 C3
Falconers Cl NN11 . . . . . .135 C3
Falconers Rise NN4 . . . . .175 A8
Falcutt Way NN2 . . . . . . .141 D5
Falkirk Cl PE9 . . . . .241 A4
Falkner's Cl OX17 . . . . . . .230 A4
Fallow Wlk NN3 . . . . .141 A6
Fallowfield NN9 . . . . .129 E8
Fallowfield Rd NN9 . . . . . .129 E8
Fallowfields NN6 . . . . . . .101 A6
Falmer Wlk NN18 . . . . .36 B4
Falster NN18 . . . . .36 A2
Fane Ct PE9 . . . . .241 D5
Far Brook NN6 . . . . .125 B8
Far Meadow Ct NN3 . . . . .142 E5
Faracre Ct NN3 . . . . .143 B1
Faraday Cl
  Daventry NN11 . . . . .135 A4
  Northampton NN5 . . . . . . .158 D5
  Wellingborough NN8 . . . . .129 A6
Faraday Ct
  Thrapston NN14 . . . . .76 E2
  Wellingborough NN8 . . . . .129 A6
Faraday Gr NN17 . . . . .37 A8
Faraday Rd CV22 . . . . . . .241 E6
Faramir Pl NN3 . . . . .143 B6
Farebrother Cl NN11 . . . . .183 D7
Fareham Ave CV22 . . . . . . .98 E8
Faringdon Cl NN3 . . . . . . .141 C4
Farm Cl Brigstock NN14 . . .55 F7
  Holcot NN6 . . . . .126 E8
  Northampton NN2 . . . . . . .141 B4
Farm Close Rd NN4 . . . . .175 E6
Farm Field Ct NN3 . . . . . .142 E5
Farm Gr CV22 . . . . .241 E6
Farm Gr Brackley NN13 . . .234 A6
  Wellingborough NN8 . . . . .129 E8
Farm Stile NN1 . . . . .182 C8
Farmbrook Ct NN3 . . . . . .142 F5
Farmers Cl NN4 . . . . .175 E5
Farmers Dr NN13 . . . . . . .233 D8
Farmfield Cl NN15 . . . . . . .91 F4
Farmhill Rd NN3 . . . . .143 A6
Farmstead Rd NN18 . . . . . .36 A3
Farnborough Cl NN15 . . . .91 D5
Farndale Ave NN17 . . . . . . .36 E7
Farndale View NN10 . . . . . .31 C2
Farndish Cl NN10 . . . . . . .131 F2
Farndish Rd NN29 . . . . . . .147 B7
Farndon Cl NN3 . . . . .142 F6
Farndon Ct LE16 . . . . .31 D2
Farndon Fields Prim Sch
  LE16 . . . . .48 E8
Farndon Rd
  Great Oxendon LE16 . . . . .48 D4
  Hinton NN11 . . . . .184 A5
  Lubenham LE16 . . . . .30 F2
  Market Harborough LE16 . .31 D4
  Marston Trussell LE16 . . . .47 D7
Farnham Dr NN10 . . . . . .147 F8
Farnworth Cl NN5 . . . . . .140 C1
Farraxton Sq NN4 . . . . . . .158 E2

Farrer Cl NN13 . . . . .223 D4
Farthinghoe Cl NN13 . . . .233 D7
Farthinghoe Prim Sch
  NN13 . . . . .223 A7
Farthinghoe Rd OX17 . . . .231 F5
Farthingstone Rd
  Litchborough NN12 . . . . . .171 B2
  Weedon NN7 . . . . .155 A1
Faugere Cl NN13 . . . . . . .233 F8
Favell Way NN3 . . . . .160 D8
Fawsley Leys CV22 . . . . . . .98 A7
Fawsley Rd
  Everdon NN11 . . . . .170 A8
  Northampton NN4 . . . . . . .159 C4
Faxton Cl NN2 . . . . .141 D4
Faxton End NN6 . . . . .107 D7
Fay Cl NN11 . . . . .184 A7
Feast Field Cl NN29 . . . . . .146 D1
Featherbed La
  Geddington NN18 . . . . .37 B1
  Rugby CV21 . . . . .80 A1
Federation Ave NN14 . . . . .50 F2
Fegans Ct MK11 . . . . .229 D6
Fell Wlk NN8 . . . . .129 D6
Fellmead Rd NN3 . . . . . . .143 C5
Fellows Cl NN29 . . . . .146 C3
Fellows Way CV21 . . . . . . .98 F8
Fengate Ct NN3 . . . . .143 C5
Fenn Cl PE8 . . . . .15 E5
Fennel Ct NN4 . . . . .175 D5
Fenners Cl NN10 . . . . .132 C5
Fenny Compton Rd
  OX17 . . . . .181 D1
Fenton Rise NN13 . . . . . . .233 D7
Fenwick Dr CV21 . . . . .99 A8
Ferguson's Cl PE8 . . . . . . .43 A3
Fergusson Rd OX16 . . . . .240 E9
Fermoy Cl NN7 . . . . .138 B4
Fermyn Pl NN18 . . . . .36 A3
Fern Dale Cl NN14 . . . . . . .54 B3
Fern Ley Cl LE16 . . . . .32 B2
Fern Rd NN10 . . . . .131 E3
Ferndale Rd NN3 . . . . . . .142 E3
Ferndown Ct CV22 . . . . . .241 A6
Ferndown Rd CV22 . . . . . .241 A6
Ferndown Terr CV22 . . . . .241 A6
Ferne Furlong MK46 . . . . .195 F5
Fernfield Cl LE16 . . . . .32 B4
Fernie Chase LE16 . . . . . . .17 A6
Fernie Cl NN15 . . . . .92 A5
Fernie Field NN3 . . . . .142 C6
Fernie Rd LE16 . . . . .31 F3
Fernie Way NN3 . . . . .129 D4
Ferrers Ct NN10 . . . . .132 C7
Ferrers Sch The NN10 . . . .132 C5
Ferrestone Rd NN8 . . . . . .130 A6
Ferris Row NN3 . . . . .160 F7
Ferro Fields NN6 . . . . . . .106 C3
Fessey Rd NN11 . . . . .183 D8
Festival Cl NN3 . . . . .113 B5
Festival Rd NN12 . . . . . . .172 D1
Fetter St NN1 . . . . .159 D5
Fettledine Rd NN9 . . . . . . .113 B5
Field Cl NN6 . . . . .102 C4
Field Cotts NN3 . . . . .53 B8
Field Rose Sq 🖪 NN3 . . . .143 C2
Field St NN16 . . . . .72 B3
Field Street Ave NN16 . . . .72 B3
Field View
  Brackley NN13 . . . . .233 D7
  Braunston NN11 . . . . .118 C1
  Marston St Lawrence
  OX17 . . . . .210 B2
Field Way NN13 . . . . .212 A5
Fieldgate Cl NN4 . . . . . . .175 F6
Fieldhead Cl LE16 . . . . . . .31 C3
Fieldmill Rd NN3 . . . . .143 B1
Fields View NN8 . . . . .130 B4
Fieldway NN3 . . . . .142 B1
Fiennes Cl NN11 . . . . .135 B6
Fiennes Rd OX16 . . . . . . .240 A6
Fiensgate NN4 . . . . .158 D1
Fife St NN5 . . . . .158 F7
Fifth Ave NN13 . . . . .238 E7
Fifth St NN13 . . . . .238 E7
Fifth St E NN13 . . . . .238 E7
Filleigh Way NN3 . . . . . . .160 C7
Finch Dr NN15 . . . . .92 A6
Finch-Hatton Dr NN17 . . . .10 C1
Finedon Hall NN9 . . . . . . .111 F5
Finedon Inf Sch NN9 . . . . .111 A6
Finedon Mulso CE Jun Sch
  NN9 . . . . .112 A5
Finedon Rd
  Burton Latimer NN15 . . . . .92 B1
  Irthlingborough NN9 . . . . .112 C3
  Irthlingborough NN9 . . . . .112 E3
  Wellingborough NN8 . . . . .130 B6
Finedon Road Ind Est
  NN8 . . . . .130 B8
Finedon St NN15 . . . . .92 B1
Finedon Station Rd
  NN9 . . . . .111 A6
Fineshade Cl
  Kettering NN15 . . . . .92 A5
  King's Cliffe PE8 . . . . .13 E7
Fineshade Gr NN17 . . . . . . .36 E7
Finland Way NN18 . . . . . . .36 A2
Fir Rd NN16 . . . . .72 D2
Fir Tree Gr NN29 . . . . . . .164 D2
Fir Tree La LE17 . . . . .62 C3
Fir Tree Wlk
  Market Harborough LE16 . .31 E4
  Northampton NN3 . . . . . . .142 E2
Firbank Cl NN3 . . . . .160 F8
Firdale Ave NN10 . . . . . . .132 B4
Fire Quarters The NN7 . . .155 C4
Firs Ct NN4 . . . . .175 F8

Firs Dr CV22 . . . . .241 B7
Firs The Daventry NN11 . . .135 C3
  Market Harborough LE16 . .31 C3
First Ave NN8 . . . . .129 D3
First La NN5 . . . . .158 F6
First St NN13 . . . . .238 F6
Firsview Dr NN5 . . . . .140 C1
Fish St NN1 . . . . .159 D6
Fisher Ave CV22 . . . . .98 E8
Fisher Cl NN14 . . . . .76 E1
Fishermans Rd MK46 . . . . .195 E4
Fishers Cl Kilsby CV23 . . . .99 F2
  Northampton NN3 . . . . . . .143 B1
Fishers Field MK18 . . . . . .240 C3
Fishpond Cl NN7 . . . . .162 B1
Fishponds Rd NN3 . . . . . . .143 B1
Fishton Cl NN15 . . . . .91 C7
Fitzroy Pl NN1 . . . . .159 B6
Fitzwilliam Dr NN15 . . . . . .92 A5
Fitzwilliam Leys NN10 . . . .132 B7
Fitzwilliam Rd
  Irthlingborough NN9 . . . . .112 C5
  Stamford PE9 . . . . .241 C5
Fitzwilliam St NN10 . . . . . .132 A2
Five Acres Fold NN4 . . . . .158 F3
Fjord Wlk NN18 . . . . .36 A2
Flaggs Mdw MK46 . . . . . .195 E4
Flamingo Gardens & Zoo
  Pk ★ MK46 . . . . .195 B3
Flatlets The NN9 . . . . .112 F2
Flavius Gate NN13 . . . . . .234 A7
Flaxland Cl LE16 . . . . .32 B3
Flaxlands Ct NN3 . . . . .142 F3
Flaxwell Ct NN3 . . . . .160 F8
Fleet Cl MK18 . . . . .240 F5
Fleet St NN16 . . . . .72 A2
Fleetwind Dr NN4 . . . . . . .175 D7
Fleetwood Cl LE16 . . . . . . .31 D1
Fleetwood Gdns LE16 . . . . .31 D1
Fleming Cl NN8 . . . . .129 B7
Fleming Rd NN17 . . . . .22 A2
Flensburg Cl NN18 . . . . . . .36 B2
Fletcher Gdns NN14 . . . . . .76 D1
Fletcher Rd NN10 . . . . . . .132 A3
Fletton Way PE8 . . . . .41 F6
Flintcomb Rise NN3 . . . . .143 B3
Flinters Cl NN4 . . . . .175 F7
Flitton Ct MK11 . . . . .229 F5
Flora Thompson Dr
  NN13 . . . . .233 E8
Flore CE Prim Sch NN7 . . .155 E5
Flore Hill NN7 . . . . .155 D5
Florence Rd NN1 . . . . .159 F7
Floribunda Dr NN4 . . . . . .158 F2
Fog Cotts NN6 . . . . .120 B5
Folly La Hartwell NN7 . . . .206 C8
  Little Brington NN7 . . . . . .138 B4
Folly Rd MK19 . . . . .228 D4
Fontwell Gdns PE9 . . . . . .241 D3
Foot La NN9 . . . . .133 C8
Ford Bank LE16 . . . . .20 D6
Ford Dr NN13 . . . . .233 D8
Ford St
  Buckingham MK18 . . . . . .240 D3
  Kettering NN16 . . . . .72 C2
Forest App PE8 . . . . .13 F7
Forest Cl NN15 . . . . .92 D3
Forest Ct NN10 . . . . .132 D3
Forest Gate Rd NN17 . . . . .36 E7
Forest Glade
  Hartwell NN7 . . . . .192 D2
  Kettering NN16 . . . . .72 C6
Forest Rd
  Hanslope MK19 . . . . .207 A6
  Hartwell NN7 . . . . .192 D2
  Northampton NN4 . . . . . . .159 C3
  Piddington NN7 . . . . .177 A1
Forest View NN7 . . . . .192 D2
Foresters Pl CV21 . . . . .99 B7
Foresters The NN9 . . . . . .114 C5
Forfar St NN5 . . . . .158 F7
Forge Ho NN11 . . . . .70 D7
Forge The NN10 . . . . .132 B1
Forrester Dr NN13 . . . . . .222 E1
Forrester Gr NN14 . . . . . . .76 E1
Forstal Cl NN18 . . . . .36 D3
Fort Pl NN1 . . . . .159 B6
Forty Foot La MK44 . . . . . .149 A1
Fosberry Cl NN4 . . . . .175 F6
Foscote Hospl OX16 . . . . .240 D6
Foscote Rise OX16 . . . . . .240 E6
Foskett Cl NN10 . . . . .132 A3
Foskitt Ct NN3 . . . . .143 B1
Fosse Cl NN8 . . . . .129 C1
Fosse Gn NN10 . . . . .132 C3
Foster Ct NN18 . . . . .36 E5
Foster's Booth Rd NN12 . .172 D1
Fothergill Cl LE16 . . . . .32 B3
Fotheringhay PE8 . . . . .27 D7
Fotheringhay Castle ★
  PE8 . . . . .27 E6
Fotheringhay Ct NN14 . . . .76 E2
Fotheringhay Rd
  Corby NN17 . . . . .36 B8
  Nassington PE8 . . . . .15 F4
Foundry Ct 🖪 NN11 . . . . .135 C1
Foundry Pl NN11 . . . . .135 C1
Foundry Rd PE9 . . . . .241 C3
Foundry St
  Banbury OX16 . . . . .240 C8
  🖪 Northampton NN1 . . . .159 C5
Foundry Wlk
  🖪 Daventry NN11 . . . . . .135 C1
  Thrapston NN14 . . . . .76 C1
Fourth Ave
  Croughton NN13 . . . . . . .238 E6
  Wellingborough NN8 . . . . .129 D3
Fourth St NN13 . . . . .238 E6

Fowey Cl NN8 ....129 C6
Fowler Rd OX16 ......240 E9
Fox Cl CV21 ....80 B1
Fox Covert Dr NN7 ...191 E3
Fox Coverts NN14 .....89 A4
Fox Dale PE9 ....241 B4
Fox Hill Rd NN3 ......143 D2
Fox La Brackley NN13 ..233 E4
   Souldern OX27 ......237 E3
Fox St NN1 ....70 C7
Fox Way MK18 ....240 E1
Fox Yd 7 LE16 ....31 E3
Foxcovert Rd NN3 .....143 B6
Foxdale Sq NN14 ......143 D2
Foxfield Way NN4 .....175 C2
Foxford Cl NN4 ....174 F8
Foxglove Ave NN11 ...184 B6
Foxglove Cl
   Buckingham MK18 ...240 C2
   Rushden NN10 ....148 C8
Foxglove Rd NN2 .....141 B4
Foxhill MK46 ....195 E5
Foxhill La OX27 ......237 E3
Foxhill Rd NN6 ....102 B3
Foxlands NN14 ....51 B2
Foxton Canal Mus★
   LE16 ....30 C7
Foxton Ct NN15 ......72 A1
Foxton Locks Ctry Pk★
   LE16 ....30 C8
Foxton Prim Sch LE16 ..30 D8
Foxton Rd Gumley LE16 ..30 D5
   Lubenham LE16 ......30 D5
Foxwell Sq NN3 ......142 F7
Foxwood Cl NN10 ....131 E2
Francis Cl NN10 ......131 E3
Francis Dickins Cl
   NN29 ....146 E3
Francis Row NN11 ....171 E6
Francis St
   8 Northampton NN1 ..159 C7
   Raunds NN9 ....114 B4
Francis Terr NN9 .....114 B4
Franciscan Cl NN10 ...147 F8
Frank Wise Sch OX16 ..240 A7
Franklin Cres NN5 ....158 D7
Franklin Fields NN17 ..37 A8
Franklin St NN5 ......158 F6
Franklin Way NN11 ...135 B5
Franklin's Cl NN6 ....143 F4
Frankston Ave MK11 ..229 E5
Fraser Cl Banbury OX16 ..240 E8
   Daventry NN11 ......135 D2
Fraser Rd NN3 ....142 D6
Frederick Press Way
   CV21 ....241 B8
Frederick St CV21 ....241 B8
Freehold St NN2 .....159 C8
Freeman Way NN7 ...112 B5
Freeman's Endowed CE Jun
   Sch NN8 ....129 E4
Freeman's La NN14 ...95 C6
Freeschool St 9 NN1 ..159 C5
Fremeaux Terr NN2 ..141 B5
French Dr NN5 ....72 F1
Frensham Cl 2 NN4 ..158 F3
Friar's Ave NN4 ......159 C1
Friar's Cl NN4 ....159 B1
Friar's Cres NN4 .....159 C1
Friars Cl NN3 ....130 A3
Friars Sch NN8 ......130 A3
Friary Cl NN11 ....135 D2
Friary The NN1 ......159 D6
Frinton Cl NN10 .....147 F8
Frisby La LE15 ....3 D8
Frobisher Cl NN11 ...135 E2
Frog Hall Brixworth NN6 ..106 A2
   Silverstone NN12 ...214 D5
Frog La NN11 ....182 C7
Front St NN14 ....95 C6
Frost Ct NN29 ....145 D6
Frosts Ct NN4 ....175 E5
Frosty Hollow NN4 ...175 C6
Froxhill Cres NN6 ....106 A1
Froxhill Wlk NN6 ....106 A1
Fuchsia Cl NN3 ......160 C6
Fulford Dr NN2 ......141 E3
Fulleburn Ct 2 NN3 ..142 E3
Fullen La NN17 ......22 D8
Fuller Rd NN3 ....142 C8
Fuller St NN16 ....72 C2
Fullers Cl NN14 ......76 F8
Fullingdale Rd NN3 ..142 B2
Fullwell Rd NN29 ....164 D4
Fulmar La NN8 ......130 A8
Fulwell Ave NN17 ....10 C1
Furber Ct NN3 ....142 D4
Furlong Rd NN14 ....51 C3
Furlongs The LE16 ...32 B3
Furnace Cotts NN9 ..111 A5
Furnace Dr NN11 ....135 A4
Furnace La Finedon NN9 ..111 B5
   Kettering NN16 ......72 A5
   Nether Heyford NN7 ..172 A8
Furnace Lane Ind Est
   NN9 ....111 B5
Furnells Cl NN9 .....114 D7
Furrow Cl CV21 .....241 F9
Furtho Cl MK19 .....229 B7
Furtho La NN12 .....217 E3
Furze Ct 5 NN4 .....159 A3
Furze Rd NN7 ....161 D2
Furze Wlk NN2 ......141 E2
Fushia Way NN10 ....148 B7
Fusilier Rd NN11 ....135 B1
Fusilier Way NN7 ....155 A4
Fyfe Rd NN17 ....36 B8
Fylingdale NN2 ......140 F5

G

Gable Cl NN11 ....135 B1
Gable Court Mews NN3 ..142 D1
Gables The NN15 .....72 B1
Gadesby Ct NN3 .....142 E3
Gainage Cl NN18 ....36 C1
Gains La PE17 ....61 D2
Gainsborough Ave NN16 ..92 A4
Gainsborough Cres CV21 ..80 B1
Gainsborough Ct NN16 ..92 A4
Gainsborough Dr NN8 ..129 F7
Gainsborough Rd
   Corby NN18 ....36 C4
   Stamford PE9 ....241 B5
Gainsborough Way
   NN11 ....135 C6
Galahad Ct NN5 .....158 A8
Galane Cl NN4 ......158 D1
Gallery Cl NN3 ......143 A6
Galley Hill MK11 ....229 F5
Gallfield Ct NN3 .....161 C8
Galliard Ct NN1 .....159 F7
Gallow Field Rd LE16 ..30 E7
Gallowhill Rd NN14 ..160 B1
Gambrel Rd NN5 ....158 D6
Gamston Wlk NN18 ..36 B6
Gander Cl NN17 .....38 A7
Gannet La NN8 ......130 A8
Ganton Cl NN11 .....135 F3
Gap The NN29 ......146 E2
Gapstile Cl NN14 ....51 A4
Garden Cl OX16 ....240 C9
Garden Fields Ct NN29 ..147 C8
Gardenfield NN10 ...132 B5
Gardenfields Cl NN9 ..113 B5
Gardens The
   East Carlton LE16 ..35 A7
   Kettering NN16 .....72 A4
Gardiner St LE16 ....31 C3
Gardner Cl NN9 .....114 C7
Gardner Rise NN13 ..233 D7
Garfield Cl NN2 .....141 C5
Garfield St Kettering NN15 ..91 B8
   Northampton NN1 ...141 B3
Garford La PE9 ......2 A5
Garners Way NN1 ...157 C7
Garrard Way NN16 ..71 F3
Garratt Rd PE9 .....241 D2
Garrick Rd NN1 .....160 B7
Garrow Cl NN9 .....112 E3
Garsdale NN2 ....140 F5
Garston Rd NN18 ...36 C1
Gas La PE9 ....241 B5
Gas St Rugby CV21 ..241 D8
   Stamford PE9 ....241 E3
Gatcombe Ho NN10 ..132 B2
Gate La NN14 ....90 B5
Gateford Ct NN18 ...36 B6
Gatehouse Cl CV21 ..99 A8
Gatehouse La LE16 ..20 F6
Gatelodge Cl NN3 ...142 E6
Gates Cl NN9 ....112 E3
Gateway Cl NN4 ....175 F6
Gatteridge St OX16 ..240 D7
Gaultney The NN14 ..51 A3
Gawcott Fields MK18 ..240 B2
Gawcott Rd MK18 ...240 B1
Gaydon Ho NN17 ...22 C1
Gayhurst Cl NN3 ....142 B7
Gayton CE Prim Sch
   NN7 ....173 E2
Gayton Rd Blisworth NN7 ..190 C8
   Eastcote NN12 .....172 F1
   Tiffield NN12 ....189 C6
Geddington CE Prim Sch
   NN14 ....54 B2
Geddington Rd NN18 ..37 D5
Gedling Cl NN3 .....160 F8
Gees Farm Cl NN7 ..179 A5
Geeston Rd PE9 .....1 B5
Geldock Rd NN3 ....143 A1
Genner Rd NN17 ....22 B1
Gentian Cl NN10 ....148 C8
George Blackall St NN17 ..36 C8
George Nutt Ct NN4 ..159 C2
George Row NN1 ...159 C5
George St Banbury OX16 ..240 C7
   Burton Latimer NN15 ..92 D3
   Corby NN17 ....36 E6
   Higham Ferrers NN10 ..132 C2
   Irthlingborough NN9 ..112 D1
   Kettering NN16 .....72 B1
   Rugby CV21 ....241 B8
   Rushden NN10 ......132 B3
   Wellingborough NN8 ..130 A5
George Yd MK11 ....229 D5
Georges Ave NN7 ...173 A4
Georges Cl NN7 .....173 A7
Gerandria Ct CV22 ..98 E8
Gerrard Gdns LE16 ..48 D8
Gervase Sq NN3 ....143 C1
Gharana Nivas NN8 ..130 B5
Gibbons Dr NN14 ...70 E7
Gibbs Rd OX16 .....240 E9
Gibbsacre Ct NN3 ...143 C1
Gibraltar Ct 23 NN1 ..159 C7
Gibson Dr Rugby CV21 ..80 A1
   Upper Benefield PE8 ..39 F7
Gibson La NN5 ......158 F8
Giffard Ct
   Market Harborough LE16 ..31 D3
   Northampton NN5 ...159 A5
Gifford Cl NN5 ......158 C8
Gifford Pl MK18 ....240 E4
Gilbert Cl LE16 .....32 B2
Gilbert Scott Ct NN12 ..203 B6

Gilberts Rugby Football
   Mus★ CV21 ....241 C8
Gilbey Cl NN9 ......110 E1
Gilchrist Ave NN17 ..37 A8
Gilkes Yd OX16 .....240 B7
Gillett Cl OX16 .....240 B7
Gillett Rd OX16 ....240 B7
Gillingham Rd NN15 ..90 F8
Gillitts Rd NN8 .....129 E3
Gillsway NN2 ....141 A4
Gilson's Cl LE15 ....3 A6
Gingles Ct CV21 ....99 A8
Gipsy La Irchester NN29 ..146 E8
   Kettering NN16 .....71 E2
Gipsy Lane Turn NN29 ..146 F7
Girton Rd PE9 ......241 C5
Gisburne Rd NN8 ...130 A6
Glade Cl
   Burton Latimer NN15 ..92 C3
   Northampton NN3 ...143 B1
Glade The NN9 .....110 E1
Gladstone Cl NN5 ..141 A1
Gladstone Ct 7 NN16 ..72 C2
Gladstone Lower Sch
   NN5 ....159 A8
Gladstone Rd NN5 ..159 A8
Gladstone St
   Desborough NN14 ..51 A4
   Kettering NN16 .....72 C2
   Market Harborough LE16 ..31 F2
   Raunds NN9 ....114 D6
   Ringstead NN14 ....95 C3
   Rothwell NN14 .....70 D7
   Rugby CV21 ....241 B9
Glaisdale Cl NN2 ...140 F5
Glaister Pl NN16 ....72 D5
Glamis Cl NN10 ....132 D1
Glan y Mor Terr NN2 ..141 C5
Glanville Cl OX16 ..240 B8
Glapthorn CE Lower Sch
   PE8 ....26 B2
Glapthorn Rd PE8 ..41 F6
Glasgow St NN5 ....158 F6
Glassbrook Rd NN10 ..132 A2
Glassthorpe La NN7 ..157 A6
Glaston Rd LE15 ....3 A5
Glastonbury Cl NN15 ..91 F8
Glastonbury Rd
   Corby NN18 ....36 A6
   Northampton NN4 ..159 D7
Glebe Ave Broughton NN14 ..90 B4
   Kettering NN15 .....91 B8
   Northampton NN4 ..175 B8
Glebe Cl Holcot NN6 ..126 E8
   Northampton NN4 ..175 E8
Glebe Cres CV21 ...241 A8
Glebe Ct PE8 ....58 A4
Glebe Dr NN13 .....234 A7
Glebe Farm Cl NN4 ..175 C4
Glebe Farm Ct NN29 ..145 E6
Glebe La
   Great Houghton NN4 ..160 E2
   Hanslope MK19 ....206 E5
   Lower Harlestone NN7 ..139 E7
   Pitsford NN6 ....125 D5
   Staverton NN11 ....152 C7
Glebe Rd
   Burton Latimer NN15 ..92 A2
   Cogenhoe NN7 .....161 E6
   Deanshanger MK19 ..228 E5
   Market Harborough LE16 ..32 A2
   Mears Ashby NN6 ..128 B2
Glebe Rise OX17 ....231 A5
Glebe The Aynho OX17 ..237 D7
   Badby NN11 ....153 A2
   Daventry NN11 .....153 C8
Glebe Way
   Cogenhoe NN7 .....161 E6
   Northampton NN4 ..175 E8
Glebeland Cres NN5 ..159 A8
Glebeland Gdns NN5 ..140 F1
Glebeland Rd NN5 ..158 F8
Glebeland Wlk 1 NN5 ..158 F8
Glebelands NN6 ....105 B1
Glen Ave NN7 ......174 B2
Glen Bank NN4 .....130 A4
Glen Baulk Rd NN14,
   NN16 ....71 C4
Glen Cres PE9 ......241 C5
Glencoe Dr NN15 ...91 E8
Glendale Ct NN3 ...143 C1
Glendon Rd NN14 ..70 E7
Glendower Cl NN11 ..135 A4
Gleneagles Cl
   Daventry NN11 .....135 E3
   Kettering NN15 .....91 F8
Gleneagles Dr NN8 ..129 D7
Glenfield Cl NN10 ...131 E2
Glenfield Dr NN29 ..145 D5
Glengary NN3 ......142 D7
Glenshee Cl NN15 ..91 E8
Glenville NN3 ....142 B4
Gloucester Ave NN4 ..159 B1
Gloucester Cl
   2 Kettering NN16 ..72 C2
   Northampton NN4 ..159 B2
   Weedon NN7 ....155 B4
Gloucester Cres
   Northampton NN4 ..159 B2
   Rushden NN10 ......132 C3
Gloucester Ct NN14 ..70 C6
Gloucester Ho NN4 ..159 C2
Gloucester Pl NN8 ..130 A4
Gloucester Rd PE9 ..241 D4
Glover Cl LE16 .....20 C1
Glovers La OX17 ...208 F1
Glyndebourne Gdns
   NN18 ....36 A4

Glynswood Rd MK18 ..240 C4
Goadby's Yd 9 NN16 ..72 B2
Gocker Wood Cl NN18 ..36 B1
Godwin Rd NN17 ...21 F3
Godwin Wlk NN5 ...140 D2
Gold St Clipston LE16 ..66 F8
   Desborough NN14 ..51 A3
   Hanslope MK19 ....207 A2
   Kettering NN16 .....72 B2
   Northampton NN1 ..159 C5
   Podington NN29 ....147 E2
   Walgrave NN6 ......108 A5
   Wellingborough NN8 ..130 A6
Gold Street Mews 6
   NN1 ....159 C5
Goldcrest Ct NN3 ...143 A4
Goldcrest Rd NN3 ..222 D1
Golden Villa Cl OX16 ..240 A7
Goldenash Ct NN3 ..142 F5
Golding Cl NN11 ...135 C2
Goldings Mid Sch NN3 ..142 F5
Goldings Rd NN3 ...142 F5
Goldsmith Dr NN17 ..36 D8
Goldsmith Rd NN8 ..129 C4
Golf La NN6 ....140 C8
Good Shepherd RC Lower
   Sch The NN3 ......141 C3
Goodacre Cl NN23 ..80 A5
Goodens La NN29 ...145 F6
Goodhew Cl NN15 ..90 F8
Goodrington Cl OX16 ..240 B8
Goodwood Ave NN3 ..141 F5
Goodwood Cl LE16 ..32 B3
Goodwood Rd NN10 ..148 D8
Goose Gn NN3 ......233 E6
Goosemere MK19 ...228 E4
Goran Ave MK11 ...229 E4
Gordon Cl Oundle PE8 ..42 A6
   Wellingborough NN8 ..130 B5
Gordon St Kettering NN16 ..72 C2
   Northampton NN2 ..159 C8
   Rothwell NN14 .....70 D6
   Rushden NN10 ......131 F2
Gordon Terr NN14 ..74 F2
Gores La LE16 ......32 A3
Gorricks MK11 .....229 D4
Gorse Cl
   Northampton NN2 ..141 B6
   Rugby CV22 ....241 A6
Gorse Rd Hinton NN11 ..184 B7
   Kettering NN16 .....72 E4
   Spratton NN6 ......124 B8
Gorseholm Ct 10 NN9 ..112 F2
Gosforth NN8 ......129 C4
Gosler The NN8 ....129 B3
Gotch Cl NN15 .....91 F4
Gotch Rd NN15 ....91 F5
Gough Cl NN15 .....72 E1
Goughs Cotts NN5 ..158 C7
Gould Cl NN11 .....118 D1
Goulds Villas OX16 ..240 A7
Goward St LE16 ....31 E3
Gower Cl NN15 .....91 C6
Gowers Yd MK19 ...229 B7
Grace Ct NN15 .....92 B1
Gracelands LE16 ...31 C2
Graeme Rd PE5 ....8 F2
Grafton Cl Hartwell NN7 ..192 D2
   Potterspury NN12 ..217 E3
   Wellingborough NN8 ..129 D7
Grafton Ct NN7 ....193 A8
Grafton Dr NN17 ...36 B8
Grafton Ho NN1 ....159 B6
Grafton Pl 10 NN1 ..159 C7
Grafton Rd Brigstock NN14 ..55 E4
   Cranford NN14 .....93 A7
   Geddington NN14 ..54 B2
   Roade NN7 ....191 C4
   Rushden NN10 ......132 D2
   Yardley Gobion NN12 ..217 F6
Grafton St Kettering NN16 ..72 A4
   Northampton NN1 ..159 C7
Grafton View NN4 ..175 E6
Grafton Way
   Northampton NN5 ..140 B2
   Rothersthorpe NN7 ..174 A7
Graham Hill NN12 ..214 D4
Graham Hill Rd NN12 ..203 C7
Graham Rd CV21 ...241 E9
Granary Cl LE16 ....31 F6
Granary Ct NN4 ....175 C7
Granary Rd NN4 ...175 C7
Granby Cl NN18 ....36 B6
Grandborough Cl NN6 ..106 C1
Grange Ave NN5 ...140 B1
Grange Cl Denton NN7 ..162 B1
   Earls Barton NN6 ..144 E5
   Irchester NN29 ....147 B7
Grange Com Sch NN16 ..72 E3
Grange Ct Brixworth NN6 ..106 B2
   Horton NN7 ....177 D1
   Stony Stratford MK12 ..227 F6
Grange Jun & Inf Schs The
   NN11 ....135 A1
Grange La Pitsford NN6 ..125 E6
   Thorpe Langton LE16 ..17 A5
Grange Pl NN16 ....72 E4
Grange Rd
   Broughton NN14 ...90 B5
   Geddington NN14 ..53 F2
   Islip NN14 ....76 B1
   Kettering NN16 .....72 A5
   Northampton NN3 ..142 C3
   Stanion NN14 ......37 C6
   Stanwick NN9 ......114 A3
   Wellingborough NN9 ..110 C1
Grange Road Workshops
   NN14 ....53 F2

Grange Way NN29 ..147 B7
Grangeway NN10 ...148 A8
Grangewood NN4 ...175 A7
Grant Cl NN15 .....90 F7
Grant Rd NN8 ......130 B5
Grantham Wlk NN18 ..36 B4
Grantown Cl NN15 ..91 E8
Granville St
   Kettering NN16 .....72 C2
   Market Harborough LE16 ..31 F2
Grasmere Gn NN8 ..129 B4
Grasmere Rd NN16 ..71 F2
Grasmere Way NN10 ..132 B8
Graspin La NN3 ....160 D8
Grass Cl NN12 .....203 B7
Grass Croft NN16 ..121 A3
Grass Slade NN6 ...106 C2
Grasscroft NN2 ....141 A4
Grassmere Ave NN3 ..142 E2
Gravel Hill NN11 ...199 D7
Gravely St NN10 ...131 F2
Gray Cl NN6 ....145 A4
Gray St Irchester NN29 ..147 A7
   Northampton NN1 ..159 E7
Gray's Cl NN17 ....36 E8
Grays Cl NN12 .....216 D8
Grays Dr NN14 ....37 E3
Grays La
   Paulerspury NN12 ..216 D8
   Yardley Gobion NN12 ..217 E6
Greasley Wlk NN18 ..36 B6
Great Addington CE Prim Sch
   NN14 ....94 B3
Great Billing CE Lower Sch
   NN3 ....143 C2
Great Billing Way NN3 ..143 C4
Great Bowden CE Sch
   LE16 ....32 A6
Great Bowden Hall LE16 ..31 E7
Great Bowden Rd LE16 ..32 A4
Great Central Walk Nature
   Trail★ CV22 ....98 D6
Great Central Way
   Rugby CV21 ....241 F9
   Woodford Halse NN11 ..184 C2
Great Cl NN6 ......124 D1
Great Creaton Prim Sch
   NN6 ....104 F4
Great Doddington Prim Sch
   NN29 ....145 E6
Great Easton Rd
   Bringhurst LE16 ...20 C6
   Caldecott LE16 ....21 A7
   Drayton NN16 .....20 A5
   Great Easton LE16 ..20 C6
Great Field Ct NN3 ..142 E5
Great Folds Rd NN18 ..35 F1
Great Gidding CE Prim Sch
   PE17 ....61 D3
Great Ground Wlk NN4 ..175 F2
Great Gull Cres NN3 ..142 F6
Great Holme Ct NN3 ..142 E5
Great La Bugbrooke NN7 ..172 F7
   Hackleton NN7 .....177 B3
Great North Rd
   Stamford PE9 ......241 A2
   Stibbington PE8 ...8 C2
   Wothorpe PE9 .....2 B8
Great Park St NN8 ..130 A5
Great Russell St NN1 ..159 D7
Great Slade MK18 ..240 D1
Greatmeadow NN3 ..143 C4
Greatmeadow Rd NN3 ..143 B4
Greatworth Prim Sch
   OX17 ....210 E2
Greaves Cl NN5 ....139 F1
Grebe Cl Hinton NN11 ..184 B6
   Thrapston NN14 ...76 E3
Green Cl NN8 ......129 C7
Green End NN2 ....141 B2
Green End La MK19 ..207 A3
Green Farm OX17 ..230 A4
Green Farm Cl CV23 ..81 A6
Green La Ashley LE16 ..18 F2
   Banbury OX16 .....240 D6
   Braybrooke LE16 ..49 F5
   Charlton OX17 .....231 E5
   Desborough NN14 ..50 D3
   Duddington PE9 ...5 B6
   Husbands Bosworth LE17 ..45 E5
   Kettering NN16 .....72 B2
   Market Harborough LE16 ..31 E1
   Northampton NN4 ..175 E5
   Silverstone NN12 ..214 D4
   Stamford PE9 ......241 D5
   Stanwick NN9 ......113 F3
   Stoke Albany LE16 ..34 B4
   Thrapston NN14 ...76 D2
   Towcester NN12 ...203 A5
   Weston by W LE16 ..18 C6
Green Oaks Lower Sch
   NN2 ....141 D4
Green Rd NN7 .....161 D4
Green St
   Milton Malsor NN7 ..174 E4
   Northampton NN1 ..159 B5
   Wollaston NN29 ...146 E2
Green The
   Abthorpe NN12 ....201 F2
   Adderbury OX17 ..230 A4
   Barby CV23 ....99 C1
   Blakesley NN12 ...187 B1
   Braunston NN11 ...118 C1
   Byfield NN11 ....183 D7
   Caldecott LE16 ....21 B8

Green The continued
Chelveston NN9 ....133 C8
Church Stowe NN7 ......171 D7
Clipston LE16 ....67 A8
Cosgrove MK19 ....218 F2
Cranford NN14 ....93 A6
Culworth OX17 ....198 C3
Deanshanger MK19 .....228 E4
Everdon NN11 ....170 A8
Flore NN7 ....155 F5
Great Bowden LE16 ......32 B6
Great Brington NN7 .....138 D7
Great Houghton NN4 ...160 E2
Hanslope MK19 ....207 A2
Helldion NN11 ....151 C1
Helmdon NN13 ....211 F4
Hollowell NN6 ....104 B4
Husbands Bosworth LE17 .45 E5
Kislingbury NN7 ....157 D3
Lilbourne CV23 ....81 A6
Little Addington NN14 ...113 B8
Lubenham LE16 ....30 C3
Lyddington LE15 ....9 D7
Marston St Lawrence
OX17 ....210 B1
Mawsley Village NN14 ....89 B4
Nether Heyford NN7 ....156 B1
Newnham NN11 ....153 D4
10 Northampton NN1 ...159 C5
Northampton NN4 ....175 F3
Northampton,Hardingstone
NN4 ....175 F8
Northampton,Kingsthorpe
NN2 ....141 B3
Orlingbury NN14 ....110 A5
Paulerspury NN12 ....216 B7
Priors Marston CV47 ....166 D7
Roade NN7 ....191 B4
Staverton NN11 ....152 B7
Titchmarsh NN14 ....77 C4
Twywell NN14 ....75 A1
Upper Harlestone NN7 ..139 D4
Wadenhoe PE8 ....58 A4
Weedon Lois NN12 ......200 C3
West Haddon NN6 ....102 A4
Weston by W LE16 ....18 B3
Woodford NN14 ....94 D6
Greenacre Dr NN10 .....148 B8
Greenacres Cvn Pk LE16 .31 C6
Greenaway Cl NN7 ......190 E7
Greenbank Ave NN15 ....72 C1
Greenbank Terr NN14 ...95 B3
Greendale Sq 8 NN3 ..143 C2
Greenfield Ave
Kettering NN15 ....71 F1
Northampton NN3 ....142 B3
Greenfield Rd NN3 ......142 A2
Greenfield Way NN10 ..132 A1
Greenfields Sch NN2 ...141 B5
Greenfinch Dr NN3 .....142 C6
Greenglades NN4 ....158 E1
Greenhill Cres NN11 ...135 B3
Greenhill Ct
Banbury OX16 ....240 D6
Long Buckby NN6 ....121 A3
Greenhill Rd Elton PE7 ..29 B6
Elton PE8 ....28 F8
Kettering NN15 ....91 A8
Long Buckby NN6 ....121 A3
Rugby CV22 ....241 B6
Greenhill Rise NN18 .....36 B5
Greenhills Cl NN2 ....141 B6
Greenhills Rd NN2 ......141 B6
Greening Rd NN14 ....70 C7
Greenland Wlk NN18 ....36 A2
Greenlaw NN8 ....129 B4
Greens Norton CE Prim Sch
NN12 ....202 D2
Greenside Blisworth NN7 190 D7
Northampton NN3 ....142 B3
Wappenham NN12 ......213 B8
Greenslade Cl NN15 ......91 B8
Greensward The OX17 ..196 E1
Greenview Dr
Northampton NN2 ....141 E3
Towcester NN12 ....203 B6
Greenway
Braunston NN11 ....118 B1
Eastcote NN12 ....173 A1
Northampton NN3 ....160 C8
Greenway Ave NN3 .....142 D4
Greenway The NN11 ....153 C8
Greenway Wlk MK18 ...240 F4
Greenwood Cl
Byfield NN11 ....183 C7
Moulton NN3 ....142 C8
Greenwood Rd NN5 ....159 A6
Greenyard The NN7 ....179 B7
Greeve Cl NN18 ....36 C1
Gregory St 8 NN1 ......159 C5
Gregory Wlk NN18 ....36 D4
Grenadier Rd NN11 .....135 B1
Grendon Ave NN17 ......36 B7
Grendon CE Prim Sch
NN7 ....163 D5
Grendon Lakes Watersports
Ctr★ NN7 ....145 C1
Grendon Rd NN6 ....144 E1
Grendon Wlk NN3 ......141 F5
Grenville Cl Corby NN17 .36 A8
Daventry NN11 ....135 E1
Rothwell NN14 ....70 E6
Grenville Comb Sch
MK18 ....240 D3
Grenville Gdns LE16 .....31 D1

Grenville Rd MK18 .....240 C4
Gresham Dr NN4 ....158 E2
Gresley Cl NN11 ....135 A4
Gresley Dr PE9 ....241 D2
Gretton Brook Rd
Corby NN17 ....21 E3
Corby NN17 ....22 C4
Gretton Ct NN8 ....129 D7
Gretton Prim Sch NN17 .22 C4
Gretton Rd Corby NN17 ..22 F3
Harringworth NN17 ....10 E7
Lyddington LE15 ....9 D5
Rockingham LE16 ....21 B5
Weldon NN17 ....38 A8
Greville Ave NN3 ....142 A4
Greville Cl NN2 ....141 C8
Greyfriars NN1 ....159 C6
Greyfriars Rd NN11 ....153 B8
Greys The NN7 ....155 B4
Grieg Wlk NN18 ....36 A2
Griffin Rd LE16 ....49 E4
Griffith St NN10 ....132 B1
Grimmer Wlk NN9 ......131 D8
Grimsbury Dr OX16 ....240 E9
Grimsbury Sq OX16 ....240 E9
Grimsby Cl NN18 ....36 C4
Grindleford Cl NN14 .....50 E3
Grizedale Cl NN16 ....72 A6
Grombold Ave NN9 ....114 C6
Grooms La NN6 ....105 A4
Grosvenor Cl NN15 ......92 A5
Grosvenor Ctr NN1 .....159 D6
Grosvenor Gdns NN2 ..141 D4
Grosvenor Ho NN2 .....141 D4
Grosvenor Pl NN13 ....233 E7
Grosvenor Rd
Banbury OX16 ....240 D7
Kettering NN15 ....92 A5
Rugby CV21 ....241 E8
Grosvenor Way NN15 ...91 F5
Groundwell Ct 1 NN3 .142 F1
Grove Farm Cl NN6 ....121 D4
Grove Farm La NN3 ...126 D2
Grove La NN12 ....199 F3
Grove Pl NN9 ....114 D5
Grove Rd
Brafield-on-t-G NN7 .....161 D3
Northampton NN1 ....159 E7
Rushden NN10 ....132 C2
Thrapston NN14 ....76 D1
Grove St Banbury OX16 .240 D7
Higham Ferrers NN10 ...132 C6
Raunds NN9 ....114 D5
Wellingborough NN8 ...129 E4
Grove The Corby NN18 ..37 C6
Kettering NN15 ....72 B1
Moulton NN3 ....126 C2
Ringstead NN14 ....95 A3
Roade NN7 ....191 E4
Wollaston NN29 ....146 D1
Grove Way NN9 ....111 E3
Grovebury Dell NN4 ....141 A4
Grovelands NN11 ....153 A8
Grundy Cl NN15 ....91 B8
Guardian Ct OX16 ......240 E8
Guildhall Rd NN1 ....159 D5
Guillemot La NN8 ......130 A7
Guilsborough CE Prim Sch
NN6 ....103 E7
Guilsborough Hill NN6 .104 B5
Guilsborough Rd
Ravensthorpe NN6 ......103 D1
West Haddon NN6 ......102 D7
Guilsborough Sch NN6 .103 D8
Guinea Orch MK46 ....195 E4
Gullet La LE16 ....18 F2
Gumley Rd LE16 ....30 C7
Gunnell Cl NN15 ....90 F8
Gunnsbrook Cl LE16 ....32 A6
Gunthorpe Pl NN18 .....36 B6
Gurston Rise NN3 ......143 C4
Gynwell NN6 ....85 B8

H

H E Bates Way NN10 ...132 A2
Hachenburg Pl NN10 ...132 C5
Hackleton Prim Sch
NN7 ....177 A3
Hackwood Rd NN11 ....153 E8
Haddon Cl
Rushden NN10 ....132 A1
Wellingborough NN8 ...129 D8
Haddon Ct NN6 ....122 C5
Haddon Rd PE9 ....241 B4
Hadfield Cl CV23 ....80 A5
Hadrian's Gate NN13 ..234 A7
Hafod Cl NN18 ....36 C2
Hagley Cl LE16 ....32 B3
Haigh Dr NN15 ....72 E1
Hailsham Ct OX17 ......220 B8
Haines Rd NN4 ....159 C3
Hale Ave MK11 ....229 E5
Halford St NN14 ....76 C1
Halford Way NN11 .....135 E8
Halfway Thorn NN6 ...124 C1
Halifax Sq NN18 ....36 B5
Hall Ave NN18 ....132 A1
Hall Cl Arthingworth LE16 .68 C7
Harpole NN7 ....157 B6
Kettering NN15 ....90 F8
Kilsby CV23 ....100 A3
Kislingbury NN7 ....157 D1
Naseby NN6 ....66 B1
Northampton NN5 ......158 C6
Old Stratford MK19 .....229 B6
Weston by W LE16 ....18 B4

Hall Dr Finedon NN9 ....111 E4
Long Buckby NN6 ....121 C4
Hall Farm Cl NN6 ......106 B3
Hall Gdns
East Haddon NN6 ....122 D5
Loddington NN14 ....70 C1
Polebrook PE8 ....43 A3
Hall Hill NN6 ....55 F7
Hall La Ashley LE16 .....18 E2
Drayton LE16 ....20 A5
Kettering NN15 ....90 F8
South Luffenham LE15 ...3 E8
Welford NN6 ....64 D6
Wittering PE8 ....7 C8
Hall Mead Ct NN7 ......172 E6
Hall Meadow Prim Sch
NN15 ....90 F7
Hall Piece Cl NN3 ....143 C3
Hall Yd Collyweston PE9 ..1 C2
King's Cliffe PE8 ....13 F7
Hall's Cl Geddington NN14 .54 B3
Weldon NN17 ....38 A8
Hall's La NN13 ....233 E6
Hallam Cl NN3 ....142 B7
Hallaton Rd LE16 ....18 F7
Hallwood Rd NN16 ......72 C5
Halse Rd NN13 ....222 F1
Halswell Ct NN3 ....142 D4
Ham La NN14 ....95 A4
Ham Meadow Dr NN3 .143 C2
Hambledon Rise NN4 ..158 E3
Hambleton Rd PE9 .....241 A2
Hamblin Ct NN10 ......132 B2
Hamilton Cl OX16 ......240 E9
Hamilton Ho Corby NN17 .36 E5
Northampton NN2 ....141 C5
Hamilton La NN7 ....138 D6
Hamlet Gn NN5 ....158 F8
Hammas Leys NN6 .....121 C4
Hammerstone La NN4 .158 F3
Hammond Way LE16 ....31 E4
Hampden Cres NN16 ....72 D3
Hampton Court Cl NN12 203 B5
Hampton Ct LE16 ....31 F3
Hampton Dr OX17 .....230 F6
Hampton Ho NN10 ....132 B2
Hampton St NN1 ....159 B7
Hamsterly Pk NN3 .....143 A6
Handcross Ct NN18 .....36 B4
Handcross Way NN10 ..132 C5
Handley Cl NN5 ....140 A1
Hanemill Ct NN3 ....143 C1
Hangerfield Ct NN3 ....142 F4
Hanover Cl NN15 ....92 A7
Hanover Ct
Northampton NN3 ......143 B4
Stamford PE9 ....241 E3
Hanover Dr NN13 ......233 E7
Hans Apel Dr NN13 ....233 D7
Hansbury Ironstone Rly
Mus★ NN4 ....158 E2
Hanslope Comb Sch
MK19 ....207 A3
Hanslope Rd MK19 .....218 F7
Harbidges La NN6 .....121 A4
Harborough Rd
Braybrooke LE16 ....49 D7
Brixworth NN6 ....106 C3
Clipston NN14 ....50 D7
Desborough NN14 ....50 D7
Dingley LE16 ....32 D5
Dingley LE16 ....32 E1
Dingley LE16 ....33 A3
East Farndon LE16 ....48 C8
Great Oxendon LE16 ....48 F4
Kelmarsh NN6 ....67 F5
Lubenham LE16 ....31 A3
Maidwell NN6 ....87 B4
Market Harborough LE16 .31 C7
Northampton NN2 ......141 C4
Rushden NN10 ....132 C1
Stoke Albany LE16 ....34 B4
Theddingworth LE17 .....30 A1
Theddingworth LE17 .....46 E8
Harborough Rd N NN2 .141 B6
Harborough Way NN10 132 C1
Harcourt Sq NN6 ....144 E4
Harcourt St
9 Kettering NN16 ....72 C2
Market Harborough LE16 .31 D3
Raunds NN9 ....114 D6
Harcourt Way NN4 .....158 E3
Hardays La NN6 ....102 B4
Harden Cl NN18 ....53 A8
Harding Cl NN15 ....72 F1
Harding Terr NN1 ......159 C7
Hardingstone La NN4 ..175 D8
Hardingstone Prim Sch
NN4 ....175 E7
Hardlands Rd NN5 .....158 C8
Hardwater Rd NN29 ...145 D4
Hardwick Cl NN8 ....129 E5
Hardwick Jun & Inf Sch
NN8 ....129 C5
Hardwick Rd
Gretton NN17 ....10 B1
Little Harrowden NN9 ..110 B3
Northampton NN4 ......175 C8
Priors Marston CV47 ...166 D7
Wellingborough NN8 ...129 A7
Wellingborough, Hatton Park
NN8 ....129 D6
Wellingborough, Hatton Park
NN8 ....129 E5
Hardy Dr NN4 ....175 F7
Hare Cl MK18 ....240 E2
Harebell Sq 1 NN3 ....143 D2
Harefield Rd NN3 ......143 B5

Harefoot Cl NN5 ....158 B8
Haresmoor Dr NN12 ...203 C4
Harksome Hill NN4 .....158 C2
Harlech NN15 ....36 C3
Harlech Ct NN14 ....76 F2
Harlestone Cl NN5 .....158 F7
Harlestone Ho NN5 ....159 A7
Harlestone Prim Sch
NN7 ....139 E5
Harlestone Rd
Church Brampton NN6 ..124 D1
Lower Harlestone NN7 ..139 F6
Northampton NN5 ......140 B2
Harley Way
Brigstock NN14 ....56 C8
Lower Benefield PE8 .....40 D3
Harmans Way NN7 ....155 B4
Harnett Dr MK12 ....229 F6
Harold St NN14 ....159 E6
Harper's Ct NN14 ....55 F7
Harpers Cl NN18 ....53 B8
Harpole Prim Sch NN7 157 D6
Harrier Pk NN4 ....175 B8
Harriers View OX16 ....240 C6
Harrington Rd
Desborough NN14 ....50 F3
Loddington NN14 ....70 D1
Old NN6 ....107 D7
Rothwell NN14 ....70 C6
Harringworth Rd NN17 ..10 C2
Harris Cl Brackley NN13 233 D8
Northampton NN4 ......175 F7
Raunds NN9 ....114 D7
Harris Dr CV22 ....241 B6
Harris Rd NN17 ....21 C1
Harris Sch CV22 ....241 B6
Harrison Cl
Market Harborough LE16 .48 D8
Rugby CV21 ....99 B8
Wellingborough NN8 ...129 D5
Harrison Ct NN7 ....172 F7
Harrod Dr LE16 ....32 A4
Harrogate Ct NN18 .....36 B4
Harrold Rd NN29 ....164 D3
Harrow La NN11 ....135 D6
Harrow Way NN2 ......140 F6
Harrowden Rd
Finedon NN9 ....111 D3
Northampton NN4 ......160 B2
Orlingbury NN14 ....110 A5
Wellingborough NN8 ...129 F6
Harrowick La NN6 .....144 E4
Harry Cl NN6 ....121 B3
Harry Potter Ho NN15 ..72 B1
Hart Cl CV21 ....241 F7
Hartburn Cl NN3 ....161 C8
Hartland Dr LE16 ....32 B3
Hartley Dr NN15 ....92 A7
Hartwell CE Prim Sch
NN7 ....192 D1
Hartwell Cl NN2 ....141 D5
Hartwell Rd Ashton NN7 205 D8
Hanslope MK19 ....206 E4
Roade NN7 ....192 A2
Hartwood Croft NN16 ..72 C6
Harvest Cl
Burton Latimer NN15 ....92 C2
Daventry NN11 ....135 D6
Harvest Way NN2 .....140 F5
Harvey Cl NN9 ....114 B5
Harvey Dr MK46 ......195 F1
Harvey La NN3 ....142 B8
Harvey Rd Rushden NN10 148 B7
Wellingborough NN8 ...129 E3
Harvey Reeves Rd NN5 159 A5
Harwood Dr NN16 ......72 A6
Haselrig Sq 4 NN4 ....158 F2
Haslemere Tramway Est
OX16 ....240 E7
Haslemere Way OX16 ..240 E7
Hassocks Hedge NN4 ..158 C2
Hastings MK11 ....229 E5
Hastings Rd NN2 ......141 D3
Hastings Wlk 4 NN18 ..36 B5
Haswell Cl CV22 ....241 E4
Hatchdoyle La PE8 ......41 D1
Hatfield Cl
6 Northampton NN4 ..175 C8
Wellingborough NN8 ...129 C7
Hathersage Cl NN14 ....50 E4
Hatton Ave NN8 ....129 F5
Hatton Cl NN3 ....142 A6
Hatton La NN17 ....10 B1
Hatton Park Rd NN8 ...129 F5
Hatton St NN8 ....129 F5
Hautboy La PE8 ....28 B3
Havelock Cotts PE8 .....42 A5
Havelock Jun Sch
Desborough NN14 ......51 A3
Havelock St
Desborough NN14 ....51 A3
Kettering NN16 ....72 C3
Wellingborough NN8 ...130 A5
Haven Cl NN5 ....159 A7
Haweswater Rd NN9 ....71 E3
Hawk Ridge NN4 ......158 F1
Hawke Rd NN11 ....135 E1
Hawkins Cl
Brackley NN13 ....233 D7
Corby NN17 ....21 B1
Daventry NN11 ....135 E2
Rothwell NN14 ....70 E7
Rugby CV22 ....241 A6
Stony Stratford MK11 ..229 D5
Hawksbeard Pl 3 NN3 .143 C2
Hawkshead NN8 ....129 B3
Hawksmoor Way NN5 .140 D1
Hawksnest NN4 ....175 A8

Hawkstone Cl NN5 .....158 D7
Hawkswood MK46 .....195 F5
Hawkwell Est MK19 ...229 B7
Hawson Cl NN15 ....91 C7
Hawthorn Cl NN15 ......92 B1
Hawthorn Dr
Brackley NN13 ....222 F1
Daventry NN11 ....135 C3
Thrapston NN14 ....76 D1
Towcester NN12 ....203 C8
Hawthorn Prim Sch
NN15 ....91 B8
Hawthorn Rd
Burton Latimer NN15 ....92 B1
Kettering NN15 ....91 B8
Northampton NN3 ......142 A1
Hawthorn Way NN8 ...129 E5
Hawthorne Cl NN11 ...184 B6
Hawthorne Rd NN9 ....112 A4
Hawthorne Wlk NN17 ..21 E1
Hawthorns The
Desborough NN14 ....51 C2
Higham Ferrers NN10 ..132 B6
Silverstone NN12 ....214 D3
Hay Cl Corby NN18 ......53 B8
Rushden NN10 ....148 B8
Hay La NN9 ....112 E1
Haycroft Wlk NN2 .....141 A5
Hayden Ave NN9 ....112 A5
Hayden Ct NN10 ......132 C2
Hayden Rd NN10 ......132 A4
Haydown Gn NN5 .....158 D8
Hayes Rd MK19 ....228 F5
Hayes Wlk PE8 ....16 D1
Hayeswood Rd NN3 ...142 F4
Hayman Rd NN13 .....233 D7
Haynes La NN6 ....105 B1
Haynes Rd NN16 ....72 D2
Hayride The NN4 ......175 A4
Haystack The NN11 ...135 D6
Hayway
Irthlingborough NN9 ....112 E1
Rushden NN10 ....132 A4
Hayway Inf Sch NN10 .132 B3
Hazel Cl Brackley NN13 222 F1
Hartwell NN7 ....192 E2
Hazel Cres NN12 ....203 B5
Hazel Croft NN11 ......118 C1
Hazel Leys Prim Sch
NN18 ....36 D4
Hazel Rd NN15 ....72 C1
Hazeland Ho NN14 .....51 A3
Hazelden Cl NN29 .....146 D1
Hazeldene Rd NN2 ....141 F3
Hazelwood NN12 ......214 C4
Hazelwood Ct 1 NN16 ..72 B1
Hazelwood La NN16 ....72 B1
Hazelwood Rd
Corby NN17 ....36 E7
Northampton NN1 ......159 D5
Hazley Wlk MK18 .....240 F4
Headingley Rd NN10 ..132 D2
Headlands
Desborough NN14 ....51 C3
Kettering NN15 ....91 B8
Headlands Lower Sch
NN3 ....142 C2
Headlands The
Market Harborough LE16 .31 F4
Northampton NN3 ......142 C2
Wellingborough NN8 ...129 F6
Headway NN18 ....53 A8
Healey Cl NN3 ....143 D4
Heart Of The Shires Sh
Village NN7 ....136 F2
Hearth St LE16 ....31 D3
Heath Gn NN5 ....140 F1
Heath Rise NN8 ....129 D6
Heath Terr NN12 ......203 C6
Heath Way
Burton Latimer NN15 ....92 C2
Rugby CV22 ....98 D8
Heathcote Gr NN14 .....50 E4
Heather Cl
Buckingham MK18 .....240 C2
Rugby CV22 ....241 A6
Heather Ct
Northampton NN4 ......159 A2
Rushden NN10 ....132 A2
Heather La NN3 ....142 E4
Heather Rd NN16 ....72 D4
Heatherbreea Gdns
NN10 ....131 F3
Heatherdale Way NN2 .141 E3
Heathers The NN29 ...146 E2
Heathfield Way NN5 ...141 A1
Heathfield Wlk NN18 ...36 B4
Heathville NN5 ....140 F1
Hecham Way NN10 ...132 B7
Hedge End NN4 ....175 C6
Hedgely Ct NN4 ....159 A2
Hedgerow Dr NN2 ....141 A5
Hedgerow Way NN11 .135 C6
Hedges The NN10 .....132 C4
Hedgeway NN4 ....175 C6
Hellidon Cl NN2 ....141 E4
Hellidon Rd CV47 .....166 D7
Helmdon NN13 ....211 F4
Helmdon Cres NN2 ...141 C4
Helmdon Prim Sch
NN13 ....211 F4
Helmdon Rd
Greatworth OX17 ......210 C2
Northampton NN2 ......141 C5
Sulgrave OX17 ....210 F7
Wappenham NN12 .....213 A8
Weston NN12 ....199 F2
Helmsley Way NN18 ...36 B5

Hemans Rd NN11 . . . . . .135 B3
Hembury Pl NN4 . . . . . . .158 F3
Hemery Way NN15 . . . . . .90 F8
Hemington Rd PE8 . . . . . .42 F2
Hemmingwell Rd NN8 . . .130 A7
Hempland Cl NN18 . . . . . .53 B8
Hemplow Dr NN6 . . . . . . .64 B2
Henders MK11 . . . . .229 E5
Henley Cl Kettering NN15 . .91 F5
Wellingborough NN8 . . . .129 C6
Henley Ct NN6 . . . . .120 C6
Henley Ho NN17 . . . . .36 E6
Henry Bird Ct NN4 . . . . .159 C4
Henry Bird Way NN4 . . . .159 C4
Henry Gotch Inf Sch
NN15 . . . . .72 D1
Henry Smith Ho 2
NN11 . . . . .135 B3
Henry St
Northampton NN1 . . . . . .159 E7
Rugby CV21 . . . . .241 C8
Henshaw Rd NN8 . . . . . .129 E6
Hensmans La NN29 . . . . .164 D3
Henson Cl NN16 . . . . .71 F5
Henson Way NN16 . . . . . .71 E4
Herbert St NN1 . . . . .159 C6
Hereford Cl NN14 . . . . . . .51 C4
Hereward Rd NN4 . . . . . .159 B2
Herford Cl NN18 . . . . .36 A2
Heritage Way Corby NN17 .22 B2
Raunds NN9 . . . . .114 E7
Hermitage Rd LE16 . . . . . .33 E3
Hermitage The PE9 . . . . .241 B3
Hermitage Way NN4 . . . .175 D7
Herne Hill Ct NN4 . . . . . .158 F2
Herne Rd PE8 . . . . .42 B4
Heron Ave NN14 . . . . .76 E3
Heron Cl
Burton Latimer NN15 . . . .92 A2
Hinton NN11 . . . . .184 B6
Towcester NN12 . . . . . .203 C3
Wellingborough NN8 . . . .130 A3
Heron Ct NN11 . . . . .135 C3
Heron Dr NN13 . . . . .222 D1
Heronsford NN4 . . . . . . .174 E8
Herrieffs Farm Rd NN13 .233 F6
Herriotts La NN8 . . . . . . .130 A5
Hertford Ct
Daventry NN11 . . . . . . .153 C7
Northampton NN3 . . . . . .143 A1
Hertford Rd NN15 . . . . . . .91 C6
Hervey Cl NN3 . . . . .142 D2
Hervey St NN1 . . . . .159 E7
Hesketh Cres NN12 . . . . .203 C4
Hesketh Rd NN12 . . . . . .217 E6
Hesperus NN8 . . . . .129 B4
Hester St NN2 . . . . .159 C8
Hever Cl Rushden NN10 . .148 C8
Thrapston NN14 . . . . . . .76 E2
Hewlett's Cl NN29 . . . . . .164 D2
Hexham Ct NN4 . . . . . . .159 A2
Heygate St LE16 . . . . .31 E4
Hiawatha NN8 . . . . .129 B4
Hibbert Cl CV22 . . . . . . .241 C6
Hibiscus Cl NN3 . . . . . . .160 C6
Hickmire NN29 . . . . .146 D3
Hicks Ct NN12 . . . . .203 D4
Hicks Rd NN12 . . . . .203 C4
Hidcote Cl
Northampton NN4 . . . . . .175 C7
Wellingborough NN8 . . . .129 D2
Hield Cl NN18 . . . . .36 C1
Higgins Sq NN4 . . . . . . .158 F2
High Acres OX16 . . . . . . .240 E6
High Barns Cl NN4 . . . . .175 E2
High Gn NN2 . . . . .141 B3
High Greeve NN4 . . . . . .176 A6
High Hill Ave NN14 . . . . . .70 C7
High Leys The NN6 . . . . .100 F4
High March NN11 . . . . . .153 E8
High March Cl NN11 . . . .153 E8
High Slade NN6 . . . . . . .125 C8
High St Adderbury OX17 . .230 A4
Astcote NN12 . . . . .188 F7
Banbury OX16 . . . . .240 D7
Blakesley NN12 . . . . . . .187 A1
Blisworth NN7 . . . . .190 D7
Bozeat NN29 . . . . .164 D2
Brackley NN13 . . . . .233 F7
Braunston NN11 . . . . . . .118 B1
Brigstock NN14 . . . . .55 F8
Brixworth NN6 . . . . .106 B3
Broughton NN14 . . . . . . .90 A4
Buckingham MK18 . . . . .240 D4
Bugbrooke NN7 . . . . . . .172 F7
Burton Latimer NN15 . . . .92 C2
Byfield NN11 . . . . .183 D7
Charwelton NN11 . . . . . .168 A4
Chelveston NN9 . . . . . . .133 C8
Clipston LE16 . . . . .67 A8
Collyweston PE9 . . . . .1 D2
Corby NN17 . . . . .37 A6
Cottingham LE16 . . . . . . .20 C1
Cranford NN14 . . . . .93 A6
Creaton NN6 . . . . .104 F4
Crick NN6 . . . . .100 F5
Croughton NN13 . . . . . . .238 C8
Culworth OX17 . . . . .198 C3
Daventry NN11 . . . . . . .135 C2
Deanshanger MK19 . . . . .228 E4
Denford NN14 . . . . .95 C6
Desborough NN14 . . . . . .51 A3
Duddington PE9 . . . . .5 B6
Earls Barton NN6 . . . . . .144 E4
Easton o t H PE9 . . . . . . .2 A5
Ecton NN6 . . . . .143 F3
Everdon NN11 . . . . .170 A8
Eydon NN11 . . . . .184 C1

High St continued
Finedon NN9 . . . . .111 F5
Flore NN7 . . . . .155 E5
Gayton NN7 . . . . .173 E2
Great Doddington NN7 . . .145 E6
Great Easton LE16 . . . . . .20 D7
Great Houghton NN4 . . . .160 E2
Greens Norton NN12 . . . .202 D8
Gretton NN17 . . . . .10 B1
Guilsborough NN6 . . . . . .103 F6
Hanslope MK19 . . . . . . .207 A2
Harpole NN7 . . . . .157 C6
Harrington NN6 . . . . .69 A5
Higham Ferrers NN10 . . . .132 B5
Husbands Bosworth LE17 . .45 E5
Irchester NN29 . . . . . . .147 B8
Irthlingborough NN9 . . . .112 E2
Islip NN14 . . . . .76 B2
Kettering NN16 . . . . .72 B2
Ketton PE9 . . . . .1 A6
Kislingbury NN7 . . . . . . .157 D4
Lamport NN6 . . . . .87 D2
Little Addington NN14 . . .113 B8
Long Buckby NN6 . . . . . .121 C4
Market Harborough LE16 . .31 E3
Middleton Cheney OX17 . .219 F8
Milton Malsor NN7 . . . . .174 E4
Morcott LE15 . . . . .3 A6
Moulton NN3 . . . . .126 C1
Naseby NN6 . . . . .85 B8
Northampton,Collingtree
NN4 . . . . .175 C4
Northampton,Great Billing
NN3 . . . . .143 C2
Northampton,Hardingstone
NN4 . . . . .175 F8
Northampton,Kingsthorpe
NN2 . . . . .141 B3
Northampton,Weston Favell
NN3 . . . . .142 D1
Northampton,Wootton
NN4 . . . . .175 E6
Olney MK46 . . . . .195 F4
Paulerspury NN12 . . . . . .216 C4
Pitsford NN6 . . . . .125 C4
Podington NN29 . . . . . . .147 E2
Pottspury NN12 . . . . . . .217 D3
Preston Capes NN11 . . . .169 D2
Pytchley NN14 . . . . .90 F2
Raunds NN9 . . . . .114 D7
Ringstead NN14 . . . . . . .95 B3
Roade NN7 . . . . .191 D4
Rothwell NN14 . . . . .70 C7
Rugby CV21 . . . . .241 C8
Rugby CV21 . . . . .99 A8
Rushden NN10 . . . . .132 B2
Rushton NN14 . . . . .52 C2
Scaldwell NN6 . . . . .106 F5
Shutlanger NN12 . . . . . .190 D1
Silverstone NN12 . . . . . .214 D4
Souldern OX27 . . . . .237 E3
Spratton NN6 . . . . .105 B1
Stamford PE9 . . . . .241 D3
Stanion NN14 . . . . .37 C2
Stanwick NN9 . . . . .113 F3
Stony Stratford MK11 . . . .229 D6
Swinford LE17 . . . . .62 B3
Syresham NN13 . . . . . . .224 B8
Thrapston NN14 . . . . . . .76 D2
Titchmarsh NN14 . . . . . . .77 D4
Twywell NN14 . . . . .74 F1
Walgrave NN6 . . . . .108 A5
Wappenham NN12 . . . . .213 B8
Weedon NN7 . . . . .155 B4
Weedon Lois NN12 . . . . .200 C2
Weldon NN17 . . . . .38 B8
Welford NN6 . . . . .64 E6
Wellingborough NN8 . . . .129 F5
Welton NN11 . . . . .119 E1
West Haddon NN6 . . . . . .102 C4
Weston NN12 . . . . .199 F2
Weston Underwood MK46 .195 B2
Whittlebury NN12 . . . . . .215 C4
Wollaston NN29 . . . . . . .146 D2
Woodford NN14 . . . . .94 D7
Woodford Halse NN11 . . .184 C6
Wymington NN10 . . . . . .148 B5
Yardley Gobion NN12 . . . .217 F6
Yardley Hastings NN7 . . . .179 B6
Yelvertoft NN6 . . . . .82 B3
High St N NN12 . . . . . . .189 D5
High St N NN14 . . . . .129 F4
High St S Olney MK46 . . . .195 F3
Rushden NN10 . . . . .132 B1
Tiffield NN12 . . . . .189 D4
High St The NN6 . . . . . . .103 D1
High Stack NN6 . . . . . . .121 C3
High Street St Martin's
PE9 . . . . .241 E2
High View
Deanshanger MK19 . . . . .228 E5
Northampton NN4 . . . . . .175 E6
High Woods NN6 . . . . . . .143 D8
Higham Cross Rd MK19 .206 E4
Higham Ferrers Jun & Inf
Schs NN10 . . . . .132 B6
Higham Park Rd NN10 . .149 A5
Higham Rd
Burton Latimer NN15 . . . .92 C1
Chelveston NN9 . . . . . . .133 B8
Little Irchester NN8,NN29 .130 D1
Rushden NN10 . . . . .132 B4
Stanwick NN9 . . . . .113 F3
Highbridge Rd NN12 . . . .213 A8
Highbrook NN18 . . . . .36 B4
Highcroft LE17 . . . . .45 E6
Highcroft Cl NN12 . . . . . .217 E6
Highcross St LE16 . . . . . . .31 C3

Highdown Cl NN4 . . . . . .158 E3
Highfield Duddington PE9 . .5 B7
Woodford NN14 . . . . .94 C7
Highfield Cotts LE15 . . . . .3 E8
Highfield Court Mews
NN13 . . . . .233 E6
Highfield Cres NN15 . . . . .91 C6
Highfield Cl NN13 . . . . . .233 E6
Highfield Gr NN17 . . . . . . .36 F7
Highfield Pk NN6 . . . . . .104 D4
Highfield Rd
Daventry NN11 . . . . . . .135 B3
Irthlingborough NN9 . . . .112 F2
Kettering NN15 . . . . .91 B7
Mears Ashby NN6 . . . . . .128 C4
Northampton NN1 . . . . . .142 A1
Rushden NN10 . . . . .131 F1
Thrapston NN14 . . . . . . .76 C2
Wellingborough NN8 . . . .130 B5
Highfield St Finedon NN9 .112 B5
Market Harborough LE16 . .31 D3
Highfield Way NN7 . . . . .179 B6
Highfields Polebrook PE8 . .42 F3
Towcester NN12 . . . . . .203 C3
Highfields Prim Sch
NN15 . . . . .91 B7
Highgate Gn PE8 . . . . . . .28 D8
Highgrove Ct NN10 . . . . .132 B2
Highgrove Gdns PE9 . . . .241 A3
Highlands Ave NN3 . . . . .142 A4
Highlands Dr NN11 . . . . .135 B5
Highlands Rd MK18 . . . . .240 D5
Highlands Way PE9 . . . . .241 B3
Highpoint NN13 . . . . . . .233 F5
Hightown Rd OX16 . . . . .240 E6
Hilda Pl NN16 . . . . .72 E4
Hill Cl NN5 . . . . .140 C2
Hill Crest NN7 . . . . .174 C1
Hill Farm Est NN14 . . . . .113 C7
Hill Farm Rise NN4 . . . . .175 A8
Hill Gdns LE16 . . . . .31 C3
Hill House Ct NN12 . . . . .172 D1
Hill House Gdns NN9 . . . .113 F3
Hill Rd NN11 . . . . .182 C5
Hill Row NN11 . . . . .134 C8
Hill St Brackley NN13 . . . .233 F7
Kettering NN16 . . . . .72 A3
Raunds NN9 . . . . .114 D6
Rugby CV21 . . . . .241 C9
Wellingborough NN8 . . . .129 F4
Hill The Aynho OX17 . . . .237 C7
Great Houghton NN4 . . . .160 E2
Middleton LE16 . . . . .35 B8
Pury End NN12 . . . . .215 F7
Syresham NN13 . . . . . . .224 B8
Hill Top NN2 . . . . .141 D4
Hill Top Rd NN9 . . . . . . .110 D4
Hill View NN11 . . . . .184 C1
Hill View Cres OX16 . . . .240 A9
Hill View Cty Prim Sch
OX16 . . . . .240 A9
Hillary Cl Daventry NN11 .135 B5
Stamford PE9 . . . . .241 F4
Hillary Rd NN10 . . . . . . .131 F1
Hillberry Rise NN3 . . . . .143 D4
Hillcrest Ave
Burton Latimer NN15 . . . .92 A1
Kettering NN15 . . . . .72 D1
Market Harborough LE16 . .31 D4
Northampton NN3 . . . . . .142 A3
Hillcrest Cl NN14 . . . . . . .76 E3
Hillcrest La NN7 . . . . .45 E5
Hillcrest Rd NN7 . . . . . . .173 E1
Hillcroft View NN12 . . . . .187 B1
Hilldrop Rd NN4 . . . . . . .175 B7
Hillesden Way MK18 . . . .240 E4
Hillfield Rd PE8 . . . . .41 E6
Hillmorton La
Clifton u D CV23 . . . . . . .80 A4
Lilbourne CV23 . . . . .80 F5
Yelvertoft NN6 . . . . .82 A4
Hillmorton Prim Sch
CV21 . . . . .99 B8
Hillmorton Rd CV22 . . . .241 B8
Hillside Chelveston NN9 . .133 B8
Daventry NN11 . . . . . . .135 C4
Great Harrowden NN9 . . .110 E4
Hartwell NN7 . . . . .192 D2
West Haddon NN6 . . . . . .102 B4
Hillside Ave
Kettering NN15 . . . . .91 C8
Silverstone NN12 . . . . . .214 E5
Hillside Cl NN29 . . . . . . .164 D2
Hillside Cotts PE28 . . . . . .97 A4
Hillside Cres
Nether Heyford NN7 . . . .156 C1
Weldon NN17 . . . . .38 A7
Hillside Rd Flore NN7 . . . .155 D6
Market Harborough LE16 . .31 F4
Nether Heyford NN7 . . . .156 C1
Piddington NN7 . . . . . . .177 B1
Wellingborough NN8 . . . .130 C7
Hillside Terr NN16 . . . . . .72 A2
Hillside Way NN3 . . . . . .160 C8
Hillstone Ct NN9 . . . . . . .113 F3
Hilltop Blisworth NN7 . . .174 C1
Dodford NN7 . . . . .154 F5
Great Harrowden NN9 . . .110 E5
Hilltop Ave
Buckingham MK18 . . . . .240 E6
Desborough NN14 . . . . . .50 F4
Kettering NN15 . . . . .91 F5
Hilltop Cl Brixworth NN6 .106 B1
Desborough NN14 . . . . . .50 F4
Hilmorton Rd CV22 . . . . .98 F8
Hilton Rd OX16 . . . . .240 B8
Hind Stile NN10 . . . . . . .132 B5
Hinton Ave NN18 . . . . . . .36 A4

Hinton Cl Hinton NN11 . .184 B6
Northampton NN2 . . . . . .141 C5
Hinton Manor Ct NN11 . .184 B6
Hinton Rd Brackley NN13 .233 E6
Hinton NN11 . . . . .184 B5
Northampton NN2 . . . . . .141 C5
Hinton's Cl NN13 . . . . . .211 F3
Hinwick Cl NN15 . . . . . . .91 D5
Hinwick Hall Coll of F Ed
NN29 . . . . .147 C1
Hinwick Rd
Podington NN29 . . . . . . .147 D1
Wollaston NN29 . . . . . . .146 D1
Hipwell Ct MK46 . . . . . . .195 F3
Hirondelle Cl NN5 . . . . . .139 C7
Historical Transport Mus★
NN10 . . . . .132 B3
History of Stamford Mus★
PE9 . . . . .241 E3
Hobbs Hill NN14 . . . . . . .70 C6
Hobby Cl NN4 . . . . .175 B8
Hocknell Cl NN4 . . . . . . .175 F6
Hockney Ave NN15 . . . . . .92 A7
Hodge Cl NN12 . . . . .188 F6
Hodge Way NN14 . . . . . .70 C6
Hodges La NN7 . . . . .157 D4
Hodnet Cl NN4 . . . . .175 C7
Hoe Way NN7 . . . . .191 C4
Hogarth Cl NN8 . . . . . . .129 F7
Hogarth Dr NN15 . . . . . . .92 A7
Hogarth Wlk NN18 . . . . . .36 E5
Hogg End OX17 . . . . .196 F6
Hogg La OX17 . . . . .231 F5
Holback La MK18 . . . . . .226 A5
Holbein Gdns NN4 . . . . . .174 E8
Holbein Wlk NN18 . . . . . .36 D5
Holbrook Ave CV21 . . . . .241 C9
Holbush Way NN9 . . . . . .112 E3
Holcot Cl NN8 . . . . .129 E8
Holcot La Scaldwell NN6 .107 A5
Sywell NN6 . . . . .127 E4
Holcot Leys CV22 . . . . . . .98 A7
Holcot Rd Brixworth NN6 .106 D2
Moulton NN3 . . . . .126 C5
Walgrave NN6 . . . . .107 F4
Holcutt Cl NN4 . . . . .175 F7
Holden Gr NN11 . . . . . . .135 B2
Holdenby Holdenby NN6 .123 D4
Kettering NN15 . . . . .91 D5
Holdenby Cl LE16 . . . . . . .32 B3
Holdenby House Gdns &
Falconry Ctr★ NN6 . . . .123 C4
Holdenby Rd
East Haddon NN6 . . . . . .122 C5
Northampton NN2 . . . . . .141 E4
Spratton NN6 . . . . .124 B8
Holdgate Cl NN13 . . . . . .222 E1
Holes La MK46 . . . . .195 F4
Holiday La MK19 . . . . . . .206 F4
Holland Rd PE9 . . . . .241 F4
Holland Rise OX17 . . . . . .230 F4
Hollands Dr NN15 . . . . . . .92 C2
Hollies The Moulton NN3 .126 B2
Wellingborough NN8 . . . .129 E5
Hollingside Dr NN2 . . . . .141 F3
Hollington Rd NN9 . . . . . .114 D6
Hollow Bank NN3 . . . . . .142 C6
Hollow The NN6 . . . . . . .103 E1
Hollow Way Aynho OX17 .237 C7
Eydon NN11 . . . . .184 B1
Hollow Wood MK46 . . . . .195 E3
Holloway Dr MK18 . . . . .240 E5
Holloway The CV47 . . . . .166 D7
Hollowell Cl NN8 . . . . . . .129 F4
Hollowell Rd NN6 . . . . . .104 E4
Holly Bush La CV47 . . . . .166 D7
Holly Cl Brackley NN13 . .222 F1
Market Harborough LE16 . .31 E4
Holly La NN4 . . . . .90 A6
Holly Lodge Dr NN2 . . . . .141 D6
Holly Rd Kettering NN16 . .72 C4
Northampton NN1 . . . . . .159 F8
Rushden NN10 . . . . .131 E3
Holly Wlk NN9 . . . . .111 D4
Hollyhill NN12 . . . . .203 B4
Holm Cl NN7 . . . . .155 A2
Holman Cl NN3 . . . . .142 D2
Holme Cl
Wellingborough NN9 . . . .110 E1
Wilbarston LE16 . . . . . . .34 C5
Holme Way CV23 . . . . . . .99 D1
Holmcross Rd NN3 . . . . .142 E5
Holmes Ave NN9 . . . . . . .114 E5
Holmes Dr NN9 . . . . .1 B5
Holmfield Dr NN9 . . . . . .114 E6
Holmfield Terr NN6 . . . . .121 A4
Holmfield Wlk NN3 . . . . .160 C8
Holmfirth Wlk NN18 . . . . .36 C4
Holmleigh Cl NN5 . . . . . .158 C7
Holmwood Cl NN5 . . . . . .140 A1
Holt Rd LE16 . . . . .19 C8
Holt The MK18 . . . . .240 E6
Holton Rd MK18 . . . . . . .240 D5
Holyoake Rd NN29 . . . . .146 D2
Holyoake Terr NN6 . . . . . .121 C4
Holyrood Ct NN5 . . . . . . .158 F7
Holyrood Rd NN5 . . . . . .158 F7
Holyrood Wlk NN18 . . . . .36 C3
Home Acre NN7 . . . . .161 B4
Home Cl Blisworth NN7 . .190 D7
Corby NN17 . . . . .36 B1
Dingley NN16 . . . . .33 A3
Eastcote NN12 . . . . .188 F8
Greens Norton NN12 . . . .202 D8
Irthlingborough NN9 . . . .131 E8
Middleton Cheney OX17 . .220 B8
Northampton NN4 . . . . . .175 E2
Silverstone NN12 . . . . . .214 D4

Home Cl continued
Staverton NN11 . . . . . . .152 C8
Towcester NN12 . . . . . . .203 C5
Home Farm Cl
Corby NN17 . . . . .53 B8
Creaton NN6 . . . . .104 F5
Northampton NN3 . . . . . .161 B8
Weedon NN7 . . . . .154 F2
Home Farm Ct
Adderbury OX17 . . . . . . .230 B4
Norton NN11 . . . . .136 C4
Home Farm Gr LE16 . . . . .68 C7
Home Farm La NN6 . . . . .125 C4
Home Farm Rd NN14 . . . .37 E2
Homefield NN11 . . . . . . .153 C8
Homestead Cl NN3 . . . . .126 D1
Homestead Ct NN2 . . . . .141 E1
Homestead Dr NN7 . . . . .173 A7
Homestead Rise NN4 . . . .175 E6
Homestead The NN14 . . . .74 F1
Homestead Way
Northampton NN2 . . . . . .141 E1
Pottspury NN12 . . . . . . .217 E3
Homewelland Ho LE16 . . .31 D4
Honey Hill Dr MK19 . . . . .228 E5
Honey Holme NN6 . . . . .106 A1
Honeypot La LE17 . . . . . .45 E5
Honeystones NN3 . . . . . .126 C1
Honeysuckle Way NN3 . .160 C6
Honiton Gdns NN18 . . . . .36 E4
Hood Cl NN17 . . . . .36 B8
Hood Rd NN11 . . . . .135 E1
Hood St NN1 . . . . .159 E7
Hood Wlk NN15 . . . . .91 D8
Hookhams Path NN29 . . .146 E2
Hope St NN29 . . . . .164 D4
Hopes Pl NN2 . . . . .141 B3
Hopmeadow Ct 2 NN3 . .143 B4
Hoppet Cl NN5 . . . . .53 A8
Hopping Hill Gdns NN5 .140 D1
Hopping Hill Lower Sch
NN5 . . . . .158 C8
Hopton Cl NN11 . . . . . . .135 D6
Hopton Fields LE16 . . . . . .48 D8
Horn La MK11 . . . . .229 D5
Hornbeam Cl
Banbury OX16 . . . . .240 B7
Podington NN29 . . . . . . .147 E2
Wellingborough NN8 . . . .129 E5
Hornbeam Ct
Desborough NN14 . . . . . .51 B3
Northampton NN3 . . . . . .142 D3
Hornby Rd NN6 . . . . .144 E5
Horncastle Cl NN11 . . . . .135 C6
Horne Cl CV21 . . . . .99 B8
Horrell Ct NN11 . . . . . . .132 A2
Horrock's Way NN15 . . . .72 F1
Horse Fair OX16 . . . . . . .240 C7
Horse Market
Kettering NN16 . . . . .72 B2
Northampton NN1 . . . . . .159 C6
Horse Shoe La LE16 . . . . .32 B6
Horse Well Ct NN3 . . . . .142 C7
Horsefair Cl LE16 . . . . . . .31 D4
Horsefair Gn MK11 . . . . .229 D5
Horselease Cl NN18 . . . . .53 A8
Horsemoor Sq 6 NN3 . .143 C2
Horsepool The CV23 . . . . .81 A7
Horseshoe Cl
Brixworth NN6 . . . . .106 C2
Creaton NN6 . . . . .104 F4
Horseshoe St NN1 . . . . . .159 C5
Horsham Wlk NN18 . . . . .36 B5
Horsley Rd NN2 . . . . .141 C5
Horton Cl OX17 . . . . .220 A7
Horton Cres
Middleton Cheney OX17 . .220 A8
Rugby CV22 . . . . .241 D7
Horton Dr OX17 . . . . .220 A8
Horton Hospl OX16 . . . . .240 D6
Horton Pk NN7 . . . . .177 E2
Horton Rd
Brafield-on-t-G NN7 . . . .177 D7
Hackleton NN7 . . . . .177 C2
Middleton Cheney OX17 . .220 A7
Hortons' La NN14 . . . . . . .76 D2
Hortonsfield Rd NN12 . . .217 F5
Hoskyn Cl CV21 . . . . .98 F8
Hospital Hill NN14 . . . . . .70 D7
Hospital of St Cross
CV22 . . . . .241 D6
Hothorpe Rd LE17 . . . . . .46 D8
Houghton Hill NN4 . . . . .160 A1
Hove Rd NN10 . . . . .132 C2
Hove St NN18 . . . . .36 B4
Howard Ave NN17 . . . . . .36 B7
Howard Biley Gdns
NN3 . . . . .142 C3
Howard Cl NN11 . . . . . . .135 D1
Howard Ct 3 NN8 . . . . .130 B5
Howard La NN2 . . . . .141 C8
Howard Rd
Banbury OX16 . . . . .240 F8
Wollaston NN29 . . . . . . .146 D2
Howard St NN16 . . . . . . .72 A2
Howard Way LE16 . . . . . .31 D1
Howard's Ct NN29 . . . . . .146 D2
Howards Mdw PE8 . . . . . .13 F7
Howcut La NN7 . . . . .178 E3
Howden Gn NN14 . . . . . . .50 E4
Howe Cres Corby NN17 . . .36 A7
Daventry NN11 . . . . . . .135 C1
Hoy Wlk NN17 . . . . .21 C1
Hoylake NN8 . . . . .129 C7
Hoylake Dr NN2 . . . . .141 F3

Hubbard Cl MK18 240 F4
Hubble Rd NN17 21 F1
Hudson Cl Corby NN18 36 C3
Daventry NN11 135 C5
Hudson Dr NN4 158 E1
Hudson Rd CV22 241 A6
Hulcote NN12 203 F8
Hulme Way NN8 129 E7
Humber Cl
Daventry NN11 134 F4
Northampton NN5 140 F2
Humber Gdns NN8 129 C6
Humber Wlk NN17 21 D2
Humfrey La NN2 141 C8
Humphries Dr NN13 233 D8
Hunsbarrow Rd NN4 158 E4
Hunsbury Cl NN4 158 F1
Hunsbury Gn NN4 158 D2
Hunsbury Hill Ave NN4 158 E3
Hunsbury Hill Country Pk★ NN4 158 F1
Hunsbury Hill Rd NN4 158 E1
Hunsbury Park Lower Sch NN4 158 F2
Hunslet La NN4 158 E2
Hunt Cl Brixworth NN6 106 B2
Towcester NN12 203 C7
Hunt St NN18 36 D5
Hunter St
Buckingham MK18 240 C3
Northampton NN1 159 D7
Rugby CV21 241 E9
Hunters Cl
Husbands Bosworth LE17 45 E6
Northampton NN2 141 D6
Hunters Rd NN17 22 E1
Hunters' Way NN6 106 B2
Hunting Way PE8 14 C4
Huntingdon Gdns LE16 31 E1
Huntingdon Rd NN14 76 E2
Huntsham Cl NN3 160 D7
Huntsmead NN3 143 D4
Hurst Cl NN15 92 C4
Husbands Bosworth CE Prim Sch LE17 45 E5
Hussar Cl NN11 135 B1
Hutchinson Ave NN14 90 B3
Hutts Cl NN11 183 D7
Huxley Cl NN8 129 A4
Huxloe Pl 13 NN16 72 B2
Huxloe Rise NN3 142 E6
Huxlow Sch NN9 112 E3
Hyacinth Way NN10 148 B7
Hyde Cl NN7 191 C4
Hyde Dr NN9 112 A5
Hyde Rd NN7 191 C4

I

Ibsen Wlk NN18 36 A2
Ibstock Cl NN3 143 A6
Icknield Dr NN4 158 E1
Ideal Bldgs 17 NN1 159 C7
Ilex Cl NN4 159 F1
Ilmor Ave NN6 106 C3
Imperial Ct NN10 132 A2
Independent St CV23 100 A3
Indmere Cl NN4 158 C1
Ingleborough Way NN5 158 D8
Inglewood Ct NN3 143 C1
Inham Cl NN18 36 C2
Inkerman Way PE8 41 F5
Inlands Cl NN11 135 D1
Inlands Rise NN11 135 D1
Inlands The NN11 135 D1
Inn Yard Ct LE16 68 C7
Insignia Cl 7 NN4 175 E7
Inwood Cl NN18 36 C2
Iona Rd NN17 36 C8
Irchester Country Pk Trail★ NN8 130 D1
Irchester Country Pk Visitor Ctr★ NN29 130 D1
Irchester Ctry Pk★ NN29 130 F1
Irchester Narrow Gauge Rly Mus★ NN8 130 D1
Irchester Prim Sch NN29 147 A8
Irchester Rd
Podington NN10 147 B4
Rushden NN10 131 F2
Wollaston NN29 146 F3
Irchester Turn NN29 131 A2
Ireton Rd LE16 31 D2
Irnham Rd PE9 241 E5
Iron Cross NN11 167 B2
Iron Duke Cl NN11 135 B4
Iron Pikes NN6 106 C1
Irondale Cl NN4 158 E3
Ironmonger St PE9 241 D3
Ironstone Ct NN9 111 F4
Ironstone La NN4 158 E3
Ironstone Way NN6 106 C3
Irthlingborough Cty Inf Sch NN9 112 E2
Irthlingborough Cty Jun Sch NN9 112 E2
Irthlingborough Rd
Finedon NN9 112 B4
Little Addington NN14 113 B7
Wellingborough NN8 130 E4
Irvine Dr NN12 203 D8
Irving Gr NN17 36 E8
Ise Com Coll NN15 72 D1
Ise Rd NN15 72 D1
Ise Vale Ave NN14 51 B3
Ise View Rd NN14 51 B3
Isebrook Ct NN15 92 A2
Isebrook Hospl NN8 130 B3
Isebrook Sch NN15 91 E7
Isham CE Prim Sch NN14 91 F1
Isham Cl NN2 141 D5
Isham Rd
Orlingbury NN14 110 A5
Pytchley NN14 91 B3
Isley Valley Ind Est NN8 130 D7
Isley Wlk NN17 36 C8
Islington Ct NN12 203 D5
Islington Rd NN12 203 D5
Ivatt Wlk OX16 240 E10
Ivens La NN12 171 C1
Ivy Ct NN11 135 B1
Ivy La NN9 111 F4
Ivy Rd Kettering NN16 72 D4
Northampton NN1 159 F8
Ivydene Terr NN14 90 A4
Ixworth Cl NN3 142 F5

J

Jackdaw Cl NN3 161 C8
Jacklin Ct NN8 129 C7
Jackson Cl
Market Harborough LE16 48 E8
Northampton NN2 141 E6
Jackson Rd CV21 80 A1
Jackson Way NN15 90 F8
Jackson's La NN8 129 F5
Jackson's Lane Flats NN8 129 F5
Jacorrin Cl NN2 141 E6
Jamb The NN17 37 A6
James Lewis Ct NN3 142 C2
James Rd NN8 130 A2
James St Irchester NN29 147 B7
Rugby CV21 241 D8
James Watt Ave NN17 37 A8
James Watt Cl NN11 135 A4
Jardine Cl NN3 142 D1
Jarman Cl MK18 240 F3
Jarretts Yd NN4 175 E6
Jarvis Ct NN13 233 F8
Jasmine Ct NN16 72 D5
Jasmine Gdns NN10 148 B7
Jasmine Rd
Kettering NN16 72 D4
Northampton NN3 143 C5
Javelin Cl NN5 158 C8
JBJ Bsns Pk NN7 174 D2
Jean Rd NN16 72 E3
Jellicoe Cl NN11 135 E1
Jenkins Rd CV21 80 A1
Jenkinson Rd NN12 203 D4
Jenner Cres NN2 141 B5
Jennings Cl
Daventry NN11 135 D1
Higham Ferrers NN10 132 B5
Jersey Cl NN8 130 B6
Jersey Ct NN3 142 F1
Jervis Cl NN11 135 E1
Jerwood Way LE16 31 F2
Jetty The Creaton NN6 104 F4
Hackleton NN7 177 B3
Wappenham NN12 213 B8
Wardington OX17 196 E1
Jeyes Cl NN3 126 B1
Jibwood NN14 89 B5
Jitty The NN14 89 B4
Joan Pyel Cl NN9 131 E8
Job's Yd NN16 72 B2
John Beverly Mews NN14 70 C6
John Clare Cl NN13 222 F1
John Clare Ct NN16 72 C6
John Clare Way NN17 36 D8
John Eagle Cl NN9 113 F4
John Gray Rd NN29 145 D6
John Hellins Prim Sch NN12 217 D3
John Pyel Rd NN9 112 E1
John Smith Ave NN14 70 E7
John St Rushden NN10 132 B2
Thrapston NN14 76 E2
John Thwaites Cl CV22 241 C7
John White Cl The NN10 132 C6
Johns Rd NN7 157 A1
Johnson Ave
Brackley NN13 233 C8
Rugby CV22 241 A7
Johnson Cl NN11 135 B3
Johnsons Field MK46 195 E4
Jones Cl NN13 233 D8
Jordan Cl LE16 32 A3
Joseph Priestley Ct 6 NN11 135 C1
Joshua Sq NN4 158 F2
Jowett Cl NN15 92 A8
Jubilee Ave NN18 36 D5
Jubilee Cl Byfield NN11 183 D7
Islip NN14 76 B3
Long Buckby NN6 121 A4
Northampton NN4 158 F3
Jubilee Cres NN8 129 F2
Jubilee Ct OX16 240 D7
Jubilee Dr NN6 108 B5
Jubilee Gdns LE16 31 F4
Jubilee Rd NN11 135 B2
Jubilee St
Irthlingborough NN9 112 E1
Jubilee St *continued*
Rothwell NN14 70 D6
Rugby CV21 241 A8
Jubilee Terr Isham NN14 110 F8
Stony Stratford MK11 229 E5
Judges Ct NN6 104 F4
Judith Rd NN16 72 E4
Julian Way NN2 141 A3
Junction Rd
Banbury OX16 240 E8
Northampton NN2 141 E1
Juniper Cl NN12 203 B4
Juniper Ct NN3 143 D3
Juniper Thorn NN6 106 C1
Jura Cl NN17 36 B8
Justin Pk LE16 48 F7
Jutland Way NN16 72 A2

K

Kane Wlk NN17 36 E8
Kangaroo Spinney NN8 130 E3
Karlstad Cl NN18 36 A2
Kathleen Dr NN16 72 E4
Katrine Cl NN17 21 B1
Kealdale Rd NN3 142 A4
Keating Cl NN15 92 A8
Keats Cl Earls Barton NN6 144 F4
Great Houghton NN4 160 F1
Keats Dr Kettering NN16 72 C6
Towcester NN12 203 B5
Keats Gr PE9 241 A3
Keats Rd Daventry NN11 135 B3
Wellingborough NN8 129 D4
Keats Way Corby NN17 36 C8
Higham Ferrers NN10 132 A5
Rushden NN10 131 E3
Keble Cl Daventry NN11 153 B8
Stamford PE9 241 C5
Keble Rd NN13 233 D8
Kedleston Cl 3 NN4 175 C8
Keeble Cl NN14 37 E2
Keepers Cl NN4 175 F3
Kelburn Cl NN4 175 B7
Keld Cl NN18 36 D2
Kelmarsh Hall★ NN6 67 F4
Kelmarsh Rd
Arthingworth LE16 68 C7
Clipston LE16 67 A7
Corby NN17 36 C7
Kelmscott Cl NN3 143 A5
Kelsall Cl NN5 158 B8
Kelthorpe Cl PE9 1 A4
Kelvin Gr NN17 37 A7
Kemp Ho NN17 21 F3
Kemps Rd OX17 230 A5
Kendal Cl
Northampton NN3 142 D4
Rushden NN10 132 D1
Wellingborough NN8 129 D6
Kendalls Cl LE16 34 D5
Kenilworth NN18 36 C3
Kenilworth Cl
Daventry NN11 135 B1
Northampton NN5 158 B8
Rushden NN10 132 C1
Kenilworth Dr NN15 91 F8
Kenilworth Gdns NN14 76 F2
Kenmore Dr NN14 51 B2
Kenmuir Ave NN2 141 F2
Kenmuir Cres NN2 141 F2
Kenmuir Gdns NN2 141 F2
Kenmuir Rd NN9 111 F4
Kennedy Cl NN11 135 E1
Kennedy Ho OX16 240 B8
Kennel Hill NN14 55 F7
Kennel Rd NN12 215 C3
Kennel Terr NN6 106 B2
Kennels Dr NN12 216 E3
Kennels The NN12 216 E3
Kennet Cl NN8 129 C6
Kennet Gn NN5 140 F2
Kensington Cl
Kings Sutton OX17 230 F6
Rushden NN10 131 E3
Towcester NN12 203 B4
Kensington Gdns NN15 91 B8
Kensington Pl MK46 195 F5
Kensington Wlk NN18 36 C3
Kent Cl Corby NN17 36 C7
Northampton NN5 158 C6
Kent Pl NN15 91 D6
Kent Rd
Northampton NN5 158 C5
Rushden NN10 132 C3
Wellingborough NN8 129 F1
Kent The CV21 80 A2
Kentford Cl NN4 175 B8
Kenton Ct NN15 92 A8
Kentstone Cl NN2 140 F4
Kerley Cl NN14 90 A3
Kerrfield Est NN5 158 C7
Kesteven Rd PE9 241 E5
Kestian Cl LE16 31 D5
Keston Way NN9 114 B5
Kestrel Cl NN3 142 D1
Kestrel Cres NN13 222 E1
Kestrel La NN8 130 A7
Kestrel Way MK18 240 E2
Keswick NN8 129 B5
Keswick Dr
Northampton NN3 142 C4
Rushden NN10 132 D3
Keswick Rd MK19 207 B2
Ketco Ave PE9 1 B7
Kettering Gdns 2 NN1 159 E6
Kettering General Hospl NN16 71 F2
Kettering Parkway NN15 91 D5
Kettering Rd
Broughton NN14 90 B5
Burton Latimer NN15 92 B3
Geddington NN14 54 A1
Great Harrowden NN9 110 E4
Isham NN14 91 E1
Islip NN14 75 E1
Market Harborough LE16 32 B2
Moulton NN3 126 F2
Northampton NN1 159 E8
Northampton,Spinney Hill NN3 142 A3
Pytchley NN14 90 F2
Rothwell NN14,NN16 70 E5
Stamford PE9 241 D2
Stanion NN14 37 E2
Walgrave NN6 108 C6
Weldon NN17 38 B7
Woodford NN14 94 B8
Wothorpe PE9 2 C8
Kettering Rd N NN3 142 C5
Kettering Sta NN15 72 A1
Kettering Town FC NN16 72 B5
Kettle End NN12 200 C3
Ketton CE Prim Sch PE9 1 A5
Ketton Rd PE9 1 C3
Kettonby Gdns NN15 91 B8
Kew Rd CV21 241 D9
Keyes Way MK18 240 E5
Keyham Ct NN3 143 A5
Keys Cl NN11 135 D1
Keys La CV47 166 E8
Keyston Rd PE18 116 D2
Keystone NN4 158 C1
Keyte's Cl OX17 230 A4
KG House Bsns Ctr 4 NN5 140 F1
Kiel Wlk NN18 36 A2
Kielder Ct NN15 92 A4
Kieldsen Cl OX17 210 B1
Kilbale Cres OX16 240 D6
Kilborn Cl NN8 129 E7
Kilborn Rd NN8 129 E6
Kilburn Pl NN10 132 B4
Kilby Cl NN8 129 E3
Kiln La
Litchborough NN12 171 C1
Welton NN11 135 E8
Kiln Way NN8 129 D4
Kilsby CE Prim Sch CV23 100 A3
Kilsby La CV21 99 C7
Kilsby Rd Barby CV23 99 C1
Crick NN6 100 F2
Watford NN6 120 B7
Kilvey Rd NN4 160 B2
Kilworth Rd
Husbands Bosworth LE17 45 D4
Rugby CV21 99 B7
Swinford LE17 62 C4
Kimberley Rd CV21 241 D9
Kimble Cl NN4 175 B8
Kimbolton Ct NN14 76 E2
Kimbolton Rd
Chelveston NN9 133 D8
Higham Ferrers NN10 132 C6
Kinewell Cl NN14 95 A3
Kinewell Lake Nature Trail★ NN14 95 A3
King Charles Cl MK18 240 E5
King Cup Cl NN10 148 C7
King Edward Rd
Northampton NN1 160 A7
Rugby CV21 241 D9
King George Cres MK11 229 E6
King John Sch The NN14 76 D1
King Richard Ct NN4 175 C6
King St Desborough NN14 51 B3
Earls Barton NN6 144 E5
Kettering NN16 72 C3
Long Buckby NN6 121 B4
Maidford NN12 186 D5
Northampton NN1 159 C6
Rugby CV21 241 C9
Stony Stratford MK11 229 E6
King Style Cl NN6 100 F6
King's Cliffe Endowed Prim Sch PE8 13 F7
King's Ct LE16 31 E4
King's Forest PE8 13 F7
King's Head Pl LE16 31 E3
King's Heath Lower Sch NN5 140 F2
King's La Flore NN7 155 F5
Little Harrowden NN9 110 B3
King's Rd Banbury OX16 240 B8
Market Harborough LE16 31 E3
King's Sutton Sta OX17 230 E5
Kingfisher Cl
Hinton NN11 184 B6
Northampton NN4 175 A7
Kingfisher Ct NN6 143 D8
Kingfisher Rd
Brackley NN13 222 E2
Buckingham MK18 240 F2
Kingfisher Way NN15 92 A2
Kingmaker Way NN4 159 A2
Kings Arms La PE8 42 F3
Kings Ave NN10 132 C7
Kings Cl NN4 175 F3
Kings Cliffe Rd PE8 14 C4
Kings Ct NN14 51 B3
Kings Gn NN11 153 C7
Kings La Barrowden LE15 3 F5
Pury End NN12 215 F7
Kings La *continued*
Yelvertoft NN6 82 B4
Kings Meadow La NN10 132 B7
Kings Meadow Sch NN3 142 C7
Kings Mill La PE9 241 D2
Kings Park Rd NN3 141 F6
Kings Pk NN7 155 A3
Kings Pl NN10 132 C2
Kings Rd Oundle PE8 42 A6
Rushden NN10 132 C2
Stamford PE9 241 D4
Kings St NN8 130 A5
Kings Stile OX17 208 F1
Kings Sutton Prim Sch OX17 231 A5
Kingsbrook NN18 36 B3
Kingsbrook Sch MK19 228 F4
Kingscroft Ct NN3 143 C1
Kingsfield Cl NN5 141 A1
Kingsfield Piece NN12 215 C4
Kingsfield Way NN5 141 A1
Kingshill Dr MK19 228 E5
Kingsland Ave NN2 141 D3
Kingsland Cl NN2 141 D3
Kingsland Gdns NN2 141 C3
Kingsley Ave
Daventry NN11 135 B1
Kettering NN16 72 B5
Rugby CV21 98 F8
Kingsley Dr NN17 36 D8
Kingsley Gdns 3 NN2 141 E1
Kingsley Lower Sch NN2 141 F2
Kingsley Park Mid Sch NN2 141 D1
Kingsley Park Terr NN2 141 F1
Kingsley Rd
Northampton NN2 141 E1
Rothwell NN14 70 C7
Silverstone NN12 214 E5
Kingsley Sch NN15 72 F1
Kingsmead
King's Cliffe PE8 13 F8
Northampton NN2 141 A5
Kingsmith Dr NN9 114 E6
Kingsthorne Distribution Pk NN16 71 E4
Kingsthorpe Ave NN17 36 B7
Kingsthorpe CE Lower Sch NN2 141 B3
Kingsthorpe Com Coll NN2 141 E5
Kingsthorpe Gr NN2 141 C2
Kingsthorpe Grove Lower Sch NN2 141 C2
Kingsthorpe Mid Sch NN2 141 B4
Kingsthorpe Rd NN2 141 C1
Kingsthorpe Sh Ctr 2 NN2 141 C3
Kingston Ave MK11 229 E5
Kingston Cl
Blakesley NN12 187 B1
Daventry NN11 135 B3
Long Buckby NN6 121 C4
Middleton Cheney OX17 220 A7
Kingston Way LE16 31 E6
Kingsway Banbury OX16 240 B7
Northampton NN2 141 B4
Rugby CV22 241 C6
Wellingborough NN8 129 E2
Kingswell Rd NN2 141 B3
Kingswell St NN1 159 C5
Kingswood Comp Sch NN18 36 A3
Kingswood Jun & Inf Sch NN18 36 C3
Kingswood Pl NN18 36 A3
Kinross Cl NN3 142 A4
Kipling Cl PE9 241 A3
Kipling Dr NN12 203 B5
Kipling Rd Corby NN17 36 D8
Kettering NN16 72 C5
Kippell Hill MK46 195 F5
Kipton Cl NN14 70 E7
Kipton Field NN14 70 E7
Kirby Cl Corby NN18 36 A3
Northampton NN4 175 F7
Kirby Ct NN15 91 C5
Kirby Hall★ NN17 23 B6
Kirby La NN17 23 C5
Kirby Rd NN17 10 C1
Kirkby Rd CV21 98 F8
Kirkhams Cl NN6 82 C3
Kirkstone Wlk 7 NN3 142 C4
Kirkwall NN17 21 C1
Kirton Cl NN3 143 B5
Kirton End NN3 143 B4
Kislingbury Prim Sch NN7 157 D4
Kislingbury Rd
Bugbrooke NN7 173 A8
Rothersthorpe NN7 174 A7
Kitchen Gdns NN14 89 F6
Kitchener Cl NN11 135 B4
Kitelee Cl MK19 207 A3
Kites Cl NN4 175 A8
Kits Cl NN7 192 D2
Knaphill Cres NN4 158 F4
Knibb Pl NN15 91 F6
Knibb St NN16 72 C2
Knight's End Rd LE16 32 B6
Knight's La NN2 141 B3
Knightlands Rd NN9 112 F3
Knightley Cl NN11 183 D7
Knightley Rd NN2 141 C1
Knighton Cl NN5 140 A3

Knightons Way NN6 . . . .106 C1
Knights Cl Bozeat NN29 .164 D2
  Corby NN18 . . . . .36 A5
  Earls Barton NN6 . . . . . .144 E4
Knights Ct
  Northampton NN1 . . . . . .159 F8
  Northampton,Little Billing
    NN3 . . . . .143 B1
  Wellingborough NN8 . . . .129 F5
Knights Hill NN6 . . . . . . .85 B8
Knightscliffe Way NN5 .140 D1
Knob The OX17 . . . . . . .231 A5
Knoll Cl LE16 . . . . .31 C3
Knoll The Brixworth NN6 .106 C2
  Grendon NN7 . . . . .163 D5
Knowle NN3 . . . . .160 C6
Knowles Cl NN10 . . . . .132 D3
Knox Cl NN8 . . . . .130 B4
Knox Rd NN8 . . . . .130 B5
Knuston Dr NN10 . . . . .131 F2
Knuston Spinney NN10 .131 E1
Knutsford La NN6 . . . . .121 C4
Krohn Cl MK18 . . . . . . .240 F3
Kylesku Cres NN15 . . . . .91 E8
Kynnesworth Gdns
  NN10 . . . . .132 C6
Kyoto Cl NN3 . . . . .142 A6

L

Laburnhum Cl NN8 . . . .129 E5
Laburnum Cl NN11 . . . .184 B6
Laburnum Cres
  Kettering NN16 . . . . .72 D4
  Northampton NN3 . . . . . .142 A3
Lace Mews MK46 . . . . .195 F4
Laceby Wlk NN3 . . . . . .142 F5
Laddermakers Yd NN7 .172 E7
Lady Cl NN11 . . . . .153 D3
Lady Croft NN11 . . . . . .135 B1
Lady Hollows Dr NN4 . .176 A6
Lady Smock Cl NN4 . . .175 F2
Lady Winefride's Wlk
  NN3 . . . . .143 B2
Lady's La
  Mears Ashby NN6 . . . . . .128 B2
  Northampton NN1 . . . . . .159 C6
Ladybower Cl NN16 . . . .71 E3
Ladybridge Dr NN4 . . . .174 E8
Lahnstein Ct 12 NN16 . . .72 B2
Lake Ave NN15 . . . . .90 F8
Lake Cres NN11 . . . . . . .135 A2
Lake Wlk
  Adderbury OX17 . . . . . . .230 B4
  Northampton NN4 . . . . . .175 C4
Lakeside
  Irthlingborough NN9 . . . .131 D7
  Northampton NN3 . . . . . .143 A7
Lakeside Bglws NN15 . . .91 E6
Lakeside Dr NN4 . . . . . . .76 D3
Lakeside Dr NN3 . . . . . .143 D3
Lakeside Lodges NN3 . .143 A7
Lakeview Gn NN3 . . . . .142 C4
Lamb's Cres OX16 . . . . .240 E6
Lambert Mews PE9 . . . .241 E2
Lambert's Cl LE15 . . . . . . .3 A6
Lambeth Wlk PE9 . . . . .241 D5
Lambourne Way OX17 . .230 B4
Lambrook Dr NN4 . . . . .175 C7
Lammas Cl
  Husbands Bosworth LE17 . .45 E5
  Orlingbury NN14 . . . . . . .110 A5
Lammas Ctyd NN17 . . . . .23 A1
Lammas Rd NN17 . . . . . .23 A1
Lamport Dr NN11 . . . . .135 A5
Lamport Hall ★ NN6 . . .87 D2
Lamport Rd NN6 . . . . . . .87 E6
Lamva Ct MK11 . . . . . .229 F5
Lancaster Cl NN29 . . . .146 C3
Lancaster Dr
  Brackley NN13 . . . . .233 E8
  Thrapston NN14 . . . . .76 F2
Lancaster Rd
  Kettering NN16 . . . . .72 C3
  Rothwell NN14 . . . . .70 E7
  Rugby CV21 . . . . .241 C9
  Stamford PE9 . . . . .241 D4
Lancaster St NN10 . . . .132 C7
Lancaster Way
  Northampton NN4 . . . . . .159 A1
  Rushden NN10 . . . . .132 C3
Lancers Way NN7 . . . . .155 B4
Lanchester Way NN11 . .134 F3
Lancum Ho NN8 . . . . . .129 E5
Landcross Dr NN3 . . . . .160 C7
Landor NN8 . . . . .129 C4
Landor Cl NN11 . . . . . . .21 D1
Landsdown Dr NN3 . . . .142 E2
Landsdowne Pl CV21 . .241 F7
Landseer Cl CV21 . . . . . .80 B1
Landseer Ct NN18 . . . . . .36 D5
Lane The Ashby St L CV23 119 B5
  Denton NN7 . . . . .178 B8
  Eastcote NN12 . . . . .173 A1
  Easton o t H PE9 . . . . .2 A5
  Grafton Regis NN12 . . . . .205 D2
  Rothersthorpe NN7 . . . . .174 B6
  Wappenham NN12 . . . . .213 B8
  Weston by W LE16 . . . . . .18 B4
Lanercost Wlk
  Northampton NN3 . . . . . .142 C4
  8 Northampton NN3 . . . .142 C4
Laneside Hollow NN4 . .175 C6
Langdale NN14 . . . . .50 F3
Langdale Gr NN17 . . . . . .36 D8
Langdale Rd NN2 . . . . .141 D3
Langdale Wlk LE16 . . . . .31 E1

Langdon Cl NN11 . . . . .135 B5
Langford Dr NN4 . . . . . .175 D5
Langham Cl NN6 . . . . . .104 F5
Langham Pl
  Northampton NN2 . . . . . .159 C8
  Walgrave NN6 . . . . .108 A5
Langham Rd NN9 . . . . .114 D7
Langley Cl NN4 . . . . . . .158 E3
Langley Cres NN9 . . . . .113 B5
Langley Ct NN15 . . . . . . .92 B2
Langley Way NN15 . . . . .91 C6
Langley Wlk NN18 . . . . .36 D5
Langport Gn NN18 . . . . .36 B6
Langsett Cl
  Kettering NN16 . . . . .71 E3
  Northampton NN3 . . . . . .142 F1
Langton Ct NN18 . . . . . .36 B6
Langton Pl NN11 . . . . . .91 E1
Langton Rd LE16 . . . . . .32 A7
Langton Rise NN11 . . . .137 C6
Lansdown Cl NN11 . . . .135 D5
Lansom Cl NN15 . . . . . .92 C3
Lapford Rd NN18 . . . . . .36 E4
Lapland Wlk NN18 . . . . .36 B2
Lapstone Ho NN5 . . . . .159 A5
Lapwing Cl NN4 . . . . . .175 A7
Larch Cl Hinton NN11 . . .184 A6
  Irchester NN29 . . . . .147 A4
Larch Dr NN11 . . . . . . .135 C5
Larch La NN5 . . . . .140 E2
Larch Rd Corby NN17 . . . .21 C1
  Kettering NN15 . . . . .72 C1
Larchwood Cl NN8 . . . .129 E5
Lark Cl MK18 . . . . .240 E2
Lark La NN4 . . . . .175 F4
Lark Rise Brackley NN13 .233 E8
  Northampton NN3 . . . . . .143 B4
Larkhall La NN7 . . . . . .157 D6
Larkhall Way NN7 . . . . .157 D7
Larkhill NN10 . . . . .132 A4
Larkin Gdns NN10 . . . . .132 A5
Larkwood Cl NN16 . . . . .72 C6
Larratt Rd NN17 . . . . . . .38 A8
Larwood Cl NN2 . . . . . .141 A5
Lasham Ct NN3 . . . . . . .143 C1
Latham Rd PE8 . . . . .41 D7
Latham St NN14 . . . . . . .55 F7
Lathbury Rd NN13 . . . . .233 D8
Lathkill St LE16 . . . . . . .31 F1
Latimer MK11 . . . . .229 E4
Latimer Cl
  Burton Latimer NN15 . . . .92 C2
  Gretton NN17 . . . . .10 C1
Latimer Cres LE16 . . . . . .31 C1
Latimer Cty Arts Coll
  NN15 . . . . .92 A6
Latimer Rd NN17 . . . . . .36 E8
Lattimore Cl NN6 . . . . .102 C5
Latymer Cl LE16 . . . . . . .49 E5
Latymer Ct 4 NN1 . . . .159 C6
Laud's Rd NN15 . . . . . .101 A5
Lauda Way NN12 . . . . .203 C8
Lauderdale Ave NN4 . . .159 A2
Laughton Rd LE16 . . . . . .30 C4
Launcelot Ct NN5 . . . . .158 A7
Launde Gdns PE9 . . . . .241 A2
Launde Pk LE16 . . . . . . .32 A2
Laundry Rd PE8 . . . . . . .14 C4
Laureate Ho NN11 . . . . .135 B4
Laurel Ct
  Northampton NN3 . . . . . .142 E3
  4 Wellingborough NN8 . .130 B5
Laurel Rd NN16 . . . . . . .72 C4
Laurel Valley NN4 . . . . .175 D4
Laurels The Ecton NN6 . .143 F3
  Moulton NN3 . . . . .126 B2
Lavant Wlk NN3 . . . . . .141 F5
Lavender Cl NN14 . . . . . .76 D3
Lavender La NN7 . . . . . .177 D1
Lavender Way NN10 . . . .148 C4
Lavendon Ct NN15 . . . . .92 A5
Lavenham Ct NN3 . . . . .142 F5
Lavery Ct NN18 . . . . . . .36 D5
Law's La PE8 . . . . .13 F7
Lawford Rd CV21,CV22,
  CV23 . . . . .241 A8
Lawns The Corby NN18 . . .36 A4
  Kettering NN16 . . . . .72 A1
  Kilsby CV23 . . . . .100 A3
  Northampton NN5 . . . . . .158 E8
Lawrence Cl
  Kettering NN15 . . . . .92 A8
  Raunds NN9 . . . . .114 B5
Lawrence Ct Corby NN18 . .36 D5
  Long Buckby NN6 . . . . . .121 B4
  22 Northampton NN1 . . .159 C7
Lawrence Rd CV21 . . . .241 F8
Lawrence Sheriff Sch
  CV21 . . . . .241 D7
Lawrence Sheriff St
  CV22 . . . . .241 C8
Laws Croft NN13 . . . . .233 D7
Laws La NN9 . . . . .111 F4
Lawson Cres NN13 . . . .143 C1
Lawson St Kettering NN16 .72 C3
  Raunds NN9 . . . . .114 D6
Lawton Rd NN10 . . . . . .132 C3
Lawyers Cl NN13 . . . . .233 E2
Laxton Cl NN17 . . . . . . .36 B8
Laxton Ct NN15 . . . . . . .92 A5
Laxton Dr PE8 . . . . .42 B7
Laxton Jun Sch PE8 . . . .42 A5
Laxton Sch PE8 . . . . . . .42 A5
Laywood Cl NN9 . . . . . .114 C7
Laywood Way NN9 . . . .131 E8
Lea Rd NN1 . . . . .159 F8
Lea Way NN8 . . . . .129 D3

Leafields NN3 . . . . .160 F8
Leah Bank NN4 . . . . . . .159 A2
Leah Cl NN18 . . . . .53 A8
Lealand The LE16 . . . . . .48 B8
Leam The NN11 . . . . . .134 F1
Leamington Way NN11 .135 A2
Leatherland St 18 NN16 . .72 B2
Leben Sq NN3 . . . . .143 C5
Leckhampstead Rd
  MK19 . . . . .228 A3
Ledaig Wlk NN3 . . . . . .142 A4
Ledbury Rd NN15 . . . . . .91 F5
Lee Way NN9 . . . . .114 D7
Lee's Way NN9 . . . . . . .114 D7
Lee's Way NN14 . . . . . . .54 A3
Lees Cl NN12 . . . . .215 C4
Lees St NN9 . . . . .112 E1
Leeson Cres NN15 . . . . .91 F6
Leeson Cl NN12 . . . . . .203 D4
Leeson Rd NN12 . . . . . .203 C4
Legg Rd PE8 . . . . .7 D8
Legion Cres NN16 . . . . . .71 F3
Leicester Cl NN9 . . . . . .72 A3
Leicester La LE16 . . . . . .31 D7
Leicester Par NN2 . . . . .159 C8
Leicester Rd
  Husbands Bosworth LE17 . .45 D7
  Market Harborough LE16 . .31 D5
Leicester St
  Kettering NN16 . . . . .72 A3
  Northampton NN1 . . . . . .159 C7
Leicester Terr 2 NN2 . . .159 C7
Leigh Gr OX16 . . . . . . .240 C7
Leighton Cl NN8 . . . . . .129 F8
Leighton Pl NN8 . . . . . .129 F4
Leighton Rd NN18 . . . . .36 D5
Leith Ct NN4 . . . . .158 E3
Lely Ct NN18 . . . . .36 D5
Lenborough Cl MK18 . . .240 C2
Lenborough Rd MK18 . .240 C2
Lennon Cl CV21 . . . . . . .99 C8
Lennox Gdns OX16 . . . .240 A6
Lennox Wlk NN5 . . . . . .140 D2
Lenthall Sq LE16 . . . . . .31 E1
Lenton Cl NN14 . . . . . . .90 A3
Leonard La 1 NN3 . . . .126 C1
Leonardo Ct NN18 . . . . .36 D5
Lerwick Way NN17 . . . . .36 C8
Leslie Rd NN2 . . . . .159 B7
Lesson Rd NN16 . . . . . .106 B1
Lester Cl OX17 . . . . . . .230 A6
Letts Rd NN4 . . . . .159 B3
Leven Way NN17 . . . . . .21 B1
Levenot Cl OX16 . . . . . .240 F8
Lever Rd CV21 . . . . .80 A1
Levitts Rd NN7 . . . . . . .173 A8
Levy Cl CV21 . . . . .241 B8
Lewin Cl NN14 . . . . .70 B7
Lewin Rd NN8 . . . . .36 B1
Lewis Ho NN14 . . . . . . .91 E1
Lewis Rd Kettering NN15 . .91 C7
  Northampton NN5 . . . . . .159 A7
Lexden Cl NN4 . . . . . . .175 F7
Lexton Gdns OX17 . . . .220 B8
Leyland Dr NN2 . . . . . .141 A5
Leyland Trad Est NN8 . .130 D4
Leyland View NN8 . . . . .130 D4
Leys Ave Desborough NN14 .51 C7
  Rothwell NN14 . . . . .70 C7
Leys Cl Denton NN7 . . . .162 B1
  Long Buckby NN6 . . . . . .121 C4
Leys Gdns NN8 . . . . . . .130 B6
Leys La NN4 . . . . .160 F1
Leys Rd Earls Barton NN6 144 D4
  Pattishall NN12 . . . . . . .172 D1
  Rugby CV21 . . . . .99 C7
  Wellingborough NN8 . . . .130 B6
Leys The Bugbrooke NN7 .172 E6
  Denton NN7 . . . . .162 B1
  Long Buckby NN6 . . . . . .121 C4
  Northampton NN2 . . . . . .141 B2
  Orlingbury NN14 . . . . . . .110 A5
  Roade NN7 . . . . .191 D4
  Upper Boddington NN11 . .182 C8
  Welford NN6 . . . . .64 E5
  Woodford NN14 . . . . .94 D7
  Yardley Hastings NN7 . . .179 A6
Leyside Ct NN3 . . . . . . .143 B5
Leyswell Ct 4 NN3 . . . .161 A8
Liberty Dr NN5 . . . . . . .140 C1
Lichfield Cl NN7 . . . . . .157 D3
Lichfield Dr NN4 . . . . . .175 B7
Liddington Way NN2 . . .141 B5
Lidsey Rd OX16 . . . . . . .240 F7
Lightfoot La LE16 . . . . . .20 B1
Lilac Cl NN14 . . . . .76 D3
Lilac Ct NN8 . . . . .129 E5
Lilac Gr NN10 . . . . .148 B7
Lilac Pl NN15 . . . . .72 D1
Lilbourne La LE17 . . . . . .62 B3
Lilbourne Rd CV23 . . . . .80 C5
Lilford Pl NN16 . . . . .72 D3
Lilford Rd NN14 . . . . . . .77 C8
Liliput Rd NN4 . . . . . . .160 C3
Lilley Homes The NN8 . .129 F2
Lilley Terr NN7 . . . . . . .112 F2
Lillington Ct NN18 . . . . .36 B6
Lilly Hill MK46 . . . . . . .195 F5
Lime Ave Banbury OX16 . .240 E6
  Buckingham MK18 . . . . .240 F2
  Eydon NN11 . . . . .184 C1
  Long Buckby NN6 . . . . . .121 C4
  Northampton NN3 . . . . . .142 A1
  Oundle PE8 . . . . .41 F7
Lime Cl Broughton NN14 . .90 B4
  Hartwell NN7 . . . . .192 C4
Lime Ct NN9 . . . . .112 F2
Lime Farm Way NN4 . . .160 F2
Lime Gr Bugbrooke NN7 .173 A7

Lime Gr continued
  Wellingborough NN8 . . . .130 A7
Lime Rd Kettering NN16 . .72 D4
  Yardley Gobion NN12 . . .217 E6
Lime St
  Irthlingborough NN9 . . . .112 F2
  Olney MK46 . . . . .195 F3
  Rushden NN10 . . . . .132 B4
Lime Terr NN9 . . . . .112 F2
Lime Tree Mews NN15 . .72 B1
Lime Trees Gr NN17 . . . .37 A6
Limefields Way NN4 . . .175 D6
Limehurst Cl NN5 . . . . .140 C1
Limehurst Rd NN5 . . . .158 C8
Limehurst Sq NN5 . . . .158 C8
Limes The
  9 Daventry NN11 . . . . . .135 C1
  11 Irthlingborough NN9 . .112 F2
  Stony Stratford MK11 . . .229 E5
  Thorpe Langton LE16 . . . .17 A5
  Thrapston NN14 . . . . .76 E2
Limlow Cl NN4 . . . . . . .158 E3
Limoges Ct NN5 . . . . . .140 A2
Linacre Cl NN3 . . . . . . .142 F6
Lincoln Cl OX16 . . . . . .240 B7
Lincoln Ct Brackley NN13 233 F5
  Market Harborough LE16 . .31 F5
Lincoln Ho NN5 . . . . . . .159 A5
Lincoln Pk NN13 . . . . . .233 F5
Lincoln Rd
  Northampton NN5 . . . . . .159 A5
  Stamford PE9 . . . . .241 E5
Lincoln St NN2 . . . . . . .141 C3
Lincoln Way Corby NN18 . .36 C4
  Daventry NN11 . . . . .153 C8
Lincoln Wlk NN18 . . . . .36 B4
Lindale Cl NN3 . . . . . . .142 B3
Linden Ave
  Higham Ferrers NN10 . . . .132 B6
  Kettering NN15,NN16 . . . .72 D1
Linden Cl NN15 . . . . . . .72 D1
Linden Rd NN3 . . . . . . .142 A1
Lindens The NN12 . . . . .203 C6
Lindisfarne Dr NN15 . . .91 F8
Lindisfarne Rd NN17 . . .21 C1
Lindisfarne Way
  Northampton NN5 . . . . . .175 C8
  Thrapston NN14 . . . . .76 F2
Lindrick Cl NN11 . . . . . .135 E2
Lindsay Ave NN3 . . . . . .142 B2
Lindsay St NN16 . . . . . .72 B3
Lindsay Terr NN3 . . . . . .142 A2
Lindsey Cl PE8 . . . . .14 F1
Lindsey Gdns LE16 . . . . .48 D8
Lindsey Rd PE9 . . . . . . .241 E4
Lingfield Terr NN2 . . . . .141 F2
Lingfield Wlk NN18 . . . .36 C2
Lings Lower Sch NN3 . .142 F4
Lings Upper Sch NN3 . .142 F2
Lings Way NN3 . . . . . . .143 A4
Lingswood Pk NN3 . . . .143 A3
Link La NN14 . . . . .89 B4
Link Rd Northampton NN2 141 B6
  Rushden NN10 . . . . .148 B7
Link The NN16 . . . . . . .240 A8
Link Way Bugbrooke NN7 173 A7
  Towcester NN12 . . . . . . .203 C5
Links Rd NN8 . . . . .130 C6
Links The NN15 . . . . . . .91 B8
Linley Dr NN14 . . . . . . .50 F4
Linley Gn NN5 . . . . .158 D8
Linnell Way NN16 . . . . . .71 F4
Linnet Cl NN8 . . . . .130 A7
Linnet Dr NN15 . . . . . . .92 A6
Linnet Rd NN12 . . . . . .203 C3
Linnetts La NN10 . . . . .132 B5
Lipscombe Dr MK18 . . .240 E4
Lismore Cl NN3 . . . . . . .143 C2
Lismore Wlk NN17 . . . . .21 C1
Lister Cl NN17 . . . . .22 A1
Lister Dr NN4 . . . . .158 E1
Lister Rd NN8 . . . . .130 A5
Litchborough Rd
  Farthingstone NN12 . . . . .170 F3
  Grimscote NN12 . . . . . . .188 A7
Litchfield Cl NN16 . . . . .72 C6
Little Back La NN11 . . . .151 D1
Little Billing Way NN3 . .143 A1
Little Bowden Cty Prim Sch
  LE16 . . . . .31 F2
Little Bowden Manor
  LE16 . . . . .31 F3
Little Casterton Rd PE9 .241 B4
Little Church St CV21 . .241 C8
Little Cl Bozeat NN29 . . .164 C2
  Chapel Brampton NN6 . . .124 D1
Little Cross St NN1 . . . .159 B6
Little Elborow St CV21 .241 C8
Little Field NN4 . . . . . . .175 E4
Little Field Cl NN12 . . . .189 A8
Little Greeve Way NN4 . .176 A6
Little Gull Cl NN3 . . . . .142 F6
Little Harrowden Com Prim
  Sch NN9 . . . . .110 C4
Little Horton House Dr
  NN7 . . . . .177 E2
Little La Aynho OX17 . . .237 C7
  Blisworth NN7 . . . . .190 D8
  Great Houghton NN4 . . . .160 D1
  Ravensthorpe NN6 . . . . .103 D1
  Stanion NN14 . . . . .37 E1
  Wollaston NN29 . . . . . . .146 D3
  Yardley Hastings NN7 . . .179 A4
Little London
  Deanshanger MK19 . . . . .228 E4
  Silverstone NN12 . . . . . .214 D5
Little Mdw NN18 . . . . . .36 B1
Little Park St 6 NN8 . . .130 A5

Little Pennington St
  CV21 . . . . .241 B8
Little Priel Rd NN7 . . . .155 B4
Little St Rushden NN10 . .132 C1
  Sulgrave OX17 . . . . .211 A8
  Yardley Hastings NN7 . . .179 B6
Littledale NN8 . . . . .129 D6
Littlewood Cl NN5 . . . . .159 A8
Littlewood St NN7 . . . . .70 E7
Livingstone Cl NN14 . . .70 F7
Livingstone Rd NN11 . . .135 C4
Llewellyn Wlk NN18 . . .36 D5
Lloyd Cl NN8 . . . . .130 B8
Lloyd's Rd NN17 . . . . . . .37 B7
Loach Cl NN3 . . . . .142 A6
Loatland St NN14 . . . . . .50 F3
Loatlands Prim Sch
  NN14 . . . . .50 F3
Lobelia Rd NN16 . . . . . .72 C4
Lock La MK19 . . . . .218 E2
Lockcroft Sq 6 NN3 . . .143 D2
Locks Gn PE8 . . . . .16 A8
Locks The CV21 . . . . . . .80 B1
Locktons Cl NN12 . . . . .201 E2
Lockwood Cl NN2 . . . . .141 C4
Loddington CE Prim Sch
  NN14 . . . . .70 D1
Loddington Rd NN14 . . .89 F7
Loddington Way NN14 . .89 B4
Lodge Ave NN4 . . . . . . .175 C4
Lodge Cl Banbury OX16 . .240 D6
  Little Houghton NN7 . . . .161 B3
  Northampton NN4 . . . . . .175 F3
  Northampton, Hopping Hill
    NN5 . . . . .140 B1
Lodge Ct 1 NN8 . . . . . .130 B5
Lodge Farm Ct MK19 . .218 F6
Lodge Farm Ind Est
  NN5 . . . . .140 C2
Lodge Flats NN6 . . . . . .122 C6
Lodge Green Rd NN17 . . .36 E8
Lodge La NN6 . . . . .121 F3
Lodge Park Tech Coll
  NN17 . . . . .21 B1
Lodge Pk NN12 . . . . . . .215 C4
Lodge Rd Daventry NN11 135 C2
  Little Houghton NN7 . . . .161 A3
  Rugby CV21 . . . . .241 D9
  Rushden NN10 . . . . .148 A8
Lodge The OX17 . . . . . .198 D2
Lodge Way
  Irthlingborough NN9 . . . .131 E8
  Northampton NN5 . . . . . .140 C3
Lodore Gdns NN3 . . . . .142 C3
Logan Cres LE16 . . . . . .31 C4
Logan Ct LE16 . . . . .31 D4
Logan St LE16 . . . . .31 D3
Logwell Rd NN3 . . . . . .142 F1
Loire Cl NN5 . . . . .140 A2
Lombard Way OX16 . . . .219 A6
Lombardy Ct NN3 . . . . .142 D3
Lomond Cl NN17 . . . . . .21 C1
Lomond Dr NN15 . . . . . .91 F8
London End
  Earls Barton NN6 . . . . . .144 D4
  Irchester NN29 . . . . .147 B8
  Titchmarsh NN14 . . . . . . .77 D3
  Upper Boddington NN11 . .182 C8
London Rd Bozeat NN29 .164 C3
  Braunston NN11 . . . . . . .118 A1
  Buckingham MK18 . . . . .240 E1
  Daventry NN11 . . . . .153 D8
  Kettering NN15 . . . . .91 C8
  Little Irchester NN8 . . . . .130 C1
  Northampton,Far Cotton
    NN4 . . . . .159 C2
  Northampton,Wootton
    NN4 . . . . .175 D5
  Old Stratford MK19 . . . . .229 C6
  Raunds NN9 . . . . .114 C6
  Roade NN7 . . . . .191 C4
  Stony Stratford MK11 . . .229 E5
  Towcester NN12 . . . . . . .203 D5
  Wansford PE8 . . . . .8 B3
  Wellingborough NN8 . . . .130 B3
  Willoughby CV23 . . . . . .117 E3
  Wollaston NN29 . . . . . . .146 D1
Lone Pine Ct NN6 . . . . .106 B2
Long Acre NN7 . . . . . . .161 D3
Long Acres 4 NN4 . . . .175 B8
Long Acres Dr NN9 . . . .112 E3
Long Barrow OX17 . . . .196 F7
Long Brimley Cl LE16 . . .32 B3
Long Buckby Inf Sch
  NN6 . . . . .121 B4
Long Buckby Jun Sch
  NN6 . . . . .121 B3
Long Buckby Rd NN6 . . .120 E5
Long Buckby Sta NN6 . .121 A2
Long Cl NN18 . . . . .36 B1
Long Croft Rd NN14,NN18 37 C3
Long Furlong CV22 . . . . .98 A8
Long La Olney MK46 . . .195 F4
  Warmington PE8 . . . . . . .28 B2
Long Mallows Rise 9
  NN3 . . . . .143 C2
Long March NN11 . . . . .153 D8
Long March Ind Est
  NN11 . . . . .153 D8
Long Marsh NN8 . . . . . .130 B2
Long Marsh Sq NN3 . . .143 A6
Long Massey MK46 . . . .195 E5
Long Mdw NN4 . . . . . . .176 B6
Long Mynd Dr NN5 . . . .158 D8

Long Row
Leckhampstead MK18 ......227 E1
Woodford NN14 ....94 D7
Long Row Cl NN11 ......170 A8
Long Street Rd MK19 ....207 A3
Long Wall NN13 ....233 E6
Longburges OX17 ....220 B8
Longcroft La NN12 ....216 C8
Longdown La CV23 ....118 B7
Longfellow Dr NN16 ......72 C6
Longfellow Rd NN8 ....129 B4
Longford Ave NN3 ....161 A8
Longland Ct NN3 ....142 B2
Longland Rd NN3 ....142 C2
Longleat Cl LE16 ....32 B3
Longleat Ct 5 NN4 ......175 C8
Longleat Gr NN15 ....91 C5
Longmead Ct NN3 ....143 B4
Longueville Ct NN3 ......142 E4
Longworth Cl OX16 ....240 E9
Lonsborough Dr NN15 ....90 E8
Lonsdale Dr
Kettering NN15 ....91 B7
Stamford PE9 ....241 A3
Loop Rd PE28 ....97 A3
Lord Burghley's Hospl
PE9 ....241 D2
Lordswood Cl NN4 ....176 A6
Lorne Cl NN17 ....36 F6
Lorne Rd NN1 ....159 C7
Lorraine Cres NN3 ....142 B5
Lorraine Dr NN3 ....142 C5
Loseby Cl NN10 ....148 A8
Lotus Ct NN15 ....72 B1
Louisa Dr NN5 ....140 E7
Louisa Lilley Homes The 7
NN9 ....112 F2
Louisberg Ct 4 NN4 .....175 E7
Louise Rd NN1 ....159 C7
Lounts Cres LE16 ....20 D7
Lovap Way NN18 ....36 B1
Lovat Dr NN5 ....158 E7
Lovell Cl NN9 ....114 A4
Lovell Ct 12 NN9 ....112 F2
Lovers La PE5 ....8 F2
Lovett Rd NN11 ....183 D8
Low Farm Pl NN3 ....141 F7
Low Greeve NN4 ....176 A6
Low March NN11 ....153 D7
Lowbury Ct NN4 ....158 E3
Lower Adelaide St NN2 .159 C7
Lower Bath St NN1 ....159 B6
Lower Cherwell St
OX16 ....240 D7
Lower Cross St NN1 ......159 B6
Lower Ecton La NN3 .....143 D1
Lower End Bradden NN12 201 F5
Hartwell NN7 ....192 C1
Pytchley NN14 ....91 A1
Lower Farm Rd NN3 ......141 F7
Lower Harding St 11
NN1 ....159 C6
Lower Hester St NN2 .....159 C8
Lower Hillmorton Rd
CV21 ....241 F7
Lower Hilmorton Rd 5
CV21 ....80 A1
Lower King St NN14 ......51 B3
Lower Meadow Ct NN3 ..142 E5
Lower Mounts NN1 ....159 D6
Lower Pastures NN3 ......53 A8
Lower Priory St NN1 .....159 B7
Lower Rd
Milton Malsor NN7 ......174 E4
Stoke Albany LE16 ....34 B5
Lower St
Desborough NN14 ....51 A3
Great Addington NN14 ...94 B2
Great Doddington NN29 .145 E6
Kettering NN16 ....72 A2
Pury End NN12 ....216 A7
Rugby CV21 ....99 C8
Twywell NN14 ....75 A1
Willoughby CV23 ....117 D4
Lower Stable Yd NN12 ....203 D5
Lower Steeping NN14 .....51 B2
Lower Thrift St NN1 ......159 F6
Lower Weald MK19 ....229 E2
Lower Wharf MK18 ....240 E4
Lowick Cl NN8 ....129 D7
Lowick Ct NN3 ....142 C7
Lowick La NN14 ....76 F7
Islip NN14 ....76 B3
Lowlands Cl NN3 ....143 C5
Lowry Cl NN8 ....129 E7
Loxton Cl NN5 ....140 A6
Loyd Rd NN1 ....160 A6
Lubenham All Saints CE Prim
Sch LE16 ....30 F3
Lubenham Hill LE16 ....31 C2
Lubenham Rd
East Farndon LE16 ....31 B1
Marston Trussell LE16 ....30 D1
Lucas Cl NN9 ....131 E8
Lucas Ct CV21 ....241 D9
Lucas La NN7 ....177 B3
Lucas Rd NN6 ....121 A3
Lucky La NN6 ....240 C7
Luddington Rd PE8,PE17 ..61 C3
Ludlow Cl NN3 ....143 A4
Luffenham Cl PE9 ....241 A3
Luffenham Rd LE15 ....3 F6
Lukes Cl NN3 ....212 A5
Lulworth Wlk NN18 ....36 A6

Lumber La NN12 ....216 B7
Lumbertubs La NN3 .....142 D5
Lumbertubs Lower Sch
NN3 ....142 F3
Lumbertubs Rise NN3 ...142 D5
Lumbertubs Way NN3 ...142 E3
Lunchfield Ct NN3 ....126 C1
Lunchfield Gdns NN3 ....126 C1
Lunchfield La NN3 ....126 C1
Lunchfield Wlk 7 NN3 ..126 C1
Lundie Cl NN9 ....114 D7
Lundy Ave NN18 ....36 E4
Lupin Cl NN16 ....72 D4
Lutterworth Rd
Northampton NN1 ....160 A6
Swinford LE17 ....62 B6
Lutton Rd PE8 ....43 C3
Lyddington Rd
Caldecott LE15, L16 ....9 D2
Gretton NN17 ....10 A1
Lydia Ct NN10 ....132 A2
Lyle Ct NN8 ....129 C7
Lyncrest Ave NN5 ....158 E7
Lyncrest Lower Sch
NN5 ....158 E7
Lyncroft Way NN2 ....141 B1
Lyndhurst Rd CV21 ....98 F8
Lyndon Way PE9 ....241 A3
Lyne Wlk NN7 ....177 B3
Lyneford Way NN10 .....147 F8
Lynmore Cl NN4 ....158 C1
Lynmouth Ave NN3 ......160 C7
Lynmouth Pl NN18 ....36 E4
Lynton Ave NN2 ....141 C6
Lynton Gr NN18 ....36 F4
Lynwood Cl NN16 ....72 B5
Lytham Cl NN2 ....141 E3
Lytham Ct NN8 ....129 C7
Lytham Rd CV22 ....241 A6
Lyttleton Rd NN5 ....159 A7
Lyveden New Bield★
PE8 ....57 A7
Lyveden Pl NN16 ....72 D3
Lyveden Rd
Brigstock NN14 ....55 F7
Northampton NN4 ....160 A1
Lyveden Way NN18 ....36 C2

M

Macadam Cl NN11 ....134 F5
Macadam Rd NN17 ....22 A1
Mackenzie Rd NN9 ....114 C5
Mackintosh Ct NN15 ......92 B1
Mackworth Dr NN9 ......111 E4
Mackworth Gn NN9 ......111 F4
Maclean Cl NN3 ....160 C7
Macmillian Way NN3 ....142 B4
Macon Cl NN5 ....139 F2
Madams Gdn NN14 ....70 D7
Madams Hill NN14 ....70 D7
Madeline Cl LE16 ....32 A5
Magdalen Cl
Daventry NN11 ....153 B8
Stony Stratford MK11 ....229 D6
Syresham NN13 ....224 C8
Magdalen Ho MK11 ......229 D6
Magdalen Mdws NN13 ..222 E1
Magdalen Rd CV23 ....117 E3
Magdalene Cl NN14 ....54 B3
Magee St NN1 ....159 F7
Magellan Cl
Daventry NN11 ....135 C5
Rothwell NN14 ....70 C6
Magnolia Cl NN3 ....160 D6
Magnolia Dr
Daventry NN11 ....135 C4
Rushden NN10 ....148 B2
Magpie La NN13 ....233 E6
Magpie Rd
Sulgrave OX17 ....210 E7
Towcester NN12 ....203 C3
Maida Cl NN4 ....175 E7
Maiden Le 2 NN8 ....241 E3
Maidencastle NN3 ....143 B3
Maidford Rd Corby NN17 ..36 C7
Farthingstone NN12 .....170 D1
Maidwell Hall (Prep Sch for
Boys) NN6 ....87 B6
Maidwell Prim Sch NN6 ..87 B6
Maidwell Rd NN6 ....87 D7
Main Dr NN12 ....217 B2
Main Rd Collyweston PE9 ...1 D2
Crick NN6 ....100 F5
Dingley LE16 ....32 F3
Earls Barton NN6 ....144 D6
Farthinghoe NN13 ....221 B4
Grendon NN7 ....163 D6
Kilsby CV23 ....99 F3
Middleton Cheney OX17 .220 A8
New Hackleton NN7 ......177 B3
Northampton, Duston NN5 158 B7
Northampton,Far cotton
NN4 ....159 B3
Shutlanger NN12 ....204 D8
Syresham NN13 ....224 C7
Upper Heyford NN7 .....156 D4
Wilby NN8 ....129 B1
Main St Abthorpe NN12 ..201 F2
Aldwincle NN14 ....76 F8
Apethorpe NN8 ....14 C4
Ashby St L CV23 ....119 C5
Ashley LE16 ....18 F2
Aston le W NN11 ....182 E2
Badby NN11 ....152 F2
Barnwell PE8 ....59 B5
Barrowden LE15 ....3 F5

Main St continued
Bradden NN12 ....201 F5
Bythorn PE28 ....97 D4
Caldecott LE16 ....21 B8
Charlton OX17 ....231 F4
Church Stowe NN7 ......171 E8
Claydon OX17 ....181 D1
Clifton u D CV23 ....80 A5
Cold Ashby NN6 ....84 B5
Cosgrove MK19 ....218 E2
Cottesbrooke NN6 ....105 A8
Denton NN7 ....162 B1
Drayton LE16 ....20 A5
East Farndon LE16 ....48 B7
East Haddon NN6 ....122 D5
Farthingstone NN12 .....170 E3
Great Addington NN14 ...94 B2
Great Bowden LE16 ....32 A6
Great Brington NN7 .....138 C7
Great Gidding PE17 ......61 D3
Great Oxendon LE16 .....48 E3
Gumley LE16 ....30 A8
Hannington NN6 ....108 C3
Hellidon NN11 ....151 D1
Holcot NN6 ....126 E8
Little Brington NN7 ......138 C4
Little Harrowden NN9 ...110 C4
Loddington NN14 ....70 C1
Lowick NN14 ....75 F6
Lubenham LE16 ....30 F3
Lyddington LE15 ....9 A7
Lyddington LE15 ....9 C7
Mawsley Village NN14 ...89 B4
Medbourne LE16 ....19 A7
Middleton LE16 ....35 C8
Orton NN14 ....70 A3
Polebrook PE8 ....43 A3
Rockingham LE16 ....21 B4
Slipton NN14 ....75 A3
Southwick PE8 ....26 B5
Sutton Bassett LE16 .....18 A1
Tansor PE8 ....27 D2
Theddingworth LE17 .....46 D8
Thorpe by Water LE15 ...10 A5
Thurning PE8 ....60 D3
Turweston NN13 ....234 C8
Upper Stowe NN7 ....171 F6
Wadenhoe PE8 ....58 A4
Wakerley LE15 ....4 A4
Watford NN6 ....120 C5
Willoughby CV23 ....117 E3
Woodend NN12 ....200 F7
Woodnewton PE8 ....14 E1
Yarwell PE8 ....15 F8
Maine Cl MK18 ....240 D2
Malabar Fields NN11 ....153 B8
Malborough Way NN12 .217 F5
Malcolm Cl NN17 ....36 F6
Malcolm Dr NN5 ....158 E7
Malcolm Rd NN1 ....141 C6
Malcolm Sargent Prim Sch
PE9 ....241 A3
Malcolm Terr NN2 ....141 F2
Malham Ct NN8 ....129 D6
Mall The NN16 ....72 B2
Mallard Cl
Earls Barton NN6 ....144 F5
Higham Ferrers NN10 ...132 C8
Northampton NN4 ....158 F2
Thrapston NN14 ....76 D3
Mallard Ct PE9 ....241 D2
Mallard Dr
Buckingham MK18 ....240 E3
Burton Latimer NN15 ....92 A2
Hinton NN11 ....184 B6
Mallery Cl NN10 ....132 D3
Mallets Cl MK11 ....229 E5
Mallory Way NN11 ......135 C5
Mallory Wlk NN3 ....141 F5
Mallows Dr NN9 ....114 C7
Malmo Cl NN18 ....36 A1
Malpas Dr NN5 ....158 B8
Malt La NN13 ....224 C8
Malt Mill Cl CV23 ....100 A2
Malt Mill Gn CV23 ....100 A2
Malthouse Cl NN9 ....112 F2
Malthouse Ct NN12 .....203 C6
Malting La NN14 ....54 A3
Malting Way NN7 ....192 D1
Malting Yd PE9 ....241 E2
Maltings PE8 ....42 A6
Maltings Rd PE8 ....10 B1
Maltings The Ashley LE16 ..18 F3
Rothwell NN14 ....70 C7
Wollaston NN29 ....146 D3
Wothorpe PE9 ....2 E8
Malton Wlk NN18 ....36 B5
Malvern Ave CV22 ....241 F6
Malvern Cl Kettering NN16 72 B7
Wellingborough NN8 ....129 D1
Malvern Dr MK11 ....229 F4
Malvern Gr NN5 ....158 D8
Malzor La NN7 ....174 E4
Manchester Rd NN29 ...146 C3
Manfield Health Campus
NN3 ....142 B4
Manfield Rd NN1 ....160 A2
Manfield Way NN3 ....142 B4
Manitoba Cl NN18 ....36 B3
Manitoba Pl NN11 ....184 C1
Manitoba Way NN11 ....184 C1
Manning Ct NN3 ....142 C7
Manning Rd NN3 ....142 C7
Manning St NN10 ....132 C1
Manning Wlk CV21 ......241 D8
Manningham Rd NN9 ....114 A4
Mannings Rise NN10 ....132 C1
Mannington Gdns NN4 .175 C7

Mannock Rd NN8 ....129 E3
Manor Cl Bozeat NN29 ..164 D3
Charwelton NN11 ....168 A4
Cosgrove MK19 ....218 E2
Great Addington NN14 ...94 B2
Great Harrowden NN9 ...110 D2
Hanslope MK19 ....207 A2
Harpole NN7 ....157 C6
Irchester NN29 ....147 B8
Isham NN14 ....110 F8
Middleton Cheney OX17 .220 B7
Roade NN7 ....191 E4
Sulgrave OX17 ....210 F8
Thrapston NN14 ....76 D2
Manor Ct Banbury OX16 .240 E9
Brackley NN13 ....233 F8
Cottingham LE16 ....20 C1
Grendon NN7 ....163 D5
Little Harrowden NN9 ...110 C4
Northampton NN2 ....141 B3
Rushden NN10 ....148 C8
2 Wellingborough NN8 .130 B5
Manor Dr Corby NN18 ....36 A4
Irthlingborough NN9 ....113 A2
Manor Farm PE8 ....14 C4
Manor Farm Cl
Barby CV23 ....99 C2
Broughton NN14 ....90 B4
Walgrave NN6 ....108 A5
Manor Farm Cotts
NN13 ....238 C8
Manor Farm Ct
Cogenhoe NN7 ....162 A6
Titchmarsh NN14 ....77 C4
Manor Farm Rd
Northampton NN3 ....143 B2
Raunds NN9 ....114 E6
Manor Gdns
Farthingstone NN12 .....170 F3
Norton NN11 ....136 C4
Pytchley NN14 ....90 F2
Stanwick NN9 ....114 A3
Manor Ho The NN14 ......76 D2
Manor House Cl NN14 ...144 E5
Manor House Gdns
NN9 ....114 D6
Manor House Mus★
Manor La Clifton u D CV23 .80 A5
Farthinghoe NN13 ....221 B4
Newnham NN11 ....153 E4
Whilton NN11 ....137 D6
Wymington NN10 ....148 A5
Manor Pk Claydon OX17 .181 D1
Nether Heyford NN7 ....156 C2
Manor Pl NN15 ....91 B8
Manor Rd Banbury OX16 .240 E9
Brackley NN13 ....233 E7
Daventry NN11 ....135 D1
Earls Barton NN6 ....144 E4
Great Bowden LE16 ......32 A6
Grendon NN7 ....163 D5
Grimscote NN12 ....188 A8
Hanging Houghton NN6 .106 C8
Hinton NN11 ....184 B6
Kilsby CV23 ....100 A3
Mears Ashby NN6 ....128 B2
Medbourne LE16 ....19 A7
Moulton NN3 ....142 C8
Northampton NN2 ....141 B3
Pitsford NN6 ....125 D5
Rothwell NN14 ....70 B7
Rugby CV21 ....241 D9
Rushden NN10 ....148 B8
Rushton NN14 ....52 C2
Spratton NN6 ....105 B1
Stanion NN14 ....37 E2
Staverton NN11 ....152 B7
Sulgrave OX17 ....210 F8
Sutton PE5 ....8 F2
Weedon NN7 ....155 B3
Manor St
Buckingham MK18 ....240 C3
Raunds NN9 ....114 D6
Manor The NN11 ....199 C7
Manor View PE9 ....1 A6
Manor Way
Higham Ferrers NN10 ...132 C5
Yardley Gobion NN12 ...217 E6
Manor Wlk
Hanging Houghton NN6 .106 C8
Market Harborough LE16 .31 E3
Nether Heyford NN7 ....156 C2
Manorfield Cl NN3 ....161 B8
Manorfield Rd NN3 ......161 B8
Manorfields Rd MK19 ...229 B6
Mansard Cl NN5 ....158 E6
Manse Cl MK11 ....229 D6
Mansefield Cl NN14 ......51 A3
Mansel Cl MK19 ....218 D2
Mansell Cl NN12 ....203 C8
Mansfield Ct NN10 ......202 D8
Mansfield St NN9 ....113 F4
Manshead Ct MK11 .....229 F5
Mansion Cl NN3 ....142 A6
Mansion Hill OX17 ....219 F8
Mantlefield Rd NN18 .....36 B6
Manton Ct NN10 ....132 C2
Manton Rd Corby NN17 ..22 C4
Irthlingborough NN9 ....112 E2
Rushden NN10 ....132 C1
Manton Spinney NN10 ..131 E2
Maple Cl Brackley NN13 .222 F1
Braunston NN11 ....118 D1
Bugbrooke NN7 ....172 F7
Hinton NN11 ....184 A6
Towcester NN12 ....203 B4

Maple Ct NN17 ....21 E1
Maple Dr NN8 ....129 E2
Maple Fields Sch NN18 ..36 D5
Maple Gr CV21 ....241 C9
Maple Rd Kettering NN16 .72 C6
Rushden NN10 ....132 C2
Maple Wood NN10 ......148 B7
Maples The NN11 ....135 D1
Mapletoft St NN5 ....114 C5
Mapperley Dr NN3 ......160 F8
March Edge MK18 ....240 E4
Marchwood Cl NN3 .....142 F6
Marconi Ctyd NN17 ......22 B1
Mare Fair NN1 ....159 C5
Mare Leys MK18 ....240 F3
Marecroft LE16 ....66 F7
Margaret Ave NN8 ......129 E2
Margaret Ct OX16 ....240 A7
Margaret Rd
Kettering NN16 ....72 E3
Twyford OX17 ....230 B5
Margaret St NN1 ....159 D7
Marion Sq NN16 ....72 E3
Maritime Way NN11 .....135 E1
Marjoram Cl 6 NN4 .....175 D6
Market Cross NN9 ......112 F2
Market Harborough CE Prim
Sch LE16 ....31 D3
Market Harborough District
Hospl LE16 ....31 D3
Market Harborough Mus★
LE16 ....31 E3
Market Harborough Sta
LE16 ....32 A3
Market Hill
Buckingham MK18 ....240 D4
Rothwell NN14 ....70 D7
Market Mall CV21 ....241 C9
Market Pl Banbury OX16 .240 D8
Brackley NN13 ....233 E6
Kettering NN16 ....72 B1
Long Buckby NN6 ....121 B4
Olney MK46 ....195 F3
Oundle PE8 ....42 A5
Rugby CV21 ....241 C8
Market Rd NN14 ....76 D2
Market Sq
Buckingham MK18 ....240 D4
3 Daventry NN11 ......135 C2
Hanslope MK19 ....207 A2
Higham Ferrers NN10 ...132 C6
Northampton NN1 ......159 C6
Stony Stratford MK11 ...229 D5
3 Wellingborough NN8 .130 A4
Market St Kettering NN16 .72 B2
Northampton NN1 ....159 E7
Rugby CV21 ....241 D9
Wellingborough NN8 ....130 A4
Market Street Mews 10
NN16 ....72 B2
Market Wlk NN1 ....159 C7
Markham Cl NN5 ....140 C1
Markham Ret Pk PE9 ....241 E5
Markham Wlk NN16 ......36 B5
Markhams Cl MK18 ......240 D3
Marks Cl NN9 ....114 A3
Marlborough Ave NN8 ..129 D7
Marlborough Cl
Kettering NN15 ....72 F1
Kings Sutton OX17 ......230 F6
Marlborough Croft
NN13 ....233 F6
Marlborough Pl OX16 ...240 C7
Marlborough Rd
Banbury OX16 ....240 D7
Northampton NN5 ......159 A6
Marlborough Way LE16 ..31 F5
Marley Ind Est OX16 ....240 D9
Marley Way OX16 ....240 C9
Marlow Cl NN11 ....135 B1
Marlow Ct Corby NN18 ...36 F7
Medbourne LE16 ....19 A8
Marlow Rd NN12 ....203 D5
Marlowe Cl NN4 ....175 B7
Marlstones NN4 ....158 D2
Marnock Sq 3 NN4 .....158 F2
Marquee Dr NN3 ....160 F7
Marriots Rd NN6 ....121 C3
Marriott Cl NN9 ....131 E8
Marriott St NN2 ....159 C8
Marseilles Cl NN5 ....139 F1
Marshall Ct 2 LE16 ......31 F2
Marshall's Rd NN9 ......114 C6
Marshleys Ct NN3 ....143 B5
Marshwell Ct 5 NN3 ....161 A8
Marsons Dr NN6 ....100 F5
Marston Hill
Marston St Lawrence
OX17 ....210 B3
Priors Marston CV47 ....166 E7
Marston Rd
Greatworth OX17 ....210 E2
Lubenham LE16 ....30 D2
Marston Trussell Rd
LE16 ....47 F7
Marston Way NN11 .....135 D6
Martel Cl NN5 ....157 F8
Martha Wallis Ct 1
NN16 ....72 B2
Martial Daire Bvd NN13 233 E8
Martin Cl
Buckingham MK18 ....240 F2
Rushden NN10 ....132 B4
Martin Rd NN15 ....91 C7
Martindale NN2 ....140 F5

Martins La NN4 ....175 E8
Martins Rd NN7 ....177 A1
Martins Yd NN5 ....159 B7
Martlet Cl NN4 ....175 E5
Marwood Cl NN3 ....160 C7
Mary Macmanus Dr
 MK18 ....240 D4
Mascord Cl OX16 ......240 A7
Mascord Rd OX16 ......240 A7
Masefield Cl NN8 ......129 C4
Masefield Dr NN10 ....131 E3
Masefield Rd NN16 ....72 C5
Masefield Way
 Corby NN17 ....36 D8
 Northampton NN2 ....141 E2
Mason Cl Oundle PE8 ..42 A5
 Thrapston NN14 ......76 D1
Massey Cl NN4 ....175 E8
Masterton Cl PE9 ......241 F5
Masterton Rd PE9 ....241 E5
Matchless Cl NN5 ....140 A1
Matlock Way NN14 ....50 E4
Matson Cl NN14 ....70 B6
Matson Ct NN9 ....114 E7
Matthews Cl NN14 ....52 C3
Mauduit Cl MK19 ......207 A3
Maunsell Rise NN14 ..70 B6
Mauntley Ave NN14 ..55 F7
Maurice Rd LE16 ......48 D8
Mawsley La NN14 ......89 C8
Maxwell Wlk NN18 ....36 E5
May Cl NN10 ....148 C7
Maybank NN11 ....153 B8
Maybush Wlk MK46 ..195 E5
Mayfield Rd
 Daventry NN11 ......135 C3
 Desborough NN14 ....51 C3
 Northampton NN3 ....142 B3
Maylan Rd NN17 ......21 F3
Mays Way NN12 ......217 D3
Mazewood Gate PE8 ..13 E7
McGibbon Wlk NN11 ..131 D8
McInnes Way NN9 ....114 D7
Mckeevor Pl OX16 ....240 E8
McKenzie Cl MK18 ....240 D3
Mdw The NN3 ....142 C1
Meacham Cl NN14 ....90 A3
Mead Rd NN15 ....90 F8
Meadow Cl
 Daventry NN11 ......135 D6
 Higham Ferrers NN10 132 D4
 Market Harborough LE16 .31 F4
 Northampton NN5 ....140 B2
 Ringstead NN14 ......95 A3
 Wellingborough NN8 ..130 D8
Meadow Ct
 6 Kettering NN16 ....72 B2
 Ravenstone MK46 ....194 D2
 Towcester NN12 ......203 C5
Meadow Dr NN10 ......132 B6
Meadow Farm Cl NN7 155 F5
Meadow Gate PE8 ....14 E2
Meadow Gdns MK18 ..240 E1
Meadow La Denford NN14 95 C6
 Little Houghton NN7 ..161 A4
 Raunds NN9 ....114 A6
 Thornhaugh PE8 ......7 F5
Meadow Rd
 Kettering NN16 ......72 A2
 Rothwell NN14 ......70 C6
Meadow Rise NN12 ..189 D4
Meadow Row MK18 ..240 D4
Meadow St LE16 ......31 E4
Meadow Sweet Rd
 NN10 ....148 C7
Meadow View
 Adderbury OX17 ....230 A4
 Banbury OX16 ......240 E6
 Great Addington NN14 ..94 C3
 Higham Ferrers NN10 ..132 A6
 Potterspury NN12 ....217 D3
Meadow Way NN9 ....112 F1
Meadow Wlk
 Buckingham MK18 ....240 D4
 Higham Ferrers NN10 ..132 B6
 9 Irthlingborough NN9 112 F2
Meadowdale Prim Sch
 LE16 ....32 B4
Meadowlands NN9 ....110 B3
Meadows The
 Northampton NN4 ....175 F2
 Wellingborough NN9 ..110 E1
Meadowside Inf Sch
 NN15 ....92 B2
Meadowside Jun Sch
 NN15 ....92 B2
Meadowsweet Wlk NN4 175 F2
Meadowvale NN9 ......112 F1
Meads Ct NN15 ....92 B1
Meadslade NN7 ......192 D2
Meadway
 Buckingham MK18 ....240 D1
 Bugbrooke NN7 ......172 A1
 Northampton NN3 ....160 D8
Meadway Cl NN15 ....91 D8
Mears Ashby Prim Sch
 NN6 ....128 B2
Mears Ashby Rd
 Earls Barton NN6 ....144 C6
 Wilby NN8 ....129 A1
Medbourne NN3 ......142 B7
Medbourne Rd
 Ashley LE16 ....18 E4
 Drayton LE16 ......19 E4
 Medbourne LE16 ....18 C8
Medellin Hill NN3 ....142 F6
Medina Rd NN17 ......21 C1
Medinah Cl NN4 ......175 D5

Medlicott Cl NN18 ....53 A8
Medway Cl
 Market Harborough LE16 .32 A3
 Northampton NN5 ....140 E2
Medway Dr
 Northampton NN5 ....140 F2
 Wellingborough NN8 ..129 C6
Medway Ho PE8 ......42 A6
Medway The NN11 ....135 A1
Medwin NN8 ....129 B4
Meeting La
 Burton Latimer NN15 ..92 C2
 Corby NN17 ....37 B7
 Irthlingborough NN9 ..112 F2
 15 Kettering NN16 ....72 B2
 Northampton NN5 ....158 C7
 Rothwell NN14 ......70 C6
 Towcester NN12 ......203 C6
Meissen Ave NN14 ....50 F3
Melbourne Ho
 Corby NN17 ....22 F1
 4 Northampton NN5 ..159 A6
Melbourne La NN5 ....158 C6
Melbourne Rd
 Northampton NN5 ....158 F6
 Stamford PE9 ....241 F4
Melbourne St 3 NN1 159 F4
Melbourne Wlk 4 NN1 159 F4
Melbury La NN3 ......143 B3
Melbury Pl NN3 ......143 B3
Melchbourne Rd NN4 149 F4
Melchester Cl NN4 ..175 E4
Meldon Cl NN4 ......175 C8
Mellish Ct CV22 ......241 A6
Mellish Rd CV22 ......241 A6
Mellor Rd CV21 ......99 B8
Melloway Rd NN10 ..131 E2
Melrose Ave NN5 ....158 E7
Melrose Cl Kettering NN15 91 F8
 Stamford PE9 ....241 A4
Meltham Cl NN3 ......142 F1
Melton Rd NN8 ......130 C5
Melton Rd N NN8 ....130 B5
Melton St NN16 ......72 B3
Melville Cl CV22 ......241 A6
Melville St NN1 ......159 F7
Membris Way NN11 ..184 A6
Memorial Gn NN7 ....191 E4
Mendip Cl NN16 ......72 B5
Mendip Ct NN11 ......135 B5
Mendip Rd NN5 ......158 D7
Meon Cl NN17 ....21 C1
Meon Way NN5 ......158 D8
Mercer Ct CV22 ......98 F8
Mercer's Row 3 NN1 159 C5
Mercia Gdns NN3 ....142 C1
Mercury Cl NN11 ....135 A4
Mercury Dr NN4 ......160 A2
Mere Cl
 Brafield-on-t-G NN7 ..161 D2
 1 Northampton NN4 ..175 B8
Mere Farm Bsns Units
 NN6 ....108 D4
Mere Way NN4 ....175 C8
Merefields NN9 ......112 E3
Merestone Ho OX17 ..210 B1
Merestone Rd NN18 ..36 D3
Mereway Lower Sch
 NN4 ....159 C1
Mereway Mid Sch NN4 175 C8
Mereway Upper Sch
 NN4 ....159 B1
Merlin Gr 5 NN4 ....175 B8
Merrivale Cl NN15 ....90 F7
Merry Tom La NN6 ..124 D4
Merrycot La NN6 ......82 B4
Merrydale Sq NN3 ..143 A6
Merryhill NN4 ....158 E2
Mersey Cl NN4 ......159 A2
Mersey Gn NN17 ......21 C1
Mershe Cl NN4 ......175 F7
Merthyr Rd NN5 ....159 A8
Merton Cl NN13 ......233 D4
Merton Rd NN11 ....153 B7
Merton St OX16 ......240 E8
Merttens Dr CV22 ..241 B7
Mescalero NN2 ......141 C4
Meshaw Cres NN3 ..160 B7
Methodist Homestead 4
 NN2 ....141 E1
Mewburn Rd OX16 ..240 B7
Mews Cotts LE16 ....48 E3
Mews The Brixworth NN6 106 B2
 Brockhall NN11 ......137 C2
 Great Bowden LE16 ..31 E7
 Long Buckby NN6 ....121 B4
 Northampton NN3 ....160 D8
 4 Rugby CV21 ......80 A1
Mickle Hill PE18 ....116 D7
Mickleborough Cl LE16 18 B3
Micklewell La NN3 ..142 F6
Middle Grass NN9 ..112 E3
Middle Greeve NN4 ..176 A6
Middle La LE16 ......34 B4
Middle March NN11 ..153 D8
Middle St Elton PE8 ..28 D8
 Foxton LE16 ....30 E8
 Isham NN14 ....110 E8
 Kilsby CV23 ....100 A3
 Nether Heyford NN7 ..156 C2
Middle Weald MK19 ..229 E1
Middledale Rd LE16 ..32 A3
Middlefield Cl MK18 ..240 F4
Middlemarch 5 NN3 143 B4
Middlemead NN3 ....143 A1
Middlemore NN3 ....142 F6
Middlethorpe NN12 ..200 B4

Millers Cl continued
 Rushden NN10 ......131 F2
Millers Gdns LE16 ..31 B2
Millers La NN8 ......145 F8
Millers Pk NN8 ......130 A1
Millers Way NN4 ....175 F3
Millfield Ave LE16 ..20 D1
Millfields PE8 ....41 F6
Millfields Ave CV21 ..98 F8
Millglade The NN14 ..91 F1
Millholm Rd NN14 ..51 B2
Mills Cl NN6 ....144 F4
Millside Cl NN2 ......141 D5
Millstone Cl NN4 ..158 D2
Millway NN5 ....158 C6
Millway Mid Sch NN5 158 D6
Millwood Way PE8 ..13 E7
Millwright Cl OX16 ..240 B8
Milner Rd NN9 ......111 F4
Milthorpe NN12 ....200 B2
Milton Ave NN8 ....129 C3
Milton Bridge NN4 ..176 A6
Milton Ct Kettering NN16 72 C5
 Milton Malsor NN7 ..174 E3
Milton Parochial Prim Sch
 NN7 ....174 E4
Milton Rd Corby NN17 ..36 C8
 Daventry NN11 ....135 B2
 Gayton NN7 ....173 F2
 Little Irchester NN8 ..130 C1
 Oundle PE8 ....41 F5
Milton St Banbury OX16 240 C7
 Higham Ferrers NN10 132 B5
 Northampton NN2 ....141 F1
Milton St N NN2 ....141 E1
Milton Terr PE8 ....44 C4
Milverton Cres NN3 ..160 D7
Mimosa Cl NN3 ......160 C6
Minden Cl NN18 ....35 F2
Minehead Cl NN18 ..36 A6
Minerva Way NN8 ..129 D5
Minshull Cl NN18 ..240 D4
Minster Ho 2 NN1 ..159 D6
Minton Cl NN14 ......50 F3
Mirfield Cl NN18 ....36 C5
Mistletoe Pl NN3 ..142 C1
Mitchell Cl NN5 ....140 D2
Mitchell Rd NN17 ..22 B2
Mitchell St NN16 ....72 C5
Mitchison Cl CV23 ..118 C8
Mitre Cl NN18 ......240 C2
Mitre St MK18 ......240 C2
Mixbury Rd NN13 ..233 F2
Moat Farm Dr CV21 ..99 A7
Moat La NN12 ......203 C6
Moat Pl NN1 ....159 B6
Moat Yd NN12 ......203 C6
Mobbs Miller Ho NN1 160 A7
Moffatt Terr NN8 ..130 A5
Mold Cres NN18 ....240 A8
Molesworth Bglws PE9 ..1 A6
Monarch Rd NN2 ..141 C1
Monarch Terr NN2 ..159 C8
Monk's Hall Rd NN1 159 F7
Monks Park Rd NN1 159 F7
Monks Pond St NN1 159 B6
Monks Rd NN29 ....146 D3
Monks Way Corby NN18 36 A4
 Crick NN6 ....101 A6
 Wellingborough NN8 ..130 A3
Monkswood NN2 ....214 C4
Monmouth Cl NN14 ..76 F2
Monmouth Rd NN5 ..159 A7
Monroe Cl LE16 ......31 D5
Monson Way PE8 ..41 E7
Montabaur Rd NN13 234 A7
Montagu Cl NN15 ..91 D5
Montagu Sch NN16 ..72 D5
Montagu St NN16 ..72 C2
Montagu Terr PE8 ..59 B6
Montague Cres NN5 ..140 C2
Montague Ct NN14 ..76 D2
Montague Dr CV23 ..100 A3
Montague St NN10 ..132 A2
Montcalm Cl NN15 ..72 F1
Montfort Cl NN5 ....158 E6
Montgomery Cl NN15 72 E1
Montrose Cl
 Market Harborough LE16 .31 D1
 Stamford PE9 ....241 A4
Montrose Rd CV22 ..241 C6
Montrose St NN17 ..36 F6
Montsaye Com Coll
 NN14 ....70 B7
Monument St OX16 ..240 C7
Moonshine Gap NN6 128 D6
Moor End PE8 ......60 D3
Moor Field NN12 ....203 B5
Moor La CV23 ....117 D3
Moor Rd NN10 ......132 A2
Moore Cl Corby NN17 ..36 D8
 Kettering NN15 ......92 A7
Moore St NN2 ......141 F1
Moorend Rd NN12 ..217 E6
Moores Cl NN7 ......172 F7
Moores Hill MK46 ..195 F5
Moorfield Cl OX16 ..240 E8
Moorfield Gn NN14 ..70 B6
Moorfield Rd NN14 ..70 B6
Moorfield Sq NN3 ..143 A6
Moorhen Way NN18 ..240 D4
Moorhouse Way NN8 ..90 A6
Moorings The
 Buckingham MK18 ..240 D1
 Woodford NN14 ......94 C6
Moorland Cl NN3 ..142 E2
Moorlands NN8 ......129 C7
Moors Cl MK19 ......228 E4

Moors Dr The OX17 ..219 F8
Moors La CV21,CV23 ..99 D8
Morby Cl NN15 ....92 B1
Morcott Rd LE15 ......3 D5
Mordaunt Cl NN14 ..75 E6
Mordaunt La NN5 ..140 D1
More Rd NN11 ......135 B4
Morehay La
 King's Cliffe PE8 ....13 E6
 King's Cliffe PE8 ....13 F7
Moreton Ave NN8 ..129 D2
Moreton Rd
 Buckingham MK18 ..240 D5
 Eydon NN11 ....184 C1
Moreton Way NN5 ..141 C5
Morgan Cl NN3 ......143 C4
Morgan Dr NN6 ......106 C3
Morgans Cl PE8 ......43 A3
Moriston Cl NN17 ..21 C1
Morland Rd NN18 ..36 E5
Morley St Kettering NN16 72 C4
 Market Harborough LE16 .31 D3
Morley Wlk NN17 ....36 C8
Morris Ave NN10 ..131 F1
Morris Cl NN8 ......129 A6
Morris Rd Daventry NN11 134 F3
 Northampton NN2 ....141 D3
Morrison Park Rd NN6 102 C5
Mortar Pit Rd NN3 ..143 C5
Mortimer Cl NN4 ..159 A2
Morton Ct CV22 ......98 F8
Morton Gdns CV21 ..241 D7
Mortons Bush NN4 ..176 A6
Moss Cl Rugby CV22 ..241 A6
 Towcester NN12 ....203 C8
Moss Wlk NN18 ......36 A2
Motala Cl NN18 ......36 A2
Motherwell Ho NN17 ..37 A8
Motspur Dr NN2 ....141 B1
Motts The NN7 ......157 B6
Moulds La NN18 ......20 D7
Moulton Coll NN3 ..126 C1
Moulton Crossing NN3 142 E8
Moulton La NN2,NN3 141 D8
Moulton Park Bsns Ctr
 NN3 ....142 A6
Moulton Prim Sch NN3 126 C1
Moulton Rd Holcot NN6 126 D7
 Pitsford NN6 ....125 D3
Moulton Sch NN3 ..126 B1
Moulton Way NN3 ..142 C6
Moulton Way N NN3 142 C6
Moulton Way S NN3 142 C6
Moultrie Rd CV21,CV22 241 D7
Mount Pleasant
 Earls Barton NN6 ....144 F4
 Harpole NN7 ....157 C7
 Wardington OX17 ..196 E1
 Woodford Halse NN11 184 D6
 Yardley Gobion NN12 217 F6
Mount Pleasant Cl
 MK18 ....240 C2
Mount Pleasant Rd LE15 3 A6
Mountbatten Ave PE9 241 C4
Mountbatten Dr NN14 95 C3
Mountbatten Ho NN11 153 E8
Mountbatten Way NN9 114 E6
Mountclair Ct NN3 ..160 E8
Mountfield Rd
 Irthlingborough NN9 ..112 F3
 Northampton NN3 ....142 A3
Mounthill Ave NN3 ..142 B3
Mounts Bsns Ctr NN1 159 D7
Mounts Ct 1 NN3 ..142 E3
Mounts La NN11 ....153 E4
Mounts The NN6 ..121 B3
Mow Mead MK46 ..195 F5
Mowsley Ct LE17 ....45 E6
Mowsley Rd
 Husbands Bosworth LE17 ..45 E6
 Theddingworth LE16 ..46 C8
Moyeady Ave CV22 ..98 E8
Muirfield Dr NN11 ..135 E2
Muirfield Rd NN8 ..129 C7
Mulberry Cl
 Northampton NN5 ..158 F7
 Wellingborough NN8 ..129 E5
Mulberry Ct LE16 ....20 A5
Mull Dr NN17 ....36 D8
Mullions The NN4 ..175 E5
Mulso Rd NN9 ......112 A4
Mumford Dr NN7 ..174 A7
Muncaster Gdns NN4 175 D7
Muncaster Way NN6 102 C5
Murcott NN6 ....121 A4
Murcott Cl NN6 ......121 A4
Murphy La NN4 ......141 D1
Murray Ho NN1 ....160 A8
Murray Rd CV21 ....241 D9
Murray Wlk NN17 ..36 E5
Murrayian Cl CV21 ..241 D8
Mursley St MK11 ..229 F5
Murswell Cl NN12 ..214 D4
Murswell La NN12 ..214 D4
Muscott La NN5 ......158 C6
Muscott St NN5 ......159 A6
Museum Way NN3 ..160 F6
Musgrave Cl NN4 ..175 F7
Mushroom Field Rd
 NN3 ....143 D2
Musk Cl NN16 ......20 D7
Musson Cl NN9 ......112 E2
Mussott Cl NN7 ......155 E6
Myers Cl OX17 ......231 F5
Myers Rd CV21 ......99 C8

Myers Way OX17 ....231 F5
Myrtle Rd NN16 ....72 D4

N

Nags Head La NN9 ......115 F2
Nairn Rd PE9 ....241 A3
Nansen Cl
  Daventry NN11 ....135 C5
  Rothwell NN14 ....70 E6
Nansen Wlk NN18 ....36 B2
Nantwich Dr NN11 .....135 D6
Naomi Cl NN3 ....142 F1
Napier Cl Daventry NN11 153 D8
  Wellingborough NN8 ....129 A4
Nares Cl CV22 ....241 A6
Narvik Rd NN18 ....36 A4
Naseby Battle & Farm Mus★
  NN6 ....85 B7
Naseby CE Prim Sch NN6 66 B1
Naseby Cl
  Market Harborough LE16 .31 E2
  Wellingborough NN8 ....129 D7
Naseby Ct MK18 ....240 E5
Naseby Dr NN11 ....135 C6
Naseby Rd Clipston LE16 .66 F8
  Corby NN17 ....36 C7
  Kettering NN16 ....72 E3
  Rugby CV22 ....241 E6
  Sibbertoft LE16 ....46 F2
  Thornby NN6 ....84 E4
  Welford NN6 ....65 C5
Naseby Sq LE16 ....31 E2
Naseby St NN2 ....159 C8
Nash Ct NN15 ....92 A8
Nasmith Ave NN17 ......37 A8
Nasmyth Rd NN11 .....134 F5
Nassington Prim Sch
  PE8 ....15 F5
Nassington Rd
  Woodnewton PE8 ....14 F1
  Yarwell PE8 ....15 F7
Navigation Row NN1 ...159 C4
Navisford Cl NN14 ......76 E3
Neale Ave NN16 ....72 B5
Neale Cl
  Northampton NN3 ......160 E8
  Wollaston NN29 ....146 C3
Needham Rd NN9 ......113 F4
Neithrop Ave OX16 ....240 B9
Neithrop Cl OX16 .....240 B9
Neithrop Cty Inf Sch
  OX16 ....240 A8
Neithrop Cty Jun Sch
  OX16 ....240 A8
Nelson Ave NN11 ......184 B6
Nelson Cl NN11 ....135 E2
Nelson Ct MK18 ....240 C3
Nelson Dr NN14 ....70 E7
Nelson Rd NN17 ....36 B8
Nelson St
  Buckingham MK18 .....240 C3
  Kettering NN16 ....72 C3
  Market Harborough LE16 ..31 D3
  24 Northampton NN1 ...159 C7
Nene Cl Kettering NN15 ..92 A5
  Raunds NN9 ....114 D7
  Wansford PE8 ....8 A3
  Wellingborough NN8 ....129 C6
Nene Cres NN17 ....21 C1
Nene Ct Thrapston NN14 ..76 D2
  Wellingborough NN8 ....130 C3
Nene Dr NN5 ....140 F2
Nene Ent Ctr NN2 .....159 C8
Nene La NN12 ....203 A6
Nene Park (Rushden &
  Diamonds FC) NN9 ....113 A2
Nene Pl NN5 ....141 A2
Nene Rd
  Burton Latimer NN15 ....92 A2
  Higham Ferrers NN10 ..132 B5
Nene Rise NN7 ....161 F6
Nene Side Cl NN11 ....152 F3
Nene Univ Coll Northampton
  NN2 ....141 E5
Nene Valley Bsns Pk PE8 42 E5
Nene Valley Ret Pk
  NN1 ....159 B4
Nene Valley Way NN3 ..160 D5
Nene View
  Irthlingborough NN14 ..112 F2
  Islip NN14 ....76 B3
  Oundle PE8 ....41 F6
Nene Way
  Kislingbury NN7 ....157 C3
  Northampton NN5 ......141 A4
  Oundle PE8 ....41 F7
  Sutton PE5 ....8 F2
Nene Whitewater Ctr★
  NN4 ....160 B3
Nene Wlk Daventry NN11 135 A1
  Northampton NN5 ......140 F2
Neneside Cl NN7 ......155 B3
Nepcote Cl NN15 ....91 D8
Nesbitt Cl NN3 ....160 E8
Nest Farm Cres NN8 ..130 A8
Nest Farm Rd NN8 ....130 A7
Nest La NN8 ....130 B7
Nether Cl NN13 ....234 A7
Nether Jackson Ct NN3 143 B4
Nether La NN14 ....155 F4
Netherfield Gr NN17 ...36 F8
Netherfield Rd NN15 ...91 C7

Nethermead Ct NN3 ...142 F4
Netherton Way NN14 ...89 B4
Nettle Gap Cl NN4 ....175 F6
Neuville Way NN14 .....50 F3
Nevill Cl MK19 ....207 B2
Nevill Holt Rd LE16 ....19 F6
Nevill Holt Sch LE16 ...19 D8
Neville Day Cl PE9 ....1 F5
Neville Ho NN17 ....36 E6
New Bldgs **7** NN16 ...72 B2
New Cotts NN17 ....24 B5
New Croft NN7 ....155 B3
New Cross Rd PE9 ....241 D4
New Forest Way NN11 .135 B4
New Hall NN11 ....153 B7
New La PE8 ....8 C1
New Post Office Sq
  NN17 ....36 E6
New Rd Banbury OX16 240 C7
  Brackley NN13 ....233 E6
  Castlethorpe MK19 ...218 F5
  Collyweston PE9 ....1 C2
  Easton o t H PE9 ....2 A5
  Farthingstone NN13 ....221 A4
  Geddington NN14 ....54 A2
  Greens Norton NN12 ..202 D8
  Maidford NN12 ....186 D6
  Northampton NN4 .....175 E6
  Oundle PE8 ....42 A6
New South Bridge Rd
  NN4 ....159 C4
New St Brixworth NN6 .106 A2
  Daventry NN11 ....135 C1
  Desborough NN14 ......51 A3
  Earls Barton NN6 .....144 F4
  Irchester NN29 ....147 B8
  Irthlingborough NN9 ..112 F2
  Oundle PE8 ....42 A5
  Rothwell NN14 ....70 D7
  Rugby CV22 ....241 A4
  Stamford PE9 ....241 D4
  Stony Stratford MK11 ..229 D5
  Weedon NN7 ....155 C3
  Wellingborough NN8 ...130 A5
New Street Ct NN29 ...147 B8
New Terr NN11 ....183 D7
New Town PE9 ....2 A5
New Town Rd **2** NN1 ..159 F6
Newark Dr NN13 ....36 C6
Newbery Dr NN13 ....233 D8
Newbold Cl
  Banbury OX16 ....240 E6
  Oundle PE8 ....41 E6
Newbold Rd CV21 ....241 C9
Newbolt Cl NN12 .....216 B8
Newbottle & Charlton CE
  Prim Sch OX17 ....231 F5
Newboults La PE9 ....241 C3
Newbridge NN8 ......136 D8
Newbridge La NN9 ....114 A3
Newbury Cl NN10 .....132 D3
Newbury Dr NN11 ....135 C6
Newby Ct NN3 ....142 C3
Newcomb Ct PE9 .....241 C3
Newcombe Dr NN5 ....159 A7
Newcombe St LE16 .....31 E2
Newcomen Rd NN8 ...130 E5
Newell Rd NN14 ....95 B3
Newgates PE9 ....241 E3
Newham Cl NN14 ....70 C7
Newham Rd PE9 ......241 C5
Newington Rd NN2 ...141 C4
Newland Pl OX16 .....240 D7
Newland St
  Banbury OX16 ....240 D7
  Walgrave NN6 ....108 A5
Newland Sq NN2 ......141 C4
Newland St
  Braybrooke LE16 ....49 E5
  Kettering NN16 ....72 B2
  Rugby CV22 ....241 A8
Newland Wlk **5** NN1 ..159 D6
Newlands Brixworth NN6 106 B2
  3 Daventry NN11 ...135 C1
  King's Sutton OX17 ...231 A6
  Naseby NN6 ....66 C1
Newlands Ctr NN16 ....72 B2
Newlands Rd NN6 .....64 E5
Newman St
  Burton Latimer NN15 ...92 B2
  Higham Ferrers NN10 ..132 C7
  6 Kettering NN16 .....72 C2
Newnham Dr NN11 ...135 A5
Newnham Prim Sch
  NN11 ....153 D4
Newnham Rd NN2 ....141 D3
Newnham Windmill★
  NN11 ....153 D7
Newport Pagnell Rd
  Horton NN7 ....177 D1
  Northampton NN4,NN7 ..176 A7
Newport Pagnell Rd W
  NN4 ....175 D8
Newport Rd
  Hanslope MK19 ....207 B2
  Northampton NN5 .....159 A7
Newstead Cl NN3 ....143 D3
Newstead Ct NN15 .....91 C5
Newstone Cres NN4 ..158 E4
Newton Cl
  Daventry NN11 ....135 A4
  Rushden NN10 ....132 D1
  Wellingborough NN8 ..129 B6
Newton Rd
  Clifton u D CV23 ....80 A7

Newton Rd continued
  Geddington NN14 ....54 A3
  Higham Ferrers NN10 ..132 E5
  Kettering NN15 ....91 F5
  Northampton NN5 .....158 D8
  Rushden NN10 ....132 E1
  Wollaston NN29 ....146 D2
Newton Road Com Prim Sch
  NN10 ....132 C2
Newton St MK46 ......195 F4
Newton Way LE16 ......49 F6
Newtown Brigstock NN14 .55 E8
  Woodford NN14 ....94 D7
Newtown Rd
  Little Irchester NN8 ...130 C1
  Raunds NN9 ....114 E5
Newtown St NN14 ......94 D7
Nibbits La NN11 ......118 C1
Nicholas Hawksmoor Prim
  Sch NN12 ....203 B5
Nicholas La NN9 ......112 A1
Nicholas Rd NN9 .....112 E1
Nicholas Way NN10 ...131 F3
Nicholls Ct NN3 .....142 E5
Nicholls Ho **1** NN4 ...159 A3
Nichols St NN14 ....51 A4
Nichols Way NN14 ....114 C7
Nielson Rd NN8 ......130 C8
Nigel Ct NN13 ....234 A5
Nightingale Cl
  Brackley NN13 ....222 E2
  Daventry NN11 ....135 D6
Nightingale La NN8 ..130 B7
Nightingale Pl MK18 .240 E4
Niort Way NN8 ....129 C8
Nippendale NN10 ....132 C2
Nithsdale Ave LE16 ....31 F2
Nithsdale Cres LE16 ...31 F2
Nithsdale Rd NN17 ....36 D7
Noble Ave NN9 ....113 A5
Nobold Ct LE16 ....66 F8
Nook The Corby NN17 ...37 B6
  Cottingham LE16 ....20 D1
  Easton o t H PE9 ....2 A5
Norbury Cl LE16 ....31 D3
Norfolk Cl NN17 ....36 C7
Norfolk Sq PE9 ......241 D4
Norfolk St NN2 ......159 C8
Norfolk Terr NN1 ....159 C8
Norman Rd NN3 ......142 B1
Norman Way
  Irchester NN29 ....147 C8
  Wellingborough NN8 ..129 D2
Norman-D-Gate NN1 .159 E5
Normandy Lodge NN13 233 E8
Normead Sq **4** NN3 ..143 D2
Norris Acre NN13 ....232 F6
Norris Cl NN15 ....92 A8
Norris Way NN10 ....131 E3
Norris Way Ind Est
  NN10 ....131 E3
Norse Wlk NN18 ....36 A2
North Ave NN15 ....92 B3
North Bar Pl OX16 ...240 C8
North Bar St OX16 ...240 C8
North Cape Wlk NN16 ..36 A2
North Cl NN11 ....118 D1
North End NN10 .....132 B7
North Field Cl NN16 ...72 A4
North Folds Rd NN8 ...35 F1
North Hayes Ct NN3 .142 A4
North Hill MK18 .....225 D2
North Holme Ct NN3 .142 D5
North La LE16 ....30 D8
North Lea LE16 ....18 B3
North Leys Ct NN3 ...142 C7
North Luffenham Rd LE15 .3 B8
North Oval NN5 ......140 F2
North Oxfordshire Coll
  OX16 ....240 B7
North Paddock Ct NN3 142 F4
North Park Dr NN16 ...72 C5
North Portway Cl NN3 142 F7
North Priors Ct NN3 .143 A4
North Rd Clifton u D CV23 .80 A6
  Earls Barton NN6 .....144 E5
  Northampton NN3 .....141 F6
  South Kilworth LE17 ....63 D8
North St Banbury OX16 240 E9
  Castlethorpe MK19 ...218 F5
  Daventry NN11 ....135 C2
  Kilsby CV23 ....99 F3
  Mears Ashby NN6 .....128 B2
  Oundle PE8 ....42 A5
  Raunds NN9 ....114 E7
  Rothersthorpe NN7 ...174 B6
  Rugby CV21 ....241 C8
  Rushden NN10 ....132 B3
  Stamford PE9 ....241 D3
  Swinford LE17 ....62 B4
  Titchmarsh NN14 ....77 C4
  Wellingborough NN8 ..129 F5
North Way
  Deanshanger MK19 ...228 E5
  Potterspury NN12 ....217 E2
North Western Ave
  NN2 ....141 A4
Northall NN6 ....108 A5
Northall Mews NN16 ...72 A4
Northall St NN16 ......72 B3
Northam Ct NN16 ......72 B4
Northampton (Sywell)
  Airport NN6 ....127 E5
Northampton Christian Sch
  NN1 ....160 A8
Northampton Coll NN3 .142 D3

Northampton General Hospl
  NN1 ....159 E5
Northampton High Sch
  NN4 ....175 E7
Northampton La N NN3 142 C8
Northampton La S NN3 142 C7
Northampton Prep Sch
  NN4 ....160 E3
Northampton Rd
  Blisworth NN7 ....174 D1
  Brackley NN13 ....223 A1
  Brixworth NN6 ....106 B1
  Broughton NN14 ....90 A3
  Chapel Brampton NN6 124 E1
  Cosgrove MK19 ......217 F7
  Denton NN7 ....178 B8
  Earls Barton NN6 .....144 D5
  Ecton NN6 ....143 F4
  Harpole NN7 ....157 C5
  Kettering NN15 ....71 F1
  Litchborough NN12 ...171 E2
  Market Harborough LE16 .31 F3
  Orlingbury NN14 .....109 F5
  Roade NN7 ....191 D5
  Rushden NN10 ....131 E4
  Towcester NN12 .....203 C7
  Welford NN6 ....64 C4
  Wellingborough NN8 ..129 D3
  West Haddon NN6 ....102 C4
  Yardley Hastings NN7 .179 A6
Northampton Sch for Boys
  NN1 ....160 A6
Northampton Sch For Girls
  NN3 ....142 A4
Northampton Sta NN1 .159 B6
Northampton Town FC
  NN5 ....158 E5
Northamptonshire Gram Sch
  NN6 ....125 C4
Northampton & Lamport Rly★
  NN6 ....124 F1
Northants County Cricket
  Club★ NN1 ....160 A8
Northants Ent Pk NN2 ..31 E3
Northbank LE16 ....31 E3
Northbrook NN18 ....36 B4
Northcot La OX16 ....240 B9
Northcote Rd CV22 ...241 B8
Northcote St NN2 ....159 C7
Northen Way NN8 ....129 F8
Northend MK46 ......194 E3
Northend Sq MK18 ...240 D4
Northern Cl NN17 ......22 B8
Northern Way NN11 ..135 D4
Northfield Ave
  Kettering NN16 ....72 A3
  Ringstead NN14 ....95 B3
Northfield Gn NN6 ...122 D5
Northfield La PE8 ......15 E5
Northfield Rd
  Broughton NN14 ....71 C1
  Northampton NN5 ....140 B1
Northfield Way NN14 .141 B4
Northfields PE9 ......241 E4
Northgate NN12 .....203 C7
Northgate Sch NN2 ..141 C2
Northlands Prim Sch
  CV21 ....241 D9
Northleigh Gr LE16 ....31 D4
Northumberland Ave
  PE9 ....241 C4
Northumberland Cl
  NN15 ....91 D6
Northumberland Ct
  OX16 ....240 E8
Northumberland Rd
  NN15 ....91 D6
Northumbria Gdns NN3 142 B1
Northway CV21 ....241 C8
Northwood Rd NN3 ...142 B2
Nortoft NN6 ....103 F7
Norton Cl NN11 ......135 D2
Norton Cres NN12 ...203 B6
Norton Leys CV22 .....98 A6
Norton Rd Corby NN17 ..36 C7
  Daventry NN11 ....135 D2
  Northampton NN2 ....141 C3
Norton St NN14 ....70 E7
Norton's Pl MK18 ....240 C3
Norway Cl NN18 ....36 A3
Notre Dame Mews **3**
  NN1 ....159 D6
Nuffield Cl NN13 ....233 D8
Nuffield Dr OX16 ....240 A10
Nunn Mills Rd NN1 ..159 E4
Nunneley Way LE16 ...31 F5
Nunnery Ave NN14 ....70 C7
Nuns La NN6 ....121 B4
Nurseries The
  Horton NN7 ....177 D1
  3 Moulton NN3 ....126 C1
  Northampton NN1 ....159 D7
Nursery Cl
  Little Houghton NN7 ..161 A4
  Maidwell NN6 ....87 B7
Nursery Ct NN6 ......128 B2
Nursery Dr
  Banbury OX16 ....240 C9
  Wellingborough NN8 ..130 B7
Nursery End LE16 .....31 C7
Nursery Gdns NN9 ...112 E2
Nursery La
  Banbury OX16 ....240 C9
  Northampton NN2 ....141 C3
Nutcote NN6 ....85 B8
Nuthall Cl NN3 ....160 F8

O

Oak Ave NN7 ....174 B1
Oak Cl Broughton NN14 ..90 B4
  Hartwell NN7 ....192 E2
  Irchester NN29 ......147 A7
  Market Harborough LE16 .31 F4
  Towcester NN12 .....203 C4
Oak Dr NN11 ....184 B6
Oak Gr NN11 ....135 C5
Oak La NN6 ....100 F6
Oak Rd Brackley NN13 222 F1
  Kettering NN15 ....72 D1
Oak St
  20 Northampton NN1 ..159 C7
  Rugby CV22 ....241 C7
  Rushden NN10 ....132 B4
  Weedon NN7 ....155 A2
Oak Terr **6** NN9 ....112 F2
Oak Tree Cl NN14 .....50 F3
Oak View NN9 ....110 F1
Oak Way NN9 ....112 F2
Oakdown Cres MK46 .195 F3
Oakfield NN10 ....132 A4
Oakfield Prim Sch CV22 241 A6
Oakfield Rd CV22 ....241 B7
Oakgrove Pl NN4 ....175 D6
Oakham Cl
  Desborough NN14 .....50 F4
  Northampton NN3 ....142 B7
  Rushden NN10 ....148 A8
Oakham La NN11 .....152 B7
Oaklands Bugbrooke NN7 173 A7
  Weedon NN7 ....155 A2
Oaklands Dr NN3 ....142 E1
Oaklands Pk **4** LE16 ..31 F2
Oakleas Rise NN16 ....76 D1
Oakleigh Cl NN9 .....114 C7
Oakleigh Dr NN5 ....140 C1
Oakley Ct NN18 ....36 A1
Oakley Dr Moulton NN3 126 D1
  Wellingborough NN8 ..129 D3
Oakley Hay Ind Est NN18 36 A1
Oakley Mews LE16 .....31 F3
Oakley Pond NN18 .....53 B8
Oakley Rd Corby NN17 ..37 A6
  Corby NN18 ....36 C3
  Corby,Pipewell NN14 ...52 D8
  Rushden NN10 ....131 F3
  Rushton NN14 ....52 E5
Oakley St Kettering NN16 72 B4
  Northampton NN1 ....159 D7
Oakmont Cl NN4 .....175 C5
Oakpark Ct NN3 .....143 A6
Oakpits Way NN10 ...132 C1
Oaks Dr NN10 ....132 B6
Oaks The NN4 ....175 F3
Oaktree Ct Aldwincle NN14 76 F8
  2 Kettering NN16 ....72 B1
Oakway NN8 ....129 F7
Oakway Jun & Inf Sch
  NN8 ....130 A7
Oakwood Cl PE8 ....27 D2
Oakwood Rd NN1 ....142 A1
Oat Hill Dr NN3 ......143 D2
Oat Hill Rd NN12 ....203 C4
Oathill Cl NN6 ....106 B1
Oathill Rise NN15 .....92 C2
Oban Cl Kettering NN15 ..91 E8
  Stamford PE9 ....241 A4
Obelisk Cl NN2 ......141 C8
Obelisk Rd NN9 .....112 A5
Obelisk Rise NN2 ....141 C6
Occupation Rd
  Corby NN17 ....36 F7
  Middleton LE16 ....20 B2
  Oundle PE8 ....42 A7
Octagon The NN17 ....37 A8
Octagon Way NN3 ...142 F2
Octavian Way NN13 .234 A7
Odeon Bldgs NN17 ....37 A7
Old A43 NN14 ....89 F2
Old Barn Ct NN3 .....142 F3
Old Brewery Wlk NN13 233 F6
Old Brickyard The NN6 102 C4
Old Carpenters Ct NN3 143 C2
Old Cl NN4 ....175 E2
Old Dairy Farm★ NN7 171 E6
Old Dry La NN14 ......55 F8
Old End NN7 ....177 A1
Old Farm La NN14 ....76 B3
Old Forge Dr NN6 ...102 C4
Old Forge La NN11 ..169 C2
Old Gaol Mus★ MK18 240 D4
Old Gn LE16 ....18 F6
Old Gorse Way NN14 ..89 A4
Old Gram School The
  NN6 ....103 F6
Old Great North Rd
  Stamford PE9 ....241 D2
  Stibbington PE8 ....8 C2
  Wothorpe PE9 ....2 F7
Old Greens Norton Rd
  NN12 ....203 B7
Old Grimsbury Rd OX16 240 E9
Old Hall La NN14 ......30 F3
Old Holt Rd LE16 ......19 A7
Old La NN13 ....221 A4
Old Leicester Rd PE8 ...8 A3
Old Manor Ct NN11 ..135 E8
Old North Rd PE8 ......8 A4
Old Oundle Rd PE8 .....7 A6
Old Parr Cl OX16 ....240 D7
Old Parr Rd OX16 ...240 D7
Old Quarry Ct NN3 ..142 E4
Old Rd Braunston NN11 134 C8
  Scaldwell NN6 ....107 A7

Old Rd *continued*
Stanion NN14 . . . . .37 E2
Walgrave NN6 . . . . .107 F5
Old Rectory Dr PE8 . . . . . .8 A6
Old Rectory Rd PE8 . . . . . .8 A4
Old Rickyard The NN11 .199 D7
Old School Cotts NN6 . .105 A6
Old School La MK18 . . . .240 C3
Old School La NN12 . . . .187 A1
Old School Mews LE16 . . . .31 E3
Old School Pl OX16 . . . .240 E8
Old Stable Yd MK19 . . . .229 C7
Old Stratford Prim Sch
MK19 . . . . .229 B6
Old Tiffield Rd NN12 . . . .203 C6
Old Towcester Rd NN4 . .159 C4
Old Town NN13 . . . . .234 A7
Old Vineyard The NN10 .132 B6
Old Yew Ct NN2 . . . . . . .141 B3
Olde Forde Cl NN6 . . . . .106 B1
Olde Hall Cl NN6 . . . . . .105 B1
Olden Rd NN3 . . . . .143 C5
Oldenburg Rd NN18 . . . . .35 F3
Oldenmead Ct NN3 . . . . .142 F3
Oldland Rd NN18 . . . . . . .36 D3
Oleander Cres NN3 . . . . .143 C4
Oliver Cl NN10 . . . . .132 C2
Oliver St
Northampton NN2 . . . . . .141 E1
Rugby CV21 . . . . .241 B8
Ollerton Wlk NN18 . . . . . .36 C5
Ollis Cl NN17 . . . . .36 E8
Olney Fst Sch NN6 . . . . .195 E3
Olney Mid Sch MK46 . . .195 F5
Olney Rd NN6 . . . . .195 F1
Olympia Cl NN4 . . . . .175 B8
Olympic Way
Kettering NN15 . . . . .91 A7
Wellingborough NN8 . . . .129 C5
Omega Pl CV21 . . . . .241 D9
Onley La CV22 . . . . .98 D6
Onley Pk CV23 . . . . .117 C8
Oransay Cl NN3 . . . . .143 C2
Orchard Cl Badby NN11 . .152 F3
Banbury OX16 . . . . .240 B8
East Haddon NN6 . . . . . .122 D5
Finedon NN9 . . . . .111 F5
Hannington NN6 . . . . . . .108 C3
Hollowell NN6 . . . . .104 B5
Milton Malsor NN7 . . . . .174 E4
Northampton NN4 . . . . . .175 E6
Orlingbury NN14 . . . . . . .110 A5
Ringstead NN14 . . . . .95 C3
Rushden NN10 . . . . .131 F3
Spratton NN6 . . . . .124 B8
Towcester NN12 . . . . . . .203 C4
Warmington PE8 . . . . .28 B3
Weedon NN7 . . . . .155 C4
Weldon NN17 . . . . .38 B8
Wilbarston LE16 . . . . .34 C5
Wollaston NN29 . . . . . . .146 D3
Yardley Gobion NN12 . . .217 F6
Yelvertoft NN6 . . . . .82 B4
Orchard Cotts NN6 . . . . .125 C5
Orchard Cres
Kettering NN16 . . . . .72 C4
Woodnewton PE8 . . . . . . .14 E2
Orchard Ct
Pattishall NN12 . . . . .172 D1
Woodford NN14 . . . . .94 C7
Orchard Dene MK18 . . . .240 D4
Orchard Est NN14 . . . . . .90 F2
Orchard Field NN14 . . . . .93 A6
Orchard Gn NN3 . . . . . . .142 C2
Orchard Hill NN3 . . . . . .143 A1
Orchard Ho NN17 . . . . . . .38 B8
Orchard La Denton NN7 . .162 B1
Gretton NN17 . . . . .10 C1
King's Cliffe PE8 . . . . .13 E7
Woodnewton PE8 . . . . . . .14 E2
Orchard Pl NN29 . . . . . . .147 A8
Orchard Rd Finedon NN9 .111 F5
Raunds NN9 . . . . .114 B5
Stamford PE9 . . . . .241 D3
Orchard Rise
Long Buckby NN6 . . . . . .121 D4
Olney MK46 . . . . .195 F3
Orchard Sch The NN16 . . .72 B5
Orchard St
Daventry NN11 . . . . .135 B2
Market Harborough LE16 . . .31 E4
3 Northampton NN5 . . .159 A6
Orchard Terr
Finedon NN9 . . . . .111 F5
Welford NN6 . . . . .64 E6
Wellingborough NN8 . . . .129 F5
Orchard The
Apethorpe PE8 . . . . .14 C4
Bozeat NN29 . . . . .164 D3
Flore NN7 . . . . .155 F5
Kislingbury NN7 . . . . . . .157 D3
Pottersbury NN12 . . . . . .217 C3
Sibbertoft LE16 . . . . .47 A2
Staverton NN11 . . . . .152 B7
Upper Boddington NN11 . .182 C7
Orchard Way
Banbury OX16 . . . . .240 B8
Cogenhoe NN7 . . . . .161 F6
Easton o t H PE9 . . . . .1 F6
Harpole NN7 . . . . .157 C6
King's Sutton OX17 . . . . .231 A5
Northampton NN5 . . . . . .158 C5
Roade NN7 . . . . .191 D4
Thrapston NN14 . . . . .76 E1
Orchards The NN6 . . . . .103 D1
Ordnance Rd NN7 . . . . . .154 F3
Oriel Rd NN11 . . . . .153 C7
Oriel Way NN13 . . . . .233 D8

Orient Way NN8 . . . . . . .130 A4
Orion Way NN15 . . . . .91 C5
Orkney Wlk NN17 . . . . . . .36 B8
Orlingbury Rd
Great Harrowden NN9 . . .110 D2
Isham NN14 . . . . .110 C7
Little Harrowden NN9 . . .110 B4
Pytchley NN14 . . . . .90 F1
Ormond Pl NN14 . . . . . . .110 E8
Orson Leys CV22 . . . . . . .98 A7
Orton Pl NN8 . . . . .129 C7
Orton Rd Kettering NN15 . .91 F5
Loddington NN14 . . . . . . .70 D2
Orwell Cl Clifton u D CV23 .80 A5
Raunds NN9 . . . . .114 D7
Wellingborough NN8 . . . .129 C6
Osborn Cl NN8 . . . . .129 E3
Osborn's Ct MK46 . . . . . .195 F3
Osborne Cl NN10 . . . . . .132 D4
Osborne Rd NN2 . . . . . . .141 C2
Osier Bed La NN17 . . . . . .24 B5
Osiers The NN12 . . . . .51 D2
Osler Cl NN2 . . . . .141 B5
Oslo Gdns NN18 . . . . .36 A3
Osmund Dr NN3 . . . . . . .143 A5
Osprey Dr NN11 . . . . . . .135 C3
Osprey La NN8 . . . . .130 B7
Osprey Rise NN4 . . . . . . .175 B8
Osprey View 6 NN4 . . . .175 B8
Osprey Wlk MK18 . . . . . .240 F2
Osterley Gr OX16 . . . . . . .240 B6
Ostlers Cl MK11 . . . . .229 D6
Ostlers Way NN15 . . . . . . .91 B7
Oswald Rd NN10 . . . . . . .132 C2
Osyth Cl NN4 . . . . .160 B2
Otters Brook MK18 . . . . .240 E3
Oulton Rise NN3 . . . . . . .141 F4
Oundle & Kings Cliffe Mid
Sch PE8 . . . . .41 E7
Oundle CE Prim Sch PE8 .41 F5
Oundle Dr NN3 . . . . .142 B7
Oundle Mus★ PE8 . . . . . .41 F5
Oundle Rd Elton PE8 . . . . .16 F1
Thrapston NN14 . . . . .76 E2
Weldon NN17 . . . . .38 E7
Woodnewton PE8 . . . . . . .14 F1
Oundle Sch PE8 . . . . .42 A5
Our Lady & Pope John RC
Sch NN16 . . . . .36 A4
Our Lady's Convent Prep Sch
NN15 . . . . .71 F1
Our Lady's Jun & Inf Schs
NN17 . . . . .36 F7
Our Lady's RC Jun & Inf Sch
NN8 . . . . .129 D3
Ouse Cl NN8 . . . . .129 D3
Ouse La NN12 . . . . .203 A6
Ousebank Way NN29 . . . .229 D5
Outlaw La NN8 . . . . .129 C5
Oval Cres NN10 . . . . .132 D2
Oval Rd Rugby CV22 . . . . .98 D8
Rushden NN10 . . . . .132 D2
Oval The Kettering NN15 . .91 B8
Market Harborough LE16 . . .31 E4
Overdale Cl LE16 . . . . .32 A3
Overfield Ave LE16 . . . . . .31 F5
Overhills MK46 . . . . .195 E4
Overleys Ct NN3 . . . . . . .143 B5
Overmead Rd NN3 . . . . .143 D2
Overn Ave MK18 . . . . . . .240 C4
Overn Cl MK18 . . . . .240 D4
Overn Cres MK18 . . . . . .240 C4
Overslade Cl NN4 . . . . . .175 A8
Overslade Ho NN4 . . . . . .175 A8
Overstone Cl NN3 . . . . . .126 E1
Overstone Cres NN6 . . . .127 B1
Overstone Cty Prim Sch
NN6 . . . . .127 A1
Overstone La NN6 . . . . . .126 F1
Overstone Park Prep & High
Sch NN6 . . . . .143 B8
Overstone Rd
Moulton NN3 . . . . .126 D1
Northampton NN1 . . . . . .159 D7
Sywell NN6 . . . . .127 D3
Overthorpe Prep Sch
OX17 . . . . .219 C8
Overthorpe Rd
Banbury OX16 . . . . .219 B6
Banbury, Grimsbury OX16 .240 F8
Ovett Cl NN15 . . . . .90 F8
Owen Cl NN8 . . . . .129 B5
Owen Mews NN8 . . . . . . .129 B5
Owen Way NN10 . . . . . . .132 A5
Owl Cl NN3 . . . . .141 F7
Owl End La NN11 . . . . . .182 C5
Owl End Way NN11 . . . . .182 C5
Oxburgh Ct 7 NN4 . . . . .175 C8
Oxendon Hall LE16 . . . . . .48 E3
Oxendon Rd
Arthingworth LE16 . . . . . .49 A1
Braybrooke LE16 . . . . .49 D5
Clipston LE16 . . . . .48 B1
East Farndon LE16 . . . . . .48 B5
Oxfield Park Dr MK19 . . .229 C7
Oxford Cl Daventry NN11 .135 C1
Earls Barton NN6 . . . . . .144 F3
Oxford Ct NN13 . . . . .233 F5
Oxford St
Adderbury OX17 . . . . . . .230 A3
Banbury OX15,OX16 . . . .240 C6
Corby NN17 . . . . .36 C6
Evenley NN13 . . . . .233 E5
Stamford PE9 . . . . .241 C5
Oxford St Daventry NN11 .135 C1
Finedon NN9 . . . . .112 B5
Kettering NN16 . . . . .72 C1
Northampton NN4 . . . . . .159 B3

Oxford St *continued*
Rothwell NN14 . . . . .70 D8
Rugby CV21 . . . . .241 E8
Stony Stratford MK11 . . . .229 D5
Wellingborough NN8 . . . .129 F4
Wymington NN10 . . . . . .148 A7
Oxfordshire Sch of Art &
Design OX16 . . . . .240 B7
Oxleys MK46 . . . . .195 E4
Oxwich Cl NN4 . . . . .160 A1

P

Packer Rd NN15 . . . . .90 E3
Packwood Ave CV21 . . . . .99 C8
Paddock Cl NN6 . . . . .103 D1
Paddock Ct LE16 . . . . .31 E3
Paddock End NN14 . . . . . .89 B4
Paddock La
Desborough NN14 . . . . . . .51 A3
Mears Ashby NN6 . . . . . .128 B2
Medbourne LE16 . . . . .19 D8
Paddock Mill Ct 1 NN3 . .143 B4
Paddock The Crick NN6 . .100 F5
Lower Boddington NN11 . .182 C5
Raunds NN9 . . . . .114 C4
Stamford PE9 . . . . .241 C3
Weedon Lois NN12 . . . . .200 B2
Welton NN11 . . . . .135 E8
Woodnewton PE8 . . . . . . .14 E2
Paddocks Cl NN6 . . . . . . .108 A5
Paddocks Rd NN10 . . . . .131 F5
Paddocks The
Brixworth NN6 . . . . .106 B3
Bugbrooke NN7 . . . . .172 F7
Moulton NN3 . . . . .126 C1
Orlingbury NN14 . . . . . . .109 F5
Shutlanger NN12 . . . . . . .204 D8
Souldern OX27 . . . . .237 E3
Paddocks Way NN3 . . . . .143 A1
Paddox Cl CV22 . . . . .98 F8
Paddox Cl CV23 . . . . .100 A3
Paddox Prim Sch
Rugby CV22 . . . . .98 D8
Rugby CV22 . . . . .98 E8
Padmans Cl NN14 . . . . . . .89 B4
Padwell Ct 2 NN3 . . . . . .161 A8
Page Hill Ave MK18 . . . . .240 E4
Pagent Cl NN12 . . . . .204 D8
Pages Wlk NN17 . . . . .37 B6
Paget Cl NN4 . . . . .160 E2
Paget Rd LE16 . . . . .30 E3
Pagnell Ct NN4 . . . . .176 A7
Palk Rd NN8 . . . . .130 B4
Palm Rd NN10 . . . . .131 E3
Palmer Ave NN9 . . . . .113 B4
Palmer Cl NN8 . . . . .129 D7
Palmer Ct NN8 . . . . .129 F5
Palmer Sq NN5 . . . . .143 C1
Palmer's Cl CV21 . . . . .99 B8
Palmerston Ct 5 NN1 . . .159 E6
Palmerston Ho 4 NN1 . . .159 E6
Palmerston Rd NN1 . . . . .159 E6
Parade Bank NN3 . . . . . . .126 C1
Parade The NN1 . . . . .159 C6
Paradise Ave NN15 . . . . . .91 D6
Paradise Ho NN8 . . . . . . .129 F5
Paradise La NN15 . . . . . . .91 D6
Paradise St CV21 . . . . . . .241 E8
Pargeter Ct OX17 . . . . . . .210 E2
Park Ave Kettering NN16 . .72 B4
Northampton NN5 . . . . . .140 A8
Northampton, Abington
NN1 . . . . .160 A8
Raunds NN9 . . . . .114 E5
Rushden NN10 . . . . .132 A5
Park Ave N NN3 . . . . .142 A1
Park Ave S NN3 . . . . .160 B7
Park Cl Badby NN11 . . . . .153 A3
Banbury OX16 . . . . .240 C8
Brafield-on-the-Gn NN7 . .161 E2
Cosgrove MK19 . . . . .218 F2
Earls Barton NN6 . . . . . .144 D4
Isham NN14 . . . . .110 F8
King's Cliffe PE8 . . . . .14 A8
Northampton NN5 . . . . . .140 A1
Sywell NN6 . . . . .127 D2
Watford NN11 . . . . .120 C6
Whittlebury NN12 . . . . . .215 C4
Park Cres 8 NN8 . . . . . . .130 A5
Park Cres E NN5 . . . . .140 F2
Park Cres W NN5 . . . . . . .140 F1
Park Dr
Market Harborough LE16 . . .31 E4
Northampton NN5 . . . . . .140 F1
Park End NN13 . . . . .238 D8
Park End Works NN13 . . .238 D7
Park Farm Barns NN7 . . .139 E6
Park Farm Ct NN14 . . . . . .77 C4
Park Farm Ind Est NN8 . .129 A5
Park Farm Way NN8 . . . . .129 A3
Park Hill Rd NN3 . . . . . . .142 D3
Park Ho LE16 . . . . .31 E4
Park Inf Sch NN9 . . . . . . .114 E6
Park Jun & Inf Schs
NN16 . . . . .72 C4
Park La Earls Barton NN6 .144 D4
Gayton NN7 . . . . .173 E2
Harpole NN7 . . . . .157 C6
Hartwell NN7 . . . . .192 C1
Northampton NN5 . . . . . .140 A2
Paulerspury NN12 . . . . . .216 B7
Stamford PE9 . . . . .241 C2
Sulgrave OX17 . . . . .210 F7
Watford NN6 . . . . .120 C6
Park Leys NN11 . . . . .135 C1
Park Lodge NN17 . . . . .36 E6

Park Mews
Market Harborough LE16 . . .31 E4
Towcester NN12 . . . . . . .203 C6
Wellingborough NN8 . . . .130 A5
Park Pl NN10 . . . . .132 B2
Park Rd Banbury OX16 . . .240 B8
Burton Latimer NN15 . . . .92 B2
Hanslope MK19 . . . . .207 B1
Hartwell NN7 . . . . .192 C1
Irthlingborough NN9 . . . .112 F1
Kettering NN16 . . . . .72 C4
Raunds NN9 . . . . .114 E6
Rugby CV21 . . . . .241 C9
Rushden NN10 . . . . .132 C1
Stony Stratford MK11 . . . .229 D5
Titchmarsh NN14 . . . . . . .77 C4
Wellingborough NN8 . . . .130 A5
Park Spinney Cl NN6 . . . . .84 A5
Park Sq NN5 . . . . .140 F2
Park St Earls Barton NN6 .144 D4
King's Cliffe PE8 . . . . .13 C7
Raunds NN9 . . . . .114 E6
Towcester NN12 . . . . . . .203 C6
Wollaston NN29 . . . . . . .146 E2
Park The PE28 . . . . .97 A3
Park View Kettering NN16 . .72 B4
Moulton NN3 . . . . .142 E8
Stamford PE9 . . . . .241 C5
Thrapston NN14 . . . . .76 D2
Wellingborough NN8 . . . .130 B4
Park View La NN11 . . . . . .126 E1
Park View Rd NN12 . . . . .203 D5
Park Wlk Brigstock NN14 . .55 E7
Easton o t H PE9 . . . . .2 A6
Northampton NN5 . . . . . .140 F2
Parker Rd PE8 . . . . .7 B8
Parkers Terr NN9 . . . . . . .111 F4
Parkfield Ave NN4 . . . . . .159 C1
Parkfield Cres NN4 . . . . .159 C2
Parkfield Rd
Brixworth NN6 . . . . .106 A1
Long Buckby NN6 . . . . . .121 A4
Rugby CV22 . . . . .241 A8
Parkham Ind Est NN10 . .131 D3
Parklands Banbury OX16 .240 B9
Crick NN6 . . . . .100 C3
Stanwick NN9 . . . . .113 F3
Sywell NN6 . . . . .127 D1
Parklands Ave NN3 . . . . .142 A5
Parklands Cl NN14 . . . . . . .70 D1
Parklands Cres NN3 . . . . .142 A5
Parklands Lower Sch
NN3 . . . . .142 A4
Parklands Mid Sch NN3 .142 A5
Parkside NN3 . . . . .143 D2
Parkside Sch NN1 . . . . . .159 E5
Parkway Nassington PE8 . .15 F5
Northampton NN3 . . . . . .142 D1
Parkway Cl PE8 . . . . .15 F5
Parkwood St NN5 . . . . . . .159 B5
Parnell Cl Rugby CV21 . . .241 B8
West Haddon NN6 . . . . . .102 C5
Parracombe Way NN3 . . .160 C7
Parson's St OX16 . . . . . . .240 D8
Parsons Cl Ecton NN6 . . . .143 F4
Nether Heyford NN7 . . . .156 C2
Parsons Gr NN17 . . . . .22 A1
Parsons Meade NN4 . . . . .158 C2
Parsons Rd
Daventry NN11 . . . . .134 F5
Irchester NN29 . . . . .147 B8
Parsons St
Adderbury OX17 . . . . . . .230 A4
Woodford Halse NN11 . . .184 C6
Parsons' Cl NN7 . . . . .163 D5
Partridge Cl
Buckingham MK18 . . . . .240 F2
Charwelton NN11 . . . . . .168 A5
Northampton NN2 . . . . . .141 A5
Partridge La NN11 . . . . . .184 C1
Parva Ct NN3 . . . . .142 E3
Pascoe Cres NN15 . . . . . .135 A4
Pashler Gdns NN14 . . . . . .76 C2
Pasteur Cl NN2 . . . . .141 B5
Pasteur Ctyd NN17 . . . . . .37 B8
Pasture The NN11 . . . . . .135 C1
Pastures The
Market Harborough LE16 . . .31 C3
Northampton NN2 . . . . . .141 A5
Wellingborough NN9 . . . .110 E1
Paterson Rd NN8 . . . . . . .130 B8
Patrick Cl NN15 . . . . .91 C6
Patrick Rd Corby NN18 . . .36 D4
Kettering NN15 . . . . .91 C6
Patrick St LE16 . . . . .31 C6
Patricks La MK19 . . . . . . .228 E4
Patterdale Wlk 1 NN3 . . .142 C4
Patterson Cl NN3 . . . . . . .142 E1
Pattishall CE Prim Sch
NN12 . . . . .188 D7
Paulerspury CE Prim Sch
NN12 . . . . .216 B8
Pavilion Dr NN4 . . . . .159 F1
Pavillion Dr PE8 . . . . .41 E6
Pavillions Way NN13 . . . .233 E8
Paxford Cl NN8 . . . . .129 E1
Paxmans Pl OX16 . . . . . . .240 C6
Paxton Cl MK46 . . . . .195 F3
Paxton Rd NN3 . . . . .142 D4
Payne's La LE16 . . . . .18 F7
Paynes Ct MK18 . . . . .240 D4
Peace Cl NN4 . . . . .158 F3
Peace Hill NN7 . . . . .172 C4
Peacock Dr NN4 . . . . .95 B3
Peacock Pl 6 NN1 . . . . . .159 D6
Peacock's Cl OX17 . . . . . .220 A8
Peak The NN7 . . . . .156 C1
Peake Cl LE16 . . . . .35 B8

Old – Pic 259

Pear Tree Cl
Bozeat NN29 . . . . .164 D3
Northampton NN3 . . . . . .143 A2
Pear Tree Gdns LE16 . . . . .31 D2
Pearmain Ave NN8 . . . . . .129 F7
Pearmain Ct NN3 . . . . . . .143 A2
Peartree Cl NN11 . . . . . . .135 C4
Peaselands NN14 . . . . .50 F4
Peat Cl CV22 . . . . .241 A6
Pebble La Brackley NN13 .233 F7
4 Wellingborough NN8 . .130 A4
Pebbleford Rd NN15 . . . . .91 D8
Peck Way NN10 . . . . .132 B4
Peg's La Clipston LE16 . . . .66 F8
Denford NN14 . . . . .95 C6
Pegasus Ct NN13 . . . . . . .233 F7
Pelham Ct NN3 . . . . .142 D4
Pell Ct NN3 . . . . .142 E3
Pells Cl NN6 . . . . .103 E7
Pemberton St NN10 . . . . .132 A3
Pembroke Cl
Rushden NN10 . . . . .132 C1
Thrapston NN14 . . . . .76 E2
Pembroke Cres NN5 . . . . .159 B8
Pembroke Gdns NN5 . . . .159 A8
Pembroke Ho MK46 . . . . .195 F3
Pembroke Rd
Northampton NN5 . . . . . .159 B8
Stamford PE9 . . . . .241 C5
Pembroke Way NN11 . . . .153 B7
Pen Ct NN1 . . . . .159 C4
Pen Gn La NN17 . . . . .37 A8
Penarth Rd NN5 . . . . .159 A8
Pendered Rd NN8 . . . . . . .130 A1
Pendle Ave NN16 . . . . .72 A6
Pendle Rd NN5 . . . . .158 C8
Pendred Rd CV22 . . . . . . .241 A8
Penfold Cl NN2 . . . . .141 B4
Penfold Dr NN3 . . . . .143 B3
Penfold Gdns NN3 . . . . . .143 C3
Penfold La NN3 . . . . .143 C3
Peninsular Cl 12 NN4 . . . .175 E7
Penistone Rd NN3 . . . . . .142 E3
Penistone Wlk 3 NN3 . . .142 E3
Penn Gdns NN5 . . . . .175 B7
Pennard Cl NN4 . . . . .160 B2
Pennine Cl NN11 . . . . . . .135 B5
Pennine Way
Kettering NN16 . . . . .72 B6
Northampton NN5 . . . . . .158 D7
Pennington Mews NN11 .241 B8
Pennington St CV21 . . . . .241 B8
Pennycress Pl NN3 . . . . . .143 D1
Penrhyn Ct NN14 . . . . . . .76 E2
Penrhyn Rd NN4 . . . . .159 C3
Penrith Dr NN8 . . . . .129 D6
Penrose Cl OX16 . . . . . . .240 A8
Penrose Dr OX16 . . . . . . .240 A8
Pentelowes The PE18 . . . .116 D2
Penthorne Cl NN11 . . . . .188 A8
Pentlands MK11 . . . . .229 F4
Penvale Rd NN4 . . . . .175 B7
Pepper Alley OX15 . . . . . .236 E4
Peppercorn Way NN4 . . . .175 D6
Perceval Cl NN5 . . . . .140 D1
Perch Cl NN11 . . . . .135 B6
Percival Rd Rugby CV22 . .241 F6
Rugby CV22 . . . . .98 D8
Percy Rd
Northampton NN1 . . . . . .159 F7
Woodford Halse NN11 . . .184 C6
Peregrine Pl NN4 . . . . . . .175 A8
Perkins Cl LE16 . . . . .31 F4
Perkins Ct 4 NN8 . . . . . . .130 A5
Perkins Rd NN9 . . . . .131 E8
Perkins Way NN11 . . . . . .153 E4
Perry Cl NN15 . . . . .91 A7
Perry St NN1 . . . . .159 F7
Pershore Cl NN8 . . . . .145 E8
Perth Ho NN17 . . . . .22 F1
Perth Rd PE9 . . . . .241 A4
Peterborough Rd
Morcott LE15 . . . . .3 D6
Wansford PE8 . . . . .8 A3
Warmington PE8 . . . . .28 C4
Petergate PE9 . . . . .241 C2
Peterhouse Cl PE9 . . . . . .241 D5
Peters La NN6 . . . . .106 F5
Pether Ave NN13 . . . . . . .233 C8
Petherton Ct NN16 . . . . . .72 B3
Pettiver Cres 2 CV21 . . . . .80 A1
Petworth Dr LE16 . . . . . . .32 B2
Petworth Gdns NN18 . . . . .36 B5
Pevensey Cl NN10 . . . . . .132 D1
Pevensey Wlk 2 NN18 . . . .36 B5
Peverel's Way NN5 . . . . . .158 E6
Peveril Cl NN10 . . . . .132 C6
Peveril Rd
Greatworth OX17 . . . . . . .210 E2
Northampton NN5 . . . . . .158 C2
Pevers La MK46 . . . . .195 A1
Pevrel Pl NN14 . . . . .50 E4
Pexley Ct PE8 . . . . .41 E5
Pheasant Way 141 A5
Pheonix Parkway NN17 . . .37 B8
Philip Way NN10 . . . . . . .132 C7
Phillips Ct PE9 . . . . .241 E2
Phillips Way NN6 . . . . . . .121 C4
Phipps Rd NN11 . . . . .184 B6
Phoenix Cl NN8 . . . . .130 B3
Phoenix Parkway NN17 . . .22 B2
Phoenix St 28 NN1 . . . . .159 C6
Piccadilly Bldgs 3 NN16 .72 B1
Piccadilly Cl NN4 . . . . . . .158 F2
Pickerings The NN6 . . . . .106 C1

Picks Cl LE16 . . . . .32 B3
Piddington La NN7 . . . . .177 A2
Pie Cnr NN6 . . . . .127 D3
Piece The Cogenhoe NN7 .161 F6
  Spratton NN6 . . . . .105 B1
Pied Bull Cl PE9 . . . . .1 A6
Pierce Cres PE8 . . . . .28 C3
Pigeon Hill NN12 . . . . . . .189 D3
Pightle Cres MK18 . . . . . .240 D6
Pightle The MK18 . . . . . .240 D6
Pightles Terr NN10 . . . . .132 C1
Pightles Wlk NN10 . . . . . .132 C1
Pigott's La NN15 . . . . .92 C2
Pike La NN1 . . . . .159 C6
Pike Rd NN18 . . . . .36 A1
Pikemead Ct NN3 . . . . . .143 B4
Pilgrim Way NN8 . . . . . . .129 F3
Pilgrims La NN7 . . . . .173 A7
Pilgrims Pl NN4 . . . . .159 C2
Pilot Rd NN17 . . . . .37 C3
Pilton Cl NN3 . . . . .143 C5
Pilton Rd PE8 . . . . .58 A4
Pincet La LE17 . . . . .45 A6
Pindar Rd NN8 . . . . .129 E2
Pindar Rise NN3 . . . . . . .142 E6
Pinders La CV21 . . . . . . .241 D9
Pine Ave NN6 . . . . .127 C3
Pine Cl Desborough NN14 . .51 C2
  Irchester NN29 . . . . .147 A7
  Northampton NN4 . . . . . .175 F3
  Rushden NN10 . . . . .148 A8
Pine Copse Cl NN5 . . . . .140 A4
Pine Cres NN6 . . . . .127 D1
Pine Ct NN7 . . . . .138 C4
Pine Gr CV21 . . . . .80 A1
Pine Rd NN15 . . . . .72 C1
Pine Ridge NN3 . . . . .142 F7
Pine Trees NN3 . . . . .142 D1
Pine Wlk NN17 . . . . .21 C1
Pineham Ave NN2 . . . . . .141 D6
Pines The LE16 . . . . .32 A6
Pinetrees Cl NN7 . . . . . . .177 B3
Pinewood Cl NN16 . . . . . .72 B6
Pinewood Rd NN3 . . . . . .142 B3
Pinfold Cl LE15 . . . . .3 E8
Pinfold La NN11 . . . . .152 F3
  Stamford PE9 . . . . .241 F3
  Stamford PE9 . . . . .241 F3
Pinfold St CV21 . . . . .241 A8
Pingle La LE15 . . . . .3 B6
Pinhill Rd OX16 . . . . .240 B9
Pioneer Ave
  Burton Latimer NN15 . . . . .92 B2
  Desborough NN14 . . . . . . .50 E7
Pioneer Cl [10] NN4 . . . . .175 E7
Piper Cl NN8 . . . . .129 F8
Piper's Hill Rd NN15 . . . . .91 C8
Pipers Cl
  Irthlingborough NN9 . . . . .112 F2
  Kettering NN15 . . . . .72 C1
Pipewell Rd
  Desborough NN14 . . . . . . .51 C4
  East Carlton LE16 . . . . . . .35 D3
Pippin Cl Cogenhoe NN7 .161 E5
  Rushden NN10 . . . . .131 B3
  Wellingborough NN8 . . . . .129 F4
Pippin La NN3 . . . . .143 A2
Pit La PE9 . . . . .1 A7
Pitchers Cl La LE16 . . . . . . .20 D7
Pitchford Ave MK18 . . . . .240 E4
Pitchford Wlk MK18 . . . . .240 E4
Pitsford & Brampton Sta★
  NN6 . . . . .124 E2
Pitsford Prim Sch NN6 . . .125 D5
Pitsford Rd
  Chapel Brampton NN6 . . . .124 E1
  Moulton NN3 . . . . .126 B2
Pitstone Rd NN4 . . . . . . .158 E3
Pitt Gn MK18 . . . . .240 F4
Pitt St NN8 . . . . .129 E4
Pittams Cl NN6 . . . . .121 B3
Pittams La NN12 . . . . . . .213 B8
Pittoms La CV23 . . . . .99 C1
Plank Hos NN12 . . . . . . .203 C5
Plantagenet Cl NN13 . . . .233 D4
Plantagenet Sq [7] NN4 .158 F2
Playford Cl NN14 . . . . . . .70 F7
Pleasant Row NN14 . . . . . .94 D7
Plessey Cl NN12 . . . . . . .203 D5
Pleydell Gdns NN4 . . . . . .159 C2
Pleydell Rd NN4 . . . . . . .159 C2
Plough Cl Daventry NN11 .135 D6
  Rothwell NN14 . . . . .70 D7
Plough La NN2 . . . . .141 A6
Plough Mews NN13 . . . . .233 F7
Ploughmans Way NN4 . . .175 F3
Ploughmans Wlk NN2 . . .141 B5
Plover Cl
  Buckingham MK18 . . . . . .240 E2
  Towcester NN12 . . . . . . .203 C3
Plowden Cl NN11 . . . . . . .182 F2
Plowman St CV21 . . . . . .241 B8
Plum Park La NN12 . . . . .216 D8
Plumpton Ct NN18 . . . . . .36 B5
Plumpton La NN11 . . . . . .199 D7
Plumpton Rd
  Weston NN12 . . . . .200 A2
  Woodend NN12 . . . . . . .200 F6
Plumtree Ave NN8 . . . . . .130 A7
Poachers Cl NN4 . . . . . . .175 F5
Poachers Way NN2 . . . . .141 B5
Pochin Dr LE16 . . . . .31 F5
Podington Rd NN10 . . . . .148 A4
Podmore Way NN14 . . . . .90 A3
Poets Way NN11 . . . . . . .153 E5

Poitiers Ct NN5 . . . . .139 F1
Pokas Cotts NN9 . . . . . . .133 C8
Polar Star Cl NN11 . . . . . .135 A4
Polebrook Airfield Nature
  Reserve★ PE8 . . . . .43 F3
Polebrook CE Prim Sch
  PE8 . . . . .43 A3
Polebrook Ct PE8 . . . . . . .42 F3
Polegate Ct NN18 . . . . . . .36 B5
Police Flats NN17 . . . . . . .36 E6
Pollard St NN16 . . . . .72 B4
Polwell La NN15 . . . . .92 A4
Pomfret Rd NN12 . . . . . . .203 C6
Pond Bank NN7 . . . . .190 D8
Pond Farm Cl NN5 . . . . . .158 C7
Pond Wood Cl NN3 . . . . .142 B6
Ponder St NN14 . . . . .70 D7
Ponds Cl NN9 . . . . .114 C6
Pool Cl NN12 . . . . .188 D8
Pool St NN11 . . . . .184 B5
Poole St NN1 . . . . .159 D7
Poolside Cl OX16 . . . . . . .240 B7
Pope Rd NN8 . . . . .129 C3
Pope St CV22 . . . . .241 B6
Popham Ct NN9 . . . . .114 C7
Poplar Cl Daventry NN11 .135 C5
  Irchester NN29 . . . . .147 A7
  Rushden NN10 . . . . .148 A8
  Towcester NN12 . . . . . . .203 A8
Poplar Ct NN3 . . . . .142 D5
Poplar Gr CV21 . . . . .241 C9
Poplar Rd
  Burton Latimer NN15 . . . . .92 C4
  Corby NN17 . . . . .21 D1
  Finedon NN9 . . . . .112 A5
  Kettering NN16 . . . . .72 D2
Poplar Rise NN12 . . . . . . .213 B8
Poplar St NN8 . . . . .130 A5
Poplar's Farm Rd NN15 . . .92 B8
Poplars Cl
  Blakesley NN12 . . . . .187 B1
  Middleton Cheney OX17 . .220 A8
  Raunds NN9 . . . . .114 C6
Poplars Ct
  Market Harborough LE16 . . .31 D4
  Scaldwell NN6 . . . . .106 C7
Poplars La NN6 . . . . .126 E8
Poplars Rd
  Buckingham MK18 . . . . . .240 D1
  Chacombe OX17 . . . . . . .208 F4
Poplars The
  Guilsborough NN6 . . . . . .103 E7
  Long Buckby NN6 . . . . . .121 B3
  Northampton NN1 . . . . . .159 C2
Poppy Cl NN10 . . . . .148 C8
Poppy Leys NN6 . . . . . . .125 B8
Poppyfield Ct
  Northampton NN3 . . . . . .142 F4
  Thrapston NN14 . . . . .76 D3
Porlock Cl NN5 . . . . .158 E8
Port Rd NN5 . . . . .140 A2
Portchester Gdns [4]
  NN3 . . . . .160 F8
Porter's Cl MK19 . . . . . . .228 E4
Porter's La PE9 . . . . .2 A5
Portfield Cl MK18 . . . . . . .240 E3
Portfield Way MK18 . . . . .240 E3
Portland Cl NN11 . . . . . . .135 D1
Portland Pl
  Northampton NN1 . . . . . .159 E6
  Rugby CV21 . . . . .241 F7
Portland Rd
  Irthlingborough NN9 . . . . .112 F3
  Rugby CV21 . . . . .241 F7
  Rushden NN10 . . . . .132 B2
Portlow La NN6 . . . . .100 F6
Portree Wlk NN17 . . . . . . .36 C8
Portstone Cl NN5 . . . . . . .140 A2
Portway Aynho OX17 . . . .237 D7
  Croughton NN13 . . . . . . .238 E7
Portway Cres NN13 . . . . .238 E7
Portway Dr NN13 . . . . . . .238 D7
Portway Gdns OX17 . . . . .237 D7
Portwey Cl NN6 . . . . .106 C1
Post Office Cl NN17 . . . . .37 B6
Postle Cl CV23 . . . . .99 F2
Potter Cl NN9 . . . . .114 A4
Potters End NN11 . . . . . . .183 D7
Potterspury Lodge Sch
  NN12 . . . . .217 A6
Pound Cl Corby NN18 . . . .36 B2
  Ringstead NN14 . . . . .95 B3
  Wicken MK19 . . . . .228 A4
Pound Ct NN3 . . . . .126 B1
Pound La Badby NN11 . . .152 F3
  Bugbrooke NN7 . . . . .173 A7
  Eastcote NN12 . . . . .172 A1
  Moulton NN3 . . . . .126 C1
  Northampton NN3 . . . . . .143 C2
Pound Pl NN9 . . . . .111 F4
Pound The
  Great Brington NN7 . . . . .138 D6
  Horton NN7 . . . . .177 E1
  Nether Heyford NN7 . . . . .156 B1
  Syresham NN13 . . . . .224 B7
Poundfield Rd NN12 . . . . .217 D2
Power Pk OX16 . . . . .240 E7
Poyntz Gdns NN5 . . . . . . .158 E8
Poyntz La NN5 . . . . .158 E8
Pratt Rd NN10 . . . . .132 C2
Premier Way NN9 . . . . . . .131 E8
Prentice Ct NN3 . . . . .143 A5
Prentice Wlk NN17 . . . . . .37 A6
Prescott Ave OX16 . . . . . .240 A8

Prescott Cl
  Banbury OX16 . . . . .240 A8
  Northampton NN3 . . . . . .143 C4
Pressland Dr NN10 . . . . . .132 C6
Prestbury Rd NN5 . . . . . .140 A1
Prestige Row NN11 . . . . .199 C7
Preston Ct
  Burton Latimer NN15 . . . . .92 C3
  Northampton NN3 . . . . . .143 C4
Preston Deanery Rd
  NN7 . . . . .176 B1
Preston Dr NN11 . . . . . . .135 C6
Preston Hedges Prim Sch
  NN4 . . . . .175 F6
Preston Rd NN11 . . . . . . .184 C2
Prestwold Way NN3 . . . . .143 B5
Prices Way NN13 . . . . . . .222 D1
Pride Pl LE16 . . . . .31 D2
Pridmore Cl PE8 . . . . .14 E2
Priestley Ct NN17 . . . . . . .22 D1
Priestwell Ct NN6 . . . . . .122 D5
Primrose Cl Corby NN18 . .36 C2
  Kettering NN16 . . . . .72 C3
Primrose Gdns NN9 . . . . .114 D5
Primrose Hill
  Daventry NN11 . . . . .135 C2
  Northampton NN2 . . . . . .159 C8
  Raunds NN9 . . . . .114 D6
Primrose Pl NN8 . . . . .130 C5
Primrose Way MK18 . . . . .240 C2
Primrose Wlk
  Hinton NN11 . . . . .184 B6
  Northampton NN5 . . . . . .175 F2
Primula Cl NN3 . . . . .160 C6
Primula Cl NN12 . . . . . . .159 C8
Prince Cl NN11 . . . . .135 B3
Prince Of Wales Row
  NN3 . . . . .126 D1
Prince Rupert Ave NN14 . .50 F3
Prince St NN6 . . . . .122 D5
Prince William Rd PE8 . . .41 E5
Prince William Sch PE8 . .41 E4
Princes Ave NN14 . . . . . . .51 B3
Princes Cl NN7 . . . . .155 A3
Princes Ct NN16 . . . . .72 B3
Princes Rd PE9 . . . . .241 D4
Princes St Kettering NN16 .72 C3
  Rugby CV21 . . . . .241 C9
Princes Wlk [4] NN1 . . . .159 D6
Princess Anne Bldg
  NN2 . . . . .141 C4
Princess Cl NN3 . . . . .160 B6
Princess Marina Hospl
  NN5 . . . . .158 B6
Princess Way NN8 . . . . . .129 E2
Princethorpe Dr
  Banbury OX16 . . . . .219 A7
  Banbury OX16 . . . . .240 F9
Princewood Rd NN17 . . . .21 E3
Printers Yd NN16 . . . . . . .72 B2
Priors Cl NN10 . . . . .147 F8
Priors Ct Corby NN17 . . . .23 A1
  Priors Marston CV47 . . . .166 D7
Priors Haw Rd NN17 . . . . .23 A1
Priors Marston Rd
  Byfield NN11 . . . . .167 B8
  Hellidon NN11 . . . . .151 C1
Priors Sch The CV47 . . . .166 D8
Priory Cl Daventry NN11 .135 D1
  Northampton NN3 . . . . . .160 B6
Priory Cres NN7 . . . . .191 F4
Priory Ct Geddington NN14 54 A2
  Weedon NN7 . . . . .155 A2
Priory Gdns PE9 . . . . . . .241 F3
Priory Ho NN1 . . . . .159 B6
Priory Rd Stamford PE9 . .241 F3
  Wellingborough NN8 . . . . .129 F3
  Wollaston NN29 . . . . . . .146 D3
Priory Vale Rd OX16 . . . . .240 F9
Pritchard Cl NN3 . . . . . . .143 C6
Probyn Cl NN3 . . . . .143 A6
Promenade The NN8 . . . .129 E6
Prospect Ave
  Irchester NN29 . . . . .147 A7
  Rushden NN10 . . . . .132 B4
Prospect Cl NN29 . . . . . . .146 D3
Prospect Ct NN10 . . . . . .217 F6
Prospect Pl MK19 . . . . . . .218 F5
Prospect Rd
  Banbury OX16 . . . . .240 D7
  Stony Stratford MK19 . . . .229 C5
Prospect Way NN11 . . . . .134 F3
Provence Cl NN5 . . . . . . .139 F1
Pudding Bag La NN29 . . .164 D3
Puddledock NN12 . . . . . . .214 D5
Purbeck Rd NN10 . . . . . . .131 D2
Purse La MK16 . . . . .207 F8
Purser Rd NN1 . . . . .159 F8
Purston Cross Rds
  OX17 . . . . .220 D6
Purvis Rd NN10 . . . . .132 A2
Pury End NN12 . . . . .205 A3
Puxley Rd MK19 . . . . .228 D5
Pye Ct CV23 . . . . .117 D4
Pyghtle The
  Earls Barton NN6 . . . . . . .144 E5
  Olney MK46 . . . . .195 F3
  Wellingborough NN8 . . . . .129 F6
Pyghtle Way NN4 . . . . . . .175 A7
Pyghtles The
  Daventry NN11 . . . . .135 B1
  Wollaston NN29 . . . . . . .146 D1
Pyke Way NN6 . . . . .101 A6
Pyket Way NN3 . . . . .160 E8
Pyramid Cl NN3 . . . . .142 E2
Pytchley Cl NN6 . . . . .106 B2
Pytchley Ct Corby NN17 . .36 B8

Pytchley Ct continued
  West Haddon NN6 . . . . . .102 C4
Pytchley Dr NN6 . . . . . . .121 B4
Pytchley Endowed CE Prim
  Sch NN14 . . . . .90 F2
Pytchley La NN15 . . . . . . .91 C5
Pytchley Lodge Ind Est
  NN15 . . . . .91 C6
Pytchley Lodge Rd NN15 91 C7
Pytchley Rd
  Kettering NN15 . . . . .91 C6
  Orlingbury NN14 . . . . . . .109 F5
  Rugby CV22 . . . . .241 E6
  Rugby CV22 . . . . .98 C8
  Rushden NN10 . . . . .131 F3
Pytchley Rise NN8 . . . . . .129 D3
Pytchley St NN1 . . . . .159 E6
Pytchley View NN3 . . . . . .126 D1
Pytchley Way
  Brixworth NN6 . . . . .106 B2
  Northampton NN5 . . . . . .140 B2
Pywell Cl NN17 . . . . .22 E2
Pywell Rd NN17 . . . . .22 E2

Q

Quakers Cl NN7 . . . . .172 F7
Quantock Cl
  Daventry NN11 . . . . .135 B5
  Kettering NN15 . . . . .92 A5
Quantock Cres NN5 . . . . .158 D8
Quarry Green Cl MK19 . . .228 B3
Quarry Park Cl NN3 . . . . .142 B6
Quarry Rd Brixworth NN6 .106 C3
  Northampton NN5 . . . . . .140 B2
Quarterstone NN4 . . . . . .158 D1
Quatercroft NN3 . . . . .142 E2
Quebec Cl Corby NN18 . . .36 C2
  [5] Northampton NN4 . . .175 E7
Queen Eleanor Comb Sch
  MK11 . . . . .229 F4
Queen Eleanor Comp Sch
  PE9 . . . . .241 D5
Queen Eleanor Lower Sch
  NN4 . . . . .159 B2
Queen Eleanor Rd
  Geddington NN14 . . . . . . .54 A3
  Northampton NN4 . . . . . .159 B2
Queen Eleanor St MK11 229 E6
Queen Eleanor Terr
  NN4 . . . . .159 C2
Queen St Bozeat NN29 . . .144 C7
  Desborough NN14 . . . . . . .51 B3
  Earls Barton NN6 . . . . . .144 F5
  Geddington NN14 . . . . . . .54 A2
  Irthlingborough NN9 . . . . .112 E2
  Kettering NN16 . . . . .72 B2
  Market Harborough LE16 . . .32 A2
  Middleton Cheney OX17 . .219 F8
  Rugby CV21 . . . . .241 C8
  Rushden NN10 . . . . .132 B2
  Stony Stratford MK11 . . . .229 E6
  Thrapston NN14 . . . . .76 E2
  Weedon NN7 . . . . .155 A2
Queen Victoria St CV21 . .241 E8
Queen's Park Par NN2 . . .141 C2
Queen's Pk NN7 . . . . .155 A3
Queen's Rd
  Banbury OX16 . . . . .240 B8
  Northampton NN1 . . . . . .159 E7
  Towcester NN12 . . . . . . .203 C6
Queen's Sq NN17 . . . . . . .36 E5
Queen's Wlk PE9 . . . . . . .241 C5
Queens Cl LE16 . . . . .34 C5
Queens Cres NN11 . . . . . .141 D2
Queens Rd
  Daventry NN11 . . . . .135 B3
  Wilbarston LE16 . . . . .34 D5
  Wollaston NN29 . . . . . . .146 D2
Queens St
  Culworth OX17 . . . . .198 D2
  Farthinghoe NN13 . . . . . .221 B4
  Stamford PE9 . . . . .241 D4
  Wellingborough NN8 . . . . .130 A5
Queensberry Rd NN15 . . . .72 B1
Queensbury Cl NN15 . . . . .72 B2
Queensland Gdns NN1 . . .141 D2
Queensway
  Banbury OX16 . . . . .240 B6
  Burton Latimer NN15 . . . . .92 B1
  Higham Ferrers NN10 . . . .132 C5
  Wellingborough NN8 . . . . .129 C4
  Wellingborough NN8 . . . . .129 D3
Queensway Prim Sch
  OX16 . . . . .240 A6
Queenswood Ave NN3 . . .142 D5
Quernstone La NN4 . . . . .158 E3
Quinton Green Cotts
  NN7 . . . . .192 C7
Quinton House Sch
  NN5 . . . . .158 B5
Quinton La NN11 . . . . . . .184 C1
Quinton Rd NN4 . . . . . . .175 F5
Quintonside NN4 . . . . . . .175 F5
Quorn Cl Kettering NN15 . .92 A5
  Wellingborough NN8 . . . . .129 D4
Quorn Rd NN10 . . . . .132 A4
Quorn Way NN1 . . . . .159 B7

R

Racecourse Rd PE9 . . . . . .2 D5
Racedown NN8 . . . . .129 B3
Radcliffe Cl PE9 . . . . .241 D3
Radcliffe Rd PE9 . . . . . . .241 C3
Radleigh Cl NN4 . . . . . . .159 A2

Radnor Way NN15 . . . . . . .92 A5
Radstone NN13 . . . . .222 F6
Radstone Rd NN13 . . . . . .222 F2
Radstone Way NN2 . . . . . .141 C5
Raeburn Rd NN2 . . . . .141 F2
Raeburn Sch NN2 . . . . . . .141 F2
Raglan Cl NN10 . . . . .132 D1
Raglan St NN1 . . . . .159 E6
Ragsdale Ct NN14 . . . . . . .70 E7
Ragsdale St NN14 . . . . . . .70 E7
Ragsdale Wlk NN3 . . . . . .142 E6
Railport App NN6 . . . . . . .100 B6
Railway Cotts
  Church Brampton NN6 . . .140 A7
  Kilsby CV23 . . . . .100 A6
  Nether Heyford NN7 . . . . .172 A8
Railway Terr CV21 . . . . . .241 D9
Railway View NN16 . . . . . .72 A2
Raincliffe Cl OX17 . . . . . .237 C7
Rainsborough Cres NN4 158 F4
Rainsborough Gdns LE16 48 D8
Rainsbrook Ave CV22 . . . .98 E8
Rainsbrook Valley Rly★
  CV22 . . . . .98 C6
Raisins Field Cl NN3 . . . .143 C3
Rakestone Cl [4] NN4 . . .175 D6
Raleigh Cl Corby NN17 . . .36 A8
  Rothwell NN14 . . . . .70 E7
Raleigh Ct NN11 . . . . . . .135 B5
Ramsay Cl NN9 . . . . .114 C7
Randall Ho NN1 . . . . .159 F7
Randall Rd NN2 . . . . .141 E1
Rands Way NN9 . . . . .114 E5
Ranelagh Rd NN8 . . . . . . .130 B4
Rankine Ho NN17 . . . . . . .36 D8
Rannoch Cl NN15 . . . . . . .91 E8
Rannoch Way NN17 . . . . . .21 C1
Ransome Rd NN4 . . . . . . .159 D3
Rathbone Cl CV21 . . . . . . .99 A8
Rathlin Cl NN17 . . . . .36 C8
Raunds Manor Sch The
  NN9 . . . . .114 E6
Raunds Rd
  Chelveston NN9 . . . . .133 C8
  Stanwick NN9 . . . . .114 A4
Raven Dr NN9 . . . . .92 A6
Ravens Croft NN4 . . . . . .175 A7
Ravens Way NN3 . . . . . . .161 C8
Ravensbank NN10 . . . . . .132 B4
Ravenscourt NN17 . . . . . .36 F8
Ravensthorpe Rd NN6 . . .122 D5
Rawley Cres NN5 . . . . . . .140 A1
Rawlings Cl NN11 . . . . . . .135 D1
Rawlins Cl OX17 . . . . . . .230 A5
Ray Cl PE8 . . . . .41 F7
Raymond Cl NN29 . . . . . .146 E1
Raymond Rd NN5 . . . . . . .159 A4
Raynsford Rd NN5 . . . . . .158 F8
Rea Cl NN4 . . . . .175 C7
Recreation Ground Rd
  PE9 . . . . .241 D3
Rectory Cl Barby CV23 . . . .99 C1
  Crick NN6 . . . . .100 F5
  Stanwick NN9 . . . . .113 F4
Rectory Ct LE16 . . . . .48 B6
Rectory Farm Ct NN9 . . . .28 D8
Rectory Farm Lower Sch
  NN3 . . . . .143 C5
Rectory Farm Mews PE8 28 D8
Rectory Farm Rd NN3 . . .143 D4
Rectory Hill NN14 . . . . . . .93 A7
Rectory La Barby CV23 . . . .99 C1
  Holcot NN6 . . . . .126 E8
  Market Harborough LE16 . . .32 A2
  Medbourne LE16 . . . . .19 A7
  Middleton Cheney OX17 . .208 F1
  Milton Malsor NN7 . . . . . .174 E3
  Orlingbury NN14 . . . . . . .110 A5
  Walgrave NN6 . . . . .108 A4
  Woodford NN14 . . . . .94 D6
  Yardley Hastings NN7 . . . .179 A7
Rectory Rd NN12 . . . . . . .132 B2
Rectory Way NN12 . . . . . .213 B8
Rectory Wlk NN15 . . . . . . .91 F7
Red Hill Cres NN29 . . . . .146 D3
Red House La NN6 . . . . . .108 E4
Red House Rd NN3 . . . . . .142 B7
Red House Wharf NN7 . . .155 C4
Red Lion Sq PE9 . . . . . . .241 D3
Red Lion St
  Kings Sutton OX17 . . . . . .230 F5
  Stamford PE9 . . . . .241 D3
Red Lodge Rd NN17 . . . . .12 A1
Red Row NN9 . . . . .114 D6
Red Wood Cl NN14 . . . . . .51 C2
Redbourn Pk NN6 . . . . . . .160 B3
Redbourne Ct MK11 . . . . .229 F5
Redcot Gdns PE9 . . . . . . .241 C4
Redding Cl NN10 . . . . . . .148 A7
Redgrave Ct NN15 . . . . . . .90 F7
Redhill Way NN9 . . . . . . .110 E1
Redhouse Rd NN14 . . . . .109 C4
Redland Cl LE15 . . . . .3 F5
Redland Dr NN2 . . . . .141 A4
Redliech Cl LE16 . . . . .32 B3
Redmile's La PE9 . . . . .1 A5
Redmoor NN12 . . . . .203 B4
Redruth Cl NN4 . . . . .159 B1
Redshaw Cl MK18 . . . . . .240 E4
Redwell Jun & Inf Sch
  NN8 . . . . .129 E7
Redwell L Ctr NN8 . . . . . .129 E7
Redwell Rd NN8 . . . . .129 F6
Redwing Ave NN3 . . . . . .142 C6
Redwood Cl NN29 . . . . . .147 A7
Reedham Ct NN5 . . . . . . .140 C1
Reedhill NN4 . . . . .158 E1
Reedway NN3 . . . . .142 A4

Reform St PE9 ....241 B3
Regal Cl NN3 ....141 F6
Regal Ct NN10 ....132 C1
Regal Dr NN16 ....72 C6
Regency Cl NN7 ....155 B4
Regency Ct 5 NN11 .....135 C2
Regent Cl NN15 ....92 A2
Regent Pl CV21 ....241 C8
Regent St NN15 ....92 A2
Regent St
  Desborough NN14 ....51 B3
  Finedon NN9 ....111 F4
  Kettering NN16 ....72 C3
  Northampton NN1 ....159 C6
  Rugby CV21 ....241 C8
  Wellingborough NN8 ....130 A5
Regents Hall MK11 .....229 D6
Regiment Cl NN4 ....175 E7
Reid Cl OX16 ....240 B8
Reigate Wlk NN18 ....36 B3
Reims Ct NN5 ....140 A2
Remus Gate NN13 ....234 A6
Rendelsham Cl NN16 ....72 A6
Rennishaw Way NN2 ....141 F3
Repton Ct NN3 ....142 D4
Reservoir Cl NN14 ....37 E3
Reservoir Hos NN6 ....125 D5
Reservoir Rd NN16 ....72 B4
Resthaven Rd NN4 ....175 D6
Restormel Cl NN10 ....132 D1
Retford Ct NN3 ....142 F4
Retreat The
  Easton o t H PE9 ....1 F5
  Stony Stratford MK11 ....229 D5
Reynard Pk NN13 ....233 F5
Reynard Way NN2 ....141 D6
Reynolds Cl
  Kettering NN15 ....92 A8
  Rugby CV21 ....80 B1
  Wellingborough NN8 ....129 F7
Reynolds Rd NN18 ....36 E5
Reynoldston Cl NN4 ....160 C1
Rhodes Cl
  Daventry NN11 ....135 C5
  Market Harborough LE16 ....31 C2
Rhosili Rd NN4 ....160 A2
Rhymer Cl MK19 ....206 F4
Rhymer Ho NN2 ....141 D5
Ribble Cl
  Northampton NN5 ....140 F2
  Wellingborough NN8 ....129 D6
Ribblesdale Ave NN17 ....36 F4
Richard Cl NN15 ....91 C6
Richardson Way NN9 ....114 D6
Richardsons La NN7 ....70 D2
Richmond Ave NN15 ....91 F8
Richmond Cl NN10 ....132 C1
Richmond Ct NN12 ....203 C5
Richmond Rd Corby NN17 36 E6
  Rugby CV21 ....241 F7
  Towcester NN12 ....203 C6
Richmond St OX17 ....231 A5
Richmond Terr NN5 ....159 B6
Rickyard Rd NN13 ....142 E3
Rickyard Wlk NN4 ....175 D6
Ridding Cl NN18 ....36 D3
Rides Ct NN3 ....142 C7
Ridge Cl OX16 ....240 D6
Ridge Dr CV21 ....241 F9
Ridge Rd NN14 ....76 C4
Ridge The NN29 ....145 E7
Ridge View LE16 ....31 E5
Ridgeway
  Northampton NN3 ....160 D8
  Stony Stratford MK11 ....229 F4
  Wellingborough NN8 ....129 F7
Ridgeway Prim Sch LE16 31 F5
Ridgeway The
  Barby CV23 ....118 E8
  Kilsby CV23 ....100 A1
  Market Harborough LE16 ....31 F5
  Welton NN11 ....119 E1
Ridgeway W LE16 ....31 F5
Ridgmont MK19 ....228 E5
Ridgmont Cl MK19 ....228 E5
Ridgway Rd NN15 ....92 B8
Riding Ct NN13 ....233 F5
Riding Rd NN13 ....233 F5
Riding The MK19 ....228 D5
Ridings The
  Brixworth NN6 ....106 C2
  Desborough NN14 ....50 E4
  Northampton NN1 ....159 D6
  Northampton NN4 ....175 D6
  Roade NN7 ....191 C4
Ridley Ct 1 NN11 ....135 C2
Ridley St Daventry NN11 .135 C2
  Kettering NN16 ....72 A4
Riggall Cl NN14 ....90 A3
Riley Cl Daventry NN11 .134 F4
  Market Harborough LE16 .31 B2
  Northampton NN3 ....143 C5
Riley Rd NN16 ....71 E4
Rillwood Ct NN3 ....142 E4
Ring The OX17 ....208 E4
Ring Way NN4 ....159 A3
Ringstead CE Prim Sch
  NN14 ....95 B3
Ringstead Cl Corby NN17 .36 B8
  Kettering NN15 ....91 F5
Ringstead Rd
  Denford NN14 ....95 C5
  Great Addington NN14 .94 C2
Ringwell Cl NN9 ....112 E3
Ringwood Cl NN2 ....141 A5
Ripley Cl LE16 ....32 B3
Ripley Rd LE16 ....20 D1
Ripley Wlk NN18 ....36 C3

Ripon Cl NN4 ....159 A2
Rise The
  Northampton NN2 ....141 B3
  Twyford OX17 ....230 A5
Ritchie Pk LE16 ....48 E8
River La PE8 ....28 C8
Rivercrest Rd MK19 ....229 B6
Riverside Banbury OX16 .240 E7
  Market Harborough LE16 .32 A4
  Oundle PE8 ....42 A4
Riverside Bsns Pk NN3 .160 E7
Riverside Cl PE8 ....42 A4
Riverside Ct
  Kislingbury NN7 ....157 D4
  Market Harborough LE16 .31 D2
  Weedon NN7 ....155 B3
Riverside Dr NN7 ....155 B3
Riverside Ind Est LE16 .32 A4
Riverside Mews MK18 .240 D3
Riverside Spinney PE8 ....8 A3
Riverside Way Islip NN14 .76 D2
  Northampton NN1 ....159 F5
Riverstone Way NN4 .....158 D2
Riverview Gdns NN14 .....143 D2
Riverwell NN8 ....143 D2
Rivetts Cl MK46 ....195 E4
Rixon Cl NN3 ....142 E1
Rixon Rd NN8 ....130 C7
RNIB Rushton Hall Sch
  NN14 ....52 B2
Roade Hill NN7 ....191 F1
Roade Prim Sch NN7 .....191 E4
Roadins Cl NN15 ....91 A3
Robb's La NN14 ....75 F6
Robbins Ct CV22 ....98 F8
Roberson Cl NN12 ....203 C4
Robert Hill Cl CV21 ....80 A1
Robert Smyth Sch LE16 .31 E5
Robert St NN1 ....159 D7
Robert's La PE8 ....42 F2
Roberts Cl MK19 ....228 E4
Roberts Field NN7 ....156 B1
Roberts St Bozeat NN29 .164 C2
  Rushden NN10 ....132 C2
  Wellingborough NN8 .....129 E4
Robertson Cl CV23 ....80 A5
Robin Cl
  Buckingham MK18 ....240 F2
  Kettering NN15 ....92 A6
  Towcester NN12 ....203 C3
Robin La NN8 ....130 A4
Robin Ride NN13 ....222 E1
Robinia Cl NN4 ....158 E3
Robins Cl NN7 ....192 C1
Robins Field PE8 ....8 A4
Robins Wood PE8 ....8 A4
Robinson Cl NN16 ....71 F4
Robinson Dr NN13 ....233 D7
Robinson Rd NN10 ....132 C2
Robinson Way NN16 ....71 F4
Robinswood OX16 ....240 A6
Roche Cl NN11 ....153 C8
Roche Way NN8 ....129 F6
Rochelle Way NN5 ....140 A4
Rochester Cl NN15 ....91 F7
Rochester Gdns LE16 ....31 D1
Rochester Way OX17 .....230 B5
Rock Hill NN14 ....70 D7
Rock Rd Finedon NN9 .....112 A5
  Oundle PE8 ....41 F6
  Stamford PE9 ....241 C6
Rock St NN8 ....129 F5
Rockcroft 3 NN4 ....175 D6
Rockhill Rd NN6 ....121 A3
Rockingham Castle & Gdns★
  LE16 ....21 B3
Rockingham Cl
  1 Daventry NN11 ....135 B4
  Thrapston NN14 ....76 E2
Rockingham Ct NN10 .....148 A8
Rockingham Hills PE8 ....41 E7
Rockingham Ind Est
  LE16 ....32 B3
Rockingham Mews NN17 .37 A7
Rockingham Motor
  Speedway Circuit★
  NN17 ....22 E4
Rockingham Paddocks
  NN16 ....72 B6
Rockingham Prim Sch
  NN17 ....37 A8
Rockingham Rd
  Caldecott LE16 ....21 B6
  Corby NN14 ....52 F5
  Corby NN17 ....21 E2
  Cottingham LE16 ....20 E2
  Gretton LE16,NN17 ....21 E7
  Kettering NN14 ....53 A3
  Kettering NN16 ....72 A5
  Market Harborough LE16 .32 A4
  Northampton NN4 ....159 C2
  Stamford PE9 ....241 A4
Rockleigh Cl NN9 ....112 A5
Roderick Way 7 NN11 .135 B4
Rodney Cl NN11 ....135 E1
Rodney Dr NN17 ....36 B8
Roe Rd NN1 ....160 A8
Rokeby Inf Sch CV22 .....98 A8
Rokeby Jun Sch CV22 .....98 A8
Rokeby St CV21 ....241 F8
Rokeby Wlk NN5 ....140 D1
Roland Way NN10 ....132 B6
Rolfe Cres NN7 ....156 B1
Rolleston Cl LE16 ....32 A3
Roman Bank PE9 ....241 B3
Roman Cl NN17 ....38 B8
Roman Dr PE8 ....8 D2

Roman Way
  Brackley NN13 ....234 A7
  Daventry NN11 ....135 C5
  Desborough NN14 ....51 B2
  Irchester NN29 ....147 B7
  Market Harborough LE16 .31 E4
  Raunds NN9 ....114 E6
  Thrapston NN14 ....76 E3
Romany Rd NN2 ....141 E2
Romney Rd NN18 ....36 E5
Romulus Way NN13 ....234 A6
Rookery La
  Northampton NN2 ....141 A5
  Stoke Bruerne NN12 .....191 B1
Rookwell Dr LE16 ....31 F1
Rope Wlk OX16 ....240 D8
Roper Cl CV21 ....99 A8
Rose Ave Rushden NN10 .131 F1
  Weldon NN17 ....38 B8
Rose Cl Broughton NN14 .90 B5
  Hartwell NN7 ....192 C3
  Rothwell NN14 ....70 C6
  Wollaston NN29 ....146 C3
Rose Cotts NN14 ....113 B7
Rose Ct Irchester NN29 .147 B8
  Weldon NN17 ....38 B8
Rose Dr NN13 ....233 D8
Rose Hall La OX17 ....220 A8
Rose Hill NN6 ....112 A5
Rose Paddock NN14 ....94 D7
Rose Terr NN14 ....94 D7
Rosebery Ave NN5 ....158 F6
Rosebery St
  Burton Latimer NN15 .....92 B1
  Kettering NN16 ....72 C2
  Ringstead NN14 ....95 B3
Rosedale Ave NN17 ....36 E6
Rosedale Rd NN2 ....141 D3
Roseholme Rd NN1 ....160 A8
Rosemoor Cl LE16 ....32 B3
Rosemoor Dr NN4 ....175 C7
Rosemount Dr NN15 ....91 C7
Rosenella Cl 3 NN4 .....158 F3
Rosette Cl NN14 ....158 C8
Rosewood Ave CV22 ....98 A8
Rosewood Cl NN11 ....135 C5
Rosewood Cl NN8 ....130 C3
Rosewood Pl NN16 ....72 C4
Rosgill Pl NN3 ....142 B2
Ross Rd NN5 ....158 E6
Rossendale Dr NN15 .....92 A2
Rossetti Rd NN18 ....36 A5
Rossiter Ho NN13 ....233 E6
Rotherhithe Cl NN4 .....158 F2
Rotherthorpe Ave NN4 159 A3
Rotherthorpe CE Prim Sch
  NN7 ....174 A6
Rotherthorpe Cres
  NN4 ....159 A3
Rotherthorpe Rd
  Kislingbury NN7 ....157 E2
  Northampton NN4 ....159 A3
Rothesay Rd NN2 ....141 F2
Rothesay Terr NN2 ....141 F2
Rothwell Grange Cotts
  NN16 ....71 B5
Rothwell Jun Sch NN16 .70 D7
Rothwell Rd
  Desborough NN14 ....51 A2
  Harrington NN6 ....69 B5
  Kettering NN14 ....71 D4
  Kettering NN16 ....71 F3
Rothwell Victoria Inf Sch
  NN14 ....70 D7
Rotten Row NN29 ....146 D2
Rotton Row NN9 ....114 D7
Roughton Cl NN15 ....91 B6
Round Cl NN11 ....119 E1
Round St CV21 ....241 B8
Roundhill Cl NN14 ....32 B2
Roundhill Rd NN15 ....91 C8
Rounds Gdns CV21 ....241 B9
Roundtown OX17 ....237 C7
Roundway The NN11 ....135 D6
Roveley Ct MK11 ....229 F5
Rowallen Way NN11 ....135 A4
Rowan Ave
  Market Harborough LE16 .31 E1
  Northampton NN4 ....175 C5
Rowan Cl Brackley NN13 .222 F1
  Northampton NN4 ....175 E2
  Towcester NN12 ....203 B4
  Wellingborough NN8 .....129 E5
Rowan Ct NN17 ....21 E1
Rowan Gate Prim Sch
  NN8 ....130 B6
Rowan Way NN11 ....184 B6
Rowans The NN15 ....135 C4
Rowden La LE16 ....17 D4
Rowell Way PE8 ....42 B4
Rowland St CV21 ....241 B8
Rowlandson Cl NN3 .....142 E1
Rowlett Cl NN10 ....132 B6
Rowlett Prim Sch NN17 ..37 B6
Rowlett Rd NN17 ....36 D8
Rowley Way NN2 ....141 E6
Rowtree Rd NN4 ....175 B6
Roxburgh Rd PE9 ....241 B4
Roxton Cl NN15 ....92 A5
Royal Cl NN11 ....135 B3
Royal Latin Sch The
  MK18 ....240 D2
Royal Oak Ind Est NN11 134 F3
Royal Oak La OX17 ....220 A8
Royal Oak Way N NN11 .134 F2
Royal Oak Way S NN11 .134 F2
Royal Star Dr NN11 ....135 A4
Royal Terr NN1 ....159 C7

Royce Cl NN17 ....21 F1
Rubens Wlk NN18 ....36 E5
Ruddington Cl NN3 ....160 E7
Rudge Mews NN5 ....157 F8
Rudgeway NN13 ....233 F2
Rufford Ave NN3 ....160 E7
Rufford Cl NN15 ....92 A5
Rufford Wlk NN18 ....36 C6
Rugby Cl LE16 ....31 D2
Rugby Rd Barby CV23 .....99 C1
  Kilsby CV21,CV23 ....99 E5
  Lilbourne CV23 ....80 F6
  South Kilworth LE17 .....62 E6
  Swinford LE17 ....62 B3
Rugby Sch CV22 ....241 C7
Rugby Sta CV21 ....241 E9
Ruins The NN12 ....203 C6
Runnell La CV21 ....15 F5
Runnymede Gdns 5
  NN3 ....142 F1
Rupert Rd LE16 ....31 E1
Ruscote Ave OX16 ....240 B9
Ruscote Sq OX16 ....240 B9
Rush Cl NN7 ....192 E2
Rushden Hospl NN10 .....148 B8
Rushden Rd
  Newton Bromswold NN10 .149 C7
  Wymington NN10 ....148 A6
Rushden Sch NN10 ....132 A4
Rushes La LE16 ....30 F3
Rushmere Ave NN1 ....160 B6
Rushmere Cl NN14 ....76 B3
Rushmere Cres NN1 .....160 B6
Rushmere Rd NN1 ....160 B5
Rushmere Way
  Northampton NN1 ....160 B6
  Rushden NN10 ....132 B4
Rushmills NN4 ....160 C6
Rushton Prim Sch NN14 .52 C2
Rushton Rd
  Desborough NN14 ....51 A8
  Rothwell NN14 ....70 E8
  Wilbarston LE16 ....34 C8
Rushton Triangular Lodge★
  NN14 ....52 A2
Rushwell Cl NN14 ....94 B3
Rushy End NN4 ....175 B6
Ruskin Ave NN8 ....129 C4
Ruskin Jun & Inf Sch
  NN8 ....129 C3
Ruskin Rd
  Daventry NN11 ....153 C8
  Northampton NN2 ....141 C4
Russell Cl NN10 ....132 B2
Russell Fst Sch MK11 .....229 D5
Russell Hill PE8 ....8 A6
Russell Rise NN7 ....155 C5
Russell Sq NN3 ....142 C6
Russell St Kettering NN16 .72 C2
  Stony Stratford MK11 .....229 D5
Russell Way NN10 ....132 B6
Russelsheim Way CV22 .241 C7
Russet Dr NN3 ....143 A2
Russett Cl LE16 ....31 F5
Ruth Gdns NN16 ....72 E3
Rutherford Ct NN17 ....22 B1
Rutherford Dr NN8 ....129 A5
Rutherford Way NN11 .....134 F4
Rutherglen Rd NN17 ....36 F7
Rutland Cl NN17 ....36 B7
Rutland Ct NN14 ....50 F4
Rutland Rd PE8 ....241 F5
Rutland St NN16 ....72 C3
Rutland Wlk
  Market Harborough LE16 .31 F5
  Northampton NN3 ....142 B7
Rycroft Cl NN8 ....129 D5
Rydal NN8 ....129 B3
Rydal Mt NN3 ....142 C3
Rydalside Kettering NN15 .72 D1
  Northampton NN4 ....158 F3
Ryder Ct NN18 ....52 F8
Ryder View NN8 ....129 C7
Rye Cl NN10 ....148 C8
Ryeburn Way NN8 ....129 E5
Ryebury Hill NN8 ....111 E2
Ryefields NN6 ....124 E8
Ryehill Cl
  Irthlingborough NN9 .....131 E8
  Isham NN14 ....91 E1
  Long Buckby NN6 ....121 A3
  Northampton NN5 ....140 C2
Ryehill Ct NN5 ....140 C2
Ryehill Rd NN3 ....142 F3
Ryeland MK11 ....229 E6
Ryeland Rd NN15 ....158 A8
Ryeland Way NN5 ....140 A1
Ryelands Mid Sch NN5 .158 A8
Ryhall Rd PE9 ....241 F5
Ryland Rd Moulton NN3 .142 C8
  Northampton NN2 ....141 E2
Rylands Cl LE16 ....32 B3
Ryle Dr NN8 ....129 A4
Rylstone The NN8 ....129 B4
Ryngwell Cl NN6 ....106 B1

S

Sackville St
  Kettering NN16 ....72 A4
  Raunds NN9 ....114 D6
  Thrapston NN14 ....76 D2
Sacrewell Farm & Ctry Ctr★
  PE8 ....8 B5
Saddleback Rd NN5 ....158 D6
Saddlers Sq NN3 ....142 E4
Saddlers The NN4 ....175 F3

Saddlers Way NN9 ....114 B5
Saffron Cl NN4 ....175 D5
Saffron Rd NN10 ....132 B6
Sage Cl NN3 ....142 E4
Saimon Cl NN13 ....233 E8
St Alban's Cl
  Kettering NN15 ....73 A1
  Northampton NN2 ....142 B3
St Alban's Rd NN3 ....142 B3
St Albans Pl NN29 ....146 D2
St Amandas Cl NN16 ....72 F2
St Andrew's CE Prim Sch
  NN16 ....72 A4
St Andrew's Cl NN14 ....77 D3
St Andrew's Ct NN14 ....90 B4
St Andrew's Ho 9 NN1 .159 C6
St Andrew's Hospl NN1 .159 F6
St Andrew's La NN14 ....93 A7
St Andrew's Rd
  East Haddon NN6 ....122 D5
  Northampton NN2 ....159 B7
St Andrew's St
  Kettering NN16 ....72 B3
  Northampton NN1 ....159 C6
St Andrew's Wlk NN17 .....37 B6
St Andrews Benn CE Prim
  Sch CV21 ....241 F9
St Andrews Cl
  Broughton NN14 ....90 B4
  Great Easton LE16 ....20 D7
St Andrews Cres
  Rugby CV22 ....98 A8
  Wellingborough NN8 .....129 E2
St Andrews Dr NN11 ....135 E3
St Andrews La NN14 ....77 D4
St Andrews Way NN14 .....90 B4
St Ann's Ct PE8 ....41 F5
St Anne's Rd
  Kettering NN15 ....73 A1
  Rugby CV22 ....241 A6
St Annes Cl
  Brackley NN13 ....233 D8
  Daventry NN11 ....153 C8
St Anthony's Hill NN14 .....51 A2
St Anthony's Rd NN15 .....72 F1
St Anthonys Cl NN11 .....153 B8
St Augustin Way NN15 .....135 D1
St Augustine's Cl NN15 .73 A1
St Augustine's RC Prim Sch
  PE9 ....241 E5
St Barnabas CE Sch
  NN8 ....129 F4
St Barnabas Ho 10 NN1 .159 C6
St Barnabas St NN8 ....129 F4
St Barnabas' Cl NN15 .....73 A1
St Bartholemews Ho 6
  NN1 ....159 C6
St Bartholomew's Cl
  NN15 ....73 A1
St Benedicts Mount
  NN4 ....158 E2
St Bernards Cl NN16 ....72 F1
St Botolph Gn PE8 ....28 E7
St Botolph's Rd NN15 .....91 F7
St Brendan's Jun & Inf Sch
  NN18 ....36 B6
St Catharine's Rd NN15 .73 A1
St Catherines Cl NN11 .153 B8
St Cecilia's Cl NN15 ....72 F1
St Chad's Cl NN15 ....73 A1
St Christopher's Cl
  NN3 ....160 B7
St Christopher's Dr PE8 .42 B4
St Christopher's Wlk
  NN3 ....160 B7
St Clement's PE9 ....241 C3
St Clements Cl NN15 ....91 B7
St Crispin Ave NN8 ....129 F2
St Crispin Cl NN15 ....92 C3
St Crispin Rd NN6 ....144 F4
St David's Cl NN15 ....72 F1
St David's Ct NN13 ....234 A8
St David's Rd
  Brixworth NN6 ....106 A1
  Northampton NN2 ....141 C2
  Rushden NN10 ....131 D3
St Davids Cl NN6 ....106 B1
St Davids RC Mid Sch
  NN2 ....141 C3
St Dunstan's Cl NN15 .....91 F8
St Dunstans Rise NN4 .....158 E1
St Edmund's Hospl NN1 159 E7
St Edmund's Rd NN1 .....159 E6
St Edmund's St NN1 ....159 E6
St Edmunds Cl NN11 .....153 C7
St Edward's RC Prim Sch
  NN15 ....91 E7
St Emilion Cl NN5 ....139 F1
St Francis Ave NN5 ....159 A8
St Francis' Cl NN15 ....73 A1
St George's Ave NN2 .....159 D8
St George's CE Prim Sch
  PE9 ....241 E5
St George's Pl NN2 ....159 C8
St George's Sq PE9 ....241 E3
St George's St
  Northampton NN1 ....159 C7
  Stamford PE9 ....241 E3
St George's Way NN10 .131 F3
St Georges Ave
  Rugby CV22 ....98 A8
  Stamford PE9 ....241 F4
St Georges Cl NN12 .....203 C5
St Georges Ho 2 NN1 .159 C6
St Gilbert CE Prim Sch
  PE9 ....241 D3

St Gilbert's CE Prim Sch
  PE9 . . . . .241 C3
St Giles Mews MK11 . . . .229 D6
St Giles' Cl NN15 . . . . .73 A1
St Giles' Sq NN1 . . . . .159 D5
St Giles' St NN1 . . . . .159 D6
St Giles' Terr NN1 . . . . . . .159 D6
St Giles's Cl NN14 . . . . .51 A3
St Gregory's RC Lower Sch
  NN3 . . . . .142 C3
St Gregory's Rd NN3 . . . .142 C3
St Helens Cl NN6 . . . . .84 D4
St Hilda's Cl NN11 . . . . . .153 C8
St Hughes Cl NN11 . . . . .153 C8
St James Cl
  2 Daventry NN11 . . . . . .135 C1
  Hanslope MK19 . . . . .207 A2
St James Inf Sch NN11 . .135 C1
St James Mill Rd E NN1 159 B4
St James Rd
  Brackley NN13 . . . . .233 F5
  Corby NN18 . . . . .37 A6
St James Ret Pk NN1 . . .159 B5
St James St NN11 . . . . . .135 C1
St James' CE Lower Sch
  NN5 . . . . .159 A6
St James' Cl
  Kettering NN15 . . . . .92 A8
  Rushden NN10 . . . . .132 C4
St James' Cres NN14 . . . .76 E2
St James' Lake Nature
  Reserve★ NN13 . . . . . . .233 E6
St James' Mill Rd NN5 . .159 A4
St James' Park Rd NN5 .159 A6
St James' Rd NN5 . . . . . .159 A6
St John St CV21 . . . . . . .241 C9
St John's Ave NN2 . . . . . .141 C6
St John's Ho **8** NN1 . . . .159 C6
St John's Cl MK19 . . . . . .228 B4
St John's Pl NN17 . . . . . . .37 B6
St John's Rd
  Banbury OX16 . . . . .240 C7
  Kettering NN15 . . . . .91 F8
St John's Sq NN11 . . . . . .135 C2
St John's St
  Northampton NN1 . . . . . .159 D5
  Stamford PE9 . . . . .241 D3
  Wellingborough NN8 . . . .129 F5
St John's Terr NN1 . . . . . .159 D5
St John's Way NN7 . . . . .177 A2
St John's Wlk NN3 . . . . . .142 D1
St Johns Cl CV22 . . . . . . .98 E8
St Johns Cl
  Daventry NN11 . . . . .153 B8
  Rothersthorpe NN7 . . . . .174 A6
St Johns Ct NN1 . . . . . . .159 D5
St Johns Rd NN12 . . . . . .189 E4
St Joseph's Cl NN15 . . . . .73 A1
St Joseph's RC Prim Sch
  LE16 . . . . .31 E3
St Josephs Cl MK46 . . . .195 F4
St Julien Cl NN5 . . . . . . .140 A2
St Katharine's Way
  NN29 . . . . .131 B1
St Katherine's Ct **25**
  NN1 . . . . .159 C6
St Katherine's Sq **27**
  NN1 . . . . .159 C6
St Katherine's St **2**
  NN1 . . . . .159 C5
St Laurence Way NN9 . . .113 F4
St Lawrence CE Jun Sch
  NN12 . . . . .203 C5
St Lawrence Ct **12** NN1 .159 E6
St Lawrence Ho **3** NN1 159 C6
St Lawrence Lower Sch
  NN10 . . . . .148 A5
St Lawrence Rd NN12 . . .203 C5
St Lawrence Rd S NN12 203 C4
St Lawrence Wlk NN10 . .148 B5
St Leonard's CE Prim Sch
  OX16 . . . . .240 F8
St Leonard's Cl
  Banbury OX16 . . . . .240 E8
  Kettering NN15 . . . . .72 F1
St Leonard's Rd NN4 . . . .159 C3
St Leonard's St PE9 . . . . .241 E3
St Leonards Cl CV47 . . . .166 D8
St Leonards Ct NN4 . . . . .159 C3
St Luke's CE Lower Sch
  NN5 . . . . .158 C6
St Luke's Cl NN15 . . . . . . .92 A8
St Luke's Ho **12** NN1 . . .159 C6
St Luke's Hospl LE16 . . . .31 C5
St Luke's Rd NN18 . . . . . .37 A5
St Lukes Cl NN6 . . . . . . .105 B1
St Magdalenes Rd NN15 .72 F2
St Margaret's Gdns **3**
  NN5 . . . . .140 F1
St Margarets Rd NN12 . . .132 A1
St Marie's RC Inf Sch
  CV22 . . . . .241 C7
St Marie's RC Jun Sch
  CV22 . . . . .241 B7
St Mark's Cl
  Kettering NN15 . . . . .73 A1
  Rushden NN10 . . . . .131 E2
St Mark's Cres NN2 . . . . .141 B6
St Mark's Rd NN18 . . . . . .37 A5
St Marks Ho **7** NN1 . . . .159 C6
St Martin's Cl PE9 . . . . . .241 E2
St Martins Cl NN2 . . . . . .141 C4
St Martins Ho **1** NN1 . . .159 C6
St Martins Yd **3** LE16 . . .31 E3
St Martyn's Way NN7 . . .155 B3

St Mary & St Giles CE Mid
  Sch MK11 . . . . .229 E6
St Mary's Ave
  Finedon NN9 . . . . .111 F5
  Rushden NN10 . . . . .132 B1
  Stony Stratford MK11 . . .229 E6
St Mary's CE Prim Sch
  Banbury OX16 . . . . .240 C8
  Burton Latimer NN15 . . . .92 C2
  Kettering NN16 . . . . .72 C2
St Mary's Cl
  Nassington PE8 . . . . .15 E5
  Priors Hardwick CV47 . . .166 A5
St Mary's Ct Finedon NN9 111 E5
  Market Harborough LE16 . .32 A4
  22 Northampton NN1 . .159 C6
St Mary's Hill PE9 . . . . . .241 D3
St Mary's Hospl NN15 . . . .72 C1
St Mary's Paddock NN8 130 C4
St Mary's Pl
  Market Harborough LE16 . .31 F3
  Stamford PE9 . . . . .241 E3
St Mary's RC Lower Sch
  NN5 . . . . .140 F1
St Mary's RC Mid Sch
  NN3 . . . . .142 C3
St Mary's RC Prim Sch
  NN11 . . . . .182 F2
St Mary's Rd
  Bozeat NN29 . . . . .164 D2
  Kettering NN15 . . . . .72 C1
  Market Harborough LE16 . .31 F3
St Mary's St
  Northampton NN1 . . . . . .159 C6
  Stamford PE9 . . . . .241 D3
St Mary's Way
  Nassington PE8 . . . . .15 E5
  Roade NN7 . . . . .191 D5
  Weedon NN7 . . . . .155 B3
St Marys Cl
  Thrapston NN14 . . . . .76 F3
  Woodnewton PE8 . . . . . . .14 E2
St Marys Ct NN7 . . . . . . .173 F2
St Marys Hill PE8 . . . . . . .14 E2
St Marys Rd NN29 . . . . . .146 E2
St Matthew's Bloxam CE Prim
  Sch CV22 . . . . .241 A7
St Matthew's Par NN2 . .141 F4
St Matthew's Rd NN15 . . .73 A1
St Matthews St CV21 . . .241 C8
St Michael's Ave NN1 . . .159 E7
St Michael's Ct NN7 . . . .205 F8
St Michael's La NN29 . . .146 D2
St Michael's Mount
  NN1 . . . . .159 E7
St Michael's Rd
  Kettering NN15 . . . . .91 C8
  Northampton NN1 . . . . . .159 D6
St Michaels Gdns NN15 . .91 C8
St Nicholas Cl
  Kettering NN15 . . . . .72 F2
  Market Harborough LE16 . .31 F2
St Nicholas Ct NN29 . . . .145 E6
St Nicholas Rd NN29 . . . .145 D6
St Nicholas Way
  Islip NN14 . . . . .76 B3
  Market Harborough LE16 . .31 F2
St Oswald's Cl NN15 . . . . .91 F8
St Osyths La PE8 . . . . . . .42 A5
St Patrick St **11** NN1 . . .159 C7
St Patrick's RC Prim Sch
  NN18 . . . . .36 D4
St Paul's CE Lower Sch
  NN2 . . . . .159 C8
St Paul's Ct
  Kettering NN15 . . . . .72 B1
  Stony Stratford MK11 . . .229 D6
St Paul's Rd NN2 . . . . . . .159 C8
St Paul's St PE9 . . . . .241 E3
St Paul's Terr NN2 . . . . . .159 C8
St Peter's Ave
  Kettering NN16 . . . . .72 C1
  Rushden NN10 . . . . .131 F3
St Peter's CE Jun Sch
  NN9 . . . . .114 E6
St Peter's Cl NN14 . . . . . . .37 F2
St Peter's Gate NN13 . . .234 A7
St Peter's Gdns NN3 . . . .142 D1
St Peter's Hill PE9 . . . . . .241 D3
St Peter's Ho **20** NN1 . .159 C6
St Peter's Ind Sch NN3 .143 A3
St Peter's Rd
  Brackley NN13 . . . . .233 F8
  Rugby CV21 . . . . .241 E8
St Peter's Sch NN15 . . . . .91 B8
St Peter's St
  Northampton NN1 . . . . . .159 B5
  Stamford PE9 . . . . .241 D2
St Peter's Vale PE9 . . . . .241 D2
St Peter's Way
  Corby NN17 . . . . .37 A6
  Irthlingborough NN9 . . . . .112 F2
  Northampton NN1 . . . . . .159 C5
  Weedon NN7 . . . . .155 B3
St Peters Cl NN11 . . . . . .153 B8
St Peters Ct NN9 . . . . . . .114 D6
St Peters Rd PE9 . . . . .41 F7
St Peters Sq **12** NN1 . . .159 C5
St Peters Way NN7 . . . . .161 F6
St Peters Wlk **5** NN1 . . .159 C5
St Philip's Cl NN15 . . . . . .73 A1
St Rumbold's La MK18 . .240 C3
St Rumbolds Dr OX17 . . .231 A5
St Saviour's Rd NN15 . . . .73 A1
St Simon's Cl NN15 . . . . . .73 A1
St Stephen's Rd NN15 . . . .73 A1
St Stephens Ho **9** NN1 .159 C6
St Swithins Cl NN15 . . . . .72 F2

St Theresa's Cl NN15 . . . .72 F1
St Thomas More RC Prim Sch
  NN16 . . . . .71 F1
St Thomas Rd NN7 . . . . .161 D3
St Valentine's Cl NN15 . . .72 F1
St Vincents Ave NN15 . . . .72 F2
St Wilfrids Rd PE8 . . . . . . .41 F7
Salcey Ave NN7 . . . . . . .192 D2
Salcey Cl
  2 Daventry NN11 . . . . .135 B4
  Hartwell NN7 . . . . .192 E2
  Kettering NN15 . . . . .92 A5
Salcey Forest Trail★
  NN7 . . . . .192 F4
Salcey Forest Trail(Rose
  Copse)★ NN7 . . . . .193 B2
Salcey Rise NN7 . . . . . . .177 B1
Salcey St NN4 . . . . .159 C2
Salcombe Rd NN18 . . . . . .36 E4
Salem Cl NN6 . . . . .121 A3
Salem La **9** NN8 . . . . . .130 A5
Salen Cl NN15 . . . . .92 B5
Salford Cl NN6 . . . . .64 E6
Salisbury Rd NN8 . . . . . .130 C5
Salisbury St
  Kettering NN16 . . . . .72 C4
  Northampton NN2 . . . . . .159 C8
Sallow Ave NN3 . . . . . . .143 C3
Sallow Rd NN17 . . . . .22 E1
Salmons La OX17 . . . . . .220 B8
Salt Pikes NN6 . . . . .125 B8
Salthouse Rd NN4 . . . . . .160 C2
Saltwell Sq **5** NN3 . . . .143 C2
Samuel Pl NN17 . . . . .37 A8
Samuels Cl NN9 . . . . .113 F3
Samwell Way NN4 . . . . . .158 C1
Sandby Rd NN18 . . . . .36 E4
Sandell Cl OX16 . . . . .240 C7
Sanders Cl
  Braunston NN11 . . . . . . .118 B1
  Wellingborough NN8 . . . .111 B1
Sanders La NN12 . . . . . . .217 D3
Sanders Lodge Ind Est
  NN10 . . . . .131 D3
Sanders Rd NN8 . . . . . . .111 B1
Sanders Terr NN6 . . . . . .121 B4
Sanderson Cl NN15 . . . . . .91 A8
Sandfield Cl NN3 . . . . . . .142 B6
Sandhill Rd **2** NN5 . . . .159 A6
Sandhills Cl NN3 . . . . . . .105 A1
Sandhills Cl NN2 . . . . . . .141 B6
Sandhills Rd NN2 . . . . . . .141 B6
Sandhurst Cl NN4 . . . . . .175 B8
Sandhurst Dr MK18 . . . . .240 C2
Sandiland Rd NN3 . . . . . .142 B2
Sandlands Ave NN14 . . . . .55 F7
Sandlands Cl NN14 . . . . . .55 F7
Sandover NN4 . . . . .175 D6
Sandown Rd CV21 . . . . . .241 E9
Sandpiper Cl NN15 . . . . . .92 A2
Sandpiper La NN8 . . . . . .130 A7
Sandringham Cl
  Brackley NN13 . . . . .233 E7
  Northampton NN1 . . . . . .160 B7
  Rushden NN10 . . . . .132 A1
  Stamford PE9 . . . . .241 D5
  Towcester NN12 . . . . . . .203 C4
  Wellingborough NN8 . . . .129 E2
Sandringham Ct NN15 . . . .91 D5
Sandringham Rd
  Kings Sutton OX17 . . . . .230 F5
  Northampton NN1 . . . . . .160 A7
Sandringham Way LE16 . .32 B3
Sands Cl NN12 . . . . .172 D1
Sandy Cl
  Buckingham MK18 . . . . .240 F3
  Wellingborough NN8 . . . .129 F6
Sandy Hill La NN3 . . . . . .126 C2
Sandy La
  Church Brampton NN6 . . .140 D8
  Harpole NN7 . . . . .157 E4
  Northampton NN5 . . . . . .139 F2
  Rugby CV21 . . . . .241 A8
Sandyhome Rd NN12 . . . .203 C5
Saneco La NN6 . . . . .106 B3
Sansom Ct NN3 . . . . .142 D4
Sansome Cl NN7 . . . . . . .177 B3
Saplings The NN16 . . . . . .72 C6
Sapphire Cl NN15 . . . . . . .72 C1
Sarek Pk NN4 . . . . .174 F7
Sargeants La NN4 . . . . . .175 C4
Sargent Rd NN18 . . . . . . .36 E4
Sargent's Ct PE9 . . . . . . .241 C4
Sarrington Rd NN17 . . . . .36 F8
Sartoris Rd NN10 . . . . . . .131 F2
Saruman La NN3 . . . . . . .143 B6
Sassoon Cl NN8 . . . . .129 C6
Sassoon Mews NN8 . . . . .129 B6
Saunders Cl NN16 . . . . . . .72 B1
Saunton Rd CV22 . . . . . .241 B6
Savill Cl NN4 . . . . .175 C7
Sawyers Cres NN9 . . . . . .133 B8
Saxby Cres NN8 . . . . . . .130 C4
Saxilby Cl NN18 . . . . .36 C4
Saxon Acre NN13 . . . . . .233 F7
Saxon Ave NN4 . . . . .175 E3
Saxon Cl
  Desborough NN14 . . . . . .51 A3
  Market Harborough LE16 . .32 C6
Saxon Dale NN15 . . . . . . .72 C6
Saxon Ho NN6 . . . . .106 B2
Saxon Rise
  Earls Barton NN6 . . . . . .144 E3
  Irchester NN29 . . . . .147 C8
  Northampton NN5 . . . . . .158 B7
Saxon St NN3 . . . . .142 B1
Saxon Way NN9 . . . . . . .114 E6
Saxon Way E NN18 . . . . . .53 A8

Saxon Way W NN18 . . . . .52 F8
Saxonlea Cl NN10 . . . . . .131 E3
Scaldwell Rd
  Brixworth NN6 . . . . .106 C4
  Old NN6 . . . . .107 C7
Scapa Cl NN17 . . . . .36 C8
Scarborough St NN9 . . . .112 E2
Scarborough Wlk NN18 . . .36 B4
Scarletwell St NN1 . . . . . .159 B6
Scarplands The NN5 . . . . .158 C6
Scharpwell NN9 . . . . .112 C3
Scholars Ct NN1 . . . . . . .159 D5
Scholars Row NN14 . . . . . .89 B4
School Cl
  Braunston NN11 . . . . . . .118 D1
  Greens Norton NN12 . . . .202 D8
  Yelvertoft NN6 . . . . .82 A4
School End OX17 . . . . . . .237 C7
School Farm Yd LE16 . . . .18 B3
School Gdns CV21 . . . . . . .80 A1
School Hill
  Irchester NN29 . . . . .147 B8
  Middleton LE16 . . . . .35 C8
  Newnham NN11 . . . . . . .153 D4
School La Abthorpe NN12 202 A2
  Badby NN11 . . . . .152 F3
  Banbury OX16 . . . . .240 C8
  Barrowden LE15 . . . . .3 F5
  Braybrooke LE16 . . . . . . .49 F5
  Buckingham MK18 . . . . .240 C3
  Bythorn PE28 . . . . .97 D4
  Castlethorpe MK19 . . . . .218 F5
  Cottingham LE16 . . . . . . .20 C1
  Denford NN14 . . . . .95 C6
  Elton PE8 . . . . .28 D8
  Evenley NN13 . . . . .233 F2
  Everdon NN11 . . . . .170 A8
  Eydon NN11 . . . . .184 C1
  Greens Norton NN12 . . . .202 D8
  Hannington NN6 . . . . . . .108 C2
  Harpole NN7 . . . . .157 B6
  Hartwell NN7 . . . . .192 D2
  Husbands Bosworth LE17 . .45 E5
  Irchester NN29 . . . . .147 A8
  Islip NN14 . . . . .76 B2
  Kettering NN16 . . . . .72 B2
  Kislingbury NN7 . . . . . . .157 D4
  Little Harrowden NN9 . . . .110 C4
  Lubenham LE16 . . . . .30 F3
  Market Harborough LE16 . .31 E3
  Morcott LE15 . . . . .3 A6
  Moulton NN3 . . . . .126 C1
  Naseby NN6 . . . . .85 B8
  Priors Marston CV47 . . . .166 D8
  Quinton NN7 . . . . .176 B1
  Rothwell NN14 . . . . .70 D7
  Scaldwell NN6 . . . . .106 F6
  Swinford LE17 . . . . .62 B4
  Titchmarsh NN14 . . . . . . .77 C4
  Wappenham NN12 . . . . .213 B8
  Warmington PE8 . . . . . . .28 B3
  Weldon NN17 . . . . .38 B8
  Wilbarston LE16 . . . . .34 C5
  Yardley Gobion NN12 . . . .217 E6
  Yelvertoft NN6 . . . . .82 B4
School Pl NN18 . . . . .36 D5
School Rd Gretton NN17 . .10 B1
  Irchester NN29 . . . . .147 A8
  Mawsley Village NN14 . . .89 B4
  Pattishall NN12 . . . . .188 F8
  Spratton NN6 . . . . .105 B1
School St Daventry NN11 135 A2
  Rugby CV21 . . . . .80 A1
  Sulgrave OX17 . . . . .210 F7
  Woodford Halse NN11 . . .184 C6
School View OX16 . . . . . .240 F8
Schoolfield Gr CV21 . . . . .241 B8
Scirocco Cl NN3 . . . . .141 E6
Scoborough Rd LE16,
  LE17 . . . . .30 A1
Scotgate
  Harringworth NN17 . . . . . .10 F7
  Stamford PE9 . . . . .241 D3
Scotia Cl NN4 . . . . .160 C2
Scotland End LE16 . . . . . .31 F1
Scotland Rd LE16 . . . . . . .32 A2
Scotland St NN16 . . . . . . .72 C3
Scotney Cl **1** NN4 . . . . .175 C8
Scotney Way NN14 . . . . . .76 E2
Scots Mere NN9 . . . . . . .112 D3
Scott Ave NN14 . . . . .70 E7
Scott Cl Daventry NN11 . .135 C4
  Market Harborough LE16 . .31 E5
  Ravensthorpe NN6 . . . . .103 D1
Scott Rd Corby NN17 . . . .37 A6
  Kettering NN16 . . . . .72 C5
  Wellingborough NN8 . . . .129 C3
Scotter Wlk NN14 . . . . . . .36 C4
Scotts La LE16 . . . . .34 C5
Scriveners La NN12 . . . . .216 A8
Scrivens Hill NN11 . . . . . .184 D6
Scully Cl **8** NN4 . . . . . .175 E7
Scythe Rd NN11 . . . . . . .135 C6
Seabroke Ave CV22 . . . . .241 B8
Seaford Wlk NN18 . . . . . .36 B5
Seagrave Ct NN3 . . . . . . .143 B5
Seagrave St NN15 . . . . . . .91 C8
Sears Cl NN7 . . . . .155 E6
Sears Ho NN11 . . . . .159 F7
Seaton Cres NN18 . . . . . . .36 E4
Seaton Dr NN3 . . . . .142 F1
Seaton Rd Barrowden LE15 .3 C4
  Harringworth NN17 . . . . . .10 E8
  Stamford PE9 . . . . .241 D2
Second Ave NN8 . . . . . . .129 D3
Second La NN5 . . . . .158 F6
Second St NN13 . . . . . . .238 E6
Sedbergh Rd NN18 . . . . . .36 C4

Sedgemoor Ct NN11 . . . .135 C6
Sedgemoor Way NN11 . . .135 C6
Sedgwick Ct NN3 . . . . . . .142 F3
Sedlescombe Pk CV22 . . . .98 A8
Seedfield Cl NN3 . . . . . . .142 E1
Selby Cl LE16 . . . . .48 E8
Selby Cl NN15 . . . . .91 F8
Selby Gdns NN29 . . . . . . .164 C2
Selby Wlk NN18 . . . . .36 B5
Selsey Rd NN18 . . . . .36 B5
Selston Wlk NN3 . . . . . . .160 D7
Selwyn Cl NN11 . . . . .153 C7
Selwyn Rd PE9 . . . . .241 C5
Semilong Ho **4** NN2 . . .159 C7
Semilong Rd NN2 . . . . . . .159 C8
Senna Dr NN12 . . . . .203 C8
Sentinel Rd NN4 . . . . . . .158 E1
Sentry Cl **6** NN4 . . . . . .175 E7
Senwick Dr NN8 . . . . . . .130 C4
Senwick Rd NN8 . . . . . . .130 C4
Setchells Yd PE8 . . . . .41 F5
Settlersfields NN15 . . . . . .91 A7
Seven Sisters Cl NN13 . . .221 B4
Severn Cl NN8 . . . . .129 C6
Severn Ct NN15 . . . . .92 B2
Severn Dr NN5 . . . . .140 F2
Severn Ho PE8 . . . . .42 A6
Severn The NN11 . . . . . . .135 A1
Severn Way NN16 . . . . . . .72 A5
Severn Wlk NN17 . . . . . . .21 C1
Sewter Gdns PE8 . . . . . . .15 E6
Sexton Cl NN11 . . . . .135 B3
Seymour Cl PE8 . . . . .41 E7
Seymour St NN5 . . . . . . .159 A6
Shackleton Cl NN14 . . . . .70 E7
Shackleton Dr NN11 . . . .135 C5
Shades The OX16 . . . . . . .240 C7
Shadowfax Dr NN3 . . . . .143 C5
Shaftesbury Rd NN18 . . . .36 B6
Shaftesbury St NN16 . . . . .72 C2
Shakespeare Ave NN11 . .135 B2
Shakespeare Dr NN15 . . . .92 A2
Shakespeare Rd
  Kettering NN16 . . . . .72 B5
  Northampton NN1 . . . . . .159 E7
  Rushden NN10 . . . . .131 E2
  Wellingborough NN8 . . . .129 C4
Shakespeare Way NN17 . .36 D8
Shale End NN5 . . . . .140 A3
Shannon Cl NN10 . . . . . . .132 D3
Shannon Ct NN18 . . . . . . .36 E4
Shannon Way NN15 . . . . . .92 B2
Shap Gn NN3 . . . . .142 C4
Shard Cl NN4 . . . . .175 D6
Sharman Cl NN11 . . . . . .135 C5
Sharman Rd
  Northampton NN5 . . . . . .159 A5
  Wellingborough NN8 . . . .129 F4
Sharman Way NN14 . . . . .70 F7
Sharmans Cl NN7 . . . . . . .162 A6
Sharpes La NN6 . . . . .121 B4
Sharplands NN7 . . . . .163 D5
Sharrow Pl **7** NN3 . . . .143 D2
Sharwood Terr NN3 . . . . .147 B8
Shatterstone **2** NN4 . . .175 D6
Shaw Cl NN8 . . . . .129 B5
Shawell Rd LE17 . . . . .62 A4
Sheaf Cl NN5 . . . . .140 B2
Sheaf St NN11 . . . . .135 C1
Shearwater La NN8 . . . . .130 A7
Shedfield Way NN4 . . . . .175 C6
Sheep Market PE9 . . . . . .241 D3
Sheep St Kettering NN16 . .72 B1
  Northampton NN1 . . . . . .159 C6
  Rugby CV21 . . . . .241 C8
  Wellingborough NN8 . . . .130 A4
Sheerwater Dr NN3 . . . . .143 D3
Sheffield Cl NN9 . . . . .114 C5
Sheffield Way NN6 . . . . . .144 E3
Sheffield Wlk NN18 . . . . . .36 B4
Sheila Pl NN16 . . . . .72 E4
Sheldons La NN6 . . . . . . .108 A5
Shelford Cl NN3 . . . . .143 B5
Shelland Cl LE16 . . . . .32 C2
Shelley Cl Daventry NN11 135 B2
  Stamford PE9 . . . . .241 A4
  Towcester NN12 . . . . . . .203 B5
Shelley Dr Corby NN17 . . .21 D1
  Higham Ferrers NN10 . . . .132 B5
Shelley Rd Kettering NN16 72 C5
  Wellingborough NN8 . . . .129 B4
Shelley St NN2 . . . . .141 F1
Shelleycotes Rd NN6 . . . .106 A1
Shelmerdine Rise NN9 . . .114 D6
Shelsley Dr NN3 . . . . .141 F4
Shelton Ct Corby NN17 . . .22 E2
  Wollaston NN29 . . . . .146 D2
Shelton Rd Corby NN17 . . .22 E2
  Raunds NN9 . . . . .114 E4
Shepherd Cl NN2 . . . . . . .141 A5
Shepherds Hill NN29 . . . .146 F1
Shepherds Wlk
  Bugbrooke NN7 . . . . .173 A6
  Harpole NN7 . . . . .157 C6
Sheppard Way NN12 . . . .213 B8
Shepperton Cl
  Castlethorpe MK19 . . . . .218 F5
  Northampton NN3 . . . . . .143 C2
Sheppey La NN7 . . . . . . .177 B3
Shepton Cl NN18 . . . . .36 A6
Sheraton Cl NN3 . . . . . . .142 C2
Sherborne Way NN14 . . . .76 E2
Sherborne Wlk NN18 . . . . .36 A6
Sheriff Rd
  Northampton NN1 . . . . . .159 F7
  Rugby CV21 . . . . .241 E8
Sherrard Rd LE16 . . . . . . .31 E5
Sherwood Ave NN2 . . . . .140 F6

Sherwood Cl Corby NN17 .36 E8
Stamford PE9 ....241 B3
Sherwood Dr
Daventry NN11 ....135 B4
Kettering NN15 ....91 F5
Shetland Way NN17 .....21 C1
Shieling Ct NN18 ......36 A1
Ship La PE8 ....41 F4
Shipton Way NN10 ....131 C3
Shire Pl NN3 ....143 C5
Shire Rd NN17 ....21 C1
Shires Bsns Pk The
NN13 ....234 A6
Shires Rd NN13 ....234 A6
Shirley Rd NN10 ......132 B3
Shoal Creek NN4 ......175 C5
Shoe Maker Cl NN12 ..188 F7
Shoemakers Ct NN10 ..132 B3
Shop La NN7 ....179 B6
Shoreham Ct NN18 .....36 B5
Short Cl PE8 ....28 B3
Short La Cogenhoe NN7 .162 A6
Thorpe Malsor NN14 ....71 B3
Wellingborough NN8 ...129 F5
Short Massey NN46 ....195 E5
Short Stocks NN10 ....132 D2
Shortlands Cl NN13 ...211 F3
Shortlands The NN9 ...113 B5
Shortwoods Cl NN9 ....114 D5
Shotwell Mill La NN14 .70 D8
Showsley Rd NN12 ....204 D8
Shrewsbury Ave LE16 ..32 B2
Shropshire Cl LE16 ....31 E4
Shropshire Pl LE16 ....31 E4
Shrubberies The NN14 .94 D7
Shrubfield Gr NN17 ....36 F8
Shuckburgh Cres CV22 .98 C3
Shuckburgh Rd CV47 ..166 D8
Shurville Rd NN6 .....144 F3
Shutlanger Rd NN12 ..190 F1
Sibbertoft Rd
Clipston LE16 ....47 E1
Husbands Bosworth LE17 .45 F2
Marston Trussell LE16 ..47 B6
Sibley Rd NN11 ....112 B4
Siddeley Way NN3 ....134 F3
Siddons Cl PE8 ....41 E7
Siddons Way NN3 ....126 D1
Sidebrook Ct NN3 ....142 F5
Sidegate La NN8 .....130 F8
Sidings Ind Ctr The
NN13 ....234 A8
Sidings The
Irthlingborough NN9 ..131 D8
Rugby CV21 ....241 D9
Sidlaw Ct MK11 ......229 F4
Sidmouth Wlk NN18 ...36 B5
Sidney Rd Rugby CV22 .98 D8
Woodford Halse NN11 .184 C6
Sillswood MK46 ......195 E4
Silver St Abthorpe NN12 .201 F2
Brixworth NN6 ....106 B3
Broughton NN14 ....90 A5
Chacombe OX17 ......208 E4
Kettering NN16 ....72 B2
Northampton NN1 ....159 C6
Stony Stratford MK11 .229 D5
Walgrave NN6 ....108 A5
Wellingborough NN8 ..130 A4
Silver St N OX17 .....208 E4
Silverdale Gr NN10 ...131 E2
Silverdale Rd NN3 ...142 D2
Silverstone CE Jun Sch
NN12 ....214 D4
Silverstone Cl NN2 ...141 D5
Silverstone Inf Sch
NN12 ....214 D5
Silverstone Motor Racing
Circuit★ NN12 .....225 E8
Silverwood Ct NN15 ...91 C8
Silverwood Rd NN15 ...91 C8
Simborough Way LE16 .32 B3
Simon de Senlis Ct
NN1 ....159 D7
Simon de Senlis Lower Sch
NN4 ....175 B8
Simon's Wlk
[17] Northampton NN1 .159 C6
Pattishall NN12 ......172 D1
Simpson Ave NN10 ...132 C7
Simpson Barracks NN4 .175 D6
Sinclair Ave OX16 ....240 A9
Sinclair Dr Banbury OX16 240 A9
Wellingborough NN8 ..129 B6
Sir Christopher Hatton Sch
NN8 ....130 A6
Sir Georges La OX17 ..230 C1
Sir John Brown Ct NN16 .72 A2
Sir John Pascoe Way
NN5 ....158 C8
Sissinghurst Dr NN14 .76 F2
Siward View NN5 ....140 D2
Six Cotts MK18 ......226 E5
Six Willows NN9 .....110 B3
Sixth St NN13 ....238 E7
Skagerrak Cl NN18 ....36 A2
Skawle Ct NN3 ......142 F3
Skeffington Ct NN14 ..54 A2
Skegness Wlk NN18 ...36 C4
Skelton Wlk [4] NN3 ..142 C4
Sketty Cl NN4 ....160 C1
Skiddaw Wlk NN3 ...142 C4
Skin Yard La NN6 ....121 B4
Skinner Ave NN5 ....158 D5
Skinner's Hill NN12 ..132 B2
Skippon Cl LE16 ......31 D2
Skipton Cl Corby NN18 .36 B4
Northampton NN4 ....175 B7

Skittle Alley OX17 ...237 C7
Skye Rd NN17 ....36 B8
Slade Cl NN14 ....54 B3
Slade Cres NN15 ......91 B7
Slade Ho NN11 ......153 C8
Slade Leas OX17 .....220 B8
Slade Rd CV21,CV22 ..241 E7
Slade The Daventry NN11 153 C8
Silverstone NN12 ....214 E5
Sladeswell Ct [1] NN3 .161 A8
Slapton Prep Sch NN12 201 E2
Slate Drift PE9 ....1 E3
Slaters Cl NN10 ......132 D2
Slawston Rd
Medbourne LE16 ......18 E7
Welham LE16 ....17 F1
Slim Cl NN15 ....72 F1
Slip The NN6 ....106 C2
Slips The NN6 ....110 E2
Slipton La NN14 ......75 A3
Small Cres MK18 ....240 F3
Smart's Cl NN13 .....233 D8
Smarts Est CV23 .....100 A3
Smith Cl NN7 ....177 A1
Smith Ct NN9 ....114 C5
Smith St NN6 ....105 A1
Smitherway NN7 ....173 A8
Smithfield Pl NN9 ...114 D6
Smithland Ct NN12 ..202 D8
Smiths Orch CV21 ...241 E8
Smiths Yd NN9 ......110 B3
Smithy The
Northampton NN3 ....142 D1
Rushden NN10 ....132 B1
Smyth Cl LE16 ....31 E5
Smyth Ct NN3 ....142 D1
Snetterton Cl NN3 ...141 F4
Snowball Sq [1] NN3 .143 C2
Soar Gn NN17 ....21 C1
Solly's Way NN3 ....203 C5
Somerby Cl PE9 .....241 D5
Somerford Rd NN8 ..129 E6
Somerset St NN1 ....159 E7
Somerton Ct NN18 ....36 A6
Somerville Ct OX17 ..230 D3
Somerville Rd
Brackley NN13 ....233 D8
Daventry NN11 ......153 B4
Stamford PE9 ....241 B4
Sondes Cl PE8 ....41 E7
Sondes Rd NN17 ......22 E2
Sopwith Way NN11 ..135 B5
Sorrel Cl Isham NN14 ..91 F1
Northampton NN4 ....175 C5
Sorrels The NN11 .....91 F1
Sotheby Rise NN3 ...143 C3
Soudan Ave NN13 ...233 E8
Sourton Pl NN11 ....135 C6
South Ave NN15 ......92 B3
South Bar St OX16 ..240 C7
South Bridge Cl PE8 ..41 F4
South Bridge Rd NN4 .159 D4
South Cl Braunston NN11 118 D1
Greatworth OX17 ....210 D1
Long Buckby NN6 ...121 B3
Rushden NN10 ......132 C1
South Copse NN4 ...175 B7
South End Jun & Inf Schs
NN10 ....148 B8
South Fields Dr NN6 .101 A5
South Folds Rd NN18 .35 F1
South Gr NN10 ......148 B5
South Holme Ct NN3 .142 E5
South Kilworth CE Prim Sch
LE17 ....63 C3
South Kilworth Rd NN6 .64 B5
South March NN11 ..153 D6
South Oval NN5 .....140 F1
South Paddock Ct NN3 .142 F4
South Pk NN10 ......132 B1
South Pl NN11 ......135 B1
South Portway Cl NN3 .142 F6
South Priors Ct NN3 .143 A3
South Rd Clifton u d CV23 .80 A5
Corby NN17 ....37 B6
Oundle PE8 ....42 A4
South St Banbury OX16 .240 E9
Castlethorpe MK19 ..218 F5
Isham NN14 ....110 F8
Northampton NN1 ...159 F6
Rugby CV21 ....241 F9
Weedon NN7 ....155 C3
Wollaston NN29 ....146 D2
Woodford Halse NN11 .184 C6
South Terr
Greens Norton NN12 .202 E8
Northampton NN1 ...159 F6
South Vale NN7 .....179 A5
South View
Brixworth NN6 ......106 B1
Harpole NN7 ....157 E5
Nether Heyford NN7 .156 B1
Roade NN7 ....191 D4
Whilton NN11 ....137 C6
South Way NN11 ...135 D1
Southall Rd NN17 ....37 B6
Southam Rd
Banbury OX16 ......240 C9
Priors Marston CV47 .166 D7
Southampton Rd NN4 159 C3
Southbrook NN18 ....36 B3
Southbrook Jun & Inf Schs
NN11 ....135 E1
Southbrook Rd CV22 .241 C6
Southcrest NN4 .....158 F1
Southcroft NN3 .....142 C7

Southfield Ave NN4 ..159 D3
Southfield Ct NN13 ..233 E6
Southfield Dr NN15 ...91 F4
Southfield Rd
Gretton NN17 ....10 C1
Northampton NN5 ...158 B4
Rugby CV22 ....241 E6
Southfield Sch for Girls
NN15 ....91 C7
Southfields NN10 ....132 C1
Southgate Dr
Kettering NN15 ....72 A2
Towcester NN12 ....203 D5
Southlands NN15 .....72 B1
Southleigh Gr LE16 ...31 D4
Southwick Hall★ PE8 .26 C5
Southwood Hill NN4 .159 A3
Sovereign Ct NN3 ...142 F6
Sovereign Pk LE16 ...31 F1
Sovereigns Ct NN16 ..72 C6
Sower Leys Rd NN18 ..36 C4
Spalding Rd NN18 ....36 C4
Spanslade Rd NN3 ..143 A1
Sparke Cl NN8 ......129 D7
Spectacle La NN3 ...125 F1
Speke Dr NN11 .....135 C5
Spelhoe St NN3 .....142 F6
Spencelayh Cl NN8 ..129 F7
Spencer Bridge Rd NN5 159 A7
Spencer Cl
Bugbrooke NN7 .....173 A8
Chapel Brampton NN6 .124 D1
Earls Barton NN6 ...144 F4
Evenley NN13 ....233 F2
Spencer Ct Corby NN17 .36 E5
Rushden NN10 ......132 A3
West Haddon NN6 ..102 C4
Spencer Gdns NN13 .233 E6
Spencer Haven NN5 .159 A7
Spencer Mid Sch NN5 .159 A7
Spencer Par
Northampton NN1 ...159 D6
Stanwick NN9 ....113 F3
Spencer Rd
Irthlingborough NN9 .112 C1
Long Buckby NN6 ...121 B3
Northampton NN1 ...159 E7
Rushden NN10 ......132 A3
Stanion NN14 ....37 E3
Spencer St
Burton Latimer NN15 ..92 B2
Kettering NN16 ....72 B6
Market Harborough LE16 .31 D3
Northampton NN5 ...159 A5
Raunds NN9 ....114 E6
Ringstead NN14 ......95 B3
Rothwell NN14 ....70 D8
Spencer Wlk NN18 ...36 E5
Spendlove Dr NN10 ..10 C1
Spenfield Ct NN3 ...142 F3
Spens Ho NN2 ......141 D5
Spenser Cres NN11 .135 A3
Spey Cl NN5 ....158 C8
Spiceball Park Rd OX16 240 D8
Spiers Dr NN13 .....233 D7
Spilsby Cl NN18 ......36 C4
Spinners Cotts OX17 .210 F7
Spinney Bank OX17 .230 F5
Spinney Cl
Boughton NN2 ......141 C7
Market Harborough LE16 .31 C3
Rushden NN10 ......131 F2
Thrapston NN14 ......76 D1
Towcester NN12 ....203 C3
Warmington PE8 ......28 B2
Spinney Dr
Kettering NN15 ....91 D7
Northampton NN4 ...175 C4
Spinney Gr NN17 .....36 E7
Spinney Hill NN11 ..118 D7
Spinney Hill Cres NN3 .142 A4
Spinney Hill Rd
Northampton NN3 ...142 A4
Olney MK46 ....195 E3
Spinney La
Kettering NN15 ....91 D7
Wellingborough NN8 .129 C2
Spinney Rd
Burton Latimer NN15 ..92 C3
Irthlingborough NN15 .112 F2
Rushden NN10 ......131 F1
Weldon NN17 ....38 C7
Spinney Rise
Daventry NN11 .....135 C1
Denford NN14 ....95 C6
Spinney St NN9 .....114 D6
Spinney Terr [8] NN9 .112 F2
Spinney The NN7 ...175 E2
Spinney Way NN3 ..142 A5
Sponne Ho NN12 ...203 C6
Sponne Sch NN12 ..203 B6
Sponnes Rd NN12 ..203 C5
Spratton CE Prim Sch
NN6 ....105 B1
Spratton Hall Sch NN6 .105 B1
Spratton Rd NN6 ...106 A2
Spring Bank LE16 ....18 F7
Spring Cl Boughton NN2 .125 C1
Daventry NN11 .....153 C8
Hollowell NN6 ......104 B4
Irthlingborough NN9 .112 C3
Kilsby CV23 ....100 A2
Spring Gdns
Burton Latimer NN15 ..92 C3
Earls Barton NN6 ...144 F4
Higham Ferrers NN10 .132 B6
Northampton NN1 ...159 D5
Rothwell NN14 ....70 D7

Spring Gdns continued
Towcester NN12 ....203 D5
Wellingborough NN8 .129 F4
Spring Ho NN8 .....129 F4
Spring La Alderton NN12 .203 D7
Flore NN7 ....155 E5
Northampton NN1 ...159 B6
Olney MK46 ....195 F3
[8] Wellingborough NN8 .130 A4
Spring Lane Lower Sch
NN1 ....159 B6
Spring Rise NN15 .....91 C7
Spring St
[4] Irthlingborough NN9 .112 F2
Rugby CV21 ....241 D8
Spring Terr
Irthlingborough NN9 .112 F2
Medbourne LE16 ......19 A6
Springbanks Way [2]
NN4 ....175 B8
Springer Straight [1]
NN4 ....158 F3
Springfield Flore NN7 .155 E5
Northampton NN3 ...175 E7
Olney MK46 ....195 F3
Springfield Ave NN14 .76 E3
Springfield Cl NN15 ..91 C7
Springfield Ct
[1] Market Harborough
LE16 ....31 F2
Northampton NN3 ...142 F3
Springfield Gdns MK19 .219 F6
Springfield Gr NN17 ..36 F8
Springfield Rd
Kettering NN15 ....91 C7
Oundle PE8 ....41 F7
Rushden NN10 ......148 D8
Walgrave NN6 ......107 F5
Wilbarston NN14 .....34 C4
Springfield St LE16 ...31 F2
Springfield Wlk NN13 .233 E8
Springfields NN12 ..203 B5
Springhill Gdns LE16 ..31 C2
Springhill Hos CV22 ..98 C8
Springs The
Northampton NN4 ...159 A3
Swinford LE17 ....62 C4
Springwell NN4 .....175 C3
Springwood Ct NN3 .142 F5
Spruce Ct
Northampton NN3 ...142 E3
Kettering NN16 ....72 C4
Spurlings PE8 ....41 F5
Spy Glass Hill NN4 ..175 B6
Square The Aynho OX17 .237 C7
Earls Barton NN6 ...144 E4
Greatworth OX17 ...210 E1
Kings Sutton OX17 ..230 E1
Market Harborough LE16 .31 E3
Moreton Pinkney NN11 .199 C7
Northampton NN4 ...175 F3
Pitsford NN6 ....125 C4
Raunds NN9 ....114 D6
South Luffenham LE15 ..3 D8
Thorpe Malsor NN14 ..71 B3
Welford NN6 ....64 E6
Yardley Hastings NN7 .179 A6
Squire Cl NN18 ......36 A4
Squires Wlk NN3 ...142 B3
Squirrel La NN5 .....158 C7
Squirrels Way MK18 .240 E2
Stable Ct Brackley NN13 .233 F7
[4] Northampton NN2 .141 C3
Pitsford NN6 ....125 D4
Stable Hill NN14 .....55 F7
Stable Yd NN14 ......70 C1
Stablegate Way LE16 .32 A3
Stables La NN6 .....140 B8
Stables The PE8 ......8 A3
Stadtpeine Ct NN17 ..36 C8
Staff Hos NN16 ......71 F2
Staffa Wlk NN17 .....36 B8
Stafford Cl NN11 ...135 D5
Stafford Pl NN3 ....141 F7
Stafford Rd NN17 ....22 C8
Staffords La NN6 ...102 B4
Stagshaw Cl [2] NN4 .175 C4
Staines Cl NN5 .....158 E6
Stalbridge Wlk NN18 .36 A6
Stamford & Rutland Hospl
PE9 ....241 F4
Stamford Bsns Pk PE9 .241 F4
Stamford Cl LE16 .....31 E2
Stamford Coll PE9 ..241 E4
Stamford High Sch PE9 .241 E4
Stamford High Sch (Welland
Ho) PE9 ....241 F4
Stamford High Sch Jun
PE9 ....241 D2
Stamford La PE8 .....28 B3
Stamford Rd
Corby NN14,NN18,NN17 .37 E4
Duddington PE9 ....5 C7
Easton o t H PE9 ......2 B5
Geddington NN14 ....54 A1
Geddington NN14 ....54 C7
Kettering NN16 ....72 E5
Ketton PE9 ....1 A5
South Luffenham LE15 ..3 D7
Weldon NN14 ....23 E2
Weldon NN17 ....38 A6
Stamford Sch PE9 ..241 E3
Stamford Stp PE9 ...241 D2
Stamford Wlk Corby NN18 36 C4
Stamford PE9 ....241 D2
Stanbridge Cl OX16 .240 A7
Stanbridge Ct MK11 .229 F5

Standens Barn Lower Sch
NN3 ....160 F8
Standens Barn Rd NN3 .142 F1
Standing Stones NN3 .143 B3
Standside NN5 ......158 F6
Stanfield Rd NN5 ...158 C6
Stanford Cl NN6 ......84 A5
Stanford Hall★ LE17 ..62 F3
Stanford Rd
Cold Ashby NN6 .....84 A5
Swinford LE17 ....62 D3
Stanford Way NN14 .175 C8
Stanhill Row NN12 ..201 F1
Stanhope Rd NN2 ...141 D1
Stanier Cl NN16 .....72 A3
Stanier Pl OX16 ....240 E9
Stanier Rd NN17 .....21 C1
Stanion CE Prim Sch
NN14 ....37 E3
Stanion La Corby NN18 ..37 B6
Corby NN18 ....37 D5
Stanion Rd NN14 .....38 C1
Stanley Boddington Ct
NN15 ....91 C8
Stanley Ct MK46 ....195 F3
Stanley Rd
Northampton NN5 ...159 A6
Wellingborough NN8 .130 B5
Stanley St
Northampton NN2 ...159 C8
Rothwell NN14 ....70 E7
Stamford PE9 ....241 E2
Stanley Way NN11 ..135 C5
Stannard Way NN6 ..106 B2
Stanton Ave NN3 ...142 A4
Stanton Cl NN8 .....111 B1
Stanway Cl LE16 .....32 A3
Stanwell Cl OX17 ...209 A1
Stanwell Dr OX17 ...209 A1
Stanwell Lea OX17 .209 A2
Stanwell Way NN8 ..129 C3
Stanwick Prim Sch NN9 114 A3
Stanwick Rd
Higham Ferrers NN10 ..132 C8
Raunds NN9 ....114 B4
Star Cnr CV23 ....99 C1
Star La PE9 ....241 E3
Starmer's Yd NN5 ..158 C7
Starmers La NN7 ...157 D4
Starvold Cl NN6 ....105 A1
Station Cl Daventry NN11 135 D2
Ecton NN3 ....143 C1
Long Buckby NN6 ...121 B3
Station Cotts NN18 ..53 D7
Station Gdns NN11 ..184 C6
Station Mews NN3 ..143 C2
Station Rd
Aynho OX15,OX17 ..237 A6
Blisworth NN7 ......174 B2
Brixworth NN6 ......106 A4
Buckingham MK18 ..240 C2
Burton Latimer NN15 .92 A2
Castlethorpe MK19 .218 F5
Clifton OX17 ....236 F5
Cogenhoe NN7 .....161 E6
Corby NN17 ....37 A6
Cottesbrooke NN6 ..105 A7
Desborough NN14 ...51 A4
Earls Barton NN6 ...144 E3
Earls Barton NN6 ...144 F1
Finedon NN9 ....111 D6
Great Bowden LE16 ..32 A6
Great Easton LE16 ...20 E6
Gretton NN17 ....10 B1
Helmdon NN13 .....211 F4
Husbands Bosworth LE17 .45 D3
Irchester MK44 .....147 C8
Irthlingborough NN9 .113 A2
Kettering NN15 ....72 B1
Ketton PE9 ....1 A5
King's Cliffe PE8 .....13 F7
Lilbourne CV23 ......81 A7
Little Houghton NN7 .161 C5
Long Buckby NN6 ...121 A2
Morcott LE15 ....3 B6
Nassington PE8 ......15 F5
North Kilworth LE17 ..45 A4
Northampton NN3 ...143 C1
Oundle PE8 ....42 A6
Raunds NN9 ....115 B7
Ringstead NN14 ......94 F2
Rushden NN10 ......132 A3
Rushton NN14 ....52 C2
Stamford PE9 ....241 D2
Stamford PE9 ....241 E2
Theddingworth LE17 ..46 C8
Watford NN11 ....120 C5
Welton NN11 ....119 E1
West Haddon NN6 ..102 B4
Woodford Halse NN11 .184 C6
Station Terr MK18 ..240 C2
Station Yard Ind Est
OX17 ....230 A2
Stavanger Cl NN18 ...36 A2
Staveley Way NN6 ..106 C3
Staverton CE Prim Sch
NN11 ....152 C7
Staverton Leys CV22 ..98 A7
Staverton Rd NN11 .135 B1
Steadfold La NN7 .....1 C8
Steam Brewery Mus★
PE9 ....241 D3
Steane View NN13 ..233 D7
Steel Cl NN14 ....76 D1
Steel Rd NN17 ....22 E2

Steele Rd NN8 . . . . .129 D4
Steele St CV22 . . . . .241 A8
Steene St NN5 . . . . .159 A6
Stefen Way NN11 . . . . . . .153 B7
Stenhouse Cl NN6 . . . . . .121 D4
Stenson St NN5 . . . . .159 A6
Stephen Bennett Cl
   NN5 . . . . .158 C8
Stephen St CV21 . . . . . . .241 B8
Stephenson Cl NN11 . . . .134 F4
Stephenson Ct
   Kilsby CV23 . . . . .99 F2
   Roade NN7 . . . . .191 C4
Stephenson Way NN17 . . .37 A8
Sterling Ct NN14 . . . . .70 C1
Sterndale Cl NN14 . . . . . . .50 E4
Stevens Cl NN6 . . . . .144 F5
Stevens St LE16 . . . . .31 D3
Stevenson St NN1 . . . . . .159 C2
Stewart Cl NN3 . . . . .126 B2
Stewart Dr NN12 . . . . . . .214 D4
Stewarts Rd NN8 . . . . . . .130 B8
Steyning Cl NN18 . . . . .36 A5
Stile Cl NN11 . . . . .135 A2
Stilebrook Rd MK46 . . . . .195 F6
Stimpson Ave NN1 . . . . . .159 F7
Stimpson Avenue Lower Sch
   NN1 . . . . .159 F7
Stinford Leys LE16 . . . . . . .32 B3
Stirling Ct PE9 . . . . .241 B3
Stirling St NN5 . . . . .158 F6
Stirrup Ho NN7 . . . . .191 C4
Stitchman Ho **8** NN5 . . .159 A6
Stock's Hill PE9 . . . . .1 A5
Stock's La NN11 . . . . .37 B6
Stockbridge Rd NN17 . . . . .22 A1
Stocken Cl MK46 . . . . . . .195 E4
Stockerston La LE16 . . . . . .20 D8
Stockholme St NN18 . . . . . .36 A2
Stocking Cl NN7 . . . . .192 D1
Stocking Green Cl
   MK19 . . . . .207 A3
Stockley St **6** NN1 . . . . .159 E6
Stockmead Rd NN3 . . . . . .161 A8
Stocks Hill Finedon NN9 . .111 E4
   Silverstone NN12 . . . . .214 D5
Stocks The NN18 . . . . . . .218 E2
Stockwell Ave NN4 . . . . . .175 D5
Stockwell Cl LE16 . . . . .32 B3
Stockwell La
   Hellidon NN11 . . . . .151 D1
   Sulgrave OX17 . . . . .210 F8
Stockwell Rd NN7 . . . . . . .174 F4
Stockwell Way NN7 . . . . . .174 F4
Stockwood Dr NN17 . . . . . .21 F1
Stoke Albany Rd LE16 . . . . .18 E1
Stoke Bruerne CE Prim Sch
   NN12 . . . . .205 A8
Stoke Doyle PE8 . . . . .41 C1
Stoke Doyle Rd PE8 . . . . . .41 D4
Stoke Firs Cl NN4 . . . . . . .175 F6
Stoke Hill Oundle PE8 . . . . .41 F5
   Stoke Albany LE16 . . . . .34 A4
Stoke Rd Ashton NN7 . . . .205 D4
   Blisworth NN7 . . . . .190 E4
   Desborough NN14 . . . . .51 A7
   Lyddington LE15 . . . . .9 C7
Stokes Rd NN18 . . . . .36 D4
Stone Circle Rd NN3 . . . . .142 E7
Stone Cl NN29 . . . . .146 D2
Stone Hill Ct NN3 . . . . . . .142 E4
Stone House Mews NN6 . . .84 E4
Stone Pit Cl MK46 . . . . . . .195 E3
Stone Way NN5 . . . . .158 B7
Stonebridge Ct NN3 . . . . .142 E3
Stonehill Way NN6 . . . . . .125 B8
Stonehouse Ct CV23 . . . . . .81 A6
Stonehurst Cl NN7 . . . . . .192 C1
Stonelea Rd NN6 . . . . . . .127 D3
Stoneleigh Chase NN5 . . .140 D1
Stonepit Dr LE16 . . . . .20 D1
Stoneway Badby NN11 . . . .152 F2
   Hartwell NN7 . . . . .192 E2
Stonewold Cl NN2 . . . . . .141 A4
Stoney Piece Cl NN29 . . . .164 C2
Stoneyhurst NN4 . . . . . . .158 F3
Stony Hill NN12 . . . . .216 C8
Stony Stratford Nature
   Reserve★ MK11 . . . . . . .229 D7
Stook The NN11 . . . . .135 C6
Storefield Cotts NN14 . . . . .53 A4
Stornoway Rd NN17 . . . . . .21 C1
Stotfold Ct MK11 . . . . . . .229 E4
Stour Rd Corby NN17 . . . . . .21 D1
   Northampton NN5 . . . . .158 F6
Stour The NN11 . . . . .153 A8
Stourhead Dr NN4 . . . . . .175 D2
Stourton Cl NN8 . . . . .129 D1
Stow Cl NN8 . . . . .129 D1
Stowe Ave MK18 . . . . .240 C4
Stowe Cl MK18 . . . . .240 C4
Stowe Rise MK18 . . . . . . .240 C4
Stowe Wlk NN3 . . . . .141 F5
Stradlers Cl NN4 . . . . .175 E5
Stratfield Way NN15 . . . . . .91 C5
Stratford Arc MK11 . . . . . .229 D5
Stratford Dr NN4 . . . . . . .175 D6
Stratford Rd
   Buckingham MK18 . . . . . . .240 E4
   Cosgrove NN12 . . . . .218 D1
   Deanshanger MK19 . . . . . . .228 E4
   Roade NN7 . . . . .191 C3
   Stony Stratford MK12 . . . . .229 F6
Strath Cl CV21 . . . . .99 A7
Strathay Wlk NN17 . . . . . . .21 C1

Stratton Cl
   Market Harborough LE16 . . .31 D1
   Northampton NN3 . . . . .160 D7
Stratton Dr NN13 . . . . . . .233 D7
Strawberry Hill NN3 . . . . .143 C3
Strawberry Hill Cotts
   MK44 . . . . .149 F2
Straws Cl NN9 . . . . .112 E1
Stream Bank Cl NN8 . . . . .129 D4
Streambank Rd NN3 . . . . .142 E6
Streatfield Rd NN5 . . . . . .159 A8
Streather Cl NN9 . . . . .114 C5
Streather Dr NN17 . . . . . . .36 E7
Street The LE15 . . . . .3 E8
Streeton Way NN6 . . . . . .144 E5
Strelley Ave NN3 . . . . .160 F8
Stringer's Hill NN14 . . . . . .90 F2
Strode Rd NN8 . . . . .130 B5
Stronglands Ct PE8 . . . . . . .41 F6
Stuart Cl Kettering NN16 . . .72 C2
   Northampton NN4 . . . . .174 F7
Stuart Cres LE16 . . . . .30 F7
Stuart Rd Brackley NN13 . .233 E8
   Corby NN17 . . . . .36 F6
   Market Harborough LE16 . . . .31 E2
Stubbing End NN18 . . . . . . .53 B8
Stubble Cl NN2 . . . . .141 A6
Stubbs Cl NN8 . . . . .129 F7
Stubbs La NN15 . . . . .92 A8
Stubbs Rd NN11 . . . . .170 B7
Stud Farm Cl OX17 . . . . . .196 E1
Studfall Ave NN17 . . . . .36 E8
Studfall Cl NN17 . . . . .36 E7
Studfall Inf Sch NN17 . . . . .36 E8
Studfall Jun Sch NN17 . . . .36 D8
Studland Rd NN2 . . . . . . .141 B1
Sturdee Cl NN11 . . . . .135 D1
Sturgess Ct NN15 . . . . .92 C2
Sturminster Way NN18 . . . .36 A6
Sturton Wlk NN18 . . . . .36 C4
Styles Pl NN1 . . . . .82 B3
Sudborough Rd
   Brigstock NN14 . . . . .56 A4
   Slipton NN14 . . . . .75 A6
Suffolk Pl NN15 . . . . .91 D6
Sulby Hall Old Dr NN6 . . . .46 B1
Sulby Rd
   Northampton NN3 . . . . .142 E6
   Welford NN6 . . . . .65 A8
Sulehay Rd PE8 . . . . .7 C1
Sulgrave Dr NN17 . . . . .36 C7
Sulgrave Manor★ OX17 211 A8
Sulgrave Rd
   Culworth OX17 . . . . .198 D1
   Northampton NN5 . . . . .158 F7
Summer Leys Nature Res★
   NN29 . . . . .145 F4
Summerfield Rd NN15 . . . . .91 C8
Summerfields NN4 . . . . . .158 D2
Summerhouse Rd NN3 . . .142 A6
Summerlee Mews NN9 . . .111 F4
Summerlee Rd NN9 . . . . . .111 F4
Summers Cl OX17 . . . . . . .230 A5
Summers Way LE16 . . . . . . .31 D2
Summit Rise NN4 . . . . . . .175 D7
Sun Hill NN14 . . . . .70 C7
Sun St CV21 . . . . .241 E8
Sun Yd NN12 . . . . .203 D5
Sunbeam Cl CV21 . . . . . . .241 E8
Sunderland St NN5 . . . . . .159 A6
Sundew Ct NN4 . . . . .158 D1
Sunley Ct NN15 . . . . .91 C8
Sunningdale Cl NN2 . . . . .141 E2
Sunningdale Dr
   Daventry NN11 . . . . .135 E3
   Rushden NN10 . . . . .148 D8
Sunny Bank NN6 . . . . .126 E8
Sunny Side NN6 . . . . .144 D4
Sunny View NN7 . . . . .179 B6
Sunnyside Ecton NN6 . . . .143 F4
   Northampton NN4 . . . . .175 E6
   Woodford NN14 . . . . .94 D7
Sunnyside Lower Sch
   NN2 . . . . .141 D6
Sunset Ct NN3 . . . . .143 A2
Surfleet Cl NN18 . . . . .36 C4
Surrey Cl NN17 . . . . .36 C6
Surrey Rd NN15 . . . . .91 D6
Surtees Way NN12 . . . . . .203 C7
Sussex Cl NN5 . . . . .158 C6
Sussex Ct **6** NN1 . . . . . .159 C6
Sussex Rd Kettering NN15 . .91 C6
   Stamford PE9 . . . . .241 D4
Sutcliffe Rd PE8 . . . . .7 D8
Sutherland Rd NN18 . . . . . .36 D4
Sutherland Way PE9 . . . . .241 B3
Sutton Acre NN7 . . . . .155 E5
Sutton Cl
   Aston le W NN11 . . . . .182 F3
   Northampton NN2 . . . . .141 D6
Sutton Ct LE16 . . . . .31 E1
Sutton Rd
   Great Bowden LE16 . . . . . . .32 B6
   Great Bowden LE16 . . . . . . .32 E7
   Oundle PE8 . . . . .42 B4
   Weston by W LE16 . . . . .18 B3
Sutton St NN7 . . . . .155 F5
Sutton's Wlk NN12 . . . . . .188 F7
Swain Cl NN3 . . . . .142 E3
Swale Cl Corby NN17 . . . . . .21 D1
   Roade NN7 . . . . .191 C4
Swale Dr
   Northampton NN5 . . . . .140 F3
   Wellingborough NN8 . . . . . .129 C6
Swallow Cl
   Brackley NN13 . . . . .222 E1
   Buckingham MK18 . . . . . . .240 E2
   Kettering NN15 . . . . .92 B6

Swallow Cl continued
   Northampton NN4 . . . . .175 A7
Swallow Dr NN10 . . . . . . .132 B5
Swan Ave NN14 . . . . .55 E8
Swan Cl Brackley NN13 . . .222 D2
   Buckingham MK18 . . . . .240 E2
   Burton Latimer NN15 . . . . . . .92 A2
   Hinton NN11 . . . . .184 B6
   Middleton Cheney OX17 . . . .219 F8
   Thrapston NN14 . . . . .76 D3
Swan Close Rd OX16 . . . .240 D7
Swan Ind Est OX16 . . . . . .240 D7
Swan St NN1 . . . . .159 D5
Swan Terr MK11 . . . . .229 D5
Swan Valley Way NN4 . . . .174 C8
Swanage Ct NN18 . . . . .36 A6
Swanhill PE8 . . . . .8 A4
Swann Dale NN11 . . . . . . .135 D1
Swann Dale Cl NN11 . . . . .135 D1
Swans La **6** NN8 . . . . . .130 A4
Swans Way NN10 . . . . . . .132 C8
Swansea Cres NN5 . . . . . .159 A7
Swansea Rd NN5 . . . . . . .159 A8
Swansgate Ctr The **9**
   NN8 . . . . .130 A4
Swanson Ho PE9 . . . . . . .241 F4
Swanspool Ct NN8 . . . . . .130 A4
Swanspool Par NN8 . . . . .130 A3
Swedish Hos NN7 . . . . . . .139 D4
Sweetacre Cl NN7 . . . . . . .163 D4
Swift Cl NN4 . . . . .175 F3
Swift Way NN13 . . . . .222 E1
Swinburne Cl NN16 . . . . . .72 C6
Swinburne Rd NN8 . . . . . .129 B4
Swinfen's Yd MK11 . . . . . .229 D5
Swinford CE Prim Sch
   LE17 . . . . .62 B4
Swinford Cnr LE17 . . . . . . .62 A8
Swinford Hollow NN1 . . . .161 A8
Swinford Rd LE17 . . . . .62 A8
Swingbridge St NN16 . . . . .30 E8
Swinnertons La NN6 . . . . . .82 B4
Swinneyford Rd NN12 . . . .203 C5
Swyncombe Gn NN7 . . . . .192 C1
Sycamore Ave NN11 . . . . .184 B6
Sycamore Cl
   Buckingham MK18 . . . . . . .240 F2
   Corby NN17 . . . . .21 C1
   Daventry NN11 . . . . .135 C5
   Kettering NN16 . . . . .72 D4
   Rushden NN10 . . . . .132 C2
   Towcester NN12 . . . . .203 C4
Sycamore Dr
   Desborough NN14 . . . . .51 D2
   Sywell NN6 . . . . .143 D8
Sycamore Gr CV21 . . . . . .241 C9
Sycamore Rd
   Greens Norton NN12 . . . . . .202 E8
   Northampton NN5 . . . . .158 C7
Sycamore Yd NN12 . . . . . .187 B1
Sycamores The LE17 . . . . . .63 D8
Sydney St NN16 . . . . .72 D2
Syers Green Cl NN6 . . . . .121 A4
Syers Green La NN6 . . . . .121 A4
Syke The NN14 . . . . .55 F7
Sykes Ct NN17 . . . . .37 A8
Syles Cl NN6 . . . . .102 B5
Sylmond Gdns NN10 . . . .148 A7
Sylvanus Ho NN3 . . . . . . .129 D5
Symington St NN5 . . . . . . .159 A7
Symington Way LE16 . . . . . .31 E3
Syresham St James CE Prim
   Sch NN13 . . . . .224 C7
Syresham Way NN2 . . . . . .141 C5
Sywell Airport Bsns Pk
   NN6 . . . . .127 F4
Sywell Ave NN8 . . . . .129 D6
Sywell CE Prim Sch
   NN6 . . . . .127 D3
Sywell Rd Holcot NN6 . . . .126 F8
   Mears Ashby NN6 . . . . .128 A1
   Overstone NN6 . . . . .127 B1
   Wellingborough NN8 . . . . . .129 C6
Sywell Resr Ctry Pk★
   NN6 . . . . .144 A7
Sywell Way NN8 . . . . .129 D6

T

Taborley Cl NN3 . . . . .142 E1
Tadcaster Cl NN11 . . . . . .135 C6
Taggies Yd NN14 . . . . . . .109 F5
Tainty Cl NN9 . . . . .111 E5
Talan Rise NN3 . . . . .143 C5
Talavera Cl NN11 . . . . . . .135 B1
Talavera Way NN11 . . . . . .142 D6
Talbot Rd
   Northampton NN1 . . . . .159 E7
   Rushden NN10 . . . . .131 F1
   Wellingborough NN8 . . . . . .130 C5
Talbot Rd N NN8 . . . . .130 C5
Talbot Yd LE16 . . . . .31 E3
Talbots Hyde MK46 . . . . . .195 E4
Tall Trees Cl NN4 . . . . . . .174 F8
Tallyfield End NN4 . . . . . .158 E3
Tamar Cl NN5 . . . . .140 E2
Tamar Gn NN17 . . . . .21 D1
Tamar Sq NN11 . . . . .135 A1
Tamarisk Dr NN3 . . . . . . .142 C6
Tancred Cl **1** NN4 . . . . .175 E7
Taney Ct PE8 . . . . .42 A5
Tanfield La NN1 . . . . .160 C5
Tanfields Gr NN11 . . . . . . .36 E8
Tanglewood NN4 . . . . .175 D4
Tann Rd NN9 . . . . .111 F5
Tanner St NN1 . . . . .159 C5
Tanner's La NN16 . . . . .72 B2

Tannery The LE15 . . . . .4 A5
Tansor Cl NN17 . . . . .36 B8
Tansy Cl NN4 . . . . .158 D1
Tantree Way NN6 . . . . . . .106 C2
Tapeley Gdns NN4 . . . . . .175 D7
Taper Way NN11 . . . . .135 B3
Tarn Croft NN3 . . . . .142 B3
Tarragon Way NN4 . . . . . .175 D6
Tarrant Cl NN3 . . . . .126 D1
Tarrant Way NN3 . . . . . . .126 D1
Tarrys End NN6 . . . . .82 B4
Tasman Way NN14 . . . . . . .70 E6
Tate Gr NN4 . . . . .175 F7
Tattersall St NN3 . . . . . . .142 A5
Taunton Ave Corby NN18 . . .36 B6
   Northampton NN3 . . . . .160 C7
Tavern La **1** NN11 . . . . .135 C1
Tavern Wlk NN18 . . . . .36 A4
Tavistock Cl **3** NN3 . . . .143 D2
Tavistock Rd NN18 . . . . . . .92 A5
Tavistock Sq NN18 . . . . . . .36 F4
Tay Cl NN11 . . . . .21 D1
Taylor Ave NN3 . . . . .142 C1
Taylor Cl NN8 . . . . .129 C7
Taylors Gn PE8 . . . . .28 B2
Teal Cl
   Burton Latimer NN15 . . . . . . .91 F2
   Daventry NN11 . . . . .135 C4
   Higham Ferrers NN10 . . . . . .132 C8
   Northampton NN4 . . . . .174 E8
Teal La NN8 . . . . .130 B7
Teasel Cl NN10 . . . . .148 C7
Tebbitt Cl NN6 . . . . .121 B4
Tebbutt Cl NN14 . . . . .70 F7
Tebbutt's Yd NN6 . . . . . . .144 E4
Tees Cl NN8 . . . . .129 C6
Teesdale NN3 . . . . .142 F6
Teesdale Rd NN17 . . . . . . .36 D7
Teeton La NN6 . . . . .104 E3
Teeton Rd
   Guilsborough NN6 . . . . .103 F5
   Ravensthorpe NN6 . . . . .103 E1
Telford Way
   Kettering NN16 . . . . .71 F4
   Northampton NN5 . . . . .158 D4
Telfords La NN17 . . . . .37 A8
Temperance Terr MK11 . . .229 C6
Templar Dr NN2 . . . . .141 A4
Templar Rd NN15 . . . . .72 F1
Temple Bar **21** NN1 . . . .159 C7
Temple St CV21,CV22 . . . .241 E7
Ten Pines NN3 . . . . .142 F7
Tenbury Way NN14 . . . . . . .70 F7
Tenby Rd NN5 . . . . .159 A8
Tenlands OX17 . . . . .219 F8
Tennyson Cl
   3 Northampton NN5 . . . .158 F8
   Towcester NN12 . . . . .203 B5
Tennyson Dr NN17 . . . . . . .36 D8
Tennyson Rd
   Daventry NN11 . . . . .135 B3
   Kettering NN16 . . . . .72 B2
   Rothwell NN14 . . . . .70 C7
   Rushden NN10 . . . . .131 F2
   Wellingborough NN8 . . . . . .129 D3
Tennyson Road Inf Sch
   NN10 . . . . .131 F2
Tennyson Way PE9 . . . . . .241 A4
Tenter Cl NN10 . . . . .132 B5
Tenter Ct PE9 . . . . .241 E2
Tenter La Finedon NN9 . . .111 F5
   Stamford PE9 . . . . .241 E3
Tenter Rd NN3 . . . . .141 F7
Tentsmuir Cl NN16 . . . . . . .72 A6
Terrace The NN13 . . . . . . .224 C5
Terrington Cl NN13 . . . . . .233 E7
Test Gn NN17 . . . . .21 D1
Tettenhall Cl NN18 . . . . . . .36 A1
Teviot Cl Corby NN17 . . . . . .21 D1
   Northampton NN5 . . . . .140 E2
Tewkesbury Cl
   Northampton NN4 . . . . .159 A1
   Wellingborough NN8 . . . . . .129 D6
Tewkesbury Dr NN10 . . . .148 D8
Tews End La NN12 . . . . . .216 C8
Thackers Cl PE8 . . . . .8 A4
Thames Ct NN15 . . . . .92 B2
Thames Rd
   Daventry NN11 . . . . .135 A1
   Northampton NN4 . . . . .175 C7
   Wellingborough NN8 . . . . . .129 C6
Thames Rise NN16 . . . . . . .72 A4
Thames Wlk NN17 . . . . . . .21 D1
Thatch Meadow Dr LE16 . .32 B3
Thatchwell Ct NN3 . . . . . .160 B8
Thebwell Rd **3** NN3 . . . .142 F1
Theddingworth Rd
   Husbands Bosworth LE17 . . .46 A6
   Lubenham LE16 . . . . .30 C2
   Marston Trussell LE16 . . . . . .47 B8
Thenford Rd OX17 . . . . . .209 C1
Thenford St NN1 . . . . .159 E6
Thetford Cl NN18 . . . . .36 B1
Third Ave NN8 . . . . .129 D3
Third St NN13 . . . . .238 E6
Thirlestane Cres NN14 . . .159 B3
Thirlestane Rd NN4 . . . . . .159 B3
Thirlmere NN8 . . . . .129 C5
Thirlmere Ave NN3 . . . . . .142 C3
Thirlmere Cl
   Daventry NN11 . . . . .135 A2
   Kettering NN16 . . . . .71 E3
Thirlmere Flats NN16 . . . . .71 E3
Thirsk Rd NN18 . . . . .36 C5
Thistle Cl **3** NN3 . . . . . .159 A3
Thistleholme Cl NN2 . . . . .141 E3
Thoday Cl NN14 . . . . .90 A3

Thomas Becket RC Upper
   Sch NN3 . . . . .142 B5
Thomas Chapman Gr
   NN4 . . . . .159 C4
Thomas Cl Byfield NN11 . .183 D6
   Corby NN18 . . . . .36 D4
   Crick NN6 . . . . .101 A6
Thomas Crewe Cl NN13 . .233 F7
Thomas Flawn Rd NN9 . . .131 D8
Thomas Rd NN15 . . . . .91 C7
Thomas Rippin Cl NN5 . . . .54 A2
Thomas St
   Northampton NN1 . . . . .159 D7
   Wellingborough NN8 . . . . . .130 B5
Thompson Way NN15 . . . . .90 F8
Thor Wlk NN18 . . . . .36 A2
Thorburn Rd NN3 . . . . . . .160 E8
Thoresby Ct NN18 . . . . . . .36 C5
Thorn Cl NN16 . . . . .72 B6
Thorn Hill NN14 . . . . .159 A3
Thornapple Cl NN3 . . . . . .143 C4
Thornborough Cl LE16 . . . .32 A2
Thornbridge Cl NN10 . . . .132 A1
Thornby Dr NN2 . . . . .141 B3
Thornby Rd NN6 . . . . .84 B5
Thorne Ct NN18 . . . . .36 C5
Thornfield NN3 . . . . .143 C4
Thorngate St NN16 . . . . . . .72 C2
Thornhill OX17 . . . . .208 F4
Thornlea Croft MK46 . . . .195 F3
Thornton Cl Crick NN6 . . . .101 A6
   Flore NN7 . . . . .155 F5
   Newnham NN11 . . . . .153 D3
Thornton Coll MK17 . . . . .235 C5
Thornton Rd
   Northampton NN2 . . . . .141 B3
   Thornton MK17 . . . . .235 F2
Thoroughsale Rd NN17 . . . .36 C5
Thorpe Cl Banbury OX16 . .219 A6
   Banbury OX16 . . . . .240 F8
   Wellingborough NN8 . . . . . .129 C5
Thorpe Ct NN14 . . . . .77 C7
Thorpe Dr Banbury OX16 . .219 A6
   Banbury OX16 . . . . .240 F8
Thorpe La OX16 . . . . .240 F8
Thorpe Langton Rd LE16 . .17 D6
Thorpe Mead OX16 . . . . . .240 F7
Thorpe Pl OX16 . . . . .240 F8
Thorpe Rd
   Chacombe OX17 . . . . .208 E4
   Earls Barton NN6 . . . . .144 E2
   Lyddington LE15 . . . . .9 D6
   Northampton NN4 . . . . .159 C3
   Thorpe Waterville NN14 . . . .77 A8
   Wardington OX17 . . . . .208 F8
Thorpe St NN9 . . . . .114 D5
Thorpe Way OX16 . . . . . . .240 F8
Thorpeville NN3 . . . . .142 D7
Thorplands Lower Sch
   NN3 . . . . .142 E5
Thrapston Prim Sch
   NN14 . . . . .76 D1
Thrapston Rd
   Finedon NN9 . . . . .112 B7
   Woodford NN14 . . . . .94 D8
Three Shires Hospl NN1 159 F5
Thrift St
   Higham Ferrers NN10 . . . . . .132 B5
   Irchester NN29 . . . . .147 A2
   Wollaston NN29 . . . . .146 D2
Thrupp Bridge NN4 . . . .176 A6
Thrush La NN8 . . . . .130 B6
Thruxton Dr NN3 . . . . .141 F4
Thurburn Cl NN14 . . . . . . .90 B5
Thurning Rd PE8,PE29 . . . .79 F7
Thursby Rd NN1 . . . . .160 B7
Thurso Wlk NN17 . . . . .21 D1
Thurspit Pl **8** NN3 . . . . .143 D2
Thurston Dr NN15 . . . . . . .91 A8
Thyme Ct NN3 . . . . .142 E3
Tibbs Way NN7 . . . . .173 A6
Tideswell Cl
   Desborough NN14 . . . . .50 E4
   Northampton NN4 . . . . .174 F8
Tiffany Gdns NN4 . . . . . . .175 C6
Tiffield CE Prim Sch
   NN12 . . . . .189 D3
Tiffield Rd NN7 . . . . .189 E8
Tilbury Rd NN6 . . . . .122 C5
Tilbury Rise NN6 . . . . .122 C5
Tilley Hill Cl PE8 . . . . .41 E7
Timber Ct CV22 . . . . .241 E7
Timken Way NN11 . . . . . . .135 A4
Timor Ct MK11 . . . . .229 D6
Timpson Cl NN16 . . . . .72 C5
Timson Cl LE16 . . . . .31 D5
Tingdene Rd NN9 . . . . . . .111 F5
Tingewick Rd MK18 . . . . .240 B3
Tingewick Road Ind Est
   MK18 . . . . .240 B3
Tinkers Cres NN6 . . . . . . .128 B2
Tinsley Cl NN3 . . . . .143 B3
Tintagel Cl NN10 . . . . . . .132 D1
Tintern Ave NN5 . . . . .159 A7
Tintern Ct NN15 . . . . .91 F8
Tinwell Rd PE9 . . . . .241 B2
Tinwell Road La PE9 . . . . .241 B2
Tippings La LE15 . . . . .3 F5
Tiptoe Cl NN3 . . . . .143 C3
Titchmarsh CE Prim Sch
   NN14 . . . . .77 C4
Tithe Barn Cl NN9 . . . . . .114 E7
Tithe Barn Rd NN8 . . . . . .130 A4
Tithe Barn Way NN4 . . . . .174 B8
Tithe Cl Holcot NN6 . . . . . .126 E8
   Ringstead NN14 . . . . .95 A3
Tithe Ct OX16 . . . . .240 A7
Tithe La OX15,OX17 . . . . .236 C6

Tithe Rd NN7 155 A2
Tithe Way NN7 191 D5
Titley Bawk Ave NN6 144 F6
Titty Ho NN9 114 C5
Tiverton Ave NN2 141 C7
Tixover Grange PE9 4 F8
Todd's Hill PE9 5 B6
Todmorden Cl NN18 36 C5
Tofts Cl NN14 77 D4
Tolethorpe Sq PE9 241 D4
Toll Bar La PE28 97 B4
Toll Bar Rd NN14 76 B2
Toll Gate Pl NN18 37 B6
Tollbar NN10 132 B5
Toller Pl NN15 91 F6
Toller St NN16 72 C3
Tollgate Cl NN2 141 B2
Tollgate Way NN5 158 D6
Tom Brown St CV21 241 E8
Tompson Cl NN11 118 C1
Toms Cl
Northampton NN4 175 C3
Theddingworth LE17 46 D8
Tonmead Rd NN3 142 E3
Top Cl NN14 76 F3
Top Dysons NN14 92 F7
Top End
Little Addington NN14 113 B7
Pytchley NN14 90 F2
Top Farm Ct NN11 184 B6
Top Farm La NN29 145 E7
Top Lodge NN17 5 A1
Top Station Rd NN13 234 A8
Top Station Road Ind Est NN13 234 A8
Top Yard Barn LE16 31 F6
Topwell Ct NN3 143 A1
Tordoff Pl NN16 72 B2
Torkington Gdns PE9 241 D3
Torkington St PE9 241 B3
Torksey Cl NN18 36 A1
Torrance Rd CV21 241 B8
Torridge Cl NN16 71 F4
Torridon Cl NN17 21 C1
Torrington Cres NN8 129 D6
Torrington Gn NN8 129 E6
Torrington Rd NN8 129 E6
Torrington Way NN8 129 E6
Torville Cres NN15 91 A8
Totnes Cl NN18 36 F4
Toulouse Cl 11 NN4 175 E7
Touraine Cl NN5 139 F2
Tove La NN12 203 A6
Tovey Dr NN11 135 D1
Towcester Dr NN12 217 B3
Towcester Inf Sch NN12 203 C5
Towcester Rd
Blisworth NN7 190 B6
Greens Norton NN12 188 E1
Litchborough NN12 171 C1
Milton Malsor NN7 174 E5
Northampton NN4 159 B2
Old Stratford MK19 229 B7
Silverstone NN12 214 E4
Towcester NN12 203 A8
Whittlebury NN12 215 C5
Tower Cl NN9 112 A4
Tower Ct Lubenham LE16 30 F3
Wollaston NN29 146 F3
Tower Field Sq NN3 143 A6
Tower Hill Cl NN4 158 E3
Tower Hill Rd NN18 36 A4
Tower Rd CV22 241 E6
Tower St NN1 159 C6
Town Cl NN9 110 C3
Town Cnr NN5 158 F6
Townley Way NN6 144 E5
Towns End NN6 121 C4
Townsend Banbury OX16 240 B8
Hinton NN11 184 B6
Townsend Cl
Hanging Houghton NN6 106 C8
Wellingborough NN8 129 F4
Townsend Ct PE8 39 E7
Townsend La
Thorpe Mandeville OX17 209 F6
Upper Boddington NN11 182 B8
Townsend Leys NN10 132 B8
Townsend Rd
Rugby CV21 241 F8
Walgrave NN6 107 F5
Towson Cl NN6 107 D7
Townwell La NN29 147 B8
Towrise OX17 210 F8
Towton Ct NN4 159 A1
Trafalgar Rd NN16 72 A2
Trafalgar Way NN11 135 D1
Trafford Rd NN10 132 D2
Traili La NN14 94 D6
Tramway Ind Est The OX16 240 E7
Tramway Rd OX16 240 E7
Treefields MK18 240 E3
Treen Cl NN14 76 F2
Treetops NN3 143 A5
Trefoil Cl NN10 148 C7
Trelawney NN8 129 B5
Trengothal Ct NN13 223 D4
Trent Cl
Northampton NN5 140 F2
Wellingborough NN8 129 C6
Trent Cres NN15 92 B1
Trent Rd Corby NN17 21 D1
Kettering NN16 72 A5
Wittering PE8 7 D8
Trent Wlk NN11 135 A1
Trentham Cl NN4 175 C7
Tresham Gn NN5 140 D1
Tresham Inst Corby NN17 36 E6
Kettering NN15 72 C1
Kettering NN15 91 D8
Wellingborough NN8 130 A5
Tresham St
Kettering NN16 72 C3
Rothwell NN14 70 D7
Trevithick Rd NN17 37 C8
Trevor Cl NN5 158 E7
Trevor Cres NN5 158 E7
Trevor White Dr CV22 241 D6
Trimley Cl NN3 160 D6
Trinity Ave NN2 141 D1
Trinity CE Lower Sch NN14 76 F8
Trinity Cl Daventry NN11 153 B8
Old Stratford MK19 229 B7
Trinity Ct NN14 70 C6
Trinity Ctr NN8 129 A7
Trinity Rd Rothwell NN14 70 C6
Stamford PE9 241 C4
Trinity Sch NN2 141 D1
Trinity Way OX17 230 D3
Trinity Wlk NN18 36 E4
Triumph Gdns NN5 139 F1
Trojan Ctr NN8 130 B8
Tromso Cl NN18 36 A2
Troon Cres NN8 129 C7
Troutbeck Wlk NN3 142 C4
Trussell Rd NN3 143 C1
Tudely Cl NN4 175 F7
Tudor Ct 4 NN16 72 C2
Tudor Gdns MK11 229 E4
Tudor Rd NN1,NN2 142 A2
Tudor Way
Brackley NN13 233 E8
Wellingborough NN8 129 E7
Tudor Wlk NN10 132 C3
Tulbrook Stones OX17 220 B7
Tulip Dr NN10 148 B7
Tunnel Hill Cotts NN4 159 A2
Tunwell La NN17 37 B7
Turn Furlong NN2 141 A5
Turnberry Ct NN8 129 C7
Turnberry La NN4 175 C5
Turnbrook Cl NN9 112 E3
Turnells Mill La NN8 130 A1
Turner Cl Kettering NN15 92 A8
Rugby CV21 99 B8
Turner Rd Corby NN18 36 E5
Wellingborough NN8 129 F7
Turner St NN1 159 F7
Turners Mus★ NN4 175 D7
Turners Yd PE8 41 F5
Turnpike Cl LE16 31 D5
Turvins Mdw CV47 166 D8
Turweston Manor NN13 234 C8
Turweston Rd NN13 223 A1
Tweed Cl
Burton Latimer NN15 92 B2
Daventry NN11 153 A8
Tweed Rd NN5 158 E6
Twickenham Ct 5 NN18 36 B5
Twigden Rd NN7 157 D3
Twistle The NN11 183 C7
Twitch Hill NN12 204 D8
Twyford Ave
Raunds NN9 114 C7
Twyford OX17 230 A6
Twyford Cl 7 NN3 161 A8
Twyford Gr OX17 230 A6
Twyford Rd OX17 230 C7
Tywell Hills & Dales Nature Res★ NN14 93 F8
Tyebeck Ct NN2 141 B3
Tyes Ct NN3 142 F3
Tyler Way NN14 76 E1
Tymecrosse Gdns LE16 31 D5
Tynan Cl NN15 92 A8
Tyne Cl NN8 129 C6
Tyne Rd Corby NN17 21 D1
Daventry NN11 153 A8
Northampton NN5 158 E6
Tyrell Cl MK18 240 C2
Tyringham Cl NN3 142 D1
Tyrrell Way NN12 203 C8
Tyson Ctyd NN18 37 E7

U

Uffington Rd PE9 241 F3
Uist Wlk NN17 21 C1
Ullswater Cl
Higham Ferrers NN10 132 B8
Wellingborough NN8 129 C5
Ullswater Rd NN16 71 E2
Underbank La NN3 142 C6
Underwood Rd NN14 70 C7
Union St Banbury OX16 240 B8
Desborough NN14 51 B3
Finedon NN9 112 A5
Kettering NN16 72 A3
Rugby CV22 241 C7
Unity Cl NN29 146 C3
Unity St NN14 51 A2
Univ Coll Northampton NN2 141 D1
Univ of Buckingham
Buckingham MK18 240 C2
Buckingham MK18 240 E2
Univ of Leicester (Annexe) NN2 159 C8
Upland Rd NN3 142 C2
Upper Astrop Rd OX17 231 A5
Upper Bath St NN1 159 C6
Upper Cross St 18 NN1 159 C6
Upper Dane NN14 50 E3
Upper George St NN10 132 C7
Upper Glen Ave NN7 174 B2
Upper Gn NN11 199 D7
Upper Green Pl LE16 32 A6
Upper Havelock St 7 NN8 130 A5
Upper High St NN7 157 C7
Upper Kings Ave NN10 132 C7
Upper Mounts NN1 159 D6
Upper Park Ave NN10 131 F1
Upper Priory St 7 NN1 159 C7
Upper Queen St NN10 132 C3
Upper St NN16 72 A2
Upper Steeping NN14 51 C3
Upper Thrift St NN1 159 F6
Upper Windsor St OX16 240 D7
Upperfield Gr NN17 36 E8
Uppingham Rd
Caldecott LE16 9 B2
Corby NN17 36 A7
Medbourne LE16 19 A8
Uppingham St NN1 159 B7
Upton Cl NN2 141 D6
Upton Way NN4, NN5 158 D3
Usher Ho NN2 141 C5

V

Vale Cl CV21 99 A8
Vale Mead Lower Sch NN3 143 A5
Vale St NN16 72 A3
Vale The NN1 141 F1
Valentine Way NN3 143 C3
Valley Cl NN13 234 A8
Valley Cres
Brackley NN13 234 A8
Northampton NN3 143 B1
Valley End NN12 172 D1
Valley Rd Banbury OX16 240 D6
Brackley NN13 234 A8
Buckingham MK18 240 F3
Northampton NN3 143 B1
Wellingborough NN8 129 F1
Weston by W LE16 18 B3
Valley Rise
Brackley NN13 233 F8
Desborough NN14 51 B2
Valley Way LE16 32 B4
Valley Wlk NN16 72 E2
Vancouver Cl NN18 36 B2
Vantage Mdw NN3 143 D3
Vara Cl NN18 36 B2
Vardon Cl NN8 129 C7
Varley Cl NN8 129 E8
Vaughan Cl LE16 48 E8
Vaux Rd NN8 111 A1
Velbert Ho NN17 21 E1
Velocette Way NN5 140 A1
Vence Cl PE9 241 C3
Venture Cl NN17 22 F1
Verdant Vale 1 NN4 175 D6
Verney Cl MK18 240 D4
Vernier Cl NN11 135 A3
Vernon Ave CV22 98 E8
Vernon Cl NN11 153 E8
Vernon Ct Kettering NN16 71 F5
10 Northampton NN1 159 F6
Vernon Rd NN12 203 D5
Vernon St NN1 159 F6
Vernon Terr NN1 159 F6
Vernon Terrace Lower Sch NN1 159 F6
Vernon Wlk 7 NN1 159 F6
Verwood Cl NN3 142 F5
Veteran Cl NN4 175 E7
Vian Way NN17 36 B8
Vicar La NN11 135 D2
Vicarage Cl
Hackleton NN7 177 A3
Northampton NN2 141 A3
Wellingborough NN8 129 D6
Whittlebury NN12 215 C5
Yardley Gobion NN12 217 E6
Vicarage Ct MK19 207 B2
Vicarage Farm Rd NN8 129 D6
Vicarage Hill NN11 153 A2
Vicarage La Denton NN7 178 B8
East Haddon NN6 122 D5
Mears Ashby NN6 128 B2
Northampton NN2 141 B3
Priors Marston CV47 166 E8
Vicarage Rd
Northampton NN5 159 A7
Rugby CV22 241 B8
Stony Stratford MK11 229 D6
Vicarage Rise NN12 200 C3
Vicarage Wlk MK11 229 D6
Viceroy Cl NN9 114 E6
Vickers Cl NN14 70 F7
Victoria Ave
Market Harborough LE16 31 D5
Rugby CV21 241 B9
Victoria Bsns Pk NN5 159 B6
Victoria Cl
Earls Barton NN6 144 E5
Rushden NN10 132 B3
West Haddon NN6 102 C5
Victoria Ct Rothwell NN14 70 D7
Rushden NN10 132 B3
Woodford NN14 94 C7
Victoria Gdns NN1 159 D5
Victoria Ho NN1 159 E6
Victoria Inf Sch NN8 130 B6
Victoria Jun Sch NN8 130 B5
Victoria Pk NN8 130 B2
Victoria Pl OX16 240 E8
Victoria Prom NN1 159 D5
Victoria Rd
Cogenhoe NN7 161 E5
Finedon NN9 111 F5
Northampton NN1 159 E6
Oundle PE8 42 A6
Rushden NN10 132 B3
Stamford PE9 241 D4
Wellingborough NN8 130 B4
Victoria Row MK18 240 C3
Victoria St
Burton Latimer NN15 92 B2
Desborough NN14 51 A3
Earls Barton NN6 144 F5
Irthlingborough NN9 112 E1
Kettering NN16 72 B2
Northampton NN1 159 D6
Rugby CV21 241 B8
Vienne Cl NN5 157 F8
Viking Cl NN16 72 C6
Viking Way NN18 36 B1
Villa Gdns NN15 92 B1
Villa La NN9 113 F3
Villa Way NN4 175 F5
Villagers Cl NN4 175 E5
Vincent Cl NN5 157 F8
Vinco Terr PE8 28 D8
Vine Cl PE8 42 A5
Vine Hill Cl NN10 132 A6
Vine Hill Dr NN10 132 B6
Vine St PE9 241 E3
Vineyard Cl OX16 240 C9
Violet Cl NN18 36 D2
Violet La Creaton NN6 104 F4
Rothwell NN14, NN16 71 C6
Viscount Rd NN3 143 C6
Vivian Rd NN8 130 B5
Vokes Cl NN3 143 A1
Volunteer Cl NN4 175 E6
Vulcan Cl NN11 135 A3
Vyse Rd NN2 141 C8

W

Wadcroft 3 NN16 72 B2
Wadd Close La NN11 137 D6
Wade Meadow Ct NN3 142 F4
Wadenhoe La PE8 57 F4
Wades Cl PE8 14 F1
Wadham Ct NN11 153 C7
Waggoners Way NN7 173 A7
Wagtail Cl NN3 142 C7
Waingrove NN3 143 B4
Wainwright Ave NN14 76 D1
Wake Way NN4 175 F3
Wakefield NN8 129 C4
Wakefield Dr NN6 64 D5
Wakefield Rd NN2 141 D4
Wakefield Way NN7 156 C1
Wakehurst Dr NN4 175 C7
Wakerley Great Wood Forest Trail★ LE15 4 C2
Wakerley Great Wood Orienteering Course★ LE15 4 B2
Wakerley Rd
Barrowden LE15 4 A4
Harringworth NN17 10 F7
Walcot Cl PE8 41 E7
Walcot Rd LE16 31 E2
Walcot Way PE9 241 A4
Walcote Rd LE17 63 C8
Wales St
Kings Sutton OX17 230 F5
Rothwell NN14 70 C7
Walford Pl CV22 98 F8
Walgrave Cl NN3 161 B8
Walgrave Prim Sch NN6 108 A5
Walgrave Rd Holcot NN6 107 E1
Old NN6 107 E6
Walgrave NN6 108 B4
Walk The NN6 124 B8
Walker Dr NN12 203 C8
Walker Sq NN8 129 C7
Walker's La 5 NN16 72 B2
Walker's Way NN9 111 F4
Walkers Acre NN6 108 A5
Walkers Field PE8 13 F8
Walkers La NN6 140 B8
Walkers Way NN4 175 E5
Walks The PE9 1 D2
Wallace Gdns NN2 141 F2
Wallace Rd NN2 141 F2
Wallace Terr NN2 141 F2
Wallbeck Cl NN2 141 C4
Walledwell Ct 4 NN3 142 F1
Wallingford End 6 NN3 161 A8
Wallis Cl NN8 129 A4
Wallis Cres NN15 91 C8
Wallis Rd NN15 91 C8
Wallwin Cl NN7 191 C4
Walmer Cl NN10 132 D1
Walnut Cl Brackley NN13 222 F1
Braunston NN11 118 D2
Clifton OX15 236 E4
Culworth OX17 198 D2
Silverstone NN12 214 D4
Weldon NN17 38 B8
Walnut Cres NN16 72 D4
Walnut Gdns OX17 181 D1
Walnut Gr NN3 142 C1
Walsingham Ave NN15 91 F8
Waltham Cl NN17 36 D8
Waltham Gdns OX16 219 A6
Walton Ave OX17 230 B5
Walton Heath Way NN2 141 E3
Walton Pl NN18 36 B6
Wansell Rd NN17 37 F8
Wansford Pl NN17 36 B8
Wansford Rd Elton PE8 16 E3
Yarwell PE8 7 F2
Wansford Sta★ PE8 16 E8
Wansford Wlk NN3 142 E6
Wantage Cl
Hackleton NN7 177 B3
Moulton NN3 126 E1
Wantage Pl NN29 147 B8
Wantage Rd
Irchester NN29 147 B8
Northampton NN1 160 A8
Wappenham Rd
Abthorpe NN12 201 F1
Helmdon NN13 212 A5
Syresham NN13 213 C2
Ward Rd NN13 234 A5
Wardens Lodge 2 NN11 135 C2
Wardington Rd OX17 208 D6
Wardle Ct NN16 72 B3
Wardle's Cl NN7 138 C7
Wardlow Cl NN4 174 F8
Wards La NN6 82 C3
Ware Orch CV23 99 C2
Ware Rd CV23 99 C2
Wareham Gn NN18 36 B6
Warehouse The LE16 31 D4
Wareing La NN7 178 B8
Warkton La NN15 73 B1
Warkton Way NN17 36 B8
Warkworth Rd OX17 219 E7
Warmington Sch PE8 28 B3
Warminster Cl NN18 36 A7
Warmonds Hill NN10 132 B5
Warners Hill NN29 164 D2
Warnham NN8 129 B5
Warren Bridge PE8 41 E5
Warren Cl
Buckingham MK18 240 E2
Irchester NN29 147 C7
Warren End
Desborough NN14 51 B4
Mawsley Village NN14 89 A4
Warren Hill NN16 71 E3
Warren La Bythorn PE28 97 D4
Clopton NN14 78 F1
Warren Rd
Northampton NN5 158 F7
Stanion NN14 37 E3
Wothorpe PE9 2 E7
Yardley Gobion NN12 217 F6
Warren The
Northampton NN4 175 F8
Thorpe Mandeville OX17 210 A6
Warren Yd MK12 229 F6
Warrenne Keep PE9 241 D2
Warrens Cl NN9 112 F2
Warrington Rd MK46 195 F5
Warth Park Way NN9 114 B7
Wartnaby St LE16 31 D3
Warwick Ave NN14 37 E3
Warwick Cl
Market Harborough LE16 31 F5
Northampton NN5 158 B8
Raunds NN9 114 D5
Warwick Ct
Daventry NN11 135 B1
Kettering NN15 91 F8
Warwick Gdns NN14 76 F2
Warwick Ho NN5 158 F7
Warwick Prim Sch NN8 129 F1
Warwick Rd
Banbury OX16 240 C8
Banbury, Ruscote OX16 240 A9
Hanslope MK19 207 A3
Upper Boddington NN11 182 C7
Wellingborough NN8 130 A2
Warwick St
Daventry NN11 135 B1
Rugby CV21,CV22 241 C7
Warwick Way NN17 36 C6
Warwickshire Coll CV21 241 F7
Washbrook Cl NN3 143 B1
Washbrook La NN6 143 F5
Washbrook Rd NN10 132 A3
Washingley La PE7 44 F6
Washington Ct NN14 76 E3
Washington Sq NN16 72 D3
Washington St NN2 141 C3
Washle Dr OX17 220 B7
Water Cl MK19 229 B7
Water La
Adderbury OX17 230 A3
Bradden NN12 201 F5
Chelveston NN9 133 B8
Cottingham LE16 35 D8
Northampton NN4 175 E6
Shutlanger NN12 204 D8
Towcester NN12 203 C5
Weldon NN17 38 A8
Water Meadow Cl NN18 36 B1
Water St Kettering NN16 72 C2
Stamford PE9 241 E2
Waterfall Way LE16 18 F6
Waterfield Pl LE16 31 E5
Waterfurlong PE9 241 C2
Watergate PE9 241 E3
Waterhouse Gdns NN15 92 A7
Watering La NN4 175 C3
Waterlee Furlong NN6 106 C1

Waterloo NN11 . . . . .135 C1
Waterloo Dr OX16 . . . . .240 E8
Waterloo Way NN9 . . . . .131 D8
Waterlow Bridge NN8 . . .111 F5
Watermeadow Dr NN3 . .142 F6
Watermill Cl NN14 . . . . . . .51 D3
Waterperry Ct OX16 . . . .240 E8
Waterpike NN6 . . . . .106 C2
Waterpump Ct NN3 . . . . .142 F5
Waters La OX17 . . . . .209 B1
Watersmeet NN1 . . . . . . .160 C6
Waterworks La NN8 . . . .129 E7
Waterworks Way LE17 . . .45 F5
Watery La Brackley NN13 234 A7
  Nether Heyford NN7 . . .156 C2
Watford Rd Crick NN6 . . .101 A2
  West Haddon NN6 . . . . .102 B3
Watkin Ct NN1 . . . . .159 D7
Watkin Terr NN1 . . . . . . .159 D7
Watling St Kilsby CV23 . .100 A3
  Potterspury NN12 . . . . .217 D3
Watling St E NN12 . . . . .203 C6
Watling St W NN12 . . . . .203 C6
Watson Ave LE16 . . . . . . .48 D8
Watson Cl Oundle PE8 . . . .41 E7
  Wellingborough NN8 . . .129 C7
Watson Rd NN6 . . . . .121 B2
Watts Cl MK19 . . . . .207 A3
Watts La CV21 . . . . .99 B8
Watts Way NN6 . . . . .121 C3
Wavell Cl NN15 . . . . .72 E1
Waveney Cl NN11 . . . . . .153 A8
Waveney Way NN5 . . . . .140 F1
Waver Cl NN18 . . . . .36 D3
Waverley Ave NN17 . . . . . .37 A6
Waverley Gdns PE9 . . . . .241 B4
Waverley Pl PE9 . . . . . . .241 B4
Waverley Rd
  Kettering NN15 . . . . .91 D8
  Northampton NN2 . . . . .141 E1
  Rugby CV21 . . . . .80 A1
Waynflete Ave NN13 . . . .233 E7
Waynflete Cl NN13 . . . . .233 E7
Waypost Cl NN3 . . . . . . .142 F3
Wayside Acres **8** NN4 . .175 B8
Weares Cl LE15 . . . . .3 B5
Weaver Cl NN16 . . . . .72 B6
Weavers End MK19 . . . . .207 B2
Weavers Rd NN8 . . . . . . .129 D4
Weavers Sch NN8 . . . . . .129 D4
Weavers The NN4 . . . . . .175 C6
Webb Cl Banbury OX16 . .240 E9
  Oundle PE8 . . . . .42 B5
Webb Ellis Bsns Pk
  CV21 . . . . .241 D9
Webb Ellis Rd CV22 . . . .241 A7
Webb Rd NN9 . . . . .114 C7
Webbs Factory NN2 . . . .141 D1
Webbs La NN6 . . . . .127 D3
Webster Cl NN7 . . . . .114 D7
Weddell Way NN4 . . . . . .160 C2
Wedgwood Cl NN14 . . . . . .50 F3
Wedmore Cl NN5 . . . . . .158 C7
Wedmore Ct NN18 . . . . . .36 B6
Weedon Bec Prim Sch
  NN7 . . . . .155 B3
Weedon La NN11 . . . . . .136 C4
Weedon Lois CE Prim Sch
  NN12 . . . . .200 B2
Weedon Rd
  Farthingstone NN12 . . .170 F3
  Kislingbury NN7 . . . . . .157 D5
  Nether Heyford NN7 . . .156 B2
  Newnham NN11 . . . . . . .153 E4
  Northampton NN5 . . . . .158 D5
Weekley Glebe Rd NN16 .72 D5
Weekley Wood La NN16 . .72 E6
Weggs Farm Rd NN5 . . . .139 F1
Weinahr Cl LE16 . . . . .34 C5
Weir Cl NN3 . . . . .129 F7
Welbeck Ct Corby NN18 . .36 C5
  Kettering NN15 . . . . .91 F8
Welbourne Ct NN9 . . . . .114 C6
Weldon CE Prim Sch
  NN17 . . . . .38 A8
Weldon Cl NN8 . . . . .129 D7
Weldon North Ind Est
  NN17 . . . . .22 F1
Weldon Rd NN17 . . . . . . .37 C7
Weldon St NN16 . . . . .72 C3
Welford Ave NN9 . . . . . .113 B5
Welford Cl NN9 . . . . .113 B5
Welford Gr NN17 . . . . . . .36 C7
Welford Rd
  Husbands Bosworth LE17 .45 E3
  Northampton NN2 . . . . .141 B4
  Rugby CV21 . . . . .241 E9
  Sibbertoft LE16 . . . . . . .46 D2
  South Kilworth LE17 . . . .63 D7
  Spratton NN6 . . . . .124 A8
  Thornby NN6 . . . . .84 D4
  Welford NN6 . . . . .64 E7
Welford Sibbertoft & Sulby
  Endowed Sch NN6 . . . .64 E5
Welham La LE16 . . . . . . .17 E8
Welham Rd
  Great Bowden LE16 . . . .32 B8
  Thorpe Langton LE16 . . .17 B5
  Welham LE16 . . . . .18 A8
  Weston by W LE16 . . . . .18 A4
Well Hill NN6 . . . . .100 F5
Well La Barnwell PE8 . . . .59 B7
  Everdon NN11 . . . . .170 A8
  Guilsborough NN6 . . . . .103 F6
  Rothwell NN14 . . . . .70 D7

Well La continued
  Staverton NN11 . . . . . . .152 B7
  Welton NN11 . . . . .119 E1
Well St Buckingham MK18 240 D3
  Finedon NN9 . . . . .111 F5
Well Yd NN2 . . . . .141 B3
Welland Ave LE16 . . . . . . .31 B8
Welland Cl Caldecott LE16 .21 C8
  Daventry NN11 . . . . . . .152 F8
  Gretton NN17 . . . . .22 B8
  Raunds NN9 . . . . .114 C7
Welland Ct
  Burton Latimer NN15 . . .92 B2
  Desborough NN14 . . . . .51 A3
  3 Market Harborough
  LE16 . . . . .31 F2
Welland Gn NN5 . . . . . . .140 F2
Welland Ind Est LE16 . . . .32 B4
Welland Mews PE9 . . . . .241 E1
Welland Park Coll LE16 . .31 E2
Welland Park Rd LE16 . . .31 E2
Welland Rd NN16 . . . . . . .72 A5
Welland Rise LE16 . . . . . . .46 F2
Welland Vale Rd NN17 . . .21 E1
Welland View Rd LE16 . . .20 D1
Welland Way NN5 . . . . . .141 A2
Welland Wlk NN5 . . . . . .140 F2
Wellesley Cl OX16 . . . . . .240 E8
Wellingborough Jun Sch
  NN8 . . . . .130 B3
Wellingborough Park Jun
  Sch NN8 . . . . .130 A5
Wellingborough Rd
  Broughton NN14 . . . . . . .90 B3
  Earls Barton NN6 . . . . .144 F6
  Finedon NN9 . . . . .111 F4
  Great Harrowden NN9 . .110 E1
  Irthlingborough NN9 . . .131 C8
  Isham NN14 . . . . .110 F8
  Little Harrowden NN9 . .110 B3
  Mears Ashby NN6 . . . . .128 C2
  Northampton NN3 . . . . .142 A1
  Olney MK46 . . . . .195 F5
  Rushden NN10 . . . . .131 F3
  Sywell NN6 . . . . .127 F4
  Wellingborough NN8 . . .111 E1
Wellingborough Sch
  NN8 . . . . .130 B3
Wellingborough Sta
  NN8 . . . . .130 C5
Wellington Ave OX16 . . .240 E9
Wellington Pl **18** NN1 . .159 C7
Wellington Rd NN9 . . . . .114 C5
Wellington St
  Kettering NN16 . . . . .72 C3
  Northampton NN1 . . . . .159 D6
Wellington Terr NN14 . . . .76 B2
Wellington Wks NN16 . . .72 C3
Wells Cl
  Husbands Bosworth LE17 .45 E5
  Kettering NN15 . . . . .90 F8
Wells Ct NN3 . . . . .142 C8
Wells Gn NN18 . . . . .36 B6
Wells St CV21 . . . . .241 D8
Wells The NN9 . . . . .111 F5
Wellspring NN7 . . . . .190 D7
Welsh Rd
  Aston le W NN11 . . . . . .182 C8
  Chipping Warden OX17 .197 C6
Welton CE Prim Sch
  NN11 . . . . .119 E1
Welton La NN11 . . . . .135 D6
Welton Pk NN11 . . . . . . .119 E1
Welton Pl CV22 . . . . .98 D8
Welton Rd
  Braunston NN11 . . . . . .118 D1
  Daventry NN11 . . . . . . .135 C3
Wenlock Way NN5 . . . . . .140 D1
Wensleydale NN2 . . . . . .140 F5
Wensleydale Pk NN17 . . .36 D8
Wentin Cl NN18 . . . . .36 C1
Wentworth Ave NN8 . . . .129 C7
Wentworth Cl NN11 . . . .135 E3
Wentworth Cotts MK18 .227 A5
Wentworth Dr PE8 . . . . . .41 E7
Wentworth Way
  Northampton NN2 . . . . .141 E3
  Stoke Bruerne NN12 . . .204 F8
Weskers Cl LE16 . . . . .67 A7
Wesley Ct NN9 . . . . .114 D6
Wesley Dr OX16 . . . . . . .240 B6
Wesley Pl OX17 . . . . .208 E4
Wesley Rd CV21 . . . . .99 A8
Wessex Cl NN16 . . . . .72 B6
Wessex Way NN3 . . . . . .142 B1
West Ave NN15 . . . . .92 B3
West Bank NN3 . . . . .142 E6
West Bar St OX16 . . . . . .240 C7
West Brook
  Blisworth NN7 . . . . .190 D8
  Newnham NN11 . . . . . . .153 D4
West Cres NN10 . . . . .131 E2
West Ct NN11 . . . . .135 C1
West End Bugbrooke NN7 172 E7
  Scaldwell NN6 . . . . .106 F5
  Silverstone NN12 . . . . .214 C4
  Welford NN6 . . . . .64 D4
  West Haddon NN6 . . . . .102 B4
West Farm Cl NN6 . . . . .108 C3
West Farm Dr LE15 . . . . . .3 E5
West Furlong NN15 . . . . . .71 F1
West Glebe Rd NN17 . . . .36 F7
West Haddon Prim Sch
  NN6 . . . . .102 B4

West Haddon Rd
  Cold Ashby NN6 . . . . . . .84 A5
  Crick NN6 . . . . .101 B6
  Guilsborough NN6 . . . . .103 D7
  Ravensthorpe NN6 . . . .103 C1
  Watford NN6 . . . . .120 D7
West Leyes CV21 . . . . . .241 C8
West Leys Ct NN3 . . . . . .142 C7
West Lodge Farm Rural Ctr★
  NN14 . . . . .51 C0
West March NN11 . . . . . .153 D7
West Mill PE9 . . . . .1 F4
West Oval NN5 . . . . .140 F1
West Paddock Ct NN14 . .142 F4
West Priors Ct NN3 . . . . .143 A4
West Ridge NN2 . . . . . . .141 D3
West Rising NN4 . . . . . . .175 D7
West Side Rise MK46 . . .195 F4
West St Banbury OX16 . .240 E9
  Broughton NN14 . . . . . . .90 A5
  Buckingham MK18 . . . .240 C4
  Earls Barton NN6 . . . . .144 E4
  Easton o t H PE9 . . . . . . .2 A5
  Ecton NN6 . . . . .143 F4
  Geddington NN14 . . . . . .54 A3
  Kettering NN16 . . . . .72 B1
  King's Cliffe PE8 . . . . . . .13 E7
  Long Buckby NN6 . . . . .121 A4
  Moulton NN3 . . . . .126 C1
  Northampton NN1 . . . . .159 F6
  Oundle PE8 . . . . .41 F5
  Raunds NN9 . . . . .114 D6
  Rushden NN10 . . . . .132 B2
  Stamford PE9 . . . . .241 C3
  Stanwick NN9 . . . . .113 E3
  Weedon NN7 . . . . .155 B3
  Welford NN6 . . . . .64 E6
  Wellingborough NN8 . . .129 E4
  Woodford NN14 . . . . . . .94 C7
West Street Gdns PE9 . .241 C2
West View Corby NN17 . . .37 B7
  Daventry NN11 . . . . . . .135 B1
West View Rd CV22 . . . . .241 A7
West Villa Rd NN8 . . . . . .129 F4
West Way
  Earls Barton NN6 . . . . .144 D5
  Weedon NN7 . . . . .155 B3
Westbeech Ct OX16 . . . .240 C7
Westbourne Gr CV22 . . .241 B6
Westbrook NN8 . . . . .129 B4
Westburgh Sq NN11 . . . .153 C8
Westbury Cl NN5 . . . . . . .158 D7
Westbury Wlk NN18 . . . . .36 B6
Westcott Way Corby NN18 36 D5
  Northampton NN3 . . . . .160 E7
Westerdale NN2 . . . . .140 F5
Western Ave
  Buckingham MK18 . . . .240 C4
  Daventry NN11 . . . . . . .153 B8
  Easton o t H PE9 . . . . . . .1 F5
  Market Harborough LE16 .31 D1
  Nether Heyford NN7 . . .156 B1
Western Cl NN11 . . . . . . .135 B2
Western Cres OX16 . . . . .240 E6
Western Dr MK19 . . . . . .207 A3
Western View NN1 . . . . .159 B5
Western Way NN8 . . . . . .129 D3
Westfield Ave
  Deanshanger MK19 . . . .228 D5
  Raunds NN9 . . . . .114 B4
  Rushden NN10 . . . . .131 F2
Westfield Barns CV47 . . .166 D7
Westfield Cl LE16 . . . . . . .31 C3
Westfield Cres NN6 . . . . .64 E6
Westfield Ctr NN13 . . . . .233 E8
Westfield Dr NN9 . . . . . .114 B4
Westfield Fst Sch CV22 .241 B7
Westfield Ho **8** NN16 . . .72 B2
Westfield Pl NN10 . . . . . .131 F2
Westfield Rd
  Northampton NN5 . . . . .158 F6
  Northampton, Duston NN5 158 B8
  Rugby CV22 . . . . .241 B7
  Wellingborough NN8 . . .129 E4
Westfields
  Buckingham MK18 . . . .240 C3
  Easton o t H PE9 . . . . . . .1 F5
  Little Harrowden NN9 . .110 B3
  Wellingborough NN8 . . .130 D3
Westfields Ave NN10 . . .132 B5
Westfields Rd NN17 . . . . .36 E8
Westfields St NN10 . . . . .132 B5
Westfields Terr NN10 . . .132 B5
Westgate La LE16 . . . . . . .30 E3
Westgate Rd NN5 . . . . . .158 D6
Westhaven PE9 . . . . .2 A5
Westhill Ave NN13 . . . . .233 E7
Westhill Cl
  Brackley NN13 . . . . .233 E7
  Kettering NN15 . . . . .71 F1
Westhill Dr NN15 . . . . . . .71 F1
Westhill Gdns NN13 . . . .233 D7
Westhorp OX17 . . . . .210 E2
Westhorpe Ashley LE16 . .18 E2
  Sibbertoft LE16 . . . . . . .46 F2
Westhorpe La NN11 . . . .183 C7
Westhorpe Mews NN11 .183 C6
Westland Cl LE16 . . . . . . .30 E3
Westlea Rd NN6 . . . . .127 D3
Westleigh Cl NN1 . . . . . .159 F8
Westleigh Pk NN1 . . . . . .141 E6
Westleigh Rd NN15 . . . . . .92 B8
Westmead St NN3 . . . . . .142 F1
Westminster Cl NN13 . . .234 A7
Westminster Cres NN13 234 A7
Westminster Croft
  NN13 . . . . .233 F7

Westminster Dr NN15 . . . .91 F7
Westminster Rd
  Brackley NN13 . . . . .233 F6
  Wellingborough NN8 . . .129 E7
Westminster Way OX16 .240 F8
Westminster Wlk NN18 . . .36 C4
Westmoreland Ct PE8 . . .15 E5
Westmorland Dr NN3 . . . .51 C4
Weston Favell CE Lower Sch
  NN3 . . . . .160 D8
Weston Favell Ctr NN3 . .142 F2
Weston Favell Upper Sch
  NN3 . . . . .142 D3
Weston Mill La NN3 . . . .160 E6
Weston Rd Ashley LE16 . .18 D3
  Olney MK46 . . . . .195 D3
  Ravenstone MK46 . . . . .194 E2
  Sulgrave OX17 . . . . .211 A8
  Sutton Bassett LE16 . . . .18 A2
  Welham LE16 . . . . .17 F5
Weston Way NN3 . . . . . .160 C8
Weston Wlk NN3 . . . . .36 C6
Westone Ave NN3 . . . . . .142 E1
Westonville PE9 . . . . .1 D2
Westover Rd NN15 . . . . . .71 F1
Westvilla Cotts NN8 . . . .129 F4
Westway Kettering NN15 . .71 F1
  Rugby CV21 . . . . .241 C8
Westway The NN1 . . . . . .153 D8
Westwood Rd CV22 . . . . .98 F7
Westwood Wlk NN18 . . . .36 C5
Wetenhall Rd NN9 . . . . .114 A4
Wetheral Cl NN3 . . . . . . .142 C4
Weymouth Cl NN18 . . . . .36 B6
Whaddon Cl NN4 . . . . . . .158 E1
Whaddon Field NN6 . . . .106 C1
Whalley Gr NN7 . . . . .161 F6
Wharf Cl MK19 . . . . .229 B7
Wharf La
  Old Stratford MK19 . . . .229 C7
  Souldern OX27 . . . . .237 B4
Wharf Rd
  Higham Ferrers NN10 . .132 B6
  Stamford PE9 . . . . .241 E3
Wharf View MK18 . . . . . .240 E4
Wharfe Gn NN5 . . . . .140 F2
Wharfedale Rd NN17 . . . .21 E1
Wharfside Pl MK18 . . . . .240 D4
Wharton Cl NN8 . . . . . . .129 F5
Wheat Cl NN11 . . . . .135 C6
Wheatcroft Gdns NN10 .132 C2
Wheatens Cl NN6 . . . . . .125 C8
Wheatfield Dr NN15 . . . . .92 C2
Wheatfield Gdns NN3 . . .142 B1
Wheatfield Rd NN3 . . . . .142 B2
Wheatfield Rd N NN3 . . .142 B2
Wheatfield Rd S NN3 . . .142 B1
Wheatfield Terr NN3 . . . .142 B1
Wheatley Ave NN17 . . . . .36 F6
Wheel La LE15 . . . . .3 F5
Wheeler's Rise NN17 . . .238 C8
Wheelwright Cl NN9 . . . .114 E7
Wheelwright Ho NN14 . . .70 D7
Wheelwrights Way
  MK19 . . . . .229 C7
Wheelwrights Yd NN29 .164 D2
Whernside NN8 . . . . .129 D6
Whernside Way NN5 . . . .158 C8
Whilton Rd
  Great Brington NN7 . . . .138 C7
  Northampton NN2 . . . . .141 D4
Whistfield Cotts NN6 . . .143 A4
Whistlets Cl NN4 . . . . . . .158 D1
Whiston Rd
  Cogenhoe NN7 . . . . . . .162 C6
  Denton NN7 . . . . .162 B2
  Northampton NN2 . . . . .141 D4
Whitby Cl NN15 . . . . .91 F8
White Cotts MK18 . . . . . .226 D4
White Delves NN8 . . . . . .129 E7
White Doe Dr NN3 . . . . .142 C7
White Hills Cres NN2 . . .141 B6
White Hills Way NN2 . . . .141 B6
White House Ct NN10 . . .132 C1
White House Ind Est
  NN6 . . . . .144 D6
White Lion Wlk OX16 . . .240 C8
White Post Ct NN17 . . . . .21 C2
White Way NN6 . . . . .144 E5
Whitecroft Gdns NN11 . .184 B7
Whitefield Rd NN5 . . . . .140 C1
Whitefield Way NN9 . . . .114 C7
Whiteford Dr NN15 . . . . . .91 C7
Whitefriars NN10 . . . . . .131 F1
Whitefriars Jun & Inf Schs
  NN10 . . . . .147 F8
Whitegates NN4 . . . . . . .158 D1
Whitehall Rd CV21 . . . . .241 D7
Whiteheart Cl NN3 . . . . .143 B2
Whitehill MK46 . . . . .195 B5
Whitehill Rd NN14 . . . . . .50 E3
Whitehills Lower Sch
  NN2 . . . . .141 A6
Whitehorse Yd MK11 . . .229 C5
Whiteland Rd NN3 . . . . . .142 C2
Whiteman La NN14 . . . . . .70 C7
Whites Rise NN9 . . . . . . .112 E1
Whitesands Way NN4 . . .158 C2
Whitfield Way NN2 . . . . .141 D5
Whiting Ct NN3 . . . . .142 C8
Whitmees Cl MK46 . . . . .195 E4
Whitmore Ct NN12 . . . . .214 D5
Whitney Rd NN15 . . . . . . .92 B1
Whitsundale Cl NN10 . . .111 F4
Whittall St OX17 . . . . . . .230 F5
Whittam Cl NN9 . . . . . . .114 C7
Whittemore Rd NN10 . . .132 D3
Whittle Cl Daventry NN11 135 A5

Whittle Cl continued
  Wellingborough NN8 . . .129 B6
Whittle Rd NN17 . . . . .37 B8
Whittlebury CE Prim Sch
  NN12 . . . . .215 C4
Whittlebury Cl NN2 . . . . .141 D5
Whittlebury Ct NN12 . . . .215 C5
Whittlebury Rd NN12 . . .214 E5
Whittles Cross NN4 . . . . .176 A6
Whittlesea Terr NN14 . . . .94 D6
Whitton Cl OX17 . . . . . . .210 E2
Whittons La NN12 . . . . . .203 C6
Whitwell Cl PE8 . . . . .41 E5
Whitworth Ave NN17 . . . .37 A8
Whitworth Cres NN6 . . .144 E5
Whitworth Rd
  Northampton NN1 . . . . .159 F7
  Wellingborough NN8 . . .130 C5
Whitworth Way
  Irthlingborough NN9 . . .131 E8
  Wellingborough NN8 . . .130 B2
Whytewell Rd NN8 . . . . .129 F6
Wick Cl NN18 . . . . .36 D3
Wicken Park Rd MK19 . .228 B1
Wicken Rd MK18 . . . . . . .227 E1
Wickery Dene NN4 . . . . .176 A6
Wicksteed Cl NN15 . . . . . .91 C6
Wicksteed L Pk★ NN15 . .91 D6
Wigston Rd **3** CV21 . . . .80 A1
Wilbarston CE Prim Sch
  LE16 . . . . .34 C5
Wilbarston Rd LE16 . . . . .34 B4
Wilberforce St **3** NN1 . .159 E6
Wilby CE Prim Sch NN8 129 B1
Wilby Cl NN17 . . . . .36 B8
Wilby La NN29 . . . . .145 D6
Wilby Rd NN6 . . . . .128 D2
Wilby St NN1 . . . . .159 F6
Wilby Way NN8 . . . . .129 D1
Wilbye Grange NN8 . . . .129 D2
Wild Cherry Cl NN11 . . .184 B6
Wildacre Rd NN10 . . . . . .131 E2
Wildern La NN4 . . . . .175 C5
Wilford Ave NN3 . . . . . . .160 F8
Wilkie Cl NN11 . . . . .90 F8
Willetts Cl NN17 . . . . .36 E8
Willey Ct MK11 . . . . .229 F4
William Rd NN6 . . . . .121 B3
William St
  Burton Latimer NN15 . . .92 B2
  Finedon NN9 . . . . .112 A4
  Kettering NN16 . . . . .72 B4
  Northampton NN1 . . . . .159 D7
  Rugby CV21 . . . . .241 D8
William Steele Way
  NN10 . . . . .132 C5
William Trigg Cl NN9 . . .131 E8
William's Way NN29 . . . .146 E1
Williams Cl MK19 . . . . . .206 F3
Williams Terr NN11 . . . . .135 B2
Williams Way NN10 . . . .132 B5
Williamscot Hill OX17 . .208 B6
Willis Way NN12 . . . . . . .203 C5
Williton Cl NN3 . . . . .160 D7
Willoughby Cl NN11 . . . .135 B3
Willoughby Pl CV22 . . . . .98 D7
Willoughby Rd
  Morcott LE15 . . . . .3 A6
  Stamford PE9 . . . . .241 E5
Willoughby Way NN7 . . .177 A1
Willow Brook Rd NN17 . .36 C8
Willow Brook Sq NN3 . . .143 D2
Willow Cl
  Desborough NN14 . . . . . .51 C3
  Hinton NN11 . . . . .184 C3
  Spratton NN6 . . . . .124 A8
  Towcester NN12 . . . . . .203 C3
Willow Cres
  Great Houghton NN4 . . .160 F2
  Market Harborough LE16 .31 C2
Willow Ct NN1 . . . . .160 A7
Willow Dr MK18 . . . . . . .240 C6
Willow Gr MK19 . . . . . . .229 B6
Willow Herb Cl NN8 . . . .148 C7
Willow La
  Great Houghton NN4 . . .160 E2
  King's Cliffe PE8 . . . . . . .13 F7
  Stanion NN14 . . . . .37 F2
  Stony Stratford MK11 . .229 C5
Willow Rd Brackley NN13 234 A6
  Kettering NN15 . . . . .72 C1
Willow Rise NN10 . . . . . .161 B8
Willow Tree Gdns CV21 . .99 A8
Willow View NN7 . . . . . . .157 C3
Willowbrook East Ind Est
  NN17 . . . . .22 E2
Willows Hill NN12 . . . . . .201 F5
Willows The
  Daventry NN11 . . . . . . .135 C3
  King's Sutton OX17 . . . .231 A6
  Little Harrowden NN9 . .110 B3
  Silverstone NN12 . . . . .214 C5
Wills Cl NN6 . . . . .103 E7
Willson Cl LE16 . . . . .32 A3
Wilmington Wlk **1** NN18 36 B5
Wilson Cl NN11 . . . . .135 A4
Wilson Cres NN9 . . . . . . .112 E1
Wilson Rd NN10 . . . . . . .132 A2
Wilson Terr NN16 . . . . . . .72 B4
Wilson Way NN6 . . . . . . .144 E3
Wilton Cl NN14 . . . . .51 A2
Wilton Rd NN15 . . . . .91 F8
Wimbledon St NN5 . . . . .159 A6
Wimborne Ave OX16 . . .240 B8
Wimborne Cl NN3 . . . . . .143 D2
Wimborne Pl NN11 . . . . .135 C5
Wimborne Wlk NN18 . . . .36 A7
Wimpole NN8 . . . . .129 C4

Wincanton Ct NN18 .....36 B6
Wincely Cl NN11 .....135 C6
Winchester Cl
  Banbury OX16 ....240 F9
  Northampton NN4 .....159 C1
Winchester House Sch
  NN13 ....233 F7
Winchester Rd
  Northampton NN4 .....159 C1
  Rushden NN10 ....132 C1
Winchilsea Dr NN17 ....10 B1
Windermere Cl NN11 ...135 B2
Windermere Dr
  Higham Ferrers NN10 ...132 B8
  Wellingborough NN8 ...129 C6
Windermere Rd NN16 ...71 F2
Windermere Way NN3 .142 C4
Windflower Pl 2 NN3 .143 D2
Windgate Way PE8 ......8 A6
Winding Way NN14 .....76 E2
Windingbrook La NN4 .175 C5
Windmill Ave
  Blisworth NN7 ....190 E7
  Kettering NN15,NN16 ...72 D2
  Raunds NN9 ....114 D6
Windmill Banks NN10 .132 C7
Windmill Bsns Ctr
  NN10 ....132 A2
Windmill Cl
  Banbury OX16 ....240 D6
  Buckingham MK18 .....240 F4
  Cottingham LE16 ......20 D1
  Wellingborough NN8 ...129 E2
  Wollaston NN29 ....146 E2
Windmill Cotts NN15 ...92 D4
Windmill Cl NN16 .....72 D3
Windmill Gdns NN11 ..152 C7
Windmill Glade NN6 ..106 A1
Windmill Gr NN9 ......114 D6
Windmill La Denton NN7 .178 B8
  Raunds NN9 ....114 D7
  Staverton NN11 ....152 C7
Windmill Prim Sch NN9 114 C7
Windmill Rd
  Irthlingborough NN9 ...112 E1
  Rushden NN10 ....132 A2
Windmill Rise LE16 ....20 D1
Windmill Terr NN2 ....141 D4
Windmill Way
  Greens Norton NN12 .202 D8
  Lyddington LE15 ....9 D6
Windrush Rd NN4 .....175 F8
Windrush Way NN5 ...141 A2
Windsor Ave NN14 .....50 F2
Windsor Cl
  Daventry NN11 ....135 B1
  Kings Sutton OX17 ...230 F6
  Long Buckby NN6 ....121 B3
  Stamford PE9 ....241 D5
  Towcester NN12 ......203 B4
  Weedon NN7 ....155 B4
  Wilbarston LE16 ......34 C4
Windsor Cres NN5 ....158 E6
Windsor Ct LE16 ......31 D4
Windsor Dr
  Brackley NN13 ....233 E8
  Thrapston NN14 ......76 E2
Windsor Gdns NN16 ...72 A2
Windsor Ho NN5 .....158 C8
Windsor Pl NN17 ......36 E5
Windsor Rd
  Rushden NN10 ....132 C3
  Wellingborough NN8 ..129 F1
Windsor St
  Banbury OX16 ....240 D7
  Rugby CV21 ....241 E8

Windsor Terr OX16 ....240 D7
Windyridge NN2 ......141 D3
Winemar Cl MK19 ....207 A3
Winfield St CV21 .....241 F8
Wing Rd LE15 ....3 A6
Wingate Cl NN15 ......72 E1
Winnington Cl NN3 ...143 C5
Winsford Way NN3 ...160 D7
Winstanley Rd NN8 ..130 B5
Winston Cl
  Nether Heyford NN7 ..156 B1
  Northampton NN3 ....142 C5
  Woodford Halse NN11 .184 D5
Winston Cres NN13 ..233 F6
Winston Dr NN14 ......91 D1
Winterbourne Ct NN18 .36 B6
Winterburn Ct NN16 ..71 E3
Winthorpe Way NN18 .36 C6
Winwick Rd PE17 ......61 D1
Winwood Cl MK19 ....228 E5
Wire La LE16 ....19 D2
Wisley Cl NN4 ....175 C7
Wisteria Cl NN10 ....148 B7
Wisteria Way NN3 ...160 C6
Witham Cl PE9 ....241 E4
Witham Gn NN5 ......140 E2
Witham Ho NN2 ......141 E1
Witham The NN11 ....134 F1
Witham Way NN5 ....140 F1
Witham Wlk NN5 ....140 F2
Witheys The NN4 ....175 F2
Withycombe Dr OX16 .240 A8
Wittmills Oak MK18 ..240 E4
Witton Rd NN5 ....158 C8
Woburn Cl Banbury OX16 240 F9
  Market Harborough LE16 .32 A3
Woburn Gate NN3 ...143 D3
Wodhams Dr NN13 ..222 E1
Wold Rd NN15 ....92 E2
Wolfe Cl NN15 ....72 F1
Wollaston Com Prim Sch
  NN29 ....146 D2
Wollaston Rd
  Bozeat NN29 ....164 C5
  Irchester NN29 ....146 F6
Wollaston Sch NN29 ..146 E2
Wollaton Gdns 3 NN3 .160 F8
Wolsey Cl NN6 ....101 A6
Wolverton Rd MK11 ..229 E6
Wood Avens Cl NN4 ..158 E1
Wood Hill NN1 ....159 D5
Wood La Hartwell NN7 .192 E2
  King's Cliffe PE8 ......13 E1
  Oundle PE8 ....41 D4
  Weston Underwood MK46 195 A2
Wood Rd PE8 ....13 F7
Wood St Corby NN17 ..36 E6
  Geddington NN14 ....54 B3
  Higham Ferrers NN10 ..132 C5
  Kettering NN16 ....72 C4
  Northampton NN1 ....159 D6
  Rugby CV21 ....241 D9
  Wellingborough NN8 .129 F4
Woodborough Gdns 5
  NN3 ....160 F8
Woodbreach Dr LE16 ..32 B3
Woodbridge Ct CV21 .241 D9
Woodcock St NN15 ...92 D3
Woodcote Ave NN3 ..142 A5
Woodcroft Cl NN12 ..203 C3
Woodfield PE9 ....1 D1
Woodfield Gr NN17 ...36 E7
Woodford CE Prim Sch
  NN14 ....94 D6
Woodford Cl NN15 ...91 F5
Woodford Glebe NN6 .64 E5

Woodford Halse CE Prim Sch
  NN11 ....184 D6
Woodford La NN14 ...75 E6
Woodford Rd
  Byfield NN11 ....183 D7
  Great Addington NN14 .94 C1
  Great Addington NN14 .94 C3
Woodford St 7 NN1 ..159 E6
Woodford Wlk 9 NN1 .159 E6
Woodgate LE16 ....30 E8
Woodgate Cl LE16 ....32 B2
Woodgate Rd NN4 ..175 F6
Woodgreen Ave OX16 .240 A7
Woodhall Cl NN4 ....158 D1
Woodhead Cl PE9 ...241 F5
Woodhill Rd NN5 ....140 C1
Woodland Ave
  Kettering NN15 ....92 A5
  Northampton NN3 ....142 A1
  Overstone NN6 ......127 A3
Woodland Cl NN5 ...140 B1
Woodland Dr NN15 ..92 C4
Woodland Hospl The
  NN16 ....71 B5
Woodland Rd NN10 ..132 A3
Woodland View Prim Sch
  NN4 ....175 E3
Woodland Wlk NN3 .143 B6
Woodlands NN3 .....175 E1
Woodlands Ave NN17 .21 F1
Woodlands Cl
  Brigstock NN14 ....55 F7
  Buckingham MK18 ...240 D5
Woodlands Cres MK18 240 D5
Woodlands Ct
  Kettering NN16 ......72 C4
  Watford NN6 ....120 C6
Woodlands Grange
  NN6 ....145 A4
Woodlands La NN18 ..53 C8
Woodlands Mews NN14 .55 F7
Woodlands Rd
  Irchester NN29 ......147 A7
  Weldon NN17 ....38 C7
Woodlands The
  Geddington NN14 ....54 B3
  Market Harborough LE16 .31 C4
  Silverstone NN12 ....214 D4
  Staverton NN11 .....152 B7
Woodley Chase NN5 .140 B1
Woodmans St MK19 ..228 E4
Woodnewton Jun & Inf Sch
  NN17 ....36 C8
Woodnewton Rd PE8 .15 D4
Woodnewton Way NN7 .36 C7
Woodpecker Cl NN13 222 D1
Woodpecker Way NN4 .174 F7
Woodroffe Rd PE8 ....7 D8
Woodrush Way NN3 ..142 C7
Woods Ct Brackley NN13 233 D7
  Rushden NN10 ....132 B3
Woods La NN12 ......217 E3
Woodside
  Stony Stratford MK11 .229 E6
  Sywell NN6 ....127 C1
Woodside Ave
  Northampton NN3 ....142 D4
  Sywell NN6 ....143 D8
Woodside Cres NN3 .142 D4
Woodside Gn NN5 ...140 F1
Woodside Pk CV21 ..241 D9
Woodside Way NN5 .140 F1
Woodside Wlk NN5 .140 E1
Woodstock Cl 12 NN1 .159 F6
Woodstock Cl NN8 ..129 E7
Woodville Cres NN12 .217 E6
Woodward Cl NN11 ..135 E1

Woodwell Cotts NN14 .94 A8
Woodwell Hill NN14 ...50 F2
Woodyard Cl NN14 ....55 F8
Wooldale Rd NN4 ....175 D8
Wooll St CV21 ....241 C8
Woolmans MK11 ....229 F4
Woolmonger St 4 NN1 159 C5
Woolrich Gdns MK11 .229 E5
Woolston Ct NN17 ....10 C1
Wooton Ct NN4 .....175 F7
Wootton Brook Cl NN4 175 C6
Wootton Hall Pk NN7 .175 D8
Wootton Hill Farm NN4 174 F8
Wootton Hope Dr NN4 .175 F6
Wootton Prim Sch NN4 175 E6
Wootton Rd NN7 .....176 A2
Worcester Cl
  Northampton NN3 ....143 B2
  West Haddon NN6 ...102 C5
Worcester Cres PE9 .241 D4
Worcester Dr LE16 ...31 E5
Worcester St CV21 ..241 C9
Worcester Way NN11 .153 C7
Wordsworth Ave NN17 .21 D1
Wordsworth Cl
  Brackley NN13 ....222 F1
  Towcester NN12 ....203 B5
Wordsworth Rd
  Daventry NN11 ......135 B3
  Kettering NN16 ......72 C5
  Wellingborough NN8 .129 B3
Works The 8 NN1 ...159 E6
Worksop Gdns NN18 ..36 B6
Wormleighton Way
  NN14 ....54 A3
Worthing Rd NN18 ...36 B5
Wothorpe Mews PE9 .241 D2
Wothorpe Rd PE9 ...241 D2
Wrekin Cl NN4 ....158 E3
Wren Cl Brackley NN13 222 D1
  Buckingham MK18 ...240 F2
  Kettering NN15 ......92 A6
  Northampton NN4 ...175 F3
  Towcester NN12 ....203 C3
Wren Spinney Sch NN15 71 F1
Wrenbury Rd NN5 ...140 A1
Wrendyke Cl LE15 ....3 A6
Wrenn Sch NN8 .....130 A3
Wright Rd NN6 ......121 B3
Wrightons Hill NN13 .211 F4
Wroe Cl NN18 ....36 C1
Wroe The NN10 .....132 B7
Wyatt St NN16 ....72 C2
Wyatt Way PE8 ......41 E6
Wychwood Cl NN5 ..140 A1
Wychwood Gdns OX16 240 A6
Wyckley Cl NN9 .....112 E3
Wycliffe Rd NN1 ....160 A6
Wye Cl NN8 ....129 C6
Wye The NN11 ......153 A8
Wykeham Rd NN10 ..132 C7
Wyman Cl NN29 .....164 D2
Wymersley Rd NN4 ..160 F2
Wymington Pk NN10 .132 B1
Wymington Rd
  Podington NN29 .....147 E3
  Rushden NN10 ......148 B8
Wyndham Way NN16 .71 A5
Wysall Rd NN3 ......143 B5

Y

Yardley Cl NN17 ......21 D1
Yardley Dr NN2 ......141 D6
Yardley Gobion CE Prim Sch
  NN12 ....217 E6

Yardley Hastings Prim Sch
  NN7 ....179 A7
Yardley Rd
  Cosgrove MK19 ......218 D2
  Grendon NN7 ....163 D4
  Olney MK46 ....195 F5
  Yardley Gobion NN12 .217 F4
Yarrow NN8 ....129 B3
Yarrow Cl NN10 .....148 C7
Yarrow Ho NN2 .....141 C5
Yarwell Ct NN15 .....91 C6
Yarwell Rd PE8 ......8 A3
Yarwell Sq NN4 ....158 F2
Yateley Dr NN15 .....92 A5
Yelden Cl NN10 .....131 F2
Yeldon Ct NN8 ......111 B1
Yelvertoft Prim Sch NN6 82 B4
Yelvertoft Rd Crick NN6 101 A8
  Lilbourne CV23 ......81 D6
  Northampton NN2 ...141 C3
  West Haddon NN6 ..102 B5
Yeoman Cl NN14 ....95 A3
Yeoman Dr NN2 .....141 B5
Yeoman Mdw NN4 ..174 F8
Yeomanry Cl NN11 ..135 B1
Yeomanry Ct LE16 ...31 E3
Yeomanry Way NN11 .135 B1
Yeomans Cl NN13 ..234 A8
Yeomans Ct NN15 ...92 C2
Yew Cl NN17 ....21 E1
Yew Tree Cl
  Kettering NN15 ......91 C8
  Middleton Cheney OX17 220 A8
Yew Tree Gdns NN7 .155 F5
Yew Tree Gr NN11 ..153 B8
Yew Tree La NN6 ...124 B8
Yew Tree Rise NN13 .238 D8
Yewtree Ct NN3 .....142 D5
York Ave NN7 ......161 F6
York Cl
  Higham Ferrers NN10 ..132 C7
  Towcester NN12 ....203 C4
York Ct NN12 ....203 C5
York Dr NN13 ....233 E8
York Rd Corby NN18 ..36 C5
  Higham Ferrers NN10 ..132 C7
  Kettering NN16 ......72 B2
  Northampton NN1 ...159 E6
  Rushden NN10 ......132 C1
  Stamford PE9 ....241 D4
  Stony Stratford MK11 .229 D5
  Wellingborough NN8 .130 B5
  Wollaston NN29 ....146 D3
York Ride NN7 .....155 B4
York St
  Market Harborough LE16 .31 F3
  Rugby CV21 ....241 B9
York Way NN9 ......114 C7
Yorke Cl NN9 ....111 E5
Yule Ct OX16 ......240 B8

Z

Zebra Cotts PE9 ....241 B3
Zion Hill NN6 ....108 A5

NG	NH	NJ	NK		
NM	NN	NO	NP		
NR	NS	NT	NU		
	NX	NY	NZ		
	SC	SD	SE	TA	
	SH	SJ	SK	TF	TG
SM	SN	SO	SP	TL	TM
SR	SS	ST	SU	TQ	TR
SW	SX	SY	SZ	TV	

Any feature in this atlas can be given a unique reference to help you find the same feature on other Ordnance Survey maps of the area, or to help someone else locate you if they do not have a Street Atlas.

The grid squares in this atlas match the Ordnance Survey National Grid and are at 500 metre intervals. The small figures at the bottom and sides of every other grid line are the National Grid kilometre values (**00** to **99** km) and are repeated across the country every 100 km (see left).

To give a unique National Grid reference you need to locate where in the country you are. The country is divided into 100 km squares with each square given a unique two-letter reference. Use the administrative map to determine in which 100 km square a particular page of this atlas falls.

The bold letters and numbers between each grid line (**A** to **F**, **1** to **8**) are for use within a specific Street Atlas only, and when used with the page number, are a convenient way of referencing these grid squares.

Example   *The railway bridge over DARLEY GREEN RD in grid square B1*

Step 1: Identify the two-letter reference, in this example the page is in **SP**

Step 2: Identify the 1 km square in which the railway bridge falls. Use the figures in the southwest corner of this square: Eastings **17**, Northings **74**. This gives a unique reference: **SP 17 74**, accurate to 1 km.

Step 3: To give a more precise reference accurate to 100 m you need to estimate how many tenths along and how many tenths up this 1 km square the feature is (to help with this the 1 km square is divided into four 500 m squares). This makes the bridge about **8** tenths along and about **1** tenth up from the southwest corner.

This gives a unique reference: **SP 178 741**, accurate to 100 m.

Eastings (read from left to right along the bottom) come before Northings (read from bottom to top). If you have trouble remembering say to yourself "Along the hall, THEN up the stairs"!

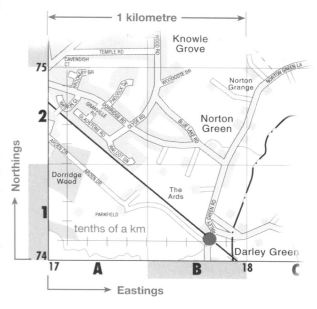

Addresses

Name and Address	Telephone	Page	Grid reference

Name and Address	Telephone	Page	Grid reference

PHILIP'S MAPS

the Gold Standard for serious driving

◆ Philip's street atlases cover every county in England and Wales, plus much of Scotland.

◆ All our atlases use the same style of mapping, with the same colours and symbols, so you can move with confidence from one atlas to the next

◆ Widely used by the emergency services, transport companies and local authorities.

◆ Created from the most up-to-date and detailed information available from Ordnance Survey

◆ Based on the National Grid

For national mapping, choose **Philip's Navigator Britain** – the most detailed road atlas available of England, Wales and Scotland. Hailed by Auto Express as 'the ultimate road atlas', this is the only one-volume atlas to show every road and lane in Britain.

Street atlases currently available

England
Bedfordshire
Berkshire
Birmingham and West Midlands
Bristol and Bath
Buckinghamshire
Cambridgeshire
Cheshire
Cornwall
Cumbria
Derbyshire
Devon
Dorset
County Durham and Teesside
Essex
North Essex
South Essex
Gloucestershire
North Hampshire
South Hampshire
Herefordshire Monmouthshire
Hertfordshire
Isle of Wight
Kent
East Kent
West Kent
Lancashire
Leicestershire and Rutland
Lincolnshire
London
Greater Manchester
Merseyside
Norfolk
Northamptonshire
Northumberland
Nottinghamshire
Oxfordshire
Shropshire
Somerset

All England and Wales coverage

Staffordshire
Suffolk
Surrey
East Sussex
West Sussex
Tyne and Wear
Warwickshire
Birmingham and West Midlands
Wiltshire and Swindon
Worcestershire
East Yorkshire Northern Lincolnshire
North Yorkshire
South Yorkshire
West Yorkshire

Wales
Anglesey, Conwy and Gwynedd
Cardiff, Swansea and The Valleys
Carmarthenshire, Pembrokeshire and Swansea
Ceredigion and South Gwynedd
Denbighshire, Flintshire, Wrexham
Herefordshire Monmouthshire
Powys

Scotland
Aberdeenshire
Ayrshire
Edinburgh and East Central Scotland
Fife and Tayside
Glasgow and West Central Scotland
Inverness and Moray

How to order

Philip's maps and atlases are available from bookshops, motorway services and petrol stations. You can order direct from the publisher by phoning **01903 828503** or online at **www.philips-maps.co.uk**
For bulk orders only, phone 020 7644 6940